The German Army

1933–1945

The German Army

1933-1945

Its Political and Military Failure

Matthew Cooper

Scarborough House/Publishers

To Mother and Father

Scarborough House/*Publishers*
Chelsea, MI 48118

FIRST SCARBOROUGH HOUSE PAPERBACK EDITION 1990

The German Army 1933-1945 was originally
published in hardcover by Stein and Day/*Publishers*.

Designed by Judy Tuke
Maps by Alec Spark

Library of Congress Cataloging-in-Publication Data

Cooper, Matthew.
    The German Army, 1933-1945
    Bibliography: p.
    Includes index.
    1. Germany. Heer. I. Title.
UA712.C66 1978   355.3′0943   77-18331
ISBN 0-8128-8519-8

Contents

PART 4: *The Years of Defeat*

Maps

Photographs follow pages 102, 198, 326 and 454

Introduction

*Things and actions are what they are, and the
consequences of them will be what they will be:
why, then, should we desire to be deceived?*

BISHOP JOSEPH BUTLER

1692–1752

'My hands are done for, and have been ever since the beginning of
December. The little finger of my left hand is missing and – what's even
worse – the three middle fingers of my right one are frozen. I can only hold
my mug with my thumb and little finger. I'm pretty hopeless; only when a
man has lost any fingers does he see how much he needs them for the very
smallest jobs. The best thing I can do with the little finger is to shoot with it.
My hands are finished. After all, even if I'm not fit for anything else, I can't
go on shooting for the rest of my life.' Thus, in January 1943, an anonymous
German soldier wrote of his condition during the battle of Stalingrad; it is
not known whether he survived, but it was unlikely. His suffering was not
unique. In the German Army alone, in the five and a half years of the Second
World War, more than 2,500,000 soldiers were killed and 5,000,000
wounded in the pursuit of an empty cause.

Although no further direct mention of the suffering of individual fighting
soldiers will be made, it is as well to remember from the outset that this, in
the final analysis, is what this book is all about. For the political and military
failure of the German Army, both in the corridors of power and on the field of
battle in the years from 1933 to 1945, had one result: the unnecessary death
of two and a half million of its men, and untold suffering for countless others.
For the world at large, the victim of Hitler's aggression, this was a cause for
great relief; for the German Army, it was a tragedy.

The Army of the Third Reich was a failure. Certainly, it won many victories:
it conquered Poland in twenty-seven days, Denmark in one, Norway in
twenty-three, Holland in five, Belgium in eighteen, France in thirty-nine,
Yugoslavia in twelve, and Greece in twenty-one. In the vast spaces of the
Soviet Union and the North African desert, although final success was to
elude it, its feats have remained remarkable to this day. Indeed, the myth
quickly developed that the German Army of the Second World War was an

excellent fighting machine, one of history's best, and that its defeat was mainly, even solely, due to Hitler burdening it with tasks far beyond its material resources. But this is to mistake appearance for reality; from the beginning there were evident beneath the façade of easy victory the seeds of later defeat, both in the headquarters of the high commands and on the field of battle. The first transient victories should not obscure this. The German Army was the prisoner of its heritage, both political and military, from which it never succeeded in breaking free. Had it not been for one man – Adolf Hitler – this need not have been so disastrous, for contemporary foreign armies were, after all, suffering the same disability. But the moment this dictator entered the European scene as Führer of the Third German Reich, the fate of the Army was sealed, and an irreversible destiny appears to have determined its descent to ultimate failure.

To understand the reasons for this failure, this book concentrates on two themes: the relationship between Hitler and the senior generals, and the strategic development of the Army. It is argued, firstly, that in their political relationship with Hitler, the generals were largely innocent of the blame that has so often been lain at their door, but that, at the same time, they inexcusably surrendered up their military responsibility and, knowingly, allowed an ungifted amateur to gain operational control of the Army, pervert its strategy and lead it to disaster; and, secondly, that the commonly accepted idea of the German Army having been well-equipped and well-trained, and having practised a revolutionary form of warfare known as *Blitzkrieg*, is a myth. Throughout, I have attempted to look at the ideas and events of 1933 to 1945 as the Army leaders themselves would have seen them, rather than as historians have tended to understand them with the advantage of hindsight. Thirty years after the end of the Second World War we may be able to see clearly where, from the beginning of his dictatorship, Hitler was leading Germany; from the relative security of contemporary western society, we find it easy to condemn all those who condoned or ignored the evils of National Socialism; and, having seen the potential of modern weapons, we believe that we can discern their use in a revolutionary strategy during the early years of the war. But are we right to expect the German generals to have done so? I think not. Their background, their heritage of political and strategic thought, was very different from ours, as was the society and age in which they lived. Only when this is realised, do the failures of the German Army under Adolf Hitler become understandable; and only when these failures are recognised, do we see how fortunate were its enemies. It is easy to believe that it was not the Germans who won the early campaigns, but the Allies who lost them, just as it was not the Allies who finally won the war, but the Germans who lost it. For the failings of the German Army under Hitler may we all be thankful; without them, the world today would be a far different place.

Those looking for a detailed, chronological account of the many campaigns undertaken by the German Army from 1939 to 1945 will be disappointed. This, they can find elsewhere. Here, I deal solely with the themes outlined above. In Part One, the reader will find portrayed the political relations between Hitler and the Army leaders from 1933 to 1939; in Part Two, the strategic basis of the Army until 1939 is analysed; in Part Three, the political and military developments in the years of victory are described, covering the campaigns in Poland, Norway, western Europe, the Balkans and the Soviet Union until early 1942; and, in Part Four, the events of the years of defeat are dealt with, showing how the German Army failed to gain victory in the Mediterranean, the east and the west, and how Hitler gained final, total, control over its operations.

This book may be likened, although, alas, not too closely, to the broad brush-sweeps of the Impressionist painters rather than to the detail of the Pre-Raphaelites. It attempts to provide for all readers, whether specialist or general, a fresh interpretation of the fortunes of the German Army from 1933 to 1945, so long overdue for revaluation; but, within the physical constraints of one book, much has had to be left out. Some may believe that my choice of subjects has been at fault, and that important aspects have been omitted; others may think that my selection of facts and quotations has been too subjective, designed only to support my own view of events. Perhaps; but, from the beginning, Napoleon's admonition was always with me: 'It is easier for the ordinary historian to build upon suppositions and to weave hypotheses together than to tell a simple story and stick to the facts. But man, and especially the historian, is all vanity; he must give full rein to his imagination, and he must hold the reader's interest, even if truth be sacrificed in the process.' Whether I have avoided this pitfall, the reader alone can judge.

No man is an island, and no author is entire in himself. The writing of this book owes much to many. Foremost among them is Miss Elaine Austin, who has given much time to reading and correcting the manuscript; her knowledge of the English language and her patience have been invaluable. Lady Liddell Hart, whose hospitality I shall always remember with gratitude, has been of great help in allowing me to work in her husband's library and among his papers; this has been of inestimable value. I should also like to thank James Lucas of the Imperial War Museum, who has been of considerable help in many ways. My editor, Michael Stevens, together with Graeme Wright, has patiently given his great experience to the production of this book; they have my warmest appreciation. Others who have made valuable contributions are Dr Anthony Clayton, of the Royal Military Academy, Sandhurst, Anthony Shadrake, of King's College, London, Terry Charman, of the Imperial War Museum, Paul Silk, of the House of Commons, Douglas Dales, Miss Elizabeth Malone-Lee, Nigel Carnelley, John Calder, Otto Kuhn and Herr L. Klein, who has been to many institutions in Germany on my behalf. Particular thanks must also go to David Henson, who occasionally let me work! Then there is the army of women who typed the manuscript: Miss Beatrix Hawkins; Miss Susan Banks, Mrs Annabelle Egremont, Miss Jane Howard, Miss Ann Power, Mrs Diana Faires, and, last but not least, Miss Julia Burn; to them all, my thanks. I should also like to express my gratitude to Brian L. Davis for the loan from his collection of the uniform and helmet for the jacket, and to all those at Macdonald and Jane's who have put so much effort into producing this book. Mention must also be made of institutions that I have used: the Library of the House of Commons, the Library of King's College, London, the War Office Library, the Department of Documents and the Library of the Imperial War Museum, and the Public Record Office. Again, may I express my gratitude to all who have helped me.

Matthew Cooper
LONDON, JUNE 1977

PART ONE

The
Political Destiny
of the German Army
1933-1939

*Must helpless man, in ignorance sedate
Roll darkling down the torrent of his fate?*

DR. JOHNSON
Vanity of Human Wishes

1

Political Heritage

Every people is the child of its history, its past, and can no more break away from it than a man can separate himself from his youth.

HANS DELBRUCK

Krieg und Politik

'It will be up to the generals to see that the Army does not in the end kiss Herr Schicklgruber's hands like hysterical women.'[1] So wrote General Wilhelm Gröner in 1932, two days after leaving his post as Reich Defence Minister and eight months before the National Socialists assumed power in Germany. It was to take just six years for his worst fears to be justified: the generals had failed; the Army had become Hitler's.

For this, the verdict of history has been harsh. The International Military Tribunal instituted by the victorious Allies immediately after the war, although it acquitted the German Army General Staff and High Command of the charge of being criminal organisations, nevertheless delivered the opinion that 'They have been responsible in large measure for the miseries and sufferings that have fallen upon millions of men, women, and children. They have been a disgrace to the honourable profession of arms. Without their military guidance the aggressive ambitions of Hitler and his fellow Nazis would have been academic and sterile. . . . they were certainly a ruthless military caste. The contemporary German militarism flourished briefly with its recent ally, National Socialism, as well or better than it had in the generations of the past.'[2]

Why, historians wonder, did the once-proud, independently minded Prusso-German Army transform itself into nothing more than the subservient military instrument of a dictator's megalomaniac will? Why, they ask, did the generals allow Hitler to take power in 1933, and then stand passively by while he proceeded to subject both Germany and her Armed Forces to his control? Surely, many argue, the Army leaders must have been aware of the enormity of the political ideas they were prepared to tolerate; and why, they moralise, did they seek to exploit this régime of unparalleled evil for their own ends, thereby allowing a reign of terror to degrade the German people and inflict on the world a war, and a genocide, of cataclysmic proportions? In answering these questions, most historians have accused Hitler of a base desire to subvert the independence of the Army, and of using every known method of guile and deceit to realise it. Moreover, they have judged the military leaders to have been, at best, moral cowards, and, at worst, calculating opportunists. One historian, a senior officer who participated in the actions of the Armed Forces High Command, believed 'that the fateful goddesses of the ancients cast over them [the German generals] their shadow and their spell: Chores, who dazzled with success, Hybris, who threatened the victims with loss of moral and intellectual equilibrium, and, finally, the Atae, who made those under the spell believe that they could achieve the impossible'.[3] Another, a famous British military historian and theorist, has compared the German officer of 1933 to 1945 to 'a modern Pontius Pilate, washing his hands of all responsibility for the orders he executed'.[4] Some have thought the Army's leaders to be vain, weak men, exemplifying the saying of the French Field-Marshal, MacMahon: 'Of all the people in the world, the generals are those who have the least courage to act',[5] while still more have seen fit to apply to them the old Latin proverb: *Quem Deus vult perdere, prius dementat* (Those whom God would damn, he first makes mad).

These judgements echo the belief of Ludwig Beck, one-time Chief of the Army General Staff, who remarked in 1937: 'The Armed Forces enjoy among our military-minded nation almost unlimited trust. The responsibility for what is to come rests almost exclusively with the Army. There is no avoiding that fact.'[6] But Beck was mistaken. Care must be taken neither to allow moral indignation to cloud vision, nor to enable emotion to take the place of cool detachment; nor to let the compulsive desire to apportion blame to distort the facts.

The question that should be asked is not, did the generals do the best for their Army and for their country, but, simply, could they have acted other than they did? If it can be proved that not only were they fully aware of the implications of the régime with which they were forced to deal, but that they also possessed the freedom to act as their individual and collective consciences dictated, then indeed they were guilty of a moral failing the like of which history has seen few parallels. If, on the other hand, it can be shown that these men were not the masters of their own destiny, that they were not capable of taking any other political path, then their innocence is assured. If choice was not theirs, history cannot condemn; it can only record their tragic failure.

The generals who were faced with National Socialism were the prisoners of their own proud heritage. The tradition bestowed on them by their predecessors was one of unconditional personal obedience to, and identification with, the autocratic Head of State, coupled with a self-imposed isolation from the world of politics – an isolation which, although elevated to the status of a military virtue, took the form of a political naïvety and ineptitude. This tradition extended back over several centuries, during which time it served both Germany and her Army well, and even after the collapse in 1918 of the social order on which it had been based, the officer corps, still fairly representative of the middle and upper classes of society, maintained a fundamental belief in its continuing relevance. This was to prove disastrous. It ensured that Germany's military caste became trapped within an ivory tower of its own making, isolated from, and incompatible with, the ever-changing, and always confusing, political realities of the twentieth century. Unconditional obedience and political inexperience were not the best of qualifications for entering the power struggle that was the dynamic of the Third Reich. Nevertheless, they were the traditions of a force in which the senior generals from 1933 to 1939 had served, on average, thirty-six years of their lives.

The German Army had long been accustomed to following an autocratic ruler. The political system of the Reich after 1871, known by the special name of Prusso-German Constitutionalism, was based on a ruling class of great landowners, and centred on the person of the Prussian King and German Emperor – the Kaiser. His power, though in theory circumscribed by the Bundesrat and the Reichstag, was in fact absolute: it was his exclusive privilege to conduct foreign affairs, hold supreme command of the Armed Forces, and declare war. In periods of acute internal dissension, he could also assume a military dictatorship. Furthermore, in his hands lay the appointment and dismissal of all senior officers. It was to such a man that the Imperial Army gave its loyalty. Article 64 of the 1871 Constitution declared: 'All German troops are obliged to obey unconditionally the commands of the Emperor. This obligation is to be incorporated in the military oath.'[7] The Prusso-German Army was the living embodiment of Plato's rule expressed through the mouth of the Athenian in *Laws XII:* 'Now, for expeditions of war much consideration and many laws are required; the great principle of all is that no one should be without a commander; nor should the mind of anyone be accustomed to do anything, either in jest or earnest, of his own motion, but in war and in peace he should look to, and follow, his leader, even in the last things being under his guidance; . . . he should . . . not teach the soul, or accustom her, to know or understand how to do anything apart from others.'[8]

The personal bond that was deemed to exist between each soldier and his Emperor was a matter of considerable pride to the Army, and it served to underline the deep commitment of the officer corps to the idea of monarchy and to the social order it represented. It became a heinous offence, punishable before a military Court of Honour, to give expression in terms contrary to the crown, reminders constantly being given that 'it is an intolerable state of affairs for officers publicly to express opinions that conflict with those which His Majesty has approved'.[9] But such regulations were totally unnecessary for the vast majority of officers, for they believed implicitly in the established order of autocratic society, and possessed, in common with their ruler, a dogged, instinctive opposition to the ideas of socialism and democracy, which threatened all they held dear. It was only among the other ranks that active Social-Democratic supporters were found.

If the Army was to remain 'a sharp, reliable weapon in the hands of its kings',[10] it was essential that disruptive influences be kept out of it. For example, although recruits were given lectures of patriotic content, the Emperor in 1907 issued an order prohibiting the discussion of political and social questions. As a result, politics became a much-neglected, even despised, subject, associated with the Social-Democrats who continually beset the authority of the Kaiser. During his interrogation by the Gestapo in 1944, Hans Oster, one of the few officers to take direct action against Hitler's dictatorship, remarked: 'During the monarchy it was really a sort of boyish enthusiasm for soldiering that sent us into the Army. It never even crossed our minds that the whole régime might collapse one day. Politics meant nothing to us. We were in uniform and that was all that mattered.'[11] In his memoirs General Gröner, Defence Minister from 1928 to 1932, commented that 'Even the senior officers [in the Army] had no political sense. . . . In the Navy it was different. Foreign travel had left the naval officers better equipped to judge political events. In the Army the only people who took an interest in politics were the military attachés.'[12]

Then came total and crushing defeat in the First World War. As Oster recorded: 'It was like being hit on the head with a hammer – the collapse in 1918 and the way the monarchy ended in a rickety affair of political parties.'[13] For a short while the distracted and divided German soldiery indulged in suicidal political strife, centred around their crudely formed anti-democratic, anti-republican, and anti-socialist beliefs. *Freikorps* (Free Corps), formed by unemployed officers, ranged the country, and crisis after crisis culminated in 1920 in the Kapp putsch, a right-wing attempt, supported by part of the Army, to overthrow the new republic. Then, in an effort to save the Army from itself, its Commander, Hans von Seeckt, firmly re-established the grand tradition of political disinterest, confirming and emphasising its status as a military necessity; with that, the Army was withdrawn from the political arena. In place of political intrigue, von Seeckt sought to foster the 'old spirit of silent, self-effacing devotion in the service of the Army'.[14] The soldiers were now ordered to ignore current politics, which most of them did with alacrity, only too glad to leave the unfamiliar, uncertain environment of Machiavellian cunning, stratagem, and guile for the sure, uncomplicated profession of soldiering, even though this might imply acceptance of the hated Weimar Republic – the democratic, republican interlude between the absolutism of the Kaiser and the dictatorship of the Führer. Unconditional obedience was reaffirmed as a fundamental of military service by Wilhelm Gröner, who announced in 1930: 'The soundness of any armed force rests upon unreserved, unlimited obedience. Soldiers who want to see whether an order suits their own ideas before they carry it out are absolutely worthless. Thoughts of that kind lead to mutiny, to the dissolution of the Reichswehr and eventually to a war of all against all.'[15]

Politics were outlawed. Von Seeckt had no doubt that the Army 'certainly must not be "political" in the party sense. "Hands off the Army!" is my cry to all parties. The Army serves the state and the state alone.'[16] Although concerned that the troops should understand what was happening around them, he refused to allow radically minded elements into the service, whatever their military prowess. He denied the soldier the right to vote, and he prohibited absolutely any connexion with political parties. As Oster said: 'We were all quite sure that under the political conditions of the times this was the only road to our objective, viz., getting the troops under discipline again, and making them the foundation and preparation for building up the Army . . . . The words "party" and "playing politics" had an unpleasant ting for us.'[17] General Siegfried Westphal recorded: 'The result was an indifferent and even uncritical attitude to political questions among the higher officers.'[18]

In such a way the small but highly influential Army became a reliable, if unthinking, pillar of the state, isolated entirely from allegiance to political creed or party. Certainly, Hitler had no cause to thank it for any assistance during his *Kampfzeit* (period of struggle) in the years leading up to his assumption of the chancellorship. Indeed, before 1933 he experienced little but opposition from its leaders: from such men as von Lossow, the Reichsheer commander in Bavaria, von Seeckt, Gröner, the Minister's successor, von Schleicher, and the Army Commander, von Hammerstein. This was demonstrated not only in November 1923, during the abortive Munich putsch when the military leaders in Bavaria refused to support Hitler's attempted coup, but also in 1930, when four young lieutenants of Leipzig were imprisoned for the dissemination of National Socialist propaganda in defiance of the ban on political action. After this last incident General Gröner felt it necessary to issue a special circular to senior officers; the action of the lieutenants, he asserted, had shattered 'faith in the Reichswehr as an unshakable rock of obedience and devotion to duty, on which is founded the whole edifice of the state'.[19] In another on the same subject, this time addressed to all officers, the Defence Minister emphasised that 'the Reichswehr is above all parties, and it serves the state alone. It must hold itself absolutely clear of party strife and of day-to-day political pressures. . . . All military measures and regulations are governed by this consideration alone.'[20] Should any officer feel unable to abide by them, resignation was his only honourable alternative. Removal was also resorted to; for example, General von Epp was dismissed because of his association with the NSDAP (he was later appointed a *Reichsleiter* [national leader] of the Party), as was Colonel Hierl (later to become Head of the Reich Labour Service), and Captain Röhm (the future SA leader). After the putsch in 1923, several officers were dismissed, and the staff of the Infantry School, who had supported Hitler, came under considerable disfavour; von Seeckt, who was given constitutional dictatorial powers during the emergency, even banned the National Socialist Party. Such was the attitude that made the Army, in

Westphal's words, 'a bulwark against threats to the republic either from the left or the right'.[21] The Reichsheer was, in short, the ideal of the non-political Army held so dear by western society.

Mighty though this principle of political independence might appear, however, it contained considerable weaknesses, the main being that isolation from politics brought with it a lack of understanding. As Hans Oster remarked: 'We were not born into the world of politics; we are not political fanatics fighting to get power in the state for one party. That is not what we were taught to do.'[22] One of the saddest victims of this political disability was Field-Marshal Wilhelm Keitel, Chief of the Armed Forces High Command from 1938 until the end of the Second World War. In the quiet, introspective atmosphere of his cell at Nuremberg in 1945, he was to write:

> 'Although the education of a professional officer is thorough, it is only one-sided; the intellectual and political education . . . is as a rule less complete. This has nothing to do with a question of intelligence . . . but I want to stress the fact that the training of a good soldier was fundamentally different from an education for a purely liberal or academic profession. The officer's profession is not a liberal profession: a soldier's cardinal virtue is obedience . . . the very opposite of criticism. . . . The consequence of all this is that . . . the one-sided education of the professional soldier described above results in a lack of ability to make a stand against theses which are not part of his real territory. Nothing is more convincing to a soldier than success.'[23]

Political ignorance resulted in a further, related, symptom: a lack of political balance. It was this that Dr Julius Leber, a leading Social-Democrat, understood when he wrote:

> 'I fear the Reichswehr has been built up on a colossal mistake of von Seeckt. He believed that discipline was enough, and that obedience to the commander's will was a sufficient guarantee for the proper functioning of the Army. But no unit in these times will place itself unreservedly in the hands of its commander. The links between the soldiers and the public are far too intimate for that. . . . It is not enough to give a soldier orders. He must have a mental image of what his task consists of. . . . He needs not only discipline but other kinds of incentive. . . . It is axiomatic nowadays that rulers and ruled, their ideas and their aims, form a single whole with a common purpose and must be sustained by common ideals. . . . If these ideals and symbols are withheld from young men in the Army, they will run after other ideals and find themselves other symbols – substitutes such as the recollection of imperial glories and patriotic language'[24]

But it was not just the young men who possessed an emotional yearning, so typical of political naivety, for something more than was offered by the republican régime; the whole Army, including the senior generals, suffered from this lack of political balance, a loss which caused it to live in the imperial past and for a new future, but not for the republican present. The historian, Herbert Rosinski, summed this up in 1939, when he wrote:

> 'To those who did not themselves experience it, it is almost impossible to convey what the First World War meant to the German people. The peaceful and prosperous development enjoyed without any serious interruption for nearly half a century was suddenly shattered and the German nation found itself overnight at war with half the world; it threw all its strength, wealth, and faith into that struggle – to wake up, after four years of unparalleled exertion and brilliant victories, not only defeated, but outlawed and branded by a world whose triumph it could not understand and who made no effort to understand it. The result was that it lost its mental balance; the economic distress after the war increased the disease and defeated all attempts at internal consolidation, until the Nazi movement, playing with considerable skill upon the psychological and material distress of the masses, rose on the ruins of the Weimar Republic and offered to the distracted nation the quack remedy of its emotional creed.'[25]

Thus, while the vast majority of soldiers within the Army held fast to the Seecktian doctrine of *Überparteilichkeit*, considering their profession to be apart from, and above, politics, they found the emergence of National Socialism, together with other nationalist creeds within Germany, not entirely unwelcome. The social composition of the Army was, after all, one that had traditionally leaned towards the right in politics. The officers came mainly either from established military families, from the nobility, or from the professional middle classes; the other ranks were recruited from the country rather than the towns, from that part of the population that was conservative rather than radical. To such men, the new movement was, at the very least, tolerable; it provided for the politically uneducated some kind of substitute for the vacuum left by the disappearance of the monarchy. It appeared to exemplify the autocratic Germanic spirit, the return of which was eagerly awaited by so many, and to provide an alternative to the decline in the fortunes of the nation and the Army. It stood against the terms of the Versailles Treaty and for general rearmament; against the atmosphere of Marxism, socialism, and pacificism, and for the respect and glory of the Reich and its Army; against the democratic 'Government of the November Criminals', and for the concepts of authority, discipline, and national regeneration. It was easy to ignore Hitler's ill-defined socialist doctrines; there were few officers who could not but feel some sympathy for a politician who promised: 'We will see to it that, when we have come to power, out of the present Reichswehr shall rise the great Army of the German people.'[26] The individual motives of those who looked favourably on the new creed ranged from ambition and pragmatism to idealism, but the general feeling was summed up by Oster, who, when under interrogation, said: 'With the upheaval of 1933 . . . the soldiers felt released from the strain which the "System" had laid on their consciences. The return to a vigorous patriotic policy, the rearmament, the reintroduction of military service – to the officers, this all meant a return to older traditions. Under the "System" soldiers had done their work because it was their duty; but these features of the National Socialists' work of reconstruction had warmed their hearts.'[27]

However, for a tiny minority of German officers, those at the very top of the military leadership, this loss of political balance was not simply a naïve sympathy for right-wing, nationalist ideas, but a desire for direct interference in the government of the nation. These men were unrepresentative of their heritage and caste, a product peculiar to the extraordinary times in which they lived. Under Bismarck, the General Staff, influential though it was, possessed no control over either the domestic or the foreign policy of Germany, the Iron Chancellor being little-inclined to allow the military to meddle in his jealously guarded province. Von Moltke's idea of a preventive war against Russia in 1887 received short shrift, while the intrigues of his deputy, von Waldersee, were purely of a personal nature and not in the tradition of the General Staff (as a result, he lasted in his post only for two years). Under Wilhelm II, this position remained unaltered, as evidenced by the relative neglect of the Army in favour of the Navy during peacetime, and it was only during the First World War that, in the absence of strong, coordinated political and military direction, the generals first took an active hand in the machinery of government. Behind the constitution of Imperial Germany there grew, from 1916, a military dictatorship of the General Staff dominated by two giants, Generals von Hindenburg and Ludendorff; only national collapse in 1918 was to bring this to an end.

After the war, following this new precedent, a few officers of no political experience, but of the highest military seniority, took the principle of *Über-parteilichkeit* one stage further. In their eyes, the soldiers' role was not that of passive onlookers, standing by while the various political parties wrought what they would with the fortunes of the nation; rather, their duty was to save Germany from the ravages of the politicians, whether of left- or right-wing persuasion, and to assist it to regain its former greatness. Von Seeckt first propounded this idea in his attempt to influence national policy. He believed that 'the Army and its leaders must be assured of their rightful position in public life . . .'.[28] In the pursuance of this aim he set his eyes on nothing less than the presidency of the Reich. But his ineptitude, together with his ill-concealed contempt for politicians, led to his downfall. The next arch-proponent of this thesis was General Kurt von Schleicher, who was appointed Reich Defence Minister on 2 June 1932. Politically ambitious, he advocated the dissolution of the despised democratic institutions of the

Republic and the creation of a virtual military dictatorship. This, he intended, would govern the nation under the authority of the President, the revered Field-Marshal von Hindenburg, by virtue of Article 48 of the Constitution, which allowed for rule by emergency decree. The idea behind this policy was explained by von Schleicher's devotee, General Curt Freiherr von Hammerstein-Equord, who wrote in 1929, one year before his elevation to command the Army: 'The revolution has taught the German Army officer to discriminate between the provisional régime of the state and its permanent identity, and to serve the latter, which is symbolised by the Reich President, elevated above ephemeral ministries and incoherent governmental bodies.'[29]

It was with such justification that a handful of the most senior generals took upon themselves the right of determining the political course of the nation. It inevitably brought them into opposition with the National Socialists: not only did they, the aristocrats, feel an instinctive dislike for the violent methods of the NSDAP and for the bombast and crudity of its leaders, but they also abhorred its challenge to von Hindenburg's authority represented by Hitler's candidature for the presidency in 1932, and the clear threat to the Army's military supremacy manifested by the party's paramilitary force, the SA, the *Sturm Abteilung*, (Storm Detachment), which, by 1933, numbered some 400,000 men. Gröner, appointed Reich Minister for the Interior in late 1931 in addition to his post as Defence Minister, warned the Army that the National Socialists 'are to be distinguished from the Communists only by the national base on which they take their footing. . . . In order to use it [the Army] for the political aims of their party, they attempt to dazzle us. . . .'[30] In opposing National Socialism, Gröner's and von Schleicher's cooperation with the government could hardly have been greater, and in order to preserve Germany from Hitler and his followers they had no hesitation in advocating the restoration of the monarchy, as well as the expansion of the Reichswehr to rival the right-wing paramilitary organisations, especially the SA.

The political machinations of the Army's leaders in the last years of the Weimar Republic have no place here; suffice it to say that by the beginning of 1933 they had come to occupy, however uncertainly, the highest offices of state. Von Schleicher, in addition to his post as Reich Defence Minister, had been appointed Reich Chancellor and Reich Commissioner for Prussia on 2 December 1932, and he was faithfully supported by the two most important men in the Army – von Hammerstein, the Commander-in-Chief, and Wilhelm Adam, Chief of the Troop Office (General Staff). The Bendlerstrasse, where the military commands were situated, and the Wilhelmstrasse, Berlin's 'Whitehall', were now as one.

Yet, within one month, von Schleicher had met his downfall, von Hammerstein had been isolated, and Hitler had been offered, and had accepted, the office of Reich Chancellor. Von Schleicher had failed in his attempt to split the National Socialist Party and suppress the SA, and, worse still, he had lost the confidence of von Hindenburg, who was disillusioned by his constant, devious, and inconsistent *politiking*. Von Hammerstein, too, had aroused the suspicions of the President, who rejected all his efforts to proffer advice. The initiative passed from the generals, and the politicians immediately made it theirs. On 28 January 1933, von Schleicher resigned together with his cabinet; within thirty-six hours Hitler had been invited to become Chancellor by von Hindenburg. The generals' brief and unsuccessful flirtation with political power was over.

This, many historians argue, was when the Army should have acted. That it failed to do so, thereby ignoring von Hammerstein's promise that 'the Reichswehr will never allow them [the National Socialists] to come to power',[31] has been seen as the first occasion on which the Army failed in its duty towards the German nation. It is claimed that, in permitting the National Socialists to take the reins of government, the generals were acting purely from their own short-term, selfish interests. Sir John Wheeler-Bennett has alleged that they:

'. . . wished to secure for the benefit of the Reichswehr, all that could be gained to advantage from the Nazi movement, while dominating and controlling it in policy. They were still dreaming in their blindness of a martial state in which the masses, galvanised and inspired by modified National Socialism, would be directed and disciplined by the Army. They may well have had it within their power in those fateful January days to combat successfully the final consummation of that National Socialist rise to power, which they, by their own equivocal policy, had helped to promote; but they did not wish to do so.'[32]

This is to misunderstand the dilemma that confronted, and entrapped, the military leaders. Isolated from the centre of power around the President, they lacked unanimity of aim and organisation, and were troubled by the thought of breaking their traditional allegience to the legally constituted political executive. Moreover, aware that a large part of the Army would be not unsympathetic to the triumph of National Socialism, they held strong fears that, as a result, the troops would refuse to obey orders to take action against the new régime. After all, no support could now be expected from von Hindenburg, their Supreme Commander. Nor did the Army leaders look on Hitler's legal assumption of power as the worst of the political alternatives then facing the country. Von Hindenburg was still President and Head of the Reichswehr, and was thought to be able to keep his Chancellor in check. Furthermore, only three of the eleven members in the new cabinet were National Socialists, and it might have been assumed they would be swamped by the eight conservatives. For this reason, it was considered safer to have Hitler in the government than out of it. Both von Schleicher and von Hammerstein believed that a National Socialist/Communist revolt would follow the creation of a right-wing nationalist government under the two main contenders, von Papen and von Hugenberg, and that the resulting civil war would leave Germany defenceless against any attack launched by Poland, an eventuality which at that time was considered to be far from remote. Moreover, the generals saw no apparent reason why Hitler would retain power any more successfully than previous chancellors, especially as the splits and factions within the NSDAP, together with its waning public support, were increasingly apparent.

Had the Army and its leaders been united in opposition to Hitler, could they at that time have prevented his accession to power? The senior generals were aware of the considerable risk of worsening the internal situation in Germany through direct military intervention; studies had shown that there existed the distinct possibility of the 100,000 strong Army, devoid of heavy artillery and tanks, being defeated in civil war by the SA, already four times its numerical strength, supported by other right-wing parties, and possibly the Communists. Even had the soldiers triumphed, there was no guarantee that the nation would return to a government and a political order any better than that which previously existed. Indeed, the reverse might have been the case: the bitterness and divisions caused within society by the Army's intervention could so easily have created an even worse situation. And, whatever the possible outcome, the fact remained that it was neither legal, nor the practice in western countries for the military to interfere in the proper constitutional workings of the nation – certainly not without the specific orders of the Head of State and Supreme Commander. The National Socialists' accession to power was entirely legal, and, moreover, was allowed and ratified by von Hindenburg. Where the Supreme Commander led, the Army was to follow.

Such was the position of the generals in January 1933. They had before them no room for manoeuvre. It would have been a matter of some surprise had the Army moved to prevent Hitler's chancellorship, and its failure to do so provides no basis for condemnation. The generals could only stand to one side of the political arena, adopt the air of interested spectators, and await events. The once-influential German Army was powerless to intervene; as a political creature, it was impotent.

2

First Years

*We cannot change politics; we must do our duty
silently.*

GENERAL WERNER VON FRITSCH
Commander-in-Chief of the German
Army, 1934–38

In 1933 there began the curious and tragic relationship between Hitler and
his senior military advisers, which, within little more than five years, led to
the subjection of the Army to the dictator's will, and, within a further seven,
to its complete destruction on the field of battle. About this process there was
an air of inevitability, as if, from the moment Hitler took office, the soldiers'
fate was sealed. But it should not be thought that, in the years leading to
1938, the dictator was the coldly calculating, devious politician so often
portrayed by historians, that his sole constancy lay in a deep contempt for
the generals and a burning desire to subvert their independence. The
opposite is nearer the truth, as Hitler's summary of his early guiding
principle illustrates: 'It has always been my view that we can achieve our
goals only with the Reichswehr, and never against it.'[1]

Only after 1938, in the middle and later years of the Third Reich, did
Hitler turn sharply from his *laissez-faire* policy towards the Army to one of
strict control and, ultimately, of complete subjection. This arose simply out
of his frustration at his generals' ever-increasing opposition to his policies, an
opposition which struck at the very basis of his long-term aims: rearmament
and foreign expansion. His faith in his military advisers weakened, he found
himself forced to render them impotent and to transform their successors
into mere executors of his will – a not unnatural action, and one achieved
with far less suffering than by other dictators.

Leaving aside his social, economic, racial, and foreign policies, Hitler's
overriding political philosophy was unequivocal: he, and he alone, would
determine the direction of the Reich, and, by so doing, would select the goals
to be attained and the methods to be used. By August 1934 he had acquired
total power within the state: as Chancellor he possessed supreme executive
authority; through the Enabling Act of 1933 he was given supreme legisla-
tive authority; and, from the merger of the office of Chancellor with that of
President on the death of von Hindenburg, he assumed supreme command

of the Armed Forces. Furthermore, the Reich Defence Law of 21 May 1935 gave him the right to declare states of emergency, mobilisation, and war. All the major decisions between 1933 and 1945 were Hitler's, and his alone; the views of Party associates, cabinet ministers, industrial magnates, Junker landowners, and generals counting for nothing if not in accord with his own ideas. Indeed, their advice was often not even sought. Reich ministers were reduced to the role of departmental heads, Party leaders to organisers. In the Byzantine power politics that characterised the Third Reich, only one law was inviolate: the Führer's authority was unchallengeable, his decision supreme. Hitler may have acknowledged his need for professional advisers to provide the Army with superior military qualities, but he nevertheless stated his intention of not allowing himself 'to be ordered about by the commanders-in-chief. I shall make war.'[3] In his opinion the generals were 'sterile . . . imprisoned in the coils of their technical knowledge',[4] and, 'in spite of the lessons of the war, they want to behave like chivalrous knights. . . . I have no use for knights. I need revolution.'[5]

From the very beginning of his chancellorship, Hitler displayed his intention to brook no interference in his policies from his military advisers. In his determinaton to eliminate political opposition, he engineered, with the active support of some of the more senior generals, the isolation and then the resignation of von Hammerstein, who left his post on 1 February 1934; and in his ambition to exercise control over Germany's rearmament and foreign policy, he created the Reich Defence Council on 4 April 1933, a body entrusted with the task of planning and coordinating the nation's activities for war. Composed of the Ministers for the Interior, Foreign Affairs, Finance, Propaganda, and Defence under the chairmanship of the Chancellor, the Council had the effect of bringing the Armed Forces more closely under the control of the government, and, therefore, of Hitler, while at the same time ending the traditional position of the military as the sole advisers to the Head of State on such matters. Satisfied with this, he took no further steps to bring the Army under his control until 1938. Until then, the position remained as Guderian summed it up: 'Any attempt to widen the General Staff corps officers' appreciation of the political situation was prevented, first by the traditional limitation of their interests to purely military matters and, secondly, by Hitler's principle according to which every fragment of the machinery which controlled the state was kept in a sort of specialised, water-tight compartment and no man might know more than was essential for the performance of his own particular job.'[6] The days of power, of Ludendorff, von Hindenburg, Gröner, von Seeckt, and von Schleicher, were now no more. This restriction of interests was met with relief by the Army, the great majority of officers believing, with Guderian, that 'policy is not laid down by soldiers, but by politicians';[7] and expressing their thanks, with General von Choltitz, for entrusting the soldier once again with the 'purely objective tasks of the service'.[8] These men understood something that historians, in their anxiety to accredit to Hitler nothing but evil intent, have overlooked: that the Führer's actions were but those of a determined politician, desirous simply of exerting his influence over national policy; that, until 1938, his attitude towards the Army and its leaders was unequivocally one of harmonious cooperation, even of friendship, the product of convenience rather than of single-minded ambition.

On assuming power, Hitler possessed not the least desire to add the running of the Army to the already onerous task of governing the nation, and, doubting their abilities as much as he feared their ambitions, he had not the slightest intention of placing the military under the control of his political subordinates. Hitler's requirement was for an Army loyal to his person, responsive to his policies, and, in common with all other organisations within the Third Reich, receptive to the ideology of National Socialism. For the rest, he intended it to be the sole bearer of arms in the defence of the nation, his chief, although not sole, adviser on military affairs, completely independent of, and impervious to, Party interference, and fully capable of ordering its own affairs as it alone thought fit. As such, Hitler's intentions were no different from those of most other political leaders. Although he recognised the importance of the Army in the political structure of the nation, he was anxious, nevertheless, to ensure that it provided no damaging opposition to his own policies. As in democracies, alike with dictatorships, the Army of the Third Reich was to be seen, not heard; its leaders, while retaining primacy over military matters, prevented from taking part in purely political debate and decision. In his attitude towards its ideological outlook, Hitler differed little from national leaders throughout history. Even in liberal parliamentary democracies with small, professional armies, the soldiers have been expected to reflect the general political and social outlook of the time, being condemned and derided should they remain hide-bound or caste-ridden. National Socialism after 1933 became not merely a party programme but a national creed, its tenets characterising the Germany of that age. It would have been strange indeed had the Army remained isolated from, or unreceptive to, its dogma.

Hitler's spirit of friendship towards the Army was evident from the moment he assumed office. Just twenty-four hours after his appointment as Chancellor, he addressed, without awaiting an invitation, troops of the Berlin garrison on the spirit of the new Germany. A few days later, on 3 February 1933, he delivered a speech of more than two hours' duration to a gathering of the leading officers of the services, in which he promised them rearmament and the 'strengthening of the will to defence by all possible means',[9] reasserted their key position within the state against the rival claims of the SA, and confirmed that they were to remain 'unpolitical and above parties'.[10] At its conclusion, as the generals emerged from the room, their suspicions radically undermined, one was overheard saying: 'At any rate, no Chancellor has ever expressed himself so warmly in favour of defence.'[11] The opening of the new Reichstag on 21 March provided Hitler with a further opportunity to display his respectful recognition of the Army's position. The ceremony was held at the old garrison church at Potsdam, the home of Prussian militarism, and Hitler made a favourable impression by bowing low before the aged Field-Marshal von Hindenburg. This occasion was seen as a symbol of the unification of the new movement with the old Prusso-German tradition, confirming the extinction of the Weimar Republic. Field-Marshal von Mackensen commented: 'We German officers used to be called representatives of reaction, whereas we were really bearers of tradition. It is in the sense of that tradition that Hitler spoke to us, so wonderfully and so directly from the heart, at Potsdam.'[12]

But it was to be Hitler's lack of interference in internal Army affairs that made the greatest impact on the soldiers. He refused to nominate his SA leader, and former Army captain, to succeed von Hammerstein, as many feared he might do; he yielded gracefully when his nominee for the post of Army Commander, von Reichenau, was rejected by the President; he made no attempt to influence the basis of promotion for officers, or to alter the judgements of courts-martial; he offered no criticisms during briefings and exercises; he usually signed unread the documents presented to him by Friedrich Hossbach, his military adjutant; he more often than not accepted unquestioningly the advice of his military subordinates; and he took no part in the planning of operations. He always gave the appearance of complete trust in his generals, and treated the new Army Commander-in-Chief, von Fritsch, with 'respectful discretion'.[13] The generals were shown only the charming side of his character, and were aware that when necessary he made a conscious effort to adapt his chaotic working routine to their needs.

Such was Hitler's praise of his servicemen that, at a meeting of senior officers and Party officials on 3 January 1935, he declared: 'The Army and the Party are the two pillars of state. . . . Then someone from the Party may come to me and say "All right, my Führer, but General So-and-So both speaks and works against you". Then I shall say "I don't believe it". And if the man says "But I can show you written evidence, my Führer", then I shall tear the scrap of paper up, for my faith in the Armed Forces is unshakable.'[14] On one occasion Hitler went so far as to admit to the generals certain failings within his own National Socialist movement: 'I know that you accuse me of many wrong things which exist in the Party. I admit that you are one hundred per cent correct, but you must remember . . . I still have to work primarily with persons of low quality.'[15] He constantly emphasised the debt he and his Party owed to the Army. At the Nuremberg rally in 1936, for example, he declared: 'The Army educated us. We have all come from the Army, those of us who became the Party storm-troops and the motor corps.'[16] He even found it within himself to ascribe to the Army a decisive role in his own success, such was his desire to court its friendship, when he remarked, quite wrongly: 'If the Reichswehr had not stood at our side during the days of the revolution, then we should not be standing here today.'[17]

Positive proof of Hitler's good intentions towards the Army came on 30

June 1934, with his eradication of the SA leadership in what has come to be known as the Night of the Long Knives. The *Sturm Abteilung,* under the command of SA *Stabschef* (Chief of Staff) Ernest Röhm, had become potentially the most powerful organisation in Germany, by 1934 numbering some three million uniformed members. As the paramilitary formation of the National Socialist Party, it had been indispensable to Hitler's rise to power, the dictator recognising this when he told his storm-troopers on 7 May 1933: 'You have been till now the Guard of the National Revolution; you have carried this revolution to victory; with your name it will be associated for all time.'[18] But the success of the SA, coupled with the beliefs and actions of its more prominent and politically extreme members, ensured its ultimate downfall. The storm-troopers had by then come to arouse considerable uneasiness, even fear, in the rest of the Party, seeming to threaten Hitler's position as effective leader of the German nation. The SA leadership saw itself as 'the incorruptible guarantors of the fulfilment of the German revolution',[19] and believed that Hitler and his supporters were betraying its basic principles. At the same time the SA was regarded by its leaders as the future German Army, a people's militia based on new principles of organisation, discipline, service, and political commitment.

Röhm, who liked to see himself as 'the new army's Scharnhorst',[20] expressed it thus: 'We have to produce something new, don't you see? . . . The generals are a lot of old fogeys. They never have a new idea.'[21] In February 1934 he felt so confident of his position that he sent a letter to the Head of the Defence Minister's Office, von Reichenau, with the pronouncement: 'I regard the Reichswehr now only as a training school for the German people. The conduct of war, and therefore of mobilisation as well, in future is the task of the SA.'[22] Armed SA headquarter guard formations were formed, and Röhm even went as far as to initiate discussions with the French military attaché in Berlin.

The Army, understandably, was deeply alarmed. So, too, was Hitler, although his concern was not entirely for his own fate. Many had been expecting Hitler to make the choice between the SA and the Army in a manner favourable to his political storm-troopers; he was, after all, the Supreme Commander of the SA. As von Fritsch was to record: 'Every thoughtful soldier, I suppose, shared my belief that the storm-troops were meant to take the Army's place. . . . I myself should have thought it perfectly natural if this had been the Führer's intention. All the same, it was frightening to think of the consequences – the total destruction of the Army's foundations. . . .'[23] In the event, Hitler unhesitatingly supported the Reichswehr in its claim to be the rightful, and sole, bearer of arms in the defence of the Reich. This was not simply a move of convenience which would serve the double aim of reassuring the generals while curtailing Röhm's power; it was a conscious choice of principle arising from his belief in maintaining the Army's traditional role. His position was made so unequivocal, and devoid of any reciprocal conditions, for it to be anything else.

Had he wished, it was not beyond Hitler's political skill at least to attempt to remove the danger to his own position posed by the SA leadership, while retaining the capacity of the SA organisation to develop into a National Socialist people's army. That he did not contemplate such a course is evidence enough that he saw nothing but impracticabilities and disaster, military as well as political, in his storm-troopers' plans. There can be little doubt that the relative levels of military expertise in the Army and the SA, and the latter's reputation as an ill-disciplined street-fighting outfit, made Hitler prefer that German youth was trained in a field-grey uniform rather than in a brownshirt.

In May 1933, after strong warnings from his Defence Minister, von Blomberg, Hitler sanctioned an agreement in military matters reached between the Reichswehr and the SA, which provided for the Army's unquestioned superiority. This he followed by a series of five speeches, each giving clear support to his soldiers. On 28 February 1934, before a conference of the Reichswehr and SA leaders in the Great Hall of the War Ministry, and in response to a plea from the Defence Minister for a ruling, Hitler, in the words of one of those present, stated:

> '. . . his decision to reject the suggestions of Röhm to form a SA militia and to affirm his resolution to build a people's army on the lines of the old army out of the Reichswehr. He based this on examples from military history, to prove that a militia, such as Röhm suggested, was not efficient for national defence. The SA would have to limit itself to political tasks. For the transitional period, he declared himself to be in agreement with the suggestion of the War Minister to employ the SA for tasks of frontier protection and for pre-military training. . . . Otherwise the Armed Forces must be the only bearer of arms of the nation. . . . After this address, the feeling of contentment reigned amongst the military audience that the Army High Command had scored a notable success over the Party organisation, and that it appeared as if Hitler wished to rely first and foremost on the Army.'[24]

Von Blomberg and Röhm were then asked to sign an agreement to confirm Hitler's policy statement. The SA leader was so furious at this, that he exclaimed to his colleagues a short while later: 'What that ridiculous corporal [Hitler] says means nothing to us. . . . I have not the slightest intention of keeping this agreement. Hitler is a traitor and at the very least must go on leave. . . . If we can't get there with him, we'll get there without him.'[25] This comment was quickly relayed to the 'ridiculous corporal', whose reaction was: 'We must allow this affair to ripen fully.'[26]

Despite Hitler's assurances, however, the Army remained apprehensive of the SA's intentions. Friction continued, especially at local level, and certain *Wehrkreise* (area commands) began preparations to meet an unspecified emergency, which was in reality the feared storm-troopers' coup. The Army dismissed Röhm, whose known homosexuality was an anathema to the military, from the officers' league, and rifles were placed by the side of desks in the Bendlerstrasse. Although most officers did not believe events would come to a fight, some actively plotted for such an outcome, believing it to be the only method of ridding themselves of the danger from the SA. From the end of April the storm-troopers' enemies had begun to prepare, and combine, their forces, while at the same time bringing increased pressure to bear on a still-reluctant Führer to act decisively. This was no easy task, for Hitler remained loyal to his old friend Röhm, and there was no truth in the suggestion that he coldly and dispassionately engineered the downfall of the man and the organisation to whom he owed so much. But, by rumour and falsehood, Heydrich, Himmler, and Göring managed at last to persuade the Führer that Röhm and his subordinates were actively planning a putsch to overthrow the new régime. On 29 June 1934, Hitler finally decided to take action. In the early hours of the following day, units of the SS, with arms and transport provided by the Army, went into action against their former comrades; by 4.00 a.m. on 2 July, when the killings ended, more than a hundred men lay dead.

The events of 30 June achieved many goals. The SA, although it remained a large Party organisation, was rendered politically and militarily impotent; Hitler's authority was extended; Göring was satisfied at the removal of a rival; Himmler was left free to develop his SS empire; and the Army was confirmed in its position as sole arms-bearer in the defence of the nation. On 13 July Hitler announced: 'My promise to him [von Hindenburg] to preserve the Army as a non-political instrument of the nation is as binding for me from innermost conviction as from my pledged word.'[27]

So much for the attitude of Hitler towards the military, but what of the Army leadership which, in January 1933, had been so antipathetic towards the National Socialists? Within a year it underwent a considerable transformation. The 'big four' – the Defence Minister, the Head of the Minister's Office, the Chief of the Army Leadership, and the Head of the Troop Office – in whose hands the direction of the Armed Forces and the Army lay, had changed. In place of von Schleicher had come von Blomberg; instead of von Bredow, there was von Reichenau; von Hammerstein had been replaced by von Fritsch; and in Adam's former post was Beck.

At the head of the German Armed Forces stood Werner Eduard Fritz von Blomberg, appointed Reich Defence Minister with the rank of *General der Infanterie* at the age of fifty-four, one day before Hitler gained the chancellorship. Von Blomberg was a strange mixture of a man. Tall, erect, blue-eyed, and radiating presence wherever he went, he was nicknamed 'the Siegfried with the monocle' because of his physical appearance, 'the Rubber Lion', because of the insubstantial personality that seemed to lie beneath his vital exterior, and 'Hitler Youth Quex', after the character of a famous propaganda film, because he idolised the Führer. Ironically, one of von Hindenburg's reasons for appointing von Blomberg to serve in the Reich Cabinet had been his belief that he, in contrast with von Schleicher, typified 'the soldier above politics'.

Frank, open, and well-liked, von Blomberg revealed considerable energy in, and dedication to, his work. His military career was impeccable: he had been awarded the much-coveted Pour le Mérite (the highest decoration of the Prussian Armed Forces) for his brilliant planning work during the First World War, and, in 1927 as a staff officer, he had reached the highest position of Chief of the Troop Office. Falling out with von Schleicher, he was transferred to command Wehrkreis I, East Prussia, in 1930, and it was while there that he was appointed leader of the German military delegation to the disarmament conference at Geneva in 1932.

Able professional soldier he might have been, but politically von Blomberg was naïve, and much restricted in his outlook. By temperament he leant towards totalitarianism, albeit for the best of motives – stability in society, the improvement in living standards, and the greatness of the nation. Lacking mental balance, von Blomberg was a combination of many strong drives; an emotional man, moody, enthusiastic and impulsive, he was at the same time vacillating and easily influenced. On a trip to the Soviet Union in 1928 he was impressed deeply by what he thought to be the qualities of its régime, so much so that he later confessed he was near to becoming a Communist. But, like so many in Germany, he found those aspects of Communism he considered so praiseworthy to be present also in National Socialism; he saw Hitler as the saviour of the nation, a man of strength and authority whom he could respect, one who propounded an ideal with which he could identify. Von Blomberg's idolisation of the man and the message was that of a romantic fantasist rather than of a hard-headed political realist. He initially gave Hitler willing and unhesitating support, fully believing that by doing so he was acting in the best interests of both the country and the Army; his reply to objections on this score was: 'The Führer is cleverer than we are, he will plan and do everything correctly.'[28]

For this, von Blomberg has incurred the censure of many, including a large number of former German officers. In his memoirs, Hossbach was particularly damning:

> 'The fund of trust which the German people, since earliest times, and since, and despite, the loss of the war in 1918, placed in the soldier involved for Blomberg the moral obligation of being the advocate of reason and of forming a barrier against totalitarian claims on the part of the state. It is the tragedy of modern German history that Blomberg was, neither as soldier nor as statesman, a strong personality, forceful and creative, guiding and leading. His intelligence lacked the foundation of a firm character.'[29]

But this is to over-emphasise the Defence Minister's weaknesses. In Nuremberg prison he wrote: 'Had I been a spineless tool in the hands of

Hitler, as some generals now assume, then he probably would have dealt differently with me [in 1938]. . . . The other generals heard nothing of my protests and showdowns with Hitler.'[30] Certainly, if von Blomberg had been the tame executor of Hitler's wishes, the dictator would have had no reason to dismiss him in 1938. The importance of von Blomberg in preserving not only the Army's independence of the Party machine but also its voice in the affairs of state should not be neglected, for, as General Warlimont stated: '. . . be it remembered that, well on into the war, Hitler was apt to give vent to his recurring dislike of generals, the General Staff and its training, and the mental outlook of the Army as a whole, in these words: "All that goes back to the time when Blomberg's broad shoulders came between me and the Wehrmacht." '[31]

Initially, however, the man who, on 29 January 1933, took charge of the Bendlerstrasse could not have suited Hitler better. Indeed, he was every political leader's dream: an able professional soldier, totally loyal to the régime, and concerned that those under his authority should be likewise. Von Blomberg immediately embarked on a reformation of the Defence Ministry, replacing von Schleicher's men with his own. His first and most important appointment was von Reichenau, who, on 1 February 1933 at the age of forty-eight, became the new Head of the Minister's Office. Formerly von Blomberg's Chief of Staff in Wehrkreis I, von Reichenau was now to be his principal assistant and deputy, and was thus chosen as much for his political beliefs as for his military and organisational abilities.

Like his chief, von Reichenau was a first-class soldier, but, in contrast, he was also an individualist, who, brimming with life, was unable to accept constraints on his actions. Although an aristocrat by birth, he had lost faith in the destiny of his own class, and, although a senior officer through well-deserved promotion, he possessed little respect for the conventions of rigid discipline and strict order that characterised the old Army. He invariably treated his men with a familiarity that did not breed contempt, and his superiors with an irreverence that aroused resentment. An anglophile, a lover of fast cars, and an athlete of considerable ability, von Reichenau was a member of the International Olympic Committee. Lacking the emotionalism of his superior, he possessed a sober, forceful personality of drive, determination, and considerable ambition, his hard exterior accurately representing an intelligent, calculating mind that delighted in taking considered decisions. Highly critical, unable to suffer fools gladly, von Reichenau was saved from isolation from the world by a magnanimity, a sense of humour, and a regard for his men which earned him high respect.

Von Reichenau's character was reflected in his political beliefs. If von Blomberg was the apotheosis of the political romantic, von Reichenau was the archetype of the political realist. Although initially an adherent of National Socialism, a frequent guest at Hitler's table, and constantly accused of being a 'Party general', he was no blind, subservient follower of the Führer. What had first attracted him to the new creed was its revolutionary outlook, with the prospect of throwing off the dead-weight of the past and substituting in its place effective action beneficial to both the Army and the nation. But he always detested the cruder aspects of National Socialist philosophy and its personalities, among whom he included the SS leaders; and, in time, he came ever more to disagree fundamentally with Hitler's policies. He attended dinners for Jewish front-fighters of the First World War; he expressed dislike for the excesses of nationalism; he explored the possibilities of instituting a youth movement to rival the Hitler Youth; he contradicted Hitler's foreign policy; and, by the beginning of the Second World War, he had become so disillusioned that he had entered into subversive opposition to the régime he once supported so ardently. For the Army, it was a tragedy that he never fulfilled his erstwhile ambition to become its Commander-in-Chief; although not recognised at the time, he, alone among the generals, possessed that combination of political insight, courage, drive, and conviction necessary to halt the progress of the later years of Hitler's dictatorship

Those selected for the posts of Army Commander and Chief of Staff were men of a different stamp, relationships between the two groups often being strained as a result. Werner Thomas Ludwig von Fritsch, who, on 1 February 1934 at the age of fifty-three, was made Chief of the Army Leadership with the rank of *General der Artillerie*, was a man of exceptional military ability, but possessing no political skill or interest whatsoever. Such qualifications, in fact, suited Hitler and von Blomberg, who, although they had pressed for von Reichenau's elevation to the post, had been forced to accept von Fritsch owing to the strenuous advocacy of von Hindenburg, whose appointment it was. In the President's eyes, von Fritsch possessed everything von Reichenau lacked: no political sympathies, a long experience of command, and the general respect of his colleagues.

Of von Fritsch, the French ambassador recorded that his 'haughty and surly exterior covered a human wit and a more amicable nature than appeared'.[32] Indeed the new Army Commander was an humanitarian with a deep, undemonstrative religious piety of a strict Protestant nature, a high personal morality, popular, and with an authority in the Army greater even than that of von Seeckt, whose friend and pupil he was. A self-contained man, von Fritsch admitted: 'I have never spoken to others about myself. I simply cannot do that.'[33] Nevertheless he exhibited considerable personal charm. Apart from his intense love of horses, von Fritsch's only other interest lay in his work, into which he sometimes appeared to retreat from the unpalatable realities of the political world around him. His monocle, needed to correct a serious weakness in his left eye, was also a feature of his personal defences. He himself said: 'I wear a monocle so that my face remains stiff, especially when I confront that man [Hitler].'[34]

Politically, von Fritsch was inadequately equipped to meet the challenges of the new National Socialist state. His belief in the ideal of the 'soldier above politics' was implicit. In 1937 he wrote: 'I have made it my guiding rule to limit myself to the military field alone, and to keep myself apart from any political activity. I lack everything necessary for politics. Furthermore, I am convinced that the less I speak in public, the more speedily I can fulfil my military task.'[35] As events were to show, von Fritsch was no easy lapdog of the politicians, shrinking from any connexion with them, so much so that he sent back the golden Party badge presented to him by Hitler as a singular honour. He made no attempt to disguise his contempt for the National Socialists, soon becoming renowned for making loud, uncomplimentary comments whenever he felt inclined. In his directives, von Fritsch avoided the clichés of National Socialism so beloved of von Blomberg, and his uncompromising attitude to the introduction of ideology into service life was well-known. Many were the soldiers he protected when they became embroiled in political scraps, his sole disciplinary action often being to warn them not to speak so loud in public again.

Like his chief, Ludwig Beck, the new Head of the Troop Office, was regarded favourably by all, even by those who sought good relations with the new régime. Appointed by von Hammerstein on 1 October 1933 during a routine reshuffle, he, too, was an excellent soldier and military thinker, his outstanding reputation coming in part from his brilliant planning of the withdrawal, under the most difficult circumstances, of German forces totalling some ninety divisions at the end of the First World War; and from his authorship of *Die Truppenführung,* the standard Army tactical manual, in which his clarity of thought and expression made a great impact on all who read it. The same age as von Fritsch, Beck also was a shy, cautious, retiring man of great honour, personal charm, and austere Christian morality. Unlike the Army Commander, with whom he nonetheless got on well and formed a strong partnership, he was a highly cultured man of poise and deliberate manner, possessing little of the stiffness traditionally associated with the German officer. Experiencing the pleasures of married life for only a brief period in 1916, before his wife died the following year, Beck led a simple existence, totally immersing himself in his chosen profession, often working up to fifteen hours a day, and experiencing his greatest pleasure in the practice of horsemanship.

Beck's political attitude has long been misunderstood; too often the charge of opportunism has been levelled against him. Welcoming the advent of National Socialism for the promise it held for the future, he nevertheless remained true to his deeply held belief in the traditional position of the Army within the state. For a time, he was able to reconcile both these views quite happily, but the moment he felt that Hitler was pursuing damaging, even destructive, policies, his conscience forced him to oppose them. Westphal recorded Beck's admonition in 1938 to a brother officer who failed in this duty:

> '. . . at a recent concert Hitler had spoken to one of the commanding generals about the attack [on Czechoslovakia]. Beck asked the latter: "Did you express your misgivings openly?" The general answered

that in view of the large number of listeners he had not thought the moment to be opportune and had been non-committal. Beck rose and said sharply: "Herr General, you were yourself once a General Staff officer. As such you should know it is the duty of a German General Staff officer to speak his mind openly and without reservation to everyone, even to the Chief of State. It is a thousand pities that you did not do so." '[36]

However, his lack of success in speaking out forced Beck into more covert opposition to National Socialism, and thence into a full-scale conspiracy which ultimately led to his death. Such an evolution was not achieved without intense moral suffering. While he remained Chief of Staff, the doctrine of political independence, the traditional loyalty to the legally constituted executive, together with his political inexperience, had served to render his opposition ineffective. It was only his well-developed honour, integrity, and courage that enabled him to escape from these binding restrictions and attempt his Führer's overthrow – an escape which few of his brother officers found possible to effect.

3

Alliance

The whole period from 1933 to 1939 was a revolutionary one, full of internal tension in all the spheres of political, international, and economic life, and it was clear that the Wehrmacht, and, above all, the old Army, was being drawn into the vortex. Every army is but a part of its own people.

GENERAL GUNTHER VON BLUMENTRITT

With the possible exception of von Reichenau, none of the military leaders in those critical years from 1933 to 1938 possessed any political ability, and all were ill-suited by their experience to meet the new conditions of the 1930s. All accepted the new régime, albeit for different reasons, and all, at the outset, served their political master faithfully. Perhaps even more important, all were condemned by fate to work in an environment that was continually, and rapidly, developing in favour of the National Socialists; for, by mid-1934, the overwhelming majority of officers had at least come to accept the new régime, even if they did not actively support it. And why should they not have done so? Von Blomberg reasoned in 1945:

> 'Hitler emphasised the *Soldatentum,* the selection of capable men, and the re-establishment of German sovereignty within the German frontiers. These were aims to which any healthy nation would give its approval after a defeat, as France had done with great success after 1870–71. . . . The German people agreed with the Hitler of those days. The masses obtained tangible advantages in the matter of social justice, the labour market, and above all an increasing importance of Germany as a political body. How could we soldiers, who had continually to deal with the masses, think otherwise?'[1]

And were not the majority of Germans of all classes at that time also blind to the logical consequences of National Socialism? The plebiscite of 12 November 1933 on Hitler's home and foreign policies had resulted in a resounding ninety-five per cent 'Yes' vote for the new Chancellor; the generals themselves, on the other hand, coming as they did from a privileged background, were regarded as reactionary by the great mass of the population, and had little or no following in the country. And had not most of the political parties come to terms with Hitler and his movement? When Hitler assumed power in 1933, he was opposed only by the Communists, and even they had flirted for a time with an alliance with the National Socialists. The Conservatives were his allies, albeit uneasily, the Centre voted with his government and suppressed its mental reservations, while the Social-Democrats, although condemning his internal programme, nevertheless supported his foreign policy. Thus, as Westphal notes, the Army leaders 'had to carry through their struggles of conscience quite alone, without being able to seek advice from members of a parliament, from a free press, or from any other responsible and independent men'.[2] Furthermore, the Army, for so long a devout believer in autocracy, had never been the champion of civil liberties, Jews, socialism, or democracy; there was, then, no reason why it should greatly perturb itself over the censorship of the press and radio, the destruction of the trades unions, the imprisonment of Communists, the emasculation of the Reichstag, the prohibition of anti-state political activity, the restrictions placed on the Jews by the Nuremburg Laws, and the dragooning of the Catholic church, although there is no doubt that these did disturb individual officers.

What of the concentration camps? As yet they were seen as nothing but rather tough internment centres necessary for the protective custody of Communists and 'socially disruptive elements', from which people were regularly released; their more ominous role was yet to come, during the war, as centres for genocide. Germany was experiencing unusual times, and these warranted unusual measures. As von Reichenau told a council of commanding officers in February 1933: 'We must recognise that we are in the midst of a revolution; what is rotten in the state must fall and it can only be brought down by terror. The Party will proceed ruthlessly against Marxism. The Army's task is to order arms. No succour if any of the persecuted seek refuge with the troops.'[3] At the same time, there was abroad a strong belief that Hitler either did not condone, or was not aware of, the worst excesses of his followers; he was only waiting for the establishment of internal stability before relaxing the strict measures he had taken in the interests of security. Distressing events though there were, they were largely unreported within Germany and, certainly, represented only a very small part of life in those early years of the Third Reich. Terror was to develop only later. The Führer, it was argued, had just taken decisive action against his SA associates, to whom he owed so much, precisely because of their excesses. Even General Halder, a future leader of the conspiracy against Hitler, could write in August 1934: 'The Chancellor's intentions are pure and inspired by idealism; but they are being abused and sometimes actually reversed in practice by the swarm of utterly incompetent – often downright useless – Party organisations . . . the Führer [wants] to build on existing values. . . .'[4]

Furthermore, was it not a fact that many of Hitler's promises were being fulfilled? Not only was the economy improving, but, most important of all, the interests of the soldiers were being respected, their autonomy preserved. Hitler had given proof of his oft-repeated assurances that the Armed Forces were to be the sole bearers of arms in the nation, and he had begun his policy of rearmament and the destruction of the Versailles Treaty. Therefore, why should the Army not acknowledge the Führer? Certainly, as events have shown, the soldiers were wrong in their political judgement, and tragically so, but this was true of almost the whole of the German nation. Indeed, it was so with much of the world.

This, then, was the situation in which the Army's leaders found themselves in the early years of Hitler's dictatorship. None of them, not even von Blomberg, was the spineless creature so often described by historians, and, certainly, none had any intention of abdicating the Army's traditional autonomy within the state. All shared the belief, seldom consciously defined and never commonly agreed on, that the only way to maintain their traditional role within the National Socialist state was to establish a close relationship between the Army and the ideals of its government, while remaining apart from its sole political party. Beck was one of the few to give expression to this; in 1938 he wrote: 'Quite apart from the fact that the Army's basis today is National Socialist, as it must be, the Party's influence must not be allowed to penetrate the Army, for it could only have a destructive effect.'[5] Such a delicately balanced policy, however, demanded a political expertise, a unity of action, and room for manoeuvre on the part of the Army leaders that were lacking completely. Without them, the generals' attempts were likely to fail, precisely because, in maintaining their independence and influence in military matters, they were brought inevitably into opposition with Hitler's rearmament and foreign policies which, in their view, were becoming increasingly dangerous to both the nation and the Army. Such opposition the Führer was not prepared to tolerate. Independence from his Party was one thing; obstruction of his aims, another.

The first outward sign of the Armed Services' acceptance of the new national creed of National Socialism was von Blomberg's order of 19 September 1933, which directed servicemen to salute uniformed members of the Party and its organisations (the SA, SS, etc.). This was followed, on 25 February 1934, by the order for the wearing of the *Wehrmachtsadler* (Armed Forces eagle) on uniforms, the bird clutching in its claws a swastika, the symbol of the National Socialist Party. It would be wrong, though, to exaggerate the importance of this: the spread-eagle was an old German symbol used extensively by the Imperial Army, and the form now adopted, although with the swastika, was by then considered to be a national, rather than a purely Party, emblem, distinct from that worn by political formations, as, indeed, was its position on the uniform. Neither von Fritsch nor Beck dissented from the order, the former expressing the hope that its introduction would give the necessary impetus to Hitler to deal with the SA. More significant than this purely outward formality was the Army's acceptance of the Aryan Paragraph in the regulations governing the appointment of state officials. As from 28 February 1934, and at the suggestion of von Blomberg, the Armed Forces accepted the imposition of racial restrictions on military appointments. Serving officers and men not of Aryan descent were to be retired, and henceforth none was to be allowed into the Armed Forces. However, relatively few Jews were dismissed, as a clause was inserted to enable those who were also war veterans to remain in service. Furthermore, the regulations of the Aryan Paragraph were not fully enforced, and they were used primarily as a device for ridding the Army of troublemakers who happened to have Jewish ancestry. In the event, only thirty-nine soldiers and eleven sailors were affected, and the affair attracted relatively little attention, few officers taking the matter as far as Colonel von Manstein, who wrote to von Reichenau complaining of the cowardly way in which the Army had surrendered to the Party. The Head of the Minister's Office was angered by this effrontery, but von Fritsch took the matter out of his hands and did nothing more about it. The whole issue was promptly forgotten.

The Army's support for Hitler during the period preceding 30 June 1934, and on the fateful Night of the Long Knives itself, was considerable, for the generals were as keen as anyone else to see the pretensions of the SA curbed. The military had no reason to take other than the most stern measures necessary to counter any threat to their autonomy – a threat which, in the case of the SA, brought into question nothing less than the continued existence of the Army. A close alliance with their protector, Adolf Hitler, was, therefore, vital. Von Blomberg announced in the Party's newspaper, *Völkischer Beobachter*, the day before the purge: 'The Armed Forces stand in close unity with the whole nation, wearing with pride the symbol of the rebirth of Germany on habit and uniform, standing in discipline and loyalty behind the leadership of the state – the Field-Marshal of the Great War, Reich President von Hindenburg, its Supreme Commander, and the Führer of the Reich, Adolf Hitler, who once came out of our ranks and who will always remain one of ours.'[6] Just four days earlier, on 25 June, von Fritsch had placed the Army on a country-wide alert and was preparing to resist any attempted putsch by Röhm and his associates. And on the 30th, despite the reluctance of some generals, including the Army Commander and Chief of General Staff, to mount an offensive rather than a defensive action against the storm-troopers, the soldiers took an active part in the capture and killing of the SA leaders. Although they did not pull the triggers, they gave rifles and ammunition to the SS men who did, provided transport and refuge for the murder squads, and were even sent by themselves to disarm certain SA units. But, most important of all, by word and deed the soldiers gave Hitler the assurance that, if the worst came to the worst, the German Army was on his side.

The climax to the Army's identification with Hitler came with the death of the Reich President and Supreme Commander, Field-Marshal von Hindenburg, on 2 August 1934. Hitler and his associates were not unprepared for this event; it had been apparent for the previous six months that the old man's life was drawing to a close, and within one hour of his death came the announcement that the office of Chancellor would henceforth be merged with the office of President. Hitler was now the undisputed head of the German Reich.

The leaders of the Armed Forces were also ready to exploit the new situation. The soldiers had always disliked the form of the oath taken under the Weimar Republic, by which they swore allegiance not to the Head of State, as in the traditional German military oath, but to the hated democratic and republican constitution. Thus, seizing the opportunity that von Hindenburg's death presented, von Reichenau, on his own initiative and without any influence being brought to bear by Hitler, composed a new oath to the Head of State which could be sworn the moment he took office. Hitler, naturally enough, was happy to agree with the change, von Blomberg was enthusiastic about it, and von Fritsch accepted it, as did Beck, but with deep foreboding. Consequently, in the afternoon and late evening of 2 August, the anniversary of the first day of German mobilisation for the First World War, at ceremonies throughout Germany, soldiers and sailors took their oath of allegiance to the new Head of State and Supreme Commander. The oath ran simply:

> *I swear by God this holy oath, that I will render to Adolf Hitler, Führer of the German Reich and People, Supreme Commander of the Armed Forces, unconditional obedience, and that I am ready, as a brave soldier, to risk my life at any time for this oath.*

By this oath, every individual serviceman of the German Armed Forces placed himself at the sole disposal of one man, Adolf Hitler, in his position as Reich Chancellor and President, the power of whose offices had been extended by the Enabling Law that swept away all legal or constitutional constraints. As a result, Hitler had to render account to no man for the use to which his soldiers were put.

The generals have been strongly criticised for having placed themselves and the Armed Forces in this position. Wheeler-Bennett has pronounced: '... the pledge which he [Hitler] exacted on 2 August 1934 was one of personal and binding loyalty and, at least in his interpretation, of blind and unreasoning obedience.'[7] Certainly a number of German officers since the Second World War have attempted to use as an excuse the point of honour that the oath entailed, so as to rid themselves of all responsibility for their actions. General Jodl was to plead, shortly after his capture in 1945: 'As a soldier I obeyed, and I believed my honour required me to maintain the obedience I had sworn. .... I have spent these five years working in silence although I often entirely disagreed and thought the orders I got were absurd and impossible. I have known since the spring of 1942 that we could not win the war.'[8] A very few recognised at the time of its introduction the possible dangers inherent in the form of the oath. Beck described 2 August as 'the blackest day of my life',[9] and his first instinct was to resign. However, as his brother later wrote, 'He appears to have let von Fritsch talk him into believing that, as things were, such a step was impossible and that the Armed Forces would not have understood it. A large number of senior generals had already thrown in their lot with Hitler, and they, at any rate, must have known what an oath to Hitler's person could bring in its wake.'[10] But if a man of Beck's intelligence and integrity could come to accept the oath, how much more possible was it for the rest of the Army?

Was the taking of this oath the criminally foolish action that is so often suggested? As has been indicated, the oath sworn personally to the Head of State was the traditional form used by the German Army throughout its history. It was the oath pledging to uphold the much-despised constitution of the Weimar Republic that was the exception. The soldiers had always preferred this personal link with their Head of State, a link they saw as the essence of their military honour, and it was a matter of great pride to them that they had publicly indicated their willingness to lay down their lives in his service. To him they pledged unconditional obedience, simply because conditional obedience was the antithesis of the discipline that formed the basis of military life. Moreover, the Weimar oath was largely meaningless because it was sworn to a little-understood and much-disliked constitution, and, owing to the legal loopholes it offered to sharp-minded soldiers to disobey orders, it had proved positively detrimental to discipline. Furthermore, the Weimar oath, although it gave 'loyalty to the constitution' and demanded services 'to protect the German nation and its lawful establishments', did specify obedience 'to the President and to . . . superiors'. Who was the final arbiter of what the constitution was, and what it demanded? One man: the President. Foreign military oaths, too, provided for personal loyalty and obedience to Heads of State and governments: the British soldier swore 'to observe and obey all orders of His Majesty, His Heirs and Successors', which, in reality, meant the government of the day; the American pledged himself 'to support and defend the constitution', but also promised 'to obey the orders of the President'; while the Soviet would 'remain obedient, unto my last breath, to my People, to my Soviet Homeland, and to the Soviet Government'. Should the fact that personal loyalty was sworn to a Head of State who was also a dictator have caused any misgiving to the German soldiers? Democracy was alien to German historical development and thought, their political beliefs having always tended towards autocracy. Up to that time, few envisaged even a part of the terrible fate that lay ahead under Hitler; the vast majority of those with any form of political awareness, even if they did not see the Führer as Germany's salvation, certainly saw him as a catalyst for improvement. Finally, those, like Beck, who feared for the consequences of such an oath but could take no immediate action, at least had the comfort of knowing that, however hard it might be, their conscience could override their oath and, if necessary, enable them to disobey or even to overthrow their Head of State. After all, an oath is but an empty form of words if the substance, the idea that lies behind it, is dead.

Hitler was unhesitating in his expression of gratitude to the Armed

Forces for the manner in which they had manifested their acceptance of him as Head of State. In a letter addressed to von Blomberg he wrote:

> '. . . I wish to express my thanks to you, and through you, to the Armed Forces, for the oath of loyalty which has been sworn to me. Just as the officers and men of the Armed Forces have obligated themselves to the new state in my person, so shall I always regard it as my highest duty to intercede for the existence and inviolability of the Armed Forces, in fulfilment of the testament of the late Field-Marshal, and in accord with my own will, to establish the Army formally as the sole bearer of arms of the nation.'[11]

The Army and the Führer now appeared as one. As Supreme Commander, Hitler ordered it to appear at the Party rally at Nuremberg in September 1934, where it performed its displays of drill, tactics, and equipment to the delight of the audience. On 9 November 1936, von Blomberg even marched in the front rank of National Socialist dignatories through the streets of Munich to commemorate the abortive 1923 putsch. On both occasions the Army lent its weight of authority and prestige to the government and to National Socialism.

Not only did the Army identify itself with the outward expression of the new régime, it also adapted itself to the ideals of the 'Germany reborn' – the ideals of National Socialism. Just as these were established in all sectors of German society, so were they extended to the Army. But the importance of this should not be exaggerated, for the Army was not turned into a political formation along the lines of the armed SS as a result. Throughout its history, the military had always shared the political outlook of the nation's rulers, and, in that respect, the Army of the 1930s was no different; traditionally, German youth had completed their education in the Armed Forces, so now it was only natural that the Army should train the young manhood in the spirit of the new Germany. Hitler, the war veteran, fully appreciated the 'system of values and decency'[12] of the front-line soldier, and it flattered the serviceman to know that in *Mein Kampf* he had written: 'Thus in the main, the period of military service shall serve as the conclusion of the normal education of the average German.'[13] This is the theme that runs throughout the political directives issued by von Blomberg. In April 1935 he decreed: 'The educational goal . . . is not only the basically trained soldier and master of a weapon, but also the man who is aware of his nationality and of his general duties towards the State. . . .'[14] In addition, Hitler saw the soldiers' acceptance of National Socialism as an insurance of their loyalty to him and to his aims during the bitter life-or-death struggle he believed lay ahead. He reasoned that political determination brought such strength to the soldier's sword as to render it invincible. For von Blomberg, National Socialism was to form the basis of the military virtues that, in his romanticism, he believed to play such an important role in the conduct of war.

The ideological infiltration of National Socialism into the Army, although inevitable, was not of itself destructive of its independence. Nor, indeed, did it on its own threaten the autonomy of the Army any more than that of the Armed Forces of other nations which also shared the general constitutional and political outlook of their governments, be they democratic, fascist, communist, or national socialist. Even in the United Kingdom today, the British Army owes loyalty to a system of political values, and unqualified allegiance to the sovereign and his or her duly elected ministers is basic to its undertaking to defend the constitutional and territorial integrity of the nation. Furthermore, the very fact that the leaders of the German Armed Forces themselves had introduced the new ideology into the ranks insured that Hitler and the Party possessed little reasonable cause for intervention.

In a series of directives, von Blomberg set out to establish the position of the Armed Forces within the newly organised structure of the Third Reich. On 25 May 1934, in a proclamation on the 'Duties of the German Soldier', signed by von Hindenburg, he defined its role as 'the bearer of arms of the German nation. It protects the German Reich and the Fatherland, as well as the people united in National Socialism, and their living space.'[15] The same day, in a decree entitled 'The Armed Forces and National Socialism', he specified the bond between the serviceman and the new ideology:

> 'National thought is the natural basis of all soldierly efforts. However, we do not wish to forget that the philosophy which fills the new state is not only national, but National Socialist. National Socialism draws its rule of conduct from the necessities of the life of the whole people, and from the duty to work in concert for the entire nation. It embraces the idea of the fellowship of blood, of the fate of all German people. It is indubitable that this principle is, and also must remain, the foundation of the duty of the German soldier, for the principles of soldierness and of National Socialism arise out of the same experiences in the Great War.'[16]

On 22 July 1935, in a secret order, the Defence Minister stipulated:

> 'As regards the state, it goes without saying that the Armed Forces accept the National Socialist view. It therefore becomes necessary to convert officers of the Reserve to the same way of thinking. In consequence no one is to be trained for, or commissioned in, the Reserve of Officers unless he sincerely accepts the National Socialist state and stands up for it in public instead of adopting an attitude of indifference or even hostility towards it.'[17]

The following year, on 16 April 1936, von Blomberg issued a further decree which explained the relationship of the Armed Forces to the state:

'With the introduction of general conscription [in March 1935], the Armed Forces again became the great school of national education. . . . The Wehrmacht owes its rebirth primarily to the Führer and Reich Chancellor, and to his political tool, the NSDAP. The Wehrmacht, SA, SS, HJ, Labour Service, Police, etc., are the parts of the whole, which, in *separate* [author's italics] fields of activity, serve the same aim. Community of purpose and comradeship must link all of these organisations.'[18]

Von Blomberg, therefore, saw the Armed Forces as a central part of the general system that was National Socialist Germany, with tasks inseparable from those of the new régime, but nevertheless preserving a separate identity. As a direct consequence, the principles of National Socialism took a direct hold on much of service life. It took just fourteen months after Hitler's rise to power for special ideological instruction to be introduced into the Army, at the time when the crisis with the SA was at its height. On 4 April 1934, von Blomberg announced:

'The first year of the National Socialist government has laid the foundations for the political and economic reconstruction of the nation. The second year places the emphasis on the spiritual saturation of the nation with the principles of the National Socialist state. Instruction in accord with this end is therefore an important task for all organisations who support the new state with their will. This applies especially to the Armed Forces. . . . I therefore order that in the future, concerning instruction in current political matters in the Armed Forces, increased significance and greater attention are to be paid to these topics by all units . . . the content of the teaching will be issued twice monthly by the Defence Ministry as "Principles for Instruction in Current Political Matters". [These were nothing more than a distillation of National Socialist propaganda.]'[19]

In 1936, political instruction became more organised. On 30 January, von Blomberg ordered the introduction of a special course of indoctrination in all Officer Training Schools, Staff Colleges, and the Armed Forces Academy, and provided for the establishment of training courses, held in Berlin by Party propagandists, for all officers who were to become instructors. Special local courses were instituted for all other officers not at the various academies. In 1937 the Party organised courses similar to those in Berlin to be held in each Wehrkreis. Once-weekly instruction was now given by officers to all NCOs and men. Simultaneously with direct political education, the Reich Ministry for Propaganda and Public Enlightenment was authorised to disseminate 'educational' literature throughout the Armed Forces; reading rooms were provided for the troops, largely stocked with propaganda; units were given funds with which to purchase the Party newspaper *Völkischer Beobachter*; and books and pamphlets produced by the

Ministry were made available free, or at very low prices. Restrictions were even placed on the newspapers allowed to be taken.

More disturbing however, had been von Blomberg's order of 26 May 1936, which directed that soldiers considered politically unreliable should be reported to the Gestapo. This was further extended, on 25 January 1938, by an order which required that especially difficult men be handed over to the Gestapo for the remainder of their period of service.

In religious matters, National Socialism at first made but little headway, although the strength of Christianity within the Armed Forces was gradually eroded. On 29 May 1935, in an 'Important Political Instruction', von Blomberg reaffirmed that attendance of soldiers at church parades was voluntary, and in April 1937 the religious instruction known as Barrack Evening Hours ceased to be obligatory, being stopped altogether for reserve troops. Chaplains found themselves increasingly restricted: on 3 December 1935 von Blomberg made a point of stating that they must use no form of compulsion, either direct or indirect, to influence non-believers; on 14 February 1936 he banned the distribution of religious material within the Armed Forces, and specified that only nominated unit chaplains could minister to the needs of servicemen; on 3 March 1936 he forbade the collection of votes on the questions of the Evangelical church, maintaining that 'it is not in accordance with the strong reserve and impartiality of the Armed Forces in religious matters';[20] and individual Army commanders took steps to restrict the freedom to discuss religion, one of them, General Dollmann, ordering: 'The Armed Forces, as one of the bearers of the National Socialist state, demand of you as chaplains at all times, a clear and unreserved acknowledgement of the Führer, State and People.'[21]

On the issue of freemasonry, von Blomberg was fully in accord with National Socialist policy. The officer corps had a strong tradition of freemasonry, traceable back to Frederick the Great, but this made no difference to his attitude. On 26 May 1934 he ordered that no serviceman might belong to a Masonic lodge, and those who did so were either to resign or be dismissed; on 7 October 1935 he went further: former freemasons were not to be considered for selection as officers unless they had resigned from their lodges before 1 October 1932 and had not taken the Third Degree, and officer-candidates were to be made to sign an affidavit declaring they had never been freemasons. Later, however, because of the pressure of numbers, von Blomberg was forced to modify this order and consider applicants on their merits.

But it was on the Jewish question that the Armed Forces' acceptance of the tenets of National Socialism took on its most ominous form. The application of the Aryan Paragraph in February 1934 has already been noted, but in one of his very few interventions in internal service affairs, Hitler, in his role as Supreme Commander, emphasised the policy of racial selection within the Armed Forces in a decree dated 13 May 1936:

'The National Socialist concept of state demands the nurturing of the idea of race, and of a specially selected group of leaders from people of pure German, or similar blood. It is therefore a natural obligation for the Armed Forces to select its professional soldiers, hence its leaders, in accordance with the strictest racial criteria above and beyond the legal regulations, and so to obtain a selection of the best of the German people in the military school of the nation.'[22]

There then followed a detailed instruction as to the application of the policy to the forces, but, as the Aryan Paragraph was already in existence, this merely served to restate the policy rather than to exert any practical effect.

Discrimination had already been extended even further by von Blomberg's order of 15 July 1935, which prohibited servicemen from using Jewish shops. It ran: 'It conflicts with the duty of the Armed Forces as one of the responsible schools of the new state when soldiers shop in non-Aryan businesses. I ask that commanders will take care, by means of oral instruction in suitable form, that the basic National Socialist attitude in this regard also becomes generally current . . . and that violations of this will be avoided in the future.'[23] After shopping came marriage. In an order dated 1 April 1936 von Blomberg stipulated that a soldier's bride must be of Aryan blood, and that if only one grandparent were Jewish, the marriage should not take place. This was confirmed by Hitler's above-mentioned decree of 13 May 1936, which expressly forbade the union of professional soldiers with non-Aryan stock.

Even in the serviceman's home life National Socialism intruded. In a decree of 6 September 1936 von Blomberg extolled the virtues of the Party's Block and Cell administration, a system whereby each and every family in the Reich came under the charge of a Party official who had the duties of propagating National Socialism, recruiting for the multitudinous Party organisations, investigating complaints or unreliable attitudes, and handling any general issue the Party might care to give him. Von Blomberg declared that he had no objection if the Party took on such an administration of soldier's families, although he specified that one area of a soldier's life which must be left free from inquiry or influence was his official military duty.

By such means the German soldier, after 1935, became subject to National Socialist ideology wherever he might turn: his barracks were named after heroes of the NSDAP; Party officials were invited to all social functions; his reading was supervised; his political attitudes were, in theory at least, controlled, watched, and, if necessary, reported to the Gestapo; his ancestry could be the subject of close scrutiny; his choice of a wife was inhibited; and even his family home was not proof against the influences of political officialdom.

4

Independence

. . . a common basic attitude was lacking. Many methods of the Party . . . did not appeal to us at all. . . . We officers were fighting a continuous battle against the influences of the Party which strove for power over our soldiers, thereby to push aside the soldierly element which we represented.

FIELD-MARSHAL ERICH VON MANSTEIN

By the beginning of 1938 it might have appeared as if the soldiers were already kissing Adolf Hitler's hands 'like hysterical women'. Not only was the Army, of necessity, in the forefront of the National Socialist policies of rearmament and national regeneration, but it had done everything possible to indicate its loyalty to the Führer. It had bound itself by an unconditional oath of obedience to his person; it had assisted in the eradication of his enemies, the SA leadership; it wore his emblem, the swastika, on its uniform; it openly lent its prestige to his government by appearing at rallies and commemorations; it officially accepted the basic tenets of his creed; and it recognised its role as the great educator of the youth of the Third Reich – Hitler's youth. Outward appearances, however, were deceptive; reality was somewhat different. The Army was far from being the subservient instrument of the dictator's will that it was later to become.

What, then, was the position of the Army within the Third Reich? At the time people said nothing had changed; that while Germany possessed a National Socialist Air Force, it still maintained an Imperial Navy and a Royal Prussian Army. While this was something of an exaggeration, there can be no doubt that the Army had abandoned to Hitler little or nothing substantial of its independence, had maintained considerable autonomy within the state, and was completely free from any Party supervision. According to paragraph 26 of the Defence Law, no soldier was allowed to undertake political activity, and this included being a member of the National Socialist Party or of its affiliated organisations. The only exceptions to this fundamental rule were minor ones: civilian members of the Armed Forces were allowed to hold Party office under certain conditions; participation in National Socialist welfare organisations was considered desirable; leading Party members could wear military uniform at Party functions during service, although they could not make speeches; and, although conscripts had to allow their membership to lapse, they could continue to pay their Party dues while in service. The Armed Forces retained full control over its own political instruction, and maintained the right to sole responsibility for its own publicity in the face of a serious challenge from the Propaganda Ministry. Just as important, the generals were successful in resisting the demands of Rudolf Hess, the Deputy Führer, for a Party Complaints Centre to be instituted within the Armed Forces to facilitate servicemen making complaints direct to the Party organisation. Furthermore, by the Army Law promulgated on 20 July 1933, the soldiers had been made independent of the jurisdiction of the civil courts. Nor was the Army responsible to any outside body for its application of the Aryan Paragraph, or of the marriage and freemasonry restrictions. And, when one of its soldiers was suspected of political unreliability, it was the Army and no other body that decided whether an investigation should be made, and, on its conclusion, whether the matter should be reported to the Gestapo.

If the Party's interference in service matters was negligible, so was Hitler's. In the later years of his rule he was often to imply that before 1938 his attitude towards the military leaders was dictated solely by his wish to undermine their hostility towards him and his creed. On one occasion he reminisced: 'Once that [conscription] was accomplished, the influx into the Armed Forces of the masses of the people, together with the spirit of National Socialism and the ever-growing power of the National Socialist movement, would, I was sure, allow me to overcome all opposition among the Armed Forces, and in particular in the corps of officers.'[1] It is on such sayings that many historians have fastened their attention, using them as proof of the thesis that, even before 1938, Hitler was scheming against his generals. But the Führer's memory was never the most truthful, and his reminiscences are usually marked by a high degree of fantasy, delighting, as he did, in conveying to those around him the idea that he was, and always had been, the all-seeing, all-powerful manipulator of the nation's destiny. Therefore it is necessary to look carefully at Hitler's actions in the five years in question, from January 1933 to January 1938, to discern whether or not he did in fact behave in a devious fashion towards the Army.

The evidence does not support the historians' contention. At no time did Hitler act against the interests of the Army's autonomy. What von Blomberg wrote in 1945 was the truth:

> 'In the early years of his régime, Hitler stressed his adherence to the historical tradition of which the *Tag von Potsdam* represented, and continued to represent, for the German people, a confession of faith. During these years we soldiers had no cause to complain to Hitler. He fulfilled hopes which were dear to all of us. If the generals no longer choose to remember this, it is obviously a case of deliberate forgetfulness. . . . Until Hitler entered upon the period of aggressive politics . . . the German people had no decisive reason for hostility to Hitler, we soldiers least of all. He had not only given us back a

position of respect in the life of the German people . . . but by the rearmament of Germany, which only Hitler could achieve, he had given the soldiers a larger sphere of influence, promotion and increased respect. . . . Up until 1938 there was no sign of hostility. . . . We soldiers had no reason to complain. . . . To sum up, I would say that Hitler in the first period, which lasted up to 1938, strove to obtain the trust of us soldiers, with complete success.'[2]

Even though he was their Supreme Commander, on no occasion did Hitler interfere in the internal affairs of the Armed Forces against the advice of his military subordinates. Indeed, he revealed nothing but complete confidence in his generals. As Field-Marshal von Manstein later recorded: 'There is no doubt that when he originally came to power he had shown the military leaders a certain deference and respected their professional abilities.'[3] Hitler's military adjutant, who was always close to the Führer, went further when he wrote:

'During this period Hitler adhered strictly to the boundaries of the area of responsibility of his military advisers. There is no substantial case in which Hitler intervened in military matters on his own authority and without previous consultaton with his Minister of War. All directives and orders which required his permission, originated in the responsible places within the War Ministry, be it on the initiative of the Ministry or after consultation between Hitler and Blomberg, and were only shown to the former for his signature after countersigning by Blomberg, and, where necessary, by the commanders of the individual services. . . . No military authority, independent of the constitutional advisers, was exercised by the Head of State until the end of January 1938.'[4]

On one occasion, for example, Hitler abandoned his, and Göring's, idea that the Army should adopt the National Socialist salute of raised arm, when Hossbach explained that it would be unpopular among the soldiers. In the light of this, it is easy to accept von Blomberg's assertion:

'. . . Hitler on several occasions approached me with the idea of training the SA as a reserve formation. He gave in to my objections . . . and the three regiments of the Waffen SS were not increased in my time – in spite of the heavy pressure on the part of Himmler. To what extent I was successful in keeping the Wehrmacht free from the influence of the Nazi Party, and from being linked up with it, has not been realised. . . . In my time the Wehrmacht stood in no sense behind the Party, but took its stand independently alongside it. The Party often sought to change this situation but did not succeed, because Hitler listened to me in those days.'[5]

A number of actions on the part of Hitler form positive proof of his good intentions towards the military. In speeches he often publicly affirmed his belief in the importance of the Army. For example, in 1934, he declared: 'Our government is supported by two organisations: politically by the community of the Volk, organised in the National Socialist movement, and in the military sphere by the Army.'[6] The next year he pronounced that the Army was 'in war the nation's great defence, in peace the splendid school of our people. It is the Army which has made men of us all, and when we looked upon the Army our faith in the future of our people was always reinforced. This old glorious Army is not dead; it only slept, and now it has risen again in you.'[7] Nor was Hitler ungenerous in awarding influence and prestige to his military advisers. For example, on 21 May 1935, he appointed von Blomberg Commander-in-Chief of the three Armed Services in addition to his ministerial responsibilities, thereby raising him to a position of military authority surpassing that of any other peacetime general in German history. Such an elevation and concentration of powers was hardly indicative of any determined policy to undermine the influence of his military advisers, and it certainly confounded his policy of 'divide and rule', which he was later to apply even to his most faithful followers. The next year, in 1936 on the occasion of his forty-seventh birthday, Hitler promoted von Blomberg to the rank of *Generalfeldmarschall,* von Fritsch (together with Göring, the Luftwaffe Commander) to *Generaloberst,* and Raeder, the Navy Commander, to *Generaladmiral.* By these promotions he was honouring 'the entire Wehrmacht, every individual officer and soldier'.[8] Hitler had wanted to bestow on his War Minister the new rank of *Reichsmarschall,* but the opinion of his military advisers was against it; instead, he had to be content with giving him the highest existing rank. Even so, von Blomberg was only the sixth German soldier to be thus honoured in peacetime, while Hitler's erstwhile political crony, Göring, had to be content with an inferior rank.

At that time, Hitler remained faithful to his declaration made in 1934, after his eradication of the SA challenge, that: 'For fourteen years I have stated consistently that the fighting organisations of the Party are political institutions and that they have nothing to do with the Army.'[9] As a result he took a leading role in protecting the military from the encroachments of Party formations. In 1933 he had ensured that the creation of the Reich Defence Council involved no opportunity to override the Army Commander-in-Chief's orders or directives. In early 1935, at the height of an SS campaign of vilification against von Fritsch and the Army, in which rumours of a military putsch were rife – Himmler had gone so far as to name the day on which the soldiers' revolt was to take place – Hitler had intervened and placed himself firmly on the side of his soldiers. The SS attacks ceased immediately, although only for the time being. A few months later, in April and May, on being told that listening devices had been found in Army telephones, and even in the *Abwehr* (military intelligence) offices, Hitler ordered that Gestapo authority should not for one moment encroach on

Armed Forces' territory. In 1936, when Himmler and Heydrich again laid charges against the Army Commander, this time accusing him of homosexuality, Hitler rejected totally the bogus evidence on which they were based, and ordered the documents to be burnt. On this occasion a senior SS officer recorded: '. . . Hitler has said that, though von Fritsch was doubtless one of the strongest and most important opponents of National Socialism, he could not be dealt with in this fashion.'[10]

In other matters Hitler was equally on the side of his soldiers. In 1935 he rejected the National Socialist Reich Labour Service's requirement for a period of two years conscription, on the grounds that it would prejudice the Army's demands on the youth of the nation, which, also, would be two years. The same year he disbanded the Defence Policy Office of the Party, giving the reason that open rearmament had rendered it superfluous, thereby freeing the Army from one aspect of outside interest (although it had never been a controlling body). In compliance with the Army's opposition, he also omitted Party-orientated sections from the draft Defence Law of 1935. And in 1936, heeding the representations of von Blomberg and von Fritsch, he refused to have instituted a 'National Socialist Soldiers' Ring', which officers and men would have been encouraged to join after their release from service. Hitler even expressed concern that von Blomberg was precipitating the introduction of National Socialist ideology into the Army; apparently he felt that 'the political permutation'[11] of the force was a matter of time and should be attempted only gradually.

Finally, some attention must be paid to Hitler's attitude to the armed SS formations being formed from 1933 onwards. In March of that year the first militarised SS unit was instituted, comprising a guard company numbering 120 men; twelve years later the armed SS contained within its order of battle some 600,000 soldiers. This, historians usually allege, is proof of the dictator's evil intent towards the military establishment, for, at the same time as he was making conciliatory, but worthless, gestures to its leaders, he was actively creating 'an élite and fanatical force, the SS, which, though . . . in its infancy, was to challenge and humiliate the Army in its own field'.[12] They claim that Hitler deliberately went back on his promise to the generals that the Armed Forces would be 'the sole arms-bearers' in the defence of the nation, and that the creation of the armed SS was a conscious act of policy on his part, the aim of which was, firstly, to foster a spirit of rivalry and division within the Armed Forces which would strengthen his position, and, secondly, to act as a substitute for the Army by providing a politically reliable military force totally subservient to his will and to the tenets of National Socialism. Such conclusions are based on misleading interpretations of Hitler's role in the development of the armed SS. Possibly, it was the long-term aim of Heinrich Himmler, as *Reichsführer SS,* to create an SS force as an élite fourth arm of the Wehrmacht, which would rival and, perhaps, one day supplant the Army in its dominant position. But that vision was never shared by Hitler, and he was the final arbiter of the fate of the SS formations.

The key to an understanding of Hitler's ideas for the armed SS within the political and military structure of the Third Reich lies in the oath, first sworn by the Führer's personal guard, the *Leibstandarte SS 'Adolf Hitler'*, in November 1933, and subsequently by every man accepted into the ranks of the armed SS. It ran:

> *I swear to you, Adolf Hitler, as Führer and Reich Chancellor, loyalty and bravery. I vow to you, and those you have appointed to command me, obedience unto death. So help me God.*

Though not generally recognised at the time, this oath had considerable significance for the future of the German Army and for the nation as a whole. It was an important step in establishing the authority of Hitler as an independent factor in German public life, for he had now instituted a body of armed men pledged to him personally, with no defined status either within the state or Party. They were at his sole disposal for use as he alone thought fit. And just as Hitler, at the junction between Party and state, represented the hazy, ill-defined relationship between the two, so also did the élite force at his command, the armed SS. Furthermore, just as his political outlook was at first dominated by internal affairs and then by external expansion, so too was the role of his SS troops.

Despite all claims to the contrary, Hitler never intended to build up the armed SS to the point it ultimately reached, and it is probable that he was entirely sincere when he promised his generals in 1934 that the Armed Forces were to be the sole bearers of arms in the defence of the Fatherland. Even Himmler, never slow to seize an opportunity for expanding his domain, was prepared in 1936 to leave it to the Wehrmacht to guarantee 'the safety of the honour, the greatness and the peace of the Reich from the exterior'.[13] Thus, the first formations of the armed SS began as purely political instruments, one of the many aspects of the paramilitary organisations of the National Socialist movement. As the task of the SS was, in Himmler's words, to 'guarantee the security of Germany from the interior', it was thought necessary that, to complement its activities in the areas of political education, secret police, counter-espionage and concentration camps, the SS should develop an armed force run on military lines for the purpose of anti-terrorist, heavy-police tasks during the periods of internal strife that were then thought likely to occur. Thus, an organisation of SS *Sonderkommandos* (Special Detachments, later renamed *Kasernierte Hundertschaften* [Barracked Hundreds] or SS *Politische Bereitschaften* [Political Readiness Squads] when they reached battalion strength) was instituted throughout Germany. In June 1934 some of these units, including the *Leibstandarte*, were sent against Hitler's internal enemies, the SA leaders.

By late 1934, the *Politische Bereitschaften* had reached such a size and state of military training that a new organisation and nomenclature was required. The Army leaders were apprised of the situation in August of that year, but they had to wait until 16 March 1935, the day Hitler announced the reintroduction of conscription, before the order officially establishing the new organisation was issued. The *Politische Bereitschaften,* consisting of three *Standarten* (regiments) modelled on the Army, made up of three battalions and motorcycle and mortar companies, each supported by a signals battalion, was henceforth known as the SS-VT, SS *Verfügungstruppen* (literally, For Disposal Troops, but better translated as Special Purpose Troops). From then on, as Hitler's attention turned from consolidating his position at home and became increasingly focused on foreign adventure, the SS-VT evolved a new role, transformed from a purely political police unit into a military force prepared to take action against its Führer's external, as well as his internal, enemies. It was a very short step from being equipped and trained for anti-terrorist duties to being organised for war. As Beck noted, 'it was interesting to observe that an organisation, which Hitler had categorically stated would never bear arms in military operations, was now taking part in every coup the Führer pulled off. Not only were they taking part, but they were, by 1938, wearing Army uniform instead of their own, except on ceremonial occasions.'[14] Units of the SS-VT took part in the occupations of the Rhineland, Austria, and the Sudetenland, and all the time their military aspect grew. From May 1935, membership of the SS-VT was officially regarded as military service with the Wehrmacht; in October 1936 the SS-VT Inspectorate, an armed SS General Staff, was instituted under the command of Paul Hausser, a former Reichsheer General (this organisation was replaced in 1940 by the SS *Führungsamt* [the Operational Office]); and by the summer of 1939 the SS-VT had completed its expansion to the strength of a division of 18,000 men with its own artillery and armoured car units. Even by November 1937 Himmler had felt confident enough to declare: 'the *Verfügungstruppen* are, according to the present standards of the Wehrmacht, prepared for war.'[15]

As a result of all this, the Army was highly suspicious of the SS-VT, viewing it as a distinct threat to its position as sole arms bearer. Von Fritsch voiced the fears of many when he wrote in early 1938: '. . . it is the *Verfügungstruppen* which, expanded further and further, must create an opposition to the Army, simply through its existence. . . . [It] develops itself totally apart, and, it appears to me, in deliberate opposition to the Army. All units report unanimously that the relationship of the SS *Verfügungstruppen* to the Army is very cool, if not hostile.'[16] Tension there was; perhaps inevitably. Relations between the SS and the Army, generally, were poor. The soldiers were indignant at what they considered to be the rivalry of political upstarts, and fearful of their future development, while the SS men were resentful of the Army's attitude, jealous of its undoubted overwhelming military superiority, arrogant of their own élite position within the Reich, and aggressive in their claims for further expansion. Both were contemptous of each other. But it would be wrong to mistake this natural mistrust, fear, and enmity as indicative of any devious intent on the part of Hitler. The SS-VT was the Führer's force, in many ways independent of Himmler and his ambitions, and was not intended to rival, supplant, or even interfere with, the Army. This, Hitler made clear time and time again. As early as 24 September 1934 a circular had been sent to the leaders of the Armed Forces outlining the purpose of the SS-VT, and stating categorically that, although it was under the command of the Reichsführer SS, in time of war it would be placed at the disposal of the Army. This position never changed, and at no time was there ever any question of the Army losing operational control over the armed SS. However, in order to remove the existing doubt concerning the SS-VT, on 2 February 1935 Hitler issued a secret order, specifically stating that 'Directives for the material outfitting and recruitment for the SS-VT will be issued by the Defence Minister'. In time of war 'The SS-VT will be incorporated into the Army. They are then subordinated to military laws which also apply to matters of recruitment. . . . The preparation of the SS-VT for employment in war will proceed even in peacetime under the responsibility of the Defence Minister to whom they are subordinate in this respect.'[17] Later that year, heeding the advice given him by von Blomberg and others, Hitler excluded from the Defence Law the draft provisions concerning the status of the armed SS, thereby maintaining the Army's position as the military training school of the nation. On 17 August 1938 he issued a further, and more comprehensive, definition of the role of the SS-VT and its relationship to the Wehrmacht. He laid down that it 'forms no part of the Wehrmacht nor of the police. It is a permanent armed force at my disposal.' As 'a formation of the NSDAP' it was to be 'recruited and trained in ideological matters by the Reichsführer SS in accordance with the directives issued by me'. In cases of emergency 'the SS-VT will be used for two purposes:

(1)   by the Commander-in-Chief of the Army within the framework of the Army. It will then be subject exclusively to military law and instructions; politically, however, it will remain a branch of the NSDAP.

(2)   at home, in case of emergency, in accordance with my instructions. It will then be under the orders of the Reichsführer SS . . . .'[18]

Such, in 1938, was the position of the armed SS, which, in Hitler's view and in reality, presented no challenge to the Army.

Consequently, at the beginning of 1938, the German Army was as independent a military force as could be found anywhere in the west. Responsive to the political mood of the nation and to the policies of its legally constituted master, the Army was for all other purposes an autonomous power within the National Socialist state. The Minister responsible for it was answerable to no one but the Head of State, who, for his part, accepted the advice of his military advisers on service matters, and did not interfere with the running of the Armed Forces. The Army was, therefore, responsible for its own discipline, promotion, training, ideological instruction, and directives. No Party organisation had the slightest control over the Army whatsoever. Only Hitler, as its Supreme Commander, possessed any authority, but he chose not to use it. As the distinguished historian, Alfred Vagts, wrote in September 1935: '. . . the National Socialist Party has ceased to be a formidable rival of the Army. . . . The reign of the Party is over.'[19] Indeed, General Westphal noted that it was still possible for the professional soldier 'to be able to keep himself clear from politics. The older officers were particularly resistant to attempts to make them adopt the National Socialist outlook; they believed they could maintain their inner independence even under Hitler's dictatorship.'[20] He went on to record that: 'The healthy instinct of the people felt that the Army was striving to remain an oasis of simplicity, uprightness, and Christian service.'[21] It was particularly this preservation of old traditions, the most suspicious feature of all in the eyes of the Party, that the politically saner part of the populace found most comforting. It was not by accident that many fled into the Army simply to escape the influence of the National Socialists.

The Army's independence of the political structure of the Reich revealed itself in a number of ways. It was clear, for example, that the troops were addressing themselves too little to the ideological training ordered by their leadership. On 17 April 1935 von Blomberg felt himself forced to issue an exhortation to the troops to take seriously the programme of political instruction. He stated: 'It has come to my attention that the "Principles for Instruction in Current Political Matters" are not being given the attention which should be given them. I determine and authorise their contents, and they are just as binding as any other official instructions.'[22]

Even more disheartening to the Defence Minister was the strong and noticeable dissatisfaction felt by the officer corps for the Party, whose interference with the privacy of family life aroused special resentment. The soldiers were distrustful of its ambitions and disgusted by the arrogance and condescension which its dignitories so often showed towards servicemen. A particular cause for complaint was that, on many occasions, former Party members serving in the Army made vindictive reports to NSDAP headquarters, complaining of matters ranging from the political unreliability of a certain officer to everyday questions of military administration. Indeed, Party organisations such as the SA and SS positively encouraged their former members to report on their officers. Their activities were formally ended in 1937, after von Blomberg had made a number of strong complaints to Hess, although they continued illegally.

The Army refused to be overawed by the politicians. In 1935 Baldur von Schirach, the Reich Leader of German Youth, who was serving his time in the Army, was refused a commission, and then was threatened with detention for complaining about it to Party headquarters. There was also grave concern at the Party's attitude to religion, many officers feeling that it was doing all it could to force a break between church and state, and to render Christianity in Germany impotent. The arrest, on 1 July 1937, of Pastor

Niemöller, widely regarded as a symbol of Christian resistance, profoundly shocked many within Germany and in the ranks of the Army (although a majority of officers were not displeased to see this man, who so constantly called for disarmament, out of the public eye). But even before then, there had begun a number of local battles to ensure that military chaplains were not compelled to accept National Socialist dogma. At least one Party official even went so far as to denounce an Army chaplain for high treason, and the whole subject aroused such ill-feeling that Keitel felt constrained to write in 1936: 'Church matters are so difficult that we only do any good if we leave them entirely alone. . . .'[23] There were many, however, including the Army Commander himself, who would not heed this advice, and, in the latter half of 1937, a wave of enthusiasm for church-attendance swept the Army, with church parades becoming unofficially obligatory in many garrisons. In November a memorandum from Protestant Army chaplains to the War Minister received much publicity, especially in the foreign press. Part of it read: 'The Party and the state today combat not only the churches. They combat Christianity. . . . The situation has become intolerable.'[24]

The National Socialist Jewish policy, too, received some resistance from the soldiers, this usually taking the form of patronising Jewish businesses, banning the vitriolic anti-Semitic paper, *Der Stürmer*, produced by Gauleiter Julius Streicher, and casting a blind eye on the non-Aryan ancestry of servicemen. Beck was one of those who attempted to assist Jewish soldiers dismissed from service, and von Fritsch, although revealing some anti-Semitic prejudice, nevertheless took action to ameliorate conditions for non-Aryan officers and their wives by prohibiting conjectures or rumours about possible ancestry. (Indeed, all von Fritsch's directives were written with a deliberate disregard for Party ideology. This was most apparent when he concerned himself with matters of the honour, the manner of living, the code of conduct, and the social responsibilities of the officers corps.) On several occasions von Blomberg pleaded with Hitler for a better treatment of Jews.

Other areas of friction were numerous. Party officials often publicly criticised the Army for being a centre of reaction, and demanded that the political attitudes of the officers be investigated. Complaints were made that soldiers did not donate enough to Party charities, such as Winter Help, and brawls in the street, even stabbings, were not unknown, Party members often overreacting to baiting by the servicemen. On one occasion soldiers shouted around the town of Braunsberg: 'First comes the Army, then nothing for a long while, then a large heap of shit, and then, perhaps, the NSDAP.'[25] On another, five young lieutenants at a dance in Neustadt gave a toast to Moscow, and received a battering for their foolishness. In particular, there was considerable vitriolic feeling between the Army and the SS and Gestapo, which arose out of the jealous and active competition of Himmler, Heydrich, and their followers against the most important and, as yet, entirely independent organisation within Germany.

The first determined onslaught by the SS against the Army's position began shortly after the events of 30 June 1934, when cooperation between the future rivals had been considerable. Every attempt was made to bring the political reliability of the Army's leadership into question, and the campaign, which had degenerated into open hatred, stopped only when Hitler personally intervened in early 1935. The truce did not last long, however, and by the summer the enmity was again marked. Von Fritsch recalled: '. . . there was scarcely a single senior officer who did not feel that he was being spied upon by the SS. Also, it became known again and again that, contrary to the expressed orders of the Deputy to the Führer [Hess], SS men who were serving in the Army had orders to report on their superiors.'[26] Gestapo surveillance penetrated the very depths of the Bendlerstrasse, even the offices of the intelligence service, and von Fritsch found himself constantly spied on, his forthrightness making him a prime target for suspicion. In Silesia, the Gestapo went as far as to undertake systematic enquiries into the political outlook of officers. In the streets, bars, cafés, restaurants, and clubs, personal relations between Army and SS were sour; SS men refused to salute officers, others attempted to exercise police authority over troops, and some even attacked lone or small groups of soldiers without provocation.

The state to which affairs had degenerated was such that a number of directives were laid down to regulate the relationship between Army and Party personnel. On 16 April 1935, in a decree, part of which has already been quoted, von Blomberg made clear that the servicemen were to be silent about any shortcomings of the Party:

> 'It would be a sign of lack of self-control and an absence of political instinct if annoyance over the defects of an individual led to derogatory criticism and remarks about institutions and organisations which are outside the Armed Forces. They . . . incriminate him who states them. . . . Everyday friction and shortcomings, which can never be avoided completely, can easily be magnified to the status of prestige matters, but this is wrong. The Armed Forces do not need to pursue prestige politics.'[27]

This had little effect. On 28 January 1936, General Dollmann, the commander of Wehrkreis IX, felt it necessary to issue a directive on Army-Party relations:

> 'In the Party, particularly in the lower ranks, some mistrust of the inner attitude and conduct of the officer corps exists. This mistrust is based on a series of incidents which are inclined to give the picture that the officer corps stood in opposition towards the concept of state and outlook represented by the Party. They believe that the officer corps inclines more to the circles who reject the present state, and hence are of the opinion that these circles regard the officer corps as their ultimate support. This is undesirable. . . . The officer corps

must have confidence in the representatives of the Party. Party opinions should not be examined or rejected.'[28]

He then went on to illustrate how relations could, and should, be improved. These included the building up of social contacts with all levels of the Party, the ending of discrimination towards National Socialists in the selection of officers, the termination of functions disapproved of by the Party – such as celebrations on the birthday of the Kaiser – and the fostering of a friendly attitude towards the NDSAP at all times. Every attempt was made by von Blomberg to settle differences between Army and SS men out of court, and thereby prevent any increase in the rivalry. On 25 January 1938 he declared: 'I stress particularly that the relationship to the SS is, like that towards the other organisations of the movement, one of conscious comradeship. Shortcomings in this regard not only damage the appearance of the Armed Forces, but at the same time constitute a severe infringement of my expressed will. I request that attention be given to this thought in the allocation of punishment.'[29]

An indication of the degree of independence possessed by the Army had been revealed by its reaction to the murder of two of its retired generals, von Schleicher, the former Chancellor, and his assistant, von Bredow, both deliberately shot in their homes by the Gestapo during the bloody events of 30 June 1934. They were murdered partly out of revenge for their former intrigues against the National Socialists and partly from the unfounded fear that they were then plotting the overthrow of the new régime. The official version of the killing, to which Hitler assented, was given by von Reichenau in a communiqué:

> 'In recent weeks it has been established that the ex-Defence Minister, General (Retired) von Schleicher has maintained treasonable relationships with foreign powers and with SA leadership circles inimical to the state. It has therefore been proved that both in word and deed he has been acting against the state and its leaders. This meant that in connexion with the general purge now in progress, his arrest was essential. When police officers came to arrest him, General (Retired) von Schleicher offered armed resistance. There was an exchange of shots as a result of which both he and his wife, who placed herself in the line of fire, were mortally wounded.'[30]

Retired, and an unpopular 'political general' though von Schleicher was, his murder aroused considerable resentment within the Army. His few admirers believed the official pronouncement to be totally false, while many others held that the whole affair besmirched the honour of the Army and set a dangerous precedent. Despite the acceptance by the officer corps of the events of 30 June, reaction within the Army to the murder of the generals was immediate and not inconsiderable. Officers spoke out privately in von Schleicher's defence, one of them, Ludwig Crüwell, a future commander of the German Africa Corps, being made the subject of a Gestapo investigation as a result of his doing so; and von Hammerstein, still on the active list, ignored von Blomberg's order not to attend von Schleicher's funeral, even insisting on carrying the decorations of the deceased. Demands for the rehabilitation of the General's honour and the punishment of his murderers were strong. Von Hammerstein and the veteran and venerated Field-Marshal von Mackensen, representative of all that was admired in the old Imperial Army, submitted a long memorandum to President von Hindenburg, which, although intending to inform him of the whole sorry affair and to complain of von Blomberg's attitude to the murder, contained criticism of Hitler's foreign policy and proposed a reconstruction of Germany's government, which in effect meant the replacement of the National Socialist régime by a military dictatorship. This was nothing more nor less than the reassertion of von Schleicher's intention of making Hitler a prisoner of the Army and reorientating foreign policy towards a favourable understanding with Poland and Russia. The memorandum was signed by some thirty generals and senior staff officers. Although it was never received by von Hindenburg, the 'Blue Book of the Reichswehr', as it came to be known, was circulated throughout the Army with ever increasing effect. The clamour for rehabilitation rose, as did Hitler's disquiet. Such was the pressure from the officer corps, which the passage of time did nothing to diminish, that, after advice from von Blomberg, Hitler felt it necessary to make some concession towards the Army. This took the unusual, indeed unique, form of an admission by Hitler that he had erred, made to a gathering of top Army and Party officials in the Berlin Opera House on 3 January 1935. He conceded that the shootings of the two generals had been wrong, and that the derogatory statements made later by himself and Göring had been based on incorrect information. He promised that the names of the two innocent men would be restored to their regimental rolls of honour. This statement, although never formally announced publicly, was reported by Field-Marshal von Mackensen to the association of former General Staff officers, the *Verein Graf Schlieffen,* on 28 February. Although the Field-Marshal's move was regretted by von Blomberg, his action was well-received by the rest of the Army. Hitler had been forced to admit his mistake because of his soldiers' pressure.

But it was over rearmament and the nation's foreign policy that the independence of the German Army within the state became most noticeable and, from Hitler's point of view, most dangerous; for it was here that the Army's most vital interest – its military autonomy – was threatened. The political outlook of its soldiers was one thing, their capacity to wage war effectively, quite another. This, on no account, was to be endangered by the government without strong protests being mounted by the Army's leadership.

Rearmament should have been the strongest link between the Army and Hitler. The soldiers rightly saw the new régime as providing the means by which they could regain their former might and ensure the defence of their homeland, while the Führer viewed the creation of a large and powerful Army as fundamental to the success of his foreign ambitions. Each was grateful for, or at the least cognisant of, the indispensable aid of the other. But here their identity of purpose ended, for Hitler proved incapable of understanding the almost unbearable strains imposed on the Army by his too rapid, and too vast, expansion. In five years the Army grew from 100,000 to 3,343,000 men. Although the size and pace of this rearmament were important in maintaining and extending the acceptance of Hitler by the officers of lower and middle ranks, it also proved to be a cause for considerable contention for the senior generals. As early as May 1934, Beck wrote in despair that the rearmament programme as then being undertaken was 'not a building-up of a peacetime army, but a mobilisation'.[31] Von Fritsch complained bitterly that the Führer's policy was 'forcing everything, overdoing everything, rushing everything far too much and destroying every healthy development'.[32] Von Blomberg, too, was deeply apprehensive, going as far as to be the sole voice in cabinet meetings speaking out against the policy. He described assurances from Hitler's foreign affairs specialist, von Ribbentrop, that there was no need to worry about foreign objections to rearmament as 'all stuff and nonsense!'[33]

The Army leaders wished to tread warily, for they feared the reaction of the major powers to Germany's efforts to establish herself as the greatest military state on the Continent, efforts in direct contradiction to the Versailles Treaty that had been established with such care just sixteen years previously. In the event, they need not have worried. The naïvety of the great powers was matched only by their inaction, but this the generals could not foresee. Of equal concern was the potentially destructive effect on the Army of too much rearmament at too high a speed, which would strike at the very roots of Hitler's declared intention of creating 'an army of the greatest possible strength and internal compactness and homogeneity at the best imaginable level of training'.[34] In June 1936 von Fritsch ordered a study of the material, manpower, and financial requirements of rearmament, which came to the conclusion that military power was being pursued with such vigour that efficiency was declining; that the money required even to maintain the armaments industry in good order after 1940 would be crippling to the economy; and that, anyway, in a major war the Army would be capable of fighting for only seven consecutive months. But, despite frequent protests, nothing was done to ameliorate the situation; the generals' military advice was powerless against Hitler's political will.

The most fundamental parting of the ways between Hitler and his senior generals, however, came over the questions of foreign policy – grand strategy, the future employment of the Army in war. Hitler's plans were aggressive and expansionist, seeing military force as an integral part of their fulfilment. Those of his generals were the opposite, summed up in von Blomberg's directive of 24 June 1937, entitled 'Unified War Preparations of the Armed Forces':

'The general political situation justifies the supposition that Germany does not have to reckon on an attack from any side. This is due mainly to the lack of desire for war on the part of all nations, especially the western powers. It is also due to the lack of military preparedness on the part of a number of states, notably Russia. Germany has just as little intention of unleashing a European war. Nonetheless, the international situation, politically unstable and not exclusive of surprising incidents, requires readiness for war on the part of the German Armed Forces, (a) so that attacks from any side may be countered: (b) so that any favourable political opportunities may be militarily exploited.'[35]

Such an attitude permeated the whole High Command. Indeed, some generals were even more cautious in answer to a request in 1935 from von Blomberg, backed by von Reichenau, to undertake a detailed study of the possibilities of making a premature attack on Czechoslovakia in the event of war, Beck replied: 'After thorough consideration, I hold it to be my duty to declare this very day that if the memorandum of the Minister is not solely concerned with the purpose of operational studies, but is aimed at the practical introduction of preparation for war, then I must express the most dutiful request to be removed from my position at the Truppenamt, because I do not feel myself to be fitted for this latter task.'[36] After a brief exploration, the Czechoslovak plan was laid to rest until 1937.

The deployment plans drawn up by the Army leadership were primarily of a defensive nature, and much emphasis was placed on the building of fortifications and defensive systems in both the east (the Heibsberg Triangle and the Oder-Warthe line) and in the west (the West Wall). Apart from a series of plans for small-scale operations to counter any Polish invasion in the 1920s, no deployment plan was prepared until late 1935. Then, under the direction of von Manstein, the Operations Department of the General Staff drew up *Aufmarsch Rot* (Deployment Red), measures to be taken in the event of what was considered then to be the most likely scene for a future conflict: a two-front war in which Germany was faced by a major attack by the French in the west, assisted by the Czechs in the east. However, the plan depended on Czechoslovakia making the military mistake of remaining primarily on the defensive; no provision was made to counter the Czechs if they chose to do the sensible thing and use their large local superiority to make a quick thrust over the 120 miles to the Reich's capital, Berlin. Therefore, in 1937, another plan, *Aufmarsch Grün* (Deployment Green) was ordered to be drawn up, this aiming to concentrate Germany's forces for a pre-emptive strike at Czechoslovakia to secure the east, before turning to deal with the French invasion which, it was expected, would by then be underway in the west. (It was the 1914 Schlieffen plan in reverse.) Beck still regarded this as militarily unsound, for the same reasons as he gave in 1935: '. . . I can regard such an operation as an act of desperation by which the German Army, as well as surrendering German soil itself, excludes itself from the direct defence of the nation, in all likelihood to find an inglorious end in a foreign land, while at home the enemy dictate their own conditions.'[37] He also believed that any invasion of Czechoslovakia would inevitably bring Britain and France together in united action against Germany. This was an attitude with which many other generals, including von Blomberg, concurred. As a result of his opposition, both *Aufmarsch Grün* and two other plans authorised by von Blomberg, *Sonderfall Otto* (a special case designed to prevent the restoration of the Habsburgs in Austria) and *Sonderfall Erweiterung Rot/Grün* (a special case enlargement of plans Red and Green aimed at checking as far as possible the intervention of Britain, Poland, and Lithuania, a situation that was regarded as fatal) were never completed. Such was the nature of the Germany Army's preparation for war before 1938: defensive, and fearful of the consequences of aggressive action.

Hitler, however, never for one moment agreed with this purely defensive attitude. From the beginning he enunciated his plans to his generals in terms that could leave them in no doubt of his intentions. On 3 February 1933, some thirty days after assuming power, Hitler told a meeting of the senior commanders that the only answer to Germany's long-term problems was the acquisition of suitable living space through armed struggle. Some were impressed; a few, like von Fritsch, apprehensive; most were thoroughly cool in their response, a reaction which Hitler did not fail to perceive. General von Leeb remarked: 'A businessman whose wares are any good, does not need to boost them in the loudest tones of a market crier.'[38] The generals thought that the realities of Germany's situation would prevent such dangerous dreaming from ever being translated into action. But a year later, on 28 February 1934 before a gathering of senior SA and Army leaders, Hitler again returned to this theme. One of those listening, General von Weichs recorded the contents of his address, which included: 'The NSDAP has overcome the unemployment. These blossoms would last only for about eight years, however, as an economic recession must ensue. This evil could be remedied only by creating living space for the surplus population. However, the western powers would not let us do this. Therefore, short, decisive blows to the west and then to the east could be necessary.'[39] Again, the reception to such remarks was cool, if not unbelieving. Von Weichs noted: '. . . one did not take at face value these war-like prophecies, which were certainly in sharp contradiction to the protestations of peace which otherwise filled the air. The soldier was accustomed not to take the words of politicians too seriously. They often chose points of view which did not have to correspond with their true intentions, in order to achieve political ends. Thus these gloomy prognostications were probably soon forgotten.'[40] But Hitler did not forget them, nor the silence of his generals.

Despite von Weich's complacency, there was by now growing disquiet over the new Chancellor's foreign policy. On 14 October 1933 he had surprised and shocked his generals by announcing, unbeknown even to von

Blomberg, Germany's withdrawal from the League of Nations and from the Geneva disarmament conference. While German diplomats were fairly sure that no counter-action would be taken by the French, the Army leadership was alarmed to read in secret orders prepared by Hitler that the Führer was quite ready to defend the Reich's borders against expected League's sanctions. As the generals knew only too well, the German Armed Forces were totally inadequate to meet these. Moreover, the fact that Hitler was prepared to run such a risk without even consulting them, quite unnerved them. This was followed ninety days later by an unexpected and dangerous development in German policy in the east. The response of the Chancellor to the threat posed to Germany by a preventive war undertaken by Poland, plans for which were known to exist in early 1933, was to reverse the foreign policy that had formed the basis of the Army's strategic thinking since the early 1920s. On 26 January 1934, Hitler signed a ten-year non-aggression pact with the Poles, and, as a consequence, the German-Soviet military pact of 1926 was allowed to lapse. The implications for the Army and the nation of abandoning the distant friendliness of Germany for the Soviet Union, and embarking on a line of rapprochement with Poland, were considerable. Not only was this pact distasteful to the generals, who continually echoed von Seeckt's pronouncement that 'Poland's existence is intolerable and incompatible with the survival of Germany. . . . With Poland collapses one of the strongest pillars of the Peace of Versailles, France's advance post of power';[41] it was also dangerous, for it would lead eventually to conflict with the USSR and – if, as seemed likely, that country were joined by the western powers (France and Czechoslovakia at the very least) – to a war on two fronts. Thus, in both the west and the east, it appeared to the Army that Hitler was courting disaster, with Germany lacking totally the military capacity with which to guarantee the success of his policies.

The first open conflict between Hitler and the Army came over the question of the military reoccupation of the Rhineland. Both regarded this as necessary for securing the vital strategic, economic, and communications centres of the Ruhr and the Rhine valley, but there their agreement ended. In March 1936 Hitler believed the time to be opportune for such a move, while his generals feared the worst. It was inconceivable to them that Britain and France would not resist such a violation of their foreign policy, one that was in direct contradiction not only to the provisions of the Versailles Treaty and the Locarno Pact, but also to the continued security of France and the stability of Europe. There had been warnings that, if such a reoccupation were attempted, both France and Britain would act; Germany would be hopelessly outnumbered and ill-prepared for a war, and would have to concede to the Allies' demands. Her emerging political strength would then be halted, her rearmament policy shattered. Hitler, however, took no heed of his generals' warnings and pressed ahead with his plans, basing all hopes of success on a gigantic bluff which would test the willingness of the signatories to the Locarno Pact to act. He believed they would not move. His generals thought differently; Jodl described the atmosphere in the General Staff at that time as 'like that of a roulette table when a player stakes his fortune on a single number'.[42] The military advisers made efforts to have their alternative policies accepted; Beck even submitted a solution to Hitler, designed to allay Allied fears, which proposed that the occupation should be accompanied by an undertaking that the Rhineland would not be fortified. Von Blomberg, on behalf of the General Staff, suggested that a bargain be made with the French whereby, in return for the Germans withdrawing their few battalions after the occupation, the French, for their part, should withdraw four or five times as many from their borders. But all opposition came to nought. On 2 March von Blomberg issued the directive for the reoccupation entitled *Winterübung* (Winter Exercise), to be followed a few days later by the date of Z day, which was set for the 7th.

At first, only three battalions of German infantry were sent across the Rhine on that day, to a jubilant reception, although by the afternoon four divisions had been raised from the well-trained *Landespolizei* of the demilitarised zone. Hitler later recorded: 'The forty-eight hours after the march . . . were the most nerve-racking in my life. If the French had then marched into the Rhineland we would have had to withdraw with our tails between our legs.'[43] But the Führer held fast to his intentions; the French did not march; no one reacted. Nevertheless, the generals were far from confident, and on 9 March, at the behest of von Fritsch and Beck, a panicky von Blomberg urged Hitler to withdraw the troops from Aachen, Trier, and Saarbrücken for fear of a strong French attack. On that day the Führer's military adjutant was summoned no less that three times to the War Minister in order to impress on Hitler the urgency of the situation, only for the dictator to dismiss these requests and, after a tense meeting with his Minister, declare that von Blomberg possessed weak nerves. He later compared him to a 'hysterical maiden'.[44]

These hesitations and fears expressed so forcibly to Hitler over the Rhineland reoccupation, however reasonable they might have been, proved fatal to the future relationship between the Führer and his generals. Hitler had proved to his own satisfaction that his will-power and intuition were immeasurably superior to the combined professional expertise of his military advisers, a 'fact' which he was often to use later in justification of his acts. More important, he was convinced that, in the field of foreign adventure, his generals were not the compliant creatures he wished for, instead holding ideas far more cautious than, and in direct contradiction to, his own. This was the beginning of a disillusionment which in 1941 he expressed thus: 'Before I became Chancellor I thought the General Staff was like a mastiff which had been held tight by the collar because it threatened all and sundry. Since then I have had to recognise that the General Staff is anything but that. It has consistently tried to impede every action that I have thought necessary. . . . It is I who have always had to goad on this mastiff.'[45]

The generals' reluctance to countenance an aggressive foreign policy became ever more apparent to Hitler. Von Manstein remembered that 'It was the War Minister, von Blomberg, who first opposed general conscription. . . . It was also von Blomberg who at the time of the march into the Rhineland advised Hitler . . . to recall the German garrisons from the left bank of the river when the French ordered a partial mobilisation.'[46] On 15 March 1935, von Blomberg distinguished himself at a cabinet meeting by being the only person present to speak out against rearmament. This continued to concern him for a long time to come. As Keitel, von Reichenau's successor as Chief of the Ministerial Office, wrote later: 'What we and von Blomberg earnestly feared at the time was the possibility of sanctions of which we had become aware from Italy's Ethiopian campaign [which began on 5 October 1935]; they continued to hang over us like the Sword of Damocles all the time our rearmament programme was still only at the organisational stage; it must be remembered that we no longer had even a seven-division army on a war-footing, as it had been split up throughout the Reich since 1 October 1935 to provide the nuclei for the formation of the new thirty-six division army.'[47] For such reasons von Blomberg took great exception to German involvement in the Spanish Civil War, which lasted from mid-1936 to March 1939. As General Warlimont recorded: 'It is . . . not generally known that . . . he [von Blomberg] had been so vigorous in his opposition to increased involvement of the Army in the Spanish Civil War that it was hardly necessary for the Commander-in-Chief of the Army to intervene.'[48] Indeed, von Blomberg was generally expressing his dissatisfaction openly, without too much regard for who heard of it. He was active against the demands of Göring for his Air Force; he was critical of von Ribbentrop, a man well-regarded by Himmler, when ambassador to London; and he was contemptuous of the Italian Army, something that upset both the head of the Luftwaffe and the chief of the SS. Unfortunately, however, von Blomberg had weakened his position when, in August 1935, he sent his closest confidant, von Reichenau, to command Wehrkreis VII, hoping thereby to give his junior additional experience in troop command in preparation for his eventual succession to the post of War Minister. In his place, von Blomberg chose Wilhelm Keitel, an easy-going, efficient subordinate, but one who lacked the personality to provide any kind of driving force for new ideas, or for opposition to the Führer's policies.

The next direct confrontation between Hitler and his military advisers occurred on 5 November 1937, at a conference at the Reich Chancellery attended by the War and Foreign Ministers and the heads of the three services. Hitler repeated the basic principles of his future policy: 'The only, perhaps dreamlike solution as it appears to us, lies in winning a greater amount of living space, an endeavour which at all times has been the cause of the building of states and of the movement of peoples.'[49] Germany would have to begin this outward movement by 1943 at the latest, for by that time her war capacity might be declining relative to that of her future enemies, and the pressure of population and economics would force direct action. If the western powers would not permit this move east, they would have to be dealt with first. History had proved that such expansion as was an essential for Germany's survival could not be achieved without risk or force. It remained only to ask 'when?' and 'how?' Hitler's adjutant, Friedrich Hossbach, records the generals' reaction, one first of astonishment and then of objection:

> 'The discussion took a very sharp form at times, above all in the differences between Blomberg and Fritsch on the one hand, and Göring on the other, and Hitler participated mainly as an attentive observer. . . . I do remember exactly that the sharpness of the opposition, both in content and in form, did not fail to make its impression on Hitler, as I could see from his changing expressions. Every detail of the conduct of Blomberg and Fritsch must have made plain to Hitler that his policies had met with only direct impersonal contradictions, instead of applause and agreement. And he knew very well that both generals were opposed to any warlike entanglement provoked from our side. It is a sin of omission before history on my part that the opinions of Blomberg and Fritsch at the conference of 5 November 1937 have not been recorded in greater detail. . . .'[50]

At best, both feared that Hitler underestimated the strength of the Czech defences, and at worst they could see nothing but disaster in any conflict in which Britain and France were Germany's enemies. On 9 November, the anniversary of the abortive Munich putsch, von Fritsch again attempted to persuade Hitler of the unpalatable military realities of the course of action he proposed, but to no avail. Such was the Führer's anger at being thus opposed, that afterwards he refused to see von Neurath, the Foreign Minister and von Fritsch's ally on this question, until mid-January 1938. Von Blomberg, however, despite his fundamental disagreement with Hitler, which was expressed in such an unexpectedly severe manner on 5 November, proceeded, as was his duty, to carry out his Supreme Commander's wishes, ordering his staff to revise the plans for the invasion of Czechoslovakia, *Aufmarsch Grün*, so that they would correspond more closely with the recently declared policy. On 13 December, von Blomberg gave Hitler a report on the military preparations in which he laid great emphasis on Germany's inability to wage war and the inadequacies of the Armed Forces, especially in their reserves of ammunition. Warlimont wrote later that 'his real reason for stressing this factor was undoubtedly opposition to this dangerous type of policy'.[51] Furthermore, Beck, fully aware of Hitler's intentions, drew up a memorandum in which he contradicted every one of the military, political, economic, and moral bases of the Führer's plans.

By the beginning of 1938, then, Hitler had become thoroughly disillusioned with his 'mastiff'. He made one further attempt to obtain the voluntary assent of the military at a meeting on 22 January at the War Ministry, directing his appeal over the heads of von Blomberg, von Fritsch, and Beck to the senior Army officers. But he was so unsure of his audience that his speech was badly delivered and his reception was unenthusiastic. Talk of the replacement of Christianity by National Socialism, of the serious plight of the Reich being solvable only by the acquisition of living space, of the domination of the world by pure-blooded nations, made little impact on the assembled generals. Frustrated abuse aimed at the audience, castigating them for their reactionary nature and their lack of foresight and positive thinking, produced nothing but antipathy. At the end, Hitler was aware he had failed to win the voluntary consent to the policies he so earnestly desired.

5

Crisis

The German officer has an abundance of pride and honour. But what use is that in these uncertain times? Politics now dominates all.

GENERAL LUDWIG BECK
Chief of the General Staff, 1933–38

By 1938, it was clear that Hitler's senior generals, who had always afforded him the loyalty owed to a legally constituted Head of State and Supreme Commander, and who had voluntarily allowed National Socialist ideology to enter the Army, were opposing the fundamentals of his future policy. Worse still, it was on their professional expertise that the success of this policy was based. Not unnaturally, Hitler's consternation, and irritation, must have been immense, although there is no evidence of any plan to rid himself of such opposition. Relations between the politician and the soldier in the Third Reich were at a stage when, in democracies, resignations would be obligatory and, in dictatorships, purges begun. The problem for Hitler, however, was not what to do – that, surely, was clear; it was how to do it. How could he eliminate the obstructions of his generals without bringing on himself the undying enmity of the instrument on which he was to rely for the success of his aims? Indeed, would not such action carry with it the very real risk of inducing an armed reaction from the Army? Was it, then, possible to get rid of his opponents at all? Contrary to the assertions of historians, the Führer was quite unprepared to take action against them. But, at this point fortune intervened, presenting to Hitler the solution of his dilemma. It took the murky guise of an unfortunate marriage to a prostitute, a case of mistaken identity with a homosexual, and the overweening ambition of two of the Führer's most ruthless political subordinates.

By 1938 the Army had reached a position broadly similar to that of the SA in 1934: both could be considered as the most powerful organisations within the National Socialist state; both were independent of the Party leadership; both were the objects of jealousy and ambition; and, most crucial of all, both had forfeited Hitler's confidence. The SS had intrigued against the Army since 1934, Himmler and his associates seeing it not only as the one important section of German society remaining free from their influence and control, but also as a powerful check to their military ambitions, then finding expression in the establishment of the SS-VT. Göring, in his capacity of Commander-in-Chief of the Luftwaffe, had long considered the generals as his rivals. He was angered by their limitation of the size and role of his Air Force, and resentful of their condescending treatment. Von Fritsch had once accused him of being a dilettante! Von Blomberg and von Fritsch made him feel small; he was their junior and, worst still, they blocked his path to the coveted post of War Minister. Consequently, at the beginning of 1938, powerful forces around Hitler were ranged against the Army leaders. All that was required was the pretext on which to act decisively.

Von Blomberg was the first to toss his fate unwittingly to fortune. On 12 January 1938, the widowed War Minister married Erna Grühn, a shorthand typist from the Reich Egg Marketing Board, who was already pregnant with his child. How von Blomberg first met her was a mystery – possibly it had been on one of his jaunts to Berlin's night-club area – but clearly he was aware that she was a girl 'with a past'. But that past, unbeknown to him, included prostitution and posing for pornographic photographs. Such a revelation, should it become public, would utterly ruin von Blomberg's career. As it was, his marriage to a mere typist outraged the officer corps; should she turn out to be a prostitute as well, his resignation or dismissal would be inevitable.

While Field-Marshal and Frau von Blomberg were happily on their honeymoon, a certain Curt Hellmuth Muller of the Reichskriminalpolizei was engaged in identifying lewd pin-up females, when he came across a photograph of the unclad body of the War Minister's wife. A further search revealed that she appeared in police records for morality crimes. From there the file on Frau von Blomberg quickly found its way onto Keitel's desk via the Berlin Police President, Count von Helldorf. But Keitel, an old friend and confidant of von Blomberg, whose daughter his son was to marry, refused to take any responsibility for the information now in his possession, and pleaded that, as he had not seen the woman in question, von Helldorf should take the matter to Göring, who, with Hitler, had acted as witness to the wedding. This the Police President undertook to do, little knowing what the result would be. The move was fatal: Göring now held the means by which to destroy his rival, and thereby to advance his own position. To secure von Blomberg's dismissal, however, was not enough; he must assure himself of the succession. Von Fritsch, the senior general in the Armed Forces, and a brilliant soldier, was von Blomberg's natural successor, and his appointment to the War Ministry would have been consistent with the tradition of installing an Army officer as the Head of State's highest military adviser. But Göring already had at hand the means by which von Fritsch could be eliminated. He had planned a brilliant double-stroke against the military leadership; one, to all outward appearances, based not on dubious political motives but on moral principles. Hitler would not refuse; the generals could not object; the public would applaud; and Göring would become War Minister. It was all so simple.

Von Fritsch's hostage to fortune was, like von Blomberg's, sexual, but, unlike the War Minister's, totally without foundation. As a middle-aged man who had never married, he was an easy target for charges of homosexuality. Both Himmler and Heydrich were eager to exploit such an opportunity, and in August 1936 had placed before the Führer an eight-page document purporting to prove von Fritsch a homosexual. Hitler, however, sensing instinctively that the allegation was utter nonsense (as did all who knew von Fritsch) and that it must have been based on false evidence (which it was), dismissed it out of hand and ordered the file to be burnt. The case of the SS revolved around a statement made under interrogation in 1935 by one Otto Schmidt, a labourer of many previous convictions who specialised in the petty blackmail of homosexuals. One cold evening in November 1933 in Berlin, near the Wannsee Station, Schmidt had witnessed a homosexual act between a man with a monocle and a youth. Masquerading as a detective he had ascertained the man's name and title from his identity card. It was, he remembered, General von Fritsch. Schmidt then proceeded to blackmail the man for a couple of thousand reichsmarks. Such was the substance of the allegation against the Army's Commander-in-Chief, and it was this that Göring had asked to be reconsidered in mid-December 1937. This was no idle speculation on the part of the Air Force Commander; his interest in the matter followed hard on von Blomberg's visit to him to ask for advice concerning his proposed marriage to Erna Grühn, when the War Minister had pointed out that not only was she a child of the people but that she also possessed a 'certain', undefined past.

Now began between Göring and Himmler an unholy alliance whose sole object was the downfall of the Army's leaders and, thereby, an end to the independence of the military. The Gestapo, who had long had von Fritsch under surveillance, keeping his file up to date, initiated a watch on Erna Grühn and detailed two agents to shadow the Army Commander on his trip to Egypt. The trap was set; all that was required was positive proof against von Blomberg. This arrived with von Helldorf on Saturday 22 January, 1938, and, on the 24th, Göring, weeping crocodile tears and lamenting his role as the bearer of bad tidings, placed the allegations against Germany's two principal generals on Hitler's desk.

There can be no doubt that the evidence against his chief military advisers hit Hitler hard. While he was clearly dissatisfied with his generals, he was totally unprepared for this blow, and, although he probably never believed the charges against von Fritsch, the scandal concerning von Blomberg's marriage bitterly revolted him. He had attended the wedding as a witness and had even shaken the bride's hand. One of his aides, Wiedemann, wrote: '. . . throughout the whole four years during which I served him, I have never seen him so downcast. He paced slowly up and down his room, bent and with his hands behind his back, mumbling that if a German Field-Marshal could do something like this, then anything in the world was possible.'[1] General von Rundstedt found the Führer 'in a fearful state of excitement such as I had never seen before. Something had cracked in him; he had lost all confidence in men.'[2] Hitler was thrown off balance, and was as yet unaware of the opportunity fate had presented him.

Indeed, it took him some time to grasp the potential of what has come to be known as the 'Blomberg–Fritsch affair'. His shock, hesitation, and indecision are proof enough that he was completely unprepared for the replacement of his generals. It is evidence, too, of his hitherto well-intentioned attitude towards them. Deviousness was lacking completely. Hitler was not even convinced immediately of the necessity of his War Minister's dismissal, and at first thought of a divorce as the answer to the problem. But Göring's machinations continued, his most effective ruse being not to inform von Blomberg of the extent of the charges brought against him, thereby ensuring Hitler's rage at what he took to be the War Minister's inability to comprehend the heinous nature of his offence. Göring then emphasised the outrage of those in the officer corps who were aware of the scandal, an outrage expressed later by Beck who declared that the Field-Marshal was not fit to command a regiment, and that he must straightway divorce his new wife or else be struck off the officer list. In any event, his career as War Minister was finished. It was bad enough that Germany's highest-ranking general should have married a typist; it was unthinkable that she should turn out to be a prostitute too. It was an insult to the very tradition of the officer corps, an affront to its honour, and a weakening of its prestige. Furthermore it would provide the Party with a subject for much criticism and mirth. To bring home to the generals the enormity of the whole affair, prostitutes throughout Germany were constantly phoning them to announce the elevation of one of their members. Von Fritsch was one of the few to take a calmer view, preferring to wait until his superior's guilt was proven, while all the time the clouds were gathering over his own future.

But, although at last convinced of the need for dismissal, Hitler had no thought of taking over von Blomberg's position himself. Indeed, from 24 to 26 January, the day of the removal, Hitler spent much time searching for a successor. On the morning of the 26th, for example, on hearing from Hossbach of von Fritsch's complete rejection of the homosexuality charges, Hitler declared with an air of relief: 'Why, then things are in order and von Fritsch can become Minister.'[3] The Army adjutant, however, replied that von Fritsch had no wish to have this honour bestowed on him, and the discussion turned to other possibilities. Finally Hitler seized on the idea of having the elderly Count von Schülenberg as his new Minister, a 'safe' man with a disinguished war record, who, as a Party supporter, held high honorary ranks in both the SA and SS. Von Schülenberg was even ordered to attend on the Führer in expectation of his appointment. Later that same morning, having informed von Blomberg of his dismissal, Hitler, still valuing his ex-Minister's advice on such matters, asked him to nominate a likely successor, excluding von Fritsch. The former War Minister suggested Göring as the most senior of those remaining, but Hitler would not for one moment entertain the idea, von Blomberg later recalling that he made 'one or two unpleasant remarks about Göring; he was too easy going – the word idle may even have been used – and in any case there was no question of him'.[4] (Hitler had already firmly decided on this point, having told his aide, Wiedemann, the day before that there was 'No question of it. That fellow Göring does not understand even how to carry out a Luftwaffe inspection.')[5] But who else? Perhaps out of spite for his former military colleagues whom he believed were now treating him so badly, or perhaps even because he genuinely believed it, von Blomberg suggested that Hitler himself should take over the post of War Minister and Commander-in-Chief of the Armed Forces. To this, Hitler made no reply.

This advice of von Blomberg was among the most significant ever given in the short history of the Third Reich, and certainly was of immense importance to the future of the Army. Hitler was presented with the solution to his problems with the military leaders, a solution which, in his five years of office, he had never seen fit to even contemplate, let alone scheme for seizing the opportunity. He immediately gave up the search for other men. The new direction his mind took was indicated by his next question to von Blomberg: whom could he suggest to head the staff? Obtaining no satisfactory answer, Hitler asked him who was in charge of his own staff. Von Blomberg replied that it was Keitel, but added 'He's nothing but the man who runs my office'. Hitler recognised immediately that he had found a man who would be an efficient *chef de bureau*, and at the same time totally subservient to his leader, possessing no independent ideas of his own. 'That's exactly the man I am looking for',[6] the dictator exclaimed, and with that, von Blomberg, having performed his greatest service for his Führer and his greatest disservice to the Army, disappeared into oblivion.

During the meeting with von Blomberg, there had been no trace of bitterness on Hitler's part. Jodl was told by Keitel that the Führer had discharged the unpleasant duty of dismissal with 'superhuman kindness' and that he had even given the Field-Marshal the promise, unfulfilled as it turned out, that 'as soon as Germany's hour comes, you shall be at my side'.[7] Hitler had told von Blomberg that he should go into voluntary exile from Germany for a year while the storm blew over, and that for this the Reichsbank would be directed to give him 50,000 reichsmarks in foreign exchange. Furthermore, as was the tradition for field-marshals, von Blomberg would continue to draw full salary and, nominally, remain on the active list. Hitler even summoned him to the Reich Chancellery for the last time on the morning of 27 January to wish him well before his exile to Italy.

For the rest of his life, von Blomberg remained faithful to his wife, only once giving any indication that he would be prepared to renounce her for a return to active duty. But till the end he was ostracised by his fellow generals, even when he lay dying in captivity after the Second World War. Surprisingly, it was Hitler who did most to ensure that his former War Minister lived out the rest of his life peacefully, and he never gave in to the Army's demand that the Field-Marshal should be brought before a specially constituted Court of Honour, the verdict of which would have been predictable and, moreover, would only have strengthened Hitler's position.

Von Blomberg's suggestion to Hitler on the morning of the 26th not only undermined the semi-autonomous position of the Army within the Reich; it also sealed von Fritsch's fate. Till then Hitler had been undecided about his Army Commander, telling Hossbach that he was aware of von Fritsch's great services and had no desire to part with him. Von Fritsch sensed this, believing the Führer would realise the allegations were false and punish their perpetrators, Göring and Himmler. With Hitler, remembering the SS attack on von Fritsch in 1936, far from convinced of his guilt, there was some justification for this hope, though it turned out to be unrealised. Furthermore, the firmness and confidence with which many of the military dismissed the evidence as false did not fail to impress the Führer. However, von Blomberg's suggestion, with all its potential, far outweighed such feelings. Now he possessed within his grasp not just the nominal control of the Wehrmacht, but its actual direction as well; he could ensure it would provide no opposition to his policies in the future. For this to become a reality, though, it was vital to have a compliant Army Commander. Von Fritsch had to go, and on what better pretext than homosexuality. Could not people believe such a charge of the bachelor Army Commander? Furthermore, if von Fritsch were removed for such a reason it would, Hitler believed, avoid any interpretation that the dismissal arose from a clash of personalities or from his own ambition to humble his military advisers.

As a result, by the afternoon on 26 January, Hitler, without any further provocation or proof, had set himself firmly against von Fritsch; by early evening he had decided that legal action would be taken against his Army Commander, not by the usual form of a military tribunal, but by a special court under the auspices of the Gestapo. There was to be no chance of von Fritsch avoiding conviction. Immediately after this decision, Hitler saw Keitel and told him that, whatever happened, he wanted a new Army Commander. Later that day, in his last act renouncing von Fritsch, Hitler called him to the Reich Chancellery, and at the meeting Göring and Himmler seized the opportunity to illustrate their allegations in a most startling manner. The blackmailer Schmidt was produced to identify von Fritsch in Hitler's presence, and the Army chief, confronted so unexpectedly by his accuser, became inarticulate with rage, a show of emotion which did much to lower him in the Führer's eyes. Göring was so well-satisfied with the outcome of the incident that all he could do was collapse on a sofa shrieking: 'He did it, he did it.'[8] Hitler asked von Fritsch for his resignation 'for reasons of health', but this was refused, and the Führer had to wait another four days before it was given.

The trial of von Fritsch opened more than a month later, on Thursday 10 March, with proceedings suspended for a week owing to the occupation of Austria. On the 18th the court returned the verdict of 'acquitted on the grounds of proven innocence'. Thus, despite all his attempts to direct the course of events against von Fritsch, even by the appointment of Göring as court president, Hitler was unable to prevent a few intrepid men, led by Count von der Goltz, the defence council, and Dr Carl Sack, the official attorney, from demonstrating that the accusation was false. They proved that, from almost the beginning, the Gestapo had been aware that the accusation was based on a case of mistaken identity; that the man Schmidt blackmailed was not the Army Commander, von Fritsch, but a retired Army captain called von Frisch, who even spelt his name differently; and that Himmler, Heydrich, and their subordinates had done all in their power to hide these facts. Only Göring, through his clever manoeuvrings, escaped open condemnation.

In the particular battle that revolved around the specific issue of von Fritsch's innocence, the Army triumphed over the Party. But in the generals' wider, and more serious, conflict against political interference, the military were soundly beaten. On 4 February the two new Commanders-in-Chief of the Armed Forces and the Army were announced, as well as a radical reorganisation of the high command structure. The new Commander of the Wehrmacht was Hitler. On that day the subjection of the German Army to the will of the Führer began.

Why did the Army not take direct action during the 'Fritsch crisis' to preserve its traditional autonomy and prestige? As von Fritsch himself noted bitterly: 'No nation ever allowed the Commander-in-Chief of its Army to be subjected to such disgraceful treatment. . . . Such treatment is not only undignified for me, at the same time it dishonours the whole Army.'[9] If its leaders were reluctant to act against Hitler because, despite all, they still maintained their previously justified belief in his good intentions towards them, could they not have moved against the evil influences surrounding him and perverting his judgement? It would not have been the first occasion in history when men had sought to save a ruler from his advisers. At that time, a united Army taking concerted action throughout the nation would almost certainly have been successful. Its only opponents would have been the Luftwaffe, still in its infancy and vulnerable to surprise occupation of the airfields, and the SS, which then possessed only 10,000 men under arms. Moreover, there were strong indications that, had the Army taken the initiative, the SA, then numbering some two and a half million men, would have joined it to exact revenge on their hated SS rivals for the events of 30 June 1934. In the event the crisis passed; the Army made no move.

At first glance it appears that such inaction was inexcusable on the part of the Army's leaders, fully justifying their condemnation by historians. Wheeler-Bennett wrote: 'The Fritsch–Blomberg crisis awakened many to the realisation of their true position, but of that many there were all too few who were prepared to take action in the cause of their own emancipation.

The majority – some because of ambition, some because of the fatal mystic spell of their own oath of loyalty, some through fear – elected to continue to support the Führer, to submit to the dictates of his "intuition" and to follow in his train.'[10] But this judgement implies a certain freedom of action possessed by the military leaders which, in reality, was not available to them. The Army found itself unable to react otherwise than submissively, despite the aggressive intentions of a few of its members; once again, it was the prisoner of its heritage.

It should not be forgotten that, for most of the officers, the Blomberg–Fritsch affair was characterised only by their complete ignorance of the events. Such was the veil of secrecy surrounding the dismissals that, outside Berlin, few officers had even the slightest indication before the beginning of February of the troubles besetting their leadership. Colonel Warlimont, for example, then an artillery regiment commander at Düsseldorf, heard not a hint of the momentous decisions being taken until Hitler's announcement on 4 February, and even by the autumn, when he was in an important post in the newly formed Armed Forces High Command, he was not much better informed. Indeed, many of those who turned up to hear the Führer deliver his speech on the 4th had heard of the reorganisation only through the morning's papers. In short, the officer corps as a whole was presented with a fait accompli of which it knew little or nothing of the facts that lay behind it. As General Guderian remarked, 'blame can be apportioned only to the few individuals in authority at the top', because for 'the majority, the true state of affairs remained obscure'.[11]

What, then, of the Army leadership referred to by Guderian? Why did it make no attempt to thwart Hitler's moves? The reasons are not hard to discern. As has been shown, the officer corps possessed none of the political experience and expertise with which to comprehend and counter the skilful machinations of the Führer during that particular period. As Westphal remarked: 'For centuries Germans had never had to suffer an internal tyranny, such as other countries had often experienced, and the Prusso-German Army had never placed itself at the disposal of a revolution. Only one famous rebel had ever risen in its ranks, General von Yorck; and he had revolted only against foreign domination.'[12] Nor were the generals personally equipped for rebellion. This, the Italian ambassador, Attolico, recognised: 'The Germans are not given to conspiracy. A conspirator needs everything they lack: patience, knowledge of human nature, psychology, tact. . . . To fight conditions here, you ought to be persevering and a good dissembler like Talleyrand and Fouché. Where will you find a Talleyrand between Rosenheim and Eydtkuhnen?'[13]

The naïvety of the generals is perhaps best illustrated by Guderian's reactions. After the Second World War he referred to 4 February as 'the second blackest day of the Army High Command' (the first, he believed was, 30 June 1934), and went on to record that 'The Fritsch case did prove the existence of a serious lack of trust between the Head of the Reich and the leaders of the Army; I was aware of this, though I was not in a position to understand what lay behind it all.'[14] This, however, contrasts strongly with what he wrote at the time. In a letter to his wife written on 7 February, Guderian stated categorically: 'The report to Hitler has provided me with the insight into things which would better not have happened. The Führer has acted, as usual, with the finest human decency. It is to be hoped that he will be approved by his colleagues.'[15] Other generals were equally credulous. They simply could not believe that Hitler, the friend and ally of the Army in the struggles against Party interference, could have turned so suddenly, and so bitterly, against his military advisers. The reversal of his attitude was too complete, and too sudden, to comprehend. As Guderian recalled: 'These serious allegations against our most senior officers, whom we knew to be men of spotless honour, cut us to the quick. They were quite incredible, and yet our immediate reaction was that the first magistrate of the German state could not simply have invented these stories out of thin air.'[16]

The general feeling was that, at worst, the Führer was the dupe of an SS intrigue, and that, once the facts were known, a full and proper rehabilitation of the former Army Commander would take place. Even von Fritsch himself had no other thought except that Hitler was acting only out of ignorance of the truth. As he later recounted: 'Yet if I had known how wholly this man is without scruple and how he gambles with the fate of the German people, I should have acted differently and taken on myself the odium of having acted through egotistic motives.'[17] As it was, von Fritsch, the one central figure in the crisis around whom the Army would have rallied, refused to take any decision. He was no political general and was incapable of acting like one; he saw the matter primarily as a personal attack on him by the Party, in accordance with past events, and had no intention of causing bloodshed for his own sake alone.

A highly sensitive man, von Fritsch was in such a state of shock at the enormity of the charges against his person that he was rendered unable to take action, whether or not he believed it correct to do so; indeed, so submissive was he, that he even gave himself to Gestapo interrogation, an unheard of thing for an Army officer to do. Beck, as Chief of the General Staff, was perhaps the only other man in a position to speak for the Army, but he was inhibited by his sense of duty, his decision to await events, and his belief in the importance of maintaining his position as a counterbalance to Hitler and his associates in the controversy over foreign policy. Furthermore, the strain on Beck was immense: his health was failing and now he had added to his already strenuous duties those of Acting Commander-in-Chief until 4 February. Gerd von Rundstedt, too, the senior Army general after von Fritsch, a most respected man who was far from being full of ardour for National Socialism, declared that he was quite assured of Hitler's (and Göring's!) sincerity and good intentions. So convinced was he that everything was satisfactory that he purposely failed to present von Fritsch's challenge of a duel to Himmler, an occasion which might have given an opportunity for wider action against the SS.

An even greater impediment to concerted Army action came from the new Army Commander-in-Chief, von Brauchitsch. For personal reasons he was the creature of his master, Adolf Hitler, and his acceptance of the post before von Fritsch's trial implied recognition and approval of the Führer's actions. His equivocal attitude towards the whole affair made it impossible for the Army to present a united front, and his only positive action during the whole period was to protest against the Gestapo's intrusion into Army barracks to interview former servants of von Fritsch. After von Fritsch's innocence had been proved, von Brauchitsch refused to lay before Hitler demands from certain senior officers calling for a reinstatement of von Fritsch, a public explanation of why he had been forced to retire, and several changes in senior SS and Gestapo appointments, including those of Himmler and Heydrich. This, too, was a missed opportunity which might have led to greater things. Nevertheless, whatever the personal and political shortcomings of these men, none of them possessed that degree of independence from his military heritage which enabled him to take decisive action against his legally constituted Head of State.

In the west, the reaction of an Army to the removal of its Commander-in-Chief had, traditionally, been one not of revolution but of obedience. Usually, every attempt was made to understand the reasons that lay behind the government's action. Indeed, the year before, Stalin had begun, unhindered, his great purges of the Red Army leadership that make Hitler's 1938 reorganisation look ridiculously mild in comparison; and the British Secretary of State for War had dismissed both the Chief of the Imperial General Staff and the Adjutant-General without any fear of reaction. Few German officers would have questioned the legally constituted executive's authority in this sphere, and, certainly, von Fritsch had no quarrel with the principle. His oath of loyalty had been given. On 25 January, he declared as soon as he heard of the charges against him: 'If Hitler wants to get rid of me then he has only to say the word and I will resign.'[18] As it was, it took him four days to do so, but this was not because he disagreed with Hitler's right to order his dismissal, but because he found the method by which he had done so distasteful, and feared that his resignation would be taken as a confession of guilt. In the end, however, von Fritsch's overriding sense of duty guided his actions. Nor could Beck find any reason for overturning the authority of the state simply because it conflicted with the interests of the military establishment. Dissatisfied as he was with the turn events had taken, Beck nevertheless found himself forced to admit: 'Mutiny and revolution are words that do not exist in the lexicon of the German soldier.'[19]

After 26 January, Hitler's handling of the Fritsch crisis was brilliant, thoroughly confounding the politically inept generals. He made every effort to avoid any issue which would unnecessarily alarm the officer corps, cause it to close ranks and enter into a direct confrontation with himself. Therefore, he did not dismiss von Fritsch instantly but allowed him several days in which to decide to resign. He submitted to fierce military opposition to the idea of a special Gestapo court to try von Fritsch, and, instead, instituted a normal military Court of Honour, making every effort to convey the impression that the crisis was not of his making and that his sole desire was simply to render justice. Indeed, Hitler did all he could to allay military suspicion of his actions: to Beck, on 26 January, he promised that he would do nothing without first consulting him; to von Rundstedt he gave assurances as to the future integrity of the Army; and to the assembled generals, on 4 February, he declared that all talk of Himmler being the future Commander-in-Chief of the Armed Forces was nonsense (as, indeed, it was) and that at some future date this post might once again be occupied by a senior Army officer.

Furthermore, there were two major distractions, one connected with, the other external to, the crisis, that diverted the attention of the senior generals away from the crucial issues at stake. First, much effort was expended on the narrow 'details' of von Fritsch's trial, his innocence and rehabilitation, and, as Guderian noted: 'Even in [this] case . . . which from the very beginning seemed not only improbable, but unthinkable, it was necessary to wait for the promulgation of the court's findings before any serious steps could be taken.'[20] Secondly, the preoccupation with the von Fritsch crisis was made to seem of little importance in the affairs of state in comparison with the momentous occupation of Austria decided on on 10 March and put into effect on 12–13 March. All thoughts were immediately turned from the postponed trial to the successful action; all eyes were now centred on the Führer in his latest glory. His popularity had never been greater; his position seemed unassailable; and the generals could bask in the reflected glory of his achievement. The best, and perhaps the only, time for action was over.

What if Germany's military leadership had been capable of ordering concerted action against Hitler and his advisers during the Fritsch crisis? Would the Army have obeyed? Some believed so. Captain Engel remembered: 'We in the Army have missed out on everything it was imperative to do. In February 1938 I was with the troops. The fury of the officers was tremendous. At that time the troops would still have obeyed us.'[21] A number advocated strong action, even force, in support of their Commander-in-Chief, including a few within the higher circles of military leadership – Halder, Beck's deputy, Hossbach, Hitler's military adjutant, von Hammerstein, the former Commander-in-Chief, Canaris, head of the Abwehr, and von Witzleben, Commander of the Wehrkreis covering the important Berlin area. Throughout the Army there was considerable feeling that things were going on that ought not be accepted. For example, General von Viehbahn was so horrified when he heard of the Gestapo interrogation of von Fritsch that he asserted that if the troops knew of it there would be a revolution – and he was far from being an ardent anti-National Socialist. It also seems quite clear that a number of units would have moved into action had they received orders to do so, among them the 9th Infantry Regiment at Potsdam, the 48th

Infantry Regiment at Döberitz, the 2nd Panzer Regiment at Eisenbach, and the 9th Cavalry Regiment. The soldiers' antagonism towards the SS was considerable; Halder believed that all ranks would have risen against the 'black ones' had the word been given, and certainly the SS men themselves were terrified at the prospect of an Army revolt. One senior SS officer recorded: 'Before the sitting of the Court of Honour that was to try General von Fritsch, I was told to report to Heydrich and to arm myself with a service pistol and an ample supply of ammunition. . . . After dinner he [Heydrich] took a large number of asperins. Then suddenly he said, without any preamble, "If they don't start marching from Potsdam during the next hour and a half, the greatest danger will have passed".'[22]

Others, however, have expressed themselves differently. They believed that neither the soldiers nor the nation would have risen against Hitler, and that only when the dictator had suffered a significant reverse, perhaps from England and France in war, would it have been the right psychological moment to strike. They also maintained that it was impossible to move solely against the SS, and that, from the beginning, it would have been a revolt against the person and the power of the Führer, because in the last resort Hitler stood or fell by the support of his Party and its organisations. Such is the view of men of the calibre of von Manstein, von Manteuffel, Warlimont, Geyr von Schweppenburg, and Heusinger, as well as of von Fritsch. Even Hossbach later came to confess that he had been wrong in advocating force as a solution. By 1938, the political complexion of the Army had altered considerably. No longer was it the tightly knit body of professionals it had been in 1933; instead, it was a loosely structured formation, undergoing fast expansion, with several years of National Socialist indoctrination and political success behind it. Gone even was the homogenity of the officer corps, which was in the process of experiencing what was to be a twenty-five-fold increase in number by 1939. National Socialist rearmament had opened up a career to talent and ambition, which had been recognised by the mass of new lieutenants, large numbers of whom had passed through the ranks of the Hitler Youth. The considerable expansion of the Army, and break-up of the old regiments during the reorganisation had particularly shattered the unity and the conservatism of the officer corps that had existed since the days of Frederick the Great, and which had formed the cornerstone of the Prusso-German military tradition. Gentlemen of the Imperial Army, former NCOs, Austrians, one-time police and SA officers, and young men fresh from the Hitler Youth rubbed shoulders one with another. Commanders complained that it was impossible to weld these heterogeneous elements together, a task which was made immeasurably more difficulty by the continued expansion and reconstruction of units. 'Dilution' was the term used by the professional officers to describe the process. This is illustrated by the changing social composition of the officer corps. In the Reichsheer, the aristocracy on average had held twenty per cent of all commissions. During the Weimar Republic the proportion of aristocrats among newly commissioned lieutenants rose from twenty-one per cent in 1922 to thirty-six per cent in 1932, and occupied sixty-one per cent of the generalships. By 1936, however, only some twenty-five per cent of generals were aristocrats, and during the war the top ranks came almost exclusively from the middle class. Although the aristocrats maintained their dominance in the *Generalfeldmarschälle*, the middle class composed twenty-one out of the twenty-six *Generalobersten* and one hundred and forty-six out of one hundred and sixty-six *Generäle der Infanterie*. Moreover, the reintroduction of conscription had brought the Army into close contact with, and dependence on, the masses, and the masses had, as yet, experienced only the benefits of National Socialism and none of its drawbacks. Gone were the days when, before 1933, the other ranks had been composed mainly of conservative peasants, and when the more radically minded townsmen were the exception. Conscription had made the Army truly representative of the people, and, as von Fritsch claimed: 'Ninety per cent of all Germans run after this man [Hitler].'[23] It also had to be considered what the Army would do after a successful revolt. For this it was totally unprepared, realising, as did von Fritsch, that 'It was not possible to rule a people like the Germans with bayonets',[24] above all a people who knew little of the generals, and had no enthusiasm for a coup, especially one which would overthrow their idol, Adolf Hitler. Obscurity and unpopularity were not the best qualifications for embarking upon a period of military rule, certainly one for which no preparations had been made.

Such, then, was the position of the Army leaders in February and March 1938, the crucial period during which the German Army was subjected to Hitler's will. What else could they have done but submit to the dictates of their Führer? The generals did not possess the historians' advantage of hindsight, nor were they blessed with the political understanding and skill required to counter a man like Hitler. They were still as much the prisoners of their heritage as they ever had been: politically naïve, unaware of Hitler's true intentions, lacking the means to stop him, and constrained by their tradition of obedience to the Head of State. When to this is added the realisation that a majority of the soldiers would not have obeyed their orders to act against Hitler, it is understandable that the generals behaved as they did. Just as in 1933, it would have been remarkable had they done anything else.

For one group of Army officers, however, the Fritsch crisis had entailed a complete and lasting break with the traditions of the Army. For those men, it was now clear that opposition to Hitler through official, constitutional channels was impossible, and that only an underground conspiracy, prepared to use violence, would suceed in ending his menace to both Germany and the world. Before 1938 most of them, while being opposed to the Party, had wondered only how to control the Führer; now they sought to remove him altogether. Perhaps the first of the military conspirators was General Erwin von Witzleben. Born in December 1881 at Breslau, he served in the

First World War as an infantry battalion commander and a General Staff officer, becoming commander of Wehrkreis III, which included Berlin, in February 1934. Although lacking the intellectual breadth of a man like Beck, he was a good, unpretentious soldier with a fund of commonsense. To von Witzleben, National Socialism was an abomination, Hitler a national disaster, the military oath a crime. On this he was prepared to act. It did not need any crisis such as the Fritsch or the later Czechoslovak affairs to make him commit himself unreservedly to conspiracy. His first moves in this direction came in the summer of 1937, when he began organising a circle of associates prepared to assume the burden of opposition, prominent among whom was General Count Erich von Brockdorff-Ahlefeld, a divisional commander. Between them, these two men undertook a careful check of all officers in command of formations, preferably those strategically placed to mount an armed coup. By 1938 their efforts were beginning to show some reward.

At the same time as von Witzleben was forming his circle in the provinces, others were at work closer to the corridors of power. This conspiracy centred on the Abwehr, the German military intelligence (part of the Armed Forces High Command after 4 February 1938), and was due primarily to the convergence of three men: Admiral Wilhelm Canaris, Head of the Abwehr, Colonel Hans Oster, his deputy, and Hans Bernhard Gisevius, an official in the Reich Ministry of the Interior.

A career naval officer who had commanded a submarine for a period in the First World War, Canaris was forty-seven when he took command of the Abwehr. A small, unassuming man of variable temperament and strange phobias (he usually disliked robust men, for example), he possessed a quick brain and a remarkable ability to judge character. A master of dissimulation, he, alone of all opponents of Hitler, managed to conceal from the dictator his real feelings. His genuine and deep goodness and humanity led him to abhor, both emotionally and intellectually, every aspect of National Socialism. By 1937 he was convinced of the necessity for its downfall and had begun to make contact with others, especially corps intelligence officers throughout Germany. His toast at the dinner table among friends was: 'We are thinking of the Führer – to rid ourselves of him.'[25]

Oster was in many ways the opposite of his master, although they got on well together. Handsome, elegant, talkative, rash, a man of the world, he was born in 1888, the son of a Dresden cleric. Although he had been dismissed from the service because of a love-affair with the wife of a fellow officer, he was able to return to the Army in 1934 on the intercession of Halder, although he was never allowed to regain his former full General Staff status. Like that of Canaris, his opposition to the National Socialist régime was that of a right-wing nationalist. The third in the triumvirate was Gisevius, a big, impetuous man with strong likes and dislikes, who had been dismissed from the Gestapo because of his ill-concealed distaste for its methods. A friend of Oser, he shared with him a disgust for the SS and the gangster methods of the régime.

As time went on, the Abwehr group enlarged the number, and improved the nature, of its contacts. Prominent among them was Arthur Nebe, Chief of the Criminal Police Office and an associate of Heydrich, Count Wolf von Helldorf, Police President of Berlin and a former SA leader, Hjalmar Schacht, former Reich Minister of Economics, Erich Schultze, a close friend of Heydrich, and Carl Goerdler, Lord Mayor of Leipzig and former Reich Price Commissioner. Contact was made also with von Witzleben. The network was beginning to spread.

The Fritsch crisis, which lasted some six weeks, acted as a catalyst among opposition circles, and was especially important in consolidating the Abwehr group, strengthening its ties with other strands of dissatisfaction, and providing it with valuable experience, especially in matters of organisation. The whole affair showed the need, and provided the opportunity, for action against the régime. It was, however, a frustrating experience. All that the Abwehr group found itself able to do was to collect information vital for the defence of von Fritsch and the proving of his innocence, being quite unable to organise any form of resistance to the régime among the Army. There were a number of reasons for this. The Abwehr group by itself commanded no one and possessed negligible influence within the Army; it was, therefore, vital for it to have not just the support, but also the leadership, of senior officers of respected authority. Von Fritsch was the obvious choice, for he alone could count on a wide, even universal, response to his appeal for action, as, to a lesser extent, could Beck. But neither would move. Weeks were wasted in the vain hope that they would be persuaded that it was not merely their own future, but the fate of the nation, that was at stake. Neither, however, possessed insight enough for the role, and while the opposition waited expectantly, the opportunity for action slipped quietly by. Time was on Hitler's side.

What of von Witzleben, whose command of the forces around Berlin placed him in a better position than all other troop commanders? He was regarded as the only one who would have a full understanding of the issues at stake. But at this critical point, von Witzleben lay ill in a Dresden sanatorium. Thus, in order to circumvent what appeared to be near paralysis at the centre of military affairs, an attempt was made to gain support from the soldiers in the provinces. Selected corps commanders were visited to get them to put pressure on von Fritsch for action and, at the same time, to rouse their colleagues. Collective resignation by the twelve corps commanders was proposed, but came to nothing. Typical of the reaction from the generals was that of General Alexander Ulex, commander of the 11th Army Corps. Personally loyal to von Fritsch, devoted to the traditions of the Army, and suspicious of the National Socialists, he refused to take part in the movement to save his chief, using as his excuse the fact that it was impossible to attain a united front, as von Reichenau and Dollman, at the very least, among the corps commanders would support Hitler. Days later his troubled conscience forced him to remark: 'It is a great burden to me to have the feeling of having failed at the decisive moment.'[26] The most rewarding feature of the conspirators' work during this period, apart from producing the evidence that proved von Fritsch's innocence, was the growth of contacts. Many were brought within their network, including Beck who had become convinced that the Fritsch crisis had 'opened up a chasm between Hitler and the officer corps . . . which can never be closed again'.[27] Even more important for the future was the fact that Beck's deputy, Halder, had now joined the conspirators. The question was, could these men, a tiny minority in the Army and the nation, hope to achieve in the future what the military establishment had signally failed to attempt – the downfall of Adolf Hitler and the destruction of National Socialism?

The final act in the Fritsch affair revolved around the struggle for the former Army Commander's rehabilitation. The energy with which many generals pursued this matter exemplifies their inability to see the wood for the trees, thereby expending their effort on periphera, in this case the honour of von Fritsch, rather than on fundamentals such as the independence of the Army. On 30 March Hitler wrote to von Fritsch in a manner which appeared to express satisfaction at the outcome of the trial, but which contained no expression of apology for the affair. The Führer had no thought of rehabilitation; it was not in his nature to trouble himself for someone who had opposed him. It has been recorded by those close to him that Hitler used to become unpleasant and bitter as soon as von Fritsch's name was mentioned. The Army, however, felt differently, seeing the issue of their former Commander-in-Chief's rehabilitation as a question not simply of his personal integrity but of the honour and integrity of the officer corps as a whole. It would also be an indictment of the SS. The rehabilitation was seen as vital for the restoration of the traditional balance between the political and the military, a balance which had been lost, irretrievably as it turned out, during the crisis.

Pressure mounted: von Brauchitsch was so besieged by troubled officers urging him to exert his influence on Hitler that he was reduced at times to seeking refuge in the house of a cousin; the venerable Field-Marshal von Mackensen sent a barrage of letters and telegrams to Hitler and prominent Army officers; and Army commanders down to regimental level were continually beset by their troubled subordinates. By May it was becoming clear that the generals might stage a collective strike. General Ulex, repenting of his previous faint-heartedness, gave written notice of his resignation from the Army should von Fritsch not receive satisfaction. He was followed by General von Kluge, whose letter of intent, though it was suppressed by Keitel (an old regimental comrade), may well have been shown to Hitler as a warning of what might happen. Even General Eugen Ritter von Schobert, commander of Wehrkreis VII and one of the generals more devoted to Hitler, announced that he was contemplating resignation. By June, according to von Kluge, no fewer than twelve Wehrkreis commanders had threatened collective resignation if their 'sharp protest' to Hitler were not heeded. It was now clear that the time was approaching when decisive action must be taken. The only question was, who would take it? In the event it was Hitler, who, sensing the danger of allowing matters to drift further, realised it was vital to direct events to his advantage. This, by brilliant timing and a superb performance, is precisely what he achieved at a meeting on the afternoon of 13 June, when he addressed Army Corps and Wehrkreis commanders at Barth on the Pommeranian coast.

Hitler was helped considerably by von Brauchitsch. The ambivalent and pusillanimous Commander-in-Chief of the Army so far had successfully managed to ward off the strongest of the military protests without giving in. On the morning of the 13th he proved himself of further inestimable value by presenting his views on the rehabilitation issue to the assembled officers at Barth. (Fortunately for him, Beck was not among them, for he would certainly have disagreed with what he had to say.) He stressed that the affair had caused him much concern, and that he had been on the point of resigning in protest at von Fritsch's treatment. By this he won his audience's sympathy; his next ploy was to shatter their nerve with a bombshell. The Führer, he informed them, had announced that there was to be an unavoidable military clash with Czechoslovakia in the near future. In such circumstances, when nothing less than national survival was in question, he could not honourably resign, and he begged his audience to follow his example. The generals were caught, off balance, on the horns of an apparently insoluble dilemma – military honour or national security.

Nor did Hitler give them time to resolve their difficulty for themselves. That same afternoon he stepped in and provided them with the solution, enabling them to reconcile the apparently irreconcilable and to set at rest their consciences. Hitler's performance was brilliant; to the Navy Commander-in-Chief, as well as to the majority of those present, he appeared 'unequivocal and convincing'.[28] Only to the few, like Ulex, who knew the intricacies of the affair, was it obvious that 'some things he concealed, some he distorted, on some he lied'.[29] In a masterful speech lasting for an hour and a half, full of pathos, Hitler played on his audience's emotions, hopes, and fears. He asked for their sympathy: he had been the victim of a shameless deception. He elaborated on the position in which the revelation of the charges against the Army Commander had placed him, charges that had shaken him to the very core, and that had been made worse by the confrontation of von Fritsch with his accuser Schmidt. He pointed out that his predicament had been made even more difficult by the man's complete exoneration 'as the result of a fortunate accident'.[30] He asked for their understanding: how could he combine compensation for von Fritsch's personal tragedy with reasons of state? For the Army's sake he had given 'bad health' as the reason for von Fritsch's retirement, and he could hardly disavow that now by contradiction. Was it not better that the public remained in ignorance of the whole sordid affair, for von Fritsch's sake as well as for the Army's? And in any case, he could not expect von Fritsch to work with him again after all that had happened. Therefore he had decided that, for the time being, the only possible way to rehabilitate the former Army Commander was to appoint him to the honorary colonelcy of his old artillery regiment, the 12th. In the future, he assured them, he would seek every way to indicate his respect for this 'irreproachable man of honour'.[31] He gave them hope: they could rest assured that such a thing would never happen again; any attack on the Armed Forces from outside their ranks would be out of the question; and changes in military personnel would be undertaken only for internal reasons and not under external pressure. He played on their vanity: he was waiting only for the next convocation of the Reichstag to compliment the Army on its fine performance during the occupation of Austria. He gave them blood: he had ordered the shooting of the blackmailer Schmidt, the real villain of the whole affair. And he concluded by asking for their support: he appealed to them not to abandon the service of the nation at such a critical time. Was not his entire confidence placed with the Wehrmacht? He begged them to place a similar trust in him. They did so.

Hitler had successfully convinced the majority of his generals of his good intention; at the very least he had shown them the need to stay at their posts. As Ulex said to a sceptical and discontented Beck: 'Neither you nor Brauchitsch can in the existing situation do anything else than stay.'[32] Von Fritsch found the honorary colonelcy offensive, believing it to be a deliberate slight; Beck was horrified at the frivolity of it all. But nevertheless, on 11 August, at the Gros Born exercise ground, von Fritsch was invested with his new appointment at an elaborate military ceremony presided over by von Brauchitsch. Hitler, unable to avoid a public congratulation, wrote a letter.

The promises made at Barth were soon forgotten. Von Fritsch received no further honour from his Führer, and his personal fate ceased to be an issue. Not for one moment did Hitler consider returning him to a post in the High Command. Instead, von Fritsch lived quietly in a house built for him by an Army subscription, attending the occasional military exercise, taking part in one or two hunts, and making rare visits to Berlin; he did little else. Retiring ever more eithin his shell, he became increasingly depressed at his treatment, at the same time resigning himself to his nation's future. His view is summed up in his oft-quoted phrase: 'This man [Hitler] is Germany's destiny for good or ill, and this destiny will run its course to the end; if it leads us into the abyss he will take us all with him – there is nothing to be done about it.'[33] Feeling strongly that he must share in his country's fate, he accompanied his regiment into the field against Poland, where, on 22 September 1939, he was struck dead by a sniper's bullet. A memorial was erected on the spot, only to be destroyed later in the war, as also was his grave. The news of his death was given to Hitler on the evening of the 22nd, when General Jodl began his daily report with the words: 'Today there fell one of the finest soldiers Germany has ever had, Generaloberst Baron von

Fritsch.'[34] Hitler gave a start, but said nothing. He later refused to attend the funeral.

Even after his death, von Fritsch still maintained some influence. The veneration that the General Staff and the whole Army felt towards this man came once more to the fore, and the indignation about his ignominious treatment was revived. Hitler condemned the obituary that von Brauchitsch issued on the occasion, and personally supervised the details of all further ceremonies in von Fritsch's honour. The German General Staff, however, mourned a man whom it had never ceased to respect. Thereafter, General Staff officers who had been especially close to General von Fritsch were regarded with particular suspicion by the Führer – as, for instance, General von Funck, who was at least twice during the war kept out of important commissions, something that would have been unheard of before January 1938. That date was, indeed, the turning point in the relationship between Hitler and his Army.

6

The First Shackles

*Few realised at the time the complete break with the
past that these events represented. The Army, quite
unprepared, embarked on a new experience. It was
not to be a happy one.*

GENERAL FRANZ HALDER
Chief of the General Staff, 1938–42

Friday, 4 February 1938 had been a day of immense importance both to the
Army and to Germany: it was the day on which Hitler had revealed to the
world a profound shift in the distribution of power within the Third Reich,
and thus began the concentration of the nation's military leadership into his
hands, a process which was to be carried still further four years later with his
assumption of the active command of the Army. At midnight of 3–4 February, the Führer's decree was read over German radio:

> 'From henceforth I exercise personally the immediate command
> over the whole Armed Forces. The former Wehrmacht Office in the
> War Ministry becomes the High Command of the Armed Forces
> [OKW], and comes immediately under my command as my military
> staff. At the head of the Staff of the High Command stands the
> former chief of the Wehrmacht Office [Keitel]. He is accorded the
> rank equivalent to that of Reichs Minister. The High Command of
> the Armed Forces also takes over the functions of the War Ministry,
> and the Chief of the High Command exercises, as my deputy, the
> powers hitherto held by the Reich War Minister. The task of preparing the unified defence of the Reich in all fields, in accordance with
> my instructions, is the function of the High Command in time of
> peace.'[1]

In addition, the resignation and dismissal of von Fritsch and von Blomberg
were announced, together with the appointment of von Brauchitsch. Consequent on this came a drastic and sweeping removal of senior officers from
their posts, and some from active service altogether. Sixteen high-ranking
generals were relieved of their commands and forty-four others, with a
number of senior field-officers, were transferred. Among those of the Army
High Command who went into the military wilderness of troop commands
were von Schwedler, head of the Personnel Office, and two of his departmen-

tal chiefs, Colonels Küntzen and Behlendorff, and von Manstein, Beck's Head of Operations in the General Staff. Some of the most prominent among these sent into retirement were: Kress von Kressenstein, a senior Wehrkreis commander; von Porgrell, Inspector of Cavalry; von Niebelschutz, Inspector of Training; and Lutz, Inspector of Mobile Troops. At the same time was announced the retirement of von Neurath, the formerly complacent, now conservative, Minister for Foreign Affairs, his replacement by the subservient von Ribbentrop, and the removal of the German ambassador in Rome, Ulrich von Hassell, an advocate of restraint known as *Il Freno* – the brake. By so many simultaneous blows, Hitler's opponents were stunned into submission. The ambitious Göring, although he had not realised his aim, was placated by being given the rank of *Generalfeldmarschall,* which, with von Brauchitsch only a *Generaloberst,* made him the senior officer of the Armed Forces. Ironically and shamefully, on this day, on the same occasion that von Fritsch's resignation was made public, Hitler announced the elevation of Walther Funk, Goebbels's Secretary of State, to the post of Minister of Economics. Funk was a notorious homosexual.

Thanks to the opportunities presented him by the foolish indiscretion of his former War Minister, by a case of mistaken identity in a sordid blackmail case, by the craven ambition of his political associates, and by the gross political naivety of his generals, Hitler had achieved an unexpected coup of considerable importance, and had laid the basis for his career as a war lord. Without any previous scheming, he had eliminated the last of the restrictions placed on his foreign policy and rearmament; he had taken direct control of the Armed Forces and, by the new command organisation and its change of personnel, had ensured their compliance to his will. Most important of all, he had humbled the Army, bringing it more fully within his sphere of influence. Thus, von Seeckt's dictum that 'The Army is the first instrument of power in the Reich'[2] was no longer true.

At first sight, the new appointments of 4 February might have seemed not unfavourable to the Army. Admittedly, Hitler was now Commander-in-Chief of the Armed Forces, but his record as Supreme Commander in the past had not been disastrous. Rather, on the contrary, his interference in service matters could hardly have been less, and the situation was better than if Göring had been appointed, a move that had been feared. As for Keitel – well, he was harmless enough; and the aristocratic von Brauchitsch, no doubt, would do what was necessary – after all he was no National Socialist and his military qualities were beyond criticism. Yet it was soon to become apparent that such hopes were ill-founded; the degree to which Hitler managed to subordinate the Armed Forces in general, and the Army in particular, may be seen in the personalities of those who now came to the leadership.

The manner by which the new Army Commander-in-Chief was chosen revealed much of Hitler's new attitude towards the military. The search was begun on 26 January and, at the beginning, the Führer's own candidate was von Reichenau, the obvious man – able, progressive, and, to all appearances, a safe 'Party general'. But Keitel, to whom Hitler turned for advice, regarded such a choice as potentially disastrous: it would provoke strong resistance from the military hierarchy, possibly even leading to mass resignation; it would also create the unfortunate, if correct, impression that there was to be a sweeping change in military policy. Keitel regarded von Reichenau's personality, too, as unsuitable, believing him to be slothful, superficial, inordinately ambitious, and unpopular with his colleagues. Instead, Keitel proposed von Rundstedt, who was thought too old by Hitler; von Leeb, of whom he did not think highly enough; and von Brauchitsch, a name put forward also by von Blomberg at his fateful meeting with the Führer on 26 January, to whom Hitler made no objection. Not only was von Brauchitsch an excellent soldier, Keitel argued, but he was well thought of in the Army and possessed no political ambition. What could be better? Later, when von Rundstedt was asked for his opinion, his immediate and complete rejection of von Reichenau made a considerable impression on the Führer; his suggestion that Beck should take command received instant and cold dismissal from Hitler, but his subsequent confirmation of the general acceptability of von Brauchitsch was listened to thoughtfully. It appears that, from that time on, the idea of von Brauchitsch as his future Army Commander gained ascendancy in Hitler's mind. Von Reichenau, from the Führer's point of view, was now seen as too much of a risk: he would needlessly antagonise the Army, and his independence of mind and political ambition might one day pose a threat to Hitler himself. Certainly he was no longer considered, the expressions of Hitler's further support for him being merely a tactical manoeuvre designed to gain the maximum concessions from von Brauchitsch in the bargaining over his appointment.

Negotiations were entered into with speed and were kept strictly secret – Keitel, for example, was not allowed to go to the Reich Chancellery other than in civilian clothes. There, he and Hitler would confer on the terms to be accepted by any future Army Commander, and Keitel would then take these proposals to von Brauchitsch, who was staying at the Hotel Continental. From time to time Keitel, occasionally accompanied by von Brauchitsch, would visit Göring at the Air Ministry. Hitler himself had three meetings with the favoured candidate. Beck, however, was furious that he was not consulted and that Keitel, an outsider, should be acting as the adviser of the new appointment; it was, however, an indication of things to come.

As it turned out, Hitler was infinitely better off having von Brauchitsch as his new Commander-in-Chief than von Reichenau. Whereas the latter was of strong personality, active, independent, and ambitious, von Brauchitsch, brave and able soldier though he might have been, was personally vulnerable, and submissive to Hitler. The impression was soon gained that he was 'ready for anything', and, indeed, the price he was forced to pay for his elevation to the command of the Army was high – the loss of his freedom of action. Three conditions were imposed on him by Hitler: he must lead the Army to a closer union with the state and its philosophy; he must, if necessary, choose a more suitable Chief of Staff (Hitler by then had come to dislike and fear Beck); and he must endorse a new structure for the Armed Forces high command. Although he took a little time to agree to the last, von Brauchitsch accepted these conditions, together with the need to remove a number of senior Army officers, prominent among whom were those directing the Army Personnel office. By 3 February the deal was settled: Hitler had gained all he wanted, and the Army, in whose name von Brauchitsch had mistakenly surrendered its most vital concerns, had lost its autonomy. The heavy load on von Brauchitsch's conscience was lightened only by the erroneous belief that by his actions he had saved the Army from a worse fate – command by von Reichenau. Silently, he was to carry in office a burden from which there was no escape.

The new Commander-in-Chief of the Army, Walter von Brauchitsch, came of a Silesian family which had provided Prussia with a dozen generals over the previous 150 years. Born in 1881 in Berlin, he possessed an aristocratic background which met with the full approval of such men as von Rundstedt – he had even been page to the Empress Augusta Victoria before entering a Guards artillery regiment. His bearing, too, was pleasing, for, as von Manstein recorded, he was 'a man of elegant appearance who . . . was never anything but dignified . . . . He was correct, courteous, and even charming, although this charm did not always leave one with an impression of inner warmth.'[3] Certainly his military record was worthy of his new position: during the First World War he had won the coveted Hohenzollern House Order; as a departmental head in the Troop Office he had distinguished himself by his experiments with aircraft and mechanisation; and while Director of Army Training and Inspector of Artillery he had pursued his profession with great energy, which continued during his command of Wehrkreis I and Fourth Army Group.

His character, however, appears to have been regarded as something of an enigma. Von Manstein remembered that: 'Just as he lacked the aggressiveness that commands an opponent's respect, or at least compels him to go warily, so did he fail to impress one as a forceful, productive personality. The general effect was one of coolness and reserve. He often appeared slightly inhibited, he was certainly rather sensitive.'[4] But Adam, not a poor judge of men, spoke of him as 'an intelligent man of determined and self-willed character'.[5] However, his record in dealing with Hitler bears eloquent testimony to the veracity of von Manstein. Von Brauchitsch was as ill-suited as any person could be to oppose or to moderate the damaging demands of the dictator. The new Army Commander-in-Chief was little more than the moral hostage of his Führer, and choosing him was the climax of Hitler's manoeuvres in 1938 to destroy the Army's independence.

The reason for this sad state of affairs goes back to 1926, when von Brauchitsch, already married, had fallen in love with a certain Charlotte

Ruffer, the divorced wife of a brother officer. His wife, however, steadfastly refused to grant a divorce without raising a scandal that would have been ruinous to his career, unless a financial settlement were made which would have been well beyond his means. By 1938 von Brauchitsch had not been living with his spouse for more than five years, and he was in a mood to sacrifice his career in order to free himself from his emotional and domestic problems. Resignation was uppermost in his mind. But, just at the point when his despair was total, he was offered the glittering prize to which all professional soldiers aspire – the command of his army. Furthermore, when he told Hitler of his marital affairs, the Führer replied that if money were the only hindrance to the divorce, then money would be provided. Göring also promised that von Brauchitsch would be shielded from criticism within the officer corps. Von Brauchitsch was undoubtedly aware of the problems such a solution might present for his future freedom of action, so beholden would he be to Hitler, who was to provide out of his own pocket a capital settlement of some 80,000 reichsmarks; but he now had within his grasp the promise of avoiding resignation and obscurity and, instead, of obtaining his divorce, marrying the woman he loved, and rising to the height of the military profession, while at the same time being protected from scandal by the most powerful men in the state. His choice was one many men would have made.

After 4 February 1938, Hitler had as his Army Commander a man under great personal obligation to him, guilty of adultery, and married to a lady with a certain past. (She had had several protectors and a husband who had died in a bath tub!) His moral probity was hardly of the highest. Nor was von Brauchitsch ever to be rid of the spectre of von Blomberg's fate; it was not for nothing that a senior British Foreign Office official, Sir Robert Vansittart, could discern: 'Hitler has a stranglehold on von Brauchitsch of some private and discreditable kind.' To make matters worse, von Brauchitsch's disposition, origin, and upbringing were not conducive to standing up to the Führer. He was often bewildered in the presence of Hitler, whose occasional coarse style of speech unnerved him, and when he did manage to summon up enough nerve to argue, he often did so in a curt, impetuous, even condescending, tone which was greatly resented. Furthermore, his new wife, a domineering woman to whom he was devoted, was, in the words of his fellow officers, '200 per cent National Socialist'. Thus, as Halder remarked, the Commander-in-Chief of the German Army stood before Adolf Hitler 'like a little cadet before his commandant'.[6] General Warlimont noted how he 'often appeared practically paralysed'.[7] Von Brauchitsch was painfully aware of this; it was a failing which greatly embarrassed him. He confessed to Halder: 'Please do not hold it against me. I know you are dissatisfied with me. When I confront this man, I feel as if someone were choking me and I cannot find another word.'[8]

From the beginning of his period in office, von Brauchitsch found himself beset by the conflict between his commitment to Hitler and his duties to the Army, and never was he able to reconcile his enslavement to the Führer with his need to gain the confidence of his colleagues. As a result, he received the respect of neither. He realised at once the impossibility of his situation when confronted with the question of von Fritsch's rehabilitation. The Army demanded he take action, but Keitel warned him that he 'should not straightway put a burden on his prestige with Hitler in this delicate matter'.[9] All he could do was make vague promises that 'There can be no talk of a reinforced influence of the Party in the internal affairs of the Armed Forces',[10] and at the same time salve his conscience towards his much-abused predecessor by placing adjutants, horses, and a car at his disposal and by authorising a collection for a house to be made among the officer corps. Von Brauchitsch managed to retain Beck as his Chief of Staff until the autumn, pleading that this was necessary because of his own unfamiliarity with the Army High Command. However, he received no recognition for this from Beck, who was continually annoyed by his chief's weakness before Hitler, and only dissatisfaction from the Führer, who became impatient at what he considered to be the continual objections to his policies still emanating from the Army Command.

Certainly von Brauchitsch maintained the resistance to any attempt by the Party organisation to interfere in military matters, and in this he was aided by Hitler who, seeing the Armed Forces now as his own inviolable province, wished to see no encroachment on his territory by anyone else. But at the same time, National Socialist doctrine became more evident in the directives and orders of the new Army Commander than it had been under von Fritsch. For example, on 18 December 1938, von Brauchitsch issued an order containing a number of Blombergesque passages: 'Adolf Hitler, our leader of genius, who has recast the great lessons of the front-line soldier in the form of the National Socialist philosophy. . . . The Armed Forces and National Socialism are of the same spiritual stem. . . . The officer corps must not be surpassed by anybody in the purity and genuineness of its National Socialist outlook . . . the officer must handle any situation in accordance with the views of the Third Reich.'[11]

The fundamental change in the relationship between Hitler and the Army was also evident in the change in the nature of the important post of the Armed Forces Adjutant to the Führer, and in the creation of a new office, Army Adjutant to the Führer. Until 1938, the Armed Forces Adjutant had been one of the most important military personages in the Army, and a far from negligible figure in the counsels of the Reich. As the Armed Forces representative to the Führer, he also possessed a special responsibility for the Army, and it was taken as automatic that he would speak for its interests. The other two services had their own separate adjutants, but not the Army. Always at Hitler's hand, he was often called on to give his Führer advice, which was usually acted on. In some ways, his influence was as great as that of the War Minister's, but, as it was always behind the scenes, it was never apparent. From 2 August 1934, the post had been held by Colonel Friedrich

Hossbach, a man much respected and liked by the officer corps and with considerable influence over an impressionable Hitler. Nicknamed 'the old Fritz', after his namesake, Frederick the Great, or 'the last Prussian', because of his unbending principles and martinet's devotion to regulations, Hossbach was extremely important to Hitler because of his high standing in the military profession. He was immune from intimidation, and gave unfailing support to von Fritsch during the crisis. On 25 January 1938, the day after the Führer had received the accusation against the Army Commander, Hossbach spent some ten hours in vehement debate with Hitler and Göring, afterwards telling von Fritsch of the charges, although strictly forbidden to do so. However, his very independence proved his downfall. Hossbach was clearly a liability on the course Hitler had now set himself, and so, on the 28th, he was dismissed from his post amid tears of rage and protestations that no German officer should be treated in such a manner.

Hossbach's successor was Major Rudolf Schmundt, a man who represented as well as anyone the type of officer with whom Hitler was determined to surround himself from that time on. Basically decent and amicable, he was nevertheless weak-willed, an insecure man who needed ideals and a hero on whom to depend. Unfortunately for his reputation, it was to Hitler that he gave his devotion (previously it had been Beck), and thus, unlike Hossbach, he ceased to function as the representative of the Wehrmacht and of the Army, becoming instead yet another docile executive instrument of the Führer's will. As his hero began to lose his majesty and infallibility, Schmundt increasingly found solace in alcohol, his personality disintegrated, and his death in the Bomb Plot of 20 July 1944 came as a merciful release.

For the Army, the loss of Hossbach and the emergence of Schmundt was a severe setback which was exacerbated by the role of Wehrmacht Adjutant changing with Hitler's assumption of the post of Commander-in-Chief. It was now reduced to a mere link between the offices now incorporated in the person of the Führer, and it was an indication of the Army's loss of status that it now felt necessary to create the new and separate post of Army Adjutant to the Führer. For his part, Hitler, not unreasonably, felt the generals were now sending someone to watch over him. The man the Army leaders chose to serve them in this important role was Captain Gerhard Engel, a talented and energetic artillery officer with an esteem for von Fritsch which was warmly reciprocated. Although no supine creature like Schmundt, Engel nevertheless was held in high opinion by Hitler, who had been briefed by him during army manoeuvres in 1937. However, although he was to prove an ardent exponent of the Army's interests, his influence was severely curtailed by the soft-cushioning that surrounded Hitler, and by the lowered prestige of the Army in the dictator's eyes.

But the greatest importance of the announcement of 4 February 1938 lay in the implications it contained for the reorganisation of the High Command.

The new Armed Forces of the 1920s and early 1930s, which rose out of the ruins of the old imperial force, had been given a concentration and coordination of command not seen since the days of Frederick the Great. Its titular head was the Head of State, the Reich President, who, as *Oberste Befehlshaber der Reichswehr* (Supreme Commander), was limited in his prerogative to protocol and making the most senior appointments. Responsible to him was the *Reichswehr Minister* (Reich Defence Minister) who had charge of the overall administration of, and policy regarding, the Armed Forces and national defence. The Reich Defence Minister's executive office was the *Ministeramt* (Ministerial Office), which was renamed the *Wehrmachstamt* (Armed Forces Office) on 13 February 1934 and *Wehrmachtamt* in October 1936. Next in the hierarchy, and arguably the man who wielded most effective power, was the *Chef der Heeresleitung* (Chief of the Army Leadership), in whose office was concentrated the entire direction of the Army, including operations, discipline, promotion, training, and equipment. Von Seeckt viewed this as the revival and continuation of that tradition of personal command on which the cohesion of the old Army had rested, and through which the independence and influences of the Army within the state were assured. The executive instrument by which this control was exerted was the *Heeresleitung* (Army Leadership), a camouflaged Army High Command which, under the provisions of the Versailles Treaty, was denied to Germany. In the event of war, it was envisaged that the Chief of Army Leadership would take the main decisions on the overall direction of the nation's effort, as did the Supreme Commander of the Army in the years 1914–18. Such was the position in 1933, one that left little room for direct interference on the part of Hitler as Reich Chancellor, even should he so wish.

As has been indicated earlier, in the first five years of his régime Hitler showed no desire to bring any direct authority to bear on the Army; his influence over von Blomberg as a member of the Reich Cabinet was sufficient for his needs at that time. Nothing was substantially altered by his assumption of the powers of Reich President with von Hindenburg's death on 2 August 1934, or by his official adoption of the title *Oberste Befehlshaber der Wehrmacht* (Supreme Commander of the Armed Forces), on 21 May 1935. Of greater significance for the future was the alteration in the status of the Reichswehr Minister. On the same day, 21 May, his post was renamed *Reichskriegsminister* (Reich War Minister) and was linked with the new title of *Oberbefehlshaber der Wehrmacht* (Commander-in-Chief of the Armed Forces). His executive instrument, the Wehrmachstamt, remained untouched. At the same time, the *Chef der Heeresleitung* became the *Oberbefehlshaber des Heeres* (Commander-in-Chief of the Army) and the *Heeresleitung* the *Oberkommando des Heeres* (Army High Command).

The significance of these changes was considerable. Through his title of Commander-in-Chief of the Wehrmacht, the War Minister could lay claim to assume responsibility for the coordinated direction of the organisation, intelligence, war propaganda, economic warfare, and, most important of all, operations of all three services. This was a claim which had been in existence ever since von Blomberg's appointment as Defence Minister in 1933, but which was further extended by this new post. Not only had the individual service chiefs to give up an important part of their prerogatives in his favour, but, for the first time, there was a superior commander interposed between the Army Commander and the Supreme Commander and Head of State. No longer would the Army Commander-in-Chief have authority to direct all fighting services, and several departments under his control in peacetime were to pass to the Wehrmacht Commander in the event of war. It was argued that the development in warfare on land, sea, and in the air that had taken place since 1918 demanded the institution of a combined Wehrmacht High Command to coordinate and direct operations in all three elements. Such a reorganisation was supported most vigorously by von Reichenau and his successor Keitel, but was hotly opposed by most of the senior Army leadership, led by Beck backed up by von Fritsch. They saw quite clearly that such a development would give increased power to the group who admired Hitler and a corresponding increase in the Führer's influence, as well as a considerable reduction in the authority of the Army, which had hitherto possessed complete autonomy in its own spheres, especially in its operations. Never, even in the Kaiser's days, had there been a superior operational command exercising authority over the Army; now the Army Commander-in-Chief was expected to hand over to a new, higher commander, interposed between him and the Head of State, a substantial part of his prerogative and freedom of action, as a consequence of which he would find himself degraded in the military hierarchy.

Apart from this loss of authority and autonomy, the creation of a unified Wehrmacht High Command was disliked by the Army leaders on purely military grounds. In a long memorandum to von Blomberg, dated August 1937, von Fritsch emphasised that the three services were not equal partners, that the Army comprised eighty per cent of the Armed Forces, and that, in the final analysis, land warfare was the decisive factor in Germany's overall strategy. The structure of the High Command ought to reflect this, and, in his words: 'Since the commands of the Army and the Armed Forces are inseparable, their separation should not consciously be caused by the creation of an Armed Forces High Command as an independent command staff.'[12] Such a creation would, in time of war, lead to considerable conflict. For the future, von Fritsch proposed that the authority of the War Minister be limited to the organisation of the whole nation in time of war, and that the Commander-in-Chief of the Army should 'be the principal adviser of the Head of State in all matters concerning the conduct of war, including naval and air matters, and must be his sole adviser on questions of land warfare'.[13]

However, the years before 1938 had seen some progress in the direction of an Armed Forces High Command, and the Wehrmachtamt had been expanded to include an embryo staff for the unified direction of the three services. How far, if at all, this was at the insistence of Hitler, it is impossible to tell; certainly no evidence has been traced that points one way or the other. Nevertheless, it may be safely assumed that the dictator was unperturbed at seeing a part of the Army's autonomy and authority taken from it and given to a higher command better disposed to his person. But this process, gradual though it was, did not proceed without considerable opposition from all three services. An Armed Forces Academy, set up in 1935 with the aim of providing suitably trained officers for such a command, was disbanded after only two years; and the practice of a new command organisation through war games, study periods, skeleton exercises and Wehrmacht manoeuvres (held in 1937), caused criticism to reach, in Warlimont's words, a state of 'well-nigh open rebellion – a most unmilitary state of affairs'.[14] So appalled was von Fritsch in early 1937 at the suggestion of forming Wehrmacht Territorial Commands to replace the Army Wehrkreis that he immediately offered his resignation, thus forcing Hitler to turn down the proposal. In June, matters were made worse by von Blomberg's directive; 'On Unified War Preparation of the Wehrmacht', over which he threatened to resign if von Fritsch protested to Hitler. Personal relationships began to suffer, and the gap between the two groupings around von Blomberg and von Fritsch widened even further.

However, the events of January 1938 brought to an abrupt halt the argument between the two men. The announcement of 4 February, although its implications were by no means immediately realised, presented the Army leaders with a fait accompli, and the reality of a considerable extension of Hitler's authority over them. With the dismissal of von Blomberg and the elimination of the post of War Minister and Commander-in-Chief of the Wehrmacht, Hitler, as Führer and Supreme Commander, assumed personal, sole, and direct command of the Armed Forces. The Wehrmachtamt became the *Oberkommando der Wehrmacht* (High Command of the Armed Forces) which also assumed both the duties of the former War Ministry and the functions of the Supreme Commander's general staff. The *Chef der Oberkommando der Wehrmacht* (Chief of OKW) was to fulfil the duties of a high-level Chief of Staff to the Supreme Commander and exercised the authority of the former War Minister. He was accorded the rank of Reich Minister and given a seat in the Reich Cabinet, the Ministerial Council for the Defence of the Reich, and the Secret Cabinet (which never met). No representative from the Army was a member of these bodies, although the Commander-in-Chief of the Luftwaffe held positions in all three, and the Commander-in-Chief of the Navy held a seat in the Secret Cabinet.

The creation of the OKW represented a fundamental change in the structure of the High Command. Previously, the War Minister and his executive arm had been primarily a military authority determined to defend its professional interests against the pressures of the politicians, and fully capable of acting on its own authority. Now it was replaced by a body which was nothing more than the military bureau of the Head of State, Supreme Commander, and Commander-in-Chief – Hitler – serving simply to carry out his wishes. As one of the OKW's functionaries, General Warlimont, wrote, those who now composed the highest echelons of the OKW '. . . made it clear that their conception of their overriding duty was to carry out Hitler's wishes and where required smooth the path for him in the military sphere. This was clearly a very different objective from that which Blomberg had set himself.'[15] From such men the Army could expect little sympathy or support in any controversy with Hitler. The character of General Staff officers had changed fundamentally. Blind, unquestioning obedience had never been one of the characteristics of the General Staff, for, while the Prussian tradition repudiated political disobedience, it nevertheless allowed for the rejection of a military order under extreme circumstances. As a general once told one of his officers: 'Sir, the King of Prussia made you a staff officer so that you should know when you ought not to obey.' Indeed, a staff officer had a responsibility to make known his objections to an order when he believed it to be misguided. Unthinking obedience in the military sphere had always been held to be inconsistent with responsibility and conscience; now, however, it was regarded as an essential. In the autumn of 1938 Hitler embodied this new principle in a special order. As Guderian records:

> '. . . there [had] existed within the Army a system by which the chiefs of staff, down to and including the chief of staff of an army corps, shared the responsibility for the decisions taken by their respective commanding generals. This system, which involved the forwarding of a report by the chief of staff should he disagree with his commander, was discontinued on Hitler's orders. . . . The system of joint responsibility . . . was one inherited from the old Prussian Army. . . . In accordance with the "leader principle" which he propagated, Hitler now logically ordered that the man who was in command must bear the entire and undivided responsibility; by this decree he automatically abolished the joint responsibility of the Chief of the Army General Staff [and of the OKW, too] in relationship to himself in his capacity as Supreme Commander of the Armed Forces.'[16]

As Keitel later recorded: 'For the execution of his [Hitler's] plans, which were unknown to us, he needed impotent tools unable to inhibit him.'[17] It was not for nothing that it was said that OKW stood for 'Oben kein Widerstand' – no resistance at the top. Its members chose to ignore the traditions of the Army, and their elevation destroyed the powerful bond of professional outlook within the senior ranks of the officer corps. Germany's generals now included a caste apart – Hitler's men.

The Führer's new military right-hand man was, from the Army's point of view, the worst possible choice. Wilhelm Bodewin Johann Gustav Keitel was born in 1882 of a middle-class Hanoverian family of landowners, to whom military traditions and tendencies were alien. Tall, good-looking, occasionally sporting a monocle, an excellent horseman with a penchant for hunting, Keitel possessed an enjoyment of the good life that was often marred by his extreme correctness and his nervousness. Conscientious, loyal, and with an insatiable appetite for work, especially of a detailed kind, he was an able staff officer whose flair for organisation was invaluable in a period of such considerable expansion. Ambitious, but lacking in exceptional talent, shrewd, but not highly intelligent, he had found promotion within the Army relatively slow until, in October 1935, von Blomberg, with the approval of von Fritsch, selected him to become his subordinate in succession to von Reichenau. The War Minister thought well of Keitel, but realised he had climbed as far up the military ladder as his capabilities would allow. Certainly he never envisaged him as a future Field-Marshal. But then came Keitel's golden opportunity with the Blomberg–Fritsch crisis. Hitler turned to him, saying: 'I rely entirely on you. You are my trusted and only counsellor in the problems of the Wehrmacht.'[18]

Only in Hitler's eyes was Keitel suitable for the post of Chief of OKW – even Keitel himself felt embarrassed by his feeling of inadequacy for the job, once declaring aloud: 'I am no Field-Marshal.'[19] His problem was that he was inordinately weak in character, infinitely preferring to serve than to dictate, so that he quickly earned for himself the nickname '*Lakaitel*' (Lackey), and he often resembled a footman running to attend to his master's every need. He was also known as the 'nodding ass'. A cynical adjutant once remarked: 'See that Field-Marshal scurrying past, with his adjutant bringing up the rear with measured tread.'[20] His insecurity was revealed in a hasty and faltering gait. Speer records his first impression of Keitel as 'a general who seconded his chief's [von Blomberg's] every word by an approving nod of his head'.[21] When he had known him for some time, his opinion became more definite: 'Basically Keitel hated his own weakness; but the hopelessness of any dispute with Hitler had ultimately brought him to the point of not even trying to form his own opinion.'[22] On more than one occasion Hitler expressed his satisfaction with the way the Chief of OKW conducted himself; Speer recorded: 'Hitler said that he could not do without Keitel because the man was "loyal as a dog" to him. Perhaps Keitel embodied most precisely the type of person Hitler needed in his entourage.'[23] As a result, Keitel exerted no influence at all on the course of operations: his function was purely executive, to carry out his master's decisions. As he himself admitted at Nuremberg after the war: 'Far from the Chief of the OKW advising Hitler, it was Hitler who advised him.'[24] Indeed, the Führer, with no respect for his military ability, was known to set little store by his judgement, often using him as little better than a doormat. Whenever Keitel raised an objection to Hitler's schemes the reply was always the same: 'I don't know why you are getting so het up by this. You are not answerable for this, the responsibility is mine alone.'[25] No wonder Keitel could call his position 'an abortion of an office'.

For the Army, Keitel was a disaster. He gave his loyalty not to his own caste but to Hitler, and thus he was unresponsive and, indeed, antagonistic to its interests. Warlimont wrote: 'He was honestly convinced that his appointment required him to identify himself unquestioningly with the wishes and instructions of his Supreme Commander, even though he might not personally agree with them. . . . He worked conscientiously to this end and apparently to no other; he was a tireless worker but had no very firm personal convictions and was therefore inclined always to seek a compromise; in his position these characteristics were fatal.'[26] The last comment may be given by Guderian: 'Field-Marshal Keitel was basically a decent individual. . . . It was [his] misfortune that he lacked the strength necessary to resist Hitler's orders. . . . He paid for this with his life at Nuremberg. His family were not permitted to mourn at his grave.'[27]

The man who was to become Hitler's foremost military adviser was Alfred Jodl, although, as Chief of the OKW *Wehrmachtführungsamt* (Operations Office), he was Keitel's subordinate. A highly gifted staff officer, Jodl, born in Aachen in 1890 of a distinguished Bavarian family, served with the artillery and the General Staff during the First World War, being wounded in the right leg in 1914. An able, ambitious, but exceptionally reserved man, he was far from being a weak nonentity; on the contrary he displayed a strong and intelligent personality in all his dealings with Hitler and his subordinates. His lack of experience of command in the field, however, was a severe drawback, and he was often unaware of the effect of his orders on the troops in the field.

Jodl was probably closer to Hitler than any other general, for not only did he brief him every day on progress in the OKW theatres of war, but, for three years after the Norwegian campaign, in which he played a leading role, he sat next to the Führer at meals. So close was his association that Jodl was regarded as the only reliable source of information on Hitler's thoughts and intentions. Unlike Keitel, however, he was not an uncritical admirer of Hitler. By 1942, Jodl was convinced that the Second World War was lost, but believing that internal dissension within the Reich had caused the defeat of the Armed Forces in the First World War, he always strove to keep his criticisms in check. As he wrote in his cell at Nuremberg: 'I made it a guiding principle to do everything in my power to combat every division, every indication of a breakdown – in short, all domestic conflicts in so far as they might affect the Wehrmacht.'[28] To Jodl, loyalty was an integral part of military high command. However, this did not mean he would never pursue the dictates of his own logic. Speer records that Jodl 'rarely contradicted Hitler openly. He proceeded diplomatically. Usually he did not express his thoughts at once, thus skirting difficult situations. Later he would persuade Hitler to yield, or even to reverse decisions already taken. His occasional deprecatory remarks about Hitler showed that he had preserved a relatively unbiased view.'[29] Indeed, on rare occasions, he could lose his patience with his Führer and, in Westphal's words, give 'free vent to his resentment'.[30]

Like his chief, though, Jodl was remarkably unsatisfactory from the Army's viewpoint. Ironically, he had been posted by Beck to von Blomberg's empire in the hope that there he would champion the Army's cause. Quite the opposite resulted. Jodl became such a staunch supporter of the idea of an Armed Forces High Command that in 1937 he refused the post of Luftwaffe Chief of Staff in order to remain at the post in which he believed so much. As a result, he became cool, if not openly hostile, towards the Army establishment, believing its criticism of the OKW and of Hitler to be infinitely damaging. An entry in his diary for 10 August 1938 described most vividly his attitude:

> 'I was summoned to the Berghof with senior officers of the Army. After dinner the Führer talked for nearly three hours explaining his line of thought on political questions. Thereafter certain of the generals tried to point out to the Führer that we were by no means ready. This was to say the least unfortunate. There are a number of reasons for this pusillanimous attitude which is unhappily fairly widespread in the Army General Staff . . . [it] is obsessed with memories of the past, and, instead of doing what it is told and getting on with its military job, thinks it is responsible for political decisions. It does get on with its job with all its old devotion, but its heart is not in it, because, in the last analysis, it does not believe in the genius of the Führer. . . . As sure as fate the result of all this belly-aching will be not only enormous political damage – for all the world knows about the differences of opinion between the generals and the Führer – but also some danger to the morale of the troops.'[31]

The third of the OKW triumvirate was Walther Warlimont, Head of Branch L – *Landesverteidigung* (National Defence) – until September 1939, when he became Deputy Chief of the Operations Staff, a man whose character differed widely from that of both Keitel and Jodl. A Rhinelander, born in 1895, he was strikingly handsome, possessing an easy, graceful manner and obvious intelligence, and was thus the social asset of the OKW, playing host to numerous military attachés and foreign diplomats. Extremely able (for nine months from November 1938, at the age of only 43, he was responsible also for the duties of the Chief of the Operations Staff while Jodl was absent), an expert in war economy, and a first-class staff officer, he was firmly convinced of the desirability of an organisation such as the OKW – so much so, indeed, that in 1937, as a Colonel in the Wehrmachtamt, he had submitted a memorandum direct to the Führer on the necessity for a unified command, without even showing it to his chiefs, Keitel and von Blomberg. However, his acute mind ensured that, while he was adamant about the advantages of an Armed Forces High Command, he was no admirer of Hitler and, by the outbreak of the war, had come to oppose his policies.

During the invasion of Poland, intense dissatisfaction with the workings of the OKW, as it was then constituted, set in, and Warlimont found himself sympathising with the position of the Army Command. In this he was not alone, for, as he afterwards wrote, 'there was a split right through OKW, and no fewer than two Chiefs of Sections, Admiral Canaris [Intelligence] and

General Thomas [Economics], together with the vast majority of their officers, were on the side of the Army'.[32] But against Keitel and Jodl they could do little. Jodl, in particular, saw the OKW not as containing officers and 'colleagues who had the right to think for themselves, to make suggestions and to advise, but as a machine for the elaboration and issue of orders'[33] – orders that came from Hitler himself.

The theory and the practice of the German High Command were two very different things. The theory was unification, centralisation, and coordination; the practice was disunity, fragmentation, and improvisation. The United States War Department *Handbook on German Military Forces*, published in 1941, noted: 'The outstanding characteristic of German military operations in the present war has been the remarkable coordination of the three sister services, Army, Navy, and Air Forces, into a unified command for definite tasks. These services do not cooperate in a campaign; rather their operations are coordinated by the High Command of the Armed Forces.'[34] This is the picture of Germany's military command structure that has been generally accepted until the present day, but one man who worked in a senior position within that High Command has given posterity a very different picture. Warlimont wrote: 'When the Second World War broke out no established headquarters existed capable of undertaking the overall direction of the German war effort.'[35] There lies the truth.

Immediately before mobilisation for war, the structure of the German High Command was headed by Adolf Hitler, Supreme Commander and effective Commander-in-Chief of the Wehrmacht; directly below him was the coordinating agency, the OKW, the head of which, Keitel, exercised the authority of the former Minister of War. The OKW consisted of the following. First, and most important, was the Armed Forces Operations Office concerned with plans, operations, communications, transport, and propaganda for the Armed Forces as a whole, whose chief, Jodl, was also Keitel's deputy. (By far the most important of its branches was the National Defence Branch in which the details of the operational planning were worked out and sent to the high commands of the three individual services.) Second in the structure of the OKW came the *Allgemeines Wehrmachtamt* (the General Armed Forces Office), concerned with matters of administration, welfare, pensions, vocational training, science, and prisoners of war. Third was the *Amt Ausland/Abwehr* (Foreign and Counter-Intelligence Office) under Canaris. Fourth came the *Wehrwirtschaftsamt* (Military Economics Office); fifth the *Wehrmacht Zentralabteilung* (Armed Forces Central Branch), concerned with mobilisation, personnel, and administration; sixth the *Wehrmachtsrechtsabteilung* (Armed Forces Legal Branch); and seventh, and last, was the *Wehrmachthaushaltsabteilung* (Armed Forces Budget Branch).

Directly beneath the OKW in the chain of command came the three service high commands – *Oberkommando des Heeres* (OKH), *Oberkommando der Kriegsmarine* (OKM) and *Oberkommando der Luftwaffe* (OKL). The Army

High Command was under the direction of the Army Commander-in-Chief, and consisted firstly, and by far the most important, of the *Generalstab des Heeres* (Army General Staff), which was concerned with operations, training, supplies, fortifications, and intelligence on foreign armies. The Chief of General Staff possessed five deputies: Assistant Chief of Staff for Operations (*Oberquartiermeister I* – Head Quartermaster I); Assistant Chief of Staff for Training (*Oberquartiermeister II*); Assistant Chief of Staff for Organisation and Technical Matters (*Oberquartiermeister III*); Assistant Chief of Staff for Foreign Armies (*Oberquartiermeister IV*); Assistant Chief of Staff for Military Science (*Oberquartiermeister V*). The second office in the OKH was the *Heeres Personalamt* (Army Personnel Office). Third came the *Allgemeines Heeresamt* (General Army Office), concerned with publications, budget, law, replacements, clothing, punishment, ordnance stores, and inspectorates of arms and services. Fourth was the *Heeres Waffenant* (Army Ordnance Office), fifth the *Heeres Verwaltungsamt* (Army Administration Office), sixth the *Inspektion der Kriegsschulen* (Inspectorate of Military Training Schools), and seventh the *Chef der Schnellen Truppen* (Chief of Mobile Troops).

Such an intricate organisation may seem confusing, but only one salient feature need be remembered: the operational ideas of the Führer and Supreme Commander were to be transmitted to the OKW Operations Office and its National Defence Branch, whence, in a detailed form combining the activities of all three services, they were to be forwarded to the various high commands, foremost among which was the OKH, where the General Staff would turn the OKW directive into operational orders for the whole of the Army. At least, such was the theory. In practice, all was confusion. At the centre of the Reich's military direction after 1938 there was only one reality: Hitler. He was the sole political authority from which all power in the Reich emanated; General Guderian wrote:

> 'Up to this time Hitler had been receptive to practical considerations, and had at least listened to advice and been prepared to discuss matters with others; now, however, he became increasingly autocratic. One example of his change in behaviour is furnished by the fact that after 1938 the Cabinet never again met. The Ministers did their work in accordance with instructions issued by Hitler to each of them singly. There was no longer any collective examination of major policy. . . . The national administration was emasculated.'[36]

Departmental ministers were given no opportunity to make their reports to Hitler for months and, finally, for years on end. Even the Party suffered, from 1937 there being no further meetings of Reichsleiters and Gauleiters. In the military sphere Hitler disregarded totally the command structure he himself had instituted. Even the OKW and its operations staff was by-passed, and, as Warlimont bitterly recorded, 'it found itself confined to an ill-defined sphere of activity, floating between the intuitive political initiatives of the dictator and their military consequences – on the one it was totally without influence, on the other its possibility of action depended on the degree of recognition accorded it by the high commands of the three services'.[37] Indeed, only a few weeks after promising he 'would never take a decision affecting the Wehrmacht without first hearing the views of his Chief of Staff ',[38] the Führer decided on the invasion of Austria without even having the courtesy to inform Keitel of his plan. The long-suffering Chief of OKW learnt of it only through a member of Hitler's personal staff. It was clear that, in Warlimont's words, the OKW 'had no authority other than that which Hitler was occasionally willing to lend'.[39]

What, then, of the position of the Army High Command during the final years leading to the outbreak of the Second World War? Although the generals' opposition to Hitler's policies had been made impotent by the events of early 1938 – revealed strikingly by their failure to make even the slightest impact on the Führer's plans for the occupation of Austria and for the attack on Czechoslovakia – there was still a considerable degree of direct contact between the Army Commander, his staff, and the dictator. This became evident during the preparations for the invasion of Poland. In March 1939, Hitler first dropped a casual hint to von Brauchitsch that he was prepared to use force against Poland, and the Chief of the OKW learnt of his intention only some days later. Once the Operations staff of the Armed Forces High Command had brought up to date the mobilisation procedure, it became nothing more than a registry for assembling the plans already drawn up by the three services. The various Commanders-in-Chiefs avoided the OKW and cultivated a personal planning relationship with their Supreme Commander, while the Chief of OKW degenerated into a go-between, 'a whipping boy who had thrust upon him . . . all those jobs which . . . no one else . . . wished to handle'.[40] The Führer dealt directly with his Army chiefs. Warlimont remembered that 'By the middle of August [1939], by which time Hitler had long been established in the Berghof, he began to give signs of increased activity in military matters; this consisted almost exclusively of the issue of a stream of new demands and requirements concerning the Army's plans for the move forward.'[41] Neither Keitel nor Jodl took any part in this.

Consequently, at the outbreak of the war it might have appeared as if, despite the February 1938 reorganisation, the Army had retained its position as the sole director, under the Supreme Commander, of military operations. But the portents for the future were ominous. There now existed an instrument, wholly under Hitler's control and occupying, in theory, the central position of the Reich's military command, which, should the dictator so wish, could wrest from the Army General Staff its traditional role as the nation's supreme operational authority. This is exactly what occurred: the OKW became one of the main instruments by which Hitler was to subject the Army to his own will as a war lord.

7

Road to War

War came upon us by stealth; only when we looked back, could we clearly see how it had come: by Hitler.

FIELD-MARSHAL ERICH VON MANSTEIN

The Austrian adventure took place in the middle of the Fritsch crisis. On 9 March 1938, the Austrian Chancellor announced that a plebiscite would be held on Sunday, 13 March, on terms disadvantageous to the National Socialists, in which the people were to declare whether they were in favour of a free, independent Austria. That evening Hitler took advice, not from his Army chiefs, nor, indeed, from the heads of OKW, but from an intimate circle consisting of Göring, von Reichenau, and two other generals known to him personally. On the 10th he summoned Beck and von Manstein, the former Chief of Operations, and, without asking for their opinion, ordered them to prepare for an immediate invasion of Austria. This they did reluctantly, having first expressed their belief to the dictator that the Army was not prepared for such a task. But, as Keitel remarked, 'their objections were summarily brushed aside by Hitler'.[1] On the 11th, OKW issued a directive which included the announcement that the Führer himself would take charge of the operations. And, on the 12th, German troops proceeded to incorporate a recalcitrant Austria into the Greater German Reich.

Both Beck and von Brauchitsch were bitterly opposed to this rushed occupation, fearing, above all, western intervention. They chose to express their main opposition through the Chief of the OKW, but, as Keitel himself recalls, they had chosen the wrong avenue of approach:

'The night [10–11 March] that followed was sheer purgatory for me: one telephone call followed another from the Army General Staff and from Brauchitsch; finally, at about four o'clock in the morning there was a call from the then Chief of the [OKW] Military Operations Staff, General von Viebahn [who was dismissed in 1938 and succeeded by Jodl]; all adjured me to persuade the Führer to call the operation off. I had no intention of asking this of the Führer even once; of course I promised them I would try, but I called them back a short time later (having made no attempt to contact him) and told each one that he had rejected their protests. This was something of which the Führer never learnt; if he had, his verdict on the Army's leadership would have been devastating, a disillusionment I wanted to spare both parties.'[2]

Against such odds, the Army leaders had little chance.

By the coup in Austria, Hitler had confirmed and consolidated his new position in the military structure of the Reich. He had demonstrated that he alone was capable of decisive leadership (although his extreme nervousness during the operation led him at one point even to cancel the march); that the opposition from the officer corps was both reactionary and groundless; and that the role of the Army leadership was merely to supply the force he required, without question.

A month later, Hitler turned his attention towards Czechoslovakia. On 21 April, the Führer summoned Keitel and explained to him the reasons why Czechoslovakia was considered to be a danger to the Reich, as well as the political principles that would be followed as preliminaries for the attack. The crux of the matter was that Czechoslovakia lay in a position that was strategically very difficult for Germany when the time came for the great reckoning with the east; the country could be used as a springboard for the Soviet forces to plunge deep into the heart of the Reich. Nevertheless, Hitler rejected the idea of an unprovoked attack because of 'hostile world opinion which might lead to a critical situation; instead they preferred lightning action based on an incident (for example, the murder of the German minister in the course of a demonstration)'.[3] Hitler then placed in the hands of the OKW the task of drawing up *Aufmarsch Grün* for the attack on Czechoslovakia, plans that the OKH had previously opposed so strongly that they had never been completed. The operation, drawn up by the OKW planning staff under Jodl, was ready for Hitler's signature on 20 May. It opened with the words: 'It is not my intention to smash Czechoslovakia by military action in the immediate future without provocation. . . .'[4]

At this point plans were overtaken by events. On that same day, 20 May, the Czech government, alarmed at rumours of a German attack and at reports of troop concentrations near the frontier, ordered a partial mobilisation of its armed forces. The British and French governments at once made strong representations to Berlin, warning of the possibility of a general war should Czechoslovakia be invaded, while France and the Soviet Union reaffirmed their promise of immediate support for the Czechs. Outraged rather than frightened at such accusations and reactions (they were, after all, groundless at that time), and unwilling to accept any loss of prestige, Hitler took a fateful decision: to solve the Czechoslovakian issue that same year, even if he thereby risked a European war. The plan for the invasion was recast, and, on 28 May, Hitler gave his signature to the new, and last, version of *Aufmarsch Grün*. Its first sentence ran: 'It is my unalterable decision to smash Czechoslovakia by military action in the near future.'[5] The date for the execution of the plan was set for 1 October.

The reaction of the Army leaders was one of utter dismay. They had always been opposed to any idea of an invasion of Czechoslovakia, and Beck had already expressed strong reservations to von Brauchitsch about the first OKW plan, which, he argued, would render a general war inevitable, a war that Germany would be bound to lose. Now that direct action had been decided on, to take place within four months, the generals' reaction was heated. At the conference of 30 May, at which Hitler communicated his decision to his Army leaders, their opposition was far from muted. Jodl noted in his diary: 'The whole contrast becomes acute once more between the Führer's intuition that we must do it this year and the opinion of the Army that we cannot do it yet as most certainly the western powers will interfere and we are not yet equal to them.'[6] But the generals faced an extreme difficulty: the plan had been drawn up by OKW without any help from them, and they were now presented with a fait accompli with no chance of reversing or, indeed, of amending it. Furthermore, their opposition was against a background of military preparation for the invasion. Events were running away from them. Beck, the leader of the opposition, produced a new memorandum for his chief on 3 June, followed by yet another on 16 July. Both were designed to convince von Brauchitsch of the disaster Germany was facing. The July document contained the following summarised sentiments that may be held to be common among the generals:

'There was no doubt that an attack on Czechoslovakia would bring France and Britain into the conflict at once . . . the outcome would be a general catastrophe for Germany, not only a military defeat. The German people did not want this war, the purpose of which they did not understand. Similar thoughts were also abroad within the Army. . . . Military preparations had attracted foreign attention. . . . Any hope of achieving surprise had thereby been dashed.'[7]

Beck ended with the following exhortation:

'I now feel in duty bound . . . to ask insistently that the Supreme Commander of the Wehrmacht should be compelled to abandon the preparations he has ordered for war, and to postpone his intention of solving the Czech problem by force until the military situation is basically changed. For the present I consider it hopeless, and this view is shared by all my Quartermasters-General and departmental chiefs of the General Staff who would have to deal with the preparations and execution of a war against Czechoslovakia.'[8]

At the same time Beck urged von Brauchitsch to organise some form of collective military, although peaceful, resistance to Hitler's policy.

Beck's attitude could hardly have been more definite. Von Brauchitsch, however, was equivocal. Although he undoubtedly shared the prevalent professional view of Hitler's plans, his political incapacity and character weakness prevented him from making anything but purely nominal appeals to the Führer. He had no desire to place himself at the head of any opposition to Hitler, for, as he later recorded: 'Why, in heaven's name, should I, of all men in the world, have taken action against Hitler? The German people had elected him, and the workers, like all other Germans, were perfectly satisfied with his successful policy.'[9] Furthermore, his relationship with Beck, strained from the beginning, was now reaching a crisis in mutual confidence; von Brauchitsch took to bypassing Beck and dealing directly with his deputy, the new Chief of Army Operations Staff, Halder, while the Chief of Staff, for his part, repeatedly offered his resignation to the Army Commander.

Von Brauchitsch, nonetheless, was worried. Although he consistently refused to convey to Hitler the generals' opposition, he did, at Beck's insistence, call a secret conference of the Army leaders on 4 August. All were in agreement that any Czechoslovak venture would be militarily foolish, and von Brauchitsch closed the meeting with the prophecy that a European war would mean the end of German culture. However, no plan of action was agreed on: Beck wanted the Army Commander to lead his generals to demand that Hitler should reverse his policy; von Reichenau believed that it would be far more effective if individual officers went to see the Führer, who would be indignant at a mass confrontation; von Rundstedt wanted von Brauchitsch to tread warily in his opposition and not to court dismissal, thereby allowing von Reichenau to take over his position; and Busch, although convinced of the folly of playing with general war, advanced the argument that this was not the province in which the soldier should interfere. In the event, it appears that when the Army Commander conveyed to Hitler the fears of his generals, albeit somewhat half-heartedly, he came up against an indignant and unbending reception. Once again, von Brauchitsch yielded to his Führer's will.

Hitler immediately mounted a counter-offensive against his discontented generalship, flatly denying the need for any anxiety. He began with a flanking movement by inviting their chiefs of staff to a dinner on 10 August to explain to them his political views. But he met with scepticism, and the occasion ended on a discordant note when, in response to an assertion that it was impossible to hold the western fortifications for more than three weeks, the enraged dictator rounded on the assembled officers, accusing them of defeatism and a lack of morale. Next, he executed a surprise manoeuvre of appeasement by formally rehabilitating von Fritsch on the 11th. His last action was a frontal attack on the 15th, when, after field manoeuvres, he informed his generals of his firm and final resolve to smash Czechoslovakia that autumn, at the same time reminding them of his prophetic gifts which, despite all advice to the contrary, had so often proved right in the past. The generals remained silent; their protest was over.

Beck, alone, was prepared for one more, final, attempt. After the meeting on the 15th, he demanded an audience with his Army Commander. Von

Brauchitsch, at the end of his patience, could take no more from his Chief of Staff and had him informed that he could not meet his request as he was just going off on a few days' leave. Beck was enraged. On the 18th, on von Brauchitsch's return, he had a stormy interview with his chief, in which he was informed of Hitler's latest order which prohibited political interference by the Army and demanded nothing less than unconditional obedience from all generals. Beck could go no further. He resigned, calling on von Brauchitsch to do likewise. The Army Commander refused, 'hitched his collar a notch higher, and said: "I am a soldier; it is my duty to obey." '[10] On the 21st, a thankful Hitler agreed to the resignation, and on 27 August Beck attended his office for the last time.

By his resignation, Beck had finally burst free of the rigid confines of the Prussian military tradition: the oath, the code of obedience to the Head of State, and the ingrained notion that the soldier was above politics, were now cast aside. He had set his reasons on paper a month previously:

> 'History will burden these [Army] leaders with blood-guilt if they do not act in accord with their specialised political knowledge and conscience. Their military obedience has a limit where their knowledge, their conscience, and their sense of responsibility forbid the execution of a command. If their warning and counsel receive no hearing in such a situation, then they have the right and duty to resign from their offices. If they all act with resolution, the execution of a policy of war is impossible. By this they have saved their country from the worst – from ruin. It is a lack of greatness and of recognition of the task if a soldier in the highest position in such times regards his duties and tasks only within the limited framework of his military instructions without being aware of the highest responsibilities towards the nation as a whole. Extraordinary times demand extraordinary measures.'[11]

Beck's act was honourable and courageous, but there it ended. Although he believed that the time had come to free Germany (and even Hitler himself) from the tyranny of the Party and secret police, and that this was possibly the last occasion on which it could be attempted, his subsequent moves ensured that his resignation would not be the catalyst for this action. Ordinarily, such a move on the part of a distinguished and respected Chief of the General Staff in the midst of a national crisis would have had a resounding impact, not only on the officer corps but on the wider, political world, both at home and abroad; disillusion and resignations would have followed. Yet Beck's action signally failed to achieve any such effect. He was supported by none of even his closest colleagues, and his act did nothing more than bring to an end his resistance to Hitler through the normal official channels. One of the reasons for this failure lies in the fact that, on Hitler's orders, Beck's resignation was not communicated either to the public or to the Army, 'for reasons of foreign policy', until the end of October, although his successor,

Franz Halder, took over his duties on 1 September. Beck, out of loyalty to his country in a time of crisis, accepted this condition; he made no attempt to turn his resignation into a burning issue around which the opposition could focus. A man of principle, he was not yet one of action. Furthermore, there were a number of men in the Armed Forces, besides Hitler, who were only too glad to see Beck leave the field. Of these Keitel was understandably one. He wrote later: 'I wept no tears over Beck in view of the shameless way he had treated me.'[12] Nor could support be expected from the Army Commander, his relationship with his Chief of Staff having long since become unworkable. Beck always looked back to this time bitterly and complained: 'Brauchitsch left me in the lurch.'[13]

As for the other generals, united resistance against Hitler was impossible. Despite their knowledge of the dangerous follies inherent in his present course of action, their political naïvety held them rigidly to their oath of obedience. Unlike Beck, they had no conception of any higher duties or wider responsibilities to the Army and to the nation, nor did they possess Beck's awareness of the nature of the régime they served, a régime in which the Army was, at that time, the only possible counterbalance to Hitler and the Party. As a result, putting their doubts firmly behind them, they immersed themselves in their work, tried to forget the vexed question of conflicting principles, breathed a sigh of relief when Germany, once again, triumphed on the international scene, and gratefully basked in the reflected glory of Hitler's success. Such was their reaction – a human one which has shaped the course of history since time began.

Beck's successor as Chief of the Army General Staff, the fifty-four year old Franz Halder, was a man who exemplified von Moltke's saying: 'Genius is diligence'. Born in 1884 to a well-known Bavarian military family, the son of a distinguished general, Halder enjoyed an outstanding career as a staff officer, rising to become, on 10 February 1938, Beck's deputy and Chief of Operations. His elevation to Chief of the Army General Staff meant a severe break with the longstanding Prussian tradition of that office, for he was a Southerner, a Bavarian. Indefatigable and cautious by nature, Halder was a man of conservative outlook, although by no means rigid or hide-bound. Dedicated to his duty as a soldier, he personified the General Staff motto: 'Achieve much, appear little', and saw himself as the 'Guardian of the Grail', declaring on one occasion: '. . . we shall not depart by one hair's breadth from this spirit of the German General Staff. . . . He to whom the mantle of honour has no more meaning than a badge of rank or an increase in pay, lives on a different plane to that on which the Prussian General Staff was founded and has grown great.'[14] Even his physical appearance denoted the ideal staff officer: his hair close-cropped, his piercing eyes made all the more noticeable by his habit of wearing pince-nez, his whole aspect, unprepossessing though it was, reflecting quiet intelligence, shrewdness, and diligence. Nor was he a colourless administrator of the mould of Keitel. On the contrary, Halder possessed wide intellectual interests, with a special liking for mathematics and botany. An unexpected vehemence destroyed any impression of a phlegmatic personality, his emotions causing him to be moved to tears on many an occasion. In addition, he possessed the independence of mind, which, contrary to the accepted view, had always characterised the German staff officer in military affairs. As von Manstein recorded: 'He was incorruptibly objective in his utterances, and I myself have known him put a criticism to Hitler with the utmost frankness. On the same occasion one also saw how fervently he stood up for the interests of the fighting troops and how much he felt for them when wrong decisions were imposed on him.'[15]

It has been said that Halder took the post of Chief of the Army General Staff only so he could best continue his opposition to Hitler, whom he detested. His beliefs and actions seem to bear out this view. During the Blomberg–Fritsch affair he was one of the few who advocated strong action, even revolt; advice that Beck rejected. When relinquishing his post to Halder, Beck admitted: 'I now realise that you were right at the time. Now all depends on you.'[16] Indeed, the changeover between the two men took on the aspect of the senior bestowing his heritage of opposition to the Führer on the junior. According to Gisevius, one of the conspirators, 'Beck had assured us . . . that he would leave a successor who was more energetic than himself, and who was firmly determined to precipitate a revolution if Hitler should decide on war. . . . on taking office, General Halder immediately took steps to start discussions on the subject with Schacht, Goerdeler, Oster, and our entire group . . . he considered that we were drifting towards war, and that he would undertake an overthrow of the government.'[17]

However, despite his deep abhorrence of all that Hitler and his régime stood for, the new Chief of the General Staff was confronted with an irreconcilable dichotomy between his role as a conspirator and his duty as a highly placed soldier. This has been sympathetically described by von Manstein:

'Now, although it may be given to a politician to play the dual role of responsible adviser and conspirator, soldiers are not usually fitted for this kind of thing. . . . As Chief of the General Staff, it was Halder's duty to strive for the victory of the Army he was jointly responsible for leading – in other words, to see that the military operations of his Commander-in-Chief were successful. In the second of his roles, however, he could not desire such a victory. There cannot be the least doubt that Halder, when confronted by this difficult choice, opted for his military duty and did everything to serve the German Army in its arduous struggle. At the same time, his other role demanded that he should at all costs hold on to the position which, he hoped, would one day enable him to bring about Hitler's removal. To that end, however, he had to bow to the latter's military decisions, even if he did not agree with them. The conflict was bound to wear him down inwardly and finally led to his downfall. One thing is certain: it was in the interest of what was at stake, and not of his own person, that . . . Halder stuck it out for so long as Chief of Staff.'[18]

As Jodl discerned, despite the removal of Beck there still remained 'a strong current of resistance to Hitler's intentions and plans . . . within the Army General Staff'.[19] The very generals in whose hands the execution of Case Green had been placed, von Reichenau and von Rundstedt, expressed their apprehension to von Brauchitsch and urged him to attempt once more the conversion of Hitler. The Army Commander's interview with the dictator and Keitel on 3 September achieved nothing more than a further opportunity for more abuse from Hitler. This was followed on the 9th, during the Nuremberg Party rally, by another meeting, this time with Halder in attendance (he shared Beck's views on the Czech venture), which lasted from 10.00 p.m. to 3.30 a.m. the next morning. The protesters again achieved nothing, and, according to Keitel, Hitler, 'who wished to bring these recalcitrants round by calmly and patiently lecturing them . . . lost his patience [and] . . . coldly and sullenly . . . dismissed the gentlemen from his presence'.[20] The strained relationship between Hitler and his Army leaders was summed up by Jodl in his diary:

> '. . . the Führer is aware that the Commander-in-Chief of the Army asked his commanders to support him in his attempt to make the Führer see sense on the subject of the adventure into which he seems determined to plunge. The Commander-in-Chief himself, so he said, unfortunately had no influence with the Führer. The atmosphere in Nuremberg was consequently cool and frosty. It is tragic that the Führer should have the whole nation behind him with the single exception of the Army generals.'[21]

However much the Army leadership might have opposed Hitler's intentions, they remained loyal to his wishes and faithful to their conception of duty. The western defences were strengthened; the plans for the deployment of five armies (36 divisions) against Czechoslovakia were expedited and presented to the Führer on 18 September; and all preparations were undertaken so that the attack could begin on 1 October.

Nevertheless, for one group within the Army, the Czechoslovak affair did serve to act as a catalyst for direct action against Hitler, action which, if successful, would have resulted in his deposition, and possibly in his death. It was a conspiracy set afoot by Canaris and Oster of the Abwehr group, and supported by a number of senior Army officers: Halder, von Witzleben, still commander of the vital Wehrkreis III, von Brockdorff-Ahlefeld, divisional commander of the Potsdam garrison, General Erich Hoepner, commander of 1st Light Division in Thuringia (a man who refused to have the statutory picture of Hitler hanging in his office), General Karl-Heinrich von Stülpnagel, Halder's successor as head of the Operations Department of the Army General Staff, von Hammerstein, and Beck. The plan was simple: Hitler would be arrested as soon as the final order for the invasion of Czechoslovakia had been given, and would later be put on trial on the charge that his activities constituted a grave danger to Germany; the Army would deal with all opposition and, unknown to him, von Brauchitsch would issue a decree to the effect that he was the supreme authority of government pending the formation of a civilian caretaker administration which would proceed to determine a new form of government acceptable to the majority. Such a scheme rested on two fundamental factors: first, that the putsch would take place at the best psychological time – the moment Hitler gave the order to attack (it was Halder's task to communicate this information as soon as he knew it); and, second, that the thesis that the Czechoslovakian adventure would escalate into a major European conflict must be shown to be correct. (To ensure foreign intervention, the conspirators sent a number of envoys to London to warn of Hitler's intentions, but they achieved nothing.) By mid-September their plans were ready, in Halder's words, 'to the last gaiter-button',[22] so carefully were they laid.

The political preparation for the invasion proceeded apace. Hitler based his aim of crushing Czechoslovakia on demands for the incorporation of the Sudetenland (that part of Czechoslovakia in which there was a large ethnic German population) into the Reich, and issued an ultimatum to that effect on 26 September. It was to expire at two o'clock on the afternoon of the 28th. Europe braced itself. Hitler announced to the British ambassador on the 27th: 'I am prepared for every eventuality. It is Tuesday today, and by next Monday we shall be at war.'[23] In Berlin, massed armour paraded down the Wilhelmstrasse; in London, trenches were dug; in Paris, there was panic. It was just as the generals had predicted: the Czechs had massed a well-trained, 800,000-strong field army behind strong defences; the French had partially mobilised and were capable of placing sixty-five divisions to face twelve of the Germans on the frontier; the British mobilised their fleet; the Soviets stated they would honour their treaty obligations; the Italians did nothing. Germany now faced the real possibility of a war on two fronts; her troops were outnumbered by those of France and Czechoslovakia alone by two to one. Perhaps even more shattering to Hitler than the prospect of facing such enemies was the painful awareness that his own people were, at best, apathetic to war. At the Berlin military parade, an American correspondent noted that the populace 'refused to look on, and the handful that did, stood at the kerb in utter silence. . . . It has been the most striking demonstration against war I've ever seen. . . . Hitler looked grim.'[24] In western Germany people rushed to leave the cities, such was the fear of air attack. Von Brauchitsch made his final attempt through Keitel to avert war, but to no avail.

But, as so often in the career of Adolf Hitler, just as Europe teetered on the edge of a general war, fate presented the German dictator with the means

The two Commanders-in-Chief: von Blomberg talking with von Fritsch at the Nuremberg Party Rally in September 1937, only a few months before their downfall.

The oath being sworn to Adolf Hitler on his assumption of the office of Reich President and Supreme Commander in August 1934.

Above: The growing military pretensions of the SS: men of Hitler's bodyguard, the Leibstandarte SS 'Adolf Hitler', who formed part of the SS Verfügungstruppe. *Below:* The occupation of the Rhineland: infantry marching out of their barracks prior to moving into the demilitarised zone, March 1936.

Above: Hitler with his commanders-in-chief: from left to right, Göring, von Brauchitsch and Raeder. *Below:* The incorporation of Austria within the Reich: soldiers of the Austrian Army, with the German national eagle already on their right breasts, march past Hitler in Vienna on 14th March 1938.

Top left: General Ludwig Beck, Chief of the General Staff, 1934–1938, shortly before his resignation over the proposed invasion of Czechoslovakia. *Top right:* Field Marshal Wilhelm Keitel, Chief of the Wehrmacht High Command, 1938–1945. *Bottom left:* One of the first of the military conspirators: Field Marshal Erwin von Witzleben, who was hanged in 1944.

Bottom right: General Alfred Jodl, Deputy Chief of the Wehrmacht High Command.

Above: The glorification of rearmament: the Army displaying its newly acquired might in the Nuremberg stadium during the National Socialist Party Rally of 1938. The anti-tank gun in this picture, however, was so ineffective that it was nicknamed the 'door-knocker'. *Left:* Early experiments: cardboard tank structures mounted on motor cars moving into the attack accompanied by infantry.

Left: The man to whom the German panzer force owed so much: General Heinz Guderian. In 1944 he became the third Chief of the General Staff during the war. *Below:* The PzKw I training tank, shown here on manœuvres in the Nuremberg Stadium, September 1938. By the time manufacture of these machines ended in 1941, 1,500 had been produced.

Left: The PzKw II, a stop-gap, training tank of which 2,000 were built. Although production ended in July 1942, the machine was used in a reconnaissance role until late 1944. *Below:* The PzKw III, intended to be Germany's main battle tank, armed with a 3.7cm gun. No less than 5,644 of these tanks, of all variants, were produced, some 5,000 being destroyed in action.

Above: The horse-drawn supply column so basic to the operation of the German Field Army. Here in the Soviet Union in 1941, wagons bring up rations to the front-line troops. *Below:* The PzKw IV, the panzer force's support-tank, armed with a short-barrelled 7.5cm gun. By 1944 the PzKw IV, with heavier armour and a more powerful gun, had become Germany's main tank, and by the end of the war 7,350 had been produced.

not only to avoid almost certain and catastrophic failure, but also to gain at least part of what he had demanded, with the prospect of the rest to come. The governments of France and Britain were still not convinced of the necessity for war, and, through the mediation of Mussolini, Hitler was persuaded to accept Chamberlain's proposal for a four-power conference on the Czechoslovak question. (Ironically, the country most concerned, Czechoslovakia, was not invited to attend.) The result of the meeting of the four leaders, Hitler, Mussolini, Chamberlain, and Daladier, which took place at Munich on 29 September, was the total acceptance of the Führer's demands. Military blackmail had worked. While Chamberlain fluttered his scrap of paper and declared 'peace in our time', German troops prepared to march, unopposed, into the Sudetenland on 1 October.

Hitler's triumph at Munich spelt ruin for the military conspirators. Their ostensible reason for undertaking the coup had been denied them: instead of the Führer appearing as the great war-monger, he now was likened to a noble statesman, ensuring Germany's rights while still maintaining the peace of Europe. Even before Munich, it had been doubtful whether the mass of the Army would have followed the lead of a few officers and shed its loyalty to Hitler in the face of external aggression; but now, amid the overwhelming rejoicing that met the Führer's achievement, an attempted coup by a few relatively unknown and obscure men would have had no chance of success. In the foreseeable future there was little hope for the conspirators. The west's surrender at Munich had made Halder extremely wary, and, despite the urgings of Bcck, Goerdeler, Canaris, and Oster, who were certain that Britain and France would act the minute Hitler occupied the rest of Czechoslovakia (had they not entered into a guarantee with the Czechs?), the Chief of the General Staff refused even to plan a putsch until the intervention had actually taken place. If war were declared over Czechoslovakia he would move, but not otherwise. Likewise von Brauchitsch, who, reportedly, before Munich was becoming sympathetic to the idea of a coup, was no longer prepared even to entertain the idea. Moreover, a great blow was dealt to the conspirators' plans by the routine removal of von Witzleben from the crucial Wehrkreis III around Berlin to command Army Group 2 based at Frankfurt-am-Main. For the time being, at least, there could be no action from this quarter.

As was predicted by the conspirators, Hitler's occupation of the Sudetenland was only a preliminary to greater things. Just three weeks later he gave the order to plan the move against the rest of Czechoslovakia, and, after a few months of political preparation, the unhappy country was occupied on 15 – 16 March on the pretext of safeguarding the order and peace of central Europe. Czechoslovakia ceased to exist, being replaced by the Protectorate of Bohemia and Moravia. On 23 March, the Memelland was also placed under German rule. Halder's fears were proved justified: the world looked on; not a finger was lifted to aid the Czechs. Hitler was confident that 'in two weeks not a soul will bother to talk about it'.[25] But on this point he was wrong; his intuition failed him. The day following Hitler's entry into Prague, Chamberlain spoke to a meeting in his constituency. 'Is this', he said, 'a step in the direction of an attempt to dominate the world by force? . . . no greater mistake could be made than to suppose that because it [Great Britain] believes war to be a senseless and a cruel thing, this nation has so lost its fibre that it will not take part to the utmost of its power in resisting such a challenge if it ever were made.'[26] Fifteen days later, the Prime Minister told a packed House of Commons: 'In the event of any action which clearly threatened Polish independence and which the Polish government accordingly considered it vital to resist with their national forces, His Majesty's government would feel themselves bound at once to lend the Polish government all support in their power. . . . I may add that the French government have authorised me to make plain that they stand in the same position . . .'[27]

Just as the Czechoslovak affair marked a turning-point in the relations between Germany and her European neighbours, so, too, did it signify the final collapse of the mutual trust and reliance between Hitler and the Army leaders. It was gone forever; one year had served to shatter it completely. Hitler now revealed a contempt for, and mistrust of, his generals not evidenced before the Blomberg–Fritsch affair. Certainly before 1938 Hossbach had detected in him a certain disillusionment with the Army leaders and their 'everlasting hesitations', and there was a noticeable decline in his consideration for Army affairs and a greater readiness to entertain suspicions and complaints from the Party. But never would he previously have said, as he did now, that all generals were cowards. The ease with which he had humbled the once-proud *Generalität* during February and March 1938 had aroused in him a deep contempt which found its outlet through continual, and ever-increasing, insulting remarks. Men who allowed themselves to be dominated like Keitel, inhibited like von Brauchitsch, and rendered impotent like von Fritsch could never hope to regain his earlier respect and deference. What he saw as their vulnerability and weakness of character made him disdainful of their whole caste. At the meeting at the War Ministry on the afternoon of 4 February 1938, Hitler had concluded by saying: 'After such sorrowful experiences I must consider anyone capable of anything. The 100,000-man Army has failed to produce any great leaders. From now on I shall concern myself with personnel matters and make the right appointments.'[28] Not a word of protest was raised at this. For the first time the generals were feeling thoroughly intimidated and shamed by Hitler. As General Curt Liebmann wrote later: 'We all had the feeling that the Army – in contrast to the Navy, the Luftwaffe, and the Party – had suffered an annihilating blow and that in future any measure directed against it would be defended with a certain justice on the plea that the generals did not deserve any confidence.'[29]

Now, with the Army leadership shown to have been so mistaken over Czechoslovakia, added to their already miserable record over rearmament,

the Rhineland, and Austria, Hitler's respect fork the professional competence of his advisers reached a new low, forcing him to exclaim: 'What kind
of generals are these whom I as the Head of State may have to propel into
war? By rights, I should be the one seeking to ward off the generals'
eagerness for war. . . .'[30] From then on his view was: 'I do not ask my
generals to understand my orders but only to carry them out.'[31] He regarded
the Army as an uncertain element in the state, even worse than the Foreign
Office and the Judiciary. Westphal wrote: 'Hitler . . . saw in the General
Staff. . . the "Public Enemy No. 1" or, as he and Göring were fond of saying,
"the last Freemasons' Lodge in Germany." '[32]

In May 1938 Hitler transferred the supervision of the building of the
West Wall from the Army to the Todt Organisation, abusing the military for
having been too slow and accusing the General Staff of sabotaging his
requirements. Outbursts became common. On hearing from Adam, then
earmarked for Commander-in-Chief in the west, that more troops were
needed to hold an attack from the French, Hitler launched into a tirade, the
butt of which was Keitel, who later wrote: 'I was obliged to stand there and
listen to him ranting at me that this general had been a bad disappointment
to him, and he would have to go; he had no use for generals like those who
had no faith in their mission from the very outset. . . . Brauchitsch had the
same lecture from him, and this outstanding soldier [Adam] was pensioned
off.'[33] This incident had a sequel on 30 January 1939, when, at a meeting
with senior officers, Hitler roundly condemned this spirit of faint-
heartedness, declaring 'I want no more warning memoranda from anybody'.[34] He announced that it was to be von Brauchitsch's task to give the
officer corps a new purpose and select only those who had faith in the Führer.
This spirit of contempt showed itself in other National Socialist leaders. In
August 1938, Göring berated an assembly of officers, telling them: 'In this
building [the War Ministry] lives the spirit of faint-heartedness. This spirit
must go.'[35] Von Manstein recorded the Luftwaffe Commander's address to
a group of high-ranking military leaders six months later: 'In the course of
his speech he quite brazenly upbraided the Army, as distinct from the other
two services, for maintaining an outlook that was steeped in tradition and
did not fit in with the National Socialist system. It was a speech which . . .
von Brauchitsch, who was among those present, should on no account have
tolerated.'[36] But he did, and there lay the rub. Even the leaders of the OKW
found it in themselves to criticise the caste from whence they sprang. Jodl, for
example, denigrated the men of the OKH for 'their pusillanimity and
smugness',[37] and, according to Warlimont, the heads of OKW 'openly
expressed their displeasure that von Brauchitsch, supported by Halder,
should try to put over his point of view even in matters of purely military
policy. They once more made it clear that their conception of their overriding duty was to carry out Hitler's wishes and where required smooth the
path for him in the military sphere.'[38]

For their part, the Army leaders, with the exception of those fundamentally opposed to the Hitler régime, were humiliated and cowed. They, the professionals, had time and time again been shown up by an amateur; they had expended their capital of goodwill with the Führer for nothing. His intuition had proved right all along. The outcome of the Czechoslovak episode stunned them. It appeared as if Hitler had achieved everything he had aimed at without firing a shot: he had saved the nation from war, and had given to it additional glory and security. To the Germans, and to the Army, this was incontrovertible proof of his consummate skill as a statesman. Jodl summed it up: 'The genius of the Führer and his determination not to shun even a world war have again achieved victory without the use of force. One hopes that the incredulous, the weak, and the doubters have been converted, and will remain so.'[39] It seemed that, yet again, the generals' expertise had been proved wrong and Hitler's instinct right. That this was almost entirely due to factors outside the Führer's control, on chance and on the weakness of Germany's enemies, was not apparent; that their worst fears had come within an ace of being fulfilled mattered not at all. Hitler's successes told a different story. As von Brauchitsch told his captors after the war, the principal point was that all foreign countries had come to recognise Germany as an equal partner, which she certainly had not been before 1933.

As a result, the majority of generals resigned themselves to the Führer, to his intransigence and dominance. The reasons were many: Hitler's achievements in foreign policy, his obvious concern to expand the Reich's military capabilities, and his belief in the soldierly virtues (even though this was limited by his own convenience) had gone far to dissipate the evil impressions gained during the crisis of the previous February. His 'genius' was clear for all to see; the 'facts' proved it, and his 'glory' was bright enough for all to bask in; the Army was, after all, the prime instrument of his successes. Of his internal policies, the success in assuaging inflation, reducing unemployment, improving economic health, building roads, raising standards of public health, maintaining order, stimulating pride in country and creating enthusiasm for military affairs, overrode those more unpleasant aspects of the regime – the bullying of the Church, the increasing persecution of the Jews, which came to a head in the 'Chrystal Night' Pogrom of November 1938, and the maintenance of the concentration camps, from which the occasional death was by then being reported. Furthermore, the continual and hectic activity entailed in the rapid and large-scale rearmament and in the frequent occurrence of foreign ventures ensured that the Army was kept off-balance, its leaders' policies degenerating into rushed improvisations, its officers' energies concentrated on military affairs. Hitler had begun with the initiative; he kept it, and exploited it. Thus, in 1939, when the clouds of war began again to gather over Europe and Hitler embarked on yet another venture that risked armed conflict, the generals did nothing. Their opposition, for a time at least, was over.

On 3 April 1939 Hitler issued a top-secret directive to his service chiefs which opened thus: 'The present attitude of Poland requires . . . the initiation of military preparations to remove, if necessary, any threat from this direction for ever.'[40] The operation was to be codenamed 'Case White', and the plans were drawn up so that the attack could be undertaken at any time from 1 September. On 7 May the Army submitted its estimate of the situation; the preparations for the attack on Poland had begun. On 23 May, the day after the signing of the Pact of Steel with Italy (a military alliance, the military terms of which were kept secret from the Army), Hitler announced his future foreign policy to fourteen senior officers from all three services. He was unequivocal about his aim: it was war. 'Further successes can no longer be attained without the shedding of blood. . . . Danzig is not the subject of the dispute at all. It is a question of expanding our living space in the east. . . . There is no question of sparing Poland and we are left with the decision: to attack Poland at the first suitable opportunity. We cannot expect a repetition of the Czech affair. There will be war. Our task is to isolate Poland.' But he was quite prepared to take on the west: France and Britain, if they did not remain neutral, and, if need be, the Soviet Union as well. Declarations of neutrality would be ignored if they got in the way of military operations. 'The aim must be to deal the enemy a smashing or a finally decisive blow right at the start. Considerations of right or wrong, or of treaties, do not enter into the matter. . . . Preparations', he announced, 'must be made for a long war as well as for a surprise attack, and every possible intervention by England on the Continent must be smashed.'[41] Not one word of dissent was heard. By 15 June Hitler had in his hands the OKH plans for the Army's operations against Poland.

Preparations for the war proceeded calmly. Few made any attempt to save Germany from the impending catastrophe. Von Brauchitsch complied with Hitler's every wish, promised him to bring the war against Poland to a conclusion within a few weeks, and even threatened to arrest Schacht if he set foot in the OKH, so infuriated was he by the man's attempt to persuade him that his former oath to the constitution did not permit the declaration of war without the consent of the Reichstag. Halder, although approached by the underground opposition, would have nothing to do with their plans, and was, in any case, anxious that Germany's strategic position be improved by reacquiring Danzig and the Corridor before discarding the Führer. The OKH, generally, worked diligently to perfect their preparations. Men of Beck's calibre were lacking: one of the very few voices raised in protest was that of General Georg Thomas, head of the OKW Economics Department, who, together with Schacht, wrote a memorandum exposing the fallacies behind the idea of a quick war and explaining that Germany lacked the resources for a long conflict. This was presented to Keitel, but the only reaction it elicited was the assurance that Hitler's genius would overcome all problems. Colonel Rudolf Gercke, head of the Transport Department of the General Staff, added his note of pessimism when he reported: 'As regards transport, Germany is at the moment not ready for war.'[42] Such warnings went unheeded. The generals, indeed the Germans as a whole, had disliked and distrusted Poland since its inception in 1919, believing that a war against that country was 'a sacred duty though a sad necessity'[43] in order to eliminate once and for all the threat of a Polish attack on East Prussia and Silesia, and to remove the desecration involved in the creation of the Polish Corridor and the inclusion of two million Germans within the Polish borders. Furthermore, the majority of the generals were confident of victory over a Poland which, they were sure, would stand alone, deserted by her allies as Czechoslovakia had been, against a Germany guided by the genius of Adolf Hitler, the victor of Munich. News that a pact was to be established with the Soviet Union was of considerable reassurance to the officers, especially to those nurtured in the Seeckt doctrine, for they believed that the removal of this potential enemy would guarantee also the neutrality of France and Britain.

Indeed, such was their confidence that neither OKW nor OKH drew up contingency plans in case of intervention from the east or the west. Despite Hitler's warlike speech of 23 May, the generals had at that time little fear of a European war. Von Manstein wrote later:

> 'We had watched Germany's precarious course along the razor's edge to date with close attention and were increasingly amazed at Hitler's incredible luck in attaining . . . all his overt and covert political aims. The man seemed to have an almost infallible instinct. Success had followed success. . . . All those things had been achieved without war. Why, we asked ourselves, should it be different this time? Look at Czechoslovakia. . . . we recalled Hitler's assertion that he would never be so rash as to unleash a war on two fronts. . . . That at least implied a man of reason. Raising that coarse voice of his, he had explicitly assured his military advisers that he was not idiot enough to bungle his way into a world war for the sake of Danzig or the Polish Corridor.'[44]

In such a climate of optimism and willing submission to the Führer's will, the military conspirators had no chance of organising a coup before war broke out. This they realised, and instead looked ahead to the time when the loyalty of the people and of the Army waned under the impact of the first disaster. Consequently, they restricted themselves to sending a number of emissaries abroad, whose purpose was to stiffen the resolve of the west through a complete exposé of Hitler's aims. They had to ensure that there would be no more Munichs; someone had to stand up to the dictator and now it could only be the democracies.

Hitler's last meeting with his senior officers before the outbreak of the European war took place on 22 August, the day von Ribbentrop flew to Moscow to sign the vital pact of non-aggression with the Soviet Union. The Führer's mood was uncompromising: 'Essentially, all depends on me, on my existence, because of my political talents.' War must come; there was no time to lose. 'Our economic situation is such that we cannot hold out more than a few years. . . . We have no other choice, we must act. . . . the political situation is favourable to us; in the Mediterranean, rivalry among Italy, France, and England; in the Orient, tension. . . . England is in great danger. France's position has also deteriorated. . . . Yugoslavia carries the germ of collapse. . . . Romania is weaker than before. . . . Turkey has been ruled by small minds. . . . All these fortunate circumstances will not prevail in two or three years.' It was highly probable that the west would not fight, but the risk had to be taken. Had this not been done before with spectacular results? Over Czechoslovakia he had carried his point when the generals had lost their nerve. The pact with the Soviet Union had rendered western intervention most unlikely. It seemed impossible that Britain and France would risk a long war alone. It was now necessary to 'test the military machine. The Army must experience actual battle before the big final showdown in the west.' The dictator ended with the words: 'Close your hearts to pity! Act brutally! Eighty million people must obtain what is their right. . . . The stronger man is right. . . . Be harsh and remorseless! Be steeled against all signs of compassion. . . . Whoever has pondered over this world order knows that its meaning lies in the success of the best by means of force. . . .'[45] The generals remained silent; only one, von Wietersheim, chief of staff of Army Group Command 2, summoned enough courage to ask questions of his Führer. Keitel, who was present, believed that Hitler realised 'he was confronted with an iron phalanx of men who inwardly refused to be swayed by any speech they though was just propaganda . . . it was a bitter disappointment to him'.[46] Von Manstetin, however, gained a more favourable impression of the whole affair and wrote: 'As a result of Hitler's address neither von Rundstedt nor I – and presumably none of the other generals either – concluded that war was now inevitable. . . there would be an eleventh hour settlement.'[47] The attack was scheduled to begin at 4.30 a.m. on 26 August.

The only setback Hitler received to his plans came not from the Army, but from abroad. On the 25 August, Great Britain, undeterred by the signing of the German–Soviet pact, gave her guarantee to Poland; France followed suit. Almost simultaneously came news from Italy that in the event of a European war she could not fulfil her part of the Pact of Steel without substantial help from Germany in the form of military supplies. Hitler, faltering, ordered a temporary postponement of the invasion while he attempted to ensure the neutrality of the west. 'The Führer is finished',[48] declared a delighted Oster, while Canaris announced: 'Peace has been saved for the next twenty years.'[49] But their high hopes came to nought. Hesitation turned to hate, and by the 28th, Hitler, anxious for revenge, had decided on armed conflict, even if it should be a two-front war. Late on the 30th he issued the order for the attack to begin at 4.45 a.m. on 1 September. Receiving this order early on the morning of the 31st, von Brauchitsch passed it to Halder who, through the efficient machinery of the Army General Staff, alerted the Army. That evening, under cover of darkness, a million and a half German troops began their final movement towards the Polish border.

PART TWO

The
Battle of Ideas

However praiseworthy it may be to uphold tradition in the field of soldierly ethics, it is to be resisted in the field of military command. For today it is not only the business of commanders to think up new techniques which will destroy the value of the old; the potentialities of warfare are themselves being continually changed by technical advance. Thus the modern army commander . . . must be able to turn the whole structure of his thinking inside out.

ERWIN ROMMEL
The Rommel Papers

8

The Myth

*Catchwords . . . are necessary for all those who are
unable to think for themselves. . . . The following
observations have no other object than to stimulate
some one . . . to think for himself and, whenever a
catchword is uttered, to confront him with the
question: Is this true?*

HANS VON SEECKT
Commander-in-Chief of The German Army,
1920–26

In September 1939 the Germans overran Poland. In April 1940 they seized almost the whole of Norway. The following May they broke through Belgium and France and reached the coast. In June they took Paris, defeated France, and turned their attention on Great Britain. The impression on contemporary minds made by these fast and devastating victories was immense; the contrast with the bitter and lengthy deadlock of the previous World War seemingly inexplicable. Writing a number of years after the event, Churchill managed to convey the atmosphere of those 'dark and evil days':

> 'Now at last the slowly gathered, long-pent-up fury of the storm broke upon us. Four or five millions of men met each other in the first shock of the most merciless of all the wars of which record has been kept. Within a week the front in France, behind which we had been accustomed to dwell through the hard years of the former war and the opening phase of this, was to be irretrievably broken. Within three weeks the long-famed French Army was to collapse in rout and ruin, and our only British Army to be hurled into the sea with all its equipment lost. Within six weeks we were to find ourselves alone, almost disarmed, with triumphant Germany and Italy at our throats, with the whole of Europe open to Hitler's power. . . .'[1]

How was this to be explained? How could the once-mighty and confident Allied Armies find themselves torn asunder in a matter of days, brushed contemptuously aside by a German Army, which, six years previously, had been only 100,000 men strong and denied all modern instruments of offence such as tanks and heavy artillery? At once the answer was believed to lie in a new form of warfare. A bewildered and fearful President of the Ministerial Council of France, Reynaud, explained on 21 May 1940, the day after the Germans had reached the Channel: 'The truth is that our classic conception of the conduct of war has come up against a new conception. At the basis of this . . . there is not only the massive use of heavy armoured divisions or cooperation between them and aeroplanes, but the creation of disorder in the enemy's rear by means of parachute raids. . . . We must think of the novel type of warfare which we are facing and take immediate decisions.'[2]

Military theorists, professionals and journalists on both sides of the Atlantic rushed immediately into print, to analyse, interpret, and catalogue the inexplicable; books, pamphlets, and articles appeared, one after another, each purporting to account for the reasons for these overwhelming victories by the Germany Army. Very quickly a coherent new theory of warfare was discerned and described in the fullest detail by the Allies. One of the best known of the contemporary writers was F. O. Miksche, an officer serving with the Free Czechoslovak Army, who wrote in 1941:

> 'Tactics have now been remade again. The new methods have been worked out and applied by Germans theorists. They are methods of "total war", first brought to the world's attention by Ludendorff's book of that name [published 1920]. . . . Using machines instead of masses of men, they attack the whole of the forces of the enemy throughout all the territory held by that enemy; or rather they threaten and disrupt those forces by penetrating deeply into the territory. And they have introduced this same method into the spheres of economics, politics, and diplomacy.'[3]

Two years later, in 1943, J. R. Lester, in his book *Tank Warfare*, wrote:

> 'What the Germans did accomplish, though, was to reduce these theories [of the military theorist and historian, Liddell Hart, and others] to definite plans, to develop them to their logical conclusions with ruthless efficiency, to set up the necessary organisations to put the plans into operation, to lay the necessary foundations of metal, to create a large body of highly trained men with the necessary spirit to attempt the tasks, and the skill to accomplish them.'[4]

From such expositions emerged three basic elements fundamental to the new German system: first, that it was revolutionary, a complete break with the past, especially with the First World War, relying on the most recent developments in mechanisation, armour, and air-power to achieve the speedy disruption and demoralisation of the enemy's command and communications, thus allowing his disorganised and bewildered troops to be easily captured or destroyed; second, that it was a coherent theory, consciously adopted by the German High Command as its strategic and tactical basis for the prosecution of the war; and, thirdly, that the Armed Forces of the Third Reich were organised and equipped to meet the requirements of this new, and demanding, form of warfare.

Since 1945, although some have questioned the degree to which the German Army was equipped to undertake this new strategy, the historians of the Second World War have but echoed the conclusions of writers such as Miksche, Wintringham, and a host of others. Sir Basil Liddell Hart, whose military writings spanned half a century, beginning in the 1920s, asserted in his *History of the Second World War* that '. . . the German High Command had, rather hesitatingly, recognised the new theory of high-speed warfare, and was willing to give it a trial',[5] and he described the battle of France as 'one of history's most striking examples of the decisive effect of a new idea, carried out by a dynamic executant'.[6] Major-General J. F. C. Fuller, also a renowned military theorist, wrote in his *Decisive Battles of the Western World*:

> 'The tactical policy of Germany was based on the offensive, and designed to overcome the linear defensive of her opponents by means of the attack by paralysation. Her army was fashioned into an armour-headed battering-ram which, under cover of fighter aircraft and dive-bombers – operating as flying field artillery – could break through its enemy's continuous front at selected points. The soul of German policy was mobility – a sharp, rapid, and short war on one front only.'[7]

And so a new form of warfare was born in the minds of men, one conceived out of bewilderment and the desire to rationalise the reasons for defeat; nurtured by those such as Liddell Hart and Fuller, who were flattered by the thought that the novel theories they had developed in the 1920s had been adopted and practised, albeit by the enemy; and wholeheartedly accepted by large numbers of historians only too glad to make use of a seemingly incontrovertible fact on which to base a whole series of assumptions about the war. To this child of the imagination, they gave the name *Blitzkrieg*.

Blitzkrieg (Lightning War) is a term inevitably linked with the German Army and the Second World War. From a convenient way of explaining the unknown, it evolved into a strict definition of a new form of warfare believed to be the basis for the devastating early victories of Hitler's Germany. The essence of *Blitzkrieg* was seen to lie not so much in the use of airborne units, which was, in any case, limited and of a purely tactical nature, nor in the activities of the dive-bomber, which were designed essentially to support the ground forces, but in the handling of the new armoured formations. As Liddell Hart wrote in a letter to Guderian: 'The secret of *Blitzkrieg* lay partly in the tactical combination of tanks and aircraft, partly in the unexpectedness of the stroke in direction and time, but *above all* in the *"follow through"* – the way that a breakthrough (the tactical penetration of the front) was exploited by a deep strategic penetration carried out by an armoured force racing ahead of the main army, and operating independently.'[8] This is a concept which, remaining intact and unquestioned for the past thirty-five years, has been raised to the status of a self-evident truth. But *Blitzkrieg* is a myth. It is a word devoid of any meaning, having substance not in fact but in fiction, serving only to mislead and to deceive. For Hitler and the German military establishment, the High Commands of the Army and the Wehrmacht, did not espouse a new, revolutionary idea of war; the German Armed Forces were not organised, equipped, or directed according to new, revolutionary principles; and the German form of war in the years 1939 to 1942 was the product not of one new, revolutionary strategy, but of two strategies – one well-defined and traditional, the other ill-expressed and novel – whose mutual conflict went far to hamper the practice of the mode of warfare popularly imagined to be *Blitzkrieg*.

The etymology of the word *Blitzkrieg* is interesting, providing good reason for regarding the idea behind it with some suspicion. As if to point to the false impression it conveys, *Blitzkrieg*, although a German word, was not a German expression. German military manuals both before and during the war may be scoured in vain for any mention of it, and it is seldom found in even the post-war memoirs of the generals who were supposed to have evolved and practised its methods. As an expressive description, 'lightning war' extends back at least as far as the fourteenth century, when the Sultan Bayazid was known as *Yilderim* (The Thunderbolt) because of his method of rapid attack. It was with that meaning in mind that the word *Blitzkrieg* was adopted in 1939 and 1940. *Time* magazine of 28 September 1939 appears to have been the first to use the expression, in an article which referred to events in Poland as 'no war of occupation, but a war of quick penetration and obliteration – *Blitzkrieg* – lightning war'.[9] As a piece of journalese the word was a great and immediate success, being highly evocative of the fast and furious campaigns then being waged by the Germans on the continent of Europe. Guderian later recorded: 'As a result of the successes of our rapid campaigns . . . our enemies coined the word *Blitzkrieg* . . .'[10] Its future was assured, and *Blitzkrieg* quickly evolved from a purely descriptive term into a whole new theory of strategy and tactics, a concept which, ever since, has pervaded all thought and writing on the Second World War. Indeed, so powerful was it that even the Germans came to use the word, Hitler believing: 'the expression *Blitzkrieg* is an Italian invention; we picked it up from the newspapers.'[11]

A further illusion, in part resulting from the idea of *Blitzkrieg*, also remains prevalent: it is that the German Army of 1939 was a well-trained force of overwhelming numbers possessing the best of modern weapons, fully prepared for a modern, mobile European war. At the time, military commentators were advancing the belief that 'The German Army is a new type of army . . . Compared with the German Army of today the armies of the western powers are terribly deficient both in numbers and equipment. Everything in the German Army today makes for mobility, striking force, and fire-power. In 1939–40 the military revolution in Germany will be complete, and by the doubling of its war material the German Army will be prepared to take the field at full strength.'[12] The same writer, Max Werner, had previously estimated German tank strength at between 6,000 and 7,000 machines, more than twice as many as they actually possessed. Such illusions before and during the war are easy to understand; they arose from the impression of overwhelming power and thorough preparedness shown by the Reich's Armed Forces through their outwardly impressive rearmament and decisive early victories, and were fostered by skilful propaganda, mass parades, and the general militarisation of society under National Socialism. Even after the war, when the reality of the Army's state in 1939 was revealed for all to see, these beliefs remained. For example, in 1956 a French writer, who had been taken prisoner in 1940, wrote of Germany as 'A nation straining at the leash, convoys of motorised troops tearing along autobahns, and an industry whose factories were working round the clock to create the most powerful war machine that Germany had ever possessed'.[13]

Nothing, however, could be further from the truth. The outbreak of a general war in 1939 took the German military leaders by surprise; the Army that marched triumphantly into Poland was one constituted not for war but for peace, and had still to be reorganised into a well-equipped, well-trained instrument of aggression. Four more years of tranquillity were required for the expansion of the period from 1933 to 1939 to be transformed from a purely numerical factor into a qualitative basis for military endeavour. Hitler's war abruptly interrupted this progression, and ensured that the Army was never to overcome the major defects with which it began the conflict. Consequently, the reasons for the German Army's initial victories lay not so much within itself, but in the weakness of its enemies. Perhaps never before in history had the countries of Europe been so ill-prepared for war.

'*Heerlos, Wehrlos, Ehrlos*' – disarmed, defenceless, dishonoured – was the constantly echoed, bitter catch-phrase of the years 1919 to 1935. By the terms of the Treaty of Versailles, signed in the palace of the same name on 28 June 1919, the Allied peacemakers had attempted to ensure that never again would Germany possess the capacity to wage aggressive war. The total military force allowed her was restricted to 100,000 long-term volunteers, of whom 4,000 were officers, organised in seven infantry and three cavalry divisions, the armament and disposition of which were minutely specified. Weapons of offence such as tanks, heavy artillery, and aeroplanes were prohibited, the army being allowed light arms and field-guns only. The General Staff and the Military Academy were both disbanded, military schools and armament factories drastically reduced in numbers, and all preparations for mobilisation, such as the maintenance of secret lists of trained military personnel, were forbidden. Strict adherence to these provisions was to be ensured by the rigorous inspection of the Inter-Allied Control Commission. But perhaps even more serious than the imposed numerical and material restrictions were the humiliations of defeat and the uncertainties of internal disruption that attended the birth of the new German Army of Peace – the *Reichsheer* (National Army). There were few soldiers who, in 1919, could have looked to the future with much confidence; and yet, by

1933, the Reichsheer, still only 100,000 strong and still without tanks and heavy artillery, was one of the most efficient military machines on the continent of Europe, and formed the nucleus, however insufficient, of the greatly expanded German Army which, within seven years, was to reach the verge of world domination.

Ironically, it was the severe restrictions imposed on the Reichsheer that contributed greatly to such an unexpected development. Thanks to the peacemakers' action, Germany's Army, freed of the dead-weight of unprofessional masses and of ageing, cumbersome equipment, was able to transform itself into a dedicated military élite, ambitious for future development and desirous of regaining lost honour and prestige. Plans for the expansion of the Reichsheer were accepted unquestioningly, and the small 100,000 strong force was regarded as *Nicht ein Soldnerheer, sondern ein Führerheer* (an army not of mercenaries but of leaders), the kernel of a greatly enlarged force within the shell of an unduly restricted one. The Reichsheer recruited only those with the highest physical attainments; it accepted and encouraged men of good education; it greatly improved the relationship between officers and other ranks, a relationship based on confidence and comradeship, which in no way prejudiced strict discipline, instead of on authority and a harsh penal code; it encouraged the closest possible cooperation between all branches within the Army, fostered by a spirit of teamwork and the development of an effective system of communications between all levels, and types, of command; it embarked on the study and development of new equipment, which included exercises with dummy tanks, the institution of such bodies as the Inspectorate of Transport Troops, the illegal establishment of fighter, reconnaissance and bomber squadrons as part of the Army's aerial capability, and general military cooperation with the Soviet Union, involving experiments with armour and heavy artillery; it represented the unification of the various German armies, the Prussian, Bavarian, Saxon, and Württembergian, which had previously been coordinated by treaty, into a single federal force; and it created the first centralised directing authority in German military history, the *Chef der Heeresleitung* – supported by the *Truppenant,* the executive organ concerned with operational and training matters – who was directly responsible to the Reichswehr Minister, a system which replaced the previous confusion of War Minister, Head of the Military Cabinet, Chief of the General Staff, and Inspector-Generals.

The man mainly responsible for these developments was General Hans von Seeckt, Chief of the Army Leadership from 27 March 1920 to 6 October 1926. His achievement, according to Sir Basil Liddell Hart, was 'in starting a train of ideas which revitalised the German Army, turned it into a new line of progress, and enabled it to add a qualitative superiority to the quantitative recovery that the victors' inertia permitted it to carry out. He gave the Reichswehr a gospel of mobility. . . .'[14] In short, von Seeckt's name has been indissolubly linked with the rising of the German Army, phoenix-like, from the ashes of impotence and defeat, and the establishment of that force on the principles of *Blitzkrieg*. As such, it was he 'who had the primary influence on the Second World War'.[15]

However, such a high estimate of his importance, which gives von Seeckt a place in German military annals ranking with that of von Moltke and von Schlieffen, mistakes not only the nature of his work but the product for which he was given responsibility. A guardsman and a brilliant staff officer – he had been the architect of significant victories over the French and the Russians in the First World War – von Seeckt was fifty-four when appointed to command the Army with the mission of neutralising 'the poison contained in the disarmament clauses of the Treaty'.[16] But however energetic he was in pursuing this objective, von Seeckt remained a conservative by inclination, and was determined to shape the Reichsheer according to the best traditions of the Imperial Army. On his assuming office, his first words to his soldiers were that they should 'salvage what is of value from the past and put it to work in the present for a brighter future'.[17]

The traditions to which von Seeckt and his Army were grateful heirs were those that spanned the centuries. From Frederick the Great, King of Prussia in the mid-eighteenth century, was inherited a sense of individual honour and pride in the regiment which not only inspired courage under fire but also made retreat unthinkable, unless it was militarily expedient. From Gerhard von Scharnhorst, the great military reformer of the Napoleonic era, came the idea of intensive training, together with the concept of discipline as the willing, intelligent, but unquestioning subordination of the individual to his superiors in the efficient exercise of the military art. From von Moltke, von Schlieffen, and the Imperial Army came the strategic doctrine of decisive manoeuvre that aimed at the total destruction of the enemy through the massive encirclement of his forces, and the acceptance of new developments in weapons and machines in the achievement of that aim. Such were to be the principles that inspired the regeneration of the German Army. But they provided no basis for any radical change in direction.

Preparations for German rearmament had begun well before Hitler's accession to power in 1933. Two five-year economic plans were adopted in 1928: the first, to be concluded by 1933, called for the provision of an Army of sixteen divisions for defence against Poland; the second envisaged equipping a force of twenty-one divisions (an Army of 300,000 men) by 1937–38, to be trebled on mobilisation, for defence against France. Owing to the shortage of raw materials, the first programme was never begun, and although the second was initiated on 7 April 1933, progress was unexpectedly slow. However, by 1932 military plans for rearmament had begun to bear fruit. At the end of the year the Reichswehr Minister had ordered that, as from 1 April 1933, the Reichsheer would be enlarged by 2,500 men in a cautious reaction to the Five-Power Declaration of 11 December, which stated that the disarmament clauses of the Versailles Treaty should be replaced by a convention in which Germany would possess equality of rights in an arrangement that would provide security for all nations. Such was the state of world opinion at that time that it only required the emergence in Germany of a political system pledged to rearmament to set the nation once again on the road to military strength.

Nonetheless, at the moment when hopes of rearmament were on the point of being realised, there was no common agreement as to the form this expansion should take. At the beginning of 1933, opinion on that point was far from uniform, von Seeckt by no means having enjoyed a monopoly of the argument. Some, a minority, wished merely to expand the Reichsheer as it stood; others, a high percentage, inclined towards von Seeckt's idea, and envisaged an extension of the Army to a small force of 200,000 effectives, fully equipped with the modern instruments of war, and a reduction in the terms of service from twelve years to six, together with a force of 20,000 officers and non-commissioned officers to train and command a large defensive militia. Such, too, had been the idea of von Seeckt's successors, Generals von Heye and von Hammerstein. And a few, led by Generals Gröner and von Schleicher, energetically supported the creation of a militia on the Swiss model, with long-service volunteers only for the armoured and technical forces. In the event, all three plans were rejected, and in their place was firmly established the traditional Continental concept of the mass army based on universal conscription. Von Seeckt had lost the argument; the ideas that had dominated the Reichsheer for the previous fourteen years were abandoned. Manpower, rather than quality, was the keynote for the future.

The reasons for the re-establishment of a mass Army along the lines of the old imperial force could be found in the new leadership that, in 1933, came to dominate Germany's military development. The new Defence Minister, von Blomberg, was an ardent admirer of Ludendorff, possessing nothing but admiration for his leadership during the First World War, and espoused, uncritically, his theories of mass armies and total warfare. He believed, as Ludendorff expressed it, that 'the fighting forces can never be ... too strong. It is a fact that victory "goes to the big battalions" ... numbers are only too often the decisive factor. It is a mistake to forget this. ... The totalitarian war demands the incorporation in the Army of every man fit to bear arms. ...'[18] But, more important, von Seeckt's idea found no favour with Adolf Hitler, whose political aims and preference called for large numbers of men under arms. In 1932 he made a speech which included the sentence: 'For whether Germany possesses an Army of 100,000 men or of 200,000 or 300,000 is in the last resort completely beside the point: the essential thing is whether Germany possesses eight million reservists whom she can transfer into her Army without any fear of falling into the same *Weltanschauliche* catastrophe as that of 1918. ...'[19] Germany's enemies, Hitler reasoned, possessed massive armies: France had 600,000 men under arms in peace and a potential war strength of 5,000,000, while Czechoslovakia and Poland could each mobilise some 1,000,000 men. Against such odds, his argument ran, what could 100,000 men, or even 250,000 as was proposed at the Geneva Disarmament Conference, hope to achieve? Equality of numerical strength, at the very least, was seen as the only answer. Furthermore, Hitler called for a mass conscript army so as to complete the education of German youth by giving them discipline and training in the soldierly ideals that were supposed to form the basis of National Socialism. Thus, Hitler's first contribution to the future downfall of the German Army was to decide on rapid and considerable expansion as the basis of the Reich's military policy.

9

The War Lord

*The value of a whole army — a mighty host of a
million men — is dependent on one man alone: such
is the influence of spirit.*

SUN TZU

The Art of War

The advent of Hitler and National Socialism was bound to have a great
impact on the German Army; the new movement provided it not only with
the means, but also with the reason, for its existence. 'Armies for the
preparation of peace do not exist', Hitler had declared in 1930, 'they exist for
triumphant exertion in war'; and war was to be the dynamic of his foreign
policy, the principles of which were established in the mid-1920s and
tragically put into practice in the late 1930s and early 1940s. It was a policy
derived from his concept of Social Darwinism, of biological determinism
summed up in the phrase: 'Might is right; the stronger nation masters and
thrives on the weaker'. The future, Hitler believed, belonged to the *Herrenvolk*
(the master race), 'the militant Nordic section which will rise again and
become the ruling element over these shopkeepers and pacifists, these
puritans and speculators and busybodies'.[2] Although no detailed plan of
conquest was ever propounded, the National Socialists nevertheless
possessed a general strategy which might be summed up in three concepts:
Grossdeutschland, Lebensraum, and *Weltmacht:* A 'greater Germany' with
sufficient 'living space' would inevitably acquire 'world power'.

In *Mein Kampf* Hitler wrote prophetically:

> 'The foreign policy of a People's State must first of all bear in mind
> the duty of securing the existence of the race which is incorporated in
> this state. And this must be done by establishing a healthy and
> natural proportion between the number and growth of the
> population on the one hand and the extent and resources of the
> territory they inhabit on the other. ... What I call a healthy
> proportion is that in which the support of a people is guaranteed by
> the resources of its own soil and subsoil. ... Our movement must
> seek to abolish the present proportion between our population and
> the area of our national territory, considering national territory as a

source of our maintenance and as the basis of political power. . . .
The confines of the Reich as they existed in 1914 were thoroughly
illogical, because they were not really complete, in the sense of
including all the members of the German nation. Nor were they
reasonable, in view of the geographical exigencies of military
defence. . . . We National Socialists must stick firmly to the aim that
we have set for our foreign policy: namely, that the German people
must be assured the territorial area which is necessary for it to exist
on this earth.'[3]

How was this to be achieved? Hitler never possessed, nor fostered, any
illusions as to this. In the second paragraph of *Mein Kampf* he wrote for all the
world to see: 'the tears of war will produce the daily bread for the generations
to come.'[4] Eight years later he was to state: 'It is impossible to build up an
Army and give it a sense of worth if the object of its existence is not the
preparation for battle.'[5] Thus the German Army of the Second World War
was one developed by its political master for the specific purpose of waging
war; it was intended primarily as an instrument of aggression.

'Hitler was a statesman. He was a dictator. He was Supreme Commander of
the Armed Forces and, from 1941, Commander-in-Chief of the Army as well.
He had unleashed the war, and it was up to him and no one else to conduct it.
He did in fact lead the war.'[6] So wrote General Jodl while a prisoner at
Nuremberg, shortly after being sentenced to death by hanging for complicity
in waging his Führer's battles. As he indicated, the 1939–45 conflict was in a
unique way Hitler's own; he began it and, until 1943 when the initiative
passed to the enemy, it was he who determined its course; he was the last of
the warlords, the prime, and often the only, political and military mover of
his country's destiny. Hitler, the former corporal of the trenches, was the
force around which Germany's war machine revolved, ultimately to such an
extent that it came to be a bitter, if apposite, jest among the officer corps that
not a single private could be moved from door to window without his
approval. Germany's Army became Hitler's Army, an instrument primarily
moulded and directed according to his principles and attitudes, with the
result that his failings and weaknesses as a military commander were
reflected in its development and in its deployment in the field.

There have been conflicting views as to Hitler's military ability. Was he,
as he himself once declared, 'the greatest strategic genius of all time',[7] or, as
Halder believed, a 'demoniac man [who] was no soldier-leader in the
German sense. And, above all, he was not a great general.'[8] Military matters
fascinated Hitler, and he was captivated by the power of modern armies. As
an Austro-German he had immense pride and respect for the traditions of
the nation's army; as a former infantry corporal, whose bravery on the
Western Front won him the Iron Cross First Class, a high distinction for one
of his rank, he possessed considerable sympathy for ordinary soldiers as well

as an understanding of their hopes, fears, and deprivations; and as a national leader whose future policy was geared to military success, he maintained considerable interest in the force upon which his fortunes depended so greatly. One of his physicians, Dr von Hasselbach, noted that 'The officers who had contact with him were continually astounded how precisely Hitler was informed about the calibre, mechanism, and range of a field piece. . . . When new weapons or vehicles were demonstrated, Hitler showed astonishing intuition concerning the advantages and flaws of their construction, and he often made helpful suggestions for improving them.'[9]

But Hitler's considerable technical knowledge, learnt somewhat parrot-fashion, was no guarantee of his ability in the wider field of military strategy. There, his inexperience, his self-education, and his amateurism were most noticeable and most fatal. His character was deficient of the application and the self-discipline necessary for acquiring anything more than a superficial military knowledge. Not that this worried the Führer; indeed, he maintained that it was a strength on his part, and, until the end, he liked to emphasise that his was a feeling, an intuition, for war, one that was immeasurably superior to the professional, but restrictive, attitude of his officers. The result was a uniquely individual appraoch to war-making. Percy Schramm, the Führer's official war-diarist from 1943 to 1945, summed it up:

'Will-power was to Hitler the dominating factor everywhere. . . . He thought that if he had ever learnt to think in the terms of a General Staff officer, at every single step he would have had to stop and calculate the impossibility of reaching the next. Consequently, he concluded, he would never even have tried to come to power, since on the basis of objective calculations he had no prospect of success in the first place. Once in power he remained a revolutionary no less in his way of acting than in his way of thinking. He regarded it as self-evident that his initial successes had created the prospect of further triumphs, insofar as they encouraged his followers and intimidated his adversaries. The Führer regarded it as proper in his military leadership, as he had in his political activity, to establish goals which were so far-reaching that the objective professionals would declare them impossible. . . . A good many of the military successes during the first part of the war had, after all, been achieved despite the predictions of the General Staff. . . . Perhaps the most decisive of all the problems of the supreme German leadership in the war was that Hitler, because of his initial successes, could say that he, and not the General Staff, which on the basis of its calculations had not established such far-reaching goals, was the true realist. He had foreseen actual developments more clearly, precisely because he had taken the incalculable into account. But then the situation changed again, and in the end the General Staff was correct in its calculations.'[10]

Acute though Schramm's observations usually were, he failed to perceive that, despite the repeated protestations to the contrary, Hitler felt his lack of training in, and familiarity with, military affairs, and that he was ever insecure in the presence of the ability and specialist knowledge displayed by his generals. As a man who was inordinately fearful of his own deficiencies, he was haunted by the ever-present spectre of failure, unable and unwilling to come to terms with the brutal facts of his own existence, with the reality behind the façade. He therefore sought refuge in the creation of visions of himself as a supreme warlord, the spiritual successor to Frederick the Great and Attila the Hun, the manipulator of powerful armies sweeping across the face of the Continent, the purveyor of mass destruction. He hid behind the self-conscious adoption of 'will-power', which, as von Manstein recognised, was the 'decisive factor in Hitler's military leadership'.[11] He was continually attempting to prove to himself, his associates, and the German people that he, above all others, possessed a nerve of iron, that his will-power alone would ensure final victory even in the face of desperate odds. His conversation was littered with such sentiments. In August 1944, for example, he embarked on a lengthy justification of his actions: 'For the past five years I have cut myself off from the other world. I have neither visited the theatre, heard a concert, nor seen a film. I live only for the single task of leading this struggle, because I know if there is not a man in there behind it who by his very nature has a will of iron, then the struggle cannot be won. . . .'[12] It was with such words that Hitler continually strove to bolster himself; perhaps after his early successes he even came to believe in them for a while. But during the war, when he was starkly confronted with failure in the form of devastating military reverses, the façade began to crack and the inadequacies reveal themselves. Fits of violent rage, which indicated total frustration and despair, even insanity, became common, and, his health steadily deteriorating, his nerves visibly faltering, Hitler withdrew further into a fantasy world of moving non-existent armies about out-of-date fields of battle, a lone, suspicious creature surrounded by nothing but desertion and defeat. What he had sought to conceal for so long, so successfully, now became a reality for all to see.

What of Hitler's understanding of the conduct of war? In 1933 he summed up his ideas as follows:

'I have the gift of reducing all problems to their simplest foundations. War has been erected into a secret science and surrounded with momentous solemnity. But war is the most natural, the most everyday matter. War is eternal, war is universal. . . . Let us go back to primitive life: the life of the savages. What is war but cunning, deception, delusion, attack, and surprise? . . . The place of artillery preparation for frontal attack by the infantry in trench warfare will in future be taken by revolutionary propaganda, to break down the enemy psychologically before the armies begin to function at all. . . . When the enemy is demoralised from within, when he stands on the brink of revolution, when social unrest threatens – that is the right moment. A single blow must destroy him. Aerial attacks, stupendous in their mass-effect, surprise, terror, sabotage, assassination from within, the murder of leading men, overwhelming attacks on all weak points in the enemy's defences, sudden attacks, all in the same second, without regard for reserves or losses: that is the war of the future. A gigantic, all-destroying blow. I do not consider consequences; I think only of this one thing. . . . I do not play at war. . . . I shall make war. I shall determine the correct moment for attack. . . . Gentlemen, let us not play at being heroes, but let us destroy the enemy. . . . I have made the doctrines of revolution the basis of my policy. . . . The next war will be unbelievably bloody and grim. But the most inhuman war, one which makes no distinction between military and civilian combatants, will be at the same time the kindest, because it will be the shortest. . . . My motto is: Destroy him by all and any means. I am the one who will wage the war.'[13]

From such superficial, egocentric bombast, historians have attempted to discern a coherent, revolutionary policy of war, the basis of *Blitzkrieg*. One of the earliest, Major-General Fuller, wrote of Hitler in 1943 as 'one of the most, if not actually the most, original soldiers in all history',[14] and in 1961 he claimed: 'As a tactical theorist, Hitler was as clairvoyant as he was astute as a politician. He had watched the last war closely and had absorbed its tactical lessons – a remarkable thing for a corporal to do. But what was more remarkable, he projected them into the future and built his military power on them. In 1939, the superiority of the German Army [lay] . . . in its tactics, which, if not devised by Hitler himself, were forced by him upon his reluctant General Staff.'[15] Such a thesis, however, is untenable. Hitler was no military theorist; he possessed no coherent, detailed strategy, and his utterances reveal no revolutionary insight into the future workings of war. For what was new or original about them? Speedy manoeuvre certainly wasn't; nor was the use of modern technology, nor the emphasis placed on psychological warfare, a weapon of war as old as mankind and which had been used systematically in the 1914–18 War. It is worth remembering that, despite his boastful predictions, Hitler never succeeded in using 'revolutionary propaganda, to break down the enemy psychologically before the armies began to function . . .',[16] and that during the invasion of the Soviet Union, when its use would have served German interests well, he conspicuously failed to exploit its potential.

Thus, instead of a revolutionary doctrine, Hitler possessed only the vaguest philosophy of war. His approach was very much that of the military illiterate and the political street-fighter: the former with his fascination for numbers, destructive power, and speed of operations; the latter with his belief in the importance of deception, brute force, and propaganda. In the place of a coherent theory of strategy and tactics, Hitler formed a pseudo-philosophy of war, the product of an amalgam of the ill-assorted, half-formed ideas so typical of National Socialism. He viewed warfare in Hobbesian terms of force and fraud, possessing the romantic vision of himself as a reincarnation of the *Furor Teutonicus*, a modern *Feldherr*, a warlord in the traditions of Attila the Hun. As such, Hitler's military thinking was limited to high-sounding, but empty, phrases. While he could state, quite unexceptionally, that 'The next war will be quite different from the last world war. Infantry attacks and mass formations are obsolete. Interlocked frontal struggles lasting for years on petrified fronts will not return, I guarantee that. They were a degenerate form of war . . .', he could also, in the next breath, indicate an alarming ignorance and misapprehension when pronouncing: '. . . strategy does not change, at least not through tactical interventions. . . . Has anything changed since the battle of Cannae? Did the invention of gunpowder in the Middle Ages change the laws of strategy? I am sceptical as to the value of technical inventions. No technical novelty has ever permanently revolutionised warfare. Each technical advance is followed by another which cancels out its effects.'[17] That such a man came to exert so decisive a control over the fortunes of the Army in the field of battle was a disaster. As a military commander, Hitler bore out to the full Gröner's warning: 'Unfortunately, strategy is a contagious disease which by preference affects heads which are not exactly filled with wisdom.'[18]

Many historians have seen in the combination of Hitler's foreign and economic policies further evidence of the existence of *Blitzkrieg*, this time as a grand strategic principle. They argue that Hitler realised that, in common with the Wilhelmine Empire, the Third Reich was incapable of winning a great war of the proportions of the 1914–18 conflict; that it simply did not possess the manpower, the raw materials, or the economic resources necessary for total war, and that, as a result, he based his grand strategy on a series of consecutive, separate, local wars which achieved their objectives in single, short, but decisive campaigns. Thus, the historians continue, Hitler's Army was consciously organised and equipped, and his economy geared, for limited lightning wars, each of no more than three months' duration. But, however attractive this thesis might be as an explanation of the unusual events of 1935–42, it possesses no basis in reality. It is true that Hitler realised that Germany could not undertake a conflict of the magnitude of the First World War, and that wars between large coalitions were to be avoided if possible. But in this he was far from being alone among the statesmen of Europe. Furthermore, no special significance should be attached to his desire to gain territorial objectives through conflicts of the shortest possible duration, for few national leaders have wished, or planned, otherwise. Indeed, it was an accepted and well established German policy to base preparations for war on such a precept, the famous Schlieffen Plan for the attack against France and Russia in 1914 being the prime example, founded as it was on a lightning victory being achieved in the west before turning east.

Such awareness and hope, alone, provides no proof of any detailed policy of *Blitzkrieg*, while even the most cursory glance at the German economy will reveal the total absence of any such systematic planning. For the German preparations for war were nothing but a chaos of competing interests and makeshift administrative methods, one of the distinguishing features of National Socialism. The Third Reich's economic resources, far from being organised according to a national plan, let alone to a well thought out strategy for war, were 'up for grabs', to use a colloquial expression which so well describes the highly competitive struggle between industrial and commercial interests, the various departments of state, the party and its organisations, especially the Labour Front, and the Armed Forces, the individual services of which were as disregarding of the others' interests as were the civilian agencies. Such a chronic condition was rendered worse by the personal nature of Hitler's dictatorship, which took little notice of the written word (the Führer was bored by paper work), but which was fairly receptive to those who had the ear of the Führer. Therefore, the Party functionaries such as Göring, Goebbels, Himmler, von Ribbentrop, and Ley had a considerable advantage over the Army and Navy chiefs in gaining support for their own schemes. This economic chaos was further complicated by the fact that the National Socialist leaders, ever fearful for their popularity, demanded, simultaneously with the large sums being spent on rearmament, the maximum prosperity for the civilian economy. Unemployment was to be eradicated, output of consumer goods greatly increased, services such as railways and roads improved, and construction of public buildings considerably expanded. Guns *and* butter, to paraphrase Göring's famous remark, was their aim. But this the economy proved incapable of providing. The result was that, while the German economy was in part geared *to* war, it was not geared *for* war. It was not until March 1940 that the Ministry of Armaments and Munitions was created, and it was 1942 before that body began to acquire the wide-ranging and overriding powers necessary for a coordinated policy of war production. The miracles of output that were then achieved are adequate proof, if proof were needed, of the gross inadequacy of the Third Reich's economic planning for war.

Thus, while Hitler and National Socialism gave the German Army the most potent reason for its existence – war – it failed miserably to provide it, at the same time, with the means necessary for its successful execution. Not only did the dictator fail to understand the strategic realities behind the Army's operation in the field, but he proved utterly incapable of ensuring that it possessed, in adequate quantities, even the most fundamental material resources essential for its tasks. Furthermore, Hitler's personal character was to ensure that his close union with the Army was not likely to be a happy one. The ancient Chinese believed that a commander in war stood for the virtues of wisdom, sincerity, benevolence, courage, and strictness; Hitler possessed none of these. His personal failings, his ignorance, and his neglect were largely the cause of the Army's struggle being hard and, ultimately, fruitless.

10

Strategic Tradition

Mobility is the keynote of war.

NAPOLEON

On 16 March 1935, Hitler announced to the world that Germany was rearming. In the fulfilment of Article 22 of the National Socialist twenty-five-point programme, which demanded the 'abolition of a mercenary army and the formation of a national army', he declared that 'service in the Wehrmacht is based on compulsory military service'.[1] This was the conclusion of the long campaign against the Versailles restrictions, and the culmination of a surreptitious expansion undertaken since 1933. Over the past two years rearmament had been proceeding apace: during 1933 the size of the Army had been increased by some ten to 20,000 men; in December of that same year the decision was taken to treble the numbers to 300,000; and, on 1 October 1934, a new organisation for the future expansion was introduced, allowing for the establishment of twenty-one infantry and three cavalry divisions, and the enlargement of Wehrkreis headquarters to army corps size. On that date, 70,000 additional men entered the Army, bringing the total of men under arms to 240,000. And then, in March 1935, seven days after the existence of the German Air Force was declared, the most decisive step was taken, one that marked a considerable extension in the rearmament policy as it had been understood by the Army until that time. Twelve months' service in the Armed Forces became compulsory for the youth of Germany, and the Army was increased to the size of thirty-six divisions. The cry that had been on the lips of nationalists for sixteen years – *'Wir wollen wieder Waffen!'* (We will have arms again) – was heard no more.

Hitler's decision, taken without any proper consultation with his military advisers, meant that the Third Reich would possess an active force of some 450,000 men, a more than four-fold increase on the number allowed by the Versailles Treaty, and half as much again as the figure regarded by the Army as tolerable for training purposes at that time. The first knowledge most of the generals had of this decision came from their radios on the morning of 16 March 1935. All were surprised. Von Manstein remembered that 'The General Staff, had it been asked, would have proposed twenty-one divisions. . . . The figure of thirty-six . . . was due to a spontaneous decision by Hitler.'[2] However, there was no sign of their misgivings the next day when, at celebrations to mark the Heroes Memorial Day, the military fervently welcomed the rebirth of their tradition, the re-establishment of the mass army. At Hitler's side in the State Opera House sat Field-Marshal von Mackensen, the aged representative of the old Army, attired in his uniform of the Death's Head Hussars, and behind them, under a massive silver and black Iron Cross, stood representatives of the new Army clad in their field grey and holding upright the war flags of the nation. It was a memorable occasion, symbolising the unity of the old and the new, manifested in the emergence of the conscript mass Army of National Socialist Germany. And on 1 June, as if to signify the complete break with the unlamented, immediate past, the Reichswehr was renamed *Die Wehrmacht* and the Reichsheer became simply *Das Heer* – the Army.

But the expansion to thirty-six active divisions announced in March 1935 was not the limit of the German peacetime army. By mid-1939, it contained no fewer than fifty-two active and fifty-one reserve divisions, which amounted to 730,000 men under arms, with another 1,100,000 in reserve. (The incorporation of Austria into the Reich in 1938 ultimately gave six active divisions to the German Army.) The 1939 peacetime figures represent a staggering 500 per cent increase in active formations in only six years, and a thousand per cent increase in total mobilised strength. In seven years, a force eighteen times the size of the original body had been trained. After mobilisation for war in September 1939, the German Army possessed 3,706,104 men under arms.

In terms of numbers, German rearmament in the six years until September 1939 had been a sizeable achievement. Indeed, it was little short of a military miracle that such a grossly expanded force could have achieved the degree of efficiency required to dominate the continent of Europe in two years of war. But numbers alone do not compose an Army. Without training, equipment, organisation, and command, the men are nothing but an ill-assorted group instead of a well-coordinated force of soldiers, finely trained to the efficient practice of warfare. At the basis of an army lies its *Kriegsführung* (war direction), the strategic doctrine that may be defined as the art of distributing and applying military means to fulfil the ends of policy. An army's strategy is the system of large-scale measures whereby its forces in the field are manoeuvred so as to bring the war to a conclusion, and it is this that gives an army its particular soul, its distinctive, unique character without which it would be just an incoherent, inanimate mass. Thus, a twentieth century force which bases its training, equipment, organisation, and command on a defensive strategy of interlocking trench and fortification systems will be radically different in composition from one which relies on an aggressive doctrine of decisive manoeuvre. On the quality of its strategic direction, then, is based the fortune of the army and, consequently, of the entire nation. An army's *Kriegsführung* is its most treasured possession.

Hitler's Army, although unmistakably a creature of the twentieth century, had the roots of its strategic direction firmly embedded in its imperial past. It was dominated by a well-established tradition extending back to the 1850s, a tradition which was to prove a greater source of strength to the commanders and troops in the field than were the numbers and quality of their equipment or the questionable tenets of their political creed. As has been seen, the link that bound the Army to its history was both immutable and indissoluble, strong enough to overcome the humiliation of defeat and the ravages of the peace treaties in 1918 and 1919. From two men in particular, Helmuth von Moltke and Alfred von Schlieffen, both renowned Chiefs of the General Staff, the German Army owed the principles that determined the nature of its wars – with only a short break – from the years 1861 to 1942, principles that placed emphasis on fast, decisive manoeuvre aimed at the encirclement and the destruction of the mass of the enemy.

Few men can have been as receptive to the opportunities presented by modern developments as von Moltke, Chief of the Prussian General Staff from 1857 to 1871. It was he who established the German military practice of exploiting the material resources and technological innovations of the age. In the mid-nineteenth century it was this readiness to use the new, and explore the unknown, that made possible not only the establishment of the Prussian Army as Europe's foremost military instrument, but also the creation by the northern state of Prussia of a united Imperial Germany. The application of the power of the industrial revolution enabled the Prussians, stimulated as they were by the desire for expansion, to spearhead the transformation of warfare from the napoleonic to the modern, leaving to subsequent generations of German soldiers the task, not of creating any new strategy, but of improving and exploiting the form already elaborated and practised to such effect. For Germany, and for the rest of the world, the revolution in war came not with the emergence of the tank or the aeroplane in the 1900s, but with the appearance of the railway, the telegraph, and the rifled weapon in the previous century. These inventions, coupled with improved standards of health, the mass production of goods, and the energy of capitalist organisation, permitted the rapid mobilisation and movement, the systematic supply, and the centralised command of considerably increased numbers of troops armed with weapons of greater accuracy and range than ever before. At first, even with the lessons of the first and terrible test of the new technology during the American Civil War in the early 1860s before them, European commanders had little idea of the impact that these developments would have on tactics and strategy. An exception, however, was von Moltke, who, with his officers, evolved new principles to suit these changed conditions – principles which, having evolved with time, were applied by his successors in the German High Command during the Second World War.

Central to this German idea of war was the concept of rapid, decisive manoeuvre. Von Moltke and his contemporaries saw that new armaments, in particular the breech-loading rifle, had made defensive fire-power the strongest single factor on the battlefield. In 1869 he wrote: 'It is absolutely beyond all doubt that the man who shoots without stirring has all the advantage of him who fires while advancing, . . . and that, if to the most spirited dash one opposes a quiet steadfastness, it is fire-effect, nowadays so powerful, which will determine the issue.'[3] As a consequence, any aggressor would have to make both time and space his servants in order to possess any chance of victory; the enemy might have more men and better guns, but speed and movement would master them. Von Moltke argued that 'Little success can be expected from a mere frontal attack, but very likely a great deal of loss. We must therefore turn towards the flanks of the enemy's position.'[4] Furthermore, the significant advances in communication and transport allowed a mobilisation and a concentration of large forces much faster than anything ever experienced before, thereby laying the enemy open to be caught off-balance before his preparations were complete. This, von Moltke saw as the means by which the dreaded result of the coalition system then gripping Europe, a war on two fronts, could be avoided. It was now possible, he argued, to deploy the main body of the army on one front, there to arrive at a speedy victory, before turning to effect a decision on the other front by an equally deft stroke. The quick concentration of force at the decisive point was indispensable, the grand sweeping movements of encirclement basic, and the total destruction of the enemy paramount.

However, von Moltke was careful not to transform his ideas about warfare into a rigid doctrine. For him the art of war lay in a combination of calculation and daring, each new conflict bringing with it new circumstances that invalidated any attempt to impose on it strict, preordained strategic principles. In his words: 'Strategy is a system of ad hoc expedients; it is more than knowledge, it is the application of knowledge to practical life, the development of an original idea in accordance with continually changing circumstances. It is the art of action, under the pressure of the most difficult conditions.'[5] It was left to von Schlieffen, the Chief of the General Staff from 1891 to 1905, to develop von Moltke's principles into well-established doctrines. Von Schlieffen's rejection of the strategy of attrition was total. For him, the only method of war was decisive manoeuvre, the extension of von Moltke's precepts to their limit. He coined the expression *Vernichtungsgedanke* (the idea of annihilation), which conveyed in a single striking term what he believed to be the end of all military endeavour – the total destruction of the enemy's forces, not by means of relatively slow, costly frontal attacks, but of swift, decisive blows from the flanks and the rear. Victory was seen to lie in strategic surprise, in the concentration of force at the decisive point, and in fast, far-reaching concentric encircling movements, all of which aimed at creating the decisive *Kesselschlachten* (cauldron battles) to surround, kill, and capture the opposing army in as short a time as possible. In his service regulations, von Schlieffen wrote: 'How is the enemy's wing to be attacked? Not with one or two corps, but with one or more armies, and the march of these armies should be directed, not against the flank, but against the enemy's line of retreat. . . . This leads immediately . . . to disorder and confusion which gives an opportunity for a battle with inverted front, a battle of annihilation, a battle with an obstacle in the rear of the enemy.'[6] Such, von Schlieffen agreed, were the lessons to be derived from history, especially from the great Carthaginian victory at Cannae in 216 B.C., a battle won by the speedy double envelopment of the numerically superior Romans, and from the Prussian success at Leuthen in 1757, when Frederick the Great's army decisively defeated an Austrian force twice its size, in what Napoleon was to call 'a masterpiece of movements, manoeuvres and resolution'. Likewise, the Germans of the nineteenth and twentieth centuries were to find their victories on the flanks and rear of their enemies. Double envelopment became their theme, *Vernichtungsgedanke* their watchword.

When compared with what had gone before, the new form of warfare as practised by the Germans was swift and efficient in the extreme. Indeed, the epithet *Blitzkrieg* might well be applied to their wars from 1866 to 1914 with as much justification as to their 1939–41 campaigns. The 1866 war against the Austro-Hungarian Empire, then generally believed to possess one of the best Continental armies, with France poised in the background, lasted just seven weeks, while the outcome of the campaign against the French in 1870–71 was decided in little more than six, although the fighting continued for another three months owing to the fierce resistance of Paris. The battle of Sadowa in 1866 had been conceived by von Moltke as one of encirclement, but there his generals failed him; the battle of Sedan four years later showed that the Prussian military establishment had learnt its lesson, and Napoleon III was forced to surrender with 104,000 men, till then the largest field force captured in modern times. In 1914 the Germans, confronted with a war on two fronts, put into practice a modified version of von Schlieffen's brilliant plan of 1905, comprised, first, of a wide manoeuvre aimed at turning the French rear which would result in the total defeat of France in a couple of months, and, then, of a switch of the armies to the east, there to face the slow but massive 'Russian Bear' with sufficient forces to bring about its death. The Germans came close to achieving this; in fewer than six weeks they advanced to within thirty miles of Paris and expected to end the campaign within a further week. But faulty decisions by their commanders both before and during the invasion, and the physical and material exhaustion that such a rapid advance occasioned, enabled the Allied armies to halt the German onslaught on the Marne.

It is at this point in the history of the German Army, in mid-September 1914, that mobility of operations temporarily gave way to a static form of war – a war of attrition in which victory would belong to the side possessing numerical and material superiority. The breakdown of the invasion plan, and the apparent failure of the all-pervasive strategy of manoeuvre, stunned the General Staff, and led to the fatal resolve to abandon, at least temporarily, the offensive, and stand on the defensive. Thus, the German Army surrendered their advantage of mobility and gave the Allies time to recover and reinforce. The resumption of the offensive came too late, and the subsequent race to the Channel in an attempt to outflank the opposition ended in stalemate. Once the deadly trio of trench, wire, and machine-gun was established in one unbroken line from the Channel coast to the Swiss border, all attempts to re-establish the strategy of swift, décisive manoeuvre failed. Their possession of time and space gone, the Germans learnt the power of the defensive that von Moltke and von Schlieffen had feared. Four weary years of deadlock and ultimate defeat were the result, a painful time made more bitter by the constant reminder of the open warfare that continued in the east until peace was made with Russia in 1917. Ironically, the superiority of German mobile strategy was never more evident than in the two whirlwind campaigns in the autumns of 1915 and 1916, by which Serbia and then Romania were humiliated, their armies swept away, and all danger from them eliminated. Thus, despite the unpleasant experience on the Western Front, *Vernichtungsgedanke* remained a principle of German strategy until the end of the war.

In the crisis of uncertainty and doubt that understandably pervaded German military thinking immediately after the bitter and humiliating defeat in 1918, the traditional strategy of decisive manoeuvre came in for some questioning. Was it still possible? If so, was it even desirable? Some feared that the 1914–18 War had shown that its days were numbered, that fire and fortification rather than movement now irrevocably dominated the battlefield. Others wanted to copy the French doctrine of the offensive, which, although slow, was safe. It presented no vulnerable flanks to the enemy and, supported by massed tanks and artillery, possessed considerable fire-power which was valuable in defence as well as in attack. But the majority remained firm – even buttressed – in their allegiance to the strategy that the Germans had rightly come to regard as their own special reserve. They believed that the experience of the war had shown the need for greater mobility, not less, and that the failure of the German Army was one of command and instrumentation rather than of doctrine. Foremost among them was von Seeckt. In a much quoted phrase he summed up his strategic principles: 'In brief, the whole future of warfare appears to me to lie in the employment of mobile armies, relatively small but of high quality, and rendered distinctly more effective by the addition of aircraft, and in the simultaneous mobilisation of the whole force, either to feed the attack or for home defence.'[7] The army of the future, he claimed 'must satisfy three main demands: first, high mobility, to be attained by the employment of numerous and highly efficient cavalry, the fullest possible use of motor transport, and the marching capacity of the infantry; second, the most effective armament; and third, continuous replacement of men and material'.

At the centre of von Seeckt's idea was the abandonment of mass armies and the adoption, instead, of small but highly mobile and well-trained striking forces to carry out the strategy of decisive manoeuvre. He argued that the past had shown that 'Mass becomes immobile: it cannot manoeuvre and therefore cannot win victories, it can only crush by sheer weight . . . A conscript mass, whose training has been brief and superficial, is "cannon fodder" in the worst sense of the word, if pitted against a small number of practised technicians on the other side.' In its place, von Seeckt wished to see a professional army possessing a higher mobility, a stronger and more flexible logistical system, and a greater degree of independence from civilian reserves, one which was capable of mobilising rapidly, taking the initiative, and moving decisively to annihilate the enemy before his preparations were complete. At the same time there would be a large-scale militia which, 'though unsuited to take part in a war of movement and seeking a decision in formal battle, is well able to fulfil the duty of home defence, and at the same time to provide from its best elements a continuous reinforcement of the regular, combatant army in the field'.[8]

Enlightened though von Seeckt's ideas were, they were by no means revolutionary. Reliance on a military mass had never been a central part of the German military tradition, but emphasis on manoeuvre and the implementation of new technology had. Von Seeckt went no further than this. His concept of war differed not at all from that of von Moltke and, especially, of von Schlieffen. In the 1920s he wrote:

> 'Graf Schlieffen is no concept for us; he typifies in head and heart the continuous life of the German General Staff, the German soldier, the German nation. We will not allow him to become a more petrified concept . . . but we will seek in him and learn from him, in new and clear form, the old eternal rules of war. Let us condense them into three sentences: The destruction of the enemy is the goal of war. . . . Every operation must be dominated by one simple clear idea. Everybody and everything must be subordinated to this idea. Decisive force must be thrown in at the decisive point; success is to be purchased only with sacrifice. Let us take to heart these doctrines of Schlieffen, the man, and then the concept "Schlieffen" will be synonymous with Victory.'[9]

Imbued with such beliefs, von Seeckt possessed no vision of any revolutionary strategy and, while he appreciated the importance of ground-support aircraft, he did not envisage the future in terms of armoured warfare. Indeed, the tank figured little in his writings, and he even wrote that 'the days of the cavalry, if trained, equipped and led on modern lines, are not numbered. . . . its lances may still flaunt their pennants with confidence in the wind of the future.'[10] Von Seeckt, in drawing his strength from the past, had failed to realise the potential of the future.

In the 1920s and 1930s, the strategic basis of the German Army for the forthcoming decade was decided. The successors to von Moltke and von

Schlieffen were the victors; the idea of *Vernichtungsgedanke* predominated, and Hitler's force was imbued with the belief in the power of the strategic initiative, manoeuvre, encirclement, and annihilation. As von Manstein, one of Germany's foremost field-marshals, wrote to Liddell Hart:

> 'Not only the German strategical but also the tactical thinking was influenced by the Schlieffen theory that a decisive success would be only reached in outflanking the enemy in connection with a frontal attack which alone would seldom lead to such a success. . . . The Schlieffen theories were also much studied in the German Army between the wars and had great influence on the strategical and tactical thinking. The idea to outflank and to encircle the enemy governed the German strategy and tactics.'[11]

The Army of the Third Reich retained its imperial heritage. The official statement of military strategic doctrine was set out in *Die Truppenführung* (the Troop Command) produced between 1931 and 1933 by a committee of officers under the chairmanship of Beck, and issued for the first time in the autumn of the latter year. *Die Truppenführung* was well-written and cogently argued, and was far from being hide-bound in its principles. On its first page was declared unequivocally: 'Even war undergoes a constant evolution. New arms give ever new forms to combat. To foresee this technical evolution before it occurs, to judge well the influence of these new arms on battle, to employ them before others, is an essential condition for success.'[12] On the question of tactics *Die Truppenführung* was a brilliant exposition of modern principles, and drew sound lessons from Germany's terrible experience in the 1914–18 War. Throughout, it emphasised the fundamental tactical role of combat teams of battalion strength composed of all arms employing every known method of the infiltration technique. Initiative, decisive manoeuvre, and envelopment were the keynotes of the German tactical doctrine, and its success in the war years was to prove it immeasurably superior to the methods of its enemies. Strategically, too, *Die Truppenführung* was far from reactionary, not only advocating the use of tanks and motorised transport to achieve the decisive destruction of the enemy, but doing so in a manner which contrasted with prevalent foreign doctrine. Instead of restricting the role of the armour merely to supporting the infantry, it emphasised that 'if tanks are too closely tied to the infantry, they lose the advantage of their speed and are liable to be knocked out by the defence'.[13]

Nevertheless, such ideas, although adapted to modern developments, were not revolutionary. The official strategic doctrine of the German Army as expressed in *Die Truppenführung* contained nothing that departed from the train of thought initiated by the first Chief of the Army General Staff some seventy years earlier. Infantry divisions, with their marching troops, horse-drawn guns, and waggons, would remain the deciding factor of the strategy of decisive encirclement, and the motorised infantry and armour would be subordinated to their needs. The new formations would serve as the 'cutting edge' of the infantry's flanking thrusts, using their superior speed, flexibility, and striking-power to penetrate the enemy's front line, destroy his artillery positions, rout his nearby reserves, and, finally, close the pincers around the opposing forces. But the emphasis would still lie on the infantry as the 'mass of decision', the means by which the ring round the enemy would be drawn tight and consolidated, and his resistance overcome. This is a theme continually expressed in the Army training manuals. The German Army *Leadership and Battles of the Infantry*, published in January 1940, proclaimed that 'The infantry is the main arm. All other arms are subsidiary to it',[14] and, in 1942, an OKW treatise on strategy in the war up to that date (the years commonly associated with the success of the panzer divisions) contained a chapter entitled 'Infantry, the Queen', in which it was claimed that the infantry still dominated the battlefield. It ended with the following paragraph:

> 'Each new weapon, so say the wiseacres, is the death of the infantry. The infantryman silently pulls on his cigarette and smiles. He knows that, tomorrow, this new weapon will belong to him. There is only one new factor in the techniques of war which remains above all other inventions. This new factor is the infantry, the eternally young child of war, the man on foot, even as Socrates himself was, the only and the eternal, who sees the whites of the enemy's eyes.'[15]

As before, and still part of their strong tradition, the Germans were eager to make full use of the development of modern weapons in order to exploit the potential of their *Vernichtungsgedanke*. Motorisation was seen as the only effective counter to increased fire-power. As one German manual put it: 'The task of military motorisation is to strive for a maximum tactical and operational mobility and speed, so that the army may be able, in the shortest possible time, to develop a maximum fighting strength at the fulcrum of the battle, in order that it may thus prove superior at the decisive point [*Schwerpunkt*], even if inferior as a whole.'[16] As far as it went, this was all to the good, for the subsequent German victories were largely the result of the happy combination of traditional strategy and modern armament. But it did not go far enough. The High Command and the senior generals failed to recognise what von Moltke had understood in the 1860s: that contemporary inventions may revolutionise the form of warfare, that they may offer possibilities, not only for the strengthening of traditional strategy, but also for its complete transformation – as with the railway, the telegraph, and the rifled weapon in the mid-nineteenth century, so with the lorry, the tank, and the aeroplane in the early twentieth century. Out of these was to emerge a new idea of war so revolutionary in its implications that few could comprehend it, and even fewer dared to use it. There was all the difference in the world between a traditional strategy using modern weapons to further its precepts, and a novel strategy based on the potential offered by those weapons to revolutionise war. This new concept may be called the 'armoured idea'.

11

Strategic Revolution

*Attacking does not merely consist in assaulting
walled cities or striking at an army in battle array;
it must include the act of assaulting the enemy's
mental equilibrium.*

SUN TZU
The Art of War

Vernichtungsgedanke and the armoured idea had much in common, a fact that
has obscured their differences and aided their obfuscation under the all-
embracing myth of *Blitzkrieg*. Both rejected any policy of attrition, both
relied on rapid, decisive movement, and both laid emphasis on the concentration of force at the crucial point. But here the similarity ended. For the
armoured idea arose not from the historic tradition of the German Army but
from the unique experience of the terrible years of deadlock on the Western
Front, and from the recognition of the revolutionary possibilities presented
by the combustion engine, the tracked weapon-platform, and the aeroplane.

The trench warfare of the years 1914–18 was both alien and distasteful to
the Germans: it was alien because a static strategy ran directly counter to
their tradition of manoeuvre, and it was distasteful because they were
painfully aware that the high cost of a struggle of attrition against an enemy
with greater resources in men and material would surely lead to ultimate
defeat. Therefore, from the beginning, every attempt was made to overcome
the stalemate; massed infantry assaults, heavy bombardments, gas and
mines were tried, but all failed; it was only with the development of a new
system of organisation and tactics that, by 1918, the Germans finally found
the method that would permit large scale breakthroughs on the Western
Front. It became known as 'infiltration'. Of it, a French staff officer wrote:
'This terrible word, which expressed the latest moves of the enemy and his
method of fighting, was feared on account of the striking light it would throw
on our present inferiority in the country and in the Army. Not only has the
word a suggestion of cunning, it expresses a treacherous action impossible to
avert, of a kind to cause alarm.'[1]

The essence of infiltration lay in the surprise, speed, and flexibility of
heavily armed groups of 'storm-troops', at any level of command up to
battalions, who, in addition to the light machine-guns, flamethrowers, and
light mortars of the infantry, were closely supported by light artillery. No

attempt was made to achieve a wide breakthrough at once, but instead, immediately after an intense, relatively short artillery bombardment, the storm-troops were sent forward to make narrow but deep penetrations in the enemy's lines, avoiding any contact with opposing strong-points. More troops were pushed, or infiltrated, through these gaps, and the remaining isolated centres of resistance, such as machine-gun nests, were then attacked from the flank and rear. Meanwhile, the original storm-troops continued to advance into the enemy's rear to pierce his vital nerve-centres – his head-quarters, communications, and supply lines. General confusion and paralysis resulted, and this, coupled with the effect on morale of the uncertainty and fear induced by the rapid and deep attack, led inevitably to the collapse of the opposition. The narrow penetration had been turned into a wide breach through which the rest of the army could advance to begin, once again, the traditional German mobile strategy. It was this method that enabled Ludendorff to achieve such success in his March–April 1918 offensives, success which, had its momentum been kept up, might well have caused the Allies to suffer total disaster.

Just as the tactics of infiltration were novel in action, so the military technical developments of the early twentieth century were revolutionary in potential. Mechanisation and air-power together permitted the addition of a new dimension to warfare, for those far-seeing enough to use it. Until the very end of the First World War, the German Army's mobile strategy had been shackled by the limited speed and endurance of its infantry, and, more fundamentally, by the restricted capacity and length of its logistical system. An advancing army could go no faster than its most important, but, at the same time, its slowest troops – the infantry. Normally, a corps could cover fifteen miles a day for three days, followed by one day of rest, but for the strategy of decisive manoeuvre this could prove woefully inadequate. Von Schlieffen's plan for the invasion of France had required of the crucial right-flanking armies a ruinous rate of continuous marching at not less than fifteen miles a day for three weeks; even more disastrous than this was the inflexible system providing for the constant supply of food, ammunition, and equipment that significantly limited the huge armies to a relatively short striking range. The size of the problem may be understood by a brief look at the logistics of the German First Army on the all-important German right wing in France in 1914. Consisting of 260,000 men, 784 artillery pieces, and 324 machine-guns, it required in fodder for its 84,000 horses, 1,848,000 pounds a day. The result of such a burden was that a corps could not operate with full efficiency over twenty-five miles from the nearest railroad, and that the horse and waggon transport system failed completely at a distance of more than fifty miles. Consequently, because of the inadequacy of the horse as a means of mass, fast transport, the Germans were forced either to restrict their range of action to the route and capacity of their enemy's railway system, which they had to repair if necessary, or to build new railroads fast enough to keep them within close operating range of the advancing armies.

Von Moltke was fully aware of this restriction, recognising that, had the nature and the dispositions of the enemy in the 1866 and 1870 campaigns been different, these limits might well have spelt ruin for the doctrine of decisive manoeuvre. This is precisely what might have happened during the great 1914 advance. Even had the German generals not made their mistakes of command, and had they found the retreating enemy's flank and rear, it is highly possible that the von Schlieffen plan, whether in its original or modified form, would have failed simply because the masses of men and horses that composed the invading armies had outdistanced their supplies and had marched themselves to exhaustion. Certainly such restrictions continually prevented the Germans from achieving the complete annihilation of the Russian armies in the east, where the enormous distances, the poor roads, and the inadequate railway system made difficult any deep penetrations or large encirclements of the enemy. In the spring offensive of 1918, too, the same limits of endurance and supply robbed the Germans of ultimate success. No mobile operation could be continued for long in the face of such harsh realities.

The advent of the lorry, the tracked-vehicle, and the aeroplane altered all this. The army now possessed the means to overcome the severe restrictions imposed on strategy by the speed and endurance of men and animals. No longer would the advancing forces be limited to a distance of between twenty-five and fifty miles from a railhead; no longer would speed and distance be dictated by marching feet or horse-drawn waggon. The motor engine and the propeller shaft would change all that. Certainly the new transport brought its own inherent difficulties, such as the necessity for a constant flow of petrol and an efficient repair system, but these were by no means insuperable, especially with the advent of air transport. Distances of thirty or forty miles a day over several weeks were now possible, and relative independence from the once-inhibiting problems of logistics presented itself. Now, the only check on the fullest exploitation of a mobile strategy would be the dispositions and the quality of the enemy.

This was a development of considerable potential, which, when allied to the tactics of infiltration, produced a strategy of revolutionary proportions – the armoured idea, or, to use a term current at the time, the 'indirect approach', an expression coined by Sir Basil Liddell Hart in the 1920s. (The Germans possessed no comparable term.) The first exposition of the idea was by another Englishman, Major-General J. F. C. Fuller, as early as May 1918, when he wrote a long service memorandum entitled 'Strategical Paralysis as the object of the Decisive Attack' (later changed to 'Plan 1919'). To quote its author, its salient points were:

> 'The fighting power of an army lies in its organisation, which can be destroyed either by wearing it down or by rendering it inoperative. The first comprises killing, wounding, and capturing the enemy soldiers – body warfare; the second in rendering inoperative his

power of command – brain warfare. To take a single man as an example; the first method may be compared with a succession of wounds which will eventually result in his bleeding to death; the second – a shot through the brain. The brains of an army are its Staff – Army, Corps, and Divisional Headquarters. Could they suddenly be removed from an extensive sector of the . . . front, the collapse of the personnel they control will be little more than a matter of hours. As our present theory is to destroy personnel, our new theory should be to destroy command, not after the enemy's personnel has been disorganised but before it has been attacked, so that it may be found in a state of disorganisation when attacked. The means proposed were a sudden eruption of squadrons of fast-moving tanks, which unheralded would proceed to the various enemy headquarters, and either round them up or scatter them. Meanwhile every available bombing machine was to concentrate on the supply and road centres. Only after these operations had been given time to mature was the enemy's front to be attacked in the normal way, and, directly penetration was effected, pursuit was to follow.'[2]

In this, Fuller was echoing an idea centuries old, one expressed thus by Sun Tzu: 'To fight and conquer in all your battles is not supreme excellence; supreme excellence consists in breaking the enemy's resistance without fighting.'

Such theories from abroad coincided with much of the experience gained by the German Army during the years of the First World War, and for some officers, a tiny minority, they came together to produce a new concept of war. From their past tradition they understood the importance of decisive man-oeuvre as the basis of strategy; from their tactics of infiltration they learnt the effectiveness of offensive action by well-armed, highly-trained mixed groups of men at any level of command attacking with vigour, speed, and flexibility to paralyse the enemy; from their failures they were forced to appreciate the necessity of full cooperation and communication between all arms of an attacking force; from their neglect, and the Allies use, of the tank, they became aware of the potential of a vehicle which possessed the unique combination of fire-power, protection, and mobility; from the developments in mechanisation and in air-power they recognised the means by which the considerable restrictions of physical exhaustion and limiting supply lines could be overcome, and a significant measure of operational freedom achieved; and from the British military theorists they found ideas that were important in broadening and welding together elements already present in their thinking. The result of this combination was a revolutionary theory seldom put into words and often inadequately presented, but which was sometimes expressed through unhesitating action in the field: action taken by men firm in the belief that they possessed within their grasp a new and potent means of victory – the armoured idea.

In the German Army, Heinz Guderian was the driving force behind the expression of this new strategy. As General von Manteuffel, who was in close touch with him from 1936, recorded:

'Guderian favoured from the beginning the strategic use of panzer forces – a deep thrust into the enemy – without worrying about a possible threat to his own unprotected and far-extended flanks. . . . It was Guderian – and at first he alone – who introduced the tank to the Army and its use as an operative weapon. It was certainly not the General Staff. . . . In peacetime he at first stood alone when he insisted that the breakthrough of tanks should be pressed long and deep, and at first without regard to the exposed flanks.'[3]

Although he cannot be credited with the introduction of tanks, Guderian certainly revolutionised strategic thinking within the Army. On 1 April, 1922, as a thirty-four-year-old *Jäger* (Rifleman) signals specialist who knew nothing about armoured vehicles, he was posted to the Motorised Transport Department of the Inspectorate of Transport Troops. At first he was reluctant to continue in his job, even asking to be returned to his regiment, but soon he came to recognise the potential that motorisation offered Germany's then limited forces. He understood that mobility could offset numerical inferiority. Although this was no new revelation, his interest was awakened, and his attention on the lorry broadened to take account of the tank. By 1929 he had evolved the idea of strategic penetration by armoured forces, and, in his own words, had become 'convinced that tanks working on their own or in conjunction with infantry could never achieve decisive importance. . . . what was needed were armoured divisions which would include the supporting arms needed to allow the tanks to fight to full effect.'[4]

Guderian committed his new ideas to paper in the form of a number of articles in military periodicals, to be republished in 1937, when there appeared his first book, *Achtung! Panzer!*, a collection of the best of his lectures and writings over the previous decade. The quality of his argument was never profound, but the ideas behind it were expressed with vigour. In an article in the *Militärwissenschaftliche Rundschau* of December 1935, for example, he wrote:

'One night the doors of aeroplane hangers and Army garages will be flung open, motors will be tuned up, and squadrons will swing into movement. The first sudden blow may capture important industrial and raw-material districts or destroy them by air attack so that they can take no part in war production. Enemy government and military centres may be crippled and his transport system disorganised. In any case, the first strategic surprise attack will penetrate more or less deeply into enemy territory according to the distances to be covered and the amount of resistance met with. The first move of air and mechanised attack will be followed up by motorised infantry divisions. They will be carried to the verge of the occupied territory and hold it, thereby freeing the mobile units for another blow. In the meantime the attacker will be raising a mass army. He has the choice of territory and time for his next big blow, and he will then bring up the weapons intended for breaking down all resistance and breaking through enemy lines. He will do his best to launch the great blow suddenly so as to take the enemy by surprise, rapidly concentrating his mobile troops and hurling his air force at the enemy. The armoured division will no longer stop when the first objectives have been reached; on the contrary, utilising their speed and their radius of action to the full, they will do their utmost to complete the breakthrough into the enemy lines of communication. Blow after blow will be launched ceaselessly in order to roll up the enemy front and carry the attack as far as possible into enemy territory. The air force will attack the enemy reserves and prevent their intervention.'[5]

To Guderian and his followers, armour, mobility, and speed were all-important. In 1937, he wrote:

'. . . until our critics can produce some new and better method of making a successful land attack other than self-massacre, we shall continue to maintain our belief that tanks – properly employed, needless to say – are today the best means available for a land attack. . . . Everything is therefore dependent on this: to be able to move faster than has hitherto been done: to keep moving despite the enemy's defensive fire and thus to make it harder for him to build up fresh defensive positions: and finally to carry the attack deep into the enemy's defences. The proponents of tank warfare believe that, in favourable circumstances, they possess the means for achieving this. . . . We believe that by attacking with tanks we can achieve a higher rate of movement than has been hitherto obtainable, and – what is perhaps even more important – that we can keep moving once a breakthrough has been made. . . . We no longer believe that other formations have the fighting ability, the speed and the manoeuvrability necessary for full exploitation of the attack and breakthrough.'[6]

The degree to which the German armour enthusiasts were inspired by the military theorists abroad was considerable. In the English edition of his memoirs, Guderian wrote selflessly:

'It was principally the books and articles of the Englishmen, Fuller, Liddell Hart and Martel, that excited my interest and gave me food for thought. These far-sighted soldiers were even then [the early 1920s] trying to make of the tank something more than just an infantry-support weapon. They envisaged it in relationship to the growing motorisation of our age, and thus they became the pioneers of a new type of warfare on the largest scale. I learned from them the concentration of armour. . . . Furthermore, it was Liddell Hart who emphasised the use of armoured forces for long-range strikes, operations against the opposing army's communications, and also proposed a type of panzer division. . . . Deeply impressed by these ideas I tried to develop them in a sense practicable for our own Army. So I owe many suggestions of our further development to Captain Liddell Hart.'[7]

Fulsome praise indeed, although in the original German language edition of Guderian's work there was no mention of Liddell Hart in this context, and in the bibliography of his pre-war *Achtung! Panzer!*, no inclusion of the Englishman's works. Guderian's son remembered that it was Fuller, rather than Liddell Hart, who had possessed the greater influence on his father before the war (and yet Guderian specifically rejected Fuller's 'all tank' theory, and adopted Liddell Hart's solution – the armoured division as a team of all arms.) Nevertheless, wherever the emphasis lay, there was no doubt of the significant impact made by the British military writers on the panzer generals, an impact which may even have been greater than that of the German theorists themselves. One of Rommel's chiefs of staff in the desert war, Fritz Bayerlein, noted:

> 'In his [Rommel's] opinion, the British could have avoided most of their defeats if only they had paid more heed to the modern theories expounded by those two writers [Liddell Hart and Fuller] before the war. During the war, in many conferences and personal talks with Field Marshal Rommel, we discussed Liddell Hart's military works, which won our admiration. Of all military writers it was Liddell Hart [not Guderian] who made the deepest impression on the Field-Marshal, and greatly influenced his tactical and strategical thinking. He, like Guderian, could in many respects be termed Liddell Hart's "pupil".'[8]

The theory and practice of the armoured idea, or the strategy of indirect approach, which developed from 1918 to 1942, may be considered as follows:

Breakthrough. The armoured force concentrates its power at the enemy's weakest point and, enjoying a local superiority in men and material, attacks with the fullest advantage of surprise. The resulting breakthrough is on a narrow front, and all opposing strong points are left for the rest of the army, which follows through, widening the gap and consolidating the gains.

Penetration. The armoured force, independently of the rest of the army, drives deep into the enemy's rear, searching not for his troops but for his line of least resistance. The main thrust is obscured by constantly developing and fading decoy threats. The speed and flexibility of the attack are of prime importance; considerations such as the security of flanks are only secondary.

The unpredictability and momentum of the force now become its primary weapon, for they not only cause considerable disarray in the opposing command, but also prevent the enemy from concentrating sufficient formations to put up an effective opposition.

Aim. The aim of the attacking force is to turn a tactical advantage into a strategic one. This is achieved by means of the indirect approach. The enemy's capacity to resist is destroyed not by the direct killing or capture of his troops, but indirectly, by the rendering inoperative of his power of command. Action without direction loses coordination; troops without headquarters, or with one that is bewildered and panic-stricken, are reduced to a mob. Just as damaging is the psychological impact – the perplexity, doubt, consternation, and sheer terror brought about by the lack of any definite appreciation of the situation, fear of the unknown, and the prospect of imminent death. The heart, as well as the head, becomes atrophied. The paralysis is complete, the victory total.

Such was the armoured idea. Throughout, it was the specialised and relatively small attacking force that set the pace of the campaign, unhindered by the slower mass of the field army, to which was given the task of mopping up the isolated pockets of resistance and capturing the large numbers of disorganised and demoralised enemy troops. This was achieved, preferably, by means of the traditional encirclement manoeuvres, made so much easier by the armoured troops' deep penetration.

The basic military organisation required to implement this new form of war was the armoured division. The division would, in theory, consist of a balanced team of all arms – tank, anti-tank, infantry, artillery and engineer – which together produced the combination of maximum striking power, high speed across country, and complete flexibility in response to enemy action demanded by the rapid, independent thrusting movements of the new concept. Modern inventions would be fully employed to give maximum freedom and speed to the force's operation, and these would include motorised transport, tracked self-propelled artillery, mechanised infantry, and aeroplanes for the dropping of supplies. As Guderian wrote in 1936:

> 'The armoured branch will include all other arms. Infantry, artillery, and engineers are necessary to the development of its action, but it will impose upon them its own methods of combat by making them dependent on the motor. Supporting infantry, artillery, and engineers will be motorised and partially armoured within the framework of the armoured division and the motorized infantry division. They will adjust their new tactical programme and employment to their new speed. An important role will be played by the engineers, who will have abundant material for crossing gaps, and who will be trained to use it rapidly and to oppose the action of enemy tanks by the rapid construction of anti-tank obstacles. The

desire to protect the armoured weapon against the counter-attack of its most dangerous enemies, the tank and the plane, will require the incorporation of numerous and powerful anti-tank and anti-aircraft weapons into the panzer division. Thus the armoured arm – minutely trained on the other hand for cooperation with the air arm – will be able to fight its own battle.'[9]

There was to be no set formula as to the relative strength of the armoured to the non-armoured forces within the field army, perhaps twenty-five per cent of the total would have been adequate, but certainly the rest of the Army, although consisting largely of infantry formations, was intended to be well-motorised and capable of swift action to consolidate the achievements of the armoured force. However, the main emphasis was to be placed upon the proper equipping and organising of the panzer arm. There lay the key to victory, which was to be gained thus: 'The attack by tanks', wrote Guderian in 1936, 'must be conducted with maximum acceleration in order to exploit the advantage of surprise, to penetrate deep into enemy lines, to prevent reserves from intervening, and to extend the tactical success into a strategical victory. Speed, therefore, is what is to be exacted above anything else from the armoured weapon.'[10] Nothing was to prevent the achievement of speed; the armoured formations were to reign supreme. This, Guderian made clear in 1937:

'We conclude that the suggestion that our tanks be divided among infantry divisions is nothing but a return to the original English tactics of 1916–17, which were even then a failure, for the English tanks were not successful until they were used in mass at Cambrai. By carrying the attack quickly into the enemy's midst, by firing our motorised guns with their protective armour direct into the target, we intend to achieve victory. It is said: "The motor is not a new weapon: it is simply a new method of carrying old weapons forward." It is fairly well-known that combustion engines do not fire bullets; if we speak of the tank as a new weapon, we mean thereby that it necessitates a new arm of the service, as happened for example in the Navy in the case of the U-boat; that, too, is called a weapon. We are convinced that we are a weapon and one whose successes in the future will leave an indelible mark on battles yet to be fought. If our attacks are to succeed, then the other weapons must be adjusted to fit in with our scale of time and space in those attacks. We therefore demand that in order to exploit our successes the necessary supporting arms be made as mobile as we are, and that even in peacetime those arms be placed under our command. For, to carry out great decisive operations, it is not the mass of the infantry but the mass of the tanks that must be on the spot.'[11]

Few proponents of armoured warfare, however, could have expressed their beliefs thus; to most, the panzer division presented only a hitherto undreamed-of potential of power and velocity which provided them with an idea of war based on speed and daring. Although such men could represent their theories only inadequately, they felt strongly that any strategic herit-age, however well-founded on the idea of mobility, was an anathema if it imposed restraint on the new instrument of war and thereby failed to recognise that 'speed, still more speed, and always speed'[12] was the secret. They placed their faith in the words of an old German proverb: 'He who dares, wins.'

The similarities of the strategy of *Vernichtungsgedanke* and of the armoured idea have been noted: decisive manoeuvre was common to both. But here all affinity ended, and the two concepts found themselves in direct conflict one with another. Physical destruction in one was supplanted by paralysis in the other as the primary aim; well-coordinated flanking and encirclement movements were replaced by unsupported thrusts deep into the enemy's rear areas as the method; guarded flanks and unbroken, if strained, supply lines gave way to velocity and unpredictability as the basic rules of opera-tion; centralisation of control was superseded by independence of action as the first condition of command; and the mass infantry armies, whether or not supported by tanks and aircraft, made way for the relatively small power-houses of the armoured divisions as the primary instrument of victory.

So fundamental were the differences between the two ideas that it is hardly surprising that the overwhelming majority of Germany's General Staff and officer corps, a body of men not noted for their radical outlook, viewed the revolutionary concept with less than favour. But could they be blamed for not recognising its potential and validity? It was, after all, a complete reversal of the rules of warfare as they knew them – extended flanks, deep, unsupported thrusts by relatively small formations which left the mass of the army in a secondary role, and which were aimed at the paralysis and not at the physical destruction of the enemy. The tradition and method of *Vernichtungsgedanke* simply could not be thrown overboard in favour of so novel a strategy as the indirect approach, centred around the actions of the, as yet, untried armoured divisions. Nevertheless, it was against this official doctrine of manoeuvre that a minority of German officers rebelled. The role they sought for armour and motorisation was one not merely of importance but of domination, to which the rest of the army was to be subordinate. As Guderian wrote in 1936: 'In the zone of action of the armour, the action of the other arms is to be based on that of the armour.'[13] The revolutionaries rejected *Vernichtungsgedanke*, and saw the dangers inher-ent in being shackled to a tradition which did not take full account of the potential of new developments. The controversy naturally enough centred around the fortunes of the armoured force. As one of the leading revolutionaries, Guderian, later recorded:

'. . . tradition is not always regarded as simply supplying ideals of behaviour, but rather as a source of practical example, as though an imitation of what was done before could produce identical results despite the fact that meanwhile circumstances and methods have completely altered. Hardly any mature institution can avoid this fallacious aspect of tradition. The Prusso-German Army and its General Staff were not immune from making this mistake in a number of ways. In consequence there was inevitably a certain internal stress between misunderstood tradition and the new tasks that had to be performed . . . so when it was a matter of setting up an independent, operational air force, or of developing the newly conceived armoured force within the Army, the Army General Staff opposed these innovations. The importance of these two technical achievements insofar as they affected the operations of the combined Armed Forces was neither sufficiently studied nor appreciated, because it was feared that they might result, in the one case, in a decrease in the importance of the Army as a whole and, in the other, in a lessening of the prestige of the older arms of that service.'[14]

As a result, the history of the German Army from the 1930s to the middle years of the Second World War became essentially the record of the unresolved conflict between the protagonists of a new strategy founded on the revolutionary use of armoured, motorised and air forces engaged in a mission of paralysis, and the adherents of the traditional strategy based on mass infantry armies, with the new arms at best treated only as equal partners, the cutting edge of the old decisive manoeuvre of encirclement and annihilation. This came to an end only in 1943 with the German loss of the initiative, their renouncement of the superiority of manoeuvre, and the return to a more or less static strategy of attrition with, as its consequence, failure on the field of battle. This was the result of the stranglehold of tradition that, together with the ineptitude of the Supreme Commander, Adolf Hitler, was to ensure the total military defeat of the much-vaunted German Army.

The battle between the two sides of German strategic thought was both bitter and unevenly matched. In conversation with Liddell Hart, General von Thoma recorded:

'It may surprise you to hear that the development of armoured forces met with much resistance from the higher generals of the German Army, as it did in yours. The older ones were afraid of developing such forces fast – because they themselves did not understand the technique of armoured warfare, and were uncomfortable with such new instruments. At the best they were interested, but dubious and cautious. We could have gone ahead much faster but for their attitude.'[15]

Rommel went further than this, his last writings before his death in 1944 revealing that his dream of armoured warfare was not a thing of the past, but still remained to be realised in the future:

> 'Nevertheless, even the German officer corps was by no means completely free of the old prejudices. There was a particular clique that still fought bitterly against any drastic modernisation of methods and clung fast to the axiom that the infantry must be regarded as the most important constituent of any army. This may be true for Germany's eastern army as it is fighting today in Russia, but it will not be true in the future, which is where our attention should be concentrated – when the tank will be the centre of all tactical thinking. The African campaign and the new aspects of warfare which it brought were never understood by men like General Halder. They stuck to their established methods and precedents, even though these often showed themselves to be outdated and hence false.'[16]

The main opponents of the new strategy were, according to Guderian, Generals Beck and Halder. Placing the blame for the rejection of his ideas squarely on the shoulders of the two Chiefs of the General Staff, Guderian condemned them for being men of the old school and dismissed them and their officers as 'Gentlemen of the Horse Artillery'. Unfairly, he criticised Beck for having 'no understanding of modern technical matters. . . . He was a paralysing element wherever he appeared.'[17] Halder he characterised as 'an officer of routine. . . . He did the inevitable, but nothing more. He did not like panzer divisions at all. In his mind infantry divisions played the leading role now and for ever.'[18] They, for their part, regarded Guderian as a mere 'technician', obsessed with modern developments to the exclusion of sober strategic realities, and thus wholly unfit for the higher operational posts that demanded a wider, more mature vision. He was not, it was constantly asserted, a 'War Academy soldier', for, although he had entered its portals in 1914, the outbreak of war had abruptly terminated his course after only a short time. His nickname, *'Brausewetter'* (Hothead) aptly summed up the prevailing attitude towards his person among the Army High Command, an attitude hardly conducive to the advancement of either his career or his ideas.

However much Guderian might inveigh against such 'reaction', he was condemned to prosecute a frustrating and, ultimately, a frustrated advocacy; the dominance of the traditional strategy was too deep-rooted within the military establishment for it to be overturned. None of those who dominated the Army's leadership could comprehend the full implications of Guderian's theories. Von Fritsch, for example, who, Guderian believed, was 'always ready to try out new ideas without prejudice and, if they seemed to him good, to adopt them',[19] was very much in agreement with Beck as to the employment of armour, and they both planned to strengthen the infantry by assigning to it packets of tanks and assault-guns, thereby contradicting

Guderian's idea of the concentration of all armour within the framework of the panzer division. Of the Army Commander, General Westphal wrote: 'Fritsch was in favour of motorising parts of the Army, but, like Beck, he considered it first necessary to gain experience before deciding finally the make-up and number of mobile divisions that were desirable. Above all it was considered necessary to bear in mind the limit imposed by the fuel factor.'[20] Von Fritsch's successor was little better, for, as Guderian recorded: 'In regard to armoured forces Field-Marshal von Brauchitsch already showed understanding before the war – from the time when he became commander of Army Group 4, in Leipzig, which embraced the motorised and mechanised forces of the Army. He had his own ideas of mechanised operations and tactics – without, however, making full use of these.'[21] The two successive Chiefs of the General Staff, although they did not, as Guderian and others have asserted, advocate the French doctrine of tying down the tanks to close support of the infantry, nevertheless possessed considerable reservations about what they saw as the indiscriminate use of armoured divisions. Certainly Guderian was correct when he recorded that since Beck 'inevitably chose men with much of his own attitude to fill the more important General Staff posts, and even more so to form his own close circle, as time went on he erected – without wishing to do so – a barrier of reaction at the very centre of the Army which was to prove very difficult to overcome'.[22] Even Hitler, fascinated as he was by the power of the panzers, proved an unstable ally in the fight for the armoured arm; General Georg Thomas was of the opinion that 'Hitler attached much importance to the possession of much heavy artillery, many mechanical weapons, and anti-tank weapons. The great importance of the tanks was not recognised until the success in the Polish campaign.'[23]

Just as deadening to the hopes of the armour enthusiasts was the resistance to radical change that came from the established arms. Foremost among these was the artillery, which, because of the higher intellectual quality of gunners and the lower mortality of artillerymen compared with that of infantrymen and cavalrymen in the First World War, came to dominate the top posts of the Army: von Fritsch, von Brauchitsch, Beck, Halder, Fromm, Keitel, Jodl and Warlimont were all from its ranks, and, by the end of the Second World War, of Germany's generals, forty per cent had begun their career in that arm (including six of the nineteen Field-Marshals). The artillery formed a closely knit fraternity, highly protective of its interests – interests that did not always coincide with those of the armour. The new idea led, in Guderian's words, to 'a demand for self-propelled artillery mounts as early as 1934; but the artillerymen did not believe in such fast-moving combat. Accustomed for five hundred years to draw their guns with the muzzle pointing backwards and to unlimber for action, they successfully opposed this proposal until the bitter experience of war taught them to follow the suggestions . . .'[24] Furthermore, as their traditional role had always lain in the provision of close support for the infantry on a basis which made them equal partners with the 'queen of the battlefield', the gunners were inclined to look with suspicion on any theory that detracted from this. Further opposition, naturally enough, came from the cavalry, whose very existence was threatened by motorisation and armour. The horse and the tank in the 1930s were uneasy bed-fellows.

The opposition to the armoured idea in the German Army was anything but unthinking or irrational. Conservative its detractors might have been, but they were far from being merely 'hide-bound'. Cogent arguments were put forward to refute the novel theories of Guderian and his associates, to meet point by point their new principles. Representative of these was an article in the *Militär Wochenblatt* of 11 October 1934. In analysing the new factors of warfare, it pointed to the quite reasonable belief (held in all European Armies) that modern developments, while they had made weapons of offence far more effective, had also strengthened the methods of defence, thus making favourable the chances of holding up the attack with comparatively small forces. It also asserted that modern armies conducting an offensive would be much more dependent on a steady supply of munitions, material and, above all, fuel-oil than were the armies of 1914, and that, therefore, they would be very sensitive to every dislocation of supplies, dislocation made all the more likely by any deep thrusts of the armoured forces with their long, unprotected flanks and supply lines. A few weeks later, the same military magazine carried an article which stated: 'A strategic raid is a very delicate matter, because although it offers a tempting chance it also represents a great and terrible risk. We must remember in particular that the loss of prestige that would result at the very beginning of a war for any country which carried out such a raid unsuccessfully would be incalculable.'[25] Such arguments gained additional force when it was realised that the German Army simply did not possess the material resources required to implement the armoured idea at a time when it was undertaking expansion into a mass conscript army along traditional lines. After all, a panzer division cost around fifteen times as much to equip and to maintain as an infantry division, and before 1939 there was no proof that the former's efficiency in battle would warrant such expenditure during a time of costly expansion.

Furthermore, the supporters of the new strategy suffered from one great weakness: they proved themselves incapable of communicating their ideas to their brother officers. They were men of action, not of the word, impatient of, and unresponsive to, what they considered shortsighted opposition. As Rommel recorded: 'My staff and I gave no regard whatsoever to all this unnecessary academic nonsense, which had long been overtaken by technical development. Consequently, many officers of the academic type, steeped in their ancient theories, failed to understand us and so took us for adventurers, amateurs, and the like.'[26] And General von Manteuffel was to admit of his much-beloved chief, Guderian, after the war: 'He may not, on some occasions, have stressed this point [the strategic use of armoured forces] very emphatically – simply because many of the older officers could not get used to these new methods, and he may not have tried to present them in a more favourable form.'[27] Moreover, these men were denied free expression of their views in the official manuals of the Army, and the few who bothered themselves to propound their messages were forced to limit themselves to professional magazines and the occasional book, none of which contained a truly lucid exposition of the new idea to equal the eloquent arguments of *Die Truppenführung*. Nor was Guderian's own character an asset in this battle of ideas. Although possessing considerable originality, energy, intelligence, determination, and tenacity, those very traits that made him a highly gifted soldier ensured that he would be, at the same time, a difficult man with whom to work. One of his former subordinates remarked later that 'He lacked the psychological faculty of feeling and sensing his way which a "leading personality" . . . should possess. . . . He had not the gift of listening calmly to his subordinates or men of his own rank. . . . He was a strong "rider", and successful as such, but he lacked the mind and psychological insight into the spirit of the "horse" which are essential in a good rider.'[28] Critical, frank, and acerbic, Guderian was not the type of man to present his argument tactfully to his superiors and persuade them of his sagacity through a combination of charm and logic. On the contrary he often appeared to be nothing other than an arrogant firebrand. This impression was forcefully expressed by Halder, who noted: 'Guderian will not tolerate any Army commander, and demands that everybody up to the highest position should bow to the ideas he produces from a restricted view point. . . . I will not give way to Guderian.'[29] Such a man was not the best person to advance a cause which was in such direct opposition to so traditional, established, and highly successful a form of war as *Vernichtungsgedanke*.

Against such odds, the outcome of the battle was a foregone conclusion. Guderian and his supporters failed; the military establishment triumphed. Although the years up to 1939 were to witness the formation of a German panzer arm, it was not one ordered to the specifications of the armour enthusiasts. By 1933 the *Inspektion der Kraftfahrtruppen* (Inspectorate of Transport Troops), under General Oswald Lutz, with Guderian as his chief of staff, had taken over from the cavalry its important reconnaissance functions; plans had been drawn up for the development of tanks, and some machines had actually been made (armoured cars had appeared); attempts were being made to establish motorised anti-tank battalions in each infantry division; and large-scale exercises had been held involving mock tank battalions and infantry regiments to test the concept of the armoured formation. In June 1934 the *Inspektion der Kraftfahrkampftruppen* (Mechanised Troops Inspectorate) was created, again with Lutz at its head and Guderian as his chief of staff, and in October the first tank unit was formed, Panzer Brigade I, equipped with light training tanks. In May 1935 a General Staff exercise studied the use of an armoured corps in the field, and in July an improvised panzer division undertook a highly successful exercise which revealed to all that the movement and control of a team of all arms, including tanks, was possible. Clearly the time was ripe for the birth of the new force, and on 27 September the *Kommando der Panzertruppen* (Armoured Troops Command) was instituted, with Lutz as its chief, followed on 15 October by the establishment of three panzer divisions. In 1938 two more armoured divisions, were formed, and on 20 November Hitler appointed Guderian *Chef der Schnellen Truppen* (Chief of Mobile Troops), a newly instituted post which had authority over the development and training of all Germany's mechanised and mounted troops, an authority denied to the former Armoured Troops Command, which had possessed control over tank-equipped units only. Finally, before the outbreak of the war, Germany's sixth armoured division, 10th Panzer, was instituted in April 1939.

The importance of Guderian and his supporters in the development of this panzer arm should not be underestimated, for it was largely through their efforts that the force that was raised from virtually nothing in 1935 had reached such a high state of readiness by 1939 that it could demonstrate to the world an unequalled degree of military proficiency on the field of battle. But such an achievement should not for one moment be represented as the triumph of the armoured idea. In the German Field Army after mobilisation, only roughly one in twenty of its divisions was panzer, and just one in ten was fully motorised (this included four light divisions and four motorised infantry divisions). Furthermore, even the existing panzer force, small as it was, suffered from neglect and misunderstanding. Despite Guderian's efforts, the German Army failed to organise its limited armour in such a way as to exploit its potential to the full. Guderian had argued that 'there could be no question for the time being of even approaching [the enemies'] standard of equipment either in quality or in quantity. We had, therefore, to attempt to compensate for these deficiencies by means of superior organisation and leadership. A tight concentration of our limited forces in large units, in divisions to be precise, and the organisation of those units as a panzer corps would, we hoped, make up for our numerical inferiority.'[30] This was not to be. In October 1937, as a result of a long-thought-out policy of the General Staff, the 4th Panzer Brigade was formed, made up of two tank regiments, a quarter of the total of such formations. This brigade, intended to provide infantry support, was followed by a second, the 6th, in 1938. That same year saw the establishment of three light divisions to add to the one incorporated from the Austrian Army. Formed in place of further armoured divisions, they were basically motorised infantry formations each with a tank battalion and a reconnaissance regiment. Therefore, although Guderian later managed to have the 4th Panzer Brigade turned into the 10th Panzer Division, out of the thirty-three tank battalions and 3,195 tanks in existence by September 1939, nine battalions and 1,251 tanks were outside the framework of the armoured division.

Equally as disturbing for Germany's armoured force was the fact that in

September 1939 ninety per cent of its tanks were obsolete. The outbreak of war had interrupted the long-term plan decided on in 1932 – and subsequently carried out with little sense of urgency – for the equipping of the panzer divisions with two main battle tanks, a light machine to form the main striking force and a medium one in support. Because of design and production problems it had been necessary to introduce a stop-gap training tank, and there emerged in 1934 a very light, six-ton machine, the PzKw I (*Panzerkampfwagen* – armoured fighting vehicle), armed with only two machine-guns. Yet it was out of date even before it made its appearance, and further delays caused another, improved, short-term, light tank, the nine-ton PzKw II, to appear. This, too, was inadequate, and by 1939 not only was its 2cm armament outclassed by similar foreign machines, but its armour was no longer proof against anti-tank weapons.

The first production models of the intended main battle tanks, the twenty-ton PzKw III and PzKw IV, were completed only in 1936, the former being armed with a 3.7cm anti-tank gun, the latter with a short-barrelled 7.5cm weapon capable of firing both high-explosive and anti-tank rounds, but at low velocity. The choice of armament for the PzKw IIIs had been the subject of much controversy; Guderian recalled that he was 'anxious that they be equipped with a 5cm weapon since this would give them the advantage over the heavier armour plate which we soon expected to see incorporated in the construction of foreign tanks. Since, however, the infantry was already being equipped with 3.7cm anti-tank guns, and since, for reasons of production simplicity, it was not considered desirable to produce more than one type of light anti-tank gun and shell, General Lutz and I had to give in.'[31] The Army Weapons Department and the Artillery Inspectorate had won the day; the needs of the panzer force were neglected. This was a story often repeated. In 1938 the Weapons Department came to realise its mistake and ordered that the PzKw III be fitted with the 5cm gun, but it was not until the middle of the French campaign that the tanks so armed made their first appearance.

After 1936, the re-equipping of the panzer units with these main tanks proceeded only slowly. In 1939, for example, output of the PzKw IV was even greatly reduced, so that only forty-five were built during the whole year. Indeed in September, the month war began, only fifty-seven tanks of all types were produced. Such was the state of the panzer arm at the time of the campaign against Poland that its main battle tank, the PzKw III, which was intended to provide threequarters of Germany's total tank strength, in reality composed only one thirty-second. Of a total of 3,195 machines on 1 September 1939, 1,445 were PzKw Is, 1,226 PzKw IIs, 215 PzKw I Command tanks, and only 98 were PzKw IIIs and 211 PzKw IVs. Germany's panzer force was committed to battle equipped mainly with training tanks.

In addition, scarce and much-needed equipment was denied to the panzer divisions and dissipated throughout the Army. Therefore, although the development of assault-guns for the infantry, the motorisation of all infantry anti-tank gun companies, and the creation of four light divisions were no doubt of value to the Army as a whole, the damage to the armoured force was considerable. As Guderian records:

> 'The development of tracked vehicles for the tank supporting arms never went as fast as we wished. It was clear that the effectiveness of the tanks would gain in proportion to the ability of the infantry, artillery, and other divisional arms to follow them in an advance across country. We wanted lightly armed half-tracks for the riflemen, combat engineers, and medical services; armoured self-propelled guns for the artillery and the anti-tank battalions; and various types of armour for the reconnaissance and signals battalions. The equipment of the divisions with these vehicles was never fully completed.'[32]

This is an understatement. In 1939, of the 2,060-odd motor vehicles in a panzer division (not including the tanks or the 200 motorcycles), not one was wholly tracked, few were half-tracked, and only one type was armoured – the SdKfz 251 (*Sonderkraftfahrzeug* – special purposes motor vehicle) half-track personnel carrier, and this was still extremely rare. Thus, by the outbreak of war, fewer than one-fifth of all vehicles in the panzer division were partially tracked and possessed a cross-country mobility approaching that of the tanks. Road-bound, unarmoured trucks did not lend themselves to the full exploitation of armoured warfare.

Lastly, the panzer troops were not given a command of sufficient status to justify their claim to supremacy. The Armoured Troops Command under Lutz, instituted in 1935, had been refused equal status with the infantry, cavalry, and artillery, and, as Guderian stated, was responsible only for looking after tank-equipped units' interests with the Chief of the General Army Office. Furthermore, a few days after its formation, Guderian was posted from his influential post as chief of staff to Lutz to become the first commander of the 2nd Panzer Division, which virtually ensured that he took little part in policy making for almost two and a half years. The fortunes of armoured and mechanised development came in 1937 to lie elsewhere, in the hands of von Brauchitsch and his successor, von Reichenau, who, as the commanders of the newly instituted Army Group Command 4, possessed operational and training control over all motorised units – the XVI Army Corps under Lutz (from 4 February 1938 under Guderian), consisting of the three panzer divisions; the XV Army Corps, made up of the light divisions; and the XIV Army Corps formed from the motorised infantry divisions.

The creation of the Chief of Mobile Troops in late 1938 did mark a theoretical improvement in the situation, for it brought the development of all mechanised and cavalry troops under the authority of one organisation. Guderian had even been given the Führer's assurance that 'Together, we'll see that the necessary modernisation is carried through'.[33] However, it was not long before Guderian and his small staff found that the powers of the new command were illusory; some even saw in his appointment a plot to deny an influential role to the protagonists of the armoured idea. Certainly Guderian himself felt that he could have been more effective had he continued as Commander of XVI Army Corps. He made no use of Hitler's promise of an alliance, believing it either worthless or improper to enlist the Führer's aid in internal Army affairs, and he was forced to expend much of his time and energy in futile battles with the traditionalists. Guderian met with obstruction from the Training Department to his draft training manuals, his proposals to modernise the cavalry received direct rejection by the General Army Office, and he failed to obtain the necessary priority for the equipping of his panzer divisions. Although the very existence of an independent command for mobile troops gave some support to the arguments of the armour enthusiasts, it was short-lived. On mobilisation in 1939, Guderian's post was dissolved, and he himself transferred to a field command as a motorised corps commander. (At one point in 1939 he had even been given a mobilisation appointment with a reserve infantry corps, and it was only with great difficulty that he managed to get it revoked.)

The interests of the panzer force came to lie with the *Inspekteur der Schnellen Truppen* (Inspector of Mobile Troops) who, along with eleven other arm and service inspectors, was directly subordinate to the Commander of the Replacement Army, General Fritz Fromm, a man not noted for his sympathy with the armoured idea. Furthermore, the Inspector possessed no command functions and little influence, his duties being merely to keep records and publish orders, directives, training manuals, and other material on behalf of the mobile troops. The Inspector, who was, until June 1942, the little-known General Kühn, was served by the *Abteilung für Panzertruppe, Kavallerie, und Heeresmotorisierung* (Department for Armoured Troops, Cavalry, and Army Motorisation) in the General Army Office, an organisation which underwent several changes before its abolition in 1943. In the Army Ordnance Office the technical concerns of the armoured force were represented by the *Kraftfahr und Motorisierungsabteilung* (Department for Motor Transport and Mechanisation), a body wholly incapable of dealing with the specialities of tank design. And, although after 10 October 1939 the three fighting arms of infantry, artillery, and engineers and fortifications troops possessed representatives, known as *Waffengeneräle* (Arm generals), attached to the General Staff in order to advise the Army Commander-in-Chief and the Chief of the Army General Staff on the organisation, training, and tactical employment of their respective branches, it was not until 5 March 1940 that a representative was appointed for the armoured troops. He was given the title *General der Schnellen Truppen beim Oberbefehlshaber des Heeres* (General of Mobile Troops with the Commander-in-Chief of the Army). The first holder of the office was General Wilhelm Ritter von Thoma, a future commander of the German Africa Corps. It was only after three years of war, when the panzer arm was on the verge of complete collapse, that a command with anything approaching sufficient authority was instituted to safeguard its interests and advance its requirements. By then it was too late; the German armoured force was broken.

Thus, at no time was the German panzer arm given the status and the special attention by the military establishment that indicated they had accepted it as the most important component of a new form of warfare. Indeed, even the creation of the first three panzer divisions in October 1935 did not differ much from contemporary developments in other European countries. The previous year, the same type of organisation, based on a tank brigade supported by an infantry brigade, had been adopted by the French in their Division Légère Mécanique, and had also been tried during the 1927–28 British Army manoeuvres. Until the outbreak of war, as well as after, the men who dominated the Army High Command kept strict control over the development of the mobile arm and took steps to ensure that the tenets of the armoured idea found no expression in the composition and employment of the panzer troops. Revolutionary reorganisation had no place in the German Army. Instead, the Third Reich's mechanised force was subordinated to the requirements of the traditional strategy of decisive manoeuvre by a mass army; the proponents of the strategy of indirect approach, whether or not they were conscious of the full implications of the theory, had lost the battle.

12

Unreadiness

Because of the many difficulties under which it laboured, the more astounding were the great successes which the Army achieved in the first years of the war.

GENERAL SIEGFRIED WESTPHAL

While the battle for the armoured divisions was being fought and, in part, lost, the formation of the mass of the Army was quietly proceeding apace. Here lay the real task of the generals, a task whose very magnitude tended to push any proper consideration of the armoured idea into the background. Out of a defence system consisting of a small professional force devoid of 'weapons of aggression', a new Army would be formed, based on universal conscription, full armament, and the utilisation of modern technology. Welcome though this must have been to the generals, they were faced, nonetheless, with the fact that it was not they who directed the pace and nature of this expansion. Just as before 1933 it had been the restrictions of the Versailles Treaty that had largely determined the size, organisation, and quality of the Army, after that year it was the policies of Adolf Hitler. In numerical terms his achievement was that, by September 1939 the peace-time Army of 730,000 men and fifty-two active divisions could be increased in a matter of a few weeks to a wartime force of 3,706,104 men and 103 divisions.

Remarkable though this was, behind the impressive façade of numbers of divisions lay certain grave weaknesses. No military force could undergo such a considerable numerical expansion without experiencing dangerous strains. In 1934, for example, there had been eighty-four infantry and twenty-four artillery battalions in existence; by 1 September 1939 there were 885 and 439 respectively. Perhaps the most serious weakness was the inability of the 100,000-man Reichsheer to provide the masses of commissioned and non-commissioned personnel necessary for the constantly expanding formations. There had been only 4,000 active officers in 1933, and of these 450, more than one in ten, were medical and veterinary personnel. Of the 3,550 actual troop and staff officers, some 500, one seventh, were released for service in the new Air Force. This meant there were only 3,000 officers to provide the nucleus of a corps which was to expand to more than 100,000 by the outbreak of war.

To meet the new Army's requirements, several expedients were used in additon to normal recruiting. The period of training required to gain a commission was shortened; 1,500 non-commissioned officers were given commissions; some 2,500 police officers from the militarised *Landespolizei* were transferred to the Army, among whom were many pre-1918 officers (the *Landespolizei* had always been used as a source of military training); officers who had been discharged since 1918 were brought back into service; the grade of *Ergänzungs-Offiziere* (officer on the supplementary list) was established for officers who, although no longer fit for duty with line units, were recalled because of their experience or specialist knowledge, and employed within the High Command, high level staffs, the Armed Forces Recruiting and Replacement Organisations, the *Grenzwacht* (frontier guard) and the *Landwehr* (territorials); some 300 legal officials were drafted from the Ministry of Justice; about 1,600 former Austrian officers came into the Army after the occupation of Austria; and, finally, an unspecified number of former SA leaders, many of whom had served in the First World War, were commissioned after only a few months' military training. Thus, by September 1939, only about one in six officers was a fully trained professional. Standards inevitably deteriorated, for five-sixths of the officer corps had neither the knowledge nor, more important, the experience required. General Wolf, commander of the 21st Infantry Division, wrote to Beck in 1935:

> 'The draft of new officers (they call them "buyers" here in East Prussia) and the bulk of the new arrivals need a great deal of "settling in", for all the good they will show. In addition we get many here who come from "small garrisons". It rather worries me to think of next winter. How are we going to inspire these officers with an intelligent interest in their profession and keep them away from the local custom of sitting night after night in the café or in the beer hall. . . .'[1]

It was even feared that the abilities of many officers were being overtaxed by being given rank beyond their capabilities; as a consequence, von Leeb went so far in 1939 as to describe the new Army as 'a blunt sword'.[2]

However, the social dilution of the officer corps possessed certain benefits. The admission of other-rankers tended to break down artificial distinction and allow good leaders to make their way in the Army. Furthermore, there was a considerable lowering of the barriers between officers and men, both on and off duty, and there were frequent meetings on equal terms on the playing fields and in the cafés, which fostered a general spirit of easy comradeship within a framework of discipline. This was to become important in the forthcoming years in maintaining morale under extremely trying conditions.

Just as there was a shortage of commissioned officers, so there was of NCOs, despite the fact that many in the Reichsheer could be used in that capacity. The situation had become so alarming by 1938 that the military authorities were forced to improve the conditions of a non-commissioned officer's career, increasing the chances of his obtaining a commission in the course of ordinary routine. Indeed, during the war, the proportion of NCOs given commissions in some regiments was as high as seventy-five per cent. Nevertheless, the desire of some to seek glory on the field as a means of self-advertisement, and their social insecurity, which often caused them to court popularity, sometimes by engaging in drinking bouts with the other ranks, were not welcomed by their subordinates and superiors alike.

Another aspect of the rapid expansion of the Army was the detrimental effect it had on the coherence of units. This was summed up by General Westphal:

> 'Even when it is taken into consideration that in peacetime each division contained on the average only one half to two-thirds of the number of battalions and batteries provided for, it can be seen that the demands on the Army were extraordinary. By 1937 the strength had been quadrupled. Every company and battery had therefore had to split up at least twice in four years so that new units could be formed from its parts. This multiple dismemberment damaged very seriously not only the coherence of the Army but also its training.'[3]

Furthermore, the Army, even expanded so greatly, proved unable to provide military training for approximately 3,250,000 men eligible for service between the ages of twenty and forty. Only thirty-eight per cent of the manpower available to the German Armed Forces was fully trained by September 1939, 1,830,000 of the 4,250,000 of the age group from twenty-one to forty-five; and even more distressing to both Hitler and the Army leadership was that this lack of training was especially high among men between the ages of twenty-one and thirty-five. Expedients thus had to be found to strengthen national defence. A frontier guard was formed from members of the border population who had received military training and were fit for service, and was given the task of border duty and manning of fortifications. On the outbreak of war this frontier guard constituted a security screen only, possessing no artillery whatever. In addition, in 1936, twenty-one Landwehr divisions were formed throughout the Reich, composed of the older age groups of reservists, from thirty to forty-five, who received summer and weekend training. These formations were, however, of poor quality by the time war broke out, for Hitler had not waited until they had been improved by the addition of trained 1914 class conscripts who would normally have left the peacetime Army and gone into the reserve.

One of the most distressing aspects of the rapid rearmament, therefore, was this shortage of trained reserves, which was further exacerbated by the extension of the period of military service from one to two years decreed on 24 August 1936 in the interests of improved training, and by the low birth-rate in the years after 1920. In September 1939, the Army possessed only 500,000 fully trained Class I reservists, and another 600,000 partially trained Class II reservists, to reinforce the 730,000 men already under arms. To provide short-term reservists, special replacement units were formed of men eligible for military service, but who were not subjected to the two-year term of service, being given instead training for three months only. The severe problems in acquiring enough officers were made more difficult by the impossibility of providing intensive training, neither the time nor the resources being available to retrain those who had seen service in the previous war, and whose assistance in the event of another could not be dispensed with. There was a shortage of instructors even for the active Army formations, and the reserve units were forced to take only what few were left. Consequently, there were 1,700,000 reservists between the ages of thirty-five and forty-five who had received no exercise in the military art since 1918. As Westphal recorded: 'For this reason it was possible to detect even in peacetime a degree of improvisation which is normally reached only in an advanced stage of a war. . . . A war-worthy army cannot be improvised. . . .'[4]

The circumstances in which the 'army troops' found themselves were poor. Although they were relatively well-provided with motorised transport (for example, in the artillery, of the two regiments and thirty-five heavy artillery battalions, only one was unmotorised), their development still had a long way to go. General Westphal wrote after the war:

> 'Apart from the large formations, a considerable number of special troops were needed outside the divisional units. The 100,000 man Army had no need of these "army troops" without which no modern army can exist, and it was therefore necessary to build them up from scratch. They consisted of heavy and very heavy artillery, sappers, railway troops, chemical warfare troops, signallers, transport, and motor transport troops. The development of these forces was only in its infancy when war broke out, and as it could not be properly completed during the war, the German Army suffered serious deficiencies in these specialised forces right up to 1945. Particularly embarrassing was the shortage of sappers. . . .'[5]

Lastly, and perhaps most important of all, the German Army in 1939 suffered from an acute shortage of military equipment, especially motorised transport. The German economy, with its desultory system of planning, had failed to keep pace with the vast numerical expansion in the size of the Armed Forces. The inadequacies of the armoured divisions have already been noted, but those of the infantry divisions were just as bad. Only four infantry divisions were fully motorised; the eighty-six others possessed fewer than one quarter of the trucks and passenger cars necessary for their transport, and, on mobilisation, fifty-one of them were equipped largely with requisitioned civilian vehicles. Horses, therefore, played a significant role in the German Army. Even the best infantry divisions each required 4,842 of the animals to supplement their 394 passenger cars and 615 trucks, while the weakest needed about 6,030 and only 330 passenger cars and 248 trucks. On

1 September 1939, the eighty-six non-motorised infantry divisions had a total of 445,500 horses. Divisional artillery, and a high percentage of the supply services, all depended on the horse, while the infantrymen had to rely on their own feet. In the infantry formations, only the anti-tank, infantry gun, signals, headquarters, medical staffs, and some pioneer units were fully motorised, and just fourteen divisions from a total of 103 within the German Army were totally independent of the horse. In this, the force committed to battle in 1939 differed little from its predecessor in 1914. During the First World War, 1,400,000 horses had passed through the German Army; in the Second, it was to be almost double that number – 2,700,000.

The quality of the equipment of the German Army at the beginning of the war left much to be desired. It had a variety of weapons of old design and numerous variants which went far to impair efficiency in the field. The lamentable condition of the tanks has already been described, but the infantry and artillery were little better off. The standard infantry weapon was the Type 98 rifle based on a design first drawn up by Mauser in 1898. The long Karabinier 98a, and its successor, the 98b, were adequate weapons but no more, and it was not until October 1941 that the Gewehr 98/40 rifle, intended to become standard, was introduced. The German soldiers were equipped with at least five types of machine-pistol – the MP 18 and 34 (Bergmann), the MP 28 and 38 (Schmeisser), and the MP 34 (Steyr-Solothurns and Ermas) prior to the general issue of the MP 38 (Schmeisser), which was to appear in 1940 in an improved, modified form, the MP 40. It was not until 1942 that the old variants were finally withdrawn from service. The machine-guns, too, were outdated. The war began before the Army was fully equipped with a standard weapon, the MG 34, and many of the soldiers were still armed with the MG 18, MG 08/15, and MG 15 light machine-guns, and the SMG 08 and ZB 26 Czechoslovak weapons. It was not until March 1941 that all these older types could be withdrawn from front-line service. The anti-tank rifles were the ineffective 7.92mm Panzerbüchse PzB 38 and 39. There was a complete absence of heavy mortars, except those used for firing smoke bombs; the only ones in existence being the 5cm Granatwerfer 36 and 8.1cm Granatwerfer 34 models, and it was not long before the lighter of both these was found to be relatively ineffective. The infantry was also provided with infantry guns for close support, weapons peculiar to the German Army, of both light and heavy variety – the 7.5cm le.IG18 and the 15cm s.IG33. The only anti-aircraft weapons issued to the Army formations were the light 2cm Flak 30 and 38, and the only anti-tank gun was the 3.7cm Pak 35/36, which came to be nicknamed the 'Army's doorknocker', so ineffective was it against contemporary armour. Furthermore, German artillery was almost uniformly competent but uninspired, the result of years of neglect. The divisional artillery of light and medium field-howitzers were modified developments of those used in the previous war – the 10.5 le.FH18 and the 15cm s.FH18. The guns (Kanonen) used by the 'army troops' were the standard 10cm K 18 (also used by the panzer divisions), the 15cm K 18, the 17cm and 21cm howitzers (termed 'mortars' by the Germans), which also dated back to the First World War. The famed 8.8cm Flak 18, 36, and 37, and the 3.7cm Flak 18, 36, and 37 were solely under Luftwaffe control, although they were used in the field to accompany the armoured formations and to protect certain vital sectors of the front.

Furthermore, there were serious shortages in arms and munitions. For example, fifty infantry divisions were without machine-pistols, light or medium mortars, 2cm anti-aircraft guns, and heavy infantry guns, while thirty-four possessed no armoured cars. Most of the formations selected for service on the Western Front as a holding force while the invasion of Poland took place, suffered from an acute lack of anti-tank and artillery guns, and many of the low quality infantry divisions were provided with old, out-of-date equipment. But perhaps the most serious deficiencies lay in the munitions required to make the weapons effective. The Army High Command based its stocks on a forecast of requirements for four months of fighting – little enough, it might be imagined. However, at the outbreak of war there was an ammunition shortage of some seventy per cent of this requirement. It lacked, for example, forty-five per cent of heavy field howitzer ammunition, sixty-five per cent of heavy infantry gun shells, seventy per cent of pistol bullet and 2cm Flak ammunition, seventy-five per cent of light infantry gun and heavy artillery ammunition, eighty-eight per cent of light and heavy artillery ammunition, eighty-eight per cent of light and ninety per cent of medium mortar shells, and a staggering ninety-five per cent of 2cm ammunition for tank guns.

The Army leadership, painfully aware of the inadequacies of the reserves of equipment and trained manpower, took steps to overcome the latter, tackling the problem with some skill. At the outset they saw before them two alternatives: either a small but highly qualified and well-equipped wartime army, or a mass army in which numbers compensated for deficiencies in material and training. Hitler, however, left them with little choice, his obsession with numbers forcing them in 1938 to adopt a compromise solution for the organisation of the wartime force. On mobilisation the Army would be divided into two: the *Feldheer* (Field Army), consisting of the divisions of the peacetime active and reserve force only slightly weakened by detaching some cadres; and the *Ersatzheer* (Replacement Army), which was organised on a broad basis without regard to the deficiences that would develop, and which was intended not only to provide trained replacement for the Field Army formations, but also to form additional field units to be committed to battle. Thus, the wartime Army of 1939 was composed of a Field Army of 2,321,266 men (plus another 426,798 construction troops formed from the Reich Labour Service) and a Replacement Army of 958,040, making a grand total of 3,706,104.

As a further aid to the solution of the problems of the wartime Army's organisation, a graduated structure of infantry divisions was formed. This was known as the *Welle* (Wave) mobilisation plan. The First Wave would consist of the thirty-five active infantry divisions that had existed in peacetime, replenished mainly from Class I reservists of the youngest age class (mountain divisions were rated as qualified for the First Wave). Second Wave divisions, which would not be activated until mobilisation had begun, but would be ready for action within some four days, would consist of sixteen reserve divisions made up of Class I reservists with a cadre, six per cent of their strength, from active divisions; they would be equipped with motor vehicles requisitioned from the national economy. Third Wave divisions, the weakest of all, which would take from four to eight weeks to become operational, were twenty-one in number and were composed only of reservists mainly from Class II and the Landwehr; somewhat deficient in armament and equipment, most would be selected either for the West Wall defences or for training centres. Lastly, the fourteen Fourth Wave divisions would also be composed mainly of reservists, but with some nine per cent of active personnel; and they would not take to the field for several weeks. The advantages of this Wave system of mobilisation were considerable, for, although complete mobilisation was no faster than that of Germany's enemies, it did allow partial mobilisation without improvisation, and ensured that the most powerful formations, the peacetime, active divisions, could mount an attack almost at once without having to wait for the completion of any lengthy process.

The Field and Replacement Armies possessed between them a grand total of 3,706,104 troops, of whom 105,394 were officers, 29,495 officials, 481,009 NCOs, and 3,090,206 men. Apart from the Army, Germany possessed other ground troops in the SS and Luftwaffe formations. At the outbreak of war the SS-VT consisted of four motorised infantry regiments (one of which had not completed its training), an artillery regiment, and independent signals, pioneer, reconnaissance, anti-aircraft machine-gun, and anti-tank battalions (one of each), together with supply and replacement units, to a total of some 23,000 men. Immediately on mobilisation, most of these units were dispersed among Army field formations. The Luftwaffe, too, contributed towards Germany's total number of ground troops in the form of the Flak Regiment Hermann Göring and the 1st *Fallschirmjäger* (Paratroop) Regiment (2 battalions), as well as numerous anti-aircraft field units. The 400,000 servicemen in the Air Force, and 50,000 in the Navy, brought the total of servicemen in the Wehrmacht on mobilisation to around 4,179,000.

But numbers were not everything. As has been shown, the paper figures, the massed parades, the manoeuvres, all served only to obscure from the world the lamentable condition in which the German Army found itself on the outbreak of the European war. Owing to the wide variety and enormous size of the tasks involved in the five-year expansion, the problem of transforming the Army on to a war-footing had been relegated to the background; Indeed, the formation of even the peacetime Army was incomplete. Of the thirty-five

First Wave divisions, one whole infantry regiment and thirty-one infantry battalions (a total of forty battalions out of 315 – twelve per cent) had still to be formed, as well as five artillery battalions, twelve artillery observation batteries, and other divisional services. Of the units that took to the field in September 1939, only between five and six per cent were fit for modern, mobile war, and even these were woefully ill-equipped. Only fourteen of the Field Army's 103 divisions were fully motorised, the other eighty-nine being dependent to a large extent on their feet, the horse, and the railway, and being hampered by serious logistical limits similar to those experienced by the old Imperial Armies. Independence from the restricting umbilical cord of supply was not granted to eighty-five per cent of the Field Army. Moreover, because of deficiencies in training and equipment, the Third and Fourth Wave divisions, which formed forty per cent of the infantry and thirty-four per cent of all field divisions, were ill-suited to the demanding conditions of a war of manoeuvre of any sort.

Such was the state of the German Army at the outbreak of the Second World War. This Army, which had expanded so rapidly since 1935, was. within two years, to be embroiled in an ever-intensifying conflict in both the east and the west, as well as in North Africa. In the early years of victory it was to prove so spectacularly successful, and in the years of defeat so tenacious in defence, that its high place in the history of warfare is assured. However, from the very beginning it possessed deficiencies so fundamental that they were never overcome – indeed, they only increased with the passage of time. Neither in its strategic basis, nor in its organisation and equipment, was the German Army prepared to adopt any new concept of war, and its imperial character – its reliance on old-fashioned infantry divisions hampered by logistical limitations, unrelieved by any thorough use of mechanisation, and directed according to the precepts of von Moltke and von Schlieffen – was not consonant with the belief that it was fashioned according to any revolutionary theory, even one so firmly founded in the imaginations of men as *Blitzkrieg*.

PART THREE

The
Years of Victory

Thou hast chosen war.
That will happen which will happen,
and what is to be we know not.
God alone knows.

GHENGHIS KHAN

13

Poland

*All units have to maintain the initiative against the
foe by quick action and ruthless attacks.*

GENERAL JOHANNES BLASKOWITZ

On 1 September 1939, the High Command of the Wehrmacht announced:
'By order of the Führer and Supreme Commander, the German Armed
Forces have taken over the active defence of the Reich. In fulfilment of their
commission to withstand the Polish menace, troops of the German Army
early today launched a counter-attack. At the same time, squadrons of the
Air Force started for Poland in order to crush Poland's military objectives.'[1]
Twenty-four days later, OKW was able to report: 'The campaign in Poland
is at an end. In a consecutive series of destructive battles . . . the Polish
Army, numbering several millions, was defeated, imprisoned, or dispersed.
Not a single one of the Polish active or reserve divisions, not one of her
independent brigades etc. escaped this fate.'[2] A decisive victory indeed, and
one gained at the cost of only 10,572 German servicemen killed, 30,322
wounded, and 3,409 missing – some three per cent of the total force engaged.
But such an achievement should not obscure two fundamental truths of the
Polish campaign: that against an enemy as deficient in the military art as the
Poles then were, the invaders were bound to win; and that the German Army
gave no demonstration of *Blitzkrieg*, but practised, instead, a traditional form
of war, *Vernichtungsgedanke*. From the outset, the armoured idea was still-
born.

It is difficult to conceive just how any force could have benefited more
from the weaknesses and mistakes of its enemy than the German Army did
from those of the Poles in 1939. In peacetime the Polish Army consisted of
some thirty infantry divisions, one cavalry division, and eleven cavalry
brigades – a force which could be doubled on mobilisation. Although well-
trained, and aggressive, the Polish soldiers were armed mainly with equipment from the 1914–18 War; they possessed little motorised transport and
only a few companies of tanks, amounting to no more than 225 machines in
all. Indeed, in modern military equipment and tactical thought, the Poles
were alarmingly deficient; they possessed only a few, obsolete aircraft and

anti-tank and anti-aircraft guns, and continued to maintain their belief in the efficiency of the cavalry charge and the attack *a l'outrance*.

Even more important than this was the nature of the disposition of these forces to meet the expected German attack. The Poles shared a common border of some 3,000 miles with the Reich and German-occupied Czechoslovakia, the western half of their country being surrounded on three sides by German territory. The terrain of this salient was flat and, except for the river Vistula and its tributaries, possessed few natural obstacles and even fewer fortifications to hinder an invader, especially if the attack was in the dry season. Furthermore, the traditionally bad relations between Poland and the Soviet Union compelled the Poles to divide their limited military resources between both their eastern and western frontiers. The Polish generals could do nothing to alter this. However, they made the situation worse by deploying their forces along the border of the western salient, directly between the German 'jaws'. Because of their intention to defend the main industrial zone, and because of their need to cover the mobilisation of the reserve, their active units were arranged west of the Vistula and near to the frontier, with a concentration in, or near, the Corridor, dangerously positioned between East and West Prussia. The Polish High Command were aware of the problems presented by these dispositions, but relied on their mobilisation being as rapid as that of the Germans, on a continuous line of defence to check any attack, and on an early French offensive against the western frontier of the Reich to deflect, or halt, the invasion. Such were the miscalculations that ensured the rapid defeat of the Poles in 1939: with these handicaps, not even a well-equipped, modern army would have possessed a good chance of victory against the Germans.

The Polish dispositions gave an immense advantage to the German Army High Command. Had the Poles massed well behind the frontier, possibly behind the Vistula, the initial German onslaught would have struck air and exhausted itself before meeting the enemy; its logistical system would have been severely overstrained by the great distances involved; the campaign would have been considerably lengthened, and its outcome less assured. As it was, OKH was offered a guarantee of a speedy victory. Not only could it undertake a grand encirclement to destroy the mass of the enemy army in one quick, decisive blow, but the relatively short distances involved west of the Vistula would ensure that the supply system need not be over-strained. The proximity of good railheads to western Poland was an added advantage, for they were positioned exactly at the proposed assembly areas, and thus facilitated the stockpiling of supplies. Furthermore, the length of time necessary for mobilisation was shortened decisively for the Germans by their 'Wave' system, which enabled them to undertake a surprise attack with their active forces before the Poles could mobilise their reserves. Moreover, the Poles initiated their mobilisation only on 30 August, two days before the invasion, whereas the Germans had begun five days earlier, on the 25th.

Such were the fundamentals on which the Army's plan for the invasion of Poland were based. The document that detailed them was Deployment Plan White, dated 15 June 1939, which, although under the signature of von Brauchitsch, was the result of the combined efforts of the General Staff and the army group planning staffs. The officers most closely associated with it were Halder, General Karl-Heinrich von Stülpnagel, Chief of Operations, Colonel Hans von Greiffenberg, Head of the Operations Section, and General Kurt von Tippelskirch, Chief of the Intelligence Section. The German plan was simple and direct:

> 'The object of the operation is to destroy the Polish Armed Forces. The political leadership demands that the war should be begun by heavy surprise blows and lead to quick success. The intention is to prevent a regular mobilisation and concentration of the Polish Army by a surprise invasion of Polish territory and to destroy the mass of the Polish Army west of the Vistula-Narev line by a concentric attack from Silesia on the one side and from Pomerania-East Prussia on the other.'[3]

To achieve this, the Germans divided their forces into two army groups – North and South. Two armies, the 3rd under von Küchler and the 4th under von Kluge, formed Army Group North (630,000 men), under von Bock, and these would advance across the Polish Corridor between East and West Prussia and strike south towards Warsaw. Three armies, the 8th under Blaskowitz, the 10th under von Reichenau, and the 14th under List, composed Army Group South (882,000 men), under von Rundstedt, and would strike north, also towards the Polish capital. There, the two arms of the pincer would meet; the final and decisive battle would be fought on the rear of the Poles, with their path of retreat blocked. To ensure that no large enemy forces succeeded in escaping over the Vistula into eastern Poland, thereby frustrating the whole design and possibly endangering the German flanks, two more thrusts, one from the north and the other from the south, would move out behind the river and its tributaries. The Polish forces, therefore, would be caught in a grand, double encirclement; destruction would be total. This was pure *Vernichtungsgedanke*; the German General Staff had represented faithfully the strategic principles of their great master, von Schlieffen.

The force of fifty-two divisions, 1,512,000 men, that marched into Poland on 1 September was the flower of the German Army. It consisted of all fourteen mechanised divisions (as well as an ad-hoc armoured unit, *Panzerverband Kempf*), twenty-three infantry divisions of the First Wave, five of the Second, and nine of the Third, together with one mountain division and one cavalry brigade. These were reinforced later during the fighting by two more infantry divisions of the First Wave, three of the Fourth, and two mountain divisions. Seventy per cent of the force that took part in the campaign were active formations of adequately trained soldiers; the reserve divisions (seventeen out of the final total of fifty-nine) acted mainly as army or army group reserves. Good units though the majority were, however, the thirty-nine infantry divisions that crossed the border on the first day of the war lacked adequate motor transport, and were dependent on some 197,000 horses, which required enough fodder each day to fill 135 railway trucks. It proved impossible to provide each infantry division with enough food for the horses to travel more than 120 miles, with rations for more than ten days in the field, or with ammunition for more than one issue – i.e. 90 rounds per infantryman, 3,750 rounds per machine-gun, and 300 rounds per artillery piece. In comparison, the mechanised formations were given enough petrol and oil to carry them 450 miles, and, because their fuel was of high efficiency in relation to its bulk, further supplies could be delivered quickly by air transport (a Junkers 52 was capable of carrying some 10,000lb). But the mass of the invasion army had no such freedom from logistical restraints; it was closely dependent on the efficient use, and the speedy extension, of the railheads and on the umbilical cord of supply transport between the trains and the advancing troops. Thus, it became dangerous to prolong operations, or to advance far beyond the termination of good railways. The longer the Army remained in the field, the more it became dependent on regular and adequate supply and reinforcement. For the Germans, time was, as it always had been, the essence of military operations.

The outcome of the campaign in Poland was decided in four days; by the seventh, Halder even began to prepare plans for the transfer of divisions to the west; and by the eighteenth all was effectively over. Seldom have military operations gone so nearly to plan as this one: the great mass of the Polish forces was trapped before it could retreat across the Vistula, and by the seventeenth day the outer pincer behind the great river had closed. On that day, too, the armies of the Soviet Union crossed Poland's eastern frontier. From that point, all that was left for the German forces to do was to complete the destruction of the remaining fortifications, which included the city of Warsaw. The Polish capital capitulated on the 27th, and the very next day the guns fell silent throughout the shattered and humiliated country.

The Armed Forces had lived up to the highest expectations. On 5 October a grateful Führer announced to his soldiers: '. . . you have fulfilled the task allotted to you. You have fought bravely and courageously.'[4] Comparisons were made with the old imperial armies, and these, however romantic, were not far off the mark. Decisive manoeuvre and encirclement had characterised the campaign on the ground. Much was made of the battle of the Bzura, the largest, self-contained action of the campaign, a giant battle of encirclement in the bend of the Vistula near Warsaw, which ended with the capture of some 170,000 Polish soldiers and the complete destruction of the Poznan Group, the only major part of the Polish Army that still remained intact and dangerous by 10 September. The traditional German strategy of *Vernichtungsgedanke* had resulted in the largest encirclement battle of annihilation in history until that date. Many more, and greater, were to follow.

The dominant force in the campaign had been the infantry divisions, which formed roughly seventy-five per cent of all formations taking part. In its report on 24 September, OKW gave them the major accolade:

'German infantry formations added one more to their list of triumphs. Their achievements on the march and their endurance of hardships were as great as their achievements on the battlefield. Their courage in attack was supplemented by indomitable and stubborn powers of resistance which no crisis could daunt. Their overwhelming powers of attack were supported by their comrades in arms. Heavy and light artillery lent them valuable assistance. Thanks to their intervention and to the work of the engineers, the fortified frontier positions of the Poles were successfully bombarded, stormed, or overrun in the shortest possible time and the enemy annihilated in a subsequent irresistible pursuit.'[5]

The mechanised forces, by comparison, were assigned second place: 'Armoured and motorised units, cavalry, anti-tank defence, and reconnoitring detachments with their magnificent *cooperation* [author's italics] more than fulfilled the expectations placed in them.'[6]

Because of the Polish dispositions, the area in which the German Army fought was relatively small. Many Polish divisions were encircled within fifty miles of the frontier, and only a few German formations were forced to cover more than 200 miles. Supply, therefore, did not become a problem, nor did the physical deterioration of the foot-bound infantry. Indeed, the marching achievements of the infantry divisions of the First Wave were remarkable, reaching standards expected of veterans. Distances of twenty miles a day were not unknown, and this compares not at all unfavourably with the average of the best performances of the mechanised divisions, which was around twenty-two. It is, perhaps, interesting that von Manstein, while recognising that 'A vital factor in the speed of . . . success was the unorthodox [*sic*] use of big, self-sufficient tank formations supported by a far superior Air Force', nevertheless believed that what was decisive was the 'spirit' of the ordinary German fighting soldiers and their staffs: 'In the German Wehrmacht it had been found possible, with the help of new means of warfare, to *reacquire* [author's italics] the true art of leadership in mobile operations . . . right down to the most junior NCO or infantryman, and in this lay the reason for our success.'[7]

What, then, of the armoured and motorised infantry divisions which, on 1 September, formed some twenty-eight per cent of the invasion force? The mechanised units were distributed along the 1,000 mile front, positioned among the armies in groupings no bigger than corps. Four motorised corps were instituted: XIX, under Guderian, with 4th Army, and XIV, under von Wietersheim, XV under Hoth, and XVI, under Hoepner, all with 10th Army, the one that was to bear the hardest fighting. At the same time *Panzerverband Kempf* and 5th Panzer Division were each given to an infantry corps; 1st Light Division was held in 10th Army's reserve; 10th Panzer was sent to Army Group North's reserve; and 4th Light and 2nd Panzer were grouped with a mountain division in an ordinary corps. The principle of concentration, so earnestly advocated by Guderian, had been disregarded. This was partially corrected shortly after the opening of the campaign, with the formation of XXII (motorised) Corps under von Kleist in 14th Army, composed of 2nd and 5th Panzer and 4th Light, but it still came nowhere near Guderian's ideal. After the war, he wrote to Liddell Hart: 'Concerning the strategy of the panzer forces, I always proposed deep thrusts operating independently of the infantry corps – and never clung with panzer forces to the flank of infantry armies. It is clear, however, that independent operations of panzer troops cannot be too far-reaching if the general disposes of only a small body of them. One or two divisions cannot execute independent operations as well as a panzer army.'[8] The composition of the motorised corps likewise proved to be unsatisfactory; XVI Corps included within its order of battle two infantry divisions, and XIV and XV Corps were composed entirely of light or of motorised infantry divisions.

The campaign was to see no use of the principles of the armoured idea. Certainly, the panzer and motorised divisions played an important role in the ground operations, spearheading three out of the five armies involved, and, certainly, the new concept found tactical expression in Hoepner's corps' advance to Warsaw which covered 140 miles in seven days, in Guderian's long thrust with one motorised and two panzer divisions, which, on one day, managed fifty miles in twelve hours; and in von Thoma's infiltration of some fifty miles by night, through undefended, but thickly wooded, hilly country, to turn the Polish flank at the important Jablunka pass. But there it ended. At every point throughout the campaign the actions of the mechanised forces were subordinated to the strategy of encirclement, and, for most of the time, the movements of the individual units were closely coordinated with those of the mass of the infantry armies to which they were attached. As Liddell Hart recognised: 'The German advance might have travelled still faster but for a lingering conventional tendency to check the mobile forces from driving far ahead of the infantry masses that were backing them up.'[9] The OKH Deployment Directive of 15 June 1939 saw the employment of the mechanised forces only in relation to the movement of the army as a whole. As an example, it stated: 'It is the task of 10th Army with its three motorised corps, using to their fullest capacities the mobility of the mechanised troops, and *in collaboration with* [author's italics] the driving power of armoured formations, to thrust across . . . to reach the Vistula without delay. . . .'[10] Thus, the role of the panzer forces was to spearhead the general advance by the whole army, not to mount any independent action. The OKH plan continued: 'This will lead to the elimination of dispersed enemy units, and the non-motorised detachments will be brought forward as quickly as possible to guard the flank and the rear of the far-advanced mechanised troops.'[11] In other words, all efforts would be made to protect

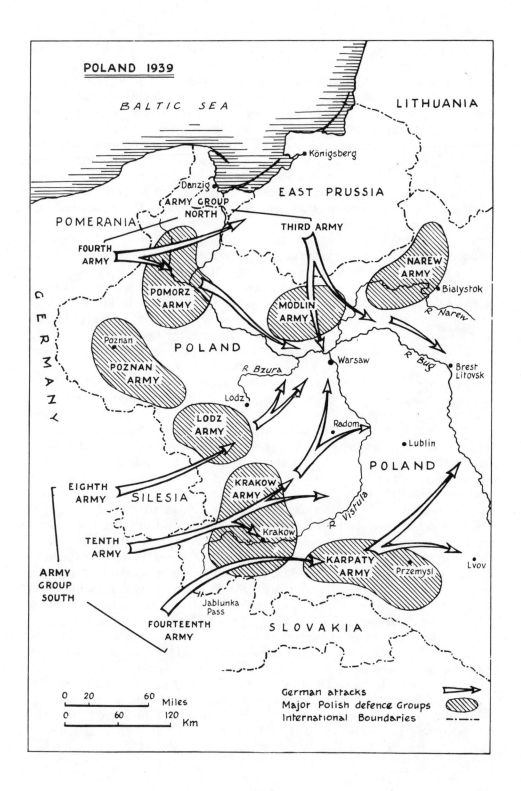

POLAND 1939

BALTIC SEA

LITHUANIA

• Königsberg

Danzig •

EAST PRUSSIA

ARMY GROUP NORTH

POMERANIA

THIRD ARMY

FOURTH ARMY

POMORZ ARMY

MODLIN ARMY

NAREW ARMY

• Bialystok

R. Narew

GERMANY

POLAND

Poznan •

POZNAN ARMY

R. Bzura

Warsaw •

R. Bug

• Brest Litovsk

Lodz •

LODZ ARMY

Radom •

• Lublin

POLAND

EIGHTH ARMY

SILESIA

KRAKOW ARMY

R. Vistula

TENTH ARMY

Krakow •

KARPATY ARMY

Przemysl •

• Lvov

ARMY GROUP SOUTH

R. Vistula

FOURTEENTH ARMY

Jablunka Pass

SLOVAKIA

0   20   60   Miles

0   60   120   Km

German attacks
Major Polish defence Groups
International Boundaries

the flanks of the advance: a sound, traditional military principle basic to *Vernichtungsgedanke*.

During the campaign, the handling of the armoured forces left much to be desired. For example, after the successful conclusion to the battle for the Danzig Corridor, the future employment orders issued by OKH for Guderian's motorised corps stipulated that it was to be kept in close attendance of 3rd Army and held back in cooperation with the infantry divisions. Fear of French intervention in the west caused the High Command to prevent any deep easterly penetration. Despite protests from Guderian and von Bock, the General Staff refused to lift their restrictions, and only after it was clear that Army Group South was not achieving the desired occupation of Warsaw was the northerly mechanised force allowed to undertake a strategic envelopment southwards towards Brest-Litovsk, more than a hundred miles east of the Polish capital. Even then, the OKH envisaged the role of XIX Corps as being merely to protect the flank of Army Group North and to make it possible to resume von Bock's advance into southern Poland without delay. Fear of enemy action against the flanks of the advance, fear which was to prove so disastrous to German prospects in the west in 1940 and in the Soviet Union in 1941, was present from the beginning of the war.

Throughout, the employment of the mechanised units revealed the idea prevalent among the senior army and army group commanders that they were intended solely to ease the advance and to support the activities of the infantry. Many were the occasions of direct cooperation between infantry and panzer. An instance of this was on 15 September, when the headquarters of 10th Army directed an infantry corps to establish a bridgehead over the Bzura to enable a motorised corps to continue the advance on the other side. Motorised divisions were often incorporated within infantry corps (for example, 10th Panzer was attached to XXI [infantry] Corps for a short period). On 15 September, von Bock even decided to divide XIX Corps into two so that it could undertake two separate tasks in conjunction with infantry formations; Guderian reacted strongly against this, but it was only on the conclusion of the campaign that the proposal was dropped. And there were a number of tactical failures in the employment of tanks. The abortive attack on the Mlawa's fortifications on the first day of the campaign, and the foolish attempt to occupy a well-defended Warsaw, in which as many as fifty-seven tanks were destroyed, are the most extreme examples, but others exist, such as a panzer division in Guderian's XIX Corps running out of fuel on only the second day of the advance.

Thus, any strategic exploitation of the armoured idea was still-born. The paralysis of command and the breakdown of morale were not made the ultimate aim of the operational employment of the German ground and air forces, and were only incidental by-products of the traditional manoeuvres of rapid encirclement and of the supporting activities of the flying artillery of the Luftwaffe, both of which had as their purpose the physical destruction of the enemy troops. Such was the *Vernichtungsgedanke* of the Polish campaign.

14

Military Impotence

'The time has come for action – but what action?'
GENERAL FRANZ HALDER
Chief of the General Staff, 1938–42

For the Army High Command, the Second World War opened very differently from the First. In 1914, the Chief of the General Staff had become automatically one of the most important personages of the state; on his abilities had rested the fortunes of the nation at war. In this, he did but follow a distinguished tradition; just as it had been von Moltke the elder and not Wilhelm I who had defeated Austria in 1866 and France in 1870, so it was von Moltke the younger, supported by the ghost of von Schlieffen, and not Wilhelm II who was responsible for the destruction of France and Russia in 1914. And in 1916, it was two generals, von Hindenburg and Ludendorff, who took over the entire war direction of the German Reich from the Kaiser and the politicians. Twenty-three years later, in 1939, the contrast could hardly have been greater. On the fourth day of the war, the Law for the Defence of the Reich was passed, specifically limiting the executive power of the Army Commander-in-Chief to the operational control of his Army, and, furthermore, leaving the definition of that limit to Adolf Hitler, in his role of Commander-in-Chief of the Wehrmacht. Any influence over the wider aspects of war policy was firmly denied to the Army.

Such a law, although of course unwelcome to the generals, merely confirmed the whole style of Hitler's dictatorship from 1938 onwards, and it occasioned little comment. War policy was, after all, a legitimate area of concern for the politicians, and during the Polish campaign it had appeared as if Hitler would limit himself to this sphere of activity and not interfere with the Army's direction of ground operations. The plan of invasion had been drawn up by the General Staff, and, although Hitler had given his agreement to it, he had not interfered in its operational precepts; the Supreme Commander had limited himself merely to planning, to the smallest detail, the attack on a bridge at Dirschau. On the third day of war the Supreme Commander boarded a train, the 'Führer Special', taking with him Keitel and Jodl (men who had contributed nothing to the operational planning of the invasion), their aides, and the liaison officers of the Army and Air Force, as well as his Party associates, 'and set off in a vaguely easterly direction with no definite destination'.[1] Hitler and his OKW chiefs spent their time visiting army and corps headquarters, and met von Brauchitsch only on two occasions. The Supreme Commander took little direct interest in the operational conduct of the Army, limiting his supervision of events to expressions of opinion and exchanges of view. Nor did the OKW act; Halder noted in his diary on 24 August: 'OKW will not interfere in the conduct of operations. OKH will report directly to the Führer.'[2] Hitler's recommendation to increase the force in East Prussia and his intervention in the conduct of von Blaskowitz's 8th Army did not take the form of definite orders, nor did they incur the displeasure of the Army High Command, while his decision to raise Warsaw by bombing, rather than to reduce it by seige, was more in the nature of a political move than a military one. The one man above all others in whose hands lay the direction of operations, the Chief of the General Staff, never even once spoke on the telephone during the entire campaign to Hitler, Keitel, Jodl, or von Vormann, the Army liaison officer on the train.

Such a state of affairs well-suited the Army. No interference from Hitler, or from his bureau, the OKW, or from the Air Force, which was acting primarily in support of the ground forces, left the Army as the dominant service and the unquestioned supreme director of military operations. However, not all was as the generals wished. During the Polish campaign, Halder had noted: 'Strict separation between the political (OKW) and military establishment (OKH) has proved a great drawback. OKH ought to have exact knowledge of the political line and of its possible variations. Otherwise, no planned action on our own responsibility is possible. OKH must not be left at the mercy of the vagaries of politics, else the Army will lose confidence.'[3] This was prophetic, for at the conclusion of one of the most successful campaigns in German history, Hitler struck yet one more blow at the Army's autonomy, this time the most serious in the political-military relationship of the Third Reich. Its importance, so often overlooked, can hardly be exaggerated; it is at this point that the moral culpability of the generals is first brought into question.

On 25 September, the day when Hitler was flying over the Polish battlefields, Halder entered in his diary the simple sentence: 'Information from Warlimont about the Führer's intention to attack the west.'[4] This was the first indication the Army leaders had been given that Hitler had any idea of taking direct military action against France. Two days later, on the day Warsaw fell, the Führer summoned his service commanders to the Reich Chancellery, where he informed them of his decision to 'attack in the west as soon as possible, since the Franco-British Army is not yet prepared'.[5] He even set the date: 12 November. And on 9 October Hitler issued 'Directive No. 6 for the Conduct of the War', which opened: 'Should it become evident in the near future that England, and, under her influence, France also, are not disposed to bring the war to an end, I have decided, without further loss of time, to go over to the offensive. . . . An offensive will be planned on the northern flank of the West Front, through Luxembourg, Belgium, and Holland. . . .'[6] In such a manner was the Army committed to a new campaign, with neither its prior knowledge nor its consent. The Army leaders were dismayed, certain that defeat or, at best, stalemate was the only prospect for such a venture. Seldom, if ever, in the history of warfare has a campaign that was to be won so decisively been entered with such reluctance by the victorious generals as that waged by the Germans in Flanders and France in May 1940.

Until that time, the Army High Command had not considered the west as a future battleground. The war was being fought in Poland, and, although France and Britain had intervened, there were no signs that these countries were prepared to take the offensive. In the final analysis, would the Men of Munich take action at all? Certainly, the generals feared the results of an Allied attack while the bulk of the German Army was occupied in the east, but they had been quite prepared to leave a force in the west of only some forty low-standard divisions sheltering behind the much-vaunted West Wall, fortifications which were, in reality, by no means impenetrable and only partly complete. Moreover, Hitler had previously given no indication that he was intending to invade the west once Poland was reduced to ruins. Indeed, his first War Directive, issued on 31 August, contained the statement '. . . it is important to leave the responsibility for opening hostilities unmistakably to England and France',[7] and on 19 September he had declared in a speech: 'I have neither toward England nor France any war claims, nor has the German nation. . . .'[8] The Army, therefore, acted accordingly. As early as 10 September Halder had begun forming his ideas about 'position warfare' in the west, and on the 24th von Stülpnagel had prepared a detailed memorandum in which he advised against attacking the French defences until the spring of 1942. Von Brauchitsch and Halder therefore resolved to conduct the war, at least for the foreseeable future, on a defensive basis; von Stülpnagel held it advisable not even to question Hitler on the matter; and von Leeb, commander on the Western Front and a leading expert in defensive strategy, submitted a report which confirmed the Army High Command's attitude. The General Staff even went so far as to draw up an order for the partial demobilisation of the Army, although this was withheld from issue at the intervention of Keitel. Then, in late September, came the bombshell: Germany would, indeed, attack in the west, and only some six weeks would be allowed for preparation. It was, as von Leeb recorded, 'insane'.

The Army chiefs' objections to launching the invasion of the west were many and reasonable, and were shared even by Göring. The remarkably successful campaign in Poland, they argued, could not be held as assurance for a future German victory against France and Britain. Halder noted in his diary: 'The technique of the Polish campaign [was] no recipe for the west. No good against a well-knit army.'[9] In contrast with the Poles, the French were generally supposed to possess the largest and strongest army on the continent of Europe, one, furthermore, which was by then fully mobilised, deployed behind the redoubtable Maginot Line, and prepared for an enemy attack. Time, the vital element in strategy, had been lost by the Germans; surprise was gone, and the year so far-advanced that good weather and ground conditions, so important for the conduct of operations, were most unlikely. Nor was the German Army prepared for an onslaught in the west: the deficiencies in supplies and equipment, especially in mechanisation, were acute; the four light divisions were about to undergo transformation into panzer formations, a lengthy process; the refitting of the armoured units which had been in Poland would not be complete for some time; and the number of fully trained men under arms was still not sufficient for such a speedy extension of the war, especially one that, in the generals' opinion, would probably lead to a costly stalemate. On 8 October, the Quartermaster-General submitted to Halder a gloomy report, of which the latter noted: 'Ammunition: We have enough for an operation with about one-third of our divisions, for fourteen combat days, then we shall have a reserve of fourteen more combat days. Current production of ammunition: one combat day for one-third of our divisions.'[10]

Moreover, the Army leaders were disturbed by Hitler's proposals for the violation of neutral Holland and Belgium, with all its unacceptable international consequences. Keitel recorded:

> 'Quite apart from their [the senior generals'] daunting recollections of the First World War, and the strength of the formidable Maginot Line against which there were then virtually no weapons of destruction, they considered that the Army was as yet not capable of launching any fresh assault after its eastern campaign, without a pause to recover, to regroup and remobilise, to finish its training, and to complete its re-equipping. Particular doubts were expressed about winter warfare, with the fog and rain, the short days and the long nights that made mobile warfare virtually impossible. In addition, the fact that the French had not exploited either the good weather or the weakness of our western defences earlier, could only lead us to conclude that they did not really want to fight, and that any attack we might launch would only foul up the prospects of peace talks – probably making them impossible. It was clear to us that the Maginot Line would oblige us to press our attack through northern France, Luxembourg, and Belgium, and possibly even through Holland, with all the consequences we had suffered in the 1914–18 war.'[11]

The decision to attack the west was Hitler's and Hitler's alone. He received advice from on one. Warlimont wrote:

'No one can say on what day the Supreme Commander reached the decision to take the offensive in the west or what influenced him to do so. One thing is quite clear: the Commander-in-Chief of the Army was the man most intimately involved; yet when von Brauchitsch appeared on the train on the 9th and again on 12 September, on the first occasion spending no fewer than two hours alone with Hitler, the latter breathed not a word to him of his intentions. . . . It is also clear that no other senior officer was consulted before the decision was made, in spite of the fact that it was tantamount to no less than a decision to embark on a second World War. . . . Even . . . the Chief of the OKW, the "sole adviser in Wehrmacht matters", had not been told by Hitler but had learnt of it through one of his aides!'[12]

At the time, von Manstein remembered: 'What horrified me was my realisation of the extent to which OKH's status had declined . . . [and] this just after it had conducted one of the most brilliant campaigns in German history!'[13] For Hitler's decision had marked a fundamental departure from what had gone before. Although the Führer had become accustomed to completely disregarding the views of his military advisers, he had hitherto confined this to the political sphere. Now, however, as von Manstein argued:

'. . . the position was quite different. It is true, of course, that the question of how the war should be continued after the defeat of Poland was a matter of *over-all war policy* which ultimately had to be decided by Hitler as the Head of State and Commander-in-Chief of the Wehrmacht. However, if the solution were to be a land offensive in the west, this must depend entirely on *how, when* and *whether* the Army would be able to tackle the task. In these three respects the primacy of the Army leadership was inalienable. Yet in all three Hitler confronted the High Command of the Army with a fait accompli. . . . Without any previous consultation with the Commander-in-Chief, he not only ordered offensive measures in the west, but even decided on the timing and method to be adopted. . . . The Commander-in-Chief of the Army was to be left with merely the technical execution of an operation on which he had deliberately not been consulted and for which, in autumn 1939 at all events, he could certainly not guarantee any prospect of decisive success.'[14]

By his decision, Hitler had extended significantly the process he began in 1938. The Army's operational autonomy was now not only threatened, it was breached. Warlimont recognised this:

'All he [Hitler] was interested in was to reinforce his position in the military field, as in all others, as the man having sole power of command; he did not want expert, responsible advice because, from the Army at any rate, that might sometimes imply opposition and warnings. . . . Instead he was determined to have "unquestioned authority downwards". He decided that during the forthcoming campaign the Commander-in-Chief of the Army should be tied to the same location as Supreme Headquarters and accompanied only by his Chief of Staff and a reduced staff; his real reason was to achieve more rapidly and more surely his object of concentrating power in his own hands, to reduce the General Staff of the Army to the level of an executive mechanism for his decisions and orders. . . .'[15]

Von Manstein moralised: 'Hitler had now taken over the functions which Schlieffen believed could at best be performed in our age by a triumvirate of king, statesman, and warlord. Now he had also usurped the role of the warlord. But had the "drop of Samuel's anointing oil", which Schlieffen considered indispensable for at least one of the triumvirs, really fallen on his head?'[16]

Faced with such a fundamental threat to their position, the reaction of the Army leaders should have been vigorous, for Hitler's intention struck at the very basis of their responsibility to both the nation and the Army. Although war might be the continuation of politics by other means, the conduct of warfare is most certainly not the conduct of politics by other means; Hitler's decision was not one simply of national policy, when it would have been the statesman, and not the soldier, who was accountable to the people for its validity; rather, it was one which directly involved military operational planning and execution, the, till-then, exclusive preserve of the highly-trained group of men at the Army High Command. In this sphere of activity, the senior officers were not to be confined by any narrow concept of unquestioning obedience to the Head of State; instead, they possessed a greater duty to the nation they served and to the troops they led. On the quality of their professional judgement lay the success or failure of their country at war, the well-being and prosperity of their fellow citizens, and the lives and welfare of their soldiers. No oath to Hitler could override this. He might have the prerogative of declaring war, but it was they who had to direct the military movements consequent upon his decision. Such a responsibility, the preserve of a professional Army Commander-in-Chief, could not be taken over by a politician and an amateur, even though he might be the constitutional 'Supreme Commander', especially by one who was so mesmerised by the power of his own intuition that he completely disregarded the military implications of his actions. To allow this to happen would, indeed, be a criminal abnegation of duty on the part of the generals.

The opposition from the military leaders to Hitler's plan for the invasion of the west was immediate. Even the Chief of the OKW could perceive the hazards of his Führer's intentions. Keitel records: '. . . the result was the first serious crisis of confidence between Hitler and myself . . . when I publicly told him what I thought, as I was bound to do, Hitler violently accused me of obstructing him and conspiring with his generals against his plans . . . he began to insult me and repeated the very offensive accusation that I was fostering an opposition group against him among the generals.'[17] If this were the case with Keitel, how much more so was it with Hitler's other military 'advisers'. On 4 October, Jodl told Halder that a 'very severe crisis is in the making' and that the Führer was 'bitter because the soldiers do not obey him'.[18] And certainly the opposition from von Reichenau was extremely disheartening. Hearing that the attack would proceed through Belgium and Holland, von Reichenau, already disillusioned with events, had declared that such a step would be 'veritably criminal'[19] and proceeded to commit himself to its prevention. Characteristically, von Reichenau's opposition was an individual act, unhampered by any ties with organised groups. He was one of the very few to stand up openly and sharply against the Führer, man to man, first on 30 October, then on the 31st, and again on 1st and 3 November. His most disheartening attempt was made on 5 November, when he realised that all was futile: his Führer's mind was fixed and closely resembled a stone wall, unassailable by argument, logical or otherwise. Subvert opposition was von Reichenau's only alternative, and he unhesitatingly adopted that attitude. The next day, the 6th, he met Goerdeler, revealing to him Hitler's plans and suggesting that Germany's enemies be informed of them. Von Reichenau hoped that Hitler would thus be persuaded to abandon his idea if the advantage of surprise could be shown to have been lost. By the 9th von Reichenau's message was on the way to London. Similarly, Warlimont attempted to induce King Leopold III of the Belgians to make an offer of mediation that the Führer would find difficult to refuse. How successful the Deputy Chief of the OKW Operations Staff was, it is impossible to say, but on 8 November the Dutch and Belgian monarchs offered their services of mediation to the belligerent powers.

In the Army High Command all was confusion. The Führer's decision found no favour with either von Brauchitsch or Halder, who were both shaken and unnerved by the situation in which they found themselves. As the days passed, the prospects for a successful attack became increasingly more distant. On 29 September, for example, General Thomas presented a brilliant analysis which revealed the inadequacies of the armament and raw material programme, foremost among which was a shortage of 600,000 tons of steel per month. Nine days later, on 8 October, Colonel Wagner, Chief Quartermaster, submitted a report which argued that the present state of munitions ruled out an offensive for some time to come; supply was enough for only one-third of the available divisions over a period of fourteen days in the field. Other reports reaching the General Staff indicated that the fighting spirit of the troops in Poland had not, in fact, been as promising as initial impressions had indicated; that training and morale in the Replacement Army were not good; that the divisions of the Third Wave could be counted on to hold their positions only if the enemy did not mount a heavy attack; that the divisions of the Fourth Wave needed considerable further training before they would be of any use for even defensive warfare; that only five armoured divisions would be ready to take the field by the middle of November; and that the French artillery was far superior to that of the Germans. Beck, who managed to see most of this information, predicted that an offensive would be turned into a stalemate after a loss of some 400,000 men killed.

By mid-October, von Brauchitsch and Halder had come to an agreement as to what must be done. Of the three choices with which they were faced – to obey orders, to await events, or to attempt a revolt – they chose the second, which would enable them to promote every argument in the cause of peace. Of the two men, von Brauchitsch was set most firmly against the idea of bringing down the régime, believing this to be a negative solution which would expose his country to the enemy. He hoped that it would be possible to dissuade Hitler of his decision, and he may have counted on the weather making it impossible to carry out the offensive until the following spring, by which time a means might have been found to end the war by a political compromise. Halder, on the other hand, was more undecided, and, as subsequent events showed, was inclined to support the idea of a military coup if he and his chief achieved nothing with their chosen option. Such, indeed, was to be the case. Von Brauchitsch made no headway in his representation to the Führer. On 11 October, for example, Halder recorded in his diary: 'Result of conference of the Army Commander with the Führer: Hopeless.'[20] The climax of the Bendlerstrasse's official opposition to Hitler came on 5 November, the day set for deciding to unleash the offensive on the 12th. Von Brauchitsch held a fatal meeting with the Führer, which von Manstein believed caused 'an irreparable breach between Hitler and the generals'.[21] The Army Commander began by reading out a memorandum summarising all his reasons against the venture in the west. Many cogent, thoroughly sensible arguments were advanced, all incontrovertible, but they included one that served to undermine completely the worth of the others. Von Brauchitsch made the mistake of criticising the performance of the infantry during the Polish campaign, accusing it of being over-cautious and insufficiently aggressive. Moreover, he went on, discipline had become exceedingly lax. Whatever the truth, or otherwise, of these assertions, they proved fatal to the Army Commander. Keitel, who was present, recorded:

> 'After the Commander-in-Chief had finished speaking, the Führer jumped up in a rage and shouted that it was quite incomprehensible to him that just because of a little lack of discipline a Commander-in-Chief should condemn his own Army and run it down. . . . he left the room, slamming the door behind him, leaving all of us just standing there. . . . It was plain to me that this signalled the break with von Brauchitsch and that what little confidence there had been between them was finally shattered.'[22]

Von Manstein realised the tactical error made by the Army Commander: 'By raising such objections in the presence of Hitler, a dictator whose self-esteem was already inflated, von Brauchitsch attained precisely the opposite of what he intended. Disregarding all von Brauchitsch's factual arguments, Hitler took umbrage at the criticism he had presumed to direct against his – Hitler's own – achievements [the creation of the new Wehrmacht].'[23] The Army Commander, came out of Hitler's chamber 'chalk white and with twisted countenance'.[24] It was the end of the official opposition.

As indicated by von Reichenau's and Warlimont's individual efforts, the subversive opposition to Hitler had been developing apace since the outbreak of war. The first to plan decisive action was General von Hammerstein, the Army Commander-in-Chief in 1933, who, on 7 September, had taken command of Army Detachment A, an ad hoc force formed for the defence of the West Wall. He spent his few weeks in active command attempting to lure Hitler to his headquarters at Cologne, there, as he later put it, 'to render him harmless once and for all – and even without judicial proceedings'.[25] But the Führer did not get within pistol-shot range of his would-be killer, and in late September von Hammerstein was transferred to the deputy command of Wehrkeis VIII, and then was soon retired.

However, the idea of killing Hitler did not end with the former Army Commander, and during October, whether, and, if so, how to manage the deed became the most widely discussed subject in opposition circles. Halder, even before the evident failure of von Brauchitsch's attempt to make Hitler see reason, began to carry a pistol in his pocket whenever he visited the Reich Chancellery but, as he confessed later, he could not 'as a human being and a Christian . . . shoot down an unarmed man'.[26] Nonetheless, he took steps to prepare for a coup: he concentrated troops within easy reach of Berlin and ordered one Lieutenant-Colonel Groscurth, a member of the Abwehr group, to institute a working party, under the general direction of von Stülpnagel, to draw up a blueprint for the overthrow of the government. Fervent preparations were also made by the other Abwehr resisters, foremost among whom was Oster, in alliance with Beck. By the beginning of November the conspiracy, which had its contacts reaching even into the Vatican, had advanced so far that Halder had committed himself to lead a coup on the 5th of that month, the day of the fatal meeting between Hitler and von Brauchitsch. He had made only one qualification: no action would be taken if the Army Commander succeeded in persuading the dictator to abandon his plans.

The support of the Chief of the General Staff, the second most influential officer in the Army, was essential to the whole conspiracy. Apart from von Brauchitsch, he was the only person in the German Army who could command general support and provide the leadership required for such momentous action. The pressures on this one man were immense. Looking back after the war, Halder felt that at that time he had been faced with two alternatives:

> 'Resignation – the way Beck went – or treacherous murder. In the making of a German officer there are deep and earnest inhibitions against the idea of shooting down an unarmed man. . . . The German Army did not grow up in the Balkans where regicide is always recurring in history. We are not professional revolutionists. Against this speaks the predominantly conservative attitude in which we grew up. I ask my critics, who are still very numerous, what should I have done, i.e. what must I have prevented? Start a hopeless coup for which the time was not ripe, or become a treacherous murderer as a German staff officer, as a top representative of the German General Staff, who would act not only for his own person but as representative of the German tradition? I say honestly, for that I was not fitted, that I have learnt. The idea that was at stake was clear to me. To burden it in the first stage with a political murder, of that as a German officer I was not capable.'[27]

But there was more to it than that. There were very severe practical implications in what Halder was preparing himself to do. Here was he, the Chief of the Army General Staff, proposing a most momentous act – the overthrow, during wartime, of the nation's legally constituted Head of State. The risks to Germany, let alone to the Army, were considerable; failure would be disastrous. Therefore, he had to be quite sure of success. The responsibility was his; history and the nation would judge him accordingly. Was Halder certain of getting the military support he so earnestly required? The Commander-in-Chief of the Army had set his face firmly against any conspiracy; the Commander-in-Chief of the Replacement Army, Fromm, had studiously fostered a non-committal attitude; and of the three army group commanders, von Rundstedt, von Bock, and von Leeb, only the last had promised to follow unreservedly any action Halder might take. Just as disturbing was the state of the Army; the war had made the conspirators position infinitely more difficult. The mass of soldiers knew nothing of their Führer other than the considerable successes under his rule. The campaign in Poland had resulted in a stunning victory, and there was no comprehension of the defeat that might so easily result from a November offensive in the west. Indeed, few had knowledge even of the possibility of that offensive. Only failure would turn the men against Hitler, and this they had yet to experience. Moreover, mobilisation had meant a further dilution of the officer corps and a massive intake of National Socialist indoctrinated youth, giddy with the Reich's victory. Even so resourceful a conspirator as von Witzleben was fearful of the officers 'drunk with Hitler', and had no idea whether, in a crisis, the soldiery would be influenced more by 'the general who attempted a coup or the troop officer babbling Nazi slogans'.[28]

In view of such weighty considerations, it is a matter of some remark that

Halder did in fact commit himself to action on the part of the conspirators. It was a decision requiring much courage, and yet one taken with many reservations. 'What if?' must continually have occupied his mind. The strain told, and by the fatal day, 5 November, his nerves were at breaking-point. At times he seemed on the verge of collapse. Little was needed to shake his resolve, and this Hitler unwittingly provided during his stormy interview with von Brauchitsch. During his tirade against the Army Commander, the dictator had screamed that he knew all about the 'spirit of Zossen' and was determined to crush it. Zossen was the wartime location of the Army High Command, and the spirit referred to was one of defeatism and cowardice. But relayed to Halder, this phrase carried a terrifying significance: Hitler knew all about the plot against him and was prepared to take action. Halder's, by now, finely balanced nerves snapped. All was lost; the conspiracy must be ended immediately, the evidence destroyed. On his return to Zossen, he unhesitatingly took the necessary action. The incriminating plans for the régime's overthrow were consigned to the fire, and all attempts by the other conspirators failed to goad the Chief of the General Staff into renewed action. Two days later, on the 7th, the weather succeeded where the generals had failed, and the western invasion was postponed, to be reconsidered daily until the middle of January, when, on the 16th, it was positively deferred until the spring.

Without the support of the Chief of the General Staff, and without the certainty of backing from the troops, the military opposition had no hope of executing a successful coup. Even the assassination of Hitler by a lone gunman was dismissed as impracticable. Oster described it as 'an act of insanity' with no more than 'one chance in a hundred. You cannot see Hitler alone. And in the antiroom in the presence of adjutants, orderlies, and visitors you would hardly get a chance to shoot.'[29] The risks involved in using a pistol or a bomb were out of all proportion to the chances of success. But what was left? The plans at Zossen had been consigned to the flames; the armoured divisions that had been kept near Berlin were transferred to the west; opposition officers who had been manoeuvred into key positions were being moved to other posts; and, as the weeks passed, the Army leaders' ideas of a putsch receded as their hopes for success in the west grew. By 7 January, after a trip to the front, Halder could record that he envisaged a series of 'really great successes'.[30] Day by day German military preparedness became more imposing, and by mid-January the prospects of a spring offensive had developed from poor to good. As a result, all further attempts to spur von Brauchitsch and Halder into action met with failure, and even the so-called 'X Report', which stated that the Pope was prepared to act as an intermediary provided the National Socialist régime was removed, had no effect. Von Brauchitsch admitted after the war: 'The whole thing was plain high treason. . . . Why should I have taken such action? It would have been action against the German people. Let us be honest. . . . The German people were all for Hitler.'[31]

By 6 November, therefore, official military opposition to Hitler's decision to invade the west was over, the underground conspiracy was effectively rendered impotent, and the Army leadership had resigned itself to carrying out the Führer's orders. Von Brauchitsch had not the personal resources with which to continue to oppose Hitler, as a conversation he held on 16 November testifies: 'But what should I do? . . . None of my generals will speak with me. . . . Will they follow me? . . . I do not know what I should do. . . . Will we again see each other alive?'[32] Halder, likewise, was so nervous and unconvinced of the success of a putsch, that his resolve, once shaken, could not be resurrected. Thus, by default, Hitler was allowed to dominate. Impervious to the formidable array of military arguments, he stuck to his intention; his only concession was to postpone the date of the attack – and then simply because of the weather, over which even the Führer of the Greater German Reich had no control. His resentment of the OKH grew, as also did his suspicion, and, after the 5th, he would not allow the Army to present the daily weather forecasts. Instead, he created a special Reporting Group headed by a top Luftwaffe meteorologist, and went so far as to prohibit the Army weather expert from attending the daily weather briefings. Even then, in case the Luftwaffe relied on meteorological information supplied by the Army officer he was invariably asked for the origin of his sources, and Hitler was always inclined to downgrade its importance. The Führer was also suspicious that the Army High Command was the source of the leak of information about the impending offensive, when it did in fact come, separately, from von Reichenau and the OKW Abwehr section.

The confrontation with von Brauchitsch on 5 November marked the final irreconcilable breach between Hitler and the Army leaders. Goebbels, Göring, and Ley, the Reich Labour Service Chief, also entered the fray. Guderian records the series of lectures organised by the first two, in which 'an almost identical train of thought was apparent, as follows: "The Luftwaffe generals . . . are entirely reliable; the admirals can be trusted to follow the Hitlerite line; but the Party cannot place unconditional trust in the good faith of the Army generals." '[33] The climax of this campaign came on 23 November, when Hitler addressed senior officers of the Wehrmacht in the imposing surroundings of the Reich Chancellery. His determination to attack was reaffirmed: 'My decision is unchangeable. . . . Breach of the neutrality of Belgium and Holland is meaningless. . . . I consider it is possible to end the war only by means of an attack.'[34] For the rest, as von Manstein put it, 'his speech constituted a massive attack not only on OKH but on the generals of the Army as a whole, whom he accused of constantly obstructing his boldness and enterprise'.[35] In one part of his speech, the Führer referred back to von Brauchitsch's blunder of 5 November: 'If the leadership in national life always had the courage expected of the infantryman, there would be no setbacks. When supreme commanders, as in 1914, already begin to have nervous breakdowns, what can one ask of the simple rifleman? . . . With the German soldier I can do everything if he is well led.'[36]

And in the early evening Hitler called back von Brauchitsch and Halder to lecture them further on the 'spirit of Zossen'. The Army Commander tendered his resignation; it was rejected. Not for nothing did Halder note in his diary that this was a 'day of crisis'.[37] OKH was finally intimidated; Hitler's disillusion irreversible.

Among the rest of the audience, reaction to Hitler's open condemnation of 23 November was mixed. Some, such as General Hermann Hoth, found the occasion inspiring, but others were profoundly depressed at the criticisms voiced. Only a very few took matters further. One, Guderian, managed to see the Führer. He told him: 'I have since talked to a number of generals. They have all expressed their astonishment and indignation that so outspoken a distrust of themselves should exist among the leading personalities of the government, despite the fact that they have only recently proved their ability and risked their lives for Germany in the Polish campaign. . . .'[38] For twenty minutes Hitler listened to him without interruption and then, on Guderian's conclusion, placed the blame entirely on von Brauchtisch's shoulders: 'It's a question of the Army Commander-in-Chief.' Replacements were suggested to Hitler, but none was found acceptable. Von Reichenau, for example, was 'quite out of the question'.[39] Then the dictator began a long tirade against his military advisers, beginning with the trouble von Fritsch and Beck had caused him over rearmament and ending with the difference of opinion over the offensive in the west. The interview was then concluded, and Guderian retired 'deeply depressed'[40] by the insight he had gained.

Hitler and his Party leaders were not the only men to range themselves against the Army command; the chiefs of the OKW did so, too. Keitel, for all his early misgivings, withdrew into silence and, along with his deputy, stood firmly behind the Supreme Commander and his decision. Jodl firmly rejected OKH's arguments, noting in his diary for 18 October: 'Even though we may act one hundred per cent contrary to the doctrine of the General Staff, we shall win this war because we have better troops, better armament, stronger nerves, and decisive leadership which knows where it is going.'[41] Warlimont, by now thoroughly disillusioned with the situation at OKW, wrote that Keitel and Jodl 'were the men who, when Blomberg departed, had worried and fought for a unified command of the Wehrmacht; yet now their actions were a major factor in destroying its solidarity'.[42] Friction between OKH and OKW mounted, the former resentful at what it considered to be unwarranted and unsound interference, the latter annoyed at what it believed to be hide-bound conservatism and lack of faith in the Führer. Indeed, the position had become extremely difficult for the Army High Command.

Hitler's decision when and how to attack the west had signalled his intention to take over command of the Army himself. As Warlimont argued:

'If this was in fact his intention he ought at the same time to have taken over OKH or the General Staff of the Army, as being by far the most effective command organisation in the Wehrmacht, and have cut OKW out of these questions. . . . it would have provided the best possible core for the Supreme Headquarters which was in process of forming, and it would have given the Army General Staff the position which it merited. The procedure adopted by Hitler in encroaching on the preserves of the Army was exactly the opposite. . . . Jodl . . clearly looked on this development as a considerable step forward in the process of cutting the Army staff down to size . . . and [seized] every opportunity to push himself into the chair of command of the Army. The door was now wide open to those "irresponsible back-stairs influences" against which Beck had warned.'[43]

Thus did the OKW begin to supplant the OKH. Hitler did not meet von Brauchitsch to discuss matters pertaining to the Army from 5 November to, at the earliest, 18 January the following year – an impossible situation for any service chief. The Army Commander possessed no automatic right of direct access to the Führer, appearing only when he was summoned. In his place came Keitel and, more important, Jodl. At the meetings where the daily situation reports were presented, Jodl became the principal reporting officer and no representative of the Army was allowed to attend; and when, on 21 October, the time came for the Army to present its intentions for Operation Yellow, the attack in the west, it was Keitel, and not von Brauchitsch, who did so (the Army Commander staying away to indicate his disagreement with the plan). Hitler's comments and alterations were then relayed back to OKH. In such a manner did the planning for the western offensive proceed, the OKW becoming the official channel for the Supreme Commander's intentions, the Army Command waiting on its every instruc-tion – and all this despite the fact that the Wehrmacht Operations Staff had neither the manpower nor the resources, nor the cooperation from the other services, required to undertake efficiently such important work. Moreover, communication between OKW and OKH was poor; Warlimont noted that although 'Jodl always treated Halder outwardly with all military courtesy . . . his diary shows that only once during these eight or nine months did he have any prolonged discussion with him. Equally, there was only one meeting between Jodl and Halder's principal subordinate, General von Stülpnagel, and this took place only after an agreement on improved cooper-ation had been reached between Keitel and Halder.'[44] Even the words used by Hitler and his OKW chiefs when addressing the Army Command, either verbally or in writing, indicated a complete disregard for its prerogatives. At one point Jodl went so far as to propose names for appointments to senior Army commands. It was not for nothing that Warlimont wrote that OKW 'had a tendency to take over responsibility for the operational plans and measures of the Army General Staff, or even . . . to cut the Army out altogether and take over the Army's job'.[45] Warlimont's words found true expression in the planning and direction of the invasions of Norway and Denmark. Here, for the first time, but not the last, OKH was totally eclipsed by OKW. Hitler had taken full operational control.

Hitler had not intended to go to war with Norway and Denmark – they were small, neutral countries posing no threat to the security of the Reich – but by the spring of 1940 several developments had made the occupation of Norway imperative. First, in November 1939, the Soviet Union had attacked Finland and there were fears that, under the pretext of aiding the Finns, the Allies might violate Norwegian neutrality and attack Germany's northern flank. Second, Norway was vital to the traffic in iron ore between Sweden and Germany, and any enemy occupation of that country would seriously disrupt the Reich's war production. Lastly, the Navy was pressing for bases beyond the North Sea so as to attack the Atlantic sea-lanes, and Admiral Raeder stressed the suitability of the Norwegian fiords and ports. The final decision to invade was taken on 19 February, following hard on the British Navy's daring raid on the *Graf Spee's* auxiliary supply ship, the *Altmark*, then stationed in Norwegian territorial waters. The inclusion of Denmark in the plan appears to have been due to the desire both to reinforce the security of the Baltic and to gain valuable advanced fighter bases for an extension of the Luftwaffe's defence network. The invasion of the two countries duly took place on 9 April; Denmark fell in a day, Norway in a month, at a cost to the Armed Forces of 1,317 killed, 2,375 missing, and 1,604 wounded. The infallibility of the Führer's judgement, and the success of his ventures, then appeared to be established beyond all reasonable doubt.

For the Army Command, however, although nine of its divisions, two of its corps headquarters, and an assortment of supporting units, including a rifle brigade and a tank battalion, took part in the battle and acquitted themselves well, the campaign was a disaster. It was excluded from all advance knowledge and planning of the operation, as well as the direction of its own troops. Hitler, through OKW, took direct control. Thus was reached the logical conclusion to the events of January-February 1938.

Hitler never set out his reasons for deliberately excluding OKH from any influence over *Weserübung* (Exercise Weser), the code designation of the operation, but they were clear enough. As Warlimont recorded: 'This had been the first attempt on the part of the dictator to subordinate the organisation for command and leadership of an operation in war to his own personal ambition and thirst for political prestige.'[46] In the pursuit of this, there was no place for the Army Command. On 13 December 1939 Hitler had ordered that 'investigations on how to seize Norway should be conducted by a very restricted staff group'[47] at OKW; by the middle of January, its study, an outline plan for the occupation of Norway, had been completed, to be further developed by a working staff headed by a Luftwaffe general, with a naval officer as chief of staff and an operations officer from the Army. Hitler rejected this arrangement, and required that the staff should be organised on the basis of equality for the three services, and be under the overall command of the Chief of OKW. On the 27th the Führer issued an OKW directive to the three service commanders, stating that the operations in the north would be carried out 'under my immediate and personal influence'.[48]

However, the operations staff at OKW were quite incapable, in numbers, organisation, and experience, to undertake the planning for such a complicated combined operation as 'Weser'. On 19 February Jodl reached the conclusion that rapid results could be achieved only by a properly organised headquarters with the necessary resources: in other words, an Army command under the guidance of the Army General Staff. Warlimont wrote:

> 'At last after all this vacillation, the Army had ... become the central factor in this undertaking. OKW did not, however, turn to the Commander-in-Chief of the Army who, in view of the special nature of the operation, would undoubtedly have detailed at least an army group or army headquarters for the job; instead they acted entirely on their own and detailed a corps headquarters, i.e. the lowest level of command organisation which could possibly have been considered. . . . Jodl and the Head of the Personnel Section saw in this an opportunity to present themselves as new-style officers on the Hitler model, as opposed to the ordinary run of Army officers, by proposing the *man* who in their view was most suitable for the job irrespective of his *rank*. OKH was merely told that "the Führer wishes to speak to General von Falkenhorst since he is an expert on Finland". This form of words was used to conceal Hitler's real intentions. . . . He [Falkenhorst] and XXI Corps headquarters [now nominated Group XXI], into which was incorporated the previous Special Staff, then set to work, still in close cooperation with Section L; this produced the extraordinary picture that the Supreme Commander relied for all matters concerning the participation of the Army in the Norwegian operation not on the Army General Staff, but on a corps headquarters, and the latter under OKW was responsible for overall command of the operation!'[49]

On 21 February, the day when von Falkenhorst presented himself to the Führer, Halder noted angrily in his diary: 'Not a single word has passed between the Führer and the Commander-in-Chief of the Army on this subject [the projected invasion]; this must be put on record for the history of the war. I shall make a point of noting down the first time the subject is broached.'[50] That date was to be 2 March, at a meeting between Keitel and von Brauchitsch, when the former presented OKW's demand for seven divisions, a motorised brigade and sundry other units, a requirement that had already been worked out with Fromm, Commander of the Replacement Army, behind OKH's back. Jodl recorded that the reaction of the Army leaders was furious.

Furious they might have been, but compared with Göring and the Luft-waffe commanders they were mildness itself. In an unconvincing jus-tification of their actions, OKW had announced that 'Headquarters XXI Corps is to be placed under OKW in order to avoid difficulties with the Luftwaffe',[51] and a few days later they subordinated the Air Force units to von Falkenhorst. Göring, his pride injured and his prerogatives endangered, would have none of this; after a short, sharp battle it was decided that the Luftwaffe formations would receive their orders from the Luftwaffe High Command, to which organisation all requests for air support would have to be addressed. The Army, on the other hand, gained no such concession, and, moreover, did not demand one. Not one point in its favour was conceded by Hitler and the OKW, who until the conclusion of the campaign maintained their determination to be directly responsible for command. The OKH lamely acquiesced. As a result, 'the Commander-in-Chief of the Army was pushed completely out into the cold; for instance, he was not even sum-moned to attend Hitler's final conference on 2 April with the Commanders-in-Chief and General von Falkenhorst. . . . Yet he raised no objections.'[52]

In such a manner did full operational control of a major operation fall to one man and his staff antipathetic to the interests of the Army. During its execution the Führer took close interest in all that went on and, as Jodl wrote, insisted 'on giving orders on every detail'.[53] But how did this man, whose proudest boast was that he possessed an intuitive appreciation of the situation in complete disregard to 'General Staff defeatism',[54] cope for the first time with the rigours of military high command? Warlimont, who was close to him that April, remembered that the periods of crisis during the campaign produced in him 'a spectacle of pitiable weakness lasting more than a week',[55] and that had it not been for Jodl, who rose to the occasion, events might have taken a somewhat different turn. Warlimont remembers a visit to the Reich Chancellery when he saw the Führer – the Supreme Commander – sitting 'hunched on a chair in the corner , unnoticed and staring in front of him, a picture of brooding gloom. He appeared to be waiting for some new piece of news which would save the situation, and in order not to lose a moment intended to take it on the same telephone line as his Chief of Operations Staff. I turned away in order not to have to look at so undignified a picture.'[56] Field-Marshal Lord Wavell once wrote that 'The first essential of a general is the quality of robustness, the ability to withstand the shocks of war';[57] Hitler lacked that, even from the beginning.

The crisis of nerves had begun on 14 April, when it was realised that General Eduard Dietl and his 3rd Mountain Division were cut off in the Norwegian port of Narvik, and that ten destroyers, an entire group, had been lost there. Jodl noted that 'Hitler became terribly agitated',[58] and Halder wrote: 'General von Brauchitsch returns from a meeting with the Führer. Result: it is not thought possible to hold Narvik. "We have had bad luck" (Hitler's words).'[59] Hitler's first reaction was that Narvik should be aban-doned and Dietl's men be made to fight their way southwards down the coast to Trondheim, an idea which Jodl rejected emphatically. The tension mounted. On the 17th the Chief of OKW Operations Staff wrote: 'Further argument regarding the orders to be given to the Narvik group. Every unfavourable piece of information makes the Führer fear the worst.'[60] To this was added controversy over the civilian administration of occupied Norway, which, on the 19th, caused Keitel to turn his back on his Führer and walk out of the room. Jodl's diary entry for the day included: 'We are once more facing complete chaos in the command system. Hitler insists on giving orders in every detail; any coordinated work by the existing military command set-up is impossible.'[61] Furthermore, when operations began to turn out badly, Hitler, for the first time, exhibited his propensity to blame everyone but himself, and during the Narvik battle he criticised the Navy for not having taken energetic action. It was a story often repeated. As events proved, Jodl was correct in his handling of the situation; the campaign was won in spite of Hitler's amateurish interventions. But, as Warlimont pointed out, it should always be remembered that had Hitler had his way, Narvik, the decisive point of the operation, would have been evacuated needlessly after only a few days, and the entire operation might well have foundered. Such a man was the Supreme Commander.

The Army leaders had lost the battle for control over ground operations. It had been an easy victory for Hitler. To the generals' political impotence was now added a far more serious charge: command impotence. From this time on, the fate of the individual soldier, of the various formations that composed the Army, and, consequently, of the entire German nation, rested on shoulders ill-suited to bear it. The senior generals had abdicated their own heavy responsibility with an acquiescence that defies justification. Not one of them resigned; not one acted decisively to prevent such a dangerous transfer of power. The judgement of history must surely be that expressed by a German, Helmut Lindemann, who wrote in 1949:

> 'It is astonishing that the generals always speak only of their military duty toward their superiors but not of their duty to the soldiers entrusted to them, most of whom were the flower of the people. One can certainly not require anyone to kill the tyrant, if his conscience forbids him to do so. But must one not require of these men that they expend the same care and scrupulousness on the life of every single man among their subordinates? The reproach of not having prevented the slaughter of many hundreds of thousands of German soldiers must weigh heavily on the conscience of every single German general.'[62]

15

The West – The Plans

'Better rashness than inertia; better a mistake than hesitation'.

DIE TRUPPENFÜHRUNG

As was consistent with Hitler's adoption of responsibility for the operational employment of the Army, the first plan drawn up by OKH for the invasion of the west followed closely the three guidelines laid down by the Supreme Commander. These were stipulated clearly in Hitler's 'Directive No. 6 for the Conduct of the War', dated 9 October 1939. First, that the offensive be carried out 'without further loss of time' (before Christmas and preferably on 12 November); second, that it take place 'on the northern flank of the Western Front, through Luxembourg, Belgium and Holland'; and third, that its purpose 'be to defeat as much as possible of the French Army and of the forces of the Allies fighting on their side, and at the same time to win as much territory as possible in Holland, Belgium, and northern France, to serve as a base for the successful prosecution of the air and sea war against England and as a wide protective area for the economically vital Ruhr'.[1] This was confirmed subsequently by other directives, in particular No. 10, issued in February 1940, which included the following: 'The objective . . . is to deny Holland and Belgium to the English by swiftly occupying them; to defeat, by an attack through Belgium and Luxembourg territory, the largest possible forces of the Anglo-French Army, and thereby to pave the way for the destruction of the military strength of the enemy.'[2]

Within these imposed limits, the original OKH plan was adequate, despite the barrage of adverse comment that it has received since the war, not only from historians but also from German generals, including, astonishingly, Halder himself. One fact, arising directly out of Hitler's specifications, should be remembered: the plan was not one aimed at the occupation of the whole of France; it was one with a limited territorial objective – the acquisition of Holland, Belgium, and northern France only. Thus, although it had some superficial similarities with the famous Schlieffen Plan carried out in 1914 (both were based on an advance through Belgium and both placed the main effort on the right wing), there was no intention of any vast encircling movement extending up to the Swiss border that would end in the total downfall of the French. Indeed, the OKW minutes for 27 September 1939 reveal that: 'From the very beginning it is the Führer's idea not to repeat the Schlieffen plan but to attack . . . through Belgium and Luxembourg under strong protection of the southern flank, and to gain the Channel Coast.'[3] Fundamentally, the plan lacked any far-reaching strategic conception; all future movements were left completely unspecified.

The OKH plan for *Fall Gelb* (Operation Yellow) was dated 19 October 1939. Its preamble reflected the Führer's directive: its intention was 'to defeat the largest possible element of the French and Allied armies and simultaneously to gain as much territory as possible in Holland, Belgium, and northern France as a basis for successful air and sea operations against England and as a broad protective zone for the Ruhr'.[4] The main objective of the initial attack was to secure central Belgium by means of a large pincer operation around Liège, with the main weight in the north. Then, the three armies (37 divisions), comprising Army Group B, were to concentrate north and south of Brussels so as to continue the offensive westwards without delay. In the second phase of the attack a thrust would be directed at Ghent and Bruges. The task of Army Group A (27 divisions) to the south would be to guard Army Group B's left flank. Meanwhile Holland would be occupied in a separate operation by Army Detachment N (North), a small force of three divisions. No attack would be made on the Maginot Line. A total of seventy-six divisions would take part in the operation, including those of the reserve. This plan, however, was a hasty improvisation, and when von Brauchitsch and Halder were summoned by Hitler on 25 October to discuss the coming offensive, they were clearly dissatisfied with it. They knew, for example, that it lacked organisational depth and made no provision for adequate reserves. Halder saw little purpose for Army Detachment N, and doubted whether it would be able to continue an advance to Amsterdam if the Dutch flooded the approaches. He also favoured a stronger concentration of motorised forces in the direction of Ghent (north of Liège) so as to carry out an encirclement manoeuvre more effectively. At the meeting with the Führer, no firm conclusions were reached, but Hitler strenuously advocated a concentration of the attack south of Liège in order to break through in a westerly direction. This meant that the operational *Schwerpunkt* (the decisive point) would be in the centre of the German front, and any hope of a wide-flanking manoeuvre, such as hoped for by Halder, would be out of the question. Hitler's somewhat vague reasoning was that, because the most important task was not to occupy the Belgian-French coast but to defeat large sections of the enemy forces, there should be a breakthrough both north and south of Liège. Further meetings took place on the 27th and 28th, when Hitler again advanced his proposal with such force that it might be regarded as a fourth stipulation to add to the three already advanced in Directive No. 6. On the 29th, a revised OKH plan was issued giving effect to the Supreme Commander's new instruction.

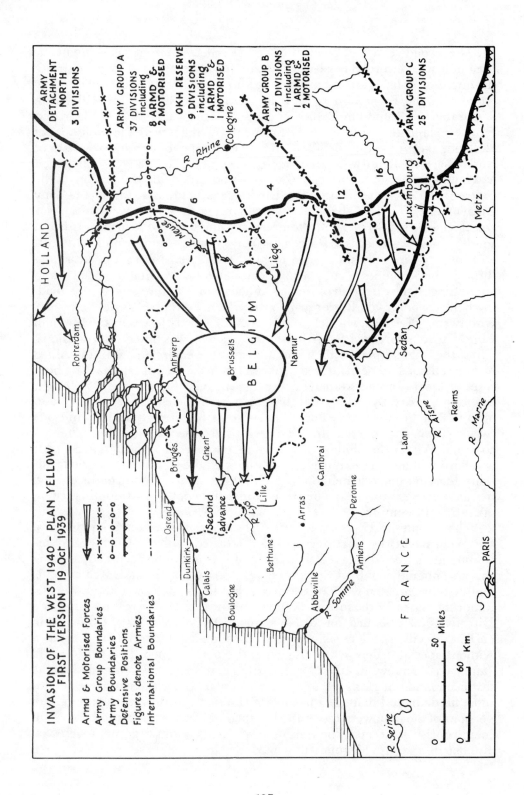

INVASION OF THE WEST 1940 - PLAN YELLOW
FIRST VERSION 19 Oct 1939

Armd & Motorised Forces
Army Group Boundaries   x—x—x—x
Army Boundaries   o—o—o—o
Defensive Positions
Figures denote Armies
International Boundaries   —·—·—·—

ARMY DETACHMENT NORTH
3 DIVISIONS

ARMY GROUP A
37 DIVISIONS including
8 ARMD & 2 MOTORISED

OKH RESERVE
9 DIVISIONS including
1 ARMD & 1 MOTORISED

ARMY GROUP B
27 DIVISIONS including
1 ARMD & 2 MOTORISED

ARMY GROUP C
25 DIVISIONS

HOLLAND

Rotterdam

R. Rhine
Cologne

R. Meuse

Liège

Luxembourg

Metz

2
6
4
12
16
I

BELGIUM

Antwerp

Brussels

Namur

Sedan

Bruges
Ghent

Osrend

Dunkirk

Calais

Boulogne

Bethune

R. Lys
Lille

Second advance

Arras

Cambrai

Peronne

Amiens

Abbeville

R. Somme

FRANCE

Laon

R. Aisne

Reims

R. Marne

PARIS

R. Seine

50 Miles
60 Km
0

The second version of Operation Yellow reflected Hitler's new intent. Its preamble was reworded to read: 'All available forces will be committed with the intention of bringing to battle on north French and Belgian soil as many sections of the French Army and its allies as possible. This will create favourable conditions for the further conduct of the war against England and France on land and in the air.'⁵ The principal changes were the avoidance of Holland, except for the so-called 'Maastricht appendix', a narrow strip of land between Belgium and Germany (this was at Halder's suggestion, which had found favour with Hitler) and, most important of all, the placing of the centre of gravity of the invasion south of Liège rather than to the north. Army Detachment N was disbanded; Army Group B, under von Bock, was enlarged to forty-two divisions (four armies) and directed to drive north and south of Liège westwards to the coast; Army Group A, under von Rundstedt, with twenty-three divisions (two armies) was given the task of attacking through the Ardennes corner of southern Belgium, crossing the Meuse and continuing in the direction of Reims-Amiens, while at the same time providing flank cover for von Bock's army group; Army Group C under von Leeb, with twenty divisions, was left to tie down the enemy forces in the Maginot Line. The total force, with ten divisions in reserve, was ninety-five divisions. Thus, the original plan, which had aimed at the encirclement of the Allied northern flank, had been altered to one that relied on a frontal attack on both sides of Liège. In von Manstein's words, the operational intention 'might best be expressed by saying that the Anglo-French elements we expected to meet in Belgium were to be floored by a (powerful) straight right, while our (weaker) left fist covered up. The territorial objective was the Channel coastline. What would follow this first punch we were not told.'⁶ Such a plan was hardly imaginative, nor was it in line with the German strategic tradition of decisive encirclement ending with the total destruction of the enemy; it was, however, the result of Hitler's interference in, and dominance of, operational planning.

The second OKH plan met with instant opposition from all quarters of the Wehrmacht; even Hitler was not satisfied with it. Göring and his commanders were dismayed that Holland was not to be occupied, arguing that this not only enabled England to take possession of the Dutch airfields and thereby threaten western Germany, but that it denied to the Luftwaffe important bases for the future conduct of the war. Thus, in reaction, Hitler's Directive No. 8, issued on 20 November 1939, stated that: 'Contrary to earlier directives, all measures planned against Holland may be taken without special orders when the general offensive opens.'⁷ At the end of January 1940 a revised OKH version of the plan specifically provided for the fast occupation of Holland, and detailed an army for the assignment. But more fundamental than the question of Holland was the criticism that both versions of the plan were too limited in their objectives and would not result in any decisive success. The leading proponents of this argument were von Rundstedt and his chief of staff, von Manstein, strongly supported by men

Left: Hitler at the Front in Poland. *Below:* Infantry and tanks in attack, Poland 1939.

Above: Obsolete equipment: old armoured cars dating from the early 1920's during the Polish campaign. *Below:* German infantrymen taking cover during the opening phase of Operation White, September 1939. The machine gun is the MG 34 in a heavy support role.

Above: A 15cm heavy infantry gun in action on the Polish plains. *Below:* German cavalry; these cavalrymen are probably engaged in reconnaissance duties, for which they were used in Poland.

Above left: Hitler takes the salute during the victory parade in Warsaw on 5th October 1939. *Above right:* The Chief of the General Staff, General Franz Halder, and the Commander-in-Chief of the Army, Walter von Brauchitsch, studying a map of Europe during the planning of the invasion of the west. *Left:* Tanks and infantry advance during the invasion of Norway, the first campaign conducted by the Wehrmacht High Command. *Opposite top:* Operation Yellow begins: infantrymen of Army Group B move, under cover of smoke, towards the enemy, May 1940. *Opposite bottom:* Crossing the Meuse under fire.

Opposite top: Tanks of Army Group A at the beginning of the advance to the Channel. The leading machine is a PzKw 35 (t) captured Czech model. *Opposite bottom:* Infantry in the attack, securing the flanks of Army Group A's thrust. *Top:* French prisoners surrendering. *Left:* A pioneer of Army Group C storming the Maginot line, June 1940.

Top right: Field Marshal Gerd von Rundstedt, the Army's most senior general and an able army group commander. Top left: Field Marshal Ewald von Kleist, who, as a general, was responsible for the armoured drive to the Channel in 1940. Bottom right: Field Marshal von Leeb. Bottom left: Field Marshal von Bock.

such as Guderian. Their fight to have their ideas accepted lasted from the end of October until mid-February, and lost none of its intensity with the passage of time.

The argument advanced by von Rundstedt and von Manstein was simple. As they saw it, the fundamental shortcoming of the existing OKH plan 'according to Hitler' was that it would lead to a frontal encounter between the German and enemy forces in Belgium; this would allow the Allies to retreat back to the Somme in northern France and, while the German attack might be able to secure the Channel coast, the Allied armies would still remain intact on a line from Sedan to the Somme estuary. A strong enemy counter-attack north-eastwards into the weak hinge of the German line centred on the northerly end of the Maginot Line might well result in the bottling-up of German forces in Belgium. Furthermore, the plan lacked the decisive advantage of strategic surprise. Allied commanders had anticipated that, in order to avoid the Maginot Line, the Germans would be forced to turn the barrier by means of an advance through Holland and Belgium, and then proceed to attack northern France to gain control of the Channel and North Sea coastline. From the outbreak of war, it had been clear that Allied deployment had been determined by anticipation of such a threat. In short, the two men believed that the plan possessed little chance of achieving a decisive victory in the German tradition, and that it was positively dangerous to German prospects. In its place von Rundstedt and von Manstein proposed moving the *Schwerpunkt* of the assault to the south, where it would be faced by relatively weak enemy forces. There, a strong Army Group A (with three armies and two strong armoured corps) would launch a surprise attack through the Ardennes, cross the Meuse at Sedan, cut through northern France to the coast below the Somme, and then encircle the Allied forces that had already been drawn into central Belgium to meet a subsidiary attack there from Army Group B. Also, a strong southern wing would be better able to check any French counter-attack from the south-east. To achieve all this, Army Group A would have to be reinforced to three armies, including a high proportion of the mechanised units. As von Rundstedt wrote in a letter to von Brauchitsch on 31 October, which marked the opening round of the 'battle', the success of the whole operation depended 'on whether it will be possible completely to defeat and annihilate the enemy forces north of the Somme, not merely to push back their front line'. Therefore 'the main effort of the whole operation . . . must be on the southern wing'.[8] In the succeeding three months, the Army High Command was to be kept constantly aware of this alternative plan for the operation, one that was contrary to Hitler's intention, but which was nevertheless true to the German strategic tradition.

For a long time, the proposals emanating from Army Group A met with nothing but scepticism from OKH. It should be remembered that, while von Rundstedt and von Manstein were advocating their proposals, the Supreme Commander and the Army Command were preparing for the offensive which, until its firm postponement in mid-January, was never more than two weeks away. Under such pressure it is difficult to change in its entirety an intricate operational plan, involving vast numbers of troops, as well as supplies and communications on a considerable scale. Moreover, the new idea called for a massive, wide-ranging sweep on the part of Army Group A which required not only good weather and good ground, but also a sufficient number of mechanised troops with which to spearhead the advance; none of these could be relied on until the spring of 1940. These dangers were minimised in the existing plan, but emphasised by the von Rundstedt-von Manstein variant. Halder foresaw other difficulties. First, the enemy intentions were not known, and there was no guarantee that their northern forces would advance into Belgium as anticipated (indeed, the Allies had no such plan until mid-November); second, there were immense logistical difficulties to any major advance through the Ardennes to the coast – one of the advantages of the OKH plan was that it placed the main effort where there were adequate roads and railways to support a major attack; and, in view of the strength of the Allies and, until early 1940 at least, the relative weakness of the Germans, a daring plan dependent on one manoeuvre, which sought total victory at the risk of total defeat, was not acceptable – the existing plan at least avoided the risk of putting all eggs into one basket. But, most important of all, the new proposals were not in accord with the Führer's stated conditions.

For his part, Hitler failed to comprehend immediately the possibilities of a southern sweep. Ironically, when meeting his Army leaders on 25 October, the Supreme Commander had asked whether it would be possible to do exactly what Army Group A proposed a few days later, namely to envelop Belgium and the enemy forces from the south, by means of a drive through the Ardennes westward and then north-westward. However, he immediately expressed his own doubts about the project, asked OKH to examine its potential, and then felt disinclined to pursue the matter when it was rejected by the Army Command. From that time on, Hitler rather fumblingly moved towards the idea that an attack through the Ardennes by way of Sedan might be advantageous, but, typically, he did not pursue this to its logical conclusion – that the main weight of the attack should be placed there from the outset – and this despite the fact that, at least from 27 November, he was aware of Army Group A's proposals. Nevertheless, he remained dissatisfied with the plan of 29 October, as did everyone else, although it met all his requirements. The day after it was issued, Jodl noted in his diary: 'The Führer comes with a new idea about having one armoured and one motorised division attack Sedan via Arlon.'[9] By 11 November this proposal had matured sufficiently for OKH to order: 'The Führer has now decreed: on the southern wing . . . a third group of mobile troops will be formed [the other two were with Army Group B, detailed to attack north and south of Liège] and will advance in the direction of Sedan.'[10] A third version of the OKH plan was accordingly issued on 15 November. The idea that the

Schwerpunkt might be shifted to the south gained momentum, and in Directive No. 8, dated 20 November, Hitler announced that: 'All precautions will be taken to enable the main weight of attack to be switched from Army Group B to Army Group A should the disposition of enemy forces at any time suggest that Army Group A could achieve greater success.'[11] This was the state in which Operation Yellow remained until 16 January, when it was definitely postponed until the spring. A fourth edition issued on 20 January did not differ materially from its predecessor. The concessions towards the southern attack continued to be totally inadequate: the one armoured formation placed there, Guderian's XIX Army Corps, was not made strong enough to exploit any success by advancing to the Channel, and the main weight of the attack remained with von Bock in Belgium, to be changed only if he ran into difficulties during the operation. However, Hitler was still subject to nagging doubts about the plan. Jodl, a staunch opponent of any *Schwerpunkt* in the south, recorded in his diary for 13 February: Führer 'says most of the gun-armed tanks have been expended on places which are not decisive. The armoured divisions with 4th Army [south of Liège] can do little in areas where there are obstructions and fortifications. They will come to a standstill on the Meuse, if not before, and will have to be withdrawn. . . . They should be concentrated in the direction of Sedan, where the enemy does not expect our main thrust.'[12]

It was at this point, in mid-February, that a number of events occurred to produce the new, and final, version of Operation Yellow. First, the forced landing in Belgium on 10 January of an aircraft carrying a staff officer with papers relating to the OKH plan produced doubt as to how much the Allies now knew of the German intentions; second, the postponement of the operation on 16 January owing to the weather, to the incident on the 10th, and to the obvious lack of surprise; and, third, OKH, dubious of its own plan and apprehensive of enemy preparations, had held map exercises at each of the army group headquarters for a ten-day period in the first half of February, and these had revealed that the present disposition of forces would result in a loss of time and opportunities in the event of an offensive.

Von Brauchitsch and Halder were at last convinced of the soundness of Army Group A's proposals and drew up new plans accordingly. Indeed, so convinced was OKH, by then, of the importance of the southern *Schwerpunkt* that it produced an outline of operations which was considerably more drastic, relying upon a greater concentration of force, than anything ever proposed by von Rundstedt and von Manstein: the line between Army Groups A and B was moved northwards; 4th Army, the strongest of von Bock's four armies, was transferred to von Rundstedt, as also were most of the mechanised formations, which were to be concentrated for a grand assault across the Meuse north of Sedan; 2nd Army was brought down, also from Army Group B, ready to be deployed in Army Group A's sector as soon as the front was broadened in attack. The Channel coast south of the Somme estuary and the Allied rear were the new objectives. To carry out this plan, the relative strengths of Army Groups A and B were reversed: von Bock was left with two armies and twenty-nine divisions, while von Rundstedt was given four armies and forty-five divisions, including threequarters of the mechanised units. This plan left open the question of the future employment of Army Group A once it had reached the coast, but at least it laid the basis for the realisation of von Schlieffen's aim of strategy – a battle of annihilation on a reversed front. The new proposals were presented by von Brauchitsch and Halder to Hitler on 18 February, the day after the Führer, at a dinner, had heard from von Manstein of his ideas. They were approved unreservedly. On the 24th, the final OKH orders for Operation Yellow were issued. The controversy was over; tradition had triumphed.

The OKH plan for Operation Yellow which had finally evolved was audacious; it relied on surprise action followed by fast, decisive manoeuvre ending in the destruction of the enemy forces. It was not, however, a plan which took any cognisance of the armoured idea – indeed, its precepts were based on ideas entirely alien to that new concept. Von Rundstedt's advance, in particular, was to be spearheaded by strong mechanised forces, but that, in itself, was no revolutionary innovation. As in Poland, Germany's armoured and motorised infantry divisions were to be tied to the armies they led, dependent for their movement on the directions emanating from army, army group and, ultimately, from Führer headquarters in accordance with traditional concepts of strategy, not on the potential for exploitation offered them by the enemy's positions and by their own power of velocity. The nearest the OKH plan of 24 February came to recognising the revolutionary value of the mechanised troops was the vague sentence: '. . . strong motorised forces are to push forward.'[13] This was not even as advanced as the thinking exhibited in the much-derided plan of 29 November 1939, which was expressed thus: 'With the release of the motorised forces for the advance, their leadership must be separated from that of the infantry divisions which are following.'[14] For the future, the armour enthusiasts might search in vain for such a far-sighted sentence to be included in any Army operational plan. Never again were the mechanised forces to be given so much independence, even in theory. The final version of Operation Yellow restrained itself to the following:

> 'Strong motorised forces are to push forward in close formation in front of the Army Group [A] towards the Meuse sector Dinant-Sedan. Their task is to rout the enemy forces brought up to southern Belgium and Luxembourg, and to gain a foothold on the western bank of the Meuse, thus creating favourable preliminary conditions for the furthering of the attack in a westerly direction [by the rest of the Army Group!]. . . . The 12th Army will break through the Belgian border fortifications on both sides of the Bastogne and, closely following the fast moving units which will go forward ahead of them, force a crossing of the Meuse. . . .'[15]

Dry phrases of OKH operational directives apart, what of the senior commanders in whose hands lay the ultimate direction of the mechanised forces? Did they understand the potential within their grasp? Were they favourably disposed to the implications of handling armour? Hitler certainly was not. Although he found the power and the success of his panzer divisions fascinating, the evolution of Operation Yellow reveals him as having no conception of the operational needs of the armoured force. At first, not only was he fully prepared to dissipate its limited strength into three widely spaced groups (by his decision of 11 November), but he was also ignorant of the limitations of such a force: for example, one army corps alone, with its two panzer divisions, one motorised infantry division, and two motorised infantry regiments, would have been quite unable to exploit any success it might have had in crossing the Meuse. Furthermore, it was clear from the OKH directive of 20 January 1940, that, in common with his Army leaders, Hitler envisaged the task of the formation as merely supporting the infantry armies. It included such phrases as: 'The task of the group will be . . . to lighten the task of 12th and 16th Armies . . . [and to create] a favourable situation for the subsequent phases of the operation. . . .'[16] On 21 January, Hitler told Halder that 'The armour whose strength is in the attack, must be closely supported by the infantry.'[17]

The commander of Army Group A, Gerd von Rundstedt, was a soldier of the old school. Widely respected throughout the German Army, and even by Hitler until the end of the war, he was known as 'the last knight.' Born in 1875 von Rundstedt was the Army's oldest serving general and, in his prime, one of Germany's most capable commanders. Chivalrous, modest, kind, humane, conscious of his subordinates' opinions and interests, he was a symbol of the old army and believed firmly in the ideal of 'duty' and in his oath of allegiance. Distasteful of National Socialism and its protagonists, he stood apart from politics in the tradition of the officer corps. He possessed a fine strategic sense, the heritage of von Moltke and von Schlieffen, and instinctively preferred cavalry to armour; confident in his own abilities and capable of understanding complicated situations in a moment, he was as forthright in expressing his military opinion as he was reserved politically. Von Rundstedt's views on the final plan of campaign accorded closely with Hitler's. As soon as it appeared that OKH would accept his, and von Manstein's, ideas, he began to worry about using armour to spearhead the attack. In his subsequent preparations for the offensive there is no impression that he understood the implications of the fact that seven panzer divisions would lead his attack; as before, he continually laid stress on a 'relentless forward drive by *all* formations'.[18] Furthermore, von Rundstedt was at that time without von Manstein, who, on 1 February, had been transferred to command an infantry corps, a long overdue field promotion.

In his place came General Georg von Sodenstern, an able General Staff officer but one who possessed no appreciation of the armoured idea. He was horrified by the prospect of using armoured forces even in the relatively limited way envisaged in the OKH plan; and, with the full approval of von Rundstedt and von Mellenthin, the army group's Chief of Operations, he expressed these fears in a memorandum to Halder, dated 5 March 1940:

> 'I have serious objections to the use of armoured and motorised forces ahead of the front line of the attacking armies. These mobile forces can have a strong effect on morale, because of their speed and heavy armament, and yet, quite apart from my basic opinion that they should be held back as operational reserves to force a decision after the enemy front has been broken [this was the role envisaged for the cavalry in the First World War], I fear that they will be unable to carry out the task allotted to them in the imminent operation.'[19]

Von Sodenstern then proceeded to list the reasons for his assertion. There was little chance of achieving surprise, he argued, and this, combined with the French fortifications, mines, and armoured forces, would ensure the exhaustion of the German attackers. 'The panzer divisions, therefore, will reach the Meuse sector, where their task really begins, with weakened fighting strength and so late that the enemy will have taken all the necessary defensive measures. The limited mobility of the heavy artillery, and that of a great number of vehicles which are usually to be found in a panzer division, must likewise be indicated in this connexion.'[20] He also feared that enemy air attack would immobilise the panzer divisions, and he was convinced that the Meuse would be so well defended that the Germans would not be able to withstand the pressure even if they managed to force a bridgehead. He continued: '. . . the panzer forces would be exhausted and need to be thoroughly refreshed before being sent in for their most important task – an operational breakthrough in a westerly or south-westerly direction.'[21] Von Sodenstern concluded that the Meuse crossing had to be forced by the infantry. 'Above all, we must have at our disposal after the breakthrough a motorised army which can be sent in for the decisive attack. This army will really spread panic among the approaching enemy reserves and the civil population and will create an effect which, I am firmly convinced, would be lacking in face of the Meuse defence.'[22] But he envisaged this advance not in terms of a deep armoured penetration, but as a fast, well-coordinated attack in which the infantry formations would play a major part. The panzer divisions would be strictly subordinated to higher control from army headquarters:

> 'I should, however, like to force this breakthrough with the 12th Army reinforced as in the case of 4th Army, by one or two panzer divisions, so that we could send the motorised divisions through the breach, followed by panzer divisions, which would in the meantime be subordinated to the 12th Army – and, if the occasion arises, to the 4th Army. This method would take most advantage of the possibilities that may be offered beyond all expectations to the armoured

forces on the Meuse, only with the difference that the conduct of operations would be in the hands of the army [headquarters], which could synchronise the movements of the armoured forces with those of the infantry. The infantry could then really follow up closely . . . and the exploitation of any armoured success in gaining a bridgehead would be ensured.'[23]

The other army group commanders held similar views. The man in charge of Army Group B, Feodor von Bock, was, like von Rundstedt, an aristocrat, an officer of the old school, and an excellent soldier. Ambitious, sarcastic, and obsessed by good manners, von Bock was noted for his eloquence and skill in conversation, and, among friends, for his dislike of the Reich's new political creed. Possessing a good traditional strategic and tactical understanding, he was energetic and elastic enough despite his years (he was born in 1880) to comprehend at least a part of the potential offered by the armoured force. In this he was aided by his readiness to take risks. However the mass of the armour was not to be placed under him for the invasion.

Born in 1876, the commander of Army Group C, Wilhelm von Leeb, was a descendant of a Bavarian Catholic family that had sent many sons into the Army. Of an ascetic, reserved and taciturn personality, he was very religious and rejected totally the philosophy of National Socialism. Politically, however, he was inhibited by the traditional sense of *'Uberparteilichkeit'* that permeated the old officer corps. His strategic abilities were well known, and he was an expert in defensive warfare, which suited the exactitude and thoroughness with which he approached military problems.

One other general of importance was the commander of 4th Army under whose command was to come the panzer group which spearheaded Army Group A's advance. Gunther von Kluge was born in 1882. In common with most other senior generals, he disliked National Socialism but did nothing about it. Energetic, ambitious, intolerant of half-measures and compromise, von Kluge had no time for the armoured idea or for its adherents. The emnity between him and Guderian was to become legendary. He enjoyed soldiering, and could often be found with the troops in battle. Although he was not generally liked, von Kluge was respected for the quickness of his decisions, his initiative in the field, his grasp of tactics and the authority with which he conducted his commands.

Such were the men in whose hands the final direction of the mechanised formations lay. Their attitude may be summed up by von Leeb who, although as commander of Army Group C possessed no armoured units under his control, wrote: 'The arguments that our mobile and armoured forces succeeded in Poland are fallacious. Not only are armoured forces dependent on the weather, but the French and the British are both equipped with armoured units and anti-tank weapons, whilst the excellence of the French Army and its commanders must not be underestimated. We cannot expect our armoured forces to maintain the same tempo here as in Poland.'[24] These men, who represented the established thinking of the great mass of the German Army, had no thought that they were being unusually conservative in their outlook; after all, they were embarking on a plan of campaign which would be as audacious as it would be decisive, and they were relying on surprise, speed, and daring manoeuvre to defeat a numerically far superior enemy. Furthermore, they believed that they were prepared to use their new mechanised and air forces to spearhead such an offensive in a manner unlike that of their more militarily hide-bound enemies. This was a feeling expressed by Halder, who wrote in reply to von Sodenstern's memorandum: 'The task the German Army faces is very difficult. In view of the given terrain and the opposing forces (especially artillery), it cannot be carried out by methods to which we became accustomed in the last war. We must use extraordinary methods and bear the risk connected with them.'[25]

But this was not enough; the generals had failed to realise the potential that the situation presented. They had already concentrated threequarters of Germany's armoured strength, by far the largest assembly of tanks ever known, at the decisive point opposite the weakest area in the Allied line, and had put them in a position to take the fullest advantage of the enemy's main dispositions to the north. Furthermore, the Allied forces facing them were restricted by rigid conceptions of war, ill-suited to the flexible response needed to combat well-directed mechanised forces. Could not the German leadership have exploited this to the full? The requirements were simple: the greatest possible concentration of the mechanised units, which included transferring to Army Group A the few divisions 'dissipated' in Army Group B; a determined attack by these units through the Ardennes, across the Meuse and westwards on to the coast. Command paralysis would bring victory, and a northern swing would then ensure the encirclement of the disorganised, demoralised enemy armies before they could escape across the Channel.

But speed and independence of action had to be the fundamentals on which all else was based. The mechanised forces should not be hampered by the slower speed of the infantry; the momentum of the panzers, supported by aircraft, must not be made dependent on the infantryman's feet. The armour enthusiasts agreed that the mass of the army had to follow at all possible speed in order to consolidate the success achieved by the armour, but argued that its slower movement should not for one moment be allowed to dictate the pace of events. Organised velocity was the key to victory. The panzer generals, however, had no chance of their proposals being accepted. Guderian wrote: 'My . . . task was to persuade my superiors and equally the men under my command that my ideas were correct and thus to achieve freedom of decision from above and confident collaboration from below. The former endeavour was only partially successful, the latter much more so.'[26] So exhausting was this struggle, that Guderian had to be granted leave in the second half of March to recover his health. He later recorded despondently: 'After years of hard struggle, I had succeeded in putting my theories into practice before the other armies had arrived at the same conclusions. The advance we had made in the organisation and employment of tanks was the primary factor on which my belief in our forthcoming success was based. Even in 1940 this belief was shared by scarcely anybody in the German Army.'[27]

The battle for the armoured idea came to be centred around the crossing of the Meuse. This was the decisive point in the campaign: a disaster here, and Army Group A's operation would be ruined almost before it began. The traditionalists saw it as the role of the mechanised forces to dash ahead from the border and throw themselves across the river, there to form a bridgehead and await the advance of the rest of the army. Halder wrote in reply to von Sodenstern:

> 'A normal advance to the Meuse and a frontal attack on this section offers no sound prospects . . . I do not consider it important that the first wave of panzer divisions should reach the Meuse in full fighting strength, but that they should attempt to gain a hold on the western bank of the Meuse quickly and with adequate forces, which will be decisive for further employment. They will be relieved by the second and third armoured waves and by the infantry divisions, which will be brought up quickly and in strength. I do not fail to appreciate that these advanced units on the west bank of the Meuse would be in great danger for some hours. . . . It is not expected that the first armoured forces that gain a foothold across the Meuse will have a direct strategic effect. The area they have reached they will clear by attacks in different directions and with changing tactical objectives, until they are relieved by the infantry divisions. Only when infantry units in sufficient strength have a firm hold on the area necessary for manoeuvring on the west bank of the Meuse can the question arise of the concentration of still serviceable armoured forces for strategic operation. . . . I believe that the consolidation of an attack over the Meuse needs so many days, if only to arrange ammunition and supply. . . .'[28]

This, too, was the view of Army Group A. On 6 March, Halder wrote: 'Phone talk with von Sodenstern; order of army group on operations of armour west of the Meuse. No distant objectives, only capture of bridgeheads (it seems that the army group has caught on to our ideas).'[29]

The armour enthusiasts, however, were far less worried at what happened before, or during, the actual crossing of the Meuse; they were concerned at what was to take place afterwards. In direct contradiction to the wishes of their superiors, they wanted to plunge forward towards the coast immediately, without waiting for the infantry to come up and consolidate the ground won. Guderian remembered the struggle with his superiors:

> '. . . I proposed [on 7 February] that on the fifth day of the campaign an attack be made with strong armoured and motorised forces to

force a crossing of the Meuse near Sedan with the objective of achieving a breakthrough which would then be expanded towards Amiens. . . . Halder, who was present, pronounced these ideas "senseless". He envisaged . . . a "unified attack" would be launched, which could not be mounted before the ninth or tenth day of the campaign. He called this "a properly marshalled attack in mass". I contradicted him strongly and repeated that the essential was that we use all the available limited offensive power of our armour in one surprise blow at one decisive point: to drive a wedge so deep and wide that we need not worry about out flanks; and then immediately to exploit any successes gained without bothering to wait for the infantry corps.'[30]

A week later, on the 14th, the same subject came under study, and Guderian, together with his fellow corps commander, von Wietersheim, became so depressed at the tone of the senior generals that they declared that under the circumstances they could have 'no confidence in the leadership of the operation'. Guderian added: 'The situation became even tenser when it became clear that not even Generaloberst von Rundstedt had any clear idea about the potentialities of tanks, and declared himself in favour of the more cautious solution. Now was the time when we needed Manstein.'[31] Halder knew of the despondency of the armoured enthusiasts; his diary for the 14th revealed that 'Guderian and von Wietersheim plainly show a lack of confidence in success. Guderian has lost confidence – the whole tank operation is planned wrong.'[32] But the controversy over the Meuse crossing was not to be resolved before the opening of the campaign. Both sides adhered to von Moltke's precept that 'no operational plan extends with any certainty beyond the first encounter with the main body of the enemy'.[33] Of this, the panzer leaders intended to make the fullest use. Guderian had told Hitler on 15 March: 'Unless I receive orders to the contrary, I intend on the next day to continue my advance westwards. . . . In my opinion the correct course is to drive past Amiens to the English Channel.'[34] Two days later, Halder observed that Hitler had 'reserved decision on further moves after the crossing of the Meuse'.[35]

Two final points concerning the disposition and command of the mechanised forces should be noted. First, the armoured divisions were distributed throughout the invasion force in a manner that left much to be desired. Army Group B was allocated three such formations, almost one-third of the total, much to the discontent of Guderian and others. They argued that this limited armoured support would have been of far greater value to the *Schwerpunkt* in the south. Furthermore, they were distributed singly to two army corps and one army reserve, only one of them being grouped with a motorised infantry division. Of the seven other panzer divisions, all in Army Group A, one came within II Army Corps, with two infantry divisions, and another within XV Army Corps, with an infantry division of the Second Wave as its partner. The remaining five, half the total, together with three motorised infantry divisions, were within a panzer group of three motorised army corps, XIV, XIX, and XLI, and formed the only satisfactory grouping of mechanised forces. Initially this did not come under the control of any infantry army commander but of Army Group A headquarters itself – in other words, it began the campaign subordinated only to von Rundstedt, and independent of the three army commanders. The question of the command of the panzer group was, however, more contentious. The most obvious candidate for the post was Guderian, whose experience was considerably greater than any of his fellow corps commanders. He was, however, outranked by a number of others, including von Wietersheim and a certain von Kleist, and, although the question of rank could have been solved in Guderian's favour, OKH preferred not to do so. Instead, Ewald von Kleist was chosen, and on 29 February approved by Hitler. Although an able general, who had commanded armour in Poland (XXII Corps), von Kleist was widely regarded as one of the old school in tactical as well as in political matters, and until that time, as Guderian acidly recorded, 'had not shown himself particularly well disposed to the armoured force'.[36]

Nor was the state of the German Army in general, and the invasion force in particular, conducive to the proper conduct of panzer operations of any type, let alone to the deep, demanding thrust of the armoured idea. Poland, which had seen ten per cent, 218, of the German tanks that took part destroyed in action, had proved beyond doubt that the PzKw I was obsolete, and that the PzKw II was effective only in a reconnaissance role. Yet on 1 April 1940, two-thirds of the Army's total tank strength was composed of these vehicles; of 3,381 machines, 1,062 were PzKw Is, 1,086 PzKw IIs, 243 PzKw I command tanks, 329 PzKw IIIs, and only 380 PzKw IVs, the tank that had impressed the panzer experts so greatly in Poland. Within their order of battle, the Germans were forced to include 143 PzKw 35(t)s and 238 PzKw 38(t)s, light Czech tanks which mounted two variants of underpowered 3.7cm anti-tank guns. For the invasion, 2,574 tanks were assembled, and of these the 349 PzKw IIIs and 278 PzKw IVs composed roughly one-seventh and one-ninth of the total; the rest, threequarters of the force, were made up of 523 PzKw Is, 955 PzKw IIs, 135 command tanks, 106 PzKw 35(t)s, and 228 PzKw 38(t)s. The lack of adequate mobility and protection for the tanks' supporting units, especially the infantry, had, on occasions, caused serious trouble in Poland, for it hindered the essential cooperation of all arms on which the fortunes of the panzer division heavily depended. Experience had proved what Guderian and his associates had argued for so long: that without infantry to support or even at times to spearhead the attack, without anti-tank guns to ward off enemy armour, without artillery to soften-up strong points, without engineers to provide passage across obstacles, and without the supply columns to bring up the all-important fuel, ammunition, and spare-parts, neither the tank nor the panzer division could operate effectively. But little was done to provide the tracked armoured transport so urgently required to produce the combination of maximum fire-power concentrated at one point, the high speed across sometimes rough country, and the complete flexibility of response to enemy action that was demanded by the rapid, ever-changing thrusting movements of armoured warfare. By May 1940, the only improvement since the outbreak of war in the provision of tracked transport and self-propelled carriages within the panzer force lay in the increasing numbers of SdKfz 251 armoured personnel-carriers for the infantry, and these were still so few in number that they appear to have been sufficient to equip only a few rifle companies. Thus, the reliance of the mechanised divisions on four-wheeled transport was as great as ever before, transport which, in the Polish campaign, had experienced a temporary breakdown rate of as high as fifty per cent at any one time. Moreover, the mounting of the Czech 4.7cm anti-tank gun on to the PzKw I chassis, to form the first *Panzerjäger* (self-propelled anti-tank gun) to enter German service, appears to have been used, again in limited numbers, by anti-tank units not of the panzer but of the infantry divisions.

The only substantial improvement in the state of the panzer arm lay in the conversion of the four light divisions into full armoured formations. The campaign in Poland had shown that these light divisions, with a single tank battalion, possessed little staying-power in sustained operations; but, with the infusion of Czech tanks, it became possible to reorganise them into panzer divisions, thus bringing the total of such formations to ten. However, these new divisions had fewer tanks than the old; Panzer Divisions 1–5 and 10 each possessed four battalions and a total of some 300 tanks, whereas Panzer Divisions 6 and 8 each had only three battalions and 210 tanks and Panzer Divisions 7 and 9, two battalions and 150 tanks. Thus the offensive capacity and endurance of the units within the panzer arm were far from uniform. In addition, the initial six armoured divisions benefited by acquiring extra motorised infantry from the motorised infantry divisons, each of which shed one of its regiments, their three-regiment organisation having proved too unwieldy.

Weak though the panzer arm might have been, the position in which the rest of the Army found itself was even worse: it was little short of chronic. The winter and spring of 1940 were, for the Germans, a time of crisis in motorisation: not only were the Reich's factories not producing enough motor transport for the Army's requirements, but the Army was not even receiving its fair share of the little that was being produced. By early February only 4,000 of the total production of 12,000 trucks per quarter went to the Armed Forces as a whole; of these, 2,500–2,600 were supposed to be sent to the Army. In fact, the Army was receiving only about 1,000 trucks per quarter – less than one per cent of its entire stocks – not enough to replace its normal losses through wear, let alone to build up a reserve to cover future losses in battle. Little hope of forming a stock for the forthcoming operation remained, because the civilian economy had already been deprived of 16,000 trucks; of these, 2,800 had gone to the Replacement Army, 5,000 to equip newly-activated units, 5,000 to replace others under repair, and 3,200 to supply existing shortages. On 4 February Halder noted: 'We have now about 120,000 trucks, with shortages reported from the field of 2,668.'[37] Even including those under repair, the Army was some 5,000 below authorised strength – a situation made even worse by the fact that many of the existing vehicles were too old to take part in combat conditions. Halder believed this meant that the Army 'cannot pull through in any operation . . . if we allow . . . two per cent [some 2,400 trucks] for the normal monthly loss (not including combat casualties), which is the normal rate, new production will cover only half that loss. The consequence is a continuous drain on our truck strength, impairing the operational efficiency of our forces.'[38] The situation was further exacerbated by the nature of vehicle production which, instead of concentrating on one or two standard types, was spread throughout a multiplicity of designs. This not only caused a relatively slow output, but also impaired efficiency in the field. The shortage was never to be overcome: indeed, it worsened as time went on and new designs and foreign vehicles were introduced.

The High Command was faced with an impossible situation. Any increase in truck production would be limited owing to rubber and steel shortages, and no more than 4,000 vehicles a quarter for all three services was counted on. Little hope could be held that Hitler would allow the Army's share of new trucks to increase, especially in face of strong opposition from Göring. The remaining resources of vehicles in the civilian economy could be tapped, and would provide a temporary solution, but within seven months normal wear alone would have cancelled out their effect. And the stocks in occupied areas, especially in the Protectorate of Bohemia and Moravia, would be insufficient to bring about any marked alleviation. By the end of April, of the 16,000 new trucks demanded by the Army, more than one quarter had not been delivered. The only permanent solution that the Chief of the Army General Staff saw lay in a de-motorisation programme, which would increase the already heavy German dependence on horse-drawn transport: 'the most important thing . . . is to start at once procuring [horse-drawn] vehicles, harness, etc., without wasting a long time for computations and conferences.'[39]

Thus, as the German Army prepared for a modern, mobile campaign against an enemy possessing large numbers of vehicles (the British Expeditionary Force, for example, was completely mechanised), it began to increase its already considerable reliance on horses. They were used wherever it was considered tactically possible to do so, although this required greater numbers of men to care for, and guide, them. They were sent especially to supply and rearward services of infantry divisions. Despite all efforts, the situation had not altered significantly by the time of the invasion. On 8 May it was established that the worst equipped divisions were lacking more than ten per cent of their establishment of vehicles. As late as March, Guderian was so appalled by the state of the motorisation of his panzer divisions that he declared that he could take no responsibility for their performance in action, and during the campaign these élite formations of the German Army were forced to rely on captured vehicles for their continued action in the field. There was no doubt that in May 1940 the German Army was incapable of undertaking anything but a short campaign, and, as Halder realised, if the fighting continued for long, 'it would be necessary to call a pause in operations in view of the impossibility [of obtaining] . . . replacement for all material losses'.[40]

Shortages made little impression on Hitler, who counted strength in terms of numbers of men and divisions rather than in quality and quantity of equipment. Thus, numerical growth continued despite the lack of resources to supply even the already existing units. The further expansion of the German Army had been decided on even before the outbreak of war. In mid-August 1939, Hitler had ordered five divisions of the Fifth Wave to be raised, and this was duly done in September, bringing the total number of divisions in the German Army to 108. In the following months until May 1940, another forty-three infantry divisions were formed: four of the Sixth Wave; thirteen of the Seventh; ten of the Eighth; nine *Landesschützen* divisions of the Ninth; and four fortification divisions. To this was added three divisions to the Second Wave and one to the Third. The grand total was now 153 divisions, for the cavalry brigade was also enlarged to divisional status. Those formations of the Fifth to Eighth Waves were organised similarly to the divisions of the First Wave, but with certain differences in equipment: Fifth and Sixth Wave divisions, for example, were equipped with Czech weapons and material, possessed no infantry guns, and only eight medium mortars. The Ninth Wave divisions were intended only for occupation and guard duties, and as such were poorly armed, as were the four fortification divisions. Immediately before the invasion of the west, orders were given for the formation of a further twelve divisions, nine of the Tenth Wave and three mountain divisions, but of these only one mountain division was ready before the end of the campaign. Thus, by May 1940, the future German Army was to consist of 144 infantry divisions of all types, six mountain divisions, one cavalry division, four motorised infantry divisions, and ten armoured divisions, making a grand total of 165, an increase of sixty-two over the number upon mobilisation. In March the strength of the Field Army, including the armed SS, was 3,300,000 men, and for the forthcoming campaign, 88 *Marsch* (Replacement) battalions from the Replacement Army were made ready, some 80,000 men in all.

The consequences of this sixty per cent expansion (which takes no account of the increase in the SS-VT formations) were detrimental. All the newly raised units faced severe shortages in equipment, and it was not possible to improve the inadequate equipment of the already established units. The critical position of the Army's motorisation has already been noted, but that of weapons and munitions was little better. Between 1 September 1939 and 1 April 1940, only 567,700 rifles, 21,100 machine-guns, 1,630 anti-tank guns, 2,172 mortars, 394 light and 55 heavy infantry guns, 536 10.5cm and 281 15cm field howitzers, and 102 21cm mortars had been added to the Army's stocks — on average only a ten per cent increase in armament.

However, the months since the outbreak of war had seen some improvements in the quality of troops within the mobilised divisions. On the whole, only the motorised and First Wave divisions had taken part in the campaign in Poland, and so the others, which were either concentrated along the quiet western frontier or assembled in training areas, had been able to improve the training of their men and to embark on the replacement of unfit personnel, in particular the First World War veterans who had been mobilised in default of younger trained reservists. By the end of the winter, several hundred thousand veterans were transferred to the service troops or other suitable units. Just as important was the battle experience gained by those units who had fought in Poland. These amounted to half the Field Army as it was then composed, and formed the great majority of those active divisions on which the offensive power of the Wehrmacht so greatly depended. Further sources for recruitment were available after September 1939 by the establishment of two new *Wehrkreise* in the annexed territory of the east and the expansion of another (East Prussia), followed by the creation of military areas in the Protectorate in Bohemia and Moravia and in the General-Government of Poland.

At the outbreak of war, the SS-VT also underwent considerable expansion. On 17 August 1938, the Führer issued a decree which, in the event of an emergency, provided for the reinforcement of the armed SS with the SS *Totenkopfverbände* (the Death's Head units, the concentration camp guards). In October 1939 this was put into effect, three *Totenkopf* infantry regiments forming the *Totenkopf* Division. Other *Totenkopf* personnel entered the *Polizei* Division, formed on Hitler's order of 18 September 1939 mainly from members of the *Ordnungspolizei*, which, although not nominally a part of the SS-VT, came under SS control. At the same time, the three SS-VT regiments — *Deutschland, Germania,* and *Der Führer* — were brought together to form the SS *Verfügungs division*. These SS divisions were larger than their Army counterparts, averaging some 21,000 men each. Hitler's guard regiment, the *Leibstandarte* SS, was reinforced with further infantry and, especially, artillery units, but otherwise remained untouched by this reorganisation. Thus, at the beginning of the campaign in the west, the SS-VT could put in the field two motorised infantry divisions (*Verfügungs* and *Totenkopf*), one division (*Polizei*) the equivalent of the Second Wave Army formations, and one strong motorised infantry regiment (*Leibstandarte*); some 70,000 men, which, together with thirteen other *Totenkopf* infantry regiments, two *Totenkopf* cavalry regiments, replacements in training, and headquarters personnel, brought the total strength of the armed SS in May 1940 to some 125,000 soldiers.

For the campaign in the west, the German Army High Command disposed its invasion force into three army groups, seven armies, and ninety-three divisions (including those of the armed SS), a number which, if the OKH reserve were taken into account, would be increased to 135 divisions and one brigade. Only sixteen were fully motorised, two-seventeenths of the total. The two army groups, A and B, on whose endeavours lay the success or failure of the plan, were composed of seventy-four divisions, fifteen, roughly one-fifth, of which were mechanised, ten of them panzer formations. Army Group A, entrusted with the vital breakthrough was made up of three armies, the 4th, 12th, and 16th, and a reserve; a total of forty-five divisions composed of twenty-two First Wave, one mountain, eight Second Wave, one Third Wave, and three Fourth Wave infantry divisions, and three motorised infantry and seven armoured divisions. Army Group B was smaller, only twenty-nine divisions in two armies, the 18th and 6th, and a reserve – ten First Wave (including one air-landing division), one Second Wave, six Third Wave, five Fourth Wave, one cavalry, two motorised infantry, and three armoured divisions. Army Group C, because of its secondary, static role, was given only nineteen infantry divisions, none of which were First Wave; four were Second Wave, two Third Wave, five Fourth Wave, four Fifth Wave, and four fortification divisions, divided into two armies, the 1st and 7th, and a reserve. The OKH Reserve was composed of forty-two infantry divisions (three First Wave and twenty-four from the Fifth to Eighth Waves) and one motorised infantry brigade. Furthermore, the Luftwaffe fielded two fully mobile Flak corps to aid the fast-moving units of 6th and 4th Armies (Panzer Group Kleist and II Army Corps). These Flak corps each included ninety-six 8.8cm anti-aircraft guns which could be used in an anti-tank role. For duty in the east, the Germans could find only ten low-grade infantry divisions; for Norway, only seven (including two mountain divisions); and for Denmark, one.

The greatest advantage the Germans possessed over their enemies in the west lay not in their own strength but in the weakness of their enemies. This was not, however, a numerical weakness. Ranged against the 135 German divisions in May 1940 were ten Dutch infantry divisions, twenty-three Belgian infantry divisions, nine British infantry divisions, and seventy-seven infantry, five cavalry, three light armoured, and three armoured French divisions, a total of 130 plus a large number of supporting units. Against 2,574 tanks, the Allies could field some 3,600 of at least equal calibre. In artillery, too, they possessed a decided advantage, with 11,500 pieces compared with 7,700. A total of 2,760,000 Germans faced 3,740,000 enemy soldiers, an unequal contest, especially when it is remembered that an attacking force is usually held to need a numerical superiority of three to one to be successful. Only in aircraft, of which they marshalled 1,200 fighters and 1,300 bombers, were the Germans markedly superior to their opponents. However, they had been brought up in the tradition that victory did not necessarily belong to the big battalions; strategic considerations could alter the balance conclusively against the numerically superior, but qualitatively inferior, enemy.

It was not that the Allies possessed worse equipment than the Germans, or less of it – neither proposition would be true. It was that they based their strategic and tactical concepts on the mistaken lessons of the deadlock of the First World War, and not on any tradition of decisive manoeuvre, let alone on the revolutionary implications of the indirect approach. The French, the Dutch, and the Belgians based their strategy on linear defence and mass attack, on fire-power rather than manoeuvre, and on a slow, organised, and 'safe' method of advance. For the French, lulled into a sense of false security behind their Maginot Line, this was especially serious. Their *Instructions for Tactical Employment of Large Units* stipulated: 'The infantry is charged with the principal mission in combat. Protected and accompanied by its own fires and by those of the artillery, perhaps preceded and supported by tanks, aviation, etc., it conquers the ground, occupies it, organises it, and holds it.'[41] Tanks were relegated to a purely supporting role; most of them were dispersed among the infantry divisions, and the few armoured divisions were scattered along the whole front. The British, although on 10 May they had no fully armoured division in France, nevertheless had some 600 tanks, half of them dispersed throughout the infantry formations and the other half massed in an unbalanced, inflexible armoured formation with too few motorised infantry to accompany them. Furthermore, the British and French armies had suffered from twenty years of neglect by parsimonious governments, and from the derision of people who blindly rejected the very possibility of war. As a result, they lacked that aggressive self-confidence so necessary for success.

The lamentable condition of the strategic and tactical thought of the Allies was made considerably more serious by the plan on which they based all their calculations to counter the expected German invasion. It could not have suited their enemy better. The Allied dispositions counted on the main thrust coming through the Belgian plain, as the original German plan had envisaged; there was no thought that the Germans might launch their *Schwerpunkt* through the Ardennes to the south. Although this was the most important point in their defences, being the hinge between the Maginot Line and the Allied northern forces, it was at the same time their weakest. Because of the wooded, hilly nature of the terrain, with its narrow, winding roads, the Allied generals believed that the Ardennes were impassable to a large army, especially a motorised one. Therefore they placed only nine divisions to face what was, unbeknown to them, the mass of the invasion force, forty-five divisions in all. The actual mechanics of the Allied plan further assisted the Germans, for they required that, once the invader set foot on Belgian soil, the British and French forces in the north would move forward sixty miles into Belgium to the Dyle river, there to form a continuous defensive front from Antwerp to the Maginot Line. Thus, while the best of the Allied armies moved into Belgium to counter Army Group B, the main German thrust, undertaken by Army Group A, began to develope from the Ardennes. Not only would the Allied move expose the southern flank of their northern armies, but it would facilitate the German thrust to the Channel and the vast, decisive encirclement of the French and British in Belgium. The state of Germany's enemies in May 1940 bore out fully the truth of Sun Tzu's saying: 'To secure ourselves from defeat lies in our hands, but the opportunity of defeating the enemy is provided by the enemy himself.'

16

The West – The Campaign

Strategy is the art of making use of time and space.
I am less chary of the latter than of the former.
Space we can recover, lost time never.

NAPOLEON

At 5.35a.m. on 10 May 1940, the German Army and Air Force attacked along the Western Front: 135 divisions, supported by 2,750 aircraft, moved against Holland, Belgium, and France. In Holland, 4,500 parachutists and 12,000 troops of an air-landing division were sent in to seize vital bridges and aerodromes and to dominate the centre of political and military leadership, The Hague, while an armoured division sped to their assistance and an army of ten divisions moved in to crush all resistance. In five days the battle for Holland was over. Against Belgium, the opening of the campaign was just as spectacular: 500 airborne troops were used to capture two bridges over the Albert Canal and the fortress of Eben Emael, which not only guarded the bridges over the wide, unfordable River Meuse, but controlled the approaches to the heart of Belgium. The invading army of fourteen infantry divisions then burst into the Belgian plains beyond. By the 15th, the Allies' position there was rendered hopeless; on the 27th, Belgium capitulated, and 500,000 troops laid down their arms.

But it was to the south that the decisive stroke was mounted. On the 10th, the spearheads of the forty-five divisions of Army Group A struck at the Ardennes, on the 13th they crossed the Meuse, and, by the evening of the 20th, the furthermost unit had reached the coast; the Allied forces had been cut in two, and more than fifty Allied divisions in Belgium faced total annihilation. By 4 June, the battle was over: the Allies had lost fifty per cent of their forces on the Continent, and more than seventy-five per cent of their best equipment. The flower of the French Army was behind wire, the majority of the British humiliated and back in Britain. On the 5th, began the final destruction of France: Paris was occupied on the 14th; on the 22nd, the German terms for an armistice was accepted, and at 1.35p.m. 25 June firing ceased. Hitler ordered that throughout the Reich the bells be rung for seven days in celebration of victory.

The campaign in the west had lasted just forty-six days and had been decided, effectively, within ten. A German Army had defeated a highly rated enemy, superior both in numbers and equipment; the defensive, so long believed to have been the strongest form of war, had been shattered by a decisive attack in which manoeuvre and organisation counted for far more than men and weapons. The speed and decisiveness of the German victors had stunned and impressed their enemies. Typical of the contemporary reactions was that of a staff officer with the Commander-in-Chief of the British Air Force in France; in his diary he made the following entry for 19 May: 'News that the panzers are in Amiens. This is like some ridiculous nightmare. . . . The Germans have taken every risk – criminally foolish risks – and they have got away with it. . . . The French General Staff have been paralysed by this unorthodox war of movement. The fluid conditions prevailing are not dealt with in the textbooks and the 1914 brains of the French Generals responsible for formulating the plans of the Allied armies are incapable of functioning in this new and astonishing lay-out.' A few days earlier he had written: 'It is the cooperation between the dive-bombers and the armoured divisions that is winning the war for Germany.'[1]

From such beginnings evolved the myth of *Blitzkrieg*. It is easy to understand why the misconception rose in relation to the campaign in Flanders and France, which had been fast, furious, and decisive, and in which modern weapons had been prominent. The exploits of the panzer divisions were considered remarkable, and it proved easy to construe them to be the result of a revolutionary, coherent system of warfare practised with supreme efficiency. General Fuller, for example, easily fell prey to this illusion. Writing in 1961, he described the exploits of Guderian's corps as '*Blitzkrieg in excelsis*'. His account was as follows:

> 'On 10 May, the attack was launched; on the 11th French advanced troops in the Ardennes were hounded westward; on the 12th Guderian stormed and took Bouillon, and before nightfall two of his divisions occupied the eastern bank of the Meuse at Sedan, while Reinhardt's corps closed in on Monthermé, and Rommel's division was at Houx. On the 13th, under cover of dive-bomber attacks, the Meuse was crossed and bridged, and by nightfall the village of Chémery, eight miles south of Sedan, was in German hands. On the night of 14th–15th, against Guderian's violent protests, the advance was halted by Kleist. Early on the 16th it was resumed, to be halted again on the 17th. From then on it became a race for the English Channel. On the 18th St Quentin was reached; on the 19th the Canal de Nord, between Douai and Péronne, was crossed, and on the 20th Montreuil, Doullers, Amiens, and Abbeville were occupied. The whole stretch of country between the Scarpe and Somme rivers was now in German hands; the British lines of communication were cut, and the way to the Channel ports opened. In eleven days the Germans had advanced 220 miles: such was *Blitzkrieg*. . . .'[2]

Liddell Hart went even further when he described the battle of France as 'one of history's most striking examples of the decisive effect of a new idea, carried out by a dynamic executant'.[3]

But the campaign was no such thing. It has already been shown that the German plan was firmly based on the traditional concept of *Vernichtungsgedanke,* in which decisive manoeuvre and encirclement by the whole attacking force, supported by the Luftwaffe's dive-bombers, were predominent; the proposals for deep, unsupported thrusts by mechanised formations, were not only actively discouraged, they were positively feared. At the outset the armour enthusiasts possessed only two advantages over the traditionalists: their major role as the 'cutting edge' of Army Group A's scythe-cut, and the freedom given to them in accordance with von Moltke's dictum that no operational plan should extend beyond the first clash with the main enemy forces. But could they exploit this, and, forging ahead from the slower infantry armies, conduct their operations according to the precepts of the armoured idea? The chances were not good. The test would come not during the advance to the Meuse, but at its crossing, and from the moment the breakout from the bridgehead began.

As the German advance into Belgium drew the Allies' attention, together with the bulk of their armoured forces, to the north, the decisive stroke was being mounted in the south. As the parachute and air-landing forces spearheading Army Group B dropped on to an unsuspecting enemy, the tanks and infantry of Army Group A quietly crossed the Luxembourg and southern Belgian borders and moved into the seventy-mile stretch of hills, streams, and forests known as the Ardennes. Flinging aside weak opposition, they emerged from that 'impassable' tract of country, crossed into France, and reached the Meuse by the fourth day of the campaign. Surprise was total. Every mile the Allies' northern armies had moved into northern Belgium was a minor victory for the Germans. Not only had the Allies failed to stop the advance of von Bock's forces, but, and more important, they had exposed more and more of their flank and rear to von Rundstedt. The German plan was working; but the greatest obstacle was yet to be overcome: the crossing of the Meuse. All depended on gaining the open country on the other side, where speedy manoeuvre would bring total victory. A halt on the Meuse, even for a few days, could prove damaging to the prospects for success. Time lost to the Germans would be time gained by the Allies, time in which to recover their balance, strengthen their defences, and switch the point of their main effort to the south. Had a counter-stroke then been possible against the advancing panzer spearheads, even if it were not particularly succcssful, the effect on the ever-fearful German Command would have been stunning, and might well have served to paralyse the advance. Indeed, even before the Meuse was reached, the Germans were showing some nervousness. As Guderian wrote to Liddell Hart after the war:

'A stroke from the direction of Montmedy [to the south] towards Kleist's left, perhaps would have caused more trouble to the German Command. When, during 11 May 1940, Kleist got the news that French cavalry tried to advance from that direction, he immediately gave orders that 10th Panzer Division – my left wing division – was to be stopped and turned against that enemy. This order, if followed, would have made nearly impracticable that attack on Sedan and an early breakthrough. I therefore ordered . . . 10th Panzer Division to continue [its] march towards Sedan on a way several kilometres north of his previous route, asking General von Kleist to safeguard my left by the units of Wietersheim's army corps and infantry units following behind.'[4]

And on 12 May, Halder noted in his diary: 'Group Kleist believes that the armour could have advanced faster if they had not to wait for the infantry to close up. Attacks should have been accompanied by armoured infantry brigades.'[5]

To the lasting credit of the generals of Army Group A, the paramount importance of the Meuse crossing was recognised. Von Blumentritt, the Operations Officer of the advancing army group, wrote:

'According to plan, the infantry corps were to attack the Meuse and force a passage for the subsequent crossing of the armoured corps. But this would have occupied nearly a week while the infantry corps were coming up, taking up their positions and making their preparations. Previous to the assault the whole of the artillery would have had to get into position *en masse* and take steps to ensure an ample supply of ammunition. Then the second miracle occurred [the first had been the weakness of the Allied air forces]. Receiving word that the panzer divisions were already in position on the heights of the Meuse north of Sedan, not only Kleist and I, but . . . Rundstedt drove forward to see them. From there we drove down to the Meuse – where the panzer engineers were already working on a bridge. Here and there a few French machine-guns were firing from small, ludicrous concrete emplacements on the west banks of the Meuse. That was all. We simply could not grasp this miracle – and feared that it was a French ruse. But in fact the dreaded Meuse position was almost non-existent, and only weakly defended. Then the panzer-race across the river began.'[6]

At 4.00p.m. on 13 May, the first soldiers of Guderian's corps crossed the Meuse, just west of Sedan, and by nightfall of the following day the bridgehead had been extended to ten miles. On the 15th the last line of defence was broken; the way to the Channel lay open. The question then was: would the military leaders follow the daring precedent they had established on the Meuse? On the answer to that lay the prospects for total victory.

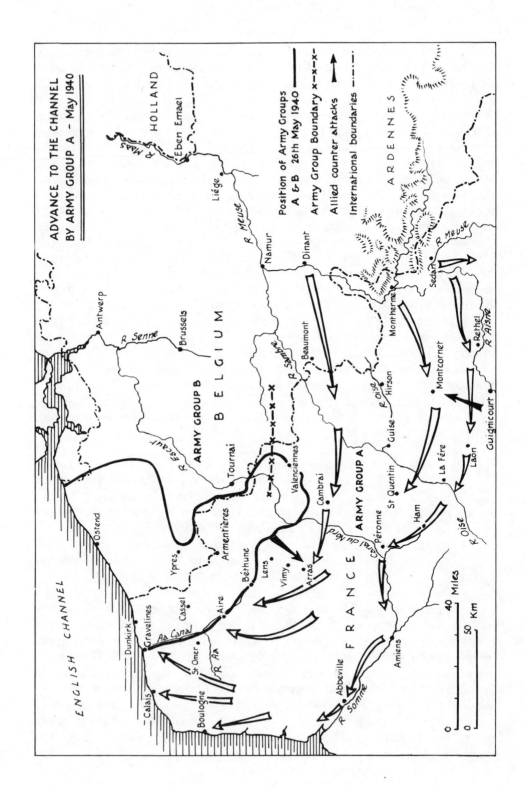

ADVANCE TO THE CHANNEL
BY ARMY GROUP A – May 1940

Position of Army Groups
A & B 26th May 1940 ——————
Army Group Boundary x–x–x–
Allied counter attacks
International boundaries —··—··—

HOLLAND

Eben Emael

R MAAS

Liége

R MEUSE

Namur

Dinant

ARDENNES

R Meuse

Sedan

Montherme

Rethel

R Aisne

Montcornet

Guignicourt

Laon

La Fére

Oise

R Oise

Hirson

Guise

Beaumont

R Sambre

St Quentin

Ham

Péronne

Canal du Nord

Antwerp

R Senne

Brussels

BELGIUM

ARMY GROUP B

R Escaut

Tournai

Valenciennes

Cambrai

ARMY GROUP A

Ostend

Ypres

Armentières

Béthune

Lens

Vimy

Arras

FRANCE

Cassel

Aire

Gravelines

Aa Canal

R Aa

St Omer

Dunkirk

Calais

Boulogne

Abbeville

R Somme

Amiens

ENGLISH CHANNEL

40 Miles

50 Km

0

0

221

However, 15 May, the day on which the advance to the Channel began, saw the Germans revert to traditional military principles; from the moment the tanks started to move west, the whole character of the future attack was set. Caution replaced daring. The progress of the mechanised forces was to be governed as much by the fears, hesitation, and conservatism of the senior generals as by the dash and brilliance of the panzer leaders. Guderian later wrote bitterly: 'The High Command's influence on my actions was merely restrictive throughout.'[7] On the morning of the 15th, although Army Group A's war diary specified von Rundstedt's intention that there should be no 'shackling' of the mechanised forces, which must be 'given every opportunity to gain ground to the west', it also recorded that the Kleist group was placed under the command of 12th Army in order to 'bring coordination between the movement of the motorised forces and the infantry divisions'.[8] A 'loose rein' was the term he used to describe the tactical control to be exercised over the armour; Guderian and his fellows wished to be rid of the harness altogether. The evening of the 15th was to witness the first warning tug on the reins, an irritation for the panzer enthusiasts which boded ill for the future. In the daylight hours the French rearward line of defence had finally collapsed, and, although no one knew it, it had been the last occasion on which von Kleist's group was to meet any solid opposition in its race for the Channel. But that evening there came an order from panzer group headquarters to halt the advance and consolidate the bridgehead. For Guderian this must have been a disheartening moment, for it seemed that Halder's idea of a 'properly marshalled attack in mass' would now be enforced. Guderian later recorded:

> 'I would not, and could not, put up with this order, as it meant forfeiting surprise and all our initial success. I therefore telephoned the Chief of Staff of the panzer group, Colonel Zeitzler, and getting no satisfaction I then telephoned General von Kleist himself to get the order cancelled. The exchange of views became very lively. . . . At last Kleist agreed to permit a continuation of the advance for another twenty-four hours in order to widen the bridgehead sufficiently to allow the infantry corps to follow us.'[9]

Guderian plunged on. The next day, the 16th, Halder began his diary entry with the exultant words: 'Our breakthrough wedge is developing in a positively classical manner. West of the Meuse our advance is sweeping on. Enemy armoured counter-attacks are being smashed in its path. The marching performance of the infantry is superb (5th Division and 1st Mountain Division).'[10] By nightfall, Guderian's and Reinhardt's units were over fifty miles west of Sedan. But however pleased Halder or Guderian might have been at the victories up to that time, there were others who saw the momentum of the attack, the cause of such success, as threatening the outcome of the campaign. As early as the 15th von Rundstedt was expressing his fears thus:

'For the first time the question has arisen whether it may not become necessary to halt temporarily the mechanised forces on the Oise [some seventy miles from Sedan]. . . . the enemy is in no circumstances to be allowed to achieve any kind of success, even if it be only a local success, on the Aisne or, later, in the Loire region [some sixty miles from the Meuse]. This would have a more detrimental effect on operations as a whole than would a temporary slowing-down of our motorised forces.'[11]

Early the next day, von Rundstedt ordered, by telephone, that a general tightening-up of the army group's formations was to take place: only advanced units were to be allowed to pass the line Beaumont-Hirson-Montcornet-Gruignicourt [forty miles from Sedan], then the furthermost limit of the offensive, although bridgeheads could be seized, but not exploited, over the Oise, some thirty miles distant. The southern flank was to be covered as the armies closed up, and all infantry formations would be moved forward at the greatest possible speed. The army group's war diary contained the following entry for the 16th:

'Army group headquarters have no doubt that, if motorised forces were to continue their push in advance of 12th Army, they would probably be able to cross the Oise between Guise and la Fère without difficulty. Their commanding officers are convinced of this and would like to act accordingly, especially Generals Guderian and von Kleist. But looking at operations as a whole, the risk involved does not appear to be justified. The extended flank between la Fère and Rethel [forty-five miles] is too sensitive, especially in the Laon area. The southern flank is simply inviting an enemy attack. . . . If the spearheads of the attack are temporarily halted, it will be possible to effect a certain stiffening of the threatened flank within twenty-four hours.'[12]

That evening, when he visited the army group headquarters, von Brauchitsch endorsed von Rundstedt's decision that no formations should pass the Oise and Sambre without specific authorisation. Consequently, early in the morning of the 17th, von Kleist ordered Guderian to halt; the eager corps commander had already pushed too far. Guderian was astonished. Later he remembered: 'After the wonderful success on 16 May it did not occur to me that my superiors might still be thinking on the same lines as before. . . .'[13] Von Kleist flew in at 7.00a.m. to inform Guderian of the decision, and a violent quarrel ensued, terminating with the panzer group commander accepting his subordinate's offer of resignation. Later that day General List, commander of 12th Army, arrived to pour oil on the troubled waters. He explained that the order to halt had come from OKH and must be obeyed, but that army group headquarters had given permission for a reconnaissance in force to be carried out, although Guderian's corps headquarters would be required to remain exactly where it then was. That evening the panzer divisions moved again, Guderian laying a wire from his stationary corps headquarters to his new and mobile 'advanced headquarters', and interpreting his 'reconnaissance in force' as loosely as was possible. As early as 9.00a.m. on the 18th, his 2nd Panzer Division had reached St Quentin, ten miles beyond the Oise, the town that was specified in von Rundstedt's order to be the objective for that day.

Von Kleist later claimed that the direction to halt had come from Hitler, and, although no documentary evidence appears to exist which corroborates this assertion, certainly the atmosphere at Führer headquarters was conducive to such an order. Hitler was fully aware of the importance of Army Group A's thrust, even to the extent of ordering , on the 16th, that the three panzer divisions of Army Group B be transferred to the south. However, his concern for the *Schwerpunkt* also included fear. Siewert, von Brauchitsch's personal assistant, recorded: 'The Führer was nervous about the risk that the main French armies might strike westward, and wanted to wait until a large number of infantry divisions had been brought up to provide flank cover along the Aisne [the southern flank of the advance].'[14] At midday on the 17th, while von Kleist's panzers were halted, Hitler told von Brauchitsch that 'he considered the principal danger to be in the south'.[15] At 1.30p.m., Army Group A received an order from the Army Commander-in-Chief urging a strong defence of the Aisne (the southern flank of the advance). By 3.00p.m., the Supreme Commander was at von Rundstedt's headquarters, only to have his anxieties confirmed. The army group's war diary reported Hitler as saying: 'At the moment, decision depends not so much on a rapid thrust to the Channel, as on the ability to secure as quickly as possible an absolutely sound defence on the Aisne in the Laon area and, later, on the Somme; the motorised forces at present employed there will thus be made available for such a thrust. All measures taken must be based on this, even if it involves a temporary delay in the advance to the west.'[16] That evening Halder wrote despondently: 'Rather an unpleasant day. The Führer is terribly nervous. Frightened by his own success, he is afraid to take any chance and so would rather pull the reins on us. Puts forward the excuse that it is all because of his concern for the left flank. Keitel's telephone calls to the army groups, on behalf of the Führer, and the Führer's personal visit to army groups have caused only bewilderment and doubts.'[17] The only man to remain calm was Halder himself, who believed that the French on the southern flank were 'too weak to attack at this time'.[18] But even his confidence might have been disastrously misplaced had he been able to exert any influence on the campaign; instead of continuing the attack west, towards the coast, he favoured a grand movement in a south-westerly direction towards Compiègne, with the possibility of subsequently wheeling south-east past Paris to take the Maginot Line in the rear. So much for the Channel!

The next day, the 18th, when Guderian's tanks were entering St Quentin, an atmosphere of near crisis still bedevilled the German Command. Jodl wrote in his diary: 'It has been a day of high tension. OKH has not carried out the instruction to build up the southern flank as rapidly as possible. . . . The Army Commander-in-Chief and General Halder were summoned at once and given the most explicit orders to take the necessary measures.'[19] Jodl then interfered directly with the Army's operations and signalled that: '1st Mountain Division and the rear elements of 4th Army to turn south.'[20] Keitel, for his part, flew to von Rundstedt to impress on him the urgency of his Führer's orders. The same day Halder noted:

> 'They have a completely different view in the Führer headquarters. The Führer is full of an incomprehensible fear about the southern flank. He rages and shouts that we are doing the best to ruin the entire operation and are running the risk of defeat. He entirely refuses to carry on the operation westwards, let alone south-west, and still clings to the plan of a north-western drive. This is the subject of a most unpleasant discussion . . . between the Führer on the one side and von Brauchitsch and myself on the other. A directive was issued on this occasion which is a confirmation in writing of our conversation which took place at 10.00a.m. Conversations between the Army Commander-in-Chief and Generaloberst von Rundstedt, and my conversation with Salmuth, produced the effects the Führer desired (sharp switch of forward divisions to the south-west, main body of motorised forces to be ready to move to the west).'[21]

Thus, on the 17th and 18th, despite the agitations of Guderian in the field and Halder at OKH, the idea of a 'properly marshalled attack in mass', with the armoured divisions as the cutting edge and with a coordinated defensive line to the south, came to dominate over the urgently expressed desire to push ahead with the panzers at all possible speed.

So strong was the control now exerted over operations by Führer Headquarters that Halder was forced to wring from Hitler his approval for further advance on the part of Army Group A's mechanised forces. At midday on the 18th Halder had become most concerned that the Allies were trying to form a defensive line between Valenciennes-Cambrai-St Quentin-la Fère, across the intended western path of the German advance. Although he knew that some elements of Guderian's command had reached these points, he was also well aware that they consisted of a 'reconnaissance in force' and not a full attack. The Chief of the General Staff therefore concluded that 'we must punch through this new line before it has a chance to consolidate'[22] and that this would require far stronger forces than were permitted. Preliminary orders were issued to that effect, and Halder went to the Führer for permission to launch the attack the following morning, the 19th. This Hitler gave, but, as Halder noted, 'in an atmosphere of bad feeling and in a form calculated to give the outside world the impression that it is a plan conceived by the OKW'.[23] Concession though this was, it amounted to very little, for already by the late evening of the 18th Guderian's advanced units had nearly reached the Oise at Péronne (still as part of his 'reconnaissance', and some eighteen miles as the crow flies from St Quentin), and the new orders specified that the corps advance units should push on to 'capture a bridgehead over the Canal du Nord [two miles from Péronne] and advance towards the line Le Mesril-Clery'.[24] This meant that the ground to be gained on the 19th would be, at most, only five miles. Furthermore the OKH order issued to Army Group A on the evening of the 18th stressed that 'The dangers of separation must be avoided'.[25] If Guderian's advance was no longer to be classified a 'reconnaissance in force', it was certainly an attack held in tight reins.

On 19 May Guderian's corps went only to the line Cambrai-Péronne-Ham. That evening, the orders for the next day's movements came in; Guderian recorded that 'the corps at last received its freedom of movement once again'.[26] Objectives were set: Amiens, some twenty-eight miles from Péronne, where a bridgehead was to be established on the south bank of the Somme, and, more ambitiously, Abbeville, also on the Somme, fifty miles from Péronne and only fourteen from the sea. By midday on the 20th the objective at Amiens had been reached, and by 7.00p.m. (Army Group A war diary gave the time as 9.00p.m.) Abbeville was in German hands. At midnight one battalion of the 2nd Panzer Division reached the Atlantic coast.

The 20th was, understandably, a day of great elation. Halder and von Brauchitsch were more than content with Guderian's achievement, and Hitler, according to Jodl, was 'beside himself with joy' and even talked 'in words of highest appreciation of the Germany Army and its leadership'.[27] But it was at the same time a day of some confusion. The predicament of the German Command was considerable: its troops were at the coast and the Allied forces were cut in two, certainly, but what of the future? Which way should Army Group A now turn – north to effect the battle of annihilation so favoured by von Rundstedt and von Manstein, or south-west to begin a vast encirclement up against the rear of the Maginot Line, as proposed by Halder, and, it seems, concurred with by von Brauchitsch? To add to this dilemma, there was the intense disquiet felt not only about the vulnerability of the southern flank, but also about the possibility of concerted Allied action coming from the north against the extended German line. The day previously, there had been great concern at OKW about Franco-British armoured attacks from Belgium, and, early on the 20th, Halder, although confident about the chance of holding off such threats, had expressed his fear of large Allied forces escaping to the south in front of von Kleist's panzer group. (Even the advance to the coast that night cannot have completely allayed his fears, as the front from Péronne to the sea was then only sparsely held.) The result of all this was that, on the 21st, the day Lord Gort, the British commander, became convinced that the BEF had to evacuate to England through the Channel ports, Guderian's panzers lay idle; no orders were forthcoming because no decision had been reached.

The 21st, then, was marked not by any further startling German advance behind the undefended flank and rear of the northern Allied armies; rather it was dominated by a British counter-attack at Arras in the evening against the northern-most armoured spearhead of Army Group A – Rommel's 7th Panzer Division, a unit of Hoth's panzer group – which succeeded in penetrating ten miles into the German line. This was regarded as the fulfilment of German fears – fears that had already been increased by the attack from the south by the French 4th Armoured Division under de Gaulle on the 19th, which had penetrated to within a mile of Guderian's advanced headquarters before being repulsed. Of the Arras affair, von Rundstedt recalled that it was 'a critical moment. . . . For a short time we feared that our armoured divisions would be cut off before the infantry divisions could come up to support them.'[28] Although the attack was delivered by only a relatively small force, with just two battalions of tanks, and although it was brought to a halt, this incident, together with Rommel's consequent failure to capture the town of Arras, had a profound psychological effect on the German command. Rommel believed himself to have been fighting against 'hundreds of enemy tanks',[29] and XIX Corps' war diary recorded that the British counter-attack had 'apparently created nervousness throughout the entire [Kleist] group area'.[30] Hitler became extremely worried by the lack of infantry divisions in the vital forward areas, and remained in the map room until 1.30a.m. the following morning. The Army Command felt forced to issue an order stating that 'the question of an attack by Army Group A in a northerly direction will only arise when the infantry divisions have gained possession of the high ground north-west of Arras'.[31]

The British counter-attack at Arras had its effect on the major event of the 21st: the decision to continue the German attack northwards, with the capture of the Channel ports as the objective. In the evening, any idea of a south-westerly attack having been rendered unthinkable by the Arras counter-attack, OKH issued its order for von Kleist's group to proceed to Boulogne and Calais, the latter being some fifty miles as the crow flies from Guderian's stationary tanks. But fear of another counter-attack similar to that at Arras caused the army group to hold back Hoth's units, and Reinhardt, commander of XXXXI Corps, felt it necessary to deploy a division eastwards as a precaution against any further counter-attacks. But most damaging to German interests was von Kleist's decision to weaken XIX Corps. Guderian explained the situation:

> 'I wanted the 10th Panzer Division to advance on Dunkirk . . . the 1st Panzer Division to move on Calais and the 2nd on Boulogne. But I had to abandon this plan since the 10th Panzer Division was withdrawn by an order of the panzer group dated 22 May, and was held back as panzer group reserve [to cover any Allied threat from

the south]. So when the advance began on the 22nd, the only divisions I commanded were the 1st and 2nd Panzer. My request that I be allowed to continue in control of all three of my divisions in order quickly to capture the Channel ports was unfortunately refused. As a result the immediate move of the 10th Panzer Division on Dunkirk could not now be carried out.'[32]

Furthermore, units of the 1st and 2nd Panzer Divisions had to be left behind to hold the Somme bridgehead until they were relieved. Thus was missed the first opportunity to cut the Allies' only means of escape. The push to Dunkirk was inhibited from the outset.

The attack by Guderian's depleted corps was to be renewed at 8.00a.m. on the 22nd, but still it was dogged by the near paralysis that had gripped the German command after Arras. At the same time as the tanks were moving out, von Rundstedt ordered that, until the situation at Arras had been cleared up, the Kleist group should not push on to Calais or Boulogne; the OKH order was to be disregarded. However, although Arras was not to fall until the evening of the next day, von Rundstedt soon thought better of his decision. The war diary of XIX Corps noted that 'for reasons unknown . . . the attack on Boulogne was only authorised by group at 12.40p.m. on the 22nd. For about five hours 1st and 2nd Panzer Divisions were standing inactive on the Amache.'[33] Such was Guderian's impatience, though, that he had sent his 2nd Panzer towards Boulogne half an hour earlier, at 12.10p.m., without waiting for orders. By the middle of the afternoon the outskirts of the town had been reached, but it was only after some thirty-six hours had elapsed that Boulogne fell to the Germans. Calais held out even longer, and it was not until the evening of the 26th that it capitulated. The XIX Corps' war diary entry of the 23rd ended with the comment: 'Corps' view is that it would have been opportune and possible to carry out its three tasks (Aa Canal [halfway between Calais and Dunkirk], Calais, Boulogne) quickly and decisively, if, on the 22nd, its total forces, i.e. all three divisions, had advanced northward from the Somme area in one united surprise strike.'[34] Time lost by the panzers was time gained by the enemy, time in which to organise defences and stiffen the resolve to fight.

On 22 May, while Guderian's divisions were battling towards Boulogne and Calais, Hitler was busily concerning himself with future operations. A quick look at his deliberations will serve to illustrate how he, and other German commanders, viewed the use of mechanised forces. His decisions have been left to posterity in a pencilled memorandum, unsigned, but dated 22 May 1940 and addressed to, and initialled by, Keitel. It ran:

> 'Führer's wishes. Free motorised divisions as fast as possible by [using] infantry divisions – the nearest ones that you can lay hands on. Panzer divisions forward – take them out of flank protection actions and defensive battles. Only motorised formations still come forward into [battle] at the right time. They will therefore be freed

from rear flank protection tasks. They will support and free the most forward armoured formations. . . . Throw forward, without delay, at least forward motorised units of infantry who are advancing to the west in forced marches. . . .'[35]

These points were probably used by the Chief of OKW when he was sent by Hitler to Army Group A to impress on von Rundstedt and his staff Hitler's desire to commit all Hoth's motorised troops on both sides of Arras and in the westward area towards the sea, while von Kleist's units on the Somme front were to be replaced as quickly as possible by the infantry divisions. In other words, the Führer wanted to relieve the mechanised forces from protection and defensive duties, and concentrate them in the spearhead so as to further the army group's advance. But this formed no indication of any sudden acceptance by Hitler of Guderian's ideas; the Keitel memorandum can be seen only in relation to Hitler's misgivings over the handling of the panzer forces exhibited during the whole campaign. Certainly, the Führer wanted fast, powerful advances by armoured spearheads, but then so did the majority of Germany's generals; what he, in common with most of the senior officers, believed were also necessary were properly constructed, secure flanks. Those would be made possible only through a coordinated attack in which the mechanised units were not allowed independence of action, but, instead, were kept in contact with the infantry. This attitude he had made clear repeatedly over the previous week. In simple terms, the form of offensive envisaged by the Supreme Commander, and also by the senior generals, was a series of moves in which the mechanised units punched their way through enemy territory and one by one fell out of the advance in order to form a continuous, secure flank extending back from the point unit to the rear of the whole army group. Meanwhile, the infantry formations would follow their faster partners with all possible speed and relieve them of their flank-guarding role, thereby allowing the motorised units to regroup and begin the attack once again. During the invasion of the Soviet Union in 1941 this method came to be known as the 'panzer raid'. In effect, the advance degenerated from the armour enthusiasts' ideal of a swift, deep thrust, ending only with the defeat of the enemy, into a succession of short, sharp jumps, with a pause between each for regrouping. Swift though this method of war was, compared with that of the enemy, it fell far short of Guderian's theories. The organised velocity of the armoured idea gave place to the initially powerful, but ever-fading, punches of the modernised *Vernichtungsgedanke*.

The dawn of 23 May witnessed the initial phase of the move on the last remaining port left open to the escaping British: Dunkirk. During the previous day, von Kleist had released 10th Panzer Division from its reserve duties, and Guderian had quickly sent it against Calais so as to relieve 1st Panzer for the attack against Dunkirk. At 10.00a.m. on the 23rd, so his orders read, the 1st Panzer would move towards 'its objective via

Gravelines'.[36] Despite meeting strong resistance, the attack continued well, and on the 24th the Aa Canal, just fifteen miles from the port, was crossed. The British reckoned that Dunkirk would fall the next day, before the main body of the BEF had managed to embark. But then, on the 24th, came the order to halt; the tanks, once again, stopped dead in their tracks and the Luftwaffe took over the entire responsibility for the fall of the port. The ground attack did not resume until the 27th, by which time the British defences had been considerably improved. Dunkirk itself did not fall until 4 June, too late: the bulk of the BEF had got back to England.

The famous 'halt order', which saved the British Army, has been a subject of much controversy. Where did the blame lie – with Hitler, the Army Command or von Rundstedt? If the fateful decision to stop the panzers outside Dunkirk is regarded as an isolated, untypical, incident of the campaign, then the answer is difficult to find. If, however, it is seen as the culmination of the fears, hesitations, and failings of the previous nine days, it becomes readily understandable. Coordination of force, and security of flanks, had been basic to the German advance so far; and on 24 May, just as they were on the verge of one of the most decisive battles of annihilation in history, Hitler and his generals chose to behave exactly as they had done for the past fourteen days. They saw no reason why they should act against their tradition.

On 23 May, von Rundstedt and his senior commanders were worried men. Certainly, they believed that, by the evening , the position of the Allies in the north was hopeless, and that there no longer existed any real urgency to their operations. But other matters, which had dogged the advance of the army group after the crossing of the Meuse, troubled them. The five armies of Army Group A were extended over some 260 miles, a huge area with widely separated fronts to secure; its ten armoured divisions were spaced far apart – the 3rd, 4th, 5th, and 7th were near Arras, the 6th and 8th were opposite Aire, the 1st at Gravelines, the 2nd and 10th at Boulogne and Calais respectively, and the 9th near the Somme. Furthermore these forces, the vital spearhead of the German Army, had suffered heavily yet would soon be needed for the forthcoming offensive into the south of France. On the morning of the 23rd von Kleist informed von Kluge, and, through him, von Rundstedt, that his group had suffered heavy losses in men and equipment, and that tank casualties amounted to more than fifty per cent. Furthermore, his much-weakened group was expected to safeguard the Somme front, establish strong bridgeheads across that river, take Boulogne and Calais, secure the territory between them, and deploy over a thirty-five-mile front for an attack in the direction of Dunkirk-Ypres. This was just not possible, he remonstrated; reinforcements and regrouping must precede any determined attack in whatever direction. Halder, who heard of von Kleist's misgivings, took an opposite view and commented that a final supreme effort should be made; the crisis would be over in forty-eight hours. The Hoth group, too, had suffered much; its XXXIX Corps' war diary noted on the 24th: 'Casualties for each armoured division [5th and 7th], approximately 50 officers and 1,500 NCOs and men, killed or wounded; armour, approximately thirty per cent. Owing to frequent encounters with enemy tanks, weapon losses are heavy – particularly machine-guns in infantry regiments.'[37]

Von Rundstedt, too, on the 23rd was of the opinion that a halt was necessary. He feared concerted action by the Allied forces to the north and south; he believed it vital that the armoured units be closed up and the northern flank consolidated immediately; and he felt that, because the southern flank was not yet secure and the ports of Boulogne and Calais had not yet fallen, the advanced units of von Kleist's and Hoth's Groups should only hold the Aa Canal line, and not attempt to cross it. At around 6.00p.m., von Kluge, commander of 4th Army which now contained both panzer groups, received from von Rundstedt a directive along these lines, and he, in turn, issued an order to the effect that 'in the main, Hoth group will halt tomorrow; Kleist group will also halt, thereby clarifying the situation and closing up'.[38] Von Kluge had himself already told his chief that the troops 'would be glad if they could close up tomorrow'[39] (the 24th), and his army's war diary confirmed his eagerness to halt 4th Army, 'in the main, tomorrow in accordance with Generaloberst von Rundstedt's order'.[40] Once again, the armour was to be closed up and the flanks secured before the attack was allowed to continue.

One final development on the 23rd was to prove of immense significance for the morrow. For the first time in the campaign, the Luftwaffe Commander exerted his influence. Warlimont related the story:

> '. . . late in the afternoon of 23 May, Göring was sitting at a heavy oak table beside his train . . . when the news arrived that the enemy in Flanders was almost surrounded. Göring reacted in a flash. Banging his great fist on the table, he shouted: "This is a wonderful opportunity for the Luftwaffe. I must speak to the Führer at once. . . ." In the telephone conversaion that followed, he used every sort of language to persuade Hitler that this was a unique opportunity for his Air Force. If the Führer would give the order that this operation was to be left to the Luftwaffe alone, he would give an unconditional assurance that he would annihilate the remnants of the enemy; all he wanted, he said, was a free run; in other words, the tanks must be withdrawn sufficiently far from the western side of the pocket to ensure that they were not in danger from our own bombing. Hitler was as quick as Göring to approve this plan without further consideration. Jeschonnek [the Luftwaffe Chief of Staff] and Jodl rapidly fixed the details, including the withdrawal of certain armoured units and the exact timing for the start of the air attack.'[41]

The reasons for Hitler's accession to Göring's forceful request are not hard to understand: the Führer was as worried as anyone about the extended flanks of Army Group A and the possibility of strong Allied counter-attacks.

Arras had proved a salutary lesson. Furthermore, as well as safeguarding the Army by allowing its units time to regroup and rest, Hitler could ensure that his very own Luftwaffe, the special creation of National Socialism, would be allowed the glory of the final decision of the campaign in which, until then, the achievements of the ground forces had necessarily played the chief part. Possibly, too, he was concerned that the watery terrain of the surrounding country was unsuitable for armoured operations. Consequently, strengthened in his new resolve, Hitler made preparations to visit Army Group A on the 24th.

The morning of 24 May saw only a very limited advance, and even that was against the letter of von Rundstedt's order, which was to halt at the Aa Canal and not cross it. However, it was consciously limited by the spirit of that order. To the south of Dunkirk; Reinhardt's corps fought to secure its bridgehead over the River Aa at St Omer, and, to the west, Guderian's 1st Panzer crossed the canal and established three bridgeheads. Both then halted, having achieved only the consolidation of a favourable position from which to continue the attack when, and if, it was ordered.

As von Kleist's group was making its final move forward, Hitler arrived at von Rundstedt's headquarters. The army group's war diary noted:

> 'At 11.30a.m. the Führer arrives and receives a summary of the situation from the Commander of the army group. He completely agrees with the opinion that the infantry should attack east of Arras while the motorised units should be held on the line Lens-Béthune-Aire-St Omer-Gravelines in order to "catch" the enemy who are being pushed back by Army Group B. He gives it added emphasis by stating that it is necessary to conserve the tank units for the coming operations and that a further narrowing of the pocket would result in an extremely undesirable restriction of Luftwaffe operations. . . .'[42]

Jodl, who had accompanied Hitler, wrote that day: 'He is very happy about the measures of the army group, which fit in entirely with his ideas.'[43] After Hitler had left, von Rundstedt issued an order at 12.31p.m., which read: 'By the Führer's orders . . . the general line Lens-Béthune-Aire-St Omer-Gravelines (Canal line) will *not* be passed.'[44] Late that day Hitler gave further substance to his decision that the panzers should halt. His Directive No. 13 stated: 'The task of the Luftwaffe will be to break all enemy resistance on the part of the surrounded forces, to prevent the escape of the English forces across the Channel. . . .'[45]

The only men of influence in the German Armed Forces who, at the time, strongly opposed von Rundstedt's decision and Hitler's order were Guderian, who confessed himself to be 'utterly speechless',[46] von Brauchitsch, although lamely, and Halder. On the morning of the 24th, the Chief of the General Staff had been confident of victory: 'The situation continues to develop favourably, even though the progress of our infantry units in the direction of Arras is taking time. But as, for the moment at least, there is no danger south of the Somme, I do not regard this as disturbing. We needn't rate the enemy's powers of resistance very high, except for local fighting. Things will take their own time; we must be patient and let them develop.'[47] But in the evening he was to comment gloomily: 'The left wing, consisting of armoured and mechanised forces, which has no enemy before it [there were some, but few and relatively disorganised] will thus be stopped dead in its tracks on the direct orders of the Führer. Finishing off the encircled enemy army is to be left to the Luftwaffe!'[48] That night Halder and his aide, Colonel von Greiffenberg, attempted to impose OKH's terms, instead of Hitler's, on the battle. In the very early hours of the 25th they sent a wireless order to both Army Groups A and B which read: 'Further to OKH's instructions of 24th May, the continuation of the attack up to the line Dunkirk- Cassel- Estaires- Armentières- Ypres- Ostend is permissible. Accordingly, the space reserved for Luftwaffe operations is correspondingly reduced.'[49] Although Army Group B agreed with this order, its arrival at Army Group A was far from welcome. On receiving it, at 12.45a.m., von Blumentritt, von Rundstedt's Operations Officer, wrote across it: 'By order of the Commander and Chief of Staff, *not* passed on to 4th Army, as the Führer has delegated control to the Commander of the army group.'[50] In the war diary the following entry was made: 'The Commander . . . considers that, even if their further advance is extremely desirable, it is in any case urgently necessary for the motorised groups to close up.'[51] So was the OKH disregarded by its own field units; such was Hitler's achievement in reducing its authority.

On the morning of 25 May, the Army High Command made one more effort to persuade Hitler to change his mind. Halder recorded in his diary:

'The day begins once again with unpleasant arguments between von Brauchitsch and the Führer concerning the future course of the battle of encirclement. I had envisaged the battle going as follows: Army Group B [with only twenty-one infantry divisions left to it] would mount a heavy frontal assault on the enemy, which would make a planned withdrawal, with the aim merely of tying them down. Army Group A [by then composed of seventy divisions, including all the panzer formations], meeting a beaten enemy, would tackle it from the rear and bring about the decision. This was to be achieved by means of the motorised troops. Now the political leadership gets the idea of transferring the final battle from Flanders to northern France. In order to disguise this political aim it is explained that the Flanders terrain with its numerous waterways is unsuitable for tanks. The tanks of the other motorised troops, therefore, had to be halted after reaching the line St Omer-Béthune. In other words the position is reversed. I wanted Army Group A to be the hammer and B to be the anvil. Now B is made the hammer and A the anvil. Since B is faced with an organised front [and was also by far the weaker of the two] this will cost a lot of blood and take a long time. Another thing, the Air Force on which hopes were pinned is completely dependent on the weather. Because of these differences of opinion, a tug-of-war has developed which is more wearying to the nerves than the whole organisation of the campaign itself.'[52]

Of the same meeting Jodl noted: 'In the morning the Commander-in-Chief of the Army arrives and asks permission for the tanks and motorised divisions to come down from the heights of Vimy-St Omer-Gravelines onto the plains towards the east. The Führer is against, and leaves the decision to Army Group A. They turn it down for the time being since the tanks must have time to recover in order to be ready for the tasks in the south. . . .'[53] Such was the divergence of views within the German Command. During the day Hitler's order of the 24th was confirmed by telephone, and then passed on to the 4th Army: 'By the Führer's orders . . . the north-western wing (Hoth and Kleist groups) will hold the favourable defensive line Lens-Béthune-Aire-St Omer-Gravelines, and allow the enemy to attack it. This line may be crossed only on express instructions from Army Group headquarters. The principal thing now is to husband the armoured formations for later and more important tasks.'[54] By the evening, 4th Army was able to report: 'The motorised groups remained – as ordered – along the canal and have closed up.'[55] The army group's war diary concluded with satisfaction: 'The battle in northern France is approaching its conclusion. There is no further possibility of any crisis except perhaps of a local nature. The task of Army Group A can be considered to have been completed in the main.'[56]

The 26th dawned, and the tanks were still motionless overlooking Dunkirk. Halder wrote despairingly in his first diary entry for the day:

'No change in the situation. Von Bock, suffering losses, is pushing slowly ahead. . . . Our armoured and mechanised forces are standing motionless on the heights of Béthune and St Omer as though they were rooted to the ground. On orders from above, they are not allowed to attack. At this rate, it can take weeks to clear up the cauldron, and that will be very damaging to our prestige and hamper future plans. All through the morning the Army Commander-in-Chief is very nervous. I can fully sympathise with him for these orders from the top just make no sense. In one area [Bock's army group] they call for a head-on attack against a front retiring in an orderly fashion and still possessing its striking power, and elsewhere they freeze the troops to the spot when the enemy rear could be cut into any time you wanted to attack.'[57]

But he concluded hopefully: 'Von Rundstedt, too, is clearly not hanging on any longer and has gone forward to Hoth and Kleist in order to get thing clear for the further advance of the mobile formations.'[58]

Even as Halder was penning these lines, the Führer himself was expressing considerable disquiet at the situation at Dunkirk, and at midday a telephone call from Führer headquarters notified OKH that Hitler had authorised the left wing to be moved to within artillery range of the town. This was followed by a summons to von Brauchitsch to attend upon the Supreme Commander. Jodl recorded the meeting: '18th and 6th Armies [Army Group B] are making only slow progress and II Corps in the south is meeting very stiff resistance. The Führer therefore agrees to a forward thrust from the west by panzer groups and infantry divisions in the direction of Tournai-Cassel-Dunkirk. . . .'[59] Halder noted that the Army Commander returned 'beaming' from this meeting at 2.30p.m. 'At last the Führer has given permission to move on Dunkirk in order to prevent further evacuations.'[60] At 3.30p.m., OKH issued orders accordingly. But the earliest the attack could resume was that night, and most units were not committed to battle for some sixteen hours. As Guderian pointed out, 'by then it was too late to achieve a great victory'.[61]

The organised opposition, with which the German ground attack now had to contend, was considerable. The War Diary of XXXIX Corps of the Hoth Group gave the reason for this: 'As foreseen, the enforced two-day halt on the southern bank of the canal produced two results on 27 May: first, the troops suffered considerable casualties when attacking across the la Bassée Canal, now stubbornly defended by the enemy; second, there was no longer time to intercept effectively the stream of French and English troops escaping westward from the Lille area towards the Channel.'[62] XXXXI Corps recorded on the 27th that 'At every position heavy fighting has developed. . . . In consequence, the corps has been unable to make any notable headway to the east or north-east. Casualties in personnel and equipment are grievous. The enemy are fighting tenaciously and, to the last man, remain at their posts.'[63] This was a new experience for the Germans in the campaign; time wasted by the Germans had been time gained by the Allies, a consequence which was in direct contradiction to the precepts of the armoured idea. Continued movement was essential, if only to keep the enemy off-balance and prevent him from organising a coherent defence. Now it was possible for Reinhardt's XXXXI Corps war diary to record that 'when engaged against enemy troops stubbornly defending a partly fortified held position, and particularly barricaded villages, the panzer division is not so suitable because it does not command sufficient infantry forces and because tanks make good targets for numbers of emplaced anti-tank weapons'.[64] Moreover, heavy rain had fallen on the 26th and 27th, and had rendered the marshy Flanders countryside around Dunkirk unsuitable for motorised units. On the 28th Guderian was forced to the conclusion that 'The infantry forces of this army [the 18th of Army Group B which was approaching from the east] are more suitable than tanks for fighting in this kind of country, and the task of closing the gap on the coast can therefore be left to them'.[65] Furthermore, in view of the forthcoming operations in the southern half of France, Guderian felt it was necessary to conserve his divisions, which had now only fifty per cent of their armoured strength, and not to pursue this 'useless sacrifice of our best troops'. Von Kleist agreed with this, and that same night, seven days before Dunkirk was to fall, orders were issued for the withdrawal and replacement of the XIX Corps. This was nothing less than a confession of failure on the part of the panzer leaders; the traditionalists had succeeded in imposing their conditions upon the battle.

The *Vernichtungsgedanke* that had been fought out in the first twenty-one days of the campaign in the west was, by any standards, an outstanding military achievement. On 4 June, OKW issued an official communiqué:

> 'The great battle of Flanders and Artois is over. It will go down in military history as the greatest battle of annihilation of all time. . . . The full extent of our victory in Holland, Belgium, and northern France can be gauged by the enemy's losses and the volume of booty captured. French, British, Belgian, and Dutch losses in terms of prisoners are in the region of 1,200,000 men. To these must be added the figure, not yet known, of killed, drowned, and wounded. The arms and equipment of some seventy-five to eighty divisions . . . have been destroyed or captured. . . . By comaprison with these figures, and in view of the scale of our success, the Wehrmacht's losses from 10 May to 1 June seem trivial: 10,252 officers, NCOs, and men killed, 8,463 missing . . . 42,523 wounded. . . . Since our adversaries persist in refusing peace, the fight will continue until they are destroyed utterly.'[66]

The Allies had lost sixty-one divisions, well over half their order of battle and the best they possessed, and three quarters of their most modern equipment. Facing the victorious Germans in the rest of France were only forty-nine divisions, many of them inadequately trained and armed, and, at most, only 200 tanks. That afternoon of the 4th, Winston Churchill for the first time publicly admitted the possibility of Germany dominating the continent of Europe.

Overwhelming though the German victory might have been, it was not decisive. On 30 May, Halder noted in his diary:

> 'He [von Brauchitsch] is angry, because the effects of the mistakes forced on us by OKW . . . are beginning to be felt now. We lost time and so the pocket with the French and British in it was sealed later than it could have been. Worse, the pocket would have been closed at the coast if only our armour had not been held back. As it is, the bad weather grounded our Air Force, and we must now stand by and watch countless thousands of the enemy get away to England right under our noses.'[67]

Some 366,000 troops, nearly a third of them Belgian and French, had been evacuated by the British from the Channel ports, principally from Dunkirk, to provide the Allies with the nucleus of an army with which to continue the war. Before the panzers had halted on the 24th, Churchill believed it would be lucky if as many as 45,000 soldiers managed to escape.

The reason for this failure on the part of the German Army was simple. It arose out of the unanimous lack of appreciation on the part of the German command of the potential of the new weapon in its armoury: the armoured force. Had Guderian and his commanders been released from the strict control imposed on them from above, had they been allowed to pursue the advance as they alone thought fit, and not been shackled to the mass of the army group, had the liberating idea of 'organised velocity' predominated over the paralysing fear of exposed flanks, then the fate of the Allied troops in the north might well have been sealed, and an important victory turned into . a total one. In the attack to the Channel, Army Group A's spearheads advanced an average of only twenty-two miles a day (the distance being measured as the crow flies) for ten days (including 17 May, when they were halted on orders for some twelve hours), a relatively slow rate considering that the last significant opposition was passed on the 15th, that the average top speed of German tanks was 25 mph, and that on the last day, the 20th, no fewer than fifty-six miles were covered by Guderian's troops. Because of the delays imposed from above on the 21st (through indecision) and on the 24th, 25th, and 26th (through considered policy), Army Group A's foremost unit advanced, on average, only nine miles per day from 22 May to 1 June. From 10 May until the 29th, when it was withdrawn from the front, Guderian's XIX Corps, as a result of the higher command's actions, was stationary for some 100 hours of the 700 it was in the field. The fears expressed by Hitler and von Rundstedt of enemy threats on the flanks were at no time proved to be justified, and the single counter-attack with any measurable success, that at Arras on the 21st, was mounted with only a small force and was never near to effecting any dislocation of the German advance. When Guderian reached the seaboard late on the 20th, there was nothing to prevent a strike eastwards up the coast at the undefended Allied rear. But the Germans proved incapable of exploiting the priceless opportunity then presented to them; consequently the events from 21 May to 4 June were for them a significant failure. The only obstacle to total victory lay not in the Allied opposition, which was, at first, negligible, or in the nature of the ground to be covered, which, before the rains, was quite adequate for any unopposed advance; it lay in the minds of the German commanders. Tradition had stifled revolution, and had ensured failure.

Even while Operation Yellow was in its initial stages, the General Staff, quite properly, was working on plans for the second, and final, phase of the destruction of France. On 21 May, the day after Guderian's troops reached the coast, the plan, known as *Fall Rot* (Operation Red) was presented to the Führer by Halder. Based on the doctrine of encirclement, OKH's proposal envisaged an attack along a broad front which spanned the 220 miles of

Army Group A's line of advance to the coast, along the Aisne and Somme rivers, and a further 200 miles along the Maginot Line and the Upper Rhine. The main thrust with nearly all the armour was to be launched west of Paris and a further attack would take place to the east. A few days later another advance would be initiated over the Upper Rhine and a secondary attack thrown against the Maginot Line near Saarbrucken. The object would be to surround and destroy the enemy forces in the Plateau de Langres south-west of Paris. Hitler, however, had other ideas; his main dissension from the OKH plan was that he wanted the bulk of the mechanised forces, and therefore the main attack, to bypass Paris on the east side. On the 31st, the final, amended OKH plan for Operation Red was issued. On 5 June, Army Group B was to attack both sides of Paris and make for the Seine; on 9 June, Army Group A was to launch its offensive, the *Schwerpunkt* of the operation, and advance east of Paris south-west through Rheims; about a week later, Army Group C was to battle its way through the Maginot Line and the Upper Rhine. The three forces would converge and, as intended originally, the great battle of annihilation would take place on the Plateau de Langres and within the bend of the Maginot Line.

The strongest part of the invasion force was Army Group B, with thirty-six infantry divisions (of which eighteen were First Wave, five Second Wave, and a mountain division), one cavalry division, four motorised infantry divisions, two motorised infantry brigades, and six panzer divisions – a total of forty-seven divisions, two brigades. Army Group A, although it was to undertake the main thrust, possessed two fewer divisions and fewer mechanised troops. Of its forty-five divisions, thirty-nine were infantry (fourteen First Wave and seven Second Wave), two were motorised infantry, and four were panzer. Both army groups had three armies, B, the 4th, 6th, and 9th, and A, the 2nd, 12th, and 16th. 18th Army, of four divisions, was to remain in the Dunkirk area for the time being. Army Group C, as befitted its secondary role, had only twenty-four infantry divisions, none of which were First Wave and only three Second Wave. OKH Reserve consisted of twenty-two infantry divisions, bringing the total in the west to 142. Only seven were left in the east, and a further seven in Norway. The mechanised units were organised into two groups, each of two corps. One group, under Guderian, spearheaded Army Group A, the other, under von Kleist, Army Group B, and one motorised Army Corps, the XV, under Hoth, was also attached to B.

Once again, the German operation was planned in accordance with traditional military precepts: decisive manoeuvre resulting in encirclement was the means to the physical destruction of the enemy. The OKH deployment order of 31 May contained no sign of any application of the armoured idea, and it made no mention of independent panzer groups which, although they were themselves the size and importance of armies, were to be subordinated to army control (Guderian to List's 12th Army, von Kleist to von Reichenau's 6th Army, and Hoth's corps to von Kluge's 4th Army). This control was to be rigidly maintained from the outset; for example, despite all Guderian's protests to the contrary, List persisted in giving the infantry corps the task of crossing the Aisne river and canal and establishing bridgeheads before the armour was released for the breakthrough. Apparently the lesson of the Meuse had not been understood; the panzers were relegated to a secondary role for the second time in the campaign (the first had been during the final advance on Dunkirk).

Although the German plan for Operation Red was unexceptional, the preparations for the final destruction of France were quite remarkable. For example, Guderian's 1st and 2nd Panzer Divisions had covered the 300-mile sweep to Dunkirk, and had then followed that by a further 200 miles to reach their starting positions for 'Red'. No wonder Guderian could record that 'Signs of extreme fatigue on the part of the troops and of wear of their vehicles began to be apparent.'[68] The troop and supply movements required for this change of front were extremely complex but, on the whole, were undertaken with high efficiency. Kesseling, commander of Luftflotte 2, later wrote: 'Anyone who watched from the air and on the ground, as I did, von Kleist's and Guderian's panzers swing round from the northern manoeuvre toward the Channel and drive south and south-east to the Somme and the Aisne, could not repress a surge of pride at the flexibility and skill of the German Army Command and the state of training of the troops.'[69]

Against this force, the remnant of the Allied armies were all but powerless. The new French commander, Weygand, faced the impossible task of defending central and southern France with an army inferior both in numbers and equipment, and with its forty-nine divisions extended from the Channel to the Maginot Line over a front of nearly 250 miles. He attempted to organise a defence in depth, a checker-board of centres of resistance based on villages, towns, and forests from which counter-attacks could be launched, continual jabs at the enemy thrusts designed to bring the German advance to a halt. But against the two hammer blows, first from the Somme and then from the Aisne, the French could do little.

At 4.00a.m. on 5 June, the Germans began the final destruction of France. After a short artillery barrage, units of Army Group B moved forward to their first main objective — the Seine. By the 9th the river was reached, in the very early morning by Hoth's mechanised corps, and roughly twelve hours later on the left by von Manstein's infantry corps. This was a remarkable achievement, not so much for the armour as for the infantry, who had advanced, while fighting, seventy-five miles in fewer than five days. By the 22nd, von Manstein's corps had covered no less than 300 miles on foot. The rest of the campaign closely followed this precedent: fast armoured advances rivalled by equally remarkable infantry manoeuvres. Indeed, Guderian recorded of his own advance with irritation: 'Our progress was made more difficult through confusion that arose from the impetuous advance of the infantry following behind us. The infantry units . . . in some cases . . . had caught up with the panzer units which were fighting their way forward. . . . Both arms of service wanted to lead the advance. The gallant infantrymen had marched day and night, so keen were they to get at the enemy.'[70] One panzer commander, von Mellenthin, remembered that the troops of the 197th Division 'gladly submitted to tramping thirty-five miles a day as everyone wanted "to be there" '.[71] Another infantry unit, the XXVI Army Corps, under General Wodrig, achieved an average rate of advance of twenty-one miles a day between 12 and 19 June from the Seine near Romilly to Moulins in the south. Such rates compared favourably with the movements of the mechanised formations such as Guderian's group, which daily averaged some forty miles.

Afterwards, as the coordinated attack increasingly took on the form of an unopposed pursuit into southern France, and as the German armies fanned out across the width of the country, the motorised and infantry components of the armies were each given different tasks, so that the infantrymen were no longer limited to following in the wake of the panzers but were instead given roles independent of the progress of the armour. For example, on 14 June, the day Paris fell, Army Group B sent its motorised forces westward to occupy the Normandy and Brittany peninsulas, while its infantry corps moved down to the south and south-west of France. Between Hoth on the Atlantic coastline and von Kleist and Guderian in Champagne, a distance of some 270 miles, there was not a single German tank to be seen, and yet the advance there continued unhesitatingly. The comment of von Bechtolsheim, the operations chief of 6th Army, concerning the earlier campaign in Flanders, was again appropriate: 'Even after the panzer group had been taken away, events proved that infantry attack was still possible without tank support – thanks to the way that the infantry had been trained, to well-controlled supporting fire, and to infiltration tactics. Widely dispersed threats create openings for concentrated thrusts.'[72]

Just as in Operation Yellow, so the handling of the mechanised forces by the higher commands in 'Red' left much to be desired. At the outset, von Kleist's group suffered the first failure experienced by German armour; its attacks north of Paris made slow progress, and on 8 June it was decided to pull it out of the line, remove it from von Reichenau's 6th Army (this was the second time this army had witnessed the removal of its armour), and attach it to 9th Army on the extreme left of von Bock's army group, near to Guderian. The cause of von Kleist's failure was simple: his troops had been thrown against the most heavily defended sector of the French front guarding their capital city, one that was relatively well-organised and of a fair depth. Furthermore, von Reichenau had gone against von Kleist's wishes and had split the two corps for a pincer stroke rather than concentrating their strength for a single *Schwerpunkt*. Thus, the armour was neither concentrated nor committed against the weakest point of the enemy, but instead was divided and sent against the strongest part of his line in an attack which was properly the province of the German infantry if, indeed, it should have been made at all.

To the east, where Army Group A lay, the offensive opened on the 9th, and immediately Guderian's formation ran into trouble. The infantry of List's army failed to cross the Aisne at Rethel, where the armour was concentrated in preparation, and it was not until late that night that elements of a panzer division managed to cross the river at another point gained by the infantry. At 6.30a.m. on the 10th, Guderian began the advance that should have started some twenty-four hours earlier — and it might well have done so had he been able to influence the planning of the operation.

During the victorious surge from the Aisne to the Marne, from there to the Swiss border and then up towards the Maginot Line, Guderian was dogged by command failures from above. The confusion resulting from the intermingling of the rapidly advancing infantry with the panzers has already been alluded to; nothing was done to alleviate it, despite the several protests made by Guderian to 12th Army headquarters. Further complications arose from the orders that continually came to the panzer group; despite the intentions of OKH to pursue Operation Red to its logical conclusion — the destruction of the enemy forces in the field — Hitler insisted on imposing his own conditions on the course of the battle. Although France's imminent fall was ensured, the Führer perversely insisted that it was necessary to secure Lorraine so as to deprive the French of their armaments industry. On 6 June, Halder wrote in desperation:

> 'The Führer thinks that changing the direction of the offensive [to the west], as proposed by me, is still too hazardous at this time. He wants to play absolutely safe. First, he would like to have a sure hold on the Lorraine iron-ore basin, so as to deprive France of her armament resources. After that, he believes it would be time to consider a drive in a westerly direction, probably having in mind a strong wing at the coast (4th Army). Here we have the same old story again. On top, there just isn't a spark of the spirit that would dare putting high stakes on a single throw. Instead, everything is done in a cheap piecemeal fashion, but with the air that we don't have to rush at all.'[73]

On the 10th, the Chief of the General Staff wrote: 'One could cry if it were not such a farce. What I recommended a few days ago is now being dispensed piecemeal and haltingly as the products of his supreme generalship.'[74] And three days later, Halder recorded: 'Führer headquarters now is slowly seeing the point of the recommendation made by me as early as 5 June, to the effect that the swing south-west should be made in the area east of Paris. . . . One could laugh about all this if that system did not always obstruct efficient work.'[75] Finally, on 19 June, Halder wrote:

> 'Some days ago I tried desperately hard to get permission to commit the armour and motorised infantry divisions on Kleist's right wing. At that time the plan was directly vetoed at top level. Now, after

those forces have been racing off in a south-easterly direction for several days, and not meeting organised resistance, they have to be reversed and ordered in a north-westerly direction. It is indeed an effort to keep calm in the face of such amateurish tinkering with the business of directing military affairs.'[76]

If the confusion at OKH was great, in the field it was greater. Fortunately for the Germans, every resistance was so weak and disorganised that their own misconduct of affairs proved not to be too dangerous. Guderian recorded:

'From now on [12 June], the panzer group received every day many mutually contradictory orders, some ordering a swing towards the east, others a continuation of the advance southward. First of all Verdun [to the east] was to be taken by means of a surprise attack, then the southward advance was to go on, then we were to swing east on St Mihiel, then again we were to move south once more. Reinhardt's corps was the one that suffered from all this vacillation; I kept Schmidt's corps on a steady course southwards, so that at least half of my panzer group was assured of continuity of purpose.'[77]

However, despite such deficiencies in the conduct of the advance, the second campaign in France went astonishingly well for the Germans. Apart from the check of von Kleist's group, everything proceeded very much as planned. On both sides of Paris the advance continued rapidly, so that, on 12 June, Weygand felt that he had no alternative but to inform the President of the Council of Ministers, M. Reynaud, that further resistance was useless and that an armistice should be sought; if not, 'chaos will take hold of the armies as it has already taken hold of the civilian population'.[78] On the 10th, Italy had entered the war on the side of the Third Reich, and on the 14th the Germans marched through Paris for the second time in seventy years. Their flanks turned, the French were dispersed to the west, shattered in the centre, and pushed up against their Maginot Line in the east. This line, upon which such hopes had been placed before the war, had already been pierced by Army Group C. There, between von Leeb's infantry and von Rundstedt's motorised formations, the final battle of annihilation took place; some 500,000 men were taken prisoner on 22 June, the day of the French acceptance of the armistice terms. Hostilities ended on the 25th, and Hitler announced to a jubilant nation: 'After fighting valiantly for six weeks, our troops have brought the war in the west to an end against a courageous enemy. Their heroic deeds will go down in history as the most glorious victory of all time.'[79] Holland, Belgium, and France had been conquered, Britain had been humiliated, and all at a cost to the Germans of 27,074 dead, 18,384 missing, and 111,034 wounded.

17

Decisions

I make decisions; I need men who obey.
ADOLF HITLER
1940

On 19 July, in celebration of Germany's great victory in the west, Hitler handed out honours by the handful to his soldiers. In doing so, he created twelve field-marshals – von Brauchitsch, Keitel, von Rundstedt, von Bock, von Leeb, List, von Kluge, von Witzleben, and von Reichenau, in order of seniority, and three from the Air Force, Milch, Kesselring, and Sperrle, – nineteen colonel-generals – among them Halder, Fromm, von Kleist, Guderian, Hoth, and Falkenhorst – and seven generals – foremost being Jodl and Dietl. Above them all came Göring, glorying in the new title of *Reichsmarschall des Grossdeutschen Reiches*. With these ranks went generous gifts of money, to allow the recipients to live as their new exalted positions demanded.

Never before in the history of the German Army had there been such a profusion of high ranks (throughout the First World War, for example, only five generals had been elevated to field-marshals). As a result, many felt that their quality and prestige had thereby been debased. Von Manstein recorded:

> 'Hitherto (apart from a few field-marshals nominated by Wilhelm II in peacetime) one needed to have led a campaign in person, to have won a battle or taken a fortress to qualify for this dignity. . . . Yet now he was creating a dozen simultaneously. They included . . . the Chief of OKW, who had held neither a command nor the post of a Chief of Staff. Another was the Under-Secretary of State for the Luftwaffe [Milch], who, valuable as his feats of organisation had been, really could not be ranked on a par with the Commander-in-Chief of the Army.'[1]

Whether Hitler deliberately intended to cheapen military rank is unknown, but he must have been aware of the deliberate slight to von Brauchitsch and to the Army by raising Göring above all other generals, and by making the

Luftwaffe Commander the sole recipient of the Grand Cross of the Knights' Cross, Germany's highest military decoration.

Awarded with high but meaningless ranks they might have been; fêted the generals certainly were not. During the First World War, victorious commanders had been accorded the status of national figures, and a man like von Hindenburg had been venerated equally with the Kaiser; now, it was Hitler the crowds greeted as the conquering hero, not the generals. Von Brauchitsch and Halder sought to reverse this position, to regain for themselves and for the officer corps the prestige of former days, aware as they were of their relative anonymity in the German nation. But Hitler, jealous of his glory, did all he could to frustrate their design; Halder recorded of von Brauchitsch in early September that he was 'very bitter about the obstacles put in his way whenever he wants to reach the public'.[2] Only a chosen few, such as Guderian or, more spectacularly, Dietl, the 'hero of Narvik', were to be publicly recognised as men who were brilliant field-commanders. In the area of strategy and in the direction of the Reich's war effort, which were the special province of the Führer, no one was to detract from his aura of genius and omnipotence; powerless anonymity was the lot of the Army's leadership.

The victory ceremony in the Reichstag on 19 July was symbolic of the relationship between Hitler and the military. The generals might sit in the balcony, glittering with gold braid and medals, all smiles and back-patting as they received their promotions, but it was one man, clad in a simple uniform of field-grey, who held the attention of the gathering, and of the nation: Hitler. His speech was not one of a Head of State gratefully thanking the authors of his country's victory; it was one of a Supreme Commander graciously acknowledging the help given to him by his assistants, an acknowledgement which served only to increase his own stature as a military leader. The plan for the downfall of France – had it not been his? The brave order for the attack – had he not given it? And the successful outcome of the campaign – had it not been due to his direction? To Keitel and Jodl, picked out for special praise, he accorded the role of playing 'the chief part in the realisation of *my* plans and ideas'.[3] The Army High Command and General Staff were thus pictured as mere automatons of their Führer's will. Bombast it might have been, but it nevertheless contained much truth. His interference in, and dictation of, the plans for Operation Yellow have already been described, as has also his continual interference in von Rundstedt's advance to the Channel. On one occasion, on the fateful 23 May, Hitler had even countermanded an order from the Army Commander-in-Chief, this being described by Halder as 'a new crisis of confidence'.[4] Indeed, during the campaign, Hitler's involvement with the direction of the ground manoeuvres had become compulsive. Keitel wrote flatteringly that 'the Führer liked to immerse himself in every detail of the practical execution of his ideas, so wide was the sweep of his unparalleled inventiveness. . . . there was no end to his questioning, intervening, and sifting of facts, until with his fantastic imagination he was satisfied that the last loophole had been plugged.'[5]

Others held a different view. Warlimont noted:

'Between the campaigns in Poland and Norway the habit had grown up of trying to run the battle in detail from the [Führer] headquarters, and the system had been tried out on a small scale in Norway. This dangerous game now continued, in spite of all Halder's warnings and in spite of the facts that we were now faced with a formidable enemy and were dealing with a rapidly changing situation. Diffuse discussion led to opinions, opinions to decisions and decisions to written directives or even direct intervention in dispositions already ordered by some military headquarters; although OKH was within a stone's throw, this was generally done without any previous reference to them. The best the Army leaders could expect was occasionally to be summoned to a briefing for some special reason but, just as in the preparatory period, they found themselves faced with preconceived ideas which only tiresome and time-wasting argument could alter. . . . There was therefore very soon an atmosphere of tension between these two neighbouring high-level headquarters. But on the side of the OKW stood Hitler, dominating everything, impatient and suspicious; he had no idea of time and space and refused to wait and let things develop; at the decisive moment, as in the case of Narvik, he would take fright at the boldness of his own decisions and then abdicate his authority and allow the situation to develop uncontrolled. Close at his side stood Keitel who, as always, considered his sole duty to be to support Hitler. . . . Jodl's influence was even greater. He . . . now seemed determined to ensure that the "Führer's genius" should win the day against the "indiscipline of the generals"; he did not appear to realise that the "pusillanimity" which he had previously ascribed to the General Staff had now become Hitler's sole prerogative.'[6]

Whatever the defects of Hitler's military leadership, after France one thing was clear: it was he, and he alone, who led the German Army. The victory in the west had confirmed his position as a military commander superior to his generals, the crowning triumph to a process that had begun in 1936 with the reoccupation of the Rhineland. The deterioration in the status of the Army High Command was thus taken one stage further; the victory of the German soldier in the field had been yet another defeat for the German general at home. The stunned submission of the Army commanders was even more complete than after the Czechoslovak affair, and they were more than content to leave decisions of peace and war to their Führer. Even the formerly sceptical Army Quartermaster-General, Eduard Wagner, could write: 'And wherein lies the secret of this victory? Indeed, in the enormous dynamism of the Führer . . . without his will it would never have come to pass.'[7]

From July to December 1940, the Army High Command was ordered to plan no less than seven operations: the invasion of England, the capture of the Azores, Canary, and Cape Verde islands, the occupation of Greece, the defence of the Finnish nickel mines, the protection of the Romanian oilfields, the support of the Italians in North Africa, and the attack against the Soviet Union. Yet throughout this period the Army leaders were not once called on to offer their advice to the Führer. As Wagner admitted, grand strategy was a subject 'of which we understand nothing, and which the Führer conducts quite alone, without any assistance, even from Göring'.[8] In July, the most important month, von Brauchitsch met Hitler on only two occasions, and between August and the end of December met him only once a month, while Halder, in the same six months, saw his Führer just eight times, and in October not at all. Hitler simply made his pronouncements, and delayed his final decisions if he so wished; the generals merely waited and obeyed. Unfortunately for the German Army, and for the Third Reich, the result was a grand strategy that was vacillating, wrong-headed, and disastrous in the long run.

Apart from the overriding importance of the proposed attack on the Soviet Union, the decision whether or not to invade Great Britain, the operation code-named *Seelöwe* (Sea-Lion), was certainly the most crucial of the period. Victory in the west had brought the Germans to the decisive turning-point of the war; in nine months they had defeated the Poles, overrun Norway and Denmark, crushed the Dutch, Belgians, and French, and forced the British to withdraw ignominiously from the Continent. Of Europe, only a part of Scandinavia, Italy, the Balkans, the Iberian peninsula, and the Soviet Union lay outside the Reich's domination, and these countries were either neutral or pro-German. Her Army exhausted, her alliances broken, Great Britain possessed only her fleet, her Channel, a far-off empire and an outnumbered air force with which to face Hitler's triumphant war-machine on an unbroken front extending from Narvik in the north to the Gironde in the south. It was an unequal struggle, and Halder had every reason for noting in his diary on 22 June 1940 that, if she continued to resist single-handed, 'the war will lead to Britain's destruction'.[9] In the summer and early autumn of 1940 Hitler held within his grasp the prize fervently sought by so many European conquerors: the conquest of Great Britain. The initiative was his, but he failed to exploit it. A year later, with Britain victorious in the air, secure round her shores, and intransigent in her aims, Hitler's attention was engrossed elsewhere – in the vast expanses of the east. The war had taken the course that in just three years was to lead to the downfall of the Third Reich.

In this momentous decision – to leave an undefeated island-fortress in the rear – and to turn instead on the Soviet Union, the German Army, which had wielded such immense influence over the course of the previous world conflict, took no part. At this, the most crucial juncture of the war, Germany's senior generals, her highest military professionals, could only say to Hitler: 'Command, and we will follow.' Advice, there was none.

From the Army's point of view, the failure to embark on the invasion of Britain represented a significant setback. Faced as it was by innumerable difficulties, foremost among which was the inadequacy of the Reich's naval resources, it is debatable whether the invasion ever possessed a reasonable chance of success. However, this is not at issue here (the question is, in any case, purely hypothetical); what is of considerable importance is the fact that the Army, alone of the three services, wanted 'Sea-Lion' to take place, and, moreover, was optimistic about its outcome. Yet in spite of this, its hopes and aspirations counted for nought in the final decision. Then, only two things mattered: Hitler's attitude, and the outcome of the Luftwaffe's performance in the skies over southern England.

Apart from a number of half-hearted service studies, the first time the idea of the invasion was contemplated as an act of policy was during a conversation between Hitler and Raeder on 21 May 1940, the day after Guderian's tanks had reached the Channel coast. But there was no attempt to prepare for a seaborne invasion after the victorious conclusion of Operation Yellow; not one voice was raised in protest at the concentration, for Operation Red, of 136 German divisions to defeat a demoralised, weak enemy less than half their size, instead of holding back certain divisions for the training of an amphibious invasion force. The question appeared to have been laid to rest on the issue of a Führer directive on 14 June, Halder noting in his diary the next day that the 'Luftwaffe and Navy alone will be carrying on the war against Britain'.[10] Then, on 25 June, Hitler unexpectedly informed the OKW Operations Staff that in a few days he wished to see studies for an invasion. From then on, the idea of a seaborne assault took shape: on 2 July an OKW directive declared that the Supreme Commander had decided an invasion might be possible, provided that air superiority could be achieved, and ordered the three services to draw up plans accordingly. On the 13th von Brauchitsch and Halder presented their proposals to Hitler, the first time they had seen him to discuss the affair; and on the 16th the Führer issued a directive 'On preparations for a landing operation against England', which stipulated: 'The Commanders-in-Chief will lead their forces, under my orders.'[11] Then, seven weeks after the Germans had reached the Channel, preparations began apace. Inter-service rivalries and lack of communication intensified, and by late August a compromise plan had been resolved, giving the Army a landing force and a landing area it believed inadequate, and the Navy a responsibility for transport which it feared to be too great. The Luftwaffe, engrossed in its private war with the RAF, gave little consideration to the matter. On 6 August Halder had noted: 'We have here the paradoxical situation where the Navy is full of apprehension, the Air Force is very reluctant to tackle a mission which at the outset is exclusively its own – and OKW, which for once has a real combined operation to direct, just plays dead. The only driving force in the whole situation comes from us. But alone we can't swing it.'[12]

The Army had embarked enthusiastically on its preparations, von

Brauchitsch regarding the whole operation a little optimistically as a 'large-scale river crossing'[13] and believing the entire operation would be concluded in a month. On 17 July, the diarist of the Naval Operations Directorate recorded: 'It appears that OKH, which a short time ago strongly opposed such an operation, has now put aside all its doubts and regards the operation as entirely practicable. . . .'[14] Indeed, the General Staff considered it of decisive importance. Even after 'Sea-Lion' had been postponed, Halder continued to regard the invasion as the surest way to hit England, and when the Army turned to move east, the senior generals were plagued by nagging doubts about the military propriety of leaving in their rear an undefeated Britain that was daily getting stronger. However, their thoughts had no effect on the supreme warlord. At no time did a hesitant Hitler commit himself irrevocably to the invasion, making it clear from the the outset that it was to be undertaken only after certain conditions had been met (most important being the victory of the Luftwaffe), and then only if necessary. In such a state of indecision were the plans and deployments for 'Sea-Lion' undertaken: on 31 July the target date of mid-August was delayed a month, to 17 September, and the final decision was put off until the results of the Luftwaffe's attack on the RAF were known; on 7 September, when the German Air Force's new mission, the complete destruction of London's docks, industries, and supplies, was announced, Hitler declared that his pronouncement on 'Sea-Lion' would depend on its outcome; on the 17th, when it was apparent that the RAF was, at the very least, surviving its desperate fight, OKW issued orders to postpone the invasion indefinitely, with options kept open for October; on 12 October, after the admitted failure of the air offensive, 'Sea-Lion' was further postponed, with the possibility of reopening it in the spring of 1941; and, on 5 December, Hitler told von Brauchitsch that the operation should be left out of the Army's considerations. On 2 March 1942, the idea of invasion was finally discarded altogether.

If the delays in the operation had been frustrating to the Army's leaders, its effective abandonment in October was a blow. But as the Army had partaken not at all in the strategic decision whether or not to invade, its enthusiasm for the operation had counted for nothing. In July, the month in which the idea and initial plans were formulated – the month, therefore, in which it was crucial to win the argument and force Hitler to commit himself to firm action – von Brauchitsch and Halder had seen Hitler only three times in all: the first, on the 13th – to present him with the OKH invasion plan, which he accepted – degenerated into an opportunity for the Führer to lecture the Chief of the General Staff on the political situation from the military angle; the second, on the 21st, was held in the presence of the service chiefs, and again Hitler regaled his audience with his view of world politics, brought up the question of attacking the Soviet Union, and pointed out the naval difficulties involved in 'Sea-Lion', while von Brauchitsch could only express his optimism; and at the third, on 31 July, when Hitler announced his decision to invade the Soviet Union and listened to Raeder's recommendation for a postponement of 'Sea Lion' until the following spring, it appears that the Army Commander and his Chief of Staff said absolutely nothing concerning the operation. At no time did von Brauchitsch have an informal conversation with his Supreme Commander, as, for example, Raeder did, and no attempt was made to submit a written memorandum on the subject. The generals confined themselves in Hitler's presence to the technical details of the operation; its strategic desirability they left to their own counsels.

Thus, the military made no attempt to counter Hitler's fears about the invasion and affect him with their enthusiasm for the idea. The Führer considered that the risks were too great, and agreed with Raeder that the invasion should be undertaken only as a last resort, carried out against an enemy already broken by blockade and air attack. A reversal on the beaches of England's south coast, although it would not have been unacceptably injurious militarily, he considered to be unthinkable politically. Any outcome other than total victory might seriously impair his personal prestige, and that he was careful to preserve above all else. Furthermore, the Army failed to challenge his assertion that the amphibious assault had to await the Luftwaffe's dominance of the skies over Britain, an idea which von Manstein later described as 'an error of leadership'.[15] Had 'Sea-Lion' been conceived not as a mopping-up operation after a successful air attack over all southeast England, but as a major offensive for conquering Britain in which each of the three services was to play an equally crucial role, then the Luftwaffe would have joined battle with the RAF over the Channel and the beaches immediately before, and during, the landings. The operational conditions would have put the German planes on a more equal operational footing with the British, and might well have led to victory in the air and, consequently, over the sea and on the land. Certainly, once ashore, the German force would have faced relatively weak opposition from the British Army. But OKH suggested nothing; it would advise only on Hitler's request, and this he did not make. At the crucial time, no attempt was made to influence Germany's war policy. Instead, Hitler's instability of purpose, his search for easy solutions, and his military naïvety were allowed to dominate unchallenged.

Nor did the Army leaders take any part in initiating, or influencing, the other grand-strategic decisions of 1940, the most important of which, apart from the invasion of the USSR, was the extension of the war against Great Britain to the periphery of Europe. The British Empire was seen as the prize, and Gibraltar and Suez especially were considered to be the immediate aims. Their occupation would seal off the Mediterranean, enabling the Reich to seize the spoils of the Near East, above all, the oil. The generals were not averse to such a course of action; von Brauchitsch even advocated limited support of the forthcoming Italian offensive on Egypt to Hitler during the conference on 31 July, to which the Führer replied that the proposal should be studied. Further pressure for some move in the Mediterranean came from

OKW and the Navy. In memoranda issued in January, March, and June, Jodl had proposed such a move, and in two private meetings with Hitler in September, Raeder supported the idea. Hitler was at last persuaded. On 27 September he concluded a tripartite pact with Italy and Japan, and then proceeded to broaden the coalition by attempting to secure the adherence of Spain and Vichy France, both of which would be valuable as a springboard for any attack in the Mediterranean area. In this, however, he was to fail. But, not to be put off, on 4 November he outlined his plans to the military commanders: he had decided not to send troops to Libya until the Italians had advanced further into Egypt, but instead – with the help of Spain – Gibraltar, the Canary Islands, and the Cape Verde Islands would be taken (in Operation 'Felix') and the Mediterranean closed to the British. Even Portugal might have to be occupied to deny the Iberian peninsula to the enemy. These decisions Hitler confirmed in his Directive No. 18, issued eight days later. The OKH, which had already surveyed the situation of Gibraltar, immediately began to draw up plans for 'Felix', and to elaborate its ideas on the future aid to Italy in North Africa. On 5 December, the day von Brauchitsch was informed that 'Sea-Lion' must be left out of his calculations, Hitler stipulated that 'Felix' should take place not later than 10 January 1941.

Then came a setback. The British counter-attacked in the desert and pushed the Italians back at lightning speed; Spain refused to enter the war on the side of Germany. Thus, on the 10th December, OKW issued an order stating that 'Felix' was abandoned, and on the same day, Hitler dictated his Directive No. 19, which proposed that Vichy France should be occupied, the western Mediterranean crossed, and French North Africa taken. This was the only decision of the many taken in those months that was directly influenced by the Army High Command. It was the product of a visit to Keitel by Halder on the 8th, and Hitler's approval of the OKH's draft plans on the 9th. The Führer did, however, reserve to himself 'the right to decide how this operation will be carried out'.[16] Ironically, the occupation of Vichy France, code-named 'Attila', never took place, for it was overtaken by events. On 31 December the German military attaché in Rome telegraphed Halder to inform him that the Italians in North Africa were completely defeated; it was then obvious that the Italian forces were in danger of collapsing. On 8-9 January 1941, Hitler held a military conference at which he stressed the importance of getting immediate aid to the Italians before Libya was overrun. This was to be seen as a stop-gap measure before the Axis offensive was resumed there in late 1942. 'Attila', therefore, was superseded by *Sonnenblume* (Sunflower), the operation to send covering forces to hold Tripolitania, although it was kept under review in case of any trouble from the Vichy government. Directive No. 22 of 11 January confirmed these decisions. Such was the genesis of the famous North African campaign.

At the same time as Hitler was planning his moves against the British Empire in the Mediterranean, he was also forced to consider action in the

Balkans. On 28 October 1940, Mussolini, much against Hitler's desires, launched his invasion of Greece. It was an inept military operation, soon to go wrong. In retaliation the British occupied the islands of Crete and Lemnos, the latter providing them with an advanced air base from which they could invade the Balkans and bomb the Romanian oil fields so vital to Germany's oil supply. Thus, the Balkans were brought sharply to the attention of Hitler and to the Army High Command. At his conference of 4 November, when he announced his decision to occupy Gibraltar, the Führer also ordered that the Romanian oilfields be protected. He requested that plans should be drawn up for an invasion of Greece to be undertaken from the German bases in Romania and Bulgaria (code-named 'Marita') so as to enable the Luftwaffe to attack targets in the eastern Mediterranean, especially Crete and Lemnos. These requirements he confirmed in his Directive No. 18 of 12 November. On 5 December, Hitler set the date for 'Marita' for early March, although the final decision as whether or not to undertake it was left open. A few days later, as the British were sweeping up the Libyan desert, the Greeks sent the Italians in Albania reeling back. On 13 December, Directive No. 20 was issued, reaffirming the importance placed on 'Marita' and stipulating the conditions on which it was to be undertaken. A month later, on 9 January 1941, at the Führer conference, Hitler ordered that the troops for 'Marita' be ready for the offensive no later than 26 March, one month later than OKH wanted. And on 11 January, the Führer's Directive No. 22, entitled 'German support for battles in the Mediterranean area', announced assistance to the Italians in Tripolitania, at the same time as a rescue operation to aid the Italians in Albania, under the code-name *Alpenveilchen* (Alpine Violet). On 17 February, predictions of bad weather in the Balkans caused a postponement of the starting date for 'Marita' until 2 April, but in spite of this hitch preparations proceeded apace. By the third week of February, the Germans had massed 680,000 men in Romania, and on the night of the 28th, in pursuance of an agreement signed twenty days earlier, troops of the 12th Army crossed the Danube and took up strategic positions in Bulgaria, which then joined the Tripartite Pact. Yugoslavia followed; on 25 March Prince-Regent Paul allied his country with the Germans and Italians. The way was open for the invasion of Greece on 1 April.

Then came the Yugoslav coup. During the night of 26–27 March, the government of Prince-Regent Paul was overthrown and the agreement with Germany repudiated. Hitler's calculations had gone awry; the dictator erupted into one of his wildest rages. On the 27th he decided 'to annihilate Yugoslavia',[17] and issued Directive No. 25 which linked the invasion of that country with operation 'Marita'. It laid down fairly detailed orders for the military moves, based on a plan known as Operation Twenty-Five drawn up by Halder and von Brauchitsch and presented to him that same afternoon. On the 29th, military cooperation between Germany and Hungarian forces was agreed on, and on 3 April Hitler's Directive No. 26 laid down guidelines for 'cooperation with our allies in the Balkans'.[18] At dawn on 6 April the German Army fell on Yugoslavia and Greece, and in three weeks all was over.

Four grand strategic decisions were taken in the year following the fall of France in June 1940. All were bound inextricably one with another; all had considerable influence on the course of the war; and all contributed in some measure to Germany's final defeat. But one was of such crucial importance that it completely overshadowed the rest. Whether or not to invade Great Britain, to become involved in North Africa, or to occupy the Balkans were, indeed, full of significance for the future; but whether or not to attack the Soviet Union was crucial. By his decision to launch the invasion, Hitler committed the German nation to a life-or-death struggle in which total defeat was the only alternative to total victory. All now would depend on the quality of the advice received from the military leaders, and on the capacity of the Führer to accept it. Should either of these conditions not prevail, disaster would result.

As was by now the accepted practice, it was Hitler alone who made the decision to move eastwards. On 21 July 1940, two days after his victory speech in the Reichstag , Hitler announced to his assembled Wehrmacht chiefs that he was considering an attack on the Soviet Union. This moment-ous declaration he approached cautiously, presenting it as a measure made necessary by Stalin's 'flirtation' with Great Britain. A plan for the invasion was proposed – by whom it is not known precisely – the aim of which Halder recorded as: 'the defeat of the Russian army, or the capture of at least as much Russia territory as necessary to prevent enemy air attacks against Berlin and the Silesian industrial areas. It would be desirable to advance far enough to attack the most important Russian centres with our Air Force.'[19] Victory would be achieved that autumn by, at most, 100 divisions.

No doubt the response expected by the Führer was, at the very least, one of scepticism, similar to that which had greeted his proposals for the military reoccupation of the Rhineland, the annexations of Austria and Czecho-slovakia, and the attack on the west. But von Brauchitsch said not a word against the new proposition. The reasons for this change of attitude were two: practical and political. The Army leaders viewed the Soviet Union, its leaders and its ideology, with a mixture of suspicion and contempt; they fully agreed with Beck, who warned that it might become 'a serious or, under certain circumstances, a deadly danger'.[20] The generals were keen to end the traditional Slavonic rivalry for the domination of Eastern Europe, and constantly expressed their fears as to the future expansionist intentions of Stalin's Soviet Union, which, even if they did not actually conflict with Germany on purely territorial questions, nevertheless posed a threat to the Reich's supremacy in Europe. Economic and psychological subversion were also considered a real risk. Therefore, after the fall of France, the attention of OKH had become ever increasingly focused on the Soviet Union, for sound grand-strategic reasons. Divisions were transferred to the east, and on 25 June it was ordered that twenty-four, including six panzer and three motorised infantry, be sent there and placed under the command of von Küchler for 'special military tasks'. It was specified that they should not *'openly* [author's italics] reveal a hostile attitude'.[21] At the beginning of July, Halder had warned that, apart from Great Britain, the other major problem still left for the Army was the delivery of 'a military blow at Russia which will force her to recognise Germany's dominant role in Europe'.[22]

However, it was not until 13 July that the OKH received the necessary impetus for the preparation of a detailed plan of action against the Soviet Union. Until then, the projected invasion of England had occupied the attentions of the generals, and probably would have continued to do so had not Hitler dropped certain hints in conversation with von Brauchitsch. Halder recorded in his diary for that day: 'The question in the forefront of the Führer's mind is why England is still unwilling to make peace; like us, he thinks that the answer is that England still has some hope of action on the part of Russia.' The Army Commander thereupon asked his Chief of the General Staff to take this problem into account so that 'OKH shall not be caught unprepared'.[23] Thus the practical merged with the political; not only did the Army leaders believe it was militarily necessary to prepare for a conflict against the Soviet Union, they also saw it as the means by which they could regain some of their influence with Hitler. Instead of pessimism, they would exude optimism; in place of doubts, they would present plans. Their Führer would have no cause to mistrust or to humiliate them; rather he would be grateful for the whole-hearted assistance given to him by the Army. Such were the considerations that lay behind OKH's initial zeal for the new foreign adventure. As a result, when on 21 July Hitler broached the subject of an eastern invasion, the Army leaders had already begun the planning of such an operation.

Shortly after the conference, Hitler asked for a memorandum on the subject from OKW; it returned the verdict that an autumn attack was totally impracticable. Hitler then decided on a campaign with a more ambitious objective – the total extinction of the Soviet Union – and a later starting date: spring 1941. This, Hitler believed, was the first and last date on which sufficient forces could safely be concentrated for an attack on such a vast scale. Any earlier, the Wehrmacht would not be ready, and the weather would be unsuitable; any later, the peak of operational efficiency would be passed and the strength of the German forces, compared with that of their enemies, would be on the wane. May 1941 was the date on which the destruction of Bolshevism was to begin.

But the Army leaders, although they were convinced of the need some day to deal with the Soviet Union – and, moreover, that Germany was capable of doing so – now, once again, became concerned at Hitler's intentions. They thought that he failed to appreciate the true priority of the Reich's grand-strategic objectives. Although they remained confident of the

Army's ability to defeat the USSR, they came to doubt the wisdom of attempting it at that time. In their opinion, the invasion of the Soviet Union should be contemplated only after Britain had been subdued. Indeed, on 30 July, von Brauchitsch and Halder had come to the conclusion that an attack on Russia in 1941, as an alternative to action against England, could be positively dangerous. The latest intelligence reports had revealed that Red Army strength was significantly greater than previously thought, while the head of Army signals, General Fellgiebel, had said that preparation of communication-networks simultaneously for both the east and for 'Sea-Lion' was impossible. Furthermore, pessimistic reports were being received about Italian chances in the North African desert. Such factors made the Army leaders realise that, instead of starting a war on two fronts, it was better for the time being to remain friendly with the Soviet Union, which showed no immediate signs of hostility, and to concentrate on attacking Great Britain and her empire with all the resources at Germany's disposal. History had shown that a defiant Britain, with her fleet intact and her empire around her, was the greatest of dangers to a Continental power; this was especially true at that time, when she had an air force capable of striking deep into the Reich's territory. Moreover, the Russians might even be induced to cooperate with the Reich, especially in connexion with their desired expansion towards the Persian Gulf. Britain before the Soviet Union, therefore, was the generals' programme of conquest. Halder noted on 30 July: 'The question whether, if a decision cannot be enforced against England and the danger exists that England allies herself with Russia, we should first wage against Russia the ensuing two-front war, must be met with the answer that we should do better to keep friendship with Russia. A visit to Stalin would be advisable. . . . We could hit the English decisively in the Mediterranean [and] drive them out of Asia. . . .'[24] Even Jodl believed that, if economic circumstances made it necessary to choose between the two courses of action, then the invasion of England should take precedence; the attack on the USSR 'could be postponed because it is not a dire necessity for the victory over Britain'.[25]

Hitler, however, did not share the views of his military advisers: he was not even aware of them. As far as can be seen from the records, only twice, on 5 and 9 December, did any representative of OKH even tentatively broach the subject, and then the first occasion was restricted merely to questioning the Luftwaffe's capacity to undertake a war on two fronts, and not the Army's. Perhaps the military leaders realised that any hesitation on their part, especially coming as it did after their unrestrained enthusiasm at the Führer conference on 21 July, would have brought into the open, once again, Hitler's mistrust and contempt for his generals, something they dare not risk. All appearance of vacillation was carefully avoided; the Army proceeded to be merely the silent executor of its Supreme Commander's will.

And so, from 21 July 1940, only eight days after the plans for 'Sea-Lion' had been approved, there began the process by which the defeat of Britain was relegated by Hitler to a lower priority than the attack on the Soviet Union. By the end of July, the Führer's mind was becoming set on dealing with Russia in the spring of 1941. From this time on, the defeat of Britain was not made a condition to the invasion of the Soviet Union, although, until the invasion, operations against 'Perfidious Albion' would continue with every hope of success. Indeed, it now became, for a short while, imperative to defeat Britain as soon as possible. On 26 July, the preparations for a landing were placed above 'Priority No. 1' of the Reich's economic objectives, and on 31 July the final decision to launch an air offensive was taken. However, failure in the skies over south England, together with Hitler's continuing doubts about the feasibility of a seaborne invasion, led to the fight in the west being relegated to the status of a side-show compared with the preparations for the move east. On 31 August, the landing ceased to have top priority in the Reich's allocation of resources; on 17 September 'Sea-Lion' was postponed indefinitely; and by the end of the month it was clear that the air offensive had been unsuccessful. Not that Hitler worried; he reasoned that Britain would still be there when he would have finished with the Soviet Union by the middle of the autumn of 1941. He did not see that his decision to turn eastwards involved a war on two fronts – the traditional German nightmare. After all, by the time the Bolshevik Empire had been destroyed, Britain would still be far from able to launch an invasion of the Continent; she would remain merely an irritation, one which an increase in U-boat production and a strengthening of the Reich's anti-aircraft defences would go far to alleviate.

Such were the thoughts behind the process of decision to invade the Soviet Union, a process that began on 21 July and ended on 18 December. On 31 July, at a conference with his military leaders, Hitler stated his belief that a decisive victory could be achieved only by the defeat of Britain, but that this might be brought about by the elimination of the Soviet Union, which, together with the neutralisation of the United States by the power of Japan, would end all hope for the little island. Halder's cryptic notes on Hitler's remarks state: 'Russia must be defeated in the course of this struggle. Spring 1941.'[26] Preparations were ordered to begin. On 28 September, Hitler issued a major directive which confirmed his orders for the preparation of the attack and for the increase in the size of the Army necessary for such an operation. On 12 November, Directive No. 18 declared: 'Political discussions for the purpose of clarifying Russia's attitude in the immediate future have already begun. Regardless of the outcome of these conversations, all preparations for the east for which verbal orders have already been given will be continued. Further directives will follow on this subject as soon as the basic operational plan of the Army has been submitted to me and approved.'[27]

After conversations with Molotov, the Soviet Foreign Minister, during the next few days, it became clear that any hope of a German-Soviet coalition against Britain was still-born. At the Führer conference of 5 December, it was clear that Hitler took it for granted that an attack on the Soviet Union would take place in spring 1941. 'Sea-Lion' was 'no longer possible';[28] the Mediterranean excursion (Operation Felix, the occupation of Gibraltar) would begin as soon as events allowed; and the preparations for the occupation of Greece (Operation Marita) were to continue. Apart from von Brauchitsch's feeble questioning, already mentioned, of the Luftwaffe's capacity to cope with such an extension of the war, no general openly doubted the wisdom of the Führer's proposed course; Halder did not even mention his fear that 'Marita' might delay the opening of the attack in the east. Instead, the Chief of the Army General Staff dutifully presented OKH's operational plan for the invasion of the Soviet Union.

It was not until 9 December that any member of OKH summed up enough courage to tackle Hitler specifically on the absolute necessity for defeating Great Britain. Halder, when called to discuss with Hitler the situation in the Mediterranean, stressed the need to concentrate on the invasion of England and to counter any strengthening of the enemy's position in North Africa or any formation of a Balkan front. Nothing, however, was said about postponing the eastern campaign, and Hitler merely expressed agreement with the Chief of the General Staff. No good came of Halder's attempt; it came far too late. The Führer's opinion had been set rigid for four months. On 18 December, he issued his Directive No. 21 for the conduct of the war. It left no doubt as to his attitude: 'The German Armed Forces must be prepared, even before the conclusion of the war against England, to crush Soviet Russia in a rapid campaign. The Army will have to employ all available formations to this end, with the reservation that occupied territories must be insured against surprise attacks. . . . Preparations [long-term ones] . . . will be concluded by 15 May 1941.'[29]

Nevertheless, OKH, as if unable to comprehend reality, was still unwilling to believe the seriousness of Hitler's intentions. Von Brauchitsch, for example, asked the Führer's Army adjutant to establish whether Hitler really intended to resort to force, or was merely bluffing. The generals' disquiet over Britain grew even more marked. In July, when they had first thought of the plans for the attack eastwards, the British were a weak enemy daily expecting invasion; by December they had successfully defeated a concerted attack by the Luftwaffe; they had bombed targets within the Reich throughout the autumn; they had inflicted serious reverses on Italy, both at sea and in North Africa; and, by their defiance, they had discouraged Spain from entering the war on the side of the Axis and had encouraged an independent attitude in the leadership of Vichy France, an independence which had even necessitated German plans for the occupation of Vichy. Thus, the OKH leaders clung stubbornly to Operation Sea-Lion, even though the conditions in which it might have been possible had passed, and Hitler had stated categorically that it was not now part of his policy. Göring and Raeder, too, although they recognised the strength of the Führer's determination, were opposed to the attack on Russia. Göring's protest was unlikely to have been strong, but Raeder's was unequivocal. On 27 December, he told Hitler that it was vital to recognise that the prime task should be the fight against Britain, to which assertion he received the same old reply: this could not be achieved until the Soviet Union had been defeated; only then could production priorities be switched from the Army to the other two services, and a seaborne invasion seriously contemplated. The Grand Admiral then realised that all further argument was completely useless. Once again, Hitler had decided on his course of action alone, and the few uncoordinated, desultory attempts to deflect him from it came to naught.

The disquiet of the generals continued to grow. On 28 January 1941, a conference between Halder and the senior administrators of the Army and Luftwaffe placed emphasis on the purely practical difficulties of any invasion in the east. Most important were the strains that would be imposed on the supply system, due in large part to enemy demolition and to the difference in gauge between the German and Soviet railways. Deficiencies in stocks of fuel and tyres, too, were disturbing, for they would restrict severely the ability of the already insufficient motor transport to provide adequate logistic support for the invasion force. That evening Halder noted gloomily in his diary:

> 'The purpose [of the operation] is not clear. We do not strike at the British, and our economic potential will not be improved. The risk in the west should not be underestimated. It is even possible that Italy might collapse after losing her colonies [at this time the Germans were not in North Africa] and we find ourselves with a southern front through Spain, Italy, and Greece. If we are then committed against Russia, our position will become increasingly difficult.'[30]

The next day, at a luncheon attended by von Brauchitsch, Halder, and the three commanders of the army groups designated for the invasion, all expressed considerable doubt about the grand-strategic position of the Reich. One of them, von Bock, observed, 'Brauchitsch gives a picture of the situation which does not please me',[31] and expressed his doubts as to whether the Red Army would be destroyed west of the Dvina-Dnepr line before it retreated virtually intact into the vast interior of the Soviet Union. Halder conceded 'that it might well turn out differently'[32] to what had been planned. Three days later, on 1 February, von Bock, a bold man, raised some of his objections with the Führer himself. Although he agreed that the Soviets would be defeated if they were made to give battle, he wondered whether they could be forced to make peace. Hitler answered that he was sure that, once Leningrad, Moscow, and the Ukraine had been captured, further resistance would be impossible. And if it were, he continued, 'I am happy that our war production is equal to any demand. We have such an abundance of material that we had to reconvert some of our war plants [to civilian production]. The Armed Forces now have more manpower than at the beginning of the war, and our economy is in an excellent condition.'[33] When the severe shortages that were then facing the Army are taken into consideration, the extent to which Hitler had already lost his grip on reality is clear.

Had the generals pressed home their doubts, the Führer might have wavered from his plan, for Hitler himself was then suffering from a growing anxiety that all was not well. On 18 December, Engel, his Army adjutant, noted: 'The Führer doesn't yet know himself how things should go. He is constantly preoccupied with mistrust towards his military leaders, uncertain over the Russians' strength and disappointed at the toughness of the British.'[34] He now began to fear attacks on the flanks of the proposed advance, and he doubted the encouraging reports he had received on the weakness of the Soviet war industry. He also expressed concern at any future British attack in Norway, especially in the light of their successful raid on the Lofoten Islands in early March, and worried about their possible support for the Russians through Murmansk, the Arctic port. In March, he wondered whether the *coup d'état* in Yugoslavia would strengthen the British influence in the Balkans. The Army leaders, however, did nothing to increase Hitler's self-induced doubts; von Bock's was a lone voice in questioning the wisdom of the plan. On 3 February, at a meeting with the Führer, Halder made no mention of the immense logistical problems; instead, he merely outlined a number of the difficulties, and then proceeded to explain how they could be overcome. Likewise, the General Staff's study of the possibility that the Pripyat Marsh might become a point of Soviet resistance in the centre of the German advance, presented to Hitler on 1 March, contained no cause for concern, declaring that only cavalry divisions and other enemy units up to regimental strength could operate there at all effectively. Moreover, when Hitler demanded that security along the coastline of Europe should be increased, thereby dissipating the Army's already limited strength, von Brauchitsch made no attempt to point out that this would weaken unduly the already minimal force committed to the east. Thus, once again, the Reich embarked on a course of action by the will of the Führer and by the default of the generals.

18

'Barbarossa' – The Plans

*The Russian colossus will be proved to be a pig's
bladder; prick it, and it will burst.*

GENERAL ALFRED JODL
Chief of Operations, OKW

The military planning for the invasion of the Soviet Union had preceded by
almost three weeks Hitler's decision to attack. On 3 July 1940, Halder had
asked Colonel von Greiffenberg, of the Operations Branch of the Army
General Staff, to study 'the requirements of a military intervention which
will compel Russia to recognize Germany's dominant position in Europe'.[1]
This was a somewhat vague order of reference, but on 21 July Hitler made it
more specific. Halder's notes on the conference include the following:

> 'German assembly will take at least four to six weeks. Object: to
> crush the Russian Army, or slice as much Russian territory as is
> necessary to bar enemy air raids on Berlin and the Silesian indus-
> tries. It is desirable to penetrate far enough to enable our Air Force to
> smash Russia's strategic areas. . . . Political aims: Ukrainian State,
> Federation of Baltic States, White Russia – Finland. . . . Strength
> required: 80 to 100 divisions; Russia has 50 to 75 . . . divisions.'[2]

The Romanian oilfields were also to be protected. At the 31 July Führer
conference, Hitler confirmed these objectives, and, according to Halder,
added:

> 'The object is the destruction of Russian manpower. The operation
> will be divided into three sections: first thrust to Kiev and secure
> flank protection on the Dnepr. Luftwaffe will destroy river crossings
> [and ?] Odessa; second thrust to Baltic States and drive on Mos-
> cow; finally, link up of northern and southern wings [presumably
> east of Moscow]. Successively: limited drive on the Baku oilfields [in
> the Caucasus].'[3]

All this would be achieved with 120 divisions.

Such were the specifications given to OKH by the Supreme Commander. The geographical objectives of the over-all advance met with little or no

dissension; but the actual strategy of the invasion, the 'lines of thrust', were by no means generally acceptable. On 26 July, after a briefing with Colonel Kinzel, of the Foreign Armies, East, Branch of the General Staff, Halder noted: 'The best chances of success lie in an operation in the direction of Moscow with flank on the Baltic Sea, which, subsequently by a drive from the north, compels the Russian concentrations in the Ukraine and on the Black Sea to accept battle on an inverted front.'[4] This bold scythe-cut, so reminiscent of von Schlieffen, might well have resulted in the greatest encirclement battle of history; whether it would have been successful is another matter. Certainly, other members of the General Staff, some of whom wanted a strong attack in the south, advised caution, and Halder agreed to defer his final decision.

On 29 July, Halder gave to General Erich Marcks, Chief of Staff to 18th Army then in the east, the special task of planning the invasion of the Soviet Union; by 1 August his plan was ready. In it, Marcks rejected the idea of a single thrust, making instead proposals corresponding closely, although unwittingly, with Hitler's specifications of the previous day. Marcks envisaged the campaign in two phases: in the first, the Germans would seek to encircle and destroy the main Soviet armies close to the frontier; in the second, the most valuable industrial areas of European Russia would be occupied – Leningrad, Moscow, and the Donets Basin of the Ukraine – and a line Archangel-Gorkiy-Rostov achieved. Two operational groups, one directed at Moscow, the other at Kiev, would be employed. Halder, while accepting the basic premises of Marcks's plan, pointed out 'that Operational Group Kiev, based on Romanian territory, is treading on very insecure political ground, and . . . that the extension of the operations of the Moscow Group into the Baltic States should be treated as a subsidiary action which must not detract from the main thrust of Moscow'.[5] Because of the economic, political, and military importance of the Soviet capital, Halder argued, it was there that the Red Army was likely to make its final stand. As the most vital aspect of the campaign was to destroy the Red Army, it was therefore necessary to concentrate the main German effort of the second, or 'pursuit', phase on Moscow, thereby relegating the drives on Leningrad and the Donets Basin to subsidiary, flanking operations.

With this in mind, Marcks produced his final plan on 5 August. The methods by which the objectives would be attained were conditioned by four factors: the strength and disposition of the Soviet forces, as estimated by German intelligence; the geographical feature of the Pripyat Marsh, a vast area of swampland, 150 miles in width from north to south and over 300 miles in length, which lay in the centre of the proposed front; the proximity to the Soviet border of the Romanian oilfields, so important to the German war economy; and the unreliability of the Balkan countries of Hungary and Romania as military allies, at least in the initial stages of the operation. Because Marcks's operational proposals distilled much of the contemporary thought among the German leadership as to the aims and methods of any attack in the east, and because it provides a base by which to evaluate the future development of the invasion plan, it is worth quoting fairly extensively from its pages.

Marcks began his appreciation with a definition of the operational aims:

> 'The purpose of the campaign is to strike the Russian Armed Forces and to make Russia incapable of entering the war as an opponent of Germany in the foreseeable future. In order to protect Germany against Russian bombers, Russia must be occupied to the line lower Don-central Volga-north Dnepr. The main centres of the Russian war economy lie in the food and raw-material producing areas of the Ukraine and Donets Basin and in the armament industries of Moscow and Leningrad. The eastern industrial regions are not yet productive enough. *Of these areas, Moscow constitutes the economic, political, and spiritual centre of the USSR. Its capture would destroy the coordination of the Russian state* [author's italics].'

Marcks continued with an appreciation of the terrain of the 'War Zone', and pointed out that the Pripyat Marsh divided the frontier zone into two separate operational areas. He then proceeded to deal with enemy intentions, foremost among which he envisaged 'a Russian breakthrough into Romania . . . in order to deprive us of oil. At the very least, strong air attacks on the Romanian oilfields must be expected.' Marcks then made an important distinction between the proposed operation and Napoleon's 1812 campaign, which had ended in disaster: '. . . the Russians cannot avoid a decision as they did in 1812. Modern armed forces of 100 divisions cannot abandon their sources of supply. It is expected that the Russian Army will stand to do battle in a defensive position protecting greater Russia and the eastern Ukraine.' He gave the strength of the Red Army as 151 infantry divisions, 32 cavalry divisions, and 38 motorised brigades, of which 96, 23, and 28 respectively were ranged against Germany. These were 'almost evenly divided south and north of the Pripyat Marsh, with a reserve around Moscow. This form of distribution can also be expected in the event of a war with Germany.' The Soviet armoured strength was negligible, and there was little doubt as to the general weakness of the army as a whole. 'Because the Russians no longer possess the superiority of numbers they had in the World War [I], it is more likely that once the long, extended line of their forces has been broken through, they will be unable to concentrate, or to coordinate counter-measures. Fighting in isolated battles, they will soon succumb to the superiority of the German troops and leadership.' Against such a weak force, he anticipated that the Germans could field 110 infantry and mountain divisions, 12 motorised infantry divisions, 24 panzer divisions, and a cavalry division – a total of 147.

Because of the size of the future combat zone, and because of its division by the Pripyat Marsh, Marcks saw that 'a decision will not be achieved in a single battle. . . . Initially, it will be necessary to divide, and advance against the two main parts of the Russian Army separately, with the object of uniting later for an operation to reach the other side of the great forest region [before Moscow, of which the Pripyat Marsh formed the southern part].' Concerning the operational intentions, Marcks was clear: there would be two thrusts, one, the more important, by Army Group North, to Moscow, the other, by Army Group South, into the Ukraine. 'The main force of the German Army will strike that part of the Russian Army in northern Russia and will take Moscow [700 miles from the border]. . . . South of the Pripyat Marsh, weaker forces [based in Galizia and southern Poland] will prevent the advance of the enemy southern group towards Romania by an attack towards Kiev and the middle Dnepr [less than 350 miles from the border]. They will also prepare for subsequent cooperation with the main forces east of the Dnepr . . . either towards Kharkov or north-eastwards.' Marcks proceeded to describe in more detail the role of the northern force:

> 'The main purpose of the offensive is to strike and destroy the mass of the Russian northern group before, within, and east of the forest area, by means of a direct thrust towards Moscow. Then from Moscow and north Russia it will turn southwards, and, in cooperation with the German southern group, conquer the Ukraine and finally reach the line Rostov-Gorkiy-Archangel. To cover the north flank of this operation, a special force will be directed across the lower Dvina towards Pskov and Leningrad [500 miles from the border].'[6]

A strong reserve, almost one-third of the total invasion force, would be brought into action as the width of the combat zone increased with the depth of the advance, thereby solving the strategic problem of the relationship of force to space.

The next development in the planning of the operation came on 3 September, with the appointment of General von Paulus as Deputy Chief of the General Staff. Straightway he was given the task of coordinating the planning for the forthcoming operation. By 17 September he had evolved a plan based on Marcks's ideas, but containing several variations. Von Paulus had created a third. army group, largely by reducing the size of Marcks's reserve, thereby providing for three independent major thrusts in the place of two – Army Group North to Leningrad, Army Group Centre to Moscow, and Army Group South to Kiev. In the south, greater emphasis was placed on an attack on Kiev from Romania in conjunction with the more northerly movement from southern Poland. However, Moscow still remained the primary objective. This became clear when, in November and December, von Paulus held a General Staff war-game to test the plan. Although it was shown that the diverging advances of the three army groups would create dangerous gaps to the north-west and south-west of Moscow, the importnace of the Soviet capital was such that it was decided that the two other· army groups should deal with these gaps, thereby allowing Army Group

Centre to continue its attack unhindered; Army Groups North and South were to converge on the flanks of Army Group Centre for the final advance on Moscow. Halder then confirmed that the capture of Leningrad and the Don Basin, beyond Kharkov, 'would depend on the progress of the general offensive against Moscow'.[7]

At the same time as OKH was working on its plan, the chiefs of staff of the three army groups then in existence, A, B and C, were ordered to undertake their own studies. Each of them reaffirmed the prime importance of Moscow as an objective; two, Generals Brennecke and von Salmuth, produced plans similar to that of von Paulus. The other, General von Sodenstern, who was extremely pessimistic about the outcome of such an invasion, however conducted, went further. Instead of first destroying the Red Army, he advocated immediate and fast advances on Moscow, Leningrad, and Kharkov with the aim of crippling the Soviet leadership. The main weight of the attack would, initially, be concentrated on the northern and southern wings, which would then converge and meet east of the Pripyat Marsh, from where they would drive on to Moscow, their flanks being covered by subsidiary thrusts north and south. Von Sodenstern, however, had no influence on OKH's deliberations, apart, perhaps, from reassuring them of their intention to push on to Moscow.

On 5 December von Brauchitsch and Halder presented the draft of their plan to Hitler. They must have been well-content with the product, for few had expressed doubts as to its operational practicability, and, moreover, it was clear that its aims were close to those stipulated by the Führer on 31 July. They little expected his dissent; nonetheless, it came. Halder noted Hitler's remarks, of which the most important were:

> 'What matters most is to prevent the enemy from falling back before our onslaught; maximum objective: occupation of an area which will render the capital [Berlin] safe from air attacks. After attainment of this objective, combined operations to destroy the sources of enemy war potential (armaments industries, mines, oilfields); aim of campaign: crushing of Russian manpower; no groups capable of recuperation must be allowed to escape. . . . make the southern group strong. The Russians must be beaten this side of the Dnepr. . . . cut off the Baltic area. . . . By striking with strong wings north and south of the Pripyat Marsh we must split the Russian front and encircle the enemy in separate pockets (similar to Poland); these two wings must be fast and strong; *Moscow is of no great importance* [author's italics].'[8]

Thus the fundamental principle on which the Army's plan was based, that the attainment of the Soviet capital should be the main objective, was reversed.

Exactly why Hitler decided on such a major alteration to the OKH's plan has never been clear, but it seems to have been due to a number of reasons; political, economic, and strategic. No doubt he was anxious, for political and psychological reasons, to capture Leningrad, the cradle of Bolshevism, and to occupy the Ukraine (and the Caucasus), the economic power-house of the Soviet Union, for the considerable material gains that would accrue to the Reich and be denied to the Soviets. Possibly, too, he feared to tread the same path as Napoleon's ill-fated expedition, which secured Moscow but allowed the Russian Army to remain intact. However, these considerations aside, Hitler's decision was also based on what he considered to be sound strategic sense. He believed that the primary objective of destroying the Soviet forces would be best achieved not by the three thrusts advocated by the Army, but by two large flanking operations, one to the north, the other to the south. Furthermore, he felt that capture of the Baltic ports would ease considerably the logistic difficulties of such a campaign. It might well have been that Hitler was influenced by the study, dated 15 September 1940, of Lieutenant-Colonel von Lossberg of the OKW. Although he had stated that the 'commitment of the main weight' was to be in the direction of Moscow, von Lossberg nevertheless proposed that it might be necessary to turn forces from the main thrust 'to the north . . . possibly east of the Dvina [some 230 miles from the border], in order to cut off the Russians facing the north wing'.[9]

However Hitler arrived at his conclusion, one thing is clear: in his Directive No. 21, dated 18 December, he stated unequivocally:

> 'In the theatre of operations . . . the main weight of the attack will be delivered in the northern area. Two army groups will be employed here. The more southerly of these two army groups (in the centre of the whole front) will have the task of advancing . . . from the area about and north of Warsaw, and routing the enemy forces in White Russia. This will make it possible for strong mobile forces to advance northwards and, in conjunction with the northern army group operating out of East Prussia in the general direction of Leningrad, to destroy the enemy forces operating in the Baltic area. Only after the fulfilment of this first essential task, which must include the occupation of Leningrad and Kronstadt, will the attack be continued with the intention of occupying Moscow, an important centre of communications and of the armaments industry. Only a surprisingly rapid collapse of Russian resistance could justify the simultaneous pursuit of both objectives.'[10]

This he confirmed on 9 January, telling von Brauchitsch that the invasion 'should on no account turn into a frontal pushing back of the Russians. . . . The most important task is the swift envelopment of the Baltic area; thus the right flank of the German forces thrusting north of the Pripyat Marsh must be made especially strong. The aims of the operation must be the destruction of the Russian Army, the seizure of the most important industrial areas and the destruction of the remaining [ones]. . . . in addition the Baku area must be occupied.'[11] Warlimont's comment was: 'So with a stroke of the pen, a new concept of the main lines of the campaign against Russia was substituted for that which the OKH had worked out as a result of months of painstaking examination and cross-checking from all angles by the best military brains available.'[12] And, just as he had radically altered the nature of the plan, so Hitler gave it a new title. Until then, OKW had used the code-name 'Fritz' and OKH, 'Otto'; on 18 December the dictator declared that he had adopted the code-name 'Barbarossa', the nickname of the Emperor Frederick I, who, according to legend, would one day return to aid Germany in her hour of need.

The Army leaders said not a word to the Führer about his fundamental change in the emphasis of their plan. There was no protest on 5 December, nor subsequently. Indeed, on 3 February 1941 Halder even agreed with Hitler on the necessity to occupy the Baltic coast as soon as possible so as to provide a secure supply base for future operations. With the exception of the Baku oilfields, Hitler's priorities were duly incorporated into the OKH's deployment directive of 31 January 1941 – and this despite the fact that the generals continued to regard Moscow as the main objective. Probably because of their dismal record in remonstrating with the Führer, von Brauchitsch and Halder preferred to pass by the question of Moscow or Leningrad for the time being and wait until the campaign was under way before making their final choice, when events would, they hoped, dictate the correct course. A conspiracy of silence descended on the subject. Warlimont remembered: 'It later became known that their reasoning was that, in time, the course of the campaign would compel even Hitler to go back to the original Army concept. This was to a certain extent taking the easy way out and it proved to be no more than self-deception.'[13]

The field commanders, who noted the vagueness with which OKH treated this crucial aspect of the plan, remonstrated with the planners about the contradiction that was clearly evident in the deployment directive. Certainly, its intentions accorded with those of the Führer. It declared unequivocally that 'Both Army Groups [North and Centre] will destroy the enemy formations in the Baltic area', and said that only if this, together with the occupation of Leningrad, was achieved unexpectedly quickly, could 'the abandonment of the turning movement [northwards by Army Group Centre] and an immediate thrust towards Moscow . . . be considered'.[14] However, the operational guidelines it then proceeded to lay down were not in accordance with the achievement of this end. Had OKH's intention indeed been to concentrate on Leningrad, the best path to be taken by that part of Army Group Centre required to cooperate with von Leeb's force would have been to turn northwards once the Dvina River had been crossed west of Vitebsk. Instead, the deployment directive laid down that the main thrust of all elements in Army Group Centre should be towards Minsk and Smolensk, eastwards on the direct route to Moscow. Only after Smolensk had been taken would any move north-west be undertaken at a point beyond the terrain best suited for it. Indeed, nowhere did the OKH directive specify any lines of advance for Army Group Centre to assist Army Group North; it limited itself to the vaguest of references to such an operation. Perhaps this was in line with the General Staff's dictum that no plan should specify exact action after the first phase of an operation; but perhaps, too, it was indicative of something more: the attempted deception of Hitler by OKH. Thus the Army leaders satisfied Hitler's desire with such vague wording as:

> '. . . Army Group Centre will commit strong mobile forces . . . to force a breakthrough towards Smolensk. This will permit the turning of strong formations to the north in order to cooperate with Army Group North. . . . It [Army Group Centre] will quickly win the area around Smolensk . . . and so achieve the prerequisites for cooperation between strong elements of its mobile troops and Army Group North. . . . At the appropriate time the OKH will order powerful mobile forces from Army Group Centre advancing on Smolensk to cooperate with Army Group North.'[15]

Thus, both the time and the place of the move away from Moscow to Leningrad would be determined by OKH, as also would the strength of the force to be so diverted. Moreover, the Army leaders declined to make any detailed planning for the establishment of a supply base on the Baltic, believing, as they did, that the campaign would be over before this was necessary. Events, they were sure, would lead them to Moscow; even Hitler, they argued, could not withstand for long such obvious military realities.

In spite of all their efforts to keep their intention hidden from the Führer, however, Hitler sensed their doubts about his plan. In December 1940 Engel, Hitler's Army Adjutant, had told von Brauchitsch of the Führer's nagging mistrust of the generals, a mistrust that was evident in his continual emphasis on the necessity for speedy, decisive action against the Soviet Union. On 9 January 1941 he reminded the Army leaders of the need for bold encircling operations that would destroy the enemy, and on 3 February, when he accepted the OKH's operational plan for the invasion, he lectured them thus: 'It is important to destroy the greater part of the enemy, not just to make them run. This will be achieved only by occupying the areas on the flanks with the strongest forces, while standing fast in the centre, and then outmanoeuvring the enemy in the centre from the flanks.' The quick capture of Leningrad, he argued, was vital 'if the Russians succeeded in conducting a large-scale withdrawal to a new defensive line further east'.[16] This theme he returned to at the military conference of 17 March, when he described the capture of Moscow as 'completely irrelevant'.[17]

At the same conference of 17 March Hitler made a further significant alteration to the operational plan of the OKH. Both the Führer and the Army leaders were disturbed by the numerical inadequacy of the German forces available for 'Barbarossa', especially in view of the dissipation of units along the European coastline, in North Africa, and in the Balkans. Halder believed the solution lay in a greater use of the armies of Romania, Slovakia, and Hungary in the south, and by allocating reserve divisions to the north. Hitler, however, would have none of this; instead, he amended the operational plan. The Romanians, he believed, lacked offensive capability; the Slovaks were best suited to occupation duties; and the Hungarians were unreliable, for they had no cause to attack the Soviet Union. Thus, he concluded, economy of force would be the only answer to the problem. As the Baltic coast was the paramount objective, no weakening of Army Groups North and Centre was possible; the Ukraine, however, was different. Using the argument that it was wrong to attack everywhere, Hitler abandoned the idea of a double envelopment to be undertaken by Army Group South, ordering instead a single main thrust north of the Carpathians towards Kiev and down the Dnepr. The German force to the south in Romania was to be reduced and relegated to a purely defensive role, safeguarding the vital Ploiesti oil-fields. Moreover, he rejected the Army's proposition that the Pripyat Marsh was an obstacle to movement, and argued that armies could progress through it. Thus, a coherent, advancing front could be maintained between Army Group Centre and Army Group South from the beginning, thereby rendering unnecessary the dispersion of forces from the south northwards, or from the north southwards, to counter any danger from the Pripyat area.

As if to emphasise his amateur's approach towards military strategy, on the same day that Hitler announced his decision to economise on force in the south, he confirmed his intention to dissipate it in the north, the area he had so long declared was vital to the whole operation. On 17 March he ordered that the garrison in northern Norway should be reinforced with two or three divisions from the west, at the expense of formations needed in Finnish Lapland for the attack on Leningrad from the north. (Finland was but 150 miles from the city.)

As had by then become the accepted form, not a word of protest or of question at Hitler's interference came from the Army leaders. Halder was critical of the decision to end the double envelopment, but no hint of this was evident at the conference. Engel noted that there was only 'cheerful agreement between the Commander-in-Chief and the Chief of the General Staff and Hitler over the deployment plan and concentrations of force'.[18] Only von Rundstedt, commander-designate of Army Group South, expressed any misgivings to Hitler. On 30 March he had heard from his Führer that 'the endless expanse of the space necessitates . . . the massive concentration of . . . forces', and that 'the fate of major German formations may not be made dependent on the staying power of Romanian formations'.[19] Von Rundstedt could not disagree with this, but he pointed out that, unless the large enemy troop concentrations were, at the very least, pinned down by attacks along the Carpathian sector, they might prove a considerable threat to the right flank of his thrust to Kiev. Hitler remained unmoved. As Warlimont noted:

'This and other interventions by Hitler in operational matters had an increasingly disturbing effect on the whole basis of the operational plan for the east, and Halder's diary shows clearly with what grumbling and distaste they were received. The effects of the Supreme Commander's determination to play the role of great war leader can be seen by the very great difficulties encountered in the advance of Army Group South during the first weeks of the campaign.'[20]

The final plan for 'Barbarossa' was as follows. The task of the Wehrmacht was 'to defeat Soviet Russia in a quick campaign'; the Army's operations would be conducted so that 'the mass of the Russian Army in western Russia will be destroyed. . . . The withdrawal of elements left intact into the depth of Russian space will be prevented.' For this to be achieved, it was assumed that 'the Russians will accept battle west of the Dnepr and Dvina at least with strong parts of their forces'. The intention of the Germany Army was 'by means of swift and deep thrusts . . . to tear open the front of the mass of the Russian Army which, it is anticipated, will be in western Russia. The enemy groups separated by these penetrations will then be destroyed.' The invasion force would be divided into three army groups, North, Centre, and South. Army Group North was to attack 'from East Prussia in the general direction of Leningrad'; Army Group Centre was to advance from northern German-occupied Poland 'to force a breakthrough towards Smolensk'. Then, these two army groups would together 'destroy the enemy formations in the Baltic area'. Army Group South was to advance from southern Poland and move through Kiev to the great bend of the lower Dnepr. After the attainment of the objectives in northern Russia, 'freedom of movement for further tasks' would be assured, 'perhaps in cooperation with the German forces in southern Russia'.[21] Only then would Moscow become an objective. The role of the Luftwaffe was, firstly, to gain command of the air and, secondly, to support the ground operations. The Navy would operate in the Baltic, primarily to prevent enemy forces from breaking out of that sea; once Leningrad had been taken, and the Soviet fleet eliminated, it would safeguard the supply of the north wing of the Army. On the flanks, Finland and Romania would give assistance at the appropriate time.

The force allocated for 'Barbarossa' was divided into three army groups. Army Group North, the smallest, was commanded by von Leeb and comprised two armies – the 16th, under Busch (eight divisions), and the 18th, under von Küchler (seven divisions) – and one panzer group – the 4th, under Hoepner (eight divisions, of which three were panzer and three motorised infantry); these, together with the three infantry and three security divisions in reserve, made a total of twenty-nine divisions. Two more OKH reserve infantry divisions were stationed behind the army group's front. Army Group Centre, the strongest force, was under von Bock, and consisted of two armies – the 4th, under von Kluge (fourteen divisions, of which two were

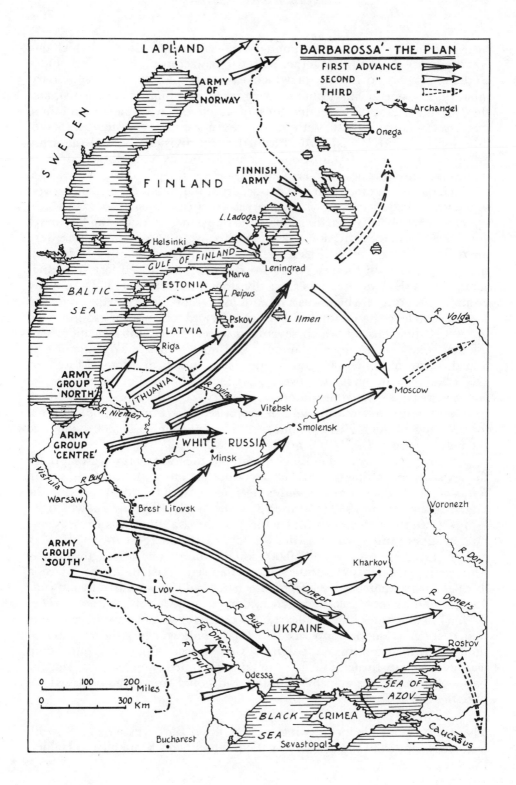

'BARBAROSSA' - THE PLAN

FIRST ADVANCE
SECOND "
THIRD "

LAPLAND

ARMY OF NORWAY

SWEDEN

FINLAND

FINNISH ARMY

Archangel

Onega

L. Ladoga

Helsinki

GULF OF FINLAND

Leningrad

Narva

BALTIC SEA

ESTONIA

L. Peipus

L. Ilmen

R. Volga

Pskov

LATVIA

Riga

ARMY GROUP 'NORTH'

LITHUANIA

R. Dvina

Vitebsk

Moscow

R. Niemen

ARMY GROUP 'CENTRE'

WHITE RUSSIA

Smolensk

Minsk

Vistula

R. Bug

Warsaw

Brest Litovsk

Voronezh

ARMY GROUP 'SOUTH'

R. Don

Lvov

Kharkov

R. Donets

R. Dnepr

R. Bug

UKRAINE

Rostov

R. Dnestr

R. Pruth

Odessa

SEA OF AZOV

0   100   200 Miles

0   300 Km

BLACK SEA

CRIMEA

CAUCASUS

Bucharest

Sevastopol

security divisions), and the 9th, under Strauss (nine divisions of which one was a security division) – together with two panzer groups – the 2nd, under Guderian (fifteen divisions, of which five were panzer, three motorised infantry, and one cavalry, plus a strong motorised infantry regiment), and the 3rd, under Hoth (eleven divisions, of which four were panzer and three motorised infantry); these, with the one division in reserve, made a total of fifty divisions. OKH disposed of a further six divisions behind the army group's front. Army Group South, commanded by von Rundstedt, was made up of three armies – the 17th, under von Stülpnagel (thirteen divisions, of which one was a mountain and two security divisions), the 6th, under von Reichenau (six divisions, of which one was a security division), and the 11th, under von Schobert (seven divisions), and one panzer group – the 1st, under von Kleist (fourteen divisions, of which five were panzer and three were motorised infantry, as well as a reinforced motorised infantry regiment); these, together with the reserve of one division, comprised forty-one divisions. The OKH held another six divisions in reserve behind the army group's front, one of which was a mountain division. Thus, on 22 June 1941 the invasion force had a total of seven armies and four panzer groups made up of 134 divisions, of which seventeen were panzer, thirteen motorised infantry, one cavalry, four mountain, and nine security. To this must be added fourteen Romanian and twenty-one Finnish divisions. Moreover, OKH had allocated a further twelve divisions to be used in the east, two of which were panzer and one motorised infantry. Four divisions, two of which were mountain and one mountain motorised, were in Finland. For the forthcoming conflict, Hitler committed no fewer than 3,050,000 soldiers to the field, supported by 7,184 artillery pieces.

An impressive array of military might, but the total German strength for the invasion, including the OKH reserve not yet moved to the east, was, in terms of numbers of divisions, only fifteen more than that committed to the attack on the west in 1940 (150 and 135 respectively). The area in which the armies were to be deployed under the 'Barbarossa' plan was roughly one million square miles, whereas the whole area conquered between 10 May and 25 June 1940 was around 50,000 square miles – one twentieth the size. Moreover, although the number of mechanised divisions in the invasion force had more than doubled, from fifteen in May 1940 to thirty-two in June 1941, the number of tanks had increased by just under a third, from 2,574 to 3,332 (758 machines in all). Clearly, the Germans would have to rely more than ever before on their superior skill. Of the importance of the mechanised units in the forthcoming campaign, all were agreed: a panzer group would lead every main thrust. But here unanimity ended, and, once again, the battle of theories was evident, with the traditional emerging an easy victor over the revolutionary.

The men responsible for drawing up Operation Barbarossa were all, with one exception, from the artillery or the infantry: von Brauchitsch, Halder, and Marcks were gunners; von Greiffenburg and Kinzel were infantrymen. Hitler, too, was a conservative in military thought. Only von Paulus was a panzer general with direct experience in the operational and administrative problems, and the potential, of mechanised forces; but he was not the type of man to question or reject what had been decided by his superiors. The invasion plan that evolved, ambitious and daring though it proved to be, was hardly revolutionary in its concept; from the outset, the traditional strategy of *Vernichtungsgedanke* dominated all thought. Foremost in the minds of the military leaders, including Hitler, appears to have been the fear that the Russians, as in 1812, would simply retreat before the invaders into their vast interior, with their forces intact, ready to counter-attack when their enemy's lines of communication had become over-extended, their troops weary, and their equipment worn out. Hence the emphasis placed on the need to destroy the Soviet army west of the Dnepr-Dvina line. Hitler, in his Directive No. 21, laid down that 'The bulk of the Russian Army stationed in western Russia will be destroyed by daring operations led by deeply penetrating armoured spearheads. Russian forces still capable of giving battle will be prevented from withdrawing into the depths of Russia.'[22] This was echoed by the Army Command in its deployment directive of 31 January 1941: 'The first intention of the OKH within the task allocated is, by means of swift and deep thrusts by strong mobile formations north and south of the Pripyat Marsh, to tear open the front of the mass of the Russian Army which it is anticipated will be in western Russia. The enemy groups separated by these penetrations will then be destroyed.'[23]

The Army's directive continued to state categorically: 'The conduct of operations will be based on the principles proved in the Polish campaign.' Foremost amongst these was the idea of the *Kesselschlacht,* the 'cauldron battle', the decisive manoeuvre of double envelopment ending with the annihilation of the enemy. A closer look at the OKH deployment directive reveals this: 'Army Group Centre will break up the enemy in White Russia by driving forward the strong forces on its wings. It will quickly win the area around Smolensk by uniting the mobile forces advancing north and south of Minsk and so achieve the prerequisites for cooperation between strong elements of its mobile troops and Army Group North in the destruction of the enemy forces fighting in the Baltic States and the Leningrad area.' These two encirclement operations, between them, were designed to destroy the mass of the Red Army in the west. To the south, the original intention for Army Group South was to carry out a bold encirclement of the enemy west of the Dnepr by two concentric attacks, one from southern Poland, the other from Romania. This, however, was amended by Hitler in mid-March, so that the destruction of Soviet troops in Galizia and in the western Ukraine would be achieved by means of a single major flanking movement emanating from southern Poland, moving to the Dnepr at, or below, Kiev and thence south-east 'along the Dnepr in order to prevent a withdrawal of the enemy . . . across the Dnepr and to destroy him by an attack from the rear'.[24] In such a manner was Hitler's specification, which he so constantly reiterated, undertaken. On 3 February 1941 he had told his Army leaders that 'It is important to destroy the greater part of the enemy, not just to make them run. This will be achieved only by occupying the areas on the flanks with the strongest forces, while standing fast in the centre, and then outmanoeuvring the enemy in the centre from the flanks.'[25] This was pure 'Schlieffen'.

Understandably, the panzer enthusiasts were unhappy. They, together with one or two generals in OKW, proposed that the panzer arm should be used independently of the rest of the army, in long-range operations aimed at paralysis rather than physical destruction. The General Staff rejected this as an 'extreme solution'.[26] Guderian, especially, 'made no attempt to conceal [his] disappointment and disgust'. He was worried that 'no single clear operational objective seemed to be envisaged'.[27] He and Hoth both wished to exploit the velocity of their armoured formations to the fullest extent, and, at the very least, to reach the Dnepr before closing the first encirclement, which OKH had decided would be nearer the frontier, at Minsk. The encirclement and destruction of the Soviet forces should be left to the infantry; the mechanised forces, stripped to their barest essentials and supplied from the air, should push on with all speed to complete the dislocation of the enemy. Moscow, the political, military, communications, and economic centre of the Soviet Union, should be the geographical objective; paralysis the strategic aim.

Von Blumentritt, Chief of Staff to 4th Army under whose control came Guderian's Panzer Group 2, recognised the essence of the disagreement when he recorded:

> 'Guderian had a different idea – to drive deep, as fast as possible, and leave the encircling of the enemy to be completed by the infantry forces that were following up. Guderian urged the importance of keeping the Russians on the run, and allowing them no time to rally. He wanted to drive straight on to Moscow, and was convinced that he could get there if no time was wasted. Russia's resistance might be paralysed by the thrust at the centre of Stalin's power. Guderian's plan was a very bold one – and meant big risks in maintaining reinforcements and supplies. But it might have been the lesser of two risks. By making the armoured forces turn in each time, and forge a ring around the enemy forces they had by-passed, a lot of time was lost.'[28]

This was similar to the view held by General von Sodenstern, the previously cautious Chief of Staff to Army Group A, who, although considering the whole idea of an invasion to be hopeless, nevertheless produced a plan which aimed not at the physical destruction of the Red Army, but at the crippling of the Soviet leadership by the capture of the three great cities of Leningrad, Kharkov, and, above all, Moscow.

The panzer generals were also unhappy at the restrictions placed on their freedom of action. Caution, rather than daring, was the keynote in the handling of the panzer groups. The OKH deployment directive, while placing emphasis on the role of the panzer groups, was careful not to give them anything approaching full independence. Thus, throughout, there are the following caveats which boded ill for those who valued freedom of operation: 'Army Group South will drive its strong left wing – with mobile forces in the lead – towards Kiev . . . The first task of Panzer Group I will be in cooperation with 17th and 6th Armies. . . . The 6th Army . . . will follow Panzer Group I . . . with all possible speed and strength. It must be ready . . . to cooperate with Panzer Group I. . . .' For Army Group Centre, OKH stipulated: 'Panzer Group 2, in cooperation with 4th Army . . . [and] Panzer Group 3, in cooperation with 9th Army, will break through the enemy forces on the frontier. . . . 4th Army [will] . . . follow advance of Panzer Group 2 . . . 9th Army will . . . follow Panzer Group 3.' In the north: 'Panzer Group 4, in cooperation with 16th and 18th Armies, will break through the enemy front . . . 16th Army will . . . follow Panzer Group 4 . . . 18th Army . . . possibly in cooperation with mobile troops north of Lake Peipus will mop up the enemy in Estonia.'[29]

Cooperation with the infantry, therefore, was to be fundamental to the operation of the panzer groups. Any attempt by the panzer leaders to push ahead and lose contact with the infantry was to be guarded against. The OKH and infantry generals urged that the armoured spearheads be held back during the initial breakthrough, which would be left to the infantry divisions, in order to conserve the strength of the panzers for the exploitation phase. The OKH deployment directive had stipulated: '4th Army will achieve the crossing of the Bug and thereby will open the way to Minsk for Panzer Group 2.'[30] They also wanted the panzer groups to be subordinate to the infantry armies. The panzer generals, however, would not agree. Guderian recorded that they 'knew from experience in France what happens. . . . at the critical moment of success the roads are covered with the endless, slow-moving, horsedrawn columns of the infantry divisions, and the panzers as a result are blocked and slowed up.'[31] Finally, a compromise was agreed on: one or two infantry corps would be placed within each panzer group for the initial attack, and the panzer groups in their turn would be subordinated to an infantry army commander for that period. In the exploitation phase, it was proposed that neither of these conditions would apply. The panzer groups would, however, have to maintain contact with the rest of the army, as laid down in the OKH directive. But this compromise solution did little to allay the tension between the panzer and the infantry generals. In his diary, on 14 March, Halder wrote: 'Panzer Group 3 and [9th] Army not yet perfect. Feel for operational requirements lacking here. Army headquarters evidently cannot assert itself over commanding-general of panzer group [Hoth] and is reluctant to place any infantry units under the command of the panzer group.'[32] And on 19 March: 'Points brought out at conference between Army Commander-in-Chief and panzer division commanders:

close control of divisions by corps . . . protection of rear communications . . . close teamwork with infantry.'[33] And, lastly, on 27 March: '. . . 9th Army and Hoth will need direct orders to get them to team up infantry divisions with panzer divisions in the jump-off.'[34] Until the end of the campaign, the panzer commanders were to complain that they were tied too closely to the slower infantry armies; independence of action was not to be theirs.

The so-called 'panzer groups', therefore, began the invasion emasculated. Only one, Panzer Group 4 in the north, was independent of control by an infantry army, even though a panzer group with its additional infantry divisions was comparable in its size to an army. Of the forty-eight divisions that composed the four groups, eighteen, over one-third, were ordinary infantry formations, one more than the total number of panzer divisions. Thus, the panzer group of 1941 was less an expression of the armoured idea than had been von Kleist's group more than a year previously.

But matters for the rest of the Army were little better. As for the invasion of the west in 1940, so for the invasion of the east in 1941: the state of the German Army was far from that required by the rigours of mobile warfare. That is not to say, however, that in the previous year there had not been a number of changes. Hitler's first idea, expressed in May 1940, even before Dunkirk was taken, was for a peacetime army in which half the 'active' divisions were to be either armoured or motorised infantry. The fall of France did not bring peace, and the Führer's intention became divided between the need to defeat Great Britain, primarily by sea and air, and his desire to attack Soviet Russia, mainly by land. Consequently, on 13 July 1940, even before he had reached his final decision to invade the east, Hitler initiated a new programme of armaments, designed to take account of the conflicting requirements of the two objectives. Production was diverted from the Army to the Luftwaffe and the Navy, so as to take care of the short-term offensive against Britain; the Army was to be reduced to 120 divisions, but at the same time its relative composition was to be altered in preparation for a mobile war. In May 1940, of the 153 divisions in the Field Army, sixteen, one-ninth, were motorised; the new plan called for thirty out of 120, one-quarter, to be motorised. This was to be achieved by increasing the number of panzer divisions from ten to twenty, and the motorised infantry divisions from six to ten. Furthermore, all infantry divisions were to be given organisation and equipment levels similar to those in the First Wave. This was confirmed on 18 July, at a meeting of the Reich Defence Council, which placed the expansion of the mechanised forces and the programmes for synthetic rubber and tyres on 'Priority level No. 1', together with production of bombers and U-boats.

Yet almost as soon as he had decided on this programme, Hitler began to repent it. Even the same day he initiated it, 13 July, he told Halder that twenty of the thirty-five divisions earmarked for disbandment should be merely sent on prolonged leave. In the event, only seventeen divisions were disbanded by the end of August, three from the Third Wave, the nine of the Ninth Wave, and the four fortification divisions. The nine infantry divisions of the Tenth Wave had never been formed, and all intention to do so was abandoned. On 31 July Hitler reversed his decision of the 13th; to the 120 divisions needed for the invasion of the Soviet Union, no less than a further sixty would be required to garrison the west and Scandinavia so as to secure Hitler's Europe from Great Britain. The new target was 180 divisions. Once again, because of Hitler's impatience and military naïvety, numbers were regarded to be of greater importance than quality. Spring 1941, the date set for 'Barbarossa', dictated both the pace of events and the nature of the invasion force. No fewer than eleven panzer divisions and four motorised infantry divisions were formed; one infantry division was added to the Seventh Wave; three mountain divisions and five more Waves were established: ten divisions were formed for the Eleventh Wave; six for the Twelfth; nine for the Thirteenth; eight for the Fourteenth; and fifteen for the Fifteenth. In addition, four light divisions (not with tanks, as before, but designed to be as independent as possible of motor transport) and nine security divisions were instituted. In the course of this expansion, nine divisions of the First Wave, together with one of the Second and one of the Third, were transformed either into panzer or motorised infantry divisions, one division of the Second Wave became classified as a formation of the First, and three divisions of the Third Wave (one of which was reactivated after its disbandment in summer 1940) became security divisions. The result of all this was that, by June 1941, the German Army consisted of 162 infantry and mountain divisions, one cavalry division, ten motorised infantry divisions, twenty-one armoured divisions, and nine security divisions – a total of 203. No fewer than eighty-four divisions had been added to the Field Army, which, with headquarters and 'army troops', brought its strength to 3,800,000 men. To this must be added the 150,000 men of the Waffen SS, disposed among five divisions – one infantry and four motorised infantry, two of which had been raised since May 1940 – and other units, including Hitler's guard formation, the *Leibstandarte*. Thus, there had been an increase of 650,000 in the ranks of the Field Army and Waffen SS since the invasion of the west, roughly an eighteen per cent expansion. The Replacement Army numbered 1,200,000 men, the Air Force 1,680,000, and the Navy 404,000. The command organisation of the Field Army was as follows: four army groups (North, Centre, South, and 'D' (in the west)), thirteen armies, four panzer groups, and fifty-eight corps commands.

This rapid and significant expansion of the Army was not accompanied by any corresponding improvement in quality, however. Indeed, it positively precluded such an improvement. The most serious deficiencies came within the panzer arm. Hitler did fulfil his aim of doubling the number of panzer divisions from ten to twenty-one (one of which was called a light division until August 1941), but the method by which he chose to do it was disastrous. When first he made his decision to raise further armoured divisions, he ordered that tank production should simultaneously be increased to 800-1,000 units per month. The Army Ordnance Office was horrified at the prospect, and informed the Führer that such an output would cost two billion marks and involve the employment of 100,000 skilled workers and specialists, already scarce, and would be detrimental to all other armament programmes. Hitler reluctantly agreed to abandon the proposal, with the result that the average monthly production of tanks rose from 182 in the last six months of 1940 to only 212 in the first six months of 1941. The total stock of tanks rose from 3,420 on 1 September 1940 to 5,262 on 1 June 1941, and, of this latter figure, the Germans considered only 4,198 fit for operational service. Thus, the number of front-line machines had risen by less than one-quarter while the divisions to which they were distributed had doubled; the result was a considerable weakening in the armoured strength of the individual panzer divisions. In May 1940 the strongest panzer division possessed 300 tanks; in June 1941 it had only 199, and the average was even lower. Most armoured divisions in 1941 had around 160, organised in one tank regiment of only two battalions (seven had three), thereby completely reversing the original ratio of tank to infantry within the panzer formations.

Such a meddling with the organisation of the armoured arm was looked on unfavourably by Guderian and the other panzer leaders, who saw the dangers that would result from this artificial inflation of the numbers of divisions. Individual formations were now far weaker than before, and the striking-power of the panzer division was severely reduced. Not only had it insufficient tanks to cover the ground, but, and more important, losses from enemy action and mechanical failure would quickly diminish an already limited armoured strength to an unacceptable low level, and disproportionately so in relation to the non-armoured troops in the rest of the division. Furthermore, an unfortunate inflation in military economics had developed; although the panzer brigade staff had been disbanded, the divisional and regimental staff had been expanded, even though the effective tank strength they administered had been reduced by half. In December 1940, Jodl commented: 'If this great campaign has to be fought soon, then it can be done just as well with twelve panzer divisions as twenty-four panzer brigades, because there won't be any more by the spring [of 1941]. We could thus save a mass of the supporting arms and rear services.'[35]

These effects were not offset by any significant improvement in the quality of the tanks, although there were some gains: by June 1941 the PzKw 35(t) had been phased out of front-line service altogether, PzKw Is and IIs figured less prominently, and there was a higher proportion of PzKw IIIs and IVs. Nevertheless, the fact remains that of the invasion force of 3,332 tanks, 1,156 were the long-obsolete PzKw Is (410) and IIs (746) while 772 were Czech PzKw 38(t)s, which equipped five divisions. In other words, 1,928, four-sevenths of the total, were machines that had never been designed to fight in the panzer divisions and, if the Germans had had their way, would never have been included within their wartime organisation.

Only 1,404, three-sevenths, were the PzKw IIIs (965) and IVs (439) that had been designed as early as 1936 to completely equip the Reich's armoured force. Although this was an improvement, however slight, on the situation in May 1940, when just under two-sevenths of the invading tanks had been PzKw IIIs and IVs, it was small compensation for the numerical dilution of the divisions. Furthermore, there had been no significant improvements in the machines themselves, with the result that they went into the field against the Soviet Union armed with the 3.7cm, the short-barrelled 5cm, and the short-barrelled 7.5cm guns, which were soon to prove woefully inadequate when compared with the best possessed by the Soviets. No action had been taken on Hitler's order that the 3.7cm gun of the PzKw III should be replaced by the long-barrelled 5cm gun, the short-barrelled variant having been preferred by the Army Ordnance Office.

In the other components of the Panzer division, few, if any, improvements had been made since the campaign in the west. A high percentage of transport continued to be wheeled, and tracks were still a rarity. This was to prove a considerable handicap in a country where only three per cent of the roads were hard-surfaced, and much of the terrain was marshy or liable to be turned into a river after a few hours of rainfall. The armoured personnel carriers, the SdKfz 250 and 251, had made but little impact, and relatively few panzer infantry companies were equipped with them (often no more than three per division). Captured foreign transport entirely equipped one panzer division. Guderian was annoyed that the four new motorised infantry divisions, none of which possessed any tracked transport, took large numbers of the scarce trucks that would have been better used in improving the standard of motorisation of the panzer formations. But even then, three of the ten motorised infantry formations had to be equipped with foreign vehicles, most of them French machines that were somewhat delicate compared with those of German make. The motorisation of the new units, too, took a long time to complete. One month before the invasion of the east, Halder noted: 'We shall be lucky if they [panzer and motorised infantry] get all the equipment through in time; training of the divisions equipped last will be incomplete in any event.'[36] Even more disturbing for the Army as a whole and for the mechanised forces in particular, was the severe shortage of tyres – up to fifty per cent of requirements – and of motor fuel, the stocks of which would permit only the concentration of the invasion force for the attack and its movement in battle for two months. On 13 June, just nine days before the start of 'Barbarossa', General Thomas reported to Halder: 'Fuel reserves will be exhausted in autumn. Aviation fuel will be down to one-half, regular fuel to one-quarter, and fuel oil to one-half requirements.'[37]

Another indication of the neglect of the mechanised force that was apparent despite the doubling of the numbers of its divisions, lay in the increased use made of the *Sturmgeschütz* (assault-gun). This machine was the brainchild of von Manstein, who envisaged it as a self-propelled, close-support gun for the infantry divisions. It was designed around the same chassis as used for the PzKw III, and mounted a short-barrelled 7.5cm gun within a well-armoured superstructure. The major difference between this machine and a tank lay in its lack of a turret with an all-round traverse, which prevented it from dealing with the unexpected situations that continually occur during attack. Design work was initiated in 1936, and production began in 1940. For the attack on France and Flanders, three batteries, each of six assault-guns, had been formed, although only one battery was ready for action by 5 May 1940. At the time of the invasion of the Soviet Union, however, there were eleven battalions (each of three batteries) and five independent batteries of assault guns; a total of 250 assault guns, out of a stock of some 390, took part in the initial offensive.

To the panzer leaders, the assault guns were unwelcome. Nor was it simply that these new machines did not behave exactly like tanks; there were more important reasons. First, they objected to the whole principle behind the assault-gun development: that of infantry-support. In effect, the establishment of assault-gun battalions was simply a reversion to the principle of panzer brigades designed to cooperate with the infantry divisions, against which Guderian and his supporters had fought so hard before the war. Second, the assault-guns came under the control not of the panzer arm but of the artillery, which meant that there was now an expanding armoured force that was not subordinate to the panzer command, but was, instead, the protégé of a rival, and a conservative, arm of service – one, moreover, that was ambitious for recognition in the field. Finally, by mid-1941, the output of assault-guns amounted to as much as one-fifth (some fifty per month) of the output of tanks. This meant that scarce production facilities and raw materials were being expended on what they considered to be a harmful diversion, instead of being concentrated on building up stocks for the badly equipped panzer force.

In the infantry formations there was some improvement in quality. The experience gained during the campaign in the west, and in subsequent training, had improved the already high standard of individual soldier generally found in the German Army. However, the same old problems still dogged the infantry. Of the grand total of 162 infantry and mountain divisions, thirty-six, well over one-fifth, were not regarded as fit for front-line service. (These were all those from the Thirteenth, Fourteenth, and Fifteenth Waves.) Furthermore, eleven of the best divisions had already gone to form the nuclei of the new mechanised formations. Transport continued to be a major problem; on 1 July 1940 Fromm told Halder that 'the activation of new panzer units required so many vehicles that motor transport columns of infantry divisions will have to cut down further'.[38] Expedients were sought; there was even a scheme to mount whole infantry divisions on bicycles, but this was rejected. On 29 September Halder noted that there were 'not enough motor vehicles on hand even to meet the most urgent minimum requirements of General Headquarter troops. We shall have to economise by curtailing the mobility of divisions of the 13th and 14th

Waves.'[39] And on 21 January 1941 his diary recorded that the signal corps alone was under-strength by no fewer than 6,000 vehicles. However, further de-motorisation and strict economies enabled the Chief of the General Staff to state on 5 May: 'Motor transport situation still tight, but better than a year ago (before campaign in the west)'[40], and three days later he noted that units assigned to 'Barbarossa' were only 1,430 trucks and 1,256 cars short on establishment and that they might receive a further 300 and 400 respectively before the onset of the campaign. Of the seventy-nine infantry divisions, almost half were equipped with foreign vehicles. The horse was more prominent than before, so for the invasion of the Soviet Union – although the Army amassed 600,000 motor vehicles (including armoured cars) – it was necessary to rely on no fewer than 625,000 of the animals.

The nature of the infantryman's equipment differed little from what it had been in September 1939. After twenty months of war, the main material difference was slight; it lay in the type of the anti-tank guns. Out of the average of seventy-two in each division, up to and including those of the Tenth Wave, six were now the new 5cm type (not in the Third Wave divisions, which had only 3.7cm guns, or in the Fourth and Eleventh Waves, which had six and nine respectively of the captured Czech 4.7cm versions). Thus, the German infantry still went into the field equipped predominantly with the ineffective 3.7cm 'doorknocker'. Moreover, although equipment levels for all divisions were now supposed to be based on those for the First Wave, there were a number of discrepancies arising from deficiencies, some of them important. Armoured cars, for example, were found only in the divisions of the First, Second, and Twelfth Waves. Instead of the seventy-five anti-tank guns, the twenty light and six heavy infantry guns, the ninety-three light and fifty-four medium mortars, the thirty-six light and twelve heavy field guns, the infantry divisions of the Thirteenth and Fourteenth Waves possessed only twenty-one anti-tank guns, a few light mortars, and twenty-four light field guns of Czech origin. The Fifteenth Wave had even fewer, their two weak infantry regiments and an artillery battalion between them possessing only thirty-six light mortars and twelve light field guns. The light divisions, also with only two infantry regiments, had forty-seven anti-tank guns, twelve light infantry guns, twenty-one light and twelve medium mortars, and twenty-eight light and eight heavy field guns. Among the other formations up to, and including, the Twelfth Wave, the discrepancies were less well-marked, and a reasonable level of equipment was maintained. Some had fewer anti-tank guns or light infantry guns, others a few more light mortars; all had the same number of field guns, medium mortars, and heavy infantry guns. The only significant difference was in the Sixth Wave, which lacked completely an infantry gun component, and in the Third Wave, whose divisions each had but forty-eight anti-tank guns.

The Army's dependence on the support of the Luftwaffe, and the relative weakness of that support, also needs mention. In Poland, in the west, and in the Balkans, the German Air Force had rendered valuable assistance to the ground forces, first by gaining control of the air, thereby allowing the armies to proceed unhindered by attack from that quarter; secondly, by destroying important parts of the enemy's communications system, thereby inducing a kind of paralysis that Guderian might well have wished had been the result of his own actions; and thirdly, by attacking enemy troop concentrations and fortifications, thereby directly assisting the progress of the field forces. Well though the Luftwaffe had performed these tasks, the Army leaders doubted whether they would continue to do so during 'Barbarossa'. But when, for the first and last time, such misgivings were openly voiced, at the Führer conference of 5 December 1940, Hitler refused to entertain any such doubts. Nevertheless, they remained valid until the end of the campaign. More than any other service at this time, the Luftwaffe had suffered from having to wage a two-front, even a three-front, war. Its responsibilities in the Mediterranean and, far more important, in the west and in the defence of the Fatherland, prevented any concentration of its resources for the campaign in the east. Against the west in 1940 it had been able to marshal 2,750 aircraft; against the Soviet Union in 1941, over a considerably larger geographical area, only 2,770 of a total front-line strength of 4,300 aircraft were available, and of these almost one-third were in need of service and repair.

Then, too, there were the Balkans. Early in the morning of 6 April the German Army moved into south-east Europe. By 2 May, Yugoslavia and Greece had been added to the growing list of Hitler's conquests, and the British had again been humbled. Most important of all, the south-eastern flank had been secured for the invasion of the Soviet Union, and the immediate danger of any air attack on the vital Romanian oilfields from bases in Greece had been removed. The plan that OKH had drawn up so hurriedly, but so well, on 27 March had succeeded totally. As in Poland, the Balkan campaign was one the German Army should have won; it was a direct result of striking with the benefit of surprise and of overwhelming material superiority. The Yugoslav Army, never fully mobilised, was crushed before effective resistance could be mounted; the Greek Army, although prepared, lacked modern armaments, especially anti-tank guns and aeroplanes. Only the British Expeditionary Force in Greece had weapons that were effective against German equipment, but its small size, and the failure of the Greeks to support it, undermined its chances of making a successful stand. The defenders failed to exploit the advantages that the mountainous country and poor roads gave them; instead, two German armies, the 2nd under von Weichs and, more important, the 12th under List, won an easy victory over a weak enemy.

The Balkan operation, quick and efficient though it was, had wider, and detrimental, effects on the forthcoming invasion of Soviet Russia. On 27 March, when the decision was taken to invade Yugoslavia and Greece, the date of 'Barbarossa' was postponed from mid-May; on 7 April an OKH order specified that the opening of the attack would be delayed by four weeks, until mid-June. Not until 17 June did Hitler approve the final date for the invasion; it was to be the 22nd. This, many have argued, imposed a delay on 'Barbarossa' that was to prove fatal and cause the Germans to run out of time during their offensive, bringing them to a halt in a premature, and especially severe, Russian winter; but for this, Moscow would have been taken. However, it seems clear that a postponement would have been necessary, Balkans or no, entirely because of the weather. The spring in east Europe had been especially wet, and the ground had suffered as a result. Von Greiffenberg, then Chief of Staff to 12th Army, remembered:

> 'East of the Bug-San line in Poland, ground operations are [always] very restricted until May, because most roads are muddy and the country generally is a morass. The many unregulated rivers cause widespread flooding. The farther one goes east the more pronounced do these disadvantages become, particularly in the boggy, forest regions of the Rokitro (Pripyat) and Berezina. Thus even in normal times movement is very restricted before mid-May. But 1941 was an exceptional year. The winter had lasted longer. As late as the beginning of June, the Bug in front of our army was over its banks for miles.'[41]

To the north, conditions were just as bad, heavy rain still continuing to fall there during early June. Therefore an attack before the middle of that month would probably have been out of the question in any case; the weather, which in 1940 had been so favourable to the Germans, was in 1941 to become their worst enemy.

The real disadvantage resulting from the Balkan campaign arose out of the diversion of formations from the build up in the east to the south-east. The problem lay not with 2nd Army in Yugoslavia, because six of the nine divisions were replaced in the east by OKH reserves, so that the infantry employed there became in effect the new reserve for 'Barbarossa'. Moreover, all the fighting divisions had been withdrawn from Yugoslavia to the east by the end of May. The situation, though, was very different for 12th Army in Greece, which had disposed of fourteen divisions, nine of them earmarked for the east – five panzer, two motorised infantry (one of them Waffen SS), and two infantry divisions. Although losses in men and equipment had been extremely small, the wear and tear on engines, especially those of the tanks, was significant and no doubt contributed to the high rate of mechanical failure experienced during 'Barbarossa'. Furthermore, the long return journey from Greece to the assembly areas in Poland imposed such delays that two panzer divisions and Hitler's motorised guard formation failed to join Army Group South by the time of the invasion. As a result, von Rundstedt's force lacked about a third of its armoured strength – two of the intended seven divisions – for its initial attack and their loss was sorely felt. Von Kleist later remembered: 'It is true that the forces employed in the Balkans were not large compared with our total strength, but the proportion of tanks employed there was high. The bulk of the tanks that came under me for the offensive . . . had taken part in the Balkan offensive, and needed overhaul, while their crews needed a rest. A large number of them had driven as far south as the Peloponnese, and had to be brought back all that way.'[42]

Two other effects, both long-term, resulted from the Balkan campaign. First, the airborne-led invasion of Crete towards the end of May, although a success, proved very costly in terms of the lives of the attackers and the destruction of their transport aircraft. It also had the effect of discouraging Hitler from attempting any further large-scale airborne operations, although there were many occasions in the forthcoming months when their use on the Eastern Front might have proved invaluable. Secondly, after the occupation of the Balkans, the necessity to guard its coasts and fight the partisans, especially in Yugoslavia, caused the Wehrmacht to expend a not inconsiderable part of its scarce resources in that area. The struggle against the guerilla fighters remained a constant drain on the Germans until the end of the war. By mid-1943 no fewer than fifteen divisions were stationed in the Balkans, and by mid-1944 this number had risen to twenty-five – one-sixth of the total committed to the invasion of the Soviet Union three years previously.

Nor were the Balkans the only area of Europe in which German formations found themselves. In the preceding months Hitler had been anxiously pressing for greater security along the coast of 'Fortress Europe'; when the invading armies crossed the Soviet frontier on 22 June, in addition to the seven divisions in the Balkans, there were eight in Norway, thirty-eight in the west, two in the Fatherland, one in Denmark, and two, both armoured, in North Africa. Thus, of the 208 divisions of the German Field Army and Waffen SS, fifty-eight, one-quarter, were committed elsewhere than in the east. Although just over half of these formations, thirty in all, were infantry divisions of the Thirteenth, Fourteenth, and Fifteenth Waves, not regarded as fit for front-line service, their very existence caused scarce-trained manpower, munitions, equipment, transport, and fuel to be used in areas other than Soviet Russia. The Army was short enough of these resources to resent every corporal and petrol-can that was not allocated to the invasion force.

Much has been made by historians of the Germans having underestimated the Soviet strength when planning 'Barbarossa'. Some have even gone so far as to call it 'the basic error'. Certainly, the initial estimate of the Red Army formations available in European Russia made by the Abwehr in late July 1940 was low – ninety infantry and twenty-three cavalry divisions, together with twenty-eight mechanised brigades. In August, the estimate was increased by six infantry divisions, and it was on this revised figure that operational planning began. It was known that the rest of the Soviet army, some fifty-five infantry divisions, eleven cavalry divisions, and ten mechanised brigades, was in the Far East, protecting Siberia from Japanese incursion, and even if they were sent to the west on the German invasion they would arrive too late to affect the outcome. The German victory, after all, was expected to take little more than two months, and the destruction of the Soviet western forces would be achieved within the first few weeks. Further intelligence reports provided for increases in the German estimates, so that by 30 January 1941, the day before the OKH deployment directive was issued, the Germans believed that the Soviets disposed of 121 infantry and twenty-five cavalry divisions and thirty-one mechanised brigades in western Russia, a total as accurate as it was then possible to obtain.

The quality of this force was an unknown factor, but the Germans thought it to be low. Hitler referred to the Soviet forces as 'a clay colossus without a head', but added that 'the Russians should not be underestimated, even now'.[43] Stalin's recent purge of his officer corps, which had meant the execution of thirteen of fifteen army commanders, had left the Red Army with a dearth of experienced leadership, and the Germans believed that this had been openly displayed during its disastrous Winter War against Finland in 1939. Equipment, too, was thought to be numerous but obsolete, as, indeed, was true. Of 24,000 tanks (the Germans estimated 10,000), only twenty-seven per cent were in running order, and only 1,475 were superior to the German machines. (These were the T34s and KVIs, of which the Germans had no knowledge.) Many of the divisions were under-strength – the mechanised formations, for example, had just half their complement of tanks – and the whole Red Army was in the process of reorganisation. The disposition of the units in the west was bad, most of them being fairly close to the frontier behind an only partially completed defence line; not one of them was in its tactical position on 22 June. The strategic doctrine of the Soviet Army was fairly crude, based on the concept of vigorous attack or counter-attack whenever possible. The plans for the use of armour were confused, some of the tanks being grouped into organisations similar to panzer divisions, while others were distributed in 'penny packets' in support of the infantry.

In mid-June 1941, immediately before the invasion, there was a significant reappraisal of Soviet numerical strength. German intelligence now believed that Russian forces in the west were composed of 154 infantry and twenty-five and a half cavalry divisions, and thirty-seven mechanised brigades, an increase of almost one-quarter over the previous assumption. These figures were probably near the truth, and it dismayed the German military leaders but little. They believed that their 136 divisions, together with those of their allies, could still defeat the enemy. The reasons for this belief were several: the superior quality of the attacking force, both in terms of equipment, training, and tactical and strategic background; the considerable advantage of achieving initial surprise; and the soundness of their invasion plan that would create the conditions by which victory would be gained before the onset of winter. However, there was one aspect of Soviet military organisation of which the Germans took no account – the highly efficient, and ruthless, Soviet mobilisation machinery. This was to succeed in putting more than a million men in the field before July was out. In this, the Osoaviakhim, a national military organisation which had thirty-six million members, thirty per cent of whom were women, played a great part. Thus, although the Germans would kill and capture some seven and a half million Red Army soldiers before the onset of winter – losses that would cripple a European country – the Soviet machine could still produce more.

Nevertheless, it would be wrong to ascribe the German failure to recognise this as the, or even a, major mistake when planning 'Barbarossa'. The magnitude of the Soviet Union's reserves of manpower, and its ability to put them under arms speedily, was not in itself sufficient to defeat the Wehrmacht. Had the German plan succeeded, and had there been a quick occupation of the Soviet Union's key industrial and armament-producing areas in European Russia following on the destruction of her original western armies, it would matter little how many men could emerge from Asiatic Russia. Without sufficient modern armaments, with the industrial area of the Urals bombing range, and denied the communications centre of Moscow, they would have posed little threat to their enemy. Time, not the underestimation of Soviet strength, was the vital factor for Germany. If the advancing armies could achieve, at least, the line Leningrad-Moscow-Rostov before the winter made further movement impossible, before the divisions from the Far East could move west, and before the Soviet mobilisation machinery could produce too many field formations, victory would indeed be possible. But should they fail to reach these objectives, then the divisions from the Far East would arrive, the new formations from the depots would move into the field in ever-increasing numbers, and the Soviet factories would continue to churn out equipment and munitions. Then the Germans, far from home, would face defeat as they stood fighting during a savage winter for every inch of Russian soil, exhausted after several months of campaigning, their supply-lines overstretched, and their losses mounting. Time was of the essence of success, and victory would be won or lost by the soundness, or otherwise, of the German operations.

19

'Barbarossa' – The Campaign

On 22 June, a door opened before us, and we didn't know
what was behind it. . . . the heavy uncertainty took me by
the throat.

ADOLF HITLER

The greatest land war in recorded history began at 3.30a.m. on 22 June 1941, the day after the 129th anniversary of Napoleon's attack on Russia in 1812. Halder began his diary entry for the day with the words: 'The morning reports indicate that all armies (except the 11th) have started the offensive according to plan. Tactical surprise of the enemy has apparently been achieved along the entire line.'[1] But beneath this calm, confident attitude lay disquiet. The generals were clearly awed by the magnitude of the task that lay ahead. Fourteen days earlier, with a trace of foreboding, the Chief of the General Staff had written: 'The imposing vastness of the spaces in which our troops are now assembling cannot fail but to strike a deep impression.'[2]

The initial German front was 995 miles long, and there was another 620 miles along the Finnish border. The main front would soon expand to 1,490 miles, and extend to a depth of over 600 miles. Into this great space of steppe, forest, and swamp marched the best of the German Army, amounting to threequarters of its field strength; by the end of the year, 3,500,000 Red Army soldiers were in captivity, and 4,000,000 had died in battle. At one time the Germans occupied some 900,000 square miles of Soviet territory. It had been an historic campaign, a remarkable achievement. But at the same time 'Barbarossa' was a significant failure for German arms. Only one of the objectives, the occupation of the Ukraine, had been achieved, and that only partly; for the rest, the Red Army had not been destroyed, Leningrad had not been reduced, and Moscow had remained Soviet. The plan of operations had proved incapable of meeting with reality. Who was responsible for this failure?

Certainly it was not the staff of the OKW. Warlimont remembered that: 'The Operations Staff of Supreme Headquarters was entirely on the touch-line. General Jodl was never once invited either as a visitor or as an observer to the large-scale war-games that the Army Staff held in the autumn of 1940, nor, as far as one knows, did he make any attempt to play any important part in the planning. . . .'³ Instead, OKW contented itself merely with collating reports for the daily briefings of Hitler, communicating the Führer's desires to the three service commands, establishing contact with Germany's allies, drawing up the time-table for the invasion build-up, and undertaking detailed studies and plans for the economic exploitation of occupied areas of the Soviet Union. The OKW was clearly the Führer's creature, and if he gave it no task to perform, it did nothing. Moreover, it was not the body to question Hitler's decisions. In August 1940 Keitel had presented a memorandum opposing a two-front war, the arguments of which the Führer bluntly refuted; Keitel then tendered his resignation, but it was not accepted. He later recalled:

> 'Hitler harshly rejected this: did he then have no right to inform me if in his view my judgement were wrong? He really would have to forbid his generals to go into a huff and ask to resign every time somebody lectured them, and in any case *he* had no chance of resigning his office either. He wanted it understood once and for all that it was nobody's right but his to relieve a person of his office if he saw fit, and until then that person would just have to put up with the job; during the previous autumn, he said, he had had to tell Brauchitsch the same as well.'⁴

From that time on, Keitel unhesitatingly and unquestioningly carried out his Führer's wishes. When, a few months later, General Thomas submitted a gloomy report on the dire logistic and economic position of the forthcoming invasion, the Chief of OKW, although no doubt sympathising with its contents, told him that 'the Führer would not allow himself to be influenced in his planning by such economic difficulties',⁵ and there exists no evidence as to whether he passed the report on to Hitler. Jodl, although preferring to deal with Great Britain before embarking on the Soviet Union, and despite his doubts about the economic basis for a war in the east, made no effort to influence his Führer once the decision to invade had been taken. Certainly there is no reason to believe, as is often asserted, that he made any attempt to suggest to the Führer the idea that Leningrad should be the primary objective of the operation. He, like Keitel, existed during the planning and invasion merely as a functionary.

Nor was the responsibility of either the Luftwaffe or the Navy Commands any greater than that of OKW. The Luftwaffe was primarily a tactical instrument of war designed to support the Army in the field, and its leaders appeared content to remain passive, ordering their deployment to the requirements of the ground forces. Göring, despite his subsequent protestations to the contrary, does not seem to have questioned either the necessity for, or the possibility of, conquering the Soviet Union; Raeder, on the other hand, until December 1940 openly maintained a critical attitude to Hitler's ideas, and consistently advocated a grand strategy for the Mediterranean and Middle East. However, as the Navy was to play only a minor role in the eastern campaign, the naval staff took but little part in the operational planning. The Army reigned supreme among the services, and it made no attempt to foster any cooperation except for the barest essentials. Commensurate with their traditional predominance in the field of operations, the generals drew up lines of march, allocated units to armies, armies to sectors, organised logistical support, and generally ensured the thorough preparation of every military aspect of the invasion. But important though that work was, the Army leaders were unable to determine the two fundamental elements upon which strategy is based: time and space. It was the Supreme Commander, Adolf Hitler, who alone decided to which objectives the armies would advance, and how long they would take to achieve them, both before and during the campaign. It was here that the fatal error lay.

This is not to absolve the generals of all responsibility for the failings of 'Barbarossa'. Both OKH and Hitler were over-confident from the beginning; both failed to realise that Germany might not emerge victorious before the onset of winter, and thus overlooked the adequate provision of special equipment and clothing; both underestimated the strain that the long distances, the rough communications, and the difficult terrain would have on the poorly mechanised, inadequately supplied German Army; both ignored the strengths of the Soviet military system and overestimated the capabilities of their own; and both rejected any use of the principles of the armoured idea, at the same time reaffirming the dominance of traditional German strategy. Independence of action, speed, and the defeat of the opposing forces by means of command paralysis were disregarded in favour of their opposites – cooperation between infantry and mechanised divisions, secure flanks and the annihilation of the enemy by means of double envelopment, and a battle on an inverted front. If at any time the Army leaders consciously recognised these failings, they omitted to make their objections known to their Supreme Commander.

For the fundamentals of the plan, however, for its allocation of time and space, Hitler must bear full responsibility. On only one aspect was he in agreement with his generals: that the Soviet forces should be destroyed west of the Dvina-Dnepr rivers. For the rest, there was intense conflict, although it was not to come into the open until the middle of the campaign. The Army planned a grand encirclement operation in the south; Hitler abandoned it in favour of a single enveloping thrust. The Army pronounced the Pripyat Marsh to be impassable; Hitler declared that it proved no obstacle. Most important of all, the Army wanted the main effort to be concentrated in the centre, on Moscow; Hitler did not. In praise of the choice of the Army Command, von Manstein wrote:

'OKH . . . rightly contended that the conquest and retention of these undoubtedly important strategic areas [the Baltic, the Ukraine, and the Caucasus] depended first on defeating the Red Army. The main body of the latter, they argued, would be met on the road to Moscow,

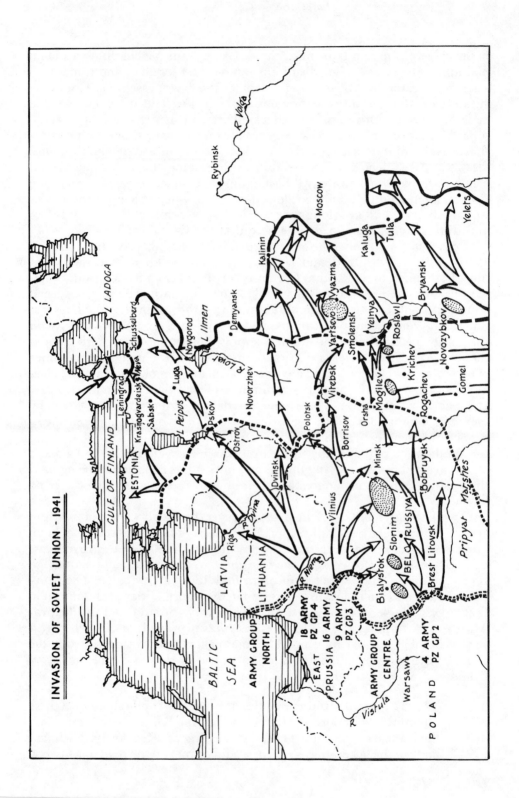

INVASION OF SOVIET UNION - 1941

R Volga

Rybinsk

L LADOGA

Schusselberg

Moscow

Kalinin

Kaluga

Tula

Yelets

Demyansk

Vyazma

Yartsevo

Bryansk

Roslavl

Novozybkov

Yalnya

Smolensk

Krichev

Gomel

L Ilmen

Novgorod

Luga

Vitebsk

Mogilev

Rogachev

Leningrad

Krasnogvardeisk

Sabsk

L Peipus

Pskov

Novorzhev

Polotsk

Orsha

Bobruysk

R Neva

R Lovat

Ostrov

Dvinsk

Borisov

Minsk

ESTONIA

R Dvina

Vilnius

Slonim

BELORUSSIA

Pripyat Marshes

Riga

Bialystok

Brest Litovsk

GULF OF FINLAND

LATVIA

LITHUANIA

R Niemen

BALTIC SEA

EAST PRUSSIA

18 ARMY PZ GP 4
16 ARMY
9 ARMY PZ GP 3

ARMY GROUP NORTH

ARMY GROUP CENTRE

4 ARMY PZ GP 2

Warsaw

R Vistula

POLAND

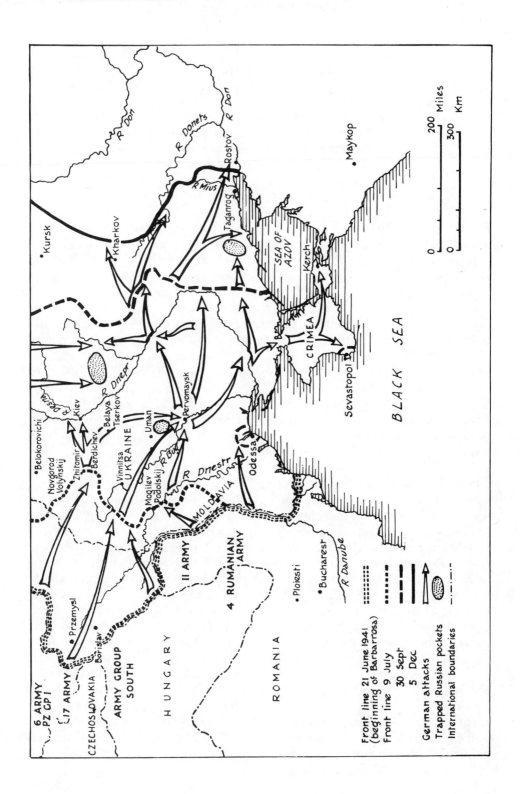

R Don

R Donets

R Don

Rostov

R Mius

Kursk

Kharkov

Taganrog

Maykop

SEA OF AZOV

Kerch

BLACK SEA

Sevastopol

CRIMEA

R Dnepr

Belokorovichi

Novgorod Volynskij

Kiev

Berdichev

Belaya Tserkov

Zhitomir

Vinnitsa

UKRAINE

Uman

Pervomaysk

Mogilev Podolskij

R Bug

R Dnestr

MOLDAVIA

Odessa

6 ARMY
PZ GP I
17 ARMY

CZECHOSLOVAKIA

Przemysl

Borislav

ARMY GROUP SOUTH

HUNGARY

II ARMY

4 RUMANIAN ARMY

ROMANIA

Ploiesti

Bucharest

R Danube

200 Miles

300 Km

0

0

Front line 21 June 1941
(beginning of Barbarossa)
Front line 9 July
30 Sept
5 Dec
German attacks
Trapped Russian pockets
International boundaries

since that city, as the focal point of Soviet power, was one whose loss the régime dare not risk. There were three reasons for this. One was that – in contrast to 1812 – Moscow really did form the political centre of Russia; another was that the loss of the armaments areas around, and east of, Moscow would at least inflict extensive damage on the Soviet war economy. The third, and possibly the most important reason from the strategic point of view, was Moscow's position as the focal point in European Russia's traffic network. Its loss would split the Russian defences in two, and prevent the Soviet command from ever mounting a single, coordinated operation.'[6]

But Hitler had rejected this choice; he had ordered that the primary objectives should lie on the flanks of the invasion, especially on the north. The capital was to him an irrelevance when compared with Leningrad and the Baltic, and with the Ukraine and the Donets Basin. This difference of opinion was to become particularly apparent during the conduct of the campaign. Hitler's choice of objectives took no account of the main advantages possessed by the enemy: the vastness of their country, the lamentable condition of their roads, and the resilience of their mobilisation system. These, the German Army, with its poor state of mechanisation and its rejection of the strategy of the armoured idea, was in any case ill-equipped to overcome. But the dissipation of its efforts to the north and south of the front, and its inability to concentrate from the outset on the single most decisive military objective, the defeat of the Soviet Army in front of Moscow and the occupation of that city, made failure certain. The responsibility for that was solely Hitler's.

The exploits of the panzer arm during 'Barbarossa' were quite remarkable; wherever the German armies advanced, the armoured divisions led the way. There can be no doubt that their fighting qualities contributed significantly to the speed of the German advance. Two examples will serve as illustration: von Manstein's LVI Panzer Corps in Army Group North covered no less than 185 miles in the first four days, and Guderian's Panzer Group 2 advanced 270 miles from Brest Litovsk to Bobruysk in the first seven, achieving seventy-two miles on the last day. But such thrusts were not the decisive factors of the campaign; the great battles of encirclement and annihilation, in which the armoured groups were but the spearheads of the mass of the army, dominated the progress of the German ground forces. Indeed, it was a strategy that yielded spectacular results. In the seven great *Vernichtungsschlachten* of Bialystok-Minsk, Smolensk, Uman, Gomel, Kiev, on the sea of Azov, and Bryansk-Vyazma, the Red Army lost around 150 divisions and a large portion of its armoured strength. These seven encirclements resulted in the capture of more than two and a quarter million soldiers and ended with the destruction or capture of 9,327 tanks and 16,179 guns. In a further thirteen minor battles of encirclement, another 736,000 Soviet soldiers were made prisoner and 4,960 tanks and 9,033 guns were captured or destroyed. Thus, in twenty encirclement operations, almost three million men, 14,287 tanks, and 25,212 guns fell into German hands; and these figures take no account of the large numbers of Red Army soldiers killed at the same time.

In the first stage of the campaign, the most decisive battles were undertaken in Belorussiya by Army Group Centre. Two closely-linked encirclement operations were planned: one, by the 4th and 9th infantry armies, was to destroy the enemy divisions in the 150-mile long Bialystok salient, the weakest point in the Soviet line which gave the Germans an ideal chance to mount a pincer operation similar to that used against the Polish forces in western Poland in 1939; the second, spearheaded by Panzer Groups 2 and 3 in conjunction with 4th and 9th Armies, was to close its jaws 100 miles further east, outside Minsk, thereby catching any enemy formations escaping into the interior of Russia. By such manoeuvres, it was expected to destroy thirty-six Soviet divisions, including ten armoured formations. At first there were delays. Hoth's Panzer Group 3 experienced difficulties in crossing the heavily wooded and virtually trackless sandy terrain, and found initial enemy resistance to be tough. Armour and infantry were concentrated on the few routes available, and close contact with the mass of the army resulted in delays to the panzer spearheads. (On one occasion, one of the panzer divisions was halted for several hours by a column of several thousand lorries belonging to the Luftwaffe.) Hoth's group did not reach the River Niemen, only forty miles beyond the German border, until midday on the 23rd, some thirty-two hours after the advance had begun. To the south, Guderian's Panzer Group 2 experienced difficulty arising from the continued resistance of the border fortress of Brest-Litovsk, which did not fall to units of 4th Army until the fourth day of the attack; congestion resulted from this blocking of a main crossing of the river Bug, and the deployment of the panzer group was adversely affected. By midday on the 26th Hoth had managed to reach a point eighteen miles to the north of Minsk, and that afternoon von Bock ordered Guderian to make contact with his fellow panzer leader and therby close the jaws of the pincer, which he did the next day. However, it was not until 3 July that resistance inside the cauldron was effectively over. Then, the final count revealed that thirty-two infantry and eight tank divisions had been caught within the Bialystok-Minsk pocket. Some 324,000 soldiers were captured, and 3,332 tanks and 1,809 artillery pieces taken or destroyed.

Success though this may have been, it gave rise to much tension between the commanders involved. As in 1940, the old question arose: how far were the armoured spearheads to advance before halting to consolidate their front and flanks, and were they to wait to be relieved by the fast-marching infantry divisions? In the first days of the campaign, the same fears and hesitations that had been so fatal the previous year were exhibited. On 24 June Hitler, fearing that Soviet troops might break out of the Bialystok pocket to the east, had told von Brauchitsch that the armoured encirclement was not tight enough; Halder noted: 'The same old song! This won't change our conduct of operations.'[7] The next day the Führer repeated his concern in written form; again the Army leaders took no notice. Guderian later wrote: 'He [Hitler] wanted to halt the panzer groups and turn them against the Russians in and about Bialystok. On this occasion, however, the OKH proved strong enough to insist on adherence to the original plan. . . .'[8] On the same day, the 25th, Hitler's Wehrmacht Adjutant, Schmundt, arrived at the headquarters of Army Group Centre to attempt to persuade von Bock to close the pincers at Novogrudok, some seventy-five miles nearer the German border than Minsk. This suggestion was stubbornly resisted.

At the same time as Hitler was pressing for a limitation on the advance of the panzer spearheads, von Bock and Hoth were advocating an extension. On the 23rd, air reconnaissance had reported that Soviet columns were retreating east from the Bialystok salient, and von Bock had become fearful that strong forces might escape the double encirclement. He therefore revived his old idea, abandoned only in May 1941, that Panzer Group 3 should not attempt to close the pincers at Minsk but instead move on 100 miles further east to the Dvina between Vitebsk and Polotsk; meanwhile the infantry of 9th Army could close the northern pincer at Minsk. Thereby, von Bock argued, the Soviet forces would be totally destroyed and the enemy prevented from building a new front on the Dvina river. Hoth, reluctant to lose time by turning in to meet Guderian and begin the inevitable wait for the infantry, agreed entirely with his chief's proposal. But OKH, as firm with von Bock as it had been with Hitler, rejected his request. Halder noted in his diary for the evening of the 23rd:

> 'In Army Group Centre everything goes according to plan. Hoth has made the farthest advance, whereas Guderian is being checked again and again. This occasions a discussion with the army group as to whether Hoth should continue his drive on Minsk, or had better strike further north for Polotsk. As a matter of fact, von Bock had from the start objected to a joint operation by the two panzer groups in the direction of Smolensk, and wanted Hoth to strike further north. That, however, would have put an almost impassable strip of water and marshland between Hoth and Guderian, enabling the enemy to beat the groups separately.'[9]

Halder was determined not to allow independent operations; cooperation in encirclement was not to be challenged.

At the same time, tension grew over the continued advance of the panzer spearhead after the closure of the pincers at Minsk. How long should the armoured divisions wait before the marching infantry had caught up with them and consolidated the ground won? Both Guderian and Hoth had pushed on to Minsk with scant regard for maintaining contact with the 4th and 9th infantry armies, under whose command they still came. Von Kluge, commander of 4th Army, urged that the further advance be halted until the cauldron battle was completed and the infantry could release the panzers from their role of securing the encirclement. This, too, accorded with the view of Hitler, who announced that he would agree to the continuation of the offensive to the Dvina and the Dnepr only after the encircled Soviet formations had been rendered sufficiently harmless. The panzer leaders, however, wished to push on with all possible speed towards Smolensk, 200 miles away. Guderian recorded: 'My views concerning the next stage of the operations were as follows: to detach the minimum amount of the panzer group for the destruction of the Russians in the Bialystok-Minsk pocket, while leaving the major part of this operation to the following infantry armies; thus our rapid, mobile, motorised forces would be able to push forward and seize the first operational objective of the campaign, the area Smolensk-Yelnya-Roslavl.'[10] This, too, was the view of von Bock, who, on the 26th, when he had ordered Panzer Group 2 to turn in towards Minsk, also specified that one of its three panzer corps should continue the advance eastwards to Bobruysk, over the Berezina river, a further eighty miles from the panzer spearhead at that time, and ninety miles south-east of Minsk. Guderian had replied that he had already given orders to that effect. On 28 June the corps reached the outskirts of Bobruysk.

Halder, too, was at first in agreement with this course of action. He had committed his view to paper as early as the 24th:

> 'The time necessary to complete this [the bringing-up of infantry to consolidate the encirclement round Bialystok] will be utilised to allow the units of Guderian's and Hoth's panzer groups to close up on the high ground around Minsk. Meanwhile, strong advanced combat teams can secure the crossings on the Upper Dnepr at Mogilev and Orsha, and on the Upper Dvina at Vitebsk and Polotsk. Continuation of the offensive [thereafter] by the combined panzer groups towards the high ground north-east of Smolensk will be allowed only after consultation with OKH.'[11]

And on 29 June, the eighth day of the offensive, in reference to Hitler's continual concern about the panzer operations, the Chief of the General Staff wrote:

> 'The Führer's worry that the panzer forces would overreach themselves in the advance has unfortunately prompted the Army Commander at a conference with Army Group Centre to refer to Bobruysk as nothing more important than the objective in a flank cover of the encirclement at Minsk. Guderian, however, quite soundly from an operational point of view, is advancing on Bobruysk with two panzer divisions and is reconnoitring in the direction of the Dnepr; he certainly does that not just to guard his flank but in order to cross the Dnepr as soon as there is an opportunity to do so. Were he not to do that, he would be making a grave mistake. . . . Let us

hope that commanders of corps and armies will do the right thing even without express orders, which we are not allowed to issue because of the Führer's instructions to the Army Commander [prohibiting the over-extension of the panzer groups' advance].'[12]

However, it must not be thought that Halder was becoming a convert to the armoured idea. He was careful to stick to the traditional method of strategy; the consolidation of the Minsk pocket remained for him the priority. On the 29th he also wrote: '. . . the outer ring formed by the panzer division is closed, but is still fairly thin, of course. It will take several days before the disposition of our forces . . . can be sufficiently reorganised to allow us to continue the [main] attack towards Smolensk on the dry route Orsha-Vitebsk (not before 4 July).'[13] The next day Halder reaffirmed his allegiance to *Vernichtungsgedanke* by writing: 'Army Group [Centre] must in particular see to it that the infantry forces are brought behind Guderian's and Hoth's panzer groups around the pocket.' To emphasise the dangers of ignoring the principles of this strategy, Halder added: 'In disregard of its orders [Guderian's panzer group] has neglected to attend to the mopping-up of the territory traversed by it, and now has its hands full with local enemy breakthroughs.' On 2 July he noted: 'Guderian is under orders not to withdraw any units from the encircled ring without orders.'[14]

As has already been mentioned, von Kluge was most unhappy at Guderian's further moves eastwards; his priority was the destruction of the pocket to the exclusion of all else. On the 26th he had ordered the panzer group to 'occupy the line Zadvorze (five miles north of Slomin)-Holynka-Zelva-the River Zelvianka, and to hold that line against the enemy advancing from Bialystok [attempting to break out of the pocket]'. By the 30th his fears about Russian breakout of the Minsk pocket had still not been allayed. Indeed, as Guderian pointed out, the fierce fighting that continued in the cauldron had:

> '. . . made such a deep impression on 4th Army that they insisted, henceforth, on the pocket being surrounded by strongly occupied and continuous lines. [On 1 July] Field-Marshal Kluge consequently forbade the departure of the 17th Panzer Division [holding the line around the pocket] in the direction of Borisov [over fifty miles on the road to Smolensk] which I had already ordered; he did this despite the fact that the 18th Panzer Division had already reached that town and had secured a bridgehead over the Berezina and that the consolidation of this bridgehead depended to a large extent on the further advance of XLVII Panzer Corps to the Dnepr.'[15]

Nevertheless, orders were orders, and Guderian transmitted von Kluge's command to his troops. But as chance would have it, part of 17th Panzer did not receive the order, and moved on towards Borisov as previously requested. On 2 July Guderian learnt of the error and immediately informed von Kluge's headquarters of the situation. However, such was von Kluge's mistrust of the panzer leaders that he threatened to have Guderian, together with Hoth, the victim of a similar incident, court-marshalled. Von Kluge believed the panzer leaders were conspiring to impose their own conditions on the battlefield, regardless of superior orders. He greatly resented the 'syphoning off' of units eastwards from the Minsk pocket, and only with difficulty did Guderian succeed in persuading him that there was no conspiracy.

On 3 July there came a further blow to the panzer leaders: both the panzer groups of Army Group Centre were placed under von Kluge, and headquarters 4th Army became known as headquarters 4th Panzer Army. The infantry formations of the former 4th Army now came under the command of von Weichs, whose 2nd Army headquarters had previously controlled no troops. The question as to the most efficient way of coordinating the operations of the two panzer groups had been deliberated for some days; Halder noted on 24 June: 'I object to putting Guderian in command of the combined panzer groups.'[16] No doubt OKH was glad to be able to put a strong, conservative general such as von Kluge in a position to control the panzer leaders, whose continual agitation to move east at all possible speed at the expense of consolidating the encirclements was not looked on at all favourably.

A further advance eastwards in the direction of Moscow had been decided on by OKH on 30 June, and Army Group Centre headquarters was told that 'a development of the operations towards Smolensk would be of decisive importance'.[17] The time was ripe for such a move; air reconnaissance had revealed that the Soviets were assembling fresh forces along the Dnepr from Mogilev to Smolensk, and, as Guderian later remarked, 'If the line of the Dnepr was to be captured without waiting for the arrival of the infantry, which would mean the loss of weeks, we would have to hurry.'[18] The next day, 1 July, OKH issued the orders for a further advance to begin on the 3rd. The new objectives were Yelnya on the Desna river for Panzer Group 2, and the region north of Smolensk for Panzer Group 3. The 2nd and 9th armies were to follow the armoured spearheads with all possible speed. The aim was the destruction of the growing Soviet forces on the Dnepr, and the acquisition of the Orsha-Vitebsk-Smolensk triangle, so vital to any continued advance on to the capital.

Accordingly, on the 3rd the general advance eastwards was resumed. Already, thanks to the impatience of Hoth and Guderian and the earlier acquiescence of Halder, a number of armoured units had moved beyond the Minsk pocket; on the right wing, the panzer corps that had crossed the Berezina at Bobruysk on 28 June was already on the way to the Dnepr at Rogachev, which it was to reach on the 4th. Another of Guderian's three corps had secured a bridgehead over the Berezina at Borisov. Units of Hoth's group were also on the way towards the Dvina around the area of Polotsk. Nonetheless, although 4th Panzer Army was well-placed to continue the attack, the fact remained that, by the 3rd, more than six days had elapsed since the armoured pincers had closed at Minsk, and only a further ninety miles had been covered in that time – and then not as part of a general advance but only as the action of individual corps. Such was the delay necessitated by *Vernichtungsgedanke*.

This pause at Minsk was unfortunate for the panzer force. The six days had allowed the Soviets to bring up troops and form some kind of defence against the attackers. On 2 July the formations that had been digging-in along the upper Dvina and upper Dnepr came under the command of Marshal Timoshenko, a martinet who was determined to stiffen Soviet resistance. Furthermore, the day the German advance to Smolensk began, the weather broke, turning the sandy tracks into rivers of mud, and the soft earth into swamp. Von Blumentritt recorded the conditions under which the advance was undertaken:

> 'It was appallingly difficult country for tank movement – great virgin forests, widespread swamps, terrible roads, and bridges not strong enough to bear the weight of tanks. The resistance also became stiffer, and the Russians began to cover their front with minefields. It was easier for them to block the way because there were so few roads. The great motor highway leading from the frontier to Moscow was unfinished – the one road a westerner would call a "road". . . . Such a country was bad enough for the tanks, but worse still for the transport accompanying them – carrying their fuel, their supplies, and all the auxiliary troops they needed. Nearly all this transport consisted of wheeled vehicles, which could not move off the roads, nor move on it if the sand turned into mud. An hour or two of rain reduced the panzer forces to stagnation. It was an extraordinary sight, with groups of them strung out over a hundred-mile stretch, all stuck – until the sun came out and the ground dried. Hoth . . . was delayed by swamps as well as bursts of rain.'[19]

Guderian's and Hoth's five corps attacked over a front of 200 miles, which the latter likened to the fingers of an open hand rather than the clenched fist it should have resembled. The reason for this sprang directly from the requirements of *Vernichtungsgedanke*; Guderian and Hoth were both obliged to advance in the same direction with their individual main objectives less than fifty miles distant from each other (Yelnya and north of Smolensk). The spread in the individual panzer groups themselves was due to the need to protect the flanks of the attacking force which, even before it had reached its objective, would, in part, halt to secure the pocket and become vulnerable to enemy counter-attacks made possible by the delay at Minsk. Hitler's interference also had its effect; the very day the advance resumed Halder privately committed his answer to the Führer's worrying to his diary: '. . . from the tactical point of view there is of course some sense in this worry about the flanks. But that is what the army and corps commanders are there for. Our commanders and staff are our strong point, but at the top they have no confidence in them because they have no conception of the strength represented by a body of commanders all of whom have been trained and educated on the same principles.'[20] Fearing the build-up of enemy forces on the weak line between Army Groups North and South, Hitler directed that Hoth keep one of his panzer corps out along the boundary. Thus, momentum was sadly dissipated and, as Hoth later argued, the broad-front advance on Smolensk became a prime example of how armoured warfare should not be conducted.

Von Kluge remained true to form and held the advance in check when it appeared to him that his panzer leaders were straining at the leash unduly. Guderian later remembered that 'What delayed us most during that time was the hindrance resulting from the doubts of Field-Marshal von Kluge. He was inclined to stop the advance of the panzers at every difficulty arising in the rear.'[21] On 9 July Halder wrote: 'Appearance of a strong and still-growing enemy group between Orsha and Vitebsk has prompted an order from 4th Army headquarters to Panzer Group 2 to put off planned attacks temporarily and instead take over cover of the left wing against enemy attacks and assure contact with Panzer Group 3.'[22] Von Kluge only reluctantly agreed to Guderian's proposal to cross the Dnepr with the panzers before waiting for the infantry divisions, which were then just arriving at the Berezina, to come up. Again von Kluge insisted that the panzer groups hold the ring around the enemy until relieved in force by the infantry, and he appears to have been not over-zealous in forcing the pace of the marching formations, which were, admittedly, tired after covering so many miles from the border, fighting for much of the way. It was not until the 16th that weak advanced-infantry units reached the Dnepr, seven days after they had arrived at the Berezina, a distance of seventy miles to the west. Not until the 20th did the infantry begin to relieve the panzer units east of the Dnepr from their task of holding the Soviet units within their bridgeheads. Guderian, who had reached the objective of Yelnya, was then keen to push on further to the east, but von Bock reminded him of his first duty: to secure the Smolensk pocket. On the 21st, when Guderian had ordered one of his panzer divisions, then on flank protection, to spearhead an attack to close the encirclement and to link up with Hoth, von Kluge intervened and without informing the panzer leader told the division to stay where it was so as not to weaken the almost-formed ring around the enemy. As a result the pocket was not closed until several days later, when Hoth succeeded in doing so from the north.

Consequently, the advance from Minsk to Smolensk had not been a spectacular affair. It took fourteen days, from 3 to 16 July, for Smolensk to be reached, a distance of 150 miles from the position of the foremost panzers on the first day of the attack, and another nineteen, until 5 August, for all resistance within the pocket to be finally subdued. Panzer Group 2 did not cross the Dnepr, some seventy miles from the Berezina, until the 10th and 11th, and was not able to close the jaws of the pincer east of Smolensk until the 26th, by which time large numbers of the enemy had escaped eastwards. Guderian did not occupy Yelnya and the surrounding area, his objective, until 20 July, which meant that his average rate of advance was less than twelve miles a day; in comparison, Minsk had been reached after an average of forty miles a day. However, the Smolensk pocket yielded a rich haul: 310,000 enemy soldiers were taken prisoner, and 3,205 tanks, together with 3,120 guns, were destroyed or captured.

Again, as at Minsk, there had been a considerable delay at Smolensk between the time the panzer divisions reached their objective and the time they were free to continue their advance. The only difference was that at Smolensk the enemy opposition was so fierce, and the control of higher command so great, that no syphoning-off of the mechanised forces eastwards was possible; all their energies were needed to guard the pocket, to attempt to close the pincer, and to ward off strong counter-attacks from the Soviet forces attempting to relieve their encircled comrades. Such was the strength of the resistance that on 30 July the enemy mounted no fewer than thirteen attacks on the Yelnya bridgehead over the Desna. Not until 27 July were there enough infantry divisions of 2nd Army east of the Dnepr to make the German positions there secure, and even then they had come not to relieve Guderian's force, but to reinforce it. Von Kluge, fearing a Soviet breakout to the south, appeared obsessed by the need to retain the enemy troops within the pocket to the exclusion of all else, even to the extent of ignoring the severe enemy pressure on the flanks to the east and south-east, especially at Roslavl. Thus from 20 July until 1 August, Army Group Centre was effectively on the defensive. No further advance was possible.

Once again, then, the requirements of *Vernichtungsgedanke* imposed a delay on the motorised forces. But as the time approached when the panzer troops would be ready to resume the advance eastwards, fresh orders came making such a course of action impossible. On 27 July Guderian had flown to Army Group Centre headquarters, expecting to be told to begin preparations for the push towards Moscow, or at least to Bryansk (some 100 miles south-east on the Desna, a possible objective during a further encirclement operation in the direction of the capital). However, he was mistaken and, to his surprise, 'learned that Hitler had ordered 2nd Panzer Group . . . to go for Gomel in collaboration with 2nd Army'. This meant that, instead of continuing east or south-east, the panzer spearhead would be swung round some 130 degrees to move in a south-westerly direction 150 miles from Smolensk towards Germany. Guderian wrote:

'. . . Hitler was anxious to encircle the eight to ten Russian divisions in the Gomel area. We were informed that Hitler was convinced that large-scale envelopments were not justified: the theory on which they were based was a false one put out by the General Staff corps, and he believed that events in France had proved his point. He preferred an alternative plan by which small enemy forces were to be encircled and destroyed piecemeal and the enemy thus bled to death. All the officers who took part in this conference were of the opinion that this was incorrect: that these manoeuvres on our part simply gave the Russians time to set up new formations and to use their inexhaustible manpower for the creation of fresh defensive lines in the rear area: even more important, we were sure that this strategy would not result in the urgently necessary, rapid conclusion of the campaign.'[23]

Halder, too, was horrified by Hitler's proposal. He wrote on 26 July:

'Such a plan implies a shift of our strategy from the operational to the tactical level. If striking at small local enemy concentrations becomes our sole objective, the campaign will resolve itself into a series of minor successes which will advance our front only by inches. Pursuing such a policy eliminates all tactical risks and enables us gradually to close the gaps between the fronts of the army groups, but the result will be that we feed all our strength into a front expanding in width at the sacrifice of depth, and end up in position warfare.'

His words were prophetic. He continued:

'The Führer's analysis, which at many points is unjustly critical of the field commanders, indicates a complete break with the strategy of large operational conceptions. You cannot beat the Russians with operational successes, he argued, because they simply do not know when they are defeated. . . . it will be necessary to destroy them bit by bit, in small encircling actions of a purely tactical nature. . . . following such a course implies letting the enemy dictate our policy and reduces our operations to a tempo which will not permit us to reach our goal, the Volga. . . . To me, these arguments mark the beginning in the decline of our initial strategy . . . and a willingness to throw away the opportunities afforded us by the impetus of our infantry and armour.'[24]

The campaign was barely a month old when Halder wrote these words. He was correct; under Hitler, even the traditional strategy of decisive manoeuvre was being bastardised and emasculated.

Guderian immediately proposed, 'regardless of what decisions Hitler now may take', to ignore the Gomel operation and instead to attack Roslavl, thereby 'to dispose of the most dangerous enemy threat to [the] right flank', and capture 'this important road centre [that] would give . . . mastery of the communications to the east, the south, and the south-west'.[25] Von Bock agreed, provided the six extra infantry divisions asked for, and made Guderian independent of von Kluge by taking his command away from 4th Panzer Army and retitling it *Armeegruppe Guderian*. At the same time a number of panzer divisions were to be withdrawn from the front line and given a few days for rest and maintenance. Furthermore, the Yelnya salient, although it was proving costly to maintain because of the fierce Soviet attacks and the supply problems resulting from its considerable distane (450 miles) from the nearest major railhead, was to be retained. By these measures a situation would be brought about whereby the advance to Moscow could be resumed. The generals' hope was that Hitler would change his mind.

On 1 August the panzers and infantry began the attack on Roslavl; by the 3rd the town was taken, and by the 8th all resistance was eliminated. Some 38,000 prisoners had been taken, and 250 tanks and 359 guns destroyed or captured in what was one of the swiftest and most complete German victories in the east. With the right flank secure, and the road to Moscow before them, the panzer spearhead of Army Group Centre was prepared to resume the advance east by mid-August. Von Bock, Hoth, and Guderian were in complete agreement on this point. Hitler, however, told these officers on 4 August that he had not yet decided on whether the next objective would be Moscow or the Ukraine. Guderian nevertheless 'decided in any case to make the necessary preparations for an attack on Moscow'.[26] In the event, it was more than seven weeks before his panzers moved again in that direction.

To the north, the advance until early August had been spectacular in terms of distance covered, though not in numbers of prisoners taken. In the first four days von Manstein's panzer corps alone had covered 185 miles on the route to Leningrad, which then lay only 340 miles distant. By 14 July, the twenty-third day of the campaign, the 'Cradle of Bolshevism' was only sixty miles from the foremost panzer spearhead of Panzer Group 4, while the 16th and 18th Armies had cleared most of the Baltic States. An average daily advance of eighteen miles had been achieved. No great battles of encirclement had taken place and, to all intents, it appeared as if Army Group North's sector was witnessing the type of warfare so urgently desired by Hoth and Guderian in the centre. Indeed, the later comments of General Charles de Beaulieu, the Chief of Staff to Panzer Group 4, appear to support this:

> 'The Commander-in-Chief of Army Group North . . . was confronted with a very different enemy employment than that facing Army Groups Centre and South [which] . . . were faced by Russian forces deployed on a wide shallow front line, with a strong concentration in the great Bialystok salient which positively invited a large-scale encircling movement. . . . But in the north the Russian deployment in the recently occupied Baltic countries, though much looser, was in much greater depth. Their reserves stretched right back into the territory of the old Russian Empire, and a large reserve of Soviet tanks was even located to the east of Pskov [more than 300

miles from the border]. At no point, therefore, did a strategy of encirclement appear feasible. Nevertheless, such a grouping on the part of an enemy still unprepared at the time should have enabled the Germans to surprise the opposition in depth and destroy it piecemeal – but for this an essential condition was superiority of speed and mobility, so that after every partial engagement a deeper and quicker thrust could be made by the attackers.'[27]

This was borne out in von Leeb's army group order of 5 May 1941, which concluded: 'Forward! Don't stop for anything. Never let the enemy consolidate once he has been thrown back.'[28]

But however clearly expressed was the intention for the deep armoured thrusts, practice, tempered as it was by inexperience in handling the panzer formations and by cautious military doctrine, was somewhat different. The first realisation of what was to happen came when a bridgehead over the Dvina at Dvinsk was gained by von Manstein's LVI Corps on 26 June. His corps was isolated 185 miles from the border, the rest of the general advance being some sixty miles distant to the west. But, as von Manstein recalled, he and his officers:

'. . . were less exercised by our present rather isolated position, which would not continue indefinitely, than by the problem of what the next move should be. . . . Instead, our enthusiasm was dampened by an order to widen the bridgehead around Dvinsk and keep the crossings open. We were to wait for XXXXI Panzer Corps and the left wing of 16th Army to move up. . . . While this was certainly the "safe", staff-college solution, we had had other ideas. As we saw it, our sudden appearance so far behind the front must have caused considerable confusion among the enemy. He would obviously make every attempt to throw us back across the river, fetching in troops from any quarter to do so. The sooner we pushed on, therefore, the less chance he would have of offering us any systematic opposition with superior forces. If we pushed on towards Pskov – while, of course, continuing to safeguard the Dvina crossings – and if, at the same time, Panzer Group headquarters pushed the other panzer corps through Dvinsk behind us [instead of fifty miles north up the river, as had already been ordered] it seemed likely that the enemy would have to keep on opposing us with whatever forces he happened to have on hand at the moment, and be incapable for the time being of fighting a set battle. As for the beaten enemy forces south of the Dvina, these could be left to the infantry armies coming up behind. It goes without saying that the further a single panzer corps – or indeed the entire panzer group – ventured into the depths of the Russian hinterland, the greater the hazards became. Against this, it may be said that the safety of a tank formation operating in the enemy's rear largely depends on its ability to keep moving. Once it comes to a halt it will immediately be assailed from all sides by the enemy's reserves.'[29]

Von Manstein was right; as his panzers remained stationary around their bridgehead, the Soviet counter-attacks increased in intensity and frequency, and when, after the sixth day of the halt, the advance began again, enemy resistance had hardened. Von Manstein made the following comment:

'A tank drive such as LVI Panzer Corps made to Dvinsk inevitably generates confusion and panic in the enemy communications zone; it ruptures the enemy's chain of command and makes it virtually impossible for him to coordinate his counter-measures. These advantages had now been waived as a result of [the] . . . decision . . . to consolidate on the Dvina. Whether we should now be fortunate enough fully to regain that lead over the enemy was doubtful, to say the least. Certainly the only chance of doing so lay in the panzer group being able to bring its forces into action as an integrated whole. As will be seen, however, this is precisely what it failed to do. . . .'[30]

From the beginning of the campaign the tactical grouping of Army Group North's forces was far from ideal. Panzer Group 4 possessed only two panzer corps, XXXXI and LVI, and both were sent forward on parallel lines of advance without even a division in reserve. A dissipation of limited armoured strength was thus brought about, further worsened by von Leeb's concept of future operations. He believed that his first task was to destroy the enemy in the Baltic region, and only then to occupy Leningrad. Therefore he proposed that Panzer Group 4 should advance as the apex of a wedge aimed at Lake Ilmen, 125 miles south-south-west of Leningrad, while 18th Army cleared the Baltic States, and 16th Army the area between the panzer group and the army goup's boundary. Hoepner, however, disagreed with this. Von Leeb's proposed advance meant that the motorised formations would have to move through an area devoid of roads and covered by forest and swamp. Moreover, the panzer leader contended that Leningrad must be the first objective, and that the armoured thrust should therefore be between the Peipus and Ilmen lakes on the direct route to the city. A compromise was then arrived at, one that satisfied Hoepner not at all. Von Manstein's LVI Panzer Corps was to advance through Novorzhev towards Lake Ilmen, while XXXXI Panzer Corps would move via Ostrov to Leningrad. Hoepner appealed to OKH, but no help came from that quarter. Halder noted in his diary for 28 June that 'the objectives were of course dependent on the directives which we had not yet issued, but which were certainly overdue'.[31] Not until 9 July would firm orders come from the Army Command; meanwhile, the advance was resumed on 2 July along the lines of von Leeb's compromise.

At first all went well with the renewed attack, due in no small measure to the surprise inflicted on the Soviets by the double thrust of Panzer Group 4. Halder noted on 8 July: 'The infantry armies are pressing on in rapid marches on a wide front and with great depth, with their advanced combat teams following closely behind the armour.'[32] Von Manstein, however, remained sceptical, for he feared the marshy and impenetrable terrain beyond the old Soviet frontier, seventy-five miles east of the Dvina. His misgivings proved correct, and after a week of inconclusive fighting any idea of a further advance through the wooded swamps towards Novorzhev had to be abandoned. On 9 July LVI Panzer Corps was accordingly diverted to Ostrov, through which XXXXI Panzer Corps had already passed five days earlier on its way to Pskov, seventy miles north, which it reached on the 8th. There XXXXI Panzer Corps rested. Now that the two parts of the panzer group were more or less reunited on the same line of attack, von Manstein 'hoped for a rapid, direct, and uniform advance on Leningrad. . . . this offered the best chance not only of effecting the quick capture of the city but also of cutting off the enemy forces retreating through Livonia into Estonia before 18th Army. The task of safeguarding this operation on its open eastern flank would have had to devolve on 16th Army as it moved up behind Panzer Group 4.'[33] It was not to be. On 7 July von Brauchitsch had approved Hoepner's plan for a bold armoured stroke on Leningrad, with XXXXI Panzer Corps proceeding directly through Luga, on the river of that name and more than 100 miles from Pskov, and LVI Panzer Corps executing a flanking movement to approach the city from the east via Lake Ilmen in order to break the line of communications between Moscow and Leningrad. Von Manstein commented: 'Important though this latter task was, these orders must once again have led to the two corps becoming widely dispersed, as a result of which each was liable to be deprived of the necessary striking power. The danger was increased by the fact that much of the country to be crossed this side of Leningrad was marshy or wooded and hardly suited for large armoured formations.'[34]

The advance began on 10 July. The XXXXI Panzer Corps immediately ran into trouble with the terrain which, on the route to Luga, was dense forest and marsh. Progress was less than seven miles a day, and on the 12th it was decided to switch the line of advance from Luga to the area of Sabsk, 100 miles north up the Luga river, where the ground was more suited to mechanised forces. Any idea of waiting for the arrival of the infantry – the only type of soldier that was of any use in the forests and swamps – was rejected by the panzer leaders and von Leeb; the idea of a fast, armoured thrust on Leningrad, decided upon on 7 July, still held good. By 14 July, XXXXI Panzer Corps had established two bridgeheads over the Luga near Sabsk; Leningrad was only sixty miles distant, across relatively easy terrain, and few enemy troops were in a position to put up any stiff resistance. Hoepner prepared for his final drive, which he reckoned could begin on 20 July. He was confident that the city could be occupied.

Again, von Manstein was unhappy about the new line of advance for XXXXI Panzer Corps. It meant that the two panzer corps were separated by more than 100 miles of nearly impenetrable wooded swamp, and there was no opportunity for mutual support. The infantry were still miles behind. The LVI Panzer Corps, moving slowly, found itself even more isolated and coming under increasing enemy pressure. Hitler, too, was growing more and more concerned. He had taken considerable interest in the tactical moves on the northern front, and Keitel had acquired the habit of telephoning or telegraphing a daily list of 'Führer worries' to army group headquarters. On 11 July the Chief of OKW had informed Halder that Hitler was worried lest Panzer Group 4 in its race to Leningrad should lose contact with the infantry, although on the same day the Chief of the General Staff noted: 'Hoepner has made some frontal advances; and now, with the infantry divisions arriving from the rear having replaced the armour on his flank, he is concentrating his forces northwards.'[35] Hitler later expressed great concern at the large gap between the two panzer corps (as also, on 14 July, did Halder). Thus, Army Group North was told to halt Hoepner's advance on the Luga; Halder complained at the time that Hitler's uninformed interference in such matters was becoming intolerable. On 19 July Hitler issued Directive No. 33, which contained the following: 'The advance on Leningrad will be resumed only when 18th Army has made contact with Panzer Group 4, and the extensive flank in the east is adequately protected by 16th Army. At the same time Army Group North must endeavour to prevent Russian forces still in action in Estonia from withdrawing to Leningrad.'[36]

Furthermore, such was the Führer's failure to allot priorities and his desire to do everything all at once, even with insufficient resources, that he denied the panzer group the infantry support it so urgently required in the marshy, forested terrain where mobility was limited, and where wheels that sank in mud became a liability. Because of the shape of the Baltic region allocated to Army Group North, the further east the invaders moved, the longer became their front. Moreover, whereas the army group was advancing north-east towards Leningrad, its neighbour, Army Group South, was moving due east in the direction of Moscow, with the result that it was becoming increasingly difficult for the two forces to keep in contact. Hitler, wishing to dominate the Baltic States as soon as possible, kept requiring that more and more infantry divisions of 18th Army should cease supporting Panzer Group 4 and move westwards to clear the region and secure the ports. He expressed the opinion that Leningrad should not be captured until the Baltic States had been cleared of all enemy troops. At the same time he insisted that, come what may, the right flank of Army Group North should be kept in close contact with Army Group Centre, and even give support to it if necessary. Thus, nearly sixty per cent of 16th Army's strength was committed to the south flank, with the result that LVI Panzer Corps was left virtually unsupported. The terrain and the opposition combined to slow down the advance and severely deplete the material resources of the panzer corps. Not until the 22nd July, when the LVI Panzer Corps had the support of an infantry corps from 18th Army, did Soltsy fall. It had taken von Manstein twelve days to cover the ninety miles from Ostrov; any further advance was then checked twelve miles west of Lake Ilmen. Von Manstein told von Paulus on 26 July that he was of the opinion that the corps should be taken out of the area where rapid movement was impossible, and instead used against Moscow. The Deputy Chief of the General Staff agreed with him. If not, von Manstein continued, it was vital to have the support of the infantry divisions until the wooded zone was cleared, otherwise the panzer corps would have no strength left for the final attack on Leningrad; he thought the best use of his corps in the north would be to combine it with XXXXI Panzer Corps on the Luga. Von Paulus again concurred wholeheartedly.

The advance of Panzer Group 4 from the Dvina to the Luga had been bedevilled by three factors: the splitting of its force; the bad, at times impassable, terrain on the approaches to Leningrad; and the lack of infantry support. Although Hoepner, supported by von Leeb, had, at least since the crossing of the Dvina, wished for a speedy armoured thrust on Leningrad, and although the Soviet forces were relatively weak, the isolation of the two corps and the forested marshes, through which they were directed, had meant that panzer divisions alone were not enough. The support of the infantry was vital: only they could master the dense, tree-covered marshes through which the bulky tanks could not pass and into which the wheeled transport just sank. But, thanks to Hitler's interference, it was not until the second half of July that this support was given, and then only by two infantry corps – one to XXXXI Panzer Corps, the other to the LVI. Army Group North then determined to resume the advance on Leningrad. On Hitler's orders, the XXXXI Panzer Corps had been standing only sixty miles from the city since 14 July, and was being subjected to increased enemy pressure. A date for the final attack was set provisionally for the 22nd, exactly one month after the invasion had begun. Hoepner hoped for success; large-scale Soviet counter-attacks were not expected, and the leaders of Leningrad were unprepared for defence. Even had the city not been occupied (Hitler had decided as early as 8 July that it should be only encircled, and then razed to the ground by the Luftwaffe, as this would save supporting the population during the winter), certainly a close encirclement would have been possible one and a half months earlier than actually happened.

However, Hitler's demands, the slowness of LVI Panzer Corps' advance, and the growing doubts about the advisability of a sudden dash by XXXXI Panzer Corps, even though reinforced by infantry, led to the postponement of the attack, first until 26 July and then until the 28th. Infantry of the 16th Army were awaited to reinforce von Manstein's force, and Hitler strongly advocated that the bulk of XXXXI Panzer Corps should be transferred to LVI Panzer Corps' area, by then around the town of Luga.

This, however, was successfully resisted by von Leeb. On the 23rd Hitler had issued his Directive No. 33a, which specified:

> 'Panzer Group 3 will come under temporary command of Army Group North to secure its right flank and to surround the enemy in the Leningrad area . . . [this] will enable Army Group North to employ strong forces of infantry for an attack in the direction of Leningrad, and to avoid expending its mobile forces in frontal attacks over difficult terrain. . . . Panzer Group 3 is to be returned to Army Group Centre on the completion of its task. The High Command of the Army will plan further operations so that large parts of Army Group North, including Panzer Group 4 . . . may be moved back to Germany.'[37]

On the 30th, this was followed by Directive No. 34:

> 'In the northern sector of the Eastern Front the main attack will continue between Lake Ilmen and Narva towards Leningrad, with the aim of encircling Leningrad and making contact with the Finnish Army. . . . The intended thrust by Panzer Group 3 against the high ground around Valdi will be postponed until armoured formations are fully ready for action. . . . Estonia must first of all be mopped up by all the forces of 18th Army. Only then may divisions advance towards Leningrad.'[38]

A delay was now inevitable. The attack had already been stayed too long, as von Leeb knew, but there was now only one course left open: to wait for the formations of 16th and 18th Armies to break through the swamp, forest, and ever-growing enemy troop concentrations. The date for the attack was set at 8 August, twenty-five days after the Luga river had been reached. The plan was for two thrusts by Panzer Group 4, one from Luga, the other from the Sabsk area, to converge on Krasnogvardeisk, twenty-five miles from Leningrad, while two army corps would attack from the west of Lake Ilmen towards Novgorod. The main emphasis of the advance would thus be on the right flank, as Hitler wished, in the most difficult of terrain, whereas before it was to have been on the left, where suitable tank country faced the XXXXI Panzer Corps. In the early morning of 8 August, just as the enemy resistance in Guderian's pocket of Roslavl to the south was collapsing, the tanks and infantry of Army Group North moved towards Leningrad. Success was not to greet their endeavours.

Events on the southern sector of the German front were less momentous than those in the north. Von Rundstedt's Army Group Centre faced the strongest concentrations of Soviet troops, for it was at this point, the Ukraine, that Stalin believed any German attack would be mounted. The invaders had disposed of only forty divisions, plus a number of Romanian and Hungarian formations, to face fifty-six, commanded by some of the most able of the Red

Army generals. The offensive capacity of von Rundstedt's force had been weakened by the allocation of units to the Balkan campaign, and further limited by Hitler's decision not to agree to OKH's proposal to mount a strong offensive movement from Romania, through ideal tank country. This, when allied with an attack from southern Poland, would have allowed a deep, double encirclement of the Soviet formations in the Borislav-Przemyśl salient similar to the advances around the Bialystok salient and beyond, to Minsk. Instead, the weak German and Romanian forces in Romania, devoid of armoured formations, did not even attack for the first seven days of the campaign but remained passive, safeguarding the vital Ploiesti oilfields and taking care not to provoke a Soviet counter-offensive. After the week had elapsed, an advance into the Ukraine and down to the Black Sea to Odessa was undertaken. The German weight in the south, therefore, fell entirely on the northern flank of the Borislav-Przemyśl salient, where von Kleist's Panzer Group 1, aided and guarded on its left flank by von Reichenau's 6th Army, under whose control it came, moved to Kiev on the Dnepr, some 270 miles from the border, and then turned south-east, following the river so as to secure bridgeheads and encircle the main Soviet forces west of its line of advance. At the same time, von Stulpnägel's 17th Army, on the right flank of the panzer group, moved through Vinnitsa, 130 miles south-west of Kiev, towards the Dnepr. By such means a double encirclement could be achieved, although not, of course, on the same grand scale as might have been possible. Furthermore, unlike the country to the south of the Ukraine, the terrain traversed by Panzer Group 1 and 6th Army was far from ideal for panzer operations; the troops were forced to advance through the woodlands of Galizia and the west Ukraine and the broken swampland south of the Pripyat.

The portents for a quick, decisive encirclement were not good, and the rate of advance of von Rundstedt's force was accordingly slow. On 23 June Halder noted in his diary: 'The situation looks more difficult on Army Group South's sector, because, in abandoning the original plan of operations based on Romania, we have thrown away our best strategic opportunity. We shall have to confine ourselves to probing for the soft spot and then drive an armoured wedge through it as hard as we can.'[39] But the soft spot was difficult to find. Panzer Group 1 and 6th Army experienced great difficulties; Halder wrote on the 25th that they were 'advancing slowly, unfortunately with considerable losses. The enemy on this front has energetic leadership.'[40] By comparison with Hoepner's achievement, the armoured spearhead of Army Group South's advance was poor. Continual Soviet attacks, designed to separate the panzer divisions from the supporting infantry formations, unsuitable ground, and the not-too-dashing leadership of von Kleist combined to produce an average advance of just under ten miles a day until 10 July, by which time Kiev had not even been reached. It took a further twenty-three days, to 2 August, to advance the 130 miles to Pervomaysk in order to meet 17th Army and seal the first encirclement around the Soviets. The *Kesselschlacht,* known as Uman, which ended on 8 August, was, by the standards of Army Group Centre, small. Only 103,000 Red Army soldiers were captured, and 317 tanks and 1,100 guns taken or destroyed. Large Soviet forces still remained to be trapped, especially those south of the Pripyat Marshes with whom 6th Army was having difficulties. Indeed, the diversion of 6th Army in this direction was the only cause for any separation between its infantry divisions and the motorised formations of Panzer Group 1; von Kleist, von Reichenau, and von Rundstedt all took care to maintain contact between the two, a fact which also contributed to the slow rate of advance which averaged only seven miles a day from 22 June until 2 August. So much for the deep, fast thrusts of armoured warfare. In the extreme south, 11th Army and the Hungarians, who began their advance on 1 July, achieved a rate of advance of only eight miles a day through the lonely, hot, wide expanses. It took two months to cross the 400 miles to the Dnepr, a distance that Panzer Group 4 in the Baltic had traversed, through more difficult terrain, in two weeks. The movement, particularly slow even for infantry, was brought about partly by daily cloudbursts, which turned the rich black soil into liquid glue, and partly by enemy action, especially by tank troops.

As in the north and the centre, there was in the south a conflict of attitudes over the handling of the advance. The question as to exactly where the main advance was to reach before turning in to encircle the enemy was considered as early as the eighth day. In his diary, Halder wrote:

> 'In the next moves, the main objective . . . must be to break through the Russian rear positions on the line Belokorivchi-Navogorod Volynskij-Mogilev Pod-mouth of the Dnestr, without engaging in major frontal attacks, and then swing south still west of the Dnepr. . . . For this breakthrough Panzer Group 1 must be furnished with infantry (which apparently were deliberately excluded when Panzer Group 1 and 6th Army were separated from each other [after the initial advance]).'[41]

On 5 July the Chief of the General Staff noted: 'Chief of Staff Army Group South sends an interesting situation estimate. It shows how widely Army Group South, which has decided to direct its main effort against Berdichev (non-existent gap in the fortified line), diverges from our plan (main concentration on the north wing).'[42] In other words, von Rundstedt proposed a wider, more ambitious encirclement than OKH were prepared to accept. On the 7th Halder wrote:

> '. . . breakthrough in the central sector of Army Group South is under way. . . . Telephone conversation with General von Sodenstern [Chief of Staff] on next moves. The thing tomorrow is to move Kleist's panzer group in such a direction that we can turn to form an "inner ring" [i.e. a tight encirclement] forthwith, resorting to an

"outer ring" [i.e. a wide encirclement] only if we are compelled to do so [i.e. by escape of the enemy eastwards]. The trouble is that the further the armour penetrates into enemy territory in such a case, the quicker our infantry loses contact with them and the enemy forces marked for destruction escape in masses through the resulting gaps.'[43]

Halder was not going to let what had happened at Minsk be repeated; the field commanders were so ambitious, so greedy for gains that they forgot such realities, or so he thought. On the 9th he noted: 'The burning question now is the further employment of Panzer Group 1. Army Group [South] states its intention to strike with its north group (III Corps) to Kiev and with the bulk of the panzer group to Belaya Tserkov, and then to push in south or south-east direction.' Now the Führer intervened; all his fears concerning wide encirclement came again to the fore. Halder continued:

'In the meantime, the Führer has called up von Brauchitsch and told him that he wants the panzer group to swing the elements that have penetrated to Berdichev [90 miles from Kiev] to the south in the direction of Vinnitsa, [75 miles to the south], in order to effect an early junction with 11th Army. At the evening situation conference this leads to an agitated exchange about the direction in which Panzer Group 1 ought to be moved. My standpoint is as follows: We must on no account ignore Kiev. There is so much evidence of enemy confusion that chances of taking Kiev by some sort of surprise thrust look good. [He added that the armour must not be risked if it was impossible to achieve surprise.] . . . Thus the ring to be formed will run from Berdichev through Belaya Tserkov and to the sector of 11th Army. Sealing the ring is the primary objective. Kiev and Dnepr crossings south of Kiev are secondary objectives. The Army Commander outlines this scheme to the Führer. He does not object, but apparently is not yet converted and emphasises that he expects nothing from the Kiev operation.'[44]

Thus, OKH and Army Group South were now in agreement about the future moves, but the Führer was unconvinced. At 1.30a.m. the following morning, 10 July, Hitler phoned von Brauchitsch, the content of his conversation being summed up by Halder:

'He cannot put his mind to rest for fear that tanks might be committed against Kiev and so needlessly sacrificed [it must be remembered that two days previously he had specified that the panzer groups should not advance into Moscow or Leningrad, but instead close round outside them and let the Air Force reduce the cities]. . . . The encircling ring is to run from Berdichev through Vinnitsa to 11th Army. Accordingly the following order goes out to Army Group South: the Führer does not want tanks to be brought to bear against

Kiev, beyond what is necessary for reconnaissance and security . . . [only those forces of Panzer Group 1 not needed for Berdichev-Vinnitsa] will strike for Belaya Tserkov and then south [the wider encirclement].'

This was the beginning of a day of frantic activity. At 11.00a.m. von Brauchitsch recalled his Chief of General Staff from the headquarters of Army Group South to tell him he had heard again from Hitler. This time the Führer, while reaffirming his intention to move south once Zhitomir-Berdichev had been reached, nevertheless granted that, if there were no large bodies of enemy troops to encircle (as von Rundstedt argued), then Panzer Group 1 could attack Kiev. Von Rundstedt believed that the ring through Vinnitsa would be too close and would miss many enemy units; it should therefore go through Belaya Tserkov astride the retreat route to Kiev, then move south-west to link up with 11th Army. If this should prove inadvisable, there were two courses of action left: to advance south-east and south-west of Dnepr, or across Dnepr at Kiev south-east and then east. The Army Commander agreed with this view, which was in effect a compromise between the Führer's two alternatives. Halder wrote: 'The Army Commander will make no decision that would not have the Führer's approval. It is now up to me to get the Führer to agree.' At 11.30a.m. his diary entry read: '. . . can't get the Führer (sleeping) to the telephone. Tell Keitel need to get as many enemy as possible and that no plan should rely on 11th Army as its capabilities are low.' At 12.30p.m. '. . . telephone call from OKW. Führer approves proposed plan, but wants to make sure nothing untoward happens on the northern flank of the panzer group [towards Kiev].'[45] At 1.00p.m. Halder informed von Brauchitsch of the Supreme Commander's views. The argument was over; Hitler's fears were to prove baseless and von Rundstedt's views were to be vindicated. The *Kesselschlacht* of Uman was the result.

20

'Barbarossa' – The Failure

*A tactical success is only really decisive if it is
gained at the strategically correct spot.*

VON MOLTKE THE ELDER
Chief of the General Staff, 1857–1871

When the first phase of 'Barbarossa' ended on 8 August, just over six weeks
after the opening of the campaign, the situation on the Eastern Front was as
follows: in the north, the Germans were within sixty miles of Leningrad and
poised for the attack that might well end with the encirclement of the city; in
the centre, two large, and one small, battles of annihilation had been won,
and Moscow lay only 200 miles away, under two weeks' advance, with few
Soviet forces to oppose the passage; and in the south, the first encirclement
battle had just been concluded and the Dnepr was only fifty miles from the
main force. The one immediate tactical worry lay in the large concentration
of Soviet forces south of the Pripyat Marsh, between Army Groups Centre
and South. Everywhere else the enemy was disorganised; roughly one and a
quarter million of his troops had been captured.

   In the east, the state of the German Army at this time was far from good.
By 31 July the Germans had suffered 213,301 casualties, around fifteen per
cent of their total invasion force, and had lost 863 tanks through enemy
action or breakdown beyond repair, nearly one-quarter of the original
number. Replacements could not keep pace with losses. The average
strength of the infantry divisions was reduced by twenty per cent, the combat
strength of the panzer divisions in Army Group Centre was down by forty
per cent, while those in Army Group South were reduced by no less than
sixty per cent. The logistical situation was more critical. The shortage of
motor fuel was made worse by the fact that the appalling roads and difficult
terrain caused the vehicles to consume almost twice the normal quantity.
(This was, however, partially offset by petrol captured from the Soviets.)
Moreover, the poor quality of much of the transport was becoming evident
on the unsurfaced roads; many of the large trucks had proved too heavy, and
by late July the high rate of mechanical breakdown and loss through enemy
action had reduced motor transport units in Army Group Centre to almost
half strength, while in the north some had as many as fifty-six per cent of

their vehicles out of action. In the south, von Rundstedt's situation was as bad, if not worse. The reliance on horses, especially on the light, agile Russian breeds, and the small *panje* wagons, became daily greater.

Even more serious was the breakdown in the railway supply system. For Army Group North there was no problem; its relatively small size and the comparatively good rail facilities in the Baltic States ensured that it received the daily average of eighteen trains a day it needed. But for Army Groups Centre and South, the position was critical. It had proved impossible to convert sufficient of the Russian rail-track to the German gauge; Yelnya, the furthest eastern point of Army Group Centre, was no less than 450 miles from the nearest adequate railhead, and 120 miles from a very inadequate one. There was also a shortage of locomotives. Thus, in late July and early August, of the twenty-five goods trains required each day, Army Group Centre received between eight and fifteen, and Army Group South's daily average was only ten. It was thus impossible to replenish losses, let alone build up stocks. The Quartermaster-General's task was made even more difficult by his uncertainty as to where the weight of the attack in the second phase would fall: in the north, as Hitler had originally intended; in the centre, the choice of OKH; or in the south, which was now attracting the Führer's attention? Certainly, Wagner knew that a simultaneous advance on all three sectors would be an impossibility, and that a pause in the attack east, however short, was necessary.

Against this background must be viewed the crucial decision of 1941. Where was the main weight of the second phase of the invasion to lie – north, centre, or south? The view of OKH was that Moscow should still remain the first objective. This had not always been so; for a short period, the early successes had served to turn attention away from the capital. As early as 3 July, when the panzer divisions were beginning their advance from Minsk to Smolensk, the opinion of the Army Command was that victory already belonged to them. Halder wrote in his diary for that day:

> 'On the whole, then, it may already be said that the aim of shattering the bulk of the Russian Army this side of the Dvina and Dnepr has been accomplished. I do not doubt the statement of the captured Russian corps general that, east of Dvina and the Dnepr, we would encounter nothing more than partial forces, not strong enough to hinder the realisation of German operational plans. It is thus probably no overstatement to say that the Russian campaign has been won in the space of two weeks. Of course, this does not yet mean that it is closed. The sheer geographical vastness of the country and the stubborness of the resistance, which is carried on with every means, will claim our efforts for many more weeks to come.'[1]

Although the Chief of the General Staff realised that hard fighting still remained ahead, he clearly believed that the pursuit phase of the operation was near at hand: 'Once we are across the Dvina and Dnepr it will be less a question of smashing enemy armies than denying the enemy the possession of his production centres.'[2] Because of the size of the success so far, and because the future appeared not to be in doubt, Halder felt there was less need to capture Moscow immediately than he had previously believed. Other priorities loomed up. As early as 30 June Halder had even suggested to Hitler that armoured formations from the central front could be diverted to the north in order to clear up the situation there before the infantry divisions had completed their concentration in the Smolensk area prior to the attack on Moscow. On 11 July, as Guderian crossed the Dnepr, Halder wrote:

> '. . . there is one question which . . . this battle of Smolensk will not settle for us, and that is the question of the enemy's armour. In every instance, large bodies, if not all, manage to escape encirclement, and, in the end, their armour may well be the only fighting force left to the Russians for carrying on the war. The [Soviet] strategy . . . would have to be visualized on the basis of operations by two or three major . . . groups of armour, supported by industrial centres and peacetime garrisons, and by the remnants of the Russian Air Force.'[3]

Thus a wide-ranging advance might be necessary. The next day he recorded: 'I am not all that wedded to the idea of hurrying the panzer groups eastwards. I can well visualise the necessity for turning considerable portions of Hoth's forces to the north. . . . Guderian must turn southwards to encircle the new enemy appearing on his southern wing. . . .' Then he added prophetically: '. . . perhaps to drive down even as far as the Kiev area. . . .'[4] Later that day, Heusinger reported to the Chief of the General Staff, who wrote: 'Planning on continuance of operations with the object of preventing a frontal retreat of the enemy and ensuring the destruction of the largest possible enemy force [no mention of Moscow]. The operations are evolved from ideas outlined to me by the Army Commander, and crystallise first of all in plans for a new drive by Panzer Group 3 aimed at liquidating the concentration of twelve to fourteen divisions now opposite von Leeb's right wing.' That evening Halder noted: 'Hoth is getting on well and is expanding his front to the north. In doing so he is anticipating our wishes.'[5] The following day, the 13th, revealed how much the views of Hitler and of OKH were now in accord. Halder's diary noted the Army's proposal: 'Next objectives. We shall temporarily halt the dash towards Moscow by Panzer Groups 2 and 3, with the object of destroying as much of the enemy strength as possible on the present front.' To this, Hitler replied: 'A quick advance east is less important than smashing the enemy's military strength. The enemy army opposite von Leeb's right wing . . . must be attacked from the rear by the motorised forces of Panzer Group 3.'[6]

But OKH's new preoccupation with the north began before the battle for the Smolensk pocket had really started. Even then, Halder had made the point that 'the prerequisite for either move is that Hoth and Guderian should break into the open to the east and so gain freedom of movement'.[7] Yet as the Smolensk *Kesselschlacht* grew in intensity, and as it became clear that a breakthrough to the east was becoming increasingly difficult, a note of alarm crept into the deliberations at the Army High Command. On 15 July Halder noted with concern: 'The Russian troops are fighting as ever with wild ferocity and enormous human sacrifice.'[8] Clearly, the Red Army was still not finished; the Germans, on the other hand, were showing signs of weariness. The 'diluted' armoured divisions, especially, were tired. On the 16th Halder wrote:

> 'The striking power of the panzer divisions is slowly declining. When the current objectives (Smolensk, Leningrad, and Uman) have been reached, a break will be necessary in order to give the units a rest, and, if advisable, to merge and refit several units. Guderian thinks he can do that in three to four days. I believe much more time will be required. The supply system of Army Group Centre will not be functioning at full capacity before 25 July. By that time the panzer groups will again be ready for new operations.'[9]

To Soviet resistance and German tiredness were added the arguments of Army Group Centre, anxious to get to Moscow. On 13 July Halder was told that von Bock 'holds that the chances are very good for our tank spearheads to smash through to Moscow. . . . He objects strongly to detaching forces in a north-easterly direction. . . . All forces must be kept together to strengthen the thrust to the east.'[10]

By the middle of July, the elation of earlier days at OKH had turned into gloom. The generals were concerned at the obvious resilience of their enemy and the ever-growing weaknesses of their own troops. The vast distances still to be covered were highlighted by the problems of closing and holding the Smolensk pocket, and by the slowness of von Rundstedt's advance in the south. On 20 July Halder wrote: 'The most visible expression is the severe depression into which [von Brauchitsch] has been plunged.'[11] Then, on the 23 July, OKH issued a memorandum drawn up several days before, which said:

> 'Decisions concerning future operations are based on the belief that once the first operational objectives [Dvina-Dnepr line] . . . have been reached, the bulk of the Russian Army capable of operational employment will have been beaten. [Then it added a note of caution.] On the other hand it must be reckoned that, by reason of his strong reserves of manpower and by further ruthless expenditure of his forces, the enemy will be able to continue to offer stubborn resistance to the German advance. In this connexion, the point of main effort of the enemy's defence may be expected to be in the Ukraine, in front of Moscow, and in front of Leningrad. The intention of the OKH is to defeat the existing or newly created enemy forces, and by a speedy capture of the most important industrial

areas in the Ukraine west of the Volga, in the area Tula-Gorkiy-Rybinsk-Moscow, and around Leningrad to deprive the enemy of the possiblity of material rearmament.'[12]

The need for further destruction of enemy troops beyond the Dvina-Dnepr line was now recognised, and the area around Moscow was restored at least to parity with Leningrad and the Ukraine. However, in a very few days, new strategic proposals from Hitler, evidence of strengthening Soviet resistance to Army Group Centre's fight for the Smolensk pocket, and further signs of increases in enemy forces, were to lead OKH back to its former position. Moscow was again to become the prime objective; by the 28th Halder was describing its attainment as 'crucial'.[13] This was justified by the old arguments: Moscow was the capital of the Soviet Union, the centre of government and communications, as well as a significant industrial base; and, most important of all, it was before Moscow that the Soviets were expected to commit the major portion of their remaining forces. It was here that the Red Army would be defeated. The brief flirtation by OKH with Hitler's operational objectives was soon over.

Hitler's view on the next objective to be pursued is less easy to comprehend. He was aware of the vital importance of the decision to be taken, and that is perhaps why he took so long in taking it, fearful as ever of committing himself irrevocably. As early as 4 July, when only success was greeting German endeavours, he recognised there were three choices confronting him: to adhere to the 'Barbarossa' plan and ensure the capture of Leningrad; to continue Army Group Centre's successful advance towards Moscow on the basis that Soviet resistance had collapsed speedily, and that Leningrad could be taken by Army Group North alone; or to switch the weight of the attack to the south for an advance deep into the Caucasus, with its oilfields as the strategic objective. In common with OKH at that time, the Führer saw no need to worry further about the Red Army's continued capacity for resistance. As Warlimont wrote: 'Hitler himself stated to his immediate entourage on 4 July: "to all intents and purposes the Russians have lost the war", and congratulated himself on what a good thing it was "that we smashed the Russian armour and air forces right at the beginning".'[14]

Hitler, like OKH, had his head turned by success. On 8 July, the seventeenth day of the campaign, Halder wrote:

> 'The Führer has in mind the following "perfect solution".... Army Group North accomplishes with its own forces the mission assigned to it in the original operational plan. Army Group Centre... will... open the way to Moscow. Once the two panzer groups have reached the areas assigned to them by the operational plan [of 31 January 1941] (a) Hoth can be halted (to assist von Leeb *if necessary* [author's italics]) or else continue operating in an easterly direction... with a view to investing Moscow.... (b) Guderian can strike in a south or

south-easterly direction east of the Dnepr cooperating with Army Group South.'[15]

This represented a considerable departure from Hitler's previous idea, which placed Leningrad above all else; now he believed that all three objectives in the north, centre, and south could be pursued concurrently.

The views of Hitler and OKH were, for a short time, not dissimilar. Contrary to what had become normal practice, Jodl was concerned to foster this, and attempted to bring OKH into the discussions on the subject. On 5 July he commented: 'Since this decision might be decisive for the whole war . . . it [is] essential that the Army Commander-in-Chief should discuss his views and intentions with the Führer. . . .'[16] The consensus of opinion resulted in Hitler's Directive No. 33, dated 19 July, which read: 'The aim of the next operations must be to prevent any further sizeable enemy forces from withdrawing into the depths of Russia, and to wipe them out.' This was to be achieved thus: in the south, one enemy troop concentration was to be 'quickly and decisively defeated and annihilated by cooperation between forces on the south flank of Army Group Centre and the northern flank of Army Group South. While infantry divisions of Army Group Centre move southward, other forces, chiefly motorised . . . will advance south-eastwards' in order to destroy Soviet forces on the east bank of the Dnepr. In the centre, von Bock's army group would continue the 'advance to Moscow with infantry formations and will use those motorised units which are not employed in the rear of the Dnepr line to cut communications between Moscow and Leningrad, and so to cover the right flank of the advance on Leningrad by Army Group North'. [17] A virtual standstill on the central front would be accompanied by reinforced manoeuvres to the north and south.

It might be thought that at this moment OKH had given Hitler, voluntarily, all he wanted concerning the implementation of his 'Barbarossa' plan. Moscow, in direct contradiction of all that the Army leaders had said previously, was now very much a secondary objective. But the Führer was not satisfied. His eyes ranged further afield, and his desire to do everything at once caused him to decide on the inclusion of the Caucasian oilfields as a new objective to be reached before winter. Thus was a further 350 miles added to Army Group South's task. On 23 July, by which time the Army leaders were reverting to their original idea, Hitler issued his Supplement to Directive No. 33 without consultation with OKH. Consensus was at an end. He now proposed to concentrate Panzer Groups 1 and 2 under the command of 4th Panzer Army which, 'with the support of infantry and mountain divisions, will occupy the Kharkov industrial area and thrust forward across the Don to Caucasia'.[18] In the centre, Hitler gave the task of the capture of Moscow to the infantry divisions of Army Group Centre, which would be devoid of armour. Panzer Group 3 would come under the command of Army Group North as already indicated. Once both Moscow and Leningrad had been captured, Panzer Group 3, again under Army Group Centre, might be used for thrusting still further east to the Volga. Once Leningrad had fallen, however, Panzer Group 4 and large parts of Army Group North were to be moved back to Germany.

The Army leaders were aghast at this radical revision of the 'Barbarossa' plan, especially in view of the stiffening Soviet opposition. At once they reverted fully to the advocacy of their first objective: Moscow. Even Jodl had attempted to prevent the adoption of the aim expressed in the Supplement. On the day it was issued, Halder saw the Führer and outlined the views of OKH. But his strong representations had no effect. He wrote in his diary for the 23rd:

> 'He has decided on his objectives and sticks to them without considering what the enemy may do, or taking account of any other points of view. This means that von Bock will have to give up his armoured groups and move on Moscow with infantry alone. In any case, the Führer right now is not interested in Moscow; all he cares about is Leningrad. This sets off a long-winded tirade on how von Leeb's operation ought to have been conducted and why Panzer Group 3 now has to be thrown into the battle to destroy the enemy at Leningrad. The chief object of the operations is viewed by him in the smashing of the enemy, a task which he believes would probably be accomplished by the time we are abreast of Moscow [at Leningrad and in the Donets Basin]. Subsequently (and into the rainy autumn season) he imagines one could drive to the Volga and into the Caucasus with panzer divisions alone. . . . I hope he is right, but all one can say is that time spent in such a conference is a sad waste.'[19]

Three days later, on the 26th, Halder again tried to convince the Führer of the errors in his views. Hitler, now advocating the Gomel operation, was prepared to hold 'long-winded and sometimes violent arguments with the Army leaders over missed opportunities for encirclement'.[20] Halder's view was that Hitler's plan would not only leave von Bock so weak as to be unable to move on to Moscow, but that it would lead to a front expanding in width but not in depth, and end in static warfare. Hitler, however, simply rejected Halder's arguments regarding the importance of Moscow without producing any real reasons against them. He merely advanced the economic argument – that it was essential for the German war effort to seize the industrial area and coalfields of the Donets Basin, and the oil of the Caucasus.

Whether because of the arguments put forward so strongly by Halder, or the unfavourable reports that were then coming in from Army Groups Centre and North, or a combination of both, Hitler changed his mind once more. On 30 July, Jodl announced to a wary Halder: 'The Führer has arrived at a new conception of the next phase of the campaign.'[21] Later that day, Hitler issued Directive No. 34, which opened: 'The development of the situation in the last few days, the appearance of strong enemy forces on the front and to the flanks of Army Group Centre, the supply position, and the need to give Panzer Groups 2 and 3 about ten days to rehabilitate their units make it necessary to postpone for the moment the further tasks and objectives laid down in Directive No. 33 of 19 July and in the supplement of 23 July.'[22] Now the attack on Leningrad was to take place without the aid of Panzer Group 3, and operations in the southern sector were to be undertaken only by formations of Army Group South. The operation into the Caucasus was abandoned, and activities were to be limited to the west of the Dnepr. On the central sector of the front, von Bock's army group was to go over to the defensive, and Panzer Groups 2 and 3 were to be withdrawn from the front line and rehabilitated. All at OKH, as at OKW, were relieved. Halder wrote: 'This solution means that all thinking soldiers are now freed from the frightful spectre of the last few days, during which time it looked as if the entire eastern operation would be bogged down as a result of the Führer's stubbornness. At last a little light on the horizon once more.'[23] However, the plan did not go far enough. No mention was made of Moscow, apart from ordering air attacks on the city, and only the vaguest of references was made to further operations on the central front. Apart from advancing north-eastwards sufficiently far to protect the right flank of Army Group North, Army Group Centre was to mount only 'attacks with limited objectives' so as 'to secure favourable springboards for our offensive against the Soviet 21st Army [to the east]'. The main emphasis remained on the flanks to the north and south. Halder noted irritably on the 31st: 'OKH issues its implementation order to the last Führer directive. Unfortunately I cannot induce the Army Commander to inject the slightest overtone expressive of a will of his own in this order. Its wording is dictated by an anxiety to avoid anything that could be suspected as opposition to his superior.'[24] As Major von Bredow, the OKH liaison officer, put it to Guderian the next day: 'The OKH and the Chief of the General Staff are engaged in a thankless undertaking, since the conduct of all operations is being controlled from the very highest level. Final decisions have not yet been taken. . . .'[25]

Hitler's mind was clearly not yet at rest. Over the next few days, the generals' fears grew unchecked. Between 4 and 6 August the Führer visited the headquarters of both Army Groups Centre and South, only to hear a unanimous plea for a resumption of the offensive towards Moscow. But in his comments to the generals, he gave them little hope. Guderian remembered:

'Hitler designated the industrial area about Leningrad as his primary objective. He had not decided whether Moscow or the Ukraine would come next. He seemed to incline towards the latter target for a number of reasons: first, Army Group South seemed to be laying the groundwork for a victory in that area; secondly, he believed that the raw materials and agricultural produce of the Ukraine were necessary to Germany for the further prosecution of the war; and finally he thought it essential that the Crimea, "that Soviet aircraft-carrier operating against the Romanian oilfields'', be neutralised. He hoped to be in possession of Moscow and Kharkov by the time winter began.'[26]

Of this conference at Army Group Centre's headquarters, Keitel recorded that Hitler:

'. . . came up against a blank wall of refusal, the two tank generals even going so far as to announce that their units were so battle-weary that they would need two or three weeks to regroup and to overhaul their tanks before they would be fully operational again. Obviously we had no means of checking these claims; the two generals remained uncooperative – despite the award to them of the Oak Leaves to their Knight's Crosses – and refused to admit any possibility of alternative employment for their units, at any rate on such remote sections of the front. Von Bock naturally had no desire to lose them and trumped the same story. All three of them were aware of the [OKH's] . . . plan of attack, and saw it as their panacea. . . . [it] had electrified them all.'[27]

At this point Jodl, who had long been in sympathy with the Army's desire to advance on Moscow, entered the fray. On 7 August he and Halder had joint talks, 'something which had not happened for as long as anybody could remember',[28] and on the 10th he presented to Hitler an OKW appreciation of the situation that was in full agreement with OKH. Warlimont recorded that:

'This began by proving . . . that the enemy was strongest opposite the centre of the front, and that therefore the most important objective was the annihilation of this enemy grouping, followed by the capture of Moscow. Operations from the centre into the areas of Army Groups North and South were attractive, but must be subordinated to the Moscow decision or postponed to a later date. The attack on Moscow would begin at the end of August, with the infantry divisions in the centre and the armoured groups on the flanks.'[29]

The early capture of Moscow became all the more urgent with the appearance of reports showing large-scale Soviet reorganisation along the central front, which indicated that field fortifications were being built in great depth, behind which mobile reserves were being formed. Halder had commented on 8 August that this enemy policy was a clear break with the past and was 'similar to that pursued by the French in the second phase of the western campaign, that is to form strong islands of resistance . . . which would serve as the backbone of . . . the new defence line'. Time was running out; the only solution was for Army Group Centre to 'concentrate its forces to the last man to destroy the main body of the enemy's strength'.[30] This was reinforced by further estimates of German weakness and Soviet strength. A day earlier, the

Chief of the General Staff had been told by Wagner that after 1 October fuel oil and petrol would be in such short supply that a further major offensive would be impossible. On 11 August Halder noted alarmingly:

> 'The whole situation makes it increasingly plain that we have underestimated the Russian colossus, which consistently prepared for war with that utterly ruthless determination so characteristic of totalitarian states. This applies to organisational and economic resources, as well as to the communications system and, most of all, to the strict military potential. At the outset of the war we reckoned with about 200 enemy divisions. Now we have already counted 360. These divisions indeed are not armed and equipped according to our standards, and their tactical leadership is often poor. But there they are, and if we smash a dozen of them, the Russians simply put up another dozen. The time factor favours them, as they are near their own resources, whereas we are moving farther and farther away from ours. And so our troops, sprawled over an immense front line, without any depth, are subjected to the enemy's incessant attacks. Sometimes these are successful, because in these enormous spaces too many gaps have to be left open.'[31]

Hitler, when he finally made his choice, decided on a compromise. On 12 August, a Supplement to Directive No. 34 was issued; this was intended to contain the final operational plan. In the north there was to be no change, as it was expected that the attack in progress would result in the encirclement of Leningrad and a junction with the Finns. In the south von Rundstedt's army group was to consolidate its position west of the Dnepr and then cross the river, destroy the Soviet forces on the east side, and occupy the Crimean peninsula, the Donets Basin, and the industrial region of Kharkov. In the centre 'the most important task' became the elimination of 'the enemy flanking positions, projecting deeply to the west, with which he is holding down large forces of infantry on both flanks of Army Group Centre. For this purpose close cooperation . . . between the adjoining flanks of Army Group South and . . . Centre is particularly important.' On the northern flank of von Bock's force the enemy was also to be defeated, and the security of Army Group North's right flank was to be achieved. Hitler continued:

> 'Only after these threats to our flanks have been entirely overcome and armoured formations have been rehabilitated, will it be possible to continue the offensive, on a wide front and with echeloning of both flanks, against the strong enemy forces which have been concentrated for the defence of the enemy. The object of operations must then be to deprive the enemy, before the coming of winter, of his government, armament, and traffic centre around Moscow, and thus prevent the rebuilding of his defeated forces and the orderly working of government control.'[32]

On the 15th the order was issued for Army Group Centre to go on the defensive; the attack on Moscow was finally abandoned for the time being, to be reopened only after movements to the north and, most important, to the south.

The Army leaders, aware of the far-reaching consequences of this decision, were far from happy at the compromise. On 13 August Halder had written: 'Attack on Moscow by Army Group Centre is approved, but approval is made conditional on so many factors . . . that the freedom of action which we need for the execution of the plan is severely restricted.'[33] Two days later, when Hitler demanded that units from Hoth's panzer group be sent to assist Army Group North which was then coming under enemy pressure at Luga, the Chief of the General Staff noted crossly: 'Once again they [OKW] are making that old mistake that has the result that an audacious thrust by a single Russian division ties up three to four German divisions – such methods are not conducive to success.' Nevertheless, he reluctantly admitted: 'So then, there will be no way of getting round issuing that order for the transfer of a motorised corps to Army Group North. To my mind it is a grave mistake for which we shall pay heavily.'[34]

Feelings among the Army leaders ran so high that they determined to put up a strong resistance such as they had not done since October and November 1939. On 18 August, while the motorised corps was on its way to the north, von Brauchitsch submitted the views of OKH to Hitler in the form of a closely argued memorandum drawn up by the Operations Section of the General Staff under Heusinger. Once again, the Army advocated a decisive thrust to Moscow:

> 'The distribution of the enemy forces indicates that at the present time, after the annihilation of the enemy forces facing Army Group South [in the battle of Uman], and with the impending successes of Army Group North, the bulk of the intact military forces of the enemy is in front of Army Group Centre. The enemy therefore appear to regard an attack by Army Group Centre in the direction of Moscow as the main threat. . . . The future objectives of Army Groups South and North are, apart from the defeat of the enemy forces confronting them, in the first instance to capture essential industrial areas and to eliminate the Russian fleet. The immediate objective of Army Group Centre, on the other hand, is, above all, the destruction of the strong enemy forces confronting it, thereby breaking down the enemy's defences. If we succeed in smashing these enemy forces, the Russians will no longer be capable of establishing a defensive position. This will create the necessary conditions for the occupation of the industrial area of Moscow. Only the elimination of this industrial area, together with the successes of Army Groups South and North, will remove the possibility of the enemy rebuilding their defeated armed forces and re-establishing them on an opera-

tionally effective basis. The decision about the operational objective for Army Group Centre must take into account the following basic points:

(a) The time factor. The offensive by Army Group Centre cannot continue after October on account of the weather conditions . . . we will not be able to push forward with the motorised units on their own without support from the infantry.

(b) Even after refuelling, the motorised units can be effective only over short distances and with diminishing combat strength. As a result, they must be used only for the essential tasks involved in the decisive operation.

(c) The suggested operation can be successful only if the forces of Army Group Centre are systematically concentrated on this single goal to the exclusion of other tactical actions which are not essential for the success of the operation. Otherwise, time and energy will not suffice to deal a decisive blow . . . during the course of this year.'[35]

On 21 August came Hitler's written reply rejecting the Army's proposal, although not answering specifically the points it raised. He argued:

'The objective of this campaign is finally to eliminate Russia as a Continental ally of Great Britain. . . . This objective can only be achieved: (a) through the annihilation of the Russian combat forces; (b) through the occupation, or at least destruction, of the economic bases which are essential for a reorganisation of the Russian forces. . . . In accordance with the initial decision on the relative importance of the individual combat zones in the east, the following are and remain the most essential points: 1) the destruction of the Russian position in the Baltic; and 2) the occupation of the Ukrainian areas and those round the Black Sea which are essential in terms of raw materials for the planned reconstruction of the Russian armed forces. 3) . . . in addition, there is concern for our own oil in Romania and the necessity of pressing on as fast as possible to a position which offers Iran at least the prospect of assistance in the foreseeable future.

As a result of the circumstances which have developed, partly because an order of mine, or rather of the OKW, was ignored, Army Group North is clearly not in a position, within a short space of time and with the forces at its disposal, to advance on Leningrad with a right-flanking movement and thereby to be certain of surrounding and destroying this base and the Russian forces defending it. The situation now demands that Army Group North should be rapidly supplied with the forces which were intended for it at the beginning of the campaign. . . . I hope that the three divisions which are being sent will suffice to enable Army Group North to achieve its objective and to deal with any crises. The cleaning-up and securing of its south-eastern flank can, however, be carried out only by forces of Army Group Centre.'

Only when its objectives had been attained would Army Group North:

'. . . help the advance of Army Group Centre on Moscow. . . . even more important is the clearing up of the situation between Army Group Centre and Army Group South. This is a strategic opportunity such as fate only very rarely provides in war. The enemy is in a salient nearly 300 kilometres long, triangular in shape and surrounded by two army groups. It can be destroyed only if at this time army group considerations are not allowed to predominate but are subordinated to the interests of the over-all conduct of the campaign. The objection that time would then be lost and that the units would no longer be technically equipped for their advance on Moscow is not decisive in view of this opportunity. . . . after the destruction of the Russian forces, which are still threatening the flank of Army Group Centre, the task of advancing on Moscow will not be more difficult, but considerably easier. For either the Russians will withdraw part of their forces from the central front to cover the gap opening up in the south, or they will immediately bring up the forces which are being created in the rear. In either event, the situation will be better than if Army Group Centre tried to advance with the undefeated Russian 5th Army as well as the Russian forces east and west of Kiev acting as a continual threat to its flanks and with the Russians able, in addition, to bring new formations from the rear as reinforcements.'[36]

The next day, the 22nd, Hitler sent a personal memorandum to von Brauchitsch, in which he criticised the Army's conduct of operations and blamed its leaders for the failure of the original 'Barbarossa' plan. The control exercised by OKH had been too loose, he argued, and the Army Commander-in-Chief had allowed his subordinates to have more influence over strategy than was desirable. The result was that the armoured forces in the centre had acted with too great a degree of independence, pushing too far ahead of the infantry, failing to surround the enemy strongly enough, and extending the advance so far eastwards as to threaten the very concept of the operation. Instead of attacking to Yelnya, beyond Smolensk, the panzer groups should have been halted after crossing the Dnepr and have been freed for flanking operations to assist Army Groups North and South, as he had always intended. Instead, the panzers had pushed on, contact with the following infantry had been lost, and many Soviet troops had managed to break out of the weakly held envelopment. After the battle for the Smolensk pocket, neither the time nor the terrain for the vital move north to Leningrad by Hoth's group was favourable. Hitler ended by comparing the Army Commander unfavourably with Göring, and accusing von Brauchitsch of lack of leadership and of not having the necessary grip on operations.

Hitler's criticisms were manifestly unfair. The OKH deployment directive of January 1941, which he had himself approved, had mentioned specifically that 'Army Group Centre . . . will quickly win the area around Smolensk' so as to 'achieve the prerequisites for cooperation between strong elements of its mobile troops and Army Group North'.[37] This is exactly what the Army leaders had done, and no more. At no point during the advance had Hitler dissented from this objective. On 8 July, for example, he had told von Brauchitsch and Halder that the ideal solution would be to leave Army Group North to gain its objective 'with its own forces'.[38] Indeed, in the first weeks of the campaign, Hitler and the Army Command were in unusual accord. Warlimont remembered that Hitler's 'appreciation of the situation . . . agreed generally with that of the Army. Accordingly during these early weeks he did not meddle with the conduct of operations in the east, apart from certain pressure and nagging at OKH to get them to close the great "pocket" [Minsk] more rapidly and securely, and later, just as in the west, being beset by "fear" for the flanks of the armoured thrusts which had driven so far ahead.'[39]

Halder's reaction to Hitler's criticisms of 22 August was immediate and strong. He wrote in his diary for the day:

> 'In my view the situation resulting from the Führer's interference is intolerable for the Army. These individual instructions from the Führer produce a situation of order, counter-order, and disorder and no one can be held responsible but he himself personally; OKH as now constituted is engaged on its fourth victorious campaign and its reputation should not be sullied by the instructions now received. In addition, the way the Commander-in-Chief has been treated is a scandal. I have accordingly suggested to [him] . . . that he should ask to be relieved of his office and propose that I should also be relieved at the same time.'[40]

At last, Halder had understood that the Führer's usurpation of the Army's operational autonomy had gone too far to bear any longer. His only fault was that he should have resolved upon such drastic action two years earlier, when Hitler had decided how and when the invasion of the west was to take place; it was now rather like shutting the stable door after the horse had bolted. Von Brauchitsch, little more than a man of straw in his master's hands, refused Halder's suggestion, giving the reason, which was probably quite correct, that 'in practice he would not be relieved and that therefore nothing would be changed'.[41] Eight days later, on the 30th, a private meeting between the Army Commander and the dictator took place, when there was a reconciliation which von Brauchitsch maintained cancelled Hitler's insulting memorandum. Warlimont, however, thought otherwise: 'For those who knew the background . . . there can be little doubt that, although for the moment he pretended to imitate it, Hitler took Brauchitsch's chivalrous attitude merely as a sign of weakness and lack of character, and considered the outcome of this encounter simply as another victory over his opponents in the Army.'[42] Halder wrote sarcastically that same day: '. . . the result is bliss and harmony! Everything is just lovely again! Of course, nothing has changed, except that we are now supposed to wait upon not only the Führer but also the Reichsmarschall with separate reports on the railways situation, supply, signal communications, and ground forces replacements.'[43]

While, on 22 August, von Brauchitsch was prepared to submit to the Führer's will, and subsequently confirmed this on the 30th, Halder was determined to make one last attempt to convince his Supreme Commander of the error of his ways. On the 23rd he informed the generals of Army Group Centre of Hitler's decision. Guderian remarked that the Chief of the General Staff 'seemed deeply upset at this shattering of his hopes'. The panzer leaders put forward their reasons why an immediate advance on Moscow was desirable, and Halder, on von Bock's suggestion, decided that Guderian should accompany him to Führer headquarters to put the arguments personally to Hitler. Guderian wrote of the meeting, which took place on the same day: 'I reported at once to . . . von Brauchitsch, who greeted me with the following words: "I forbid you to mention the question of Moscow to the Führer. The operation to the south has been ordered. The problem now is simply how it is to be carried out. Discussion is pointless." ' However, during the meeting, at which neither von Brauchitsch nor Halder was present, Hitler himself brought up the subject, and Guderian was able to put forward his reasons, which were listened to without interruption. In reply, the Führer again reiterated the economic importance of the Ukraine, declaring 'My generals know nothing about the economic aspects of war.' Guderian noted that he 'saw for the first time that . . . all those present nodded in agreement with every sentence that Hitler uttered'.[44] Guderian, having failed in his impossible mission, then returned to his command. That night, OKH sent an order to Army Group Centre concerning future operations, the object of which was 'to destroy as much of the strength of the Russian 5th Army as possible, and to open the Dnepr crossings for Army Group South with maximum speed'.[45] The final aim was a grand double encirclement operation, in which the inner jaws would be closed by 2nd, 6th, and 17th Armies, and the outer by Panzer Groups 1 and 2. The cauldron was to be 130 miles in width and depth. Once again, the German Army would perform in the classic tradition of *Vernichtungsgedanke*; it was to be the greatest battle of annihilation in history. Four enemy armies were largely destroyed, together with parts of two others. By the time the battle of Kiev was over on 26 September, the Germans had captured 665,000 prisoners and destroyed or taken 884 tanks and 3,178 guns.

The drive south had already been begun by Guderian's group before the decision of 23 August. After the encirclement at Roslavl, one of his panzer corps had continued to Krichev, a few miles to the south, where a further

16,000 prisoners were taken by 14 August. Against his better judgement, Guderian had been ordered by OKH to exploit this success by pushing on to Gomel to destroy the enemy there in cooperation with 2nd Army, in pursuance of Hitler's order of 26 July. The panzer leader commented: 'As I saw it, such a march to the south-west would constitute a step backwards.'[46] However, by the 24 August the panzer corps had captured Novozybkov, more than 100 miles south-west of Roslavl, and was well positioned to embark on the advance ordered by Hitler the day before.

From the beginning of the Kiev encirclement, Guderian was bedevilled with interference from higher command. He wished to pursue his advance southwards with all his forces as he alone thought best; he was particularly keen to attack strongly on his eastern, left flank, where the enemy threatened his movements. But Halder, feeling that the panzer leader had given way to Hitler during the meeting on the 23 August, and had therefore betrayed the Army's intention, was in no mood to allow the headstrong Guderian any latitude; OKH would control operations firmly, and contact would not be lost between the panzers and the infantry. As early as the 25th, the Chief of the General Staff wrote in his diary: 'The intention of the panzer group to strike out . . . with its left wing . . . leads too far eastwards. Everything depends on its assisting 2nd Army [to the west] across the Desna and then the 6th Army across the Dnepr.'[47] On the 27th Halder asked Army Group Centre 'not to allow Guderian to run east, but keep him in readiness for the 2nd Army's crossing of the Desna'. Moreover, despite his strong protests, one third of Guderian's force was kept back in reserve for the central sector, then under enemy attack. Again, on the 27th, Halder recorded a message from von Bock: 'Guderian rages, since he fails to make progress because of being attacked from the right and left flanks, and demands reinforcement in the form of the rest of the fast units of his group. Von Bock feels unable to do this. . . . I am of the same opinion and request him not to give way to Guderian. . . . In addition, I ask him to keep a tight rein on Guderian.'[48] The next day, after von Paulus had pleaded the panzer leader's case for the release of the panzer corps, Halder commented: 'I realise the difficulty of the situation. But in the final analysis all war consists of difficulties. Guderian will not tolerate any army commander and demands that everybody up to the highest position should bow to the ideas he produces from a restricted point of view. Regrettably, von Paulus has allowed himself to be caught. I will not give way to Guderian. He has got himself into this fix. Now he can get himself out of it.'[49]

Seldom had Guderian come under such vitriolic attack; OKH had never been firmer in holding out against the pressures of this 'firebrand'. The advance was to be properly conducted according to well-established military principles. The panzer group would not be allowed to overreach itself; it would maintain contact with the infantry; it would adhere to its task of assisting 2nd and 6th Armies instead of pushing the encirclement too far to the east so as to secure its flank; and a mobile reserve would be kept back at

Top: The bugler sounds the cease-fire after one of the German Army's most spectacular campaigns. *Left:* The opening stage of Barbarossa: German infantrymen around a burning Soviet tank during the battle for the Minsk pocket.

Top left: The commander of an infantry regiment and his staff outside a captured Soviet bunker during the attack on the weakly fortified 'Stalin Line'. *Top right:* A light infantry gun and its crew in action, central front. *Bottom:* An 8.8cm anti-aircraft/anti-tank gun in action in the Ukraine.

Top: The autumn mud: a motor-cycle combination rider of a Waffen SS unit behind a light panje wagon. *Bottom right:* Winter draws on: an infantry attack during Operation Typhoon. *Bottom left:* A 5cm anti-tank gun in a defensive position during the Soviet counter-attacks in the winter of 1941/42.

Opposite top: Winter conditions on the Eastern front: horse-drawn transport finds the snow heavy going. *Opposite bottom left:* Field Marshal von Kluge, who succeeded von Bock as commander of Army Group Centre. *Left:* A German armoured car on reconnaissance duties in North Africa. *Above:* Exhaustion in the desert: members of the Africa Corps rest after the conclusion of the Gazala battles, May 1942. *Right:* Field Marshal Erwin Rommel, the 'Desert Fox'. *Above right:* A 10.5cm field howitzer in action in a southern Italian village street, August 1943.

Above and left: Two studies of German soldiers in the east in 1942. *Opposite:* The German 6th Army inside Stalingrad, October 1942.

Above: The advanced guard in the foothills of the Caucasus. *Below left:* Field Marshal von Paulus, commander of 6th Army and defender of the Stalingrad pocket. *Below right:* Field Marshal List, commander of Army Group A in the drive to the Caucasus.

the disposal of the army group, to be committed whenever necessary (there might well have been an idea that this panzer corps should be preserved for the advance on Moscow). If, as had happened, Guderian should want to advance in a direction that OKH believed would threaten the coordination of the general advance, no help would be given him to continue to do so. Between 24 and 26 August, when a bridgehead across the Desna was effected, Guderian's foremost panzer corps covered more than eighty miles; in the view of the Chief of the General Staff, he had needlessly overreached himself and exposed his flank. Halder's diary provides a full record of the controversy. For 29 August it contains the following entry:

> 'Guderian's situation is none too pretty. He is being very hard-pressed from the west by enemy elements evading the thrust of 2nd Army, from the east by the newly armed enemy forces, and on top of that has to cope with frontal opposition. And this front consists of only 3rd Panzer and 10th Motorised Infantry Divisions, which are rather far apart at that. It's all Guderian's fault. He devised this plan of attack [a reference to Guderian's meeting with Hitler on the 23rd] and even the most naïve enemy could not be expected to stand passively by while an enemy flank is parading past his front. So the attacks from the east are only what he might have expected. Moreover, with Guderian straining away from 2nd Army instead of keeping close to it, a gap has developed through which the enemy is escaping to the east, that in turn accounts for the attacks against Guderian from the west.'[50]

And on the 31st: '. . . his movements are paralysed. Now he is blaming everyone in sight for his predicament and hurls accusations and recriminations in all directions. . . . Personal relationships between von Bock and Guderian are increasingly deteriorating. Guderian is striking a tone which von Bock cannot tolerate on any account. He even appeals to the Führer for a decision, so as to get his head. This is unparalleled cheek.'[51]

For his part, Guderian felt that the advance on his left flank should be pursued at all costs, for there, he was convinced, he had found a weak spot, if not a gap, in the enemy's defences; he was not to be tied to an infantry army and thereby forced to give up any idea of exploiting this opportunity. But for success he needed his divisions held back in reserve. His continual pleading for reinforcement began to bear fruit only as late as 2 September, and even then the trickle that was allowed satisfied him not at all. On 1 September he demanded from the Führer that he be sent the whole of his panzer corps kept in reserve, but OKH intercepted his radio call and listened to what he said. This resulted, in Guderian's words, 'in a positive uproar'.[52] On 4 September, Lieutenant-Colonel Nagel, an OKH liaison officer, was even dismissed for daring to advocate Guderian's argument, being described as a 'loudspeaker and propagandist',[53] and von Bock asked OKH to relieve

Guderian of his command. By this time, Hitler, too, was 'very exasperated'[54] with the panzer leader. The consequence was, in Guderian's words:

'A telephone message from army group had informed us that OKW was dissatisfied with the operations of the panzer group and particularly with the employment of XLVII Panzer Corps on the eastern bank of the Desna. A report . . . was demanded. That night an order came from OKH in which it was stated that the attack by XLVII Panzer Corps was to be discontinued, and the corps transferred back to the west bank of the Desna. These orders were cast in an uncouth language which offended me. The effect of the order on XLVII Panzer Corps was crushing . . . [it believed itself] to be on the brink of victory. The withdrawal of the corps and its redeployment on the west bank would require more time than was needed for the completion of the attack.'[55]

As a result of the interference from OKH, von Bock, and the Führer, Guderian found himself forced to conduct the attack south against strong opposition to meet von Kleist with just one panzer corps, the XXIV, spearheaded by a single armoured division, 3rd Panzer. The requirements of the higher commands to maintain contact with 2nd Army on the right, to keep back a corps in reserve, and to refrain from advancing too far on the left, had brought about this absurd situation. On 16 September, when Guderian's group finally met with von Kleist's, the 3rd Panzer Division had but ten tanks left fit for action, of which six were PzKw IIs.

On 23 August Hitler had taken a firm decision to turn his main effort away from Moscow and disperse it to the two ends of the 1,000-mile eastern front, to the Baltic and to the Ukraine. The weary armoured formations of Army Group Centre, just 200 miles from the Soviet capital, were ordered to advance more than 400 miles to the north and to the south, while the equally tired infantry consolidated the front and fought off ever more violent enemy counter-attacks. On 5 September, only thirteen days later, Hitler decided that the emphasis of the German advance should be changed again. In his Directive No. 35 of the following day, he stated:

'Combined with the progressive encirclement of the Leningrad area, the initial successes against the enemy forces in the area between the flanks of Army Groups South and Centre have provided favourable conditions for a decisive operation against the Timoshenko army group which is attacking on the central front. This army group must be defeated and annihilated in the limited time which remains before the onset of winter weather. For this purpose it is necessary to concentrate all the forces of the Army and Air Force which can be spared on the flanks and which can be brought up in time.'[56]

On 19 September the OKH deployment order gave the code-name *Taifun* (Typhoon) to the forthcoming operation towards Moscow.

The planning for Operation Typhoon was undertaken by OKH, in conjunction with Army Group Centre, and was subject to Hitler's approval. The offensive was to be carried out by seventy divisions, of which just under one-third were mechanised (14 panzer and 8 motorised infantry). This was the highest proportion of mechanised units to infantry units ever to be achieved by an attacking force of the German Army in the years of victory. Moreover, efforts had been made to re-establish the panzer groups to full strength, at least in tanks – Panzer Groups 2, 3, and 4 now possessed 50, 75, and 100 per cent respectively of their established tank complements. As a result, 1,500 tanks would spearhead the offensive. However, this did not betoken any conversion to the principles of the armoured idea. Yet again, the panzer groups were to be subordinated to infantry armies; and again double encirclement was seen to be the method by which victory would be achieved. There exists no evidence that a direct thrust to Moscow by the mechanised forces was ever even contemplated. The plan that evolved was pure *Vernichtungsgedanke*. The main operation would take place opposite the capital; there the northern pincer, consisting of 9th Army and Panzer Group 3, would meet the southern pincer, made up of 4th Army and Panzer Group 4, at Vyazma, eighty miles in the Soviet rear and more than 100 miles west of Moscow. Once this was achieved, a second similar operation would invest the enemy capital. To the south, 2nd Army and a part of Panzer Group 2 (or 2nd Panzer Army as it was to be designated after 6 October) would undertake a subsidiary encirclement operation, the pincers meeting at Bryansk, some thirty-seven miles behind the Soviet front, while the rest of Guderian's force would proceed to Tula, 105 miles to the south of Moscow, an advance which not only protected the flank of the main operation, but also put the panzer group in a good position for the subsequent envelopment of the capital. Thus, the attack on Moscow would be undertaken over an initial front of 400 miles, the unusual length being made necessary by the inability of Panzer Group 2 to return any further north by the time the offensive was to begin. The role of Army Groups North and South in 'Typhoon' would be restricted to operations that would secure the flanks of the central advance.

Time was crucial to the whole operation. On the central sector of the front, two relatively dry summer months had passed without any advance at all; indeed, there had actually been a small withdrawal, when on 5 September, in order to save casualties, the Germans had yielded up the Yelnya salient. Now, in the middle of autumn, Hitler proposed to cross the 200 miles to Moscow, in face of stronger enemy opposition, and at a time when the weather did not favour mobile operations. In this part of the Soviet Union, heavy rains usually come in late September or early October, turning the earth and tracks into a sea of mud; at the end of October and in November, frost hardens the ground, and in December· snow begins to settle. To an Army equipped to meet these vicissitudes, a wet autumn and a hard winter need not have rendered operations impossible. Only in the most extreme conditions would tracked vehicles be unable to move in mud or in snow; only if denied adequate food and clothing would soldiers be incapable of action in the extreme cold; and only if special preparations, such as antifreeze for vehicle radiators, were not available would transport and guns cease to function in deep winter. But the German Army was not so equipped: tracked vehicles were a rarity; winter clothing was scarce; winter precautions were minimal. All this was made infinitely worse by the lack of any comprehensive system of surfaced roads in the Soviet Union. The effects of rainfall had already been experienced by the Germans from almost the very beginning of 'Barbarossa', but it was not until early September that the heavy rains began, although intermittently. For example, Guderian recorded of the Kiev encirclement:

> 'During the whole night it poured with rain. My drive . . . on the 11th [September], therefore, proved very difficult. I had covered 100 miles in ten hours, on the 11th eighty miles in ten and a quarter hours. The boggy roads made any faster progress impossible. These time-wasting drives gave me sufficient insight into the difficulties that lay ahead of us. Only a man who has personally experienced what life on those canals of mud we called roads was like can form any picture of what the troops and their equipment had to put up with, and can truly judge the situation at the front and the consequent effect on our operations.'[57]

And yet Hitler and OKH were pinning their hopes of success on good weather in a season not noted for it. Guderian summed it up: 'It all depended on this: would the German Army, before the onset of winter and, indeed, before the autumn mud set in, still be capable of achieving decisive results? . . . Was there still sufficient time . . . to succeed?'[58]

At first all went extraordinarily well. On 30 September, in bright sunshine, 2nd Army and Panzer Group 2 began their advance; by 3 October Guderian had taken Orël, 130 miles in the Soviet rear, and by the 9th he had linked up with 2nd Army to complete the Bryansk pocket. All resistance in the 'cauldron' was eliminated by the 20th. To the north, the main offensive began on 2 October, also in good weather; by 7 October the pincers had met at Vyazma, and the fighting around the pocket ended on the 14th. These two encirclements gave the Germans no less than 673,000 Soviet prisoners, and ensured the capture or destruction of 1,242 tanks and 5,412 guns. Orders for the exploitation of this success were not slow in coming, and on 7 October von Bock had set the next objectives, which included the encirclement, but not the capture, of Moscow. Speed was urged on the soldiers, although, as usual, the mechanised forces were not allowed to push ahead from the pockets until relieved by the infantry divisions. Confidence was high. On the 8th Halder found it possible to write: 'To save Moscow the enemy will try to bring up reinforcements, especially from the north. But any such miscellaneous force, scraped together in an emergency, will not suffice against our superior strength, and, provided our strategy is any good at all (and provided the weather is not too bad), we shall succeed in investing Moscow.'[59]

It was not to be. Even before Halder had written these words, the weather broke. Guderian was the first to experience the consequences, when, on the night of 6–7 October, snow fell on his part of the front. At first it did not settle, but was followed by incessant rain. Guderian wrote: '. . . the roads rapidly became nothing but canals of bottomless mud, along which our vehicles could advance only at snail's pace and with great wear to the engines. . . . The next few weeks were dominated by the mud. Wheeled vehicles could advance only with the help of tracked vehicles. These latter, having to perform tasks for which they were not intended, rapidly wore out.'[60] The supply of the armoured spearheads now became a considerable problem, with which the Luftwaffe, for all its effort, was simply not equipped to deal. Those tracked vehicles that survived the mud were in great danger of coming to a standstill through lack of petrol. By the 28th, Guderian remembered, 'We could advance only as fast as our supply situation would allow. Travelling along the now completely disintegrated Orël-Tula road our vehicles could occasionally achieve a maximum speed of twelve miles per hour.' In response to Hitler's instructions concerning 'fast-moving units', Guderian noted: 'There were no "fast-moving units" any more. Hitler was living in a world of fantasy.'[61] On average, Guderian's foremost units were now advancing only five miles a day. It was not until mid-October that the weather broke on the rest of Army Group Centre's front, with the same results. Whole divisions came to a halt; thousands of horses died of over-exertion; guns and vehicles sank in the mud; troops went without proper rations for days; infantrymen's boots fell to pieces, or were lost in the mire. The attack quickly foundered, and made hardly any progress in the latter half of the month. Moscow lay only fifty miles away, but until the ground hardened it was impassible in the face of ever-increasing enemy opposition. On the 30 October OKH ordered a halt.

The situation in which the German Army found itself was by far the most critical of the war up to that date. Losses had been high; an OKH assessment of 6 November estimated that the 101 infantry divisions in the east possessed a fighting strength equivalent to sixty-five divisions at full strength, while the seventeen panzer divisions had been reduced to the effectiveness of only six. In all, the combat power of the invasion force of the 136 battered German divisions was now equal to only eighty-three. Only thirty per cent of the trucks were still in working order. Moreover, of the thirty-one supply trains required daily by Army Group Centre, only sixteen were being provided. Fuel was low; reliance on horses was high, and increasing. Winter clothing for the troops was almost completely lacking. Furthermore, because there were only three major approach routes to the capital in von Bock's area of operations, there was considerable confusion in the supply lines of the advancing forces – 4th and 9th Armies and Panzer Group 3 all competed for space on two roads, while 2nd Army and Panzer Group 4 shared the other. Against this background, a decision had to be made whether to continue the advance or to retreat. General Fromm even believed it was time to make peace proposals. Others did not go so far as this, advocating rather a move back to the positions the army group had held during the summer months, where some form of a defensive line had been constructed and where the supply of the troops would be considerably easier. There the troops could take up winter quarters, beat off Soviet counter-attacks, re-form, and plan a spring offensive.

The Army leaders, however, took a different view. Von Brauchitsch and Halder were convinced that the Red Army must be at the end of its tether; that one further advance was all that was needed to gain the capital. They argued that the acquisition of the Moscow-Vologda-Saratov line would be decisive. Not only would it mean the loss to the Soviets of any rail communication between the main theatres of operation, the Caucasus, the Urals, and the incoming Allied seaborne aid from the Baltic, it would also deprive the enemy of a main industrial and armament area and so prevent any full re-equipping of his armed forces. Furthermore, because of the area's importance, it was here that the last stand of the Red Army was expected; it was here, therefore, that it would be finally encircled and destroyed. Von Bock, who, like the OKH generals, had always attached the greatest importance to the capture of Moscow, also advocated continued advance. On 13 November a conference was held at Orsha between the commanders and the chiefs of staff of the army groups and the armies subordinate to them. After a discussion, and despite opposition, the order for the resumption of the attack was issued. The objectives were far-reaching: 2nd Panzer Army, for example, was assigned the city of Gorkiy, 250 miles east of Moscow, which led von Liebenstein, the chief of staff, to protest that 'This was not the month of May and [they] were not fighting in France!' Guderian immediately informed von Bock that his panzer army 'was no longer capable of carrying out the orders that had been issued it'.[62] One of his panzer corps, which had an establishment of 600 tanks, had only fifty left. On further protests from von Kluge, who believed that such an advance was a fantasy at that time of the year, von Bock came to share his opinion, saying he believed that it was almost impossible to reach the capital 'in view of the condition of his troops',[63] let alone to carry the offensive beyond. Because of the importance of attacking before the deep snow fell, a more limited attack aimed directly at Moscow was ordered, even before the Germans had built up their strength.

The Army leaders had taken a bold decision, a gamble that was fully justified by the facts as they knew them. The Red Army had already suffered catastrophic losses in front of Moscow; the capital lay only fifty miles distant; and the importance of the objective had diminished not at all. Furthermore, the abandonment of the advance after the greatest victory of the campaign – the Vyazma-Bryansk encirclements – and when Moscow was so near, would never have been accepted by the Führer. Success was now a question of one final effort – in von Bock's words, 'the last battalion will decide the issue'.[64]

On 15 November the new offensive opened on the left wing, followed on the 17th by the right wing. The ground had indeed become hard, but the furthest advance was but fifty miles, and that not in the direction of Moscow. This time it was not rain that paralysed the attack; it was the tremendous drop in temperature. Even before the 15th the cold was becoming crippling; on the night of 3–4 November the first frost set in; on the 12th the temperature dropped to $+5°F$, and the next day to $-8°F$. Guderian remembered some of its effects: 'Ice was causing a lot of trouble, since the calks for the tanks had not yet arrived. The cold made the telescopic sights useless; the salve which was supposed to prevent this also had not arrived. In order to start the engines of the tanks, fires had to be lit beneath them. Fuel was freezing on occasions, and the oil became viscous.'[65] Vehicles were frozen into the snow up to their axles; when halted, their engines had to be started up every four hours, and their transmissions operated, so that the strain on the metal, made brittle by the cold, was eased. Owing to the lack of antifreeze, some would even seize while running. Oil became like tar; the plates of vehicle batteries buckled; guns of all types became inoperable as the oil in their recoil systems solidified – only one in five of the tank guns could fire; and the narrow tracks of the German tanks sank deep into the soft snow, giving them a poor performance compared with their Soviet counterparts. Small arms, too, froze solid; the grenade was the only weapon that retained its efficiency. On 21 November Guderian wrote to his wife: 'The icy cold, the lack of shelter, the shortage of clothing, the heavy losses of men and equipment, the wretched state of our fuel supplies, all this makes the duties of a commander a misery, and the longer it goes on the more I am crushed by the responsibility which I have to bear. . . .'[66] After the war, he remembered: 'Only he who saw the endless expanse of Russian snow during this winter of our misery, and felt the icy wind that blew across it, burying in snow every object in its path; who drove for hour after hour through no-man's land only at last to find too thin shelter with insufficiently clothed, half-starved men; and who also saw by contrast the well-fed, warmly clad, and fresh Siberians [the Soviet reinforcements recently arrived], fully equipped for winter fighting – only a man who knew all that can truly judge the events which now occurred.'[67]

Yet the offensive continued; the endurance of the German soldiers, most of whom were without winter clothing, was magnificent. By 27 November the advanced units of Panzer Group 3 were only nineteen miles from the capital; but the field commanders, quite rightly, were convinced that further advance was impossible. On 29 November von Bock reported to Halder that 'if within a few days they do not force the front north-west of Moscow to collapse, the offensive must be abandoned. It would merely lead to a soulless frontal struggle with an enemy who apparently still had large reserves of men and material.'[68] Two days later he wrote:

'After further bloody struggles the offensive will bring a restricted gain of ground and it will destroy part of the enemy's forces, but it is most unlikely to bring about strategic success. The idea that the enemy facing the army group was on the point of collapse was, as the fighting of the last fortnight shows, a pipe-dream. To remain outside the gates of Moscow, where the rail and road systems connect with almost the whole of eastern Russia, means heavy defensive fighting for us against an enemy vastly superior in numbers. Further offensive action therefore seems to be senseless and aimless, especially as the time is coming very near when the physical strength of the troops will be completely exhausted.'[69]

The Army High Command, however, was reluctant to concede failure. When Guderian spoke to von Brauchitsch by telephone on 23 November, he noted that 'The Commander-in-Chief of the Army was, plainly, not allowed to make a decision. In his answer he ignored the actual difficulties, refused to agree to my proposals [to go over to the defensive], and ordered the attack to continue.'[70] But OKH could not withstand reality for long; on 27 November Wagner reported to Halder and the senior officers of the General Staff that 'we are at an end of our resources in both personnel and material. We are about to be confronted with the dangers of deep winter. . . . Situation is particularly difficult north of Moscow. . . . Horses – situation very serious; distressing lack of forage. Clothing – very bad, no means of improvement in sight.'[71] Three days later Halder noted 'total losses on the Eastern Front (not counting sick) 743,112 [since 22 June], i.e. 23.12 per cent of the average total strength of 3.2 million. . . . On the Eastern Front the Army is short of 340,000 men, i.e. 50 per cent of the fighting strength of the infantry. Companies have a fighting strength of 50-60 men. At home there are only 33,000 men available. Only at most 50 per cent of load-carrying vehicles are runners. Time needed for the rehabilitation of an armoured division is six months. . . . We cannot replace even 50 per cent of our motorcycle losses.' Of the 500,000 trucks that had begun the campaign, 150,000 were total losses, and a further 275,000 needed repair. After the obvious failure of the last, desperate push in the first few days of December, OKH was finally convinced of the hopelessness of the situation. On the 4th it allowed the commander of Army Group Centre the discretion whether to carry on with the offensive or not; on the 5th, the 167th day of the campaign, von Bock called off the attack and ordered a withdrawal from over-exposed positions, and the Army leaders approved his move. Halder noted: 'They are at the end of their strength.'[73] Von Brauchitsch, his health broken, determined on resignation.

The next day, at a conference with the Führer, the Army Commander and his Chief of General Staff did all they could to impress on Hitler the dire straits in which Army Group Centre found itself. Halder noted that 'he refuses to take any account of comparative figures of strengths. To him our superiority is proved by the number of prisoners taken.'[74] Although Hitler reluctantly agreed that there should be a pause in the attack, he insisted that the objectives should be maintained and pursued as soon as possible. It was not until 8 December that he was forced to realise that the offensive should be abandoned completely. In Directive No. 39 he conceded defeat: 'The severe winter weather which has come surprisingly early in the east, and the consequent difficulties in bringing up supplies, compel us to abandon immediately all major offensive operations and go over to the defensive.'[75] Only in the extreme north and south was offensive action to continue; the lower Don-Donets line and Sevastopol were to be captured as soon as possible, and Leningrad encircled. Meanwhile, every attempt would be made to bring the eastern armies up to strength for the 1942 campaign, although the resources of the Army in the west were to be only temporarily weakened and would be maintained so that it was still capable of coastal defence and of carrying out the occupation of Vichy France.

The attack on Moscow was over; but the fighting certainly was not. On the night of 5 December, the day Army Group Centre had come to a halt, the Red Army launched the first of a series of counter-attacks which were to last until March. Of this period, Guderian wrote: 'We had suffered a grievous defeat in the failure to reach the capital which was to be seriously aggravated during the next few weeks thanks to the rigidity of our Supreme Command: despite all our reports, these men far away in East Prussia could form no true concept of the real conditions of the winter war in which their soldiers were now engaged. This ignorance led to repeatedly exorbitant demands being made on the fighting troops.'[76]

After 5 December there were two courses of action open to the military leaders: either a withdrawal until the following spring to a suitable defensive line, where positions had already been prepared, or an unyielding defence outside the gates of Moscow, in which any retreat was strictly forbidden. There were arguments for both courses. Von Bock's sixty-seven exhausted divisions were committed to a wide front that curved in a large, extended 600-mile salient, exposed to attack, difficult to defend, and for which there were no reserves to meet the Soviet counter-offensive. This problem could have been solved by a withdrawal to prepared positions nearer the supply bases, which would have had the effect of shortening the front and allowing a higher ratio of force to space. Moreover, the shelter afforded by these prepared positions would have prevented the high casualties brought about by the intense cold – by 8 December the temperature had fallen to −30°C. Had the Germans moved back to either Vyazma or Smolensk, the enemy would be forced to fight a major battle at the end of a 200-mile line of communication in deep snow, which the Soviet Army was ill-equipped to do. Such a withdrawal was favoured by all the front-line generals almost without exception. Initially, too, Hitler appears to have favoured some sort of a rearward move. In his Directive No. 39 of 8 December he specified three factors that should be observed when the Army went over to the defensive; areas 'of great operational or economic importance to the enemy' were to be held; the soldiers were to be allowed 'to rest and recuperate as much as possible'; and 'Conditions suitable for the resumption of large-scale offensive operations in 1942' were to be established. None of these precluded a withdrawal. Hitler continued: 'The main body of the Army . . . will, as soon as possible, go over to the defensive along a lightly tenable front to be fixed by the Commander-in-Chief of the Army. . . . Where the front had been withdrawn without being forced by the enemy, rear areas will be established in advance which offer troops better living conditions and defensive possibilities than the former positions. . . . The front line must be chosen with an eye to easy quartering and defence, and simplification of supply problems. . . .'[77]

Soon the Führer was to contradict himself. On 13 December, in accordance with Hitler's will, von Brauchitsch issued an order to commanders telling them to break off contact with the enemy and withdraw ninety miles; the very next day the Führer countermanded this. On the 15th von Brauchitsch again proposed a withdrawal, which Hitler overrode the next day, ordering: 'A general withdrawal is out of the question. The enemy has made substantial penetration only in a few places. The idea that we should prepare rear positions is just drivelling nonsense. The only trouble at the front is that the enemy outnumbers us in soldiers. He does not have any more artillery. His soldiers are not nearly as good as ours.'[78] A fanatical resistance was to be undertaken, without regard to the enemy on the flanks or the rear. Hitler was concerned that any withdrawal under enemy pressure would soon degenerate into a rout which would end, at the best, in the loss of most heavy equipment and, at the worst, in the destruction of Army Group Centre. Just as important in the Führer's eyes was the impact that any retreat would entail on the morale of the German nation, and the lowering of his status as a warlord in the eyes of the world. Moreover, he was convinced that 'will power' could override the crisis; that rigidity and tenacity would suffice to stem the Soviet tide. Keitel was fully in agreement with his Führer's decision: '. . . he correctly realised that to withdraw even by only a few miles, was synonymous with writing off all our heavy armaments; in which case the troops themselves could be considered lost. . . .'[79] Others, however, disagreed, and a large number of generals were replaced for acting on their convictions. Both Guderian and Hoepner were dismissed in disgrace for having dared pull their troops back without approval from the Führer.

The views of the military amateur were not in accord with those of the professionals. As it was, the front was forced back in a series of piecemeal withdrawals over distances of between 100 and 200 miles in the five weeks from 5 December, and losses in men and equipment were extremely high. By Christmas Eve Guderian had only forty tanks left in action. Between December 1941 and the middle of March 1942 Army Group Centre lost 256,000 men, and suffered a crippling sickness rate of some 350,000 men, a large proportion being the result of frostbite. In the same period it lost around 55,000 motor vehicles, 1,800 tanks, 140 heavy infantry guns, and so on down to 10,000 machine-guns. Material losses were considerably higher than during the summer victories. For example, during the first six months of 'Barbarossa', the average monthly loss of trucks was 1,223, and of light and heavy field howitzers, 193; in the following four months of winter, no less that 5,095 and 391 respectively were destroyed or captured. The suffering of the individual soldier, from cold and lack of food, to say nothing of the shortage of weapons and ammunition, was immense. On 2 February an agitated Halder noted: 'The scenes in this battle . . . are absolutely grotesque and testify to the degree to which this war has degenerated into a sort of slogging-bout which has no resemblance whatever to any form of warfare we have known.'[80] Yet in spite of this the German line did not break; by mid-March the Soviet offensive, at the end of its resources, came to a halt. There is no reason to suppose that a well-conducted, staged withdrawal, as was attempted by several first-class commanders at the time, would not have succeeded with, at most, the same loss that was in any case suffered, and probably with far less.

Moreover, the Germans were extremely fortunate not to suffer greater casualties, and to succeed in avoiding the enemy's repeated attempts at envelopment. Von Blumentritt gave a graphic description of what might have happened to 4th Army had it not been for mistakes on the part of the enemy:

> 'Following the final check before Moscow . . . von Kluge advised the Supreme Command that it would be wise to make a general withdrawal to the Ugra, between Kaluga and Vyazma, a line which had already been partially prepared. There was prolonged deliberation at the Führer's headquarters over this proposal before reluctant permission was granted. Meanwhile the Russian counter-offensive developed in a menacing way, especially on the flanks. The withdrawal was just beginning when a fresh order came from the Führer, saying: "The 4th Army is not to retire a single step." . . . 4th Army became isolated in its forward position, and in imminent danger of encirclement. . . . Soon the danger became acute, for a Russian cavalry corps pressed round our right flank well to the rear of it. . . . Such was the grim situation of 4th Army on 24 December – and it had arisen from Hitler's refusal to permit a timely step back. . . . I and my staff spent Christmas Day in a small hut . . . with tommy-guns on the table and sounds of shooting all around us. Just as it seemed that nothing could save us from being cut off, we found that the Russians were moving on westward, instead of turning up north astride our rear. They certainly missed their opportunity.'[81]

It was the endurance of the German soldier, the skill of his front-line generals, and the mistakes of the enemy that saved Army Group Centre, not

Hitler. The utter ineptitude of his military leadership is revealed in the following extracts from the Chief of the General Staff's diary:

> '19 December . . . [Hitler] orders to hold present positions. Not worried about any threats to the flanks. . . . 9 January . . . Several phone calls with von Kluge and Jodl. We have reached the point where a decision on taking back the front is absolutely essential, but the Führer cannot make up his mind yet and wants to talk to von Kluge directly. So, to our great distress, the decision on this burning question is put off again, while we lose precious time. . . . 10 January . . . owing to adverse weather, von Kluge could not fly to the Führer. The decisive conference on the continuation of the operations is therefore put off [to the next day]. . . . 11 January . . . The whole day with von Kluge at Führer headquarters. The Führer upholds his order to defend every inch of the ground. . . . The situation is now becoming really critical. . . . 14 January . . . von Kluge reports that he must move back if he wants to extricate himself. . . . The Führer appreciates the necessity for taking back the front, but will make no decision. This kind of leadership can only lead to the annihilation of the Army . . . 20 January . . . The front is being taken back gradually.'[82]

Halder's comment after the war was most apposite: 'Events proved stronger than Hitler's order. In spite of the superhuman efforts of the troops, the front was pressed back step by step and in some places even torn open. When the force of the Russian attack had finally been spent, the battered army held a deeply bulging line, and even had to accept the fact that a substantial body of its troops was cut off.'[83] By the time the Soviet counter-offensive drew to a close, the German front had stabilised along a line similar to, although more unfavourable than, that proposed by von Bock four months earlier. Even Hitler could not contravene reality; his attempt to do so, however, had been costly in the lives of his soldiers.

21

The New
Commander-in-Chief

'I can take no more'

FIELD-MARSHAL WALTHER von BRAUCHITSCH

Commander-in-Chief of the German
Army, 1938–41

The assault on Moscow had failed; the fears of the generals, expressed so forcibly in the summer, had been realised in the winter. The campaign that had opened with such high hopes in June had come to a bitter end just six months later. Keitel, in an effort to understand the reasons for this, wrote:

> '. . . during the summer of 1941 it almost seemed as though the eastern colossus would succumb to the mighty blows inflicted by the German Army, for the first and probably the best Soviet front-line army had, in fact, been all but wiped out by that autumn. . . . One wonders what army in the world could have withstood such annihilating blows, had the vast expanse of Russia, her manpower reserves, had the Russian winter not come to its assistance?'[1]

Perhaps, but von Bock's sober assessment, written on 7 December 1941, shows a clearer grasp of the reasons for failure:

> 'Three things have led to the present crisis: 1) the setting-in of the autumn mud season. . . . 2) the failure of the railways. . . . 3) the underestimation of the enemy's resistance and of his reserves of men and material. The Russians have understood how to increase our transport difficulties by destroying almost all the bridges on the main lines and roads to such an extent that the front lacks the basic necessities of life and of fighting equipment. . . . The Russians have managed in a surprisingly short time to reconstitute divisions which had been smashed, to bring new ones from Siberia, Iran, and the Caucasus up to the threatened front, and to replace the artillery which had been lost by numerous rocket launchers. There are now twenty-four more divisions in the sector of this army group than there were on 15 November. By contrast, the strength of the German divisions has sunk to less than a half as a result of the unbroken fighting and of the winter . . . the fighting strength of the tanks is

even less. The losses of officers and NCOs are terribly high, and at the moment replacements for them are even more difficult to get than new troops.'[2]

Where lay the responsibility for these three reasons for failure? They lay with Hitler. Had he listened to the advice of his generals in August, he would probably have been in the capital by October. But, as has been seen, he took another course. Time, the most valuable of commodities, had been lost; time in which the autumn mud season had drawn perilously near, in which the effect of the failure of the railways had had time to accumulate, and, most important, in which the enemy could build up his strength. By the middle of July, when von Bock was reporting that his chances were good for capturing Moscow by means of quick armoured thrusts, the Soviets had no tanks defending the Yartsevo-Vyazma-Moscow axis, and their divisions averaged fewer than 6,000 men in strength. No more than 50,000 soldiers could have stood between the Germans and the capital. By October the position had changed radically; no fewer than 800,000 men and 770 tanks, half the entire strength of the Red Army in the west, faced von Bock's offensive, and three defensive lines that had not been there in August had been erected around the capital. Operation Typhoon did indeed suceed in annihilating this force; by mid-November, after suffering losses of up to 700,000 men, the Soviets had but 90,000 men and only a few tanks defending Moscow. But then, at this decisive point, the weather broke. The Germans, exhausted by their efforts over the previous months, and denied adequate supplies, were unable to cross the hundred miles to Moscow, even against such weak opposition. Time was again on the side of the Red Army, and by the middle of November sixty rifle divisions, seventeen tank brigades, and fourteen cavalry divisions faced thirty-eight infantry, thirteen panzer, and seven motorised infantry divisions. Many of the Soviet formations might have been understrength, but all of the Germans were exhausted. When it became clear that the Japanese would not attack in Siberia, divisions from the Far East began to arrive in large numbers, composed of men highly trained and well-equipped for operating in the intense cold of a Russian winter. By early December, on the eve of their counter-attack, the Soviets had 718,000 men, 7,985 guns and mortars, and 721 tanks, mostly T34s, on their central front. The Germans, outnumbered and ill-equipped for winter warfare, proved incapable of reaching their objective. The result was the first major defeat for German arms in the war.

It is, of course, a purely hypothetical question whether the German Army could have reached Moscow in the autumn had Hitler allowed it to attempt to do so. All that can be said is that the chances seemed good; certainly this was the consensus of military opinion at the time. It is only possible to guess at the impact that the loss of Moscow would have had on the Soviet colossus, but the argument of Kesselring appears not unreasonable:

'If on conclusion of the encirclement battle of Smolensk . . . the offensive had been continued against Moscow after a reasonable breather, it is my belief that Moscow would have fallen into our hands before the winter and before the arrival of the Siberian divisions. The capture of Moscow would have been decisive in that the whole of Russia in Europe would have been cut off from its Asiatic potential and the seizure of the vital economic centres of Leningrad, the Donets Basin, and the Maykop oilfields in 1942 would have been no insoluble task.'[3]

Such was the potential that Hitler had lost; more crucially, he had also paved the way for the total defeat of the German Army in the field.

On the flanks of the German Eastern Front, operations had continued during the final advance on Moscow. In the south, von Rundstedt's weakened army group had been given new tasks by the Führer, despite the fact that it now possessed only forty German divisions, of which three were panzer and two motorised infantry, and had suffered severe shortages of supplies, especially petrol. Von Rundstedt recalled:

'After accomplishing my first objective, which was the encirclement and destruction of the enemy forces west of the Dnepr, I was given my second objective. It was to advance eastwards and take Maykop and Stalingrad. We laughed aloud when we received these orders, for winter had already come and we were almost 700 kilometres away from these cities. Hitler thought that with the frost making the roads hard we could advance towards Stalingrad very quickly. At the same time I was told to advance towards Maykop because oil was urgently needed, and I was also expected to clean up the Crimea in order to deprive the Russians of their airfields in this area.'[4]

Thus, Army Group South was expected to be capable of achieving three objectives at once. None was achieved in 1941; in the Crimea, Sevastopol continued its stubborn resistance, and 11th Army was forced to waste its energies which would have been spent more properly on the main attack to the Caucasus; in the Ukraine the Germans managed to get no further than Rostov, the 'gateway' to the Caucasus; and on the road to Stalingrad, they only passed Kharkov, still on the west bank of the Donets. Their inability to gain these three objectives simultaneously need not be regarded as a failure, for they were certainly too ambitious for a force with the limited resources of Army Group South.

However, in their main attack the Germans were to experience their first setback of the war, at Rostov-on-the-Don. The advance south-east to the Caucasus was led by von Kleist's Panzer Group 1, renamed 1st Panzer Army on 5 October, with 17th and 6th Armies in support. Halder was concerned that such an advance would leave a dangerous gap between Army Groups

Centre and South, and von Rundstedt was disturbed by the risks of advancing a further 400 miles beyond the Dnepr and exposing and over-stretching his left flank. Hitler dismissed these fears with the confident argument that the Soviets were by then incapable of offering any serious opposition. However, as in the central sector of the front, so in the south. On 6 October the weather broke and the ground turned to mire; by the 11th, 6th and 17th Armies were at a standstill. But it was not until the 14th that 1st Panzer Army was similarly affected, with the result that the supporting infantry armies were kept from maintaining close contact with the vulnerable, but still advancing, spearhead. Nevertheless the attack continued. On the 17th Taganrog fell; on the 30th Kharkov was reached, and on 20 November Rostov was entered. Although their achievement was hailed as a great victory by Germany's propaganda machine, von Rundstedt and his officers knew that the reality of their position was other than Geobbels would have it.

With insufficient resources, an over-extended flank, and a rate of advance that was far too slow to keep the enemy off balance, the army group was vulnerable to Soviet counter-attack. At the end of November this came, with, as its object, the severance of 1st Panzer Army from the rest of von Rundstedt's army group. As 6th Army was stuck in the mud, and 17th Army too far back to relieve the armoured spearheads, there was nothing for it but to evacuate Rostov and fall back over the Mius to Taganrog. On 28 November the Germans left the city. But on the 30th Hitler ordered 'no retreat'. Von Rundstedt remembered:

> 'The Russians attacked at Rostov from the north and south about the end of November, and, realising that I couldn't hold the city, I ordered it to be evacuated. I had previously asked for permission to withdraw this extended armoured spearhead to the Mius river, about 100 kilometres west of Rostov. I was told that I could do this and we began to withdraw very slowly, fighting all the way. Suddenly an order came to me from the Führer: "Remain where you are, and retreat no further", it said. I immediately wired back: "It is madness to attempt to hold. In the first place the troops cannot do it, and in the second place if they do not retreat they will be destroyed. I repeat that this order be rescinded or that you find someone else." That same night the Führer's reply arrived: "I am acceding to your request", it read, "please give up your command". I then went home.'[5]

Von Rundstedt was replaced by von Reichenau. The attacks continued unabated, and Halder wrote in his diary for 1 December: '1st Panzer Army is convinced intermediate position [between Rostov and Taganrog] cannot be held. . . . It cannot understand why our troops should stand here and have the enemy punch through their line when five miles back there is a much better position.'[6] Nor could von Reichenau. His request to the Führer for a withdrawal met with compliance; in the afternoon of 1 December, less than twenty-four hours after von Rundstedt had been relieved of his command, permission was given to move back across the Mius. Halder noted wryly: 'We have arrived where we were yesterday evening. Meanwhile we have lost energy and time, and von Rundstedt.'[7]

To the north , too, the Germans had suffered a major setback, although this was not at first apparent to them. Leningrad had not fallen; it had not even been fully encircled. As Warlimont said later: 'Hitler gave another fateful halt order just when the vanguards of Army Group North had reached the outskirts of the city [on 10 September]. Apparently he thereby wanted to avoid the loss of human life and material to be expected from fighting in the streets and squares of this Soviet metropolis against an outraged population, and hoped to gain the same ends by cutting off the city from all lines of supply.'[8] But although all road and rail communications to the city had been cut, the Lake of Ladoga, which froze over on 18 November, still remained in Soviet hands as the vital lifeline to Leningrad. On 25 November the Germans went over to the defensive; deprived of Panzer Group 4, then in the central sector of the front, von Leeb was left with only one Spanish and thirty German divisions to withstand the inevitable Soviet counter-offensive. When this broke, the ring round Leningrad remained intact, but Hitler's 'no withdrawal' order ensured that other parts of the front were penetrated, and troops encircled, much to von Leeb's disquiet. The most renowned of these pockets was at Demyansk, where 90,000 men in an area forty by twenty miles were kept supplied for two and a half months by the Luftwaffe until, by 21 April 1942, a corridor was forced through to the defenders. This had been a notable achievement by the Air Force, which succeeded in getting a daily average of 273 tons of supplies to the troops, and it won the Führer's praise. Demyansk, above all other battles during the Soviet counter-offensive, proved to Hitler's own satisfaction that his policy of 'no withdrawal' was correct, and with this as his justification he was to embark on exactly the same course the following winter. It was to result in the débâcle at Stalingrad.

Failure at the gates of Moscow, the first significant setback suffered by Hitler since 1933, inevitably brought with it serious consequences for the Army leadership, innocent though it was of the causes. Relations between the Supreme Commander and OKH, which had blown hot and cold during the campaign, were at their lowest level. On 7 December, Halder noted in his diary: 'The experiences of today have been shattering and humiliating. The Commander-in-Chief is little more than a post-box. The Führer is dealing over his head with commanders-in-chief of army groups.'[9] Already Hitler had dismissed one army group commander, von Rundstedt, without even consulting OKH; now he was personally directing the battle as well. On 6 December von Brauchitsch, weakened considerably from ill-health (he had been suffering heart-attacks since November) and torn between his conceptions of duty and honour, had offered his resignation, only to be told by the Führer that he was too busy with more important matters to be bothered by it. Eleven days later the Army Commander was summoned to Hitler's presence and informed that he was to be relieved. All suggestions of a successor were rejected with the exception of one, when Schmundt proposed what was no doubt already in the dictator's mind – that Hitler himself should be the new Commander-in-Chief. On the 19th von Brauchitsch's retirement was announced, and the Führer informed his soldiers that henceforth he would assume active command of the Army. He told Halder: 'Anyone can do the little job of directing operations in war. The task of the Commander-in-Chief is to educate the Army to be National Socialist. I do not know any Army general who can do this as I want it done. I have therefore decided to take over command of the Army myself.'[10] At the same time, although Halder was to maintain his position as Chief of the General Staff, Keitel was to take over all the other 'administrative functions' of OKH. Thus, in mid-December 1941 Hitler concluded a process which had begun in early 1938. Then, the political independence of the soldiers had received a significant setback, and was soon to exist no more; now the operational autonomy of the Army, already severely breached on many occasions, was to end abruptly. The corporal of the First World War had, indeed, become the warlord of the Second.

Hitler's disillusion with, and contempt for, his generals reached a high point at the end of 1941. Three months later he could speak of von Brauchitsch 'only in terms of contempt. A vain cowardly wretch who could not appraise the situation, much less master it. By his constant interference and consistent disobedience he completely spoiled the entire plan. . . .'[11] Of the other generals, too, the Führer had a low opinion: 'The senior officers who have risen from the General Staff are incapable of withstanding severe strain and major tests of character.'[12] During the winter crisis his temper grew shorter, and his dislike more marked. Halder's diary for this period is full of the Führer's outbursts. For example, on 30 November, as von Rundstedt was pulling back from Rostov, Halder noted: 'The interview [between Hitler and von Brauchitsch] appears to have been more than disagreeable, with the Führer doing all the talking, pouring out reproaches and abuse, and shouting orders as fast as they came into his head.'[13] On 2 January Halder wrote: 'The withdrawals of 9th Army [under extreme pressure] against the will of the supreme Commander occasion mad outbursts on his part at the morning conference. OKH is charged with having introduced parliamentary procedures into the Army [a high abuse!], and with lacking incisiveness of direction. These ravings, interspersed with utterly baseless accusations, waste our time and undermine any effective cooperation.'[14] And the next day: 'Another dramatic scene with the Führer, who calls into question the generals' courage to make hard decisions.'[15]

Thus, between December 1941 and April 1942 there came about a considerable transformation in the leadership of the German Army. On 1 December von Rundstedt was removed, and von Reichenau put in his place; on 18 December von Bock, suffering from a bad stomach, left Army Group Centre, and was succeeded by von Kluge; on 19 December von Brauchitsch was replaced by Hitler; on 16 January von Leeb, frustrated by his loss of operational freedom, was relieved of his command as requested, to be replaced by von Küchler; on 17 January von Reichenau died of a stroke, and von Bock returned to the front to take up command of Army Group South. In addition, thirty-five army, corps, and divisional generals, including Guderian and Hoepner, were dismissed. Gone with them was the respect that had traditionally been accorded to members of the Army General Staff. From then on, none of its members was to be safe from the Führer's wrath. Warlimont remembered one instance of this:

> 'In the Reich Chancery . . . Brauchitsch's departure was followed by a busy perusal of the list of generals and their chiefs of staff whom Brauchitsch might have seen on his trip. Then Hitler came across the name of Hossbach, his former aide-de-camp, whom he had dismissed on 4 February 1938, and very brusquely transferred him to field duty. Hitler added, as I learned later, that Hossbach was "one of those defeatist General Staff officers" who should not be allowed to influence an able commander (General Strauss). Under the circumstances this incident made a painful and lasting impression among the older General Staff officers.'[16]

This was but one of the manifestations of the Army's political and operational impotence; the most damaging were Hitler's inflated regard for himself as a military leader, and the power he had come to possess over the Army, which he was determined to exercise to the full. The impotence of the Army High Command in operational matters was the end of a process that had begun so innocently with the several suggestions made by the Führer during the Polish campaign. The offensives against Norway and the west had further extended this precedent to unacceptable limits, while the invasion of the Soviet Union had seen the matter taken to its logical conclusion with the choice of objectives. By September 1941, it was clear that the General Staff could never hope to prevail against Hitler's direction of the battle; and by the end of the year the Army leaders were even isolated from their generals in the field. Von Brauchitsch was Army Commander-in-Chief only in name; Hitler had already assumed his power. The transfer of his title was but a formality. After December 1941 and the bitter fighting of the winter of early 1942, Hitler placed the weight of the blame for the failure in front of Moscow on the military commanders, both in OKH and in the field; he was convinced that his 'no retreat' order had saved the Army. This was but the last of a number of events stretching back to 1936, in which he believed that his intuition had shown itself to be immeasurably superior to the professional expertise of the generals. This, he was convinced, would continue; he would take no heed of their advice or warnings.

The fact that Hitler had assumed the full authority of the Army Commander, was, in itself, no reason why OKH should continue to lose its importance relative to OKW. There were two other solutions to the problem as to how the division of operational responsibility should be divided between the commands: either the merger of the two staffs, both of whom were now directly answerable to Hitler, or the absorption of OKW into the larger, and better equipped, OKH. However, neither of these courses was to be followed; combination of the two offices would have been against one of Hitler's fundamental political principles – the division of authority. Furthermore, the dominance of the Army Command, after all its supposed opposition to his wishes, would have been highly distasteful to him. Hitler's suspicion of OKH and his dislike of its methods were ingrained. He once remarked: 'General Staff officers do too much thinking for me. They make everything too complicated. That goes even for Halder. It is a good thing that I have done away with the joint responsibility of the General Staff.' As Warlimont noted: 'Hitler did not want unity; he preferred diversity, such unity as there was being concentrated in his person alone.'[17]

Ironically, however, it had been the Army itself that, in the period between July 1940 and June 1941, had first extended the authority of OKW. Von Brauchitsch, still resentful at OKW's role during the Norwegian campaign, and no doubt annoyed by Hitler's interference in the plans for the Army of Norway, had declared on 18 March 1941 that 'he was leaving it to the OKW to issue all orders'[18] for the operations in Finnish Lapland. Halder disagreed, but to no avail. The result was that OKW controlled the operations of the Army units in that theatre, but, because it had not the organisation for the job, it left their supply, replacements, and organisation to OKH. This situation was made even more bizarre by the fact that OKH continued to advise Marshal Mannerheim, the Finnish Commander, on operational matters. Of this peculiar arrangement, Warlimont commented: '. . . a second "OKW theatre of war" was set up in Finland [to add to Norway] . . . now the Commander-in-Chief of the Army of his own accord surrendered to OKW, in other words to Hitler, his responsibility for, and his powers of command over, a considerable number of Army formations in a purely land theatre of war.'[19] Once again the Army had yielded its operational autonomy, but this time without being ordered, or even asked, to do so. It was a poor reflection on the quality of von Brauchitsch's leadership.

During 'Barbarossa', the influence of OKW, which during the planning of the invasion had been negligible, began to grow. Instead of remaining in Berlin, or surrounding himself with the Operations Staff of OKH, Hitler chose to situate his well-guarded Führer headquarters, code-named the *Wolfschanze* (Wolf's Lair), in East Prussia, a lonely place, remote from the front, far from the capital, and an hour away, by road, from the Army

Command. Surrounding the Führer were the officers of OKW, who provided him with his daily briefings, and received and passed on his orders. Von Brauchitsch, Halder, and von Paulus met with Hitler only twenty-two times between 22 June and 19 December, whereas Keitel and Jodl saw and ate with him every day. Such an environment suited Hitler's temperament – especially his suspicion, his determination to exercise his authority as warlord, his inadequacies in military training, and his capacity to subordinate reality to wishful thinking. The OKW staff did nothing except foster this. Warlimont remembered: 'His permanent entourage . . . believing as they did that he had second sight and could not go wrong, egged him on rather than restraining him; moreover he was actually confirmed in his determination to play the part of supreme military leader by the fact that in Norway and northern Finland he was in direct command; the buffer of OKH did not exist there, and he could run affairs as he pleased.'[20] Furthermore, there still remained within the circle around Hitler that distrust and contempt for the Army Command of old, which so pleased the dictator. For example, Goebbels wrote in his diary that 'Schmundt complained bitterly about the indolence of a number of senior officers who either do not want, or in some cases are unable, to understand the Führer'.[21] At least for the moment, Hitler had no fear of the OKW and OKH combining to thwart his wishes.

The OKW, then, suited Hitler well, despite the fact that it was ill-equipped for its growing responsibilities. From the early summer of 1941 he began to use it in the place of OKH as his command organisation in all theatres of war except in the east. Warlimont wrote: 'He was entirely unmoved by the obvious disadvantages of this peculiar command organisation, and apparently encountered no objection from any quarter.'[22] On 15 October 1941 Hitler instituted the post of Commander-in-Chief of the Armed Forces, South-East, to control the Balkans, the Aegean, and Crete up to Dalmatia; he was to receive his orders from, and report to, OKW. From the autumn the Mediterranean also became an OKW theatre. Although supreme command there nominally belonged to the Italians, the importance of Rommel's activities in North Africa and the problems of communications across the Mediterranean caused Hitler to attempt to exert more influence over that area. Although no order was issued specifically transferring responsibility from OKH to OKW, the Führer made greater use of the latter at the expense of the former. On 1 December the Luftwaffe general, Kesselring, was made Commander-in-Chief, South, directly responsible to OKW. This was similar to the position as it developed in the west; again, no specific order was ever given, but on 20 October command was effectively moved from OKH to OKW by the Führer's direction to the Wehrmacht Command to build up the defence of the occupied English Channel Islands. This was followed in December by Hitler's decision to build a new West Wall to protect the Arctic, North Sea, and Atlantic coasts, the responsibility for which he gave to OKW. The Commander-in-Chief, West, was also made responsible to the Wehrmacht Command. By such means OKW was provided with a role; as a command organisation responsible for the over-all direction of the war it was impotent, but as one concerned with the individual services in individual theatres, it was to have an influence at least as great, or as little, as that of OKH.

By mid-December 1941 the OKW had replaced OKH as the responsible command in Norway, Finland, the west, the south-east, and the Mediterranean, and Hitler had succeeded in taking full control of the conduct of ground operations in the Eastern Front in place of von Brauchitsch and his staff. Thus, because of the division of authority between OKW and OKH, no single organisation possessed command over all the units of the Army in all the theatres of operation; this power was in the hands of just one man: Adolf Hitler. He was in every sense the supreme warlord. It was his tragedy, and the Army's, that he was to pay no heed to von Moltke's dictum: 'Only humility leads to victory; arrogance and self-conceit to defeat.'

PART FOUR

The
Years of Defeat

*An army is of little value in the field unless there
are wise counsels at home.*

CICERO
De Officiis

22

North Africa — The Scene

The German High Command, brought up to think in terms of continental warfare, did not find the overseas theatre congenial. It failed altogether to understand the importance of the Mediterranean and the inherent difficulties of the war in Africa. It did not originate or follow any clear-cut plan, but allowed its hand to be forced by fits and starts.

FIELD-MARSHAL ALBERT KESSELRING
Commander-in-Chief, South

The beginning of 1941 saw Germany, albeit half-heartedly, become involved in Italy's desultory little war along the North African coast. For the Führer and his two High Commands, whose attention was becoming ever-increasingly focussed on the vast, open spaces of the Soviet Union, the affair remained a side-show, and often an annoying one, until its end in 1943; but for those who had to fight the British and Commonwealth forces in the desert, the campaign took on an importance the potential of which rivalled anything that might have been achieved on the Eastern Front. Under interrogation after the war, Halder admitted that 'on the whole we regarded the matter as a fight for time', and he even dismissed the renowned exploits of Rommel, the German commander in North Africa, as 'such an unholy muddle that I doubt whether anyone will ever be able to make head or tail of it'.[1] Rommel was bitter at such treatment, and wrote shortly before his death in 1944:

> 'The German High Command . . . failed to see the importance of the African theatre. They did not realise that, with relatively small means, we could have won victories in the Near East which, in their strategic and economic value, would have far surpassed the conquest of the Don Bend [the aim of the 1942 German offensive in the Soviet Union]. Ahead of us lay territories containing an enormous wealth of raw materials . . . which could have freed us from all our anxieties about oil. A few more divisions for my army, with supplies for them guaranteed, would have sufficed to bring about the complete defeat of the entire British forces in the Near East.'[2]

He even went so far as to envisage the final strategic objective as an attack through Persia and Iraq into southern USSR to take Baku and its oilfields. But this remained a pipe-dream. Although Rommel, initially at least, had a large measure of control over his forces in the field, and although this resulted in a brilliant tactical exposition of the armoured idea, the neglect by Hitler and the Axis High Commands, their half-hearted support, and their wrong-headed interference ensured his ultimate, and costly, strategic failure.

Defeat came hard for Rommel, his previous career having been marked only by success. During the First World War, as a battle-group commander on the Italian front, he had won the coveted Pour le Mérite which, when granted to a junior officer, was comparable with the Victoria Cross; in the late 1930s he had written a well-received infantry training-manual, *Infanterie Greift An*, which, when read by Hitler, had won him command of the *Führerbegleitbattalion*, the military bodyguard, during the occupation of the Sudetenland and the invasion of Poland; and in May and June of 1940 he had command of 7th Panzer Division, which, by its outstanding exploits, earned itself the nickname of 'Ghost Division'. In early 1941, at the age of 49 and with the rank of *Generalleutnant*, he was given the small, but independent command of German troops in Libya, and within two years he was to be a *Generalfeldmarschall*, renowned the world over as the 'Desert Fox'. Even an enemy Prime Minister, Winston Churchill, could refer to him in the House of Commons thus: 'We have a very daring and skilful opponent against us, and, may I say across the havoc of war, a great general.'[3]

Rommel had his faults. He was vain, ambitious, and, occasionally, perversely obstinate. Like Guderian, he was deficient in the diplomacy necessary to convert sceptical superiors to the wisdom of his argument. Perhaps, too, he lacked that breadth of intellect which belongs to the truly great commanders of history, a failing which revealed itself in the political deficiencies common to the German officer corps, as well as in an inability to escape from the front-line mentality in which he excelled and to translate his unusual tactical brilliance into an equally remarkable strategic vision. However, as General Westphal, his chief of staff in Africa, noted: 'All who worked with him were constantly astounded at the rapidity with which he summed up the most complex situations and came to the heart of the matter. He therefore has the right to be considered one of the outstanding soldiers of the Second World War. He was an upright and a brave man.'[4]

Such was the general who 'was not only the soul but also the motive power of the North African war'.[5] Rommel's intuitive grasp of the principles and potential of armoured warfare was remarkable, and it served to place him among the foremost exponents of the new idea, a position for which his personal qualities well-qualified him. He was brave, quick, and daring in his decisions as well as in his leadership, and possessed a superabundance of that energy, aggression, and robustness without which no commander can withstand the rigours of war. He was one of the few generals in history who was capable of creating victory out of the near-certainty of defeat, a man who was at his best when in a tight corner or taking a dangerous gamble. This was reflected in his attitude to warfare; he understood that victory for the armoured force lay in the 'art of concentrating strength at one point, forcing a breakthrough, rolling up and securing the flanks on either side, and then penetrating like lightning, before the enemy has time to react, deep into his rear'.[6] Rommel realised the potential that had been given him. He was later to record:

> 'Of all the theatres of operation, North Africa was probably the one where the war took on its most modern shape. Here were opposed fully motorised formations for whose employment the flat desert, free of obstructions, offered hitherto unforeseen possibilities. Here only could the principles of motorised and tank warfare, as they had been taught before 1939, be fully applied, and, what was more important, further developed. Here only did the pure tank battle between large armoured formations actually occur.'[7]

His leadership was brilliant. Although outnumbered and outgunned, almost immediately on landing in Tunisia in March 1941 he advanced some 350 miles in just twelve days, winning back everything, with the exception of the vital part of Tobruk, that Wavell, the British commander, had taken fifty days to capture from the Italians. But then, at the end of the year, in the first of the desert 'seesaws', he was forced to retreat in his turn to within fifty miles of his initial starting-point. In 1942, still outnumbered, he again pushed back the British and Commonwealth forces, this time 550 miles, taking Tobruk, crossing the Egyptian border, and advancing to the small village of El Alamein, 150 miles from Cairo. By means of swift night marches, deft flanking movements, audacious swoops on the enemy's rear, and by the unhesitating acceptance of the most distant of objectives, Rommel had been brought to within striking distance of victory. No wonder that Churchill could pace his office crying: 'Rommel, Rommel, Rommel, Rommel . . . what else matters but beating him.'[8]

Nevertheless, brilliant though Rommel's generalship may have been, on its own it was not enough to secure him victory. As von Thoma remarked after the war: 'In modern mobile warfare . . . tactics are not the main thing. The decisive factor is the organisation of one's resources – to maintain the momentum.'[9] And this, through no fault of his own, Rommel was unable to achieve: the material resources of his force were outside his control. They lay in the hands of Hitler, Mussolini, and the Axis High Commands. As a result, the desert campaign degenerated from a war of manoeuvre to a war of material, in which ultimate victory would go to the side best able to maintain or to build up its battle-strength. However spectacular an offensive by Rommel might be, failure would most surely result simply because the neglect of the military leaders in Germany ensured the material exhaustion, and, on occasions, the material collapse, of his force. Thus, eleven months after reaching El Alamein, the battered remnants of the once-victorious Panzer Army Africa, cornered on the Tunisian coast, passed into Allied captivity.

From the beginning, the German venture in North Africa was viewed from Berlin and the Führer headquarters as merely a holding operation, a stop-gap intended to guard against total Italian collapse rather than as initiating a great surging advance that might result in the Axis domination of the Near East. On 24 October 1940, after a reconnaissance mission in Libya, von Thoma had given a report to Hitler about the possibility of operations in North Africa. The general later recalled that he had:

> '. . . emphasised that the supply problem was the decisive factor – not only because of the difficulties of the desert, but because of the British Navy's command of the Mediterranean. I said it would not be possible to maintain a large German army there as well as the Italian army. My conclusion was that, if a force was sent by us, it should be an armoured force. Nothing less than four armoured divisions would suffice to ensure success – and this, I calculated, was also the maximum that could be effectively maintained with supplies in an advance across the desert to the Nile valley.'

Hitler, however, rejected this argument, saying that 'he could not spare more than one armoured division. At that, I [von Thoma] told him that it would be better to give up the idea of sending any force at all. My remark made him angry.'[10] Defence rather than offence was Hitler's idea. A few days later the Führer confirmed his own view in Directive No. 18, dated 12 November, when he ordered: 'One armoured division . . . will stand by for service in North Africa.'[11] However, the exhilarating scent of their own victory in the desert caused the Italians to be lukewarm about German help, and in December it was decided to stand-down the panzer division assigned for North Africa. Then came rapid Italian defeat; the need for German assistance was never more urgent. On 9 January 1941 Hitler decided to send a 'blocking detachment' to aid his ally, although his Directive No. 22, dated 11 January, made no attempt to stipulate the size of the force. It stated merely that the 'Army Commander will provide covering forces sufficient to render valuable service to our allies in the defence of Tripolitania. . . .'[12] In fact, it had already been decided to send a number of troops and equipment from the 3rd Panzer Division, foremost among which would be the 5th Panzer Regiment, which would be reorganised with a new formation, the 5th Light Division. Under-strength in motorised infantry, the first contingents had arrived in Tripoli on 14 February, and all the armour landed by the 20th. The first contact made with the enemy was on the 24th.

This small force alone was clearly insufficient. An OKH memorandum of the previous year had specified that, if necessary, a panzer corps of two divisions should be sent, a view confirmed by General Funck, who had returned from a visit to North Africa in January 1941, and by General von Rintelen, the senior German military attaché in Rome. These men favoured the adoption of the role of 'aggressive defence', which could be mounted only by a formation of, at least, two divisions. On 3 February von Brauchitsch formally asked the Führer for permission to send a further panzer division. However, Hitler, although approving of the idea of 'aggressive defence', would allow only another tank regiment, though he promised that the rest of a panzer division would follow later. This promise was confirmed on the 19th, when OKW issued a directive stating that 'OKH should tranfer a full panzer division to Tripolitania in addition to 5th Light Division'.[13] Units of this second force, the 15th Panzer Division, began to arrive in late April 1941, the whole transfer being completed by the middle of June, by which time Rommel's first advance had ended and the German-Italian troops had gone over to the defensive.

From the outset, Rommel was acutely aware of the limitations imposed on him by the higher command. On 3 April 1941, at the height of victory, he wrote to his wife: 'We've been attacking since the 31st with dazzling success. There'll be consternation among our masters in Tripoli and Rome, perhaps in Berlin too. I took the risk against all orders because the opportunity seemed favourable. No doubt it will all be pronounced good later, and they'll all say they'd have done exactly the same in my place.'[14] From the beginning the military authorities had been at pains to make clear to Rommel the precise limitations imposed on his freedom of action; at his OKH briefing in January 1941, it had been stressed that his mission was merely to stiffen the Italian resolve to defend what was left of Cyrenaica and to maintain the port of Tripoli. 'Aggressive defence' did not mean the licence to pursue an all-out advance. Thus, for tactical purposes, Rommel would be subordinate to the uninspiring Italian Commander-in-Chief in North Africa, Marshal Gariboldi, who was succeeded by Bastico before the Germans arrived. However, following his first discussions with the Italian leaders, Rommel promptly decided to disregard his instructions and take command at the front as soon as possible. This move was against the advice of von Rintelen, who had warned him not to pursue too energetic a policy, for 'that was the way to lose both honour and reputation'.[15] After his initial, limited advance in late February and early March 1941, Rommel returned to Germany and reported to OKH on 19 March. Halder had already gained Hitler's consent to his own proposals for a defensive strategy based on limited forces in North Africa, and two days earlier the Führer had approved his rejection of Rommel's appeal for two further panzer divisions. Of the meeting with the heads of the Army, Rommel remembered: 'The Commander-in-Chief of the Army informed me that there was no intention of striking a decisive blow in Africa in the near future, and that for the present I could expect no reinforcements. . . . I was not very happy at the efforts of . . . von Brauchitsch and . . . Halder to keep down the numbers of troops sent to Africa and leave the future of this theatre of war to chance.'[16]

On his return to the desert Rommel decided again to throw all caution to the winds and make his bid to seize the whole of Cyrenaica. The advance began on 31 March. On 3 April an agitated Führer sent a despatch to Rommel:

'Recognition of accomplishments and reminder not to be reckless, as Air Force units are being withdrawn and arrival of 15th Panzer Division will be delayed; moreover, the Italians now need all their strength against Yugoslavia, and so have nothing left for North Africa. Under these circumstances there is a danger of English counter-attack on [flanks]. Further advance authorised only when sure that British armoured elements have been taken out of the area.'[17]

When the message arrived, Rommel was in heated discussion with Gariboldi, who was also objecting to the advance because of logistical problems and the lack of authority from Rome. Seizing on the despatch, and totally misrepresenting its contents, Rommel declared that Hitler had given him complete freedom of action in the desert and that he would move accordingly. By 14 April the Africa Corps had passed the port of Tobruk and was asking for OKH's permission to drive on to Suez. Hitler, by then carried away by Rommel's heady success, was toying with the idea of sending more units to North Africa to exploit the potential now so unexpectedly presented, but Halder and von Brauchitsch, together with Jodl, managed to persuade him otherwise. Neither extra troops nor sufficient air cover was available, they argued, and Rommel should remain on the Egyptian border, build up a strong front, and undertake only limited raids. In 1941 the Germans in Africa advanced no further. Another offensive, planned by Rommel for November, was prevented by the British attack that same month, which ended in the retreat of the German and Italian forces.

Spectacular though Rommel's advance in April had been, OKH had been dismayed by its extent; Halder noted smugly in his diary on 15 April 1941: 'Now, at last, he is constrained to state that his forces are not sufficiently strong to allow him to take full advantage of the "unique opportunities" afforded by the over-all situation. That is the impression we have had for quite some time over here.'[18] The Chief of the General Staff then turned his attention to the Balkans. But the problem of North Africa could not be dismissed; Tobruk, although isolated, was still holding out and the British were still active on the Egyptian border. After the Greek surrender, OKH was again forced to consider Rommel's predicament. Complaining that Rommel had not sent back a single 'clear-cut report all these days', Halder had the 'feeling things [were] in a mess', and noted: 'Reports from officers coming from this theatre . . . show that Rommel is in no way equal to his task. He rushes about all day between the widely scattered units, stages reconnaissance raids, and fritters away his forces. No one has any idea of their dispositions and battle-strength. The only certainty is that the troops are widely dispersed and their battle-strength reduced.'[19] Halder even contemplated going out to North Africa to see things for himself, but in the event contented himself with sending his deputy, von Paulus, who had 'enough personal influence to head off this soldier gone stark mad'.[20]

Von Paulus, arriving in Africa on 27 April, immediately suspended the attack on Tobruk, about which the General Staff had considerable reservations. After a discussion with Gariboldi, who advocated Rommel's plan, the Deputy Chief of the General Staff sanctioned a renewal of the battle, which duly began on 30 April. Halder, however, insisted that in no circumstances was the advance to penetrate into Egypt further than Siwa-Sollum. On 3 May, when it was clear that the assault on Tobruk was coming to nought, von Paulus ordered Rommel not to resume the attack on the port unless it offered chances of quick success, instructing him that his main mission was to defend Cyrenaica from the British. Approving this, Halder and von Brauchitsch sent a number of reinforcements in the form of independent motorised infantry battalions to Africa to bolster the defence. Halder wrote: 'Paulus remains in Africa in compliance with my teletype message. I am glad he is there to act as a guardian of our ideas, which also have the blessing of the Führer.'[21]

However, OKH was still far from satisfied with the German position in North Africa, defensive though it then was. Rommel did not please them, and they had no faith in his armoured tactics. On 7 May Halder wrote: 'At last, a decent situation map. It shows that Rommel has broken up his units in a wild pattern and conducts a campaign with very scanty forces on a widely extended front which cannot be measured by European standards.'[22] Two months later, the Chief of the General Staff recorded the feeling of resentment at OKH: 'Personal relations are complicated by General Rommel's character and his inordinate ambition. . . . Rommel's character defects make him extremely hard to get along with, but no one cares to come out in open opposition because of his brutality and the backing he has at top level.'[23] On 11 May von Paulus had made his report to Halder on Rommel's prospects, and as a result the Chief of the General Staff concluded that 'by overstepping his orders, Rommel has brought about a situation for which our present supply capabilities are insufficient. . . . Rommel cannot cope with the situation.'[24] The next day, a British convoy arrived in Alexandria bringing with it 200 tanks, thereby completely changing the balance of power in the desert and allowing General Wavell to prepare for a major offensive to be launched in mid-June. A gloomy Halder then held a conference with von Brauchitsch, during which a reorganisation of the German command in North Africa was decided on: Rommel was to be subordinated to a new headquarters whose general would be entitled 'Commander of German Troops in North Africa'. This most dangerous threat to Rommel's autonomy, however, was thwarted by higher authority. On 14 May OKH referred the proposal to OKW, who replied with certain ideas of their own. It soon became clear that Hitler himself was protecting Rommel's command, and, as von Paulus informed Halder, 'all the Führer cares about is that Rommel should not be hampered by any superior headquarters put over him'.[25] In the event, OKW predictably won the day, and the affair was settled by the appointment of Colonel Alfred Gause to act as the German

Liaison Officer at Italian headquarters in Libya. Gause was to help solve supply problems and reconnoitre the possibilities for a larger German presence in Africa. Rommel, highly suspicious of him at first, demanded that he place himself entirely under his command, which Gause did, and the two men finally came to establish good working and personal relationships. The threat to Rommel's position was over for a time, although the disenchantment between him and the military leaders remained, as evidenced by several letters written by the desert commander to his wife at the end of May and in early June 1941. On 26 May he wrote: 'Yesterday I received a considerable rocket from Brauchitsch, the reason for which completely passes my comprehension. Apparently the reports I send back, stating the conditions as they exist, don't suit their book. The result will be that we'll keep our mouths shut and only report in the briefest form.'[26] Three days later he added: 'I'm not going to take it lying down, and a letter is already on its way to von Brauchitsch.'[27] On 2 June he continued: 'My affair with the OKH is under way. Either they've got confidence in me or they haven't. If not, then I'm asking them to draw their own conclusions. . . . It's easy enough to bellyache when you aren't sweating it out here.'[28] And on the 11th: 'They were mad at me in the OKH because my reports had gone to the OKW as well. But that was Rintelen's fault, who was acting in accordance with his duty. I've had no reply to my letter to Brauchitsch.'[29]

On 15 June the long-awaited British counter-attack broke on Rommel's positions around Sollum and Halfaya Pass, but the fears of OKH were not to be fulfilled. By 1 June the British were thoroughly worsted; Rommel's brilliant armoured tactics had won the day. The German defences remained intact and the enemy withdrew, leaving eighty-seven burnt-out tanks on the battlefield. Desert success had come just at the right time for Hitler and the Army High Command, for now they could safely remove their anxious gaze from North Africa and concentrate it, to the exclusion of all else, on the forthcoming conflict in the east. A week after the battle at Sollum, Germany invaded the Soviet Union with 134 divisions and more than 3,000,000 men. The great clash of political tyrannies and cultures had begun; in comparison North Africa was an unwanted side-show.

Consequently, even when Hitler planned future ambitious offensive action in North Africa, he refused to acknowledge that this demanded any significant resources in men and material. In his Directive No. 32, dated 11 June 1941 and entitled 'Preparations for the period after "Barbarossa" ', he had envisaged that 'The struggle against the British positions in the Mediterranean and in Western Asia will be continued by converging attacks launched from Libya through Egypt, from Bulgaria through Turkey and in certain circumstances from Transcaucasia through Iran.' The attack in North Africa should be planned for November 1941 'on the understanding that the German Africa Corps will be by then brought to the highest possible efficiency in personnel and equipment and with adequate reserves of all kinds under its own hand . . .'. How was this to be achieved? '. . . by the conversion of 5th Light Division into a full armoured division . . . so that it is not necessary to move any further large German formations to North Africa.'[30] Thus, partly because the far-reaching advance would be accompanied by operations from Bulgaria and, possibly, Transcaucasia aimed at the Suez Canal, Hitler did not believe that the German forces in Africa would ever require more than two divisions. His attitude was confirmed by an OKW memorandum of 13 September 1941, which stated: 'Only after the exclusion of Russia as a power factor will it be feasible to concentrate on the battle in the Atlantic and in the Mediterranean against Britain. . . . Even if Russia was largely crushed by the end of the year, the army and air forces necessary for decisive operations in the Mediterranean, the Atlantic, and on the Spanish mainland will not be available until the spring of 1942.'[31]

The two divisions available to Rommel, the 5th Light and 21st Panzer, together with a number of individual units such as an anti-tank battalion and two Flak battalions, were grouped together in the renowned *Deutches Afrikakorps* (German Africa Corps), instituted on 19 February 1941. On 15 August under a new leader, General Ludwig Crüwell, the corps became part of the larger command formed on that date: Panzer Group 'Africa', under Rommel. The panzer group, renamed Panzer Army 'Africa' on 30 January 1942, coordinated the Africa Corps, the Africa Division z.b.V (*zur besonderen Verfügung* – for special duties), and six Italian divisions, one of which was armoured (these were formed into two corps, the XX and XXI). The Africa Division z.b.V was formed in early August, consisting of a number of formerly independent units serving in Africa, together with a new intake from Europe, and was renamed 90th Light Division on 27 November. Although motorised, this division had no armour; tanks were possessed only by the 5th Light and 21st Panzer (two battalions each). On 1 October 1941, the 5th Light was redesignated a panzer division – the 21st. These were the only German divisions in North Africa until the end of the decisive advance to El Alamein that ground to a halt at the beginning of August 1942. Then the 164th Light Africa Division, without transport (it was not fully motorised until early January 1943), and the Ramke Parachute Brigade, also lacking motor vehicles, arrived. Neither of these units contained a single tank. The only Italian reinforcements to arrive were a second armoured division, in May 1942, and the Folgore Parachute Division, in August. At El Alamein, the panzer army faced an enemy many times its strength.

From January 1941 to the end of the battle in Egypt and Libya, therefore, the only German units assigned to Rommel were two panzer and two light divisions, a parachute brigade, and various supporting 'army troops' (including an artillery command) – at full strength only some 90,000 men. Of the eight Italian divisions, four were non-motorised infantry, and the two armoured were equipped with slow, obsolete tanks nicknamed 'tin-coffins'. Little need be said about the Italian force in Panzer Army Africa, except that it only artificially inflated the size of Rommel's command. As Westphal wrote: 'In addition to the disadvantages of his [the Italian's] Latin temperament, his inferiority in fire-power, equipment, and training, and the absence of any inspiring war aim combined from the start to push the Italian armed forces hopelessly into the background.'[32]

Yet Rommel's battle with Hitler and the Army High Command lay not so much in the provision of more field units but in the proper supply of those he already possessed. He summed up the importance of this thus: 'In a mobile action, what counts is material, as the essential complement to the soldier. The finest fighting man has no value in mobile warfare without tanks, guns, and vehicles. Thus a mobile force can be rendered unfit for action by the destruction of its tanks, without . . . serious casualties in manpower.'[33] This would be the fate of the Panzer Army Africa on many an occasion, for the severe restrictions of the early months soon degenerated into the crippling shortages that were to render Rommel's advances but empty victories, a mere record of ground covered at the expense of exhaustion and, consequently, of ultimate defeat.

Even during the early period of the German presence in Africa, when enemy dislocation of the supply line across the Mediterranean was at a minimum, it proved impossible for sufficient material – equipment, rations and, above all, petrol – to reach the Axis forces. In the first half of 1941, when they consumed some 70,000 tons of supplies every four weeks, in one month (May, when only 69,331 tons were delivered) even the normal needs could not be met; in three months only modest stockpiling was possible (some forty-five tons in all); and in only July (when 125,076 tons were delivered) was there a generous build-up of supplies for any forthcoming offensive action. Nevertheless, these were halcyon days compared with what was to come. Bayerlein, the Africa Corps Chief of Staff, estimated that in September only one-third of the troops and one-seventh of the supplies required did in fact arrive. Sinkings increased. Whereas in June only six per cent of the cargo embarked at Italian ports was lost in transit, in November, a particularly bad month, sixty-two per cent found its way to the bottom of the Mediterranean. In November and December the amount of cargo arriving in Libya decreased by half, and, at the same time, over the preceeding four months, the percentage lost was more than doubled. In November, for example, only 30,000 tons arrived, compared with 83,000 tons in August. In the last six months of 1941, more than 280,000 tons of military cargo had been sunk on the way to North Africa. The resulting shortage of fuel was especially serious; in August, for example, 37,000 tons of fuel had been delivered to the Axis forces, but in November only 2,500 tons. Rationing was, in consequence, strict. The following year, 1942, saw considerable fluctuations in supply. The best month was April, when 150,000 tons came across the Mediterranean; the worst was March, when only 18,000 arrived. Although after March strenuous efforts were made to ensure that the convoys got through, the establishment of Axis air superiority over the Mediterranean was but short-lived, and in the second half of the year sinkings again began to increase, to forty-four per cent in October and fifty-two per cent in December. Not once during the entire year, with the possible exception of July, did military supplies to North Africa ever meet even minimal requirements. Moreover, the tonnage actually reaching the panzer army was only a part of the tonnage that was shipped over the Mediterranean. By the late summer of 1942, for example, there were 146,000 Italian soldiers in North Africa, of whom only 54,000 were under Rommel's command, the rest being used for security duties in Cyrenaica and Tripolitania. These men, as well as the Italian civilian administration, took more than their fair share of supplies. It was the old story of the troops in the rear areas living well while the fighters at the front went short.

Rommel was unequivocal as to where lay the blame: 'The fact is that there were men in high places who, though not without the capacity to grasp the facts of the situation, simply did not have the courage to look them in the face and draw the proper conclusions. They preferred to put their heads in the sand, live in a sort of military pipe-dream, and look for scapegoats whom they usually found in the troops or field commanders.'[34] The Army High Command, for its part, was convinced that Rommel was ignoring the realities of the situation, and that the proper supply of his forces when undertaking such fast, deep advances along the North African coastline was an impossibility. After the war Halder remembered:

> 'I last talked to Rommel about this subject in the spring of 1942. At that time he told me that he would conquer Egypt and the Suez Canal, and then he spoke of East Africa. I could not restrain a somewhat impolite smile and asked him what he would need for the purpose. He thought he would want another two armoured corps. I asked him, "Even if we had them, how would you supply and feed them?" To this question his reply was, "That's quite immaterial to me; that's your problem." As events in Africa grew worse, Rommel kept demanding more and more aid. Where it was to come from didn't worry him.'[35]

The argument put forward by OKH was both simple and forceful; at first glance it appeared to possess considerable truth. Its essence was as follows: effective operations in North Africa could not be begun without first creating a well-developed supply base, and this could not be achieved without careful conservation of the forces in the field – in other words, a major offensive should not even be contemplated, let alone undertaken, for some time. Should Rommel disobey his instructions and, by his independent actions, force Germany to prosecute an aggressive war in North Africa, it would prove impossible to maintain even his small army in the essentials of material. Germany was becoming deeply embroiled in its war against the Soviet Union, which demanded huge resources in men and material undreamt of in the African theatre; diversion from this overriding task was neither possible nor desirable. The route of supply from Italy to the Axis base at Tripoli (the main port), and from there to the front, precluded any large movement of resources to the panzer army. Its very length, alone, was an immense drawback. The normal route of the convoys at that time was round the western coast of Sicily, across the Mediterranean to eastern Tunisia and then, hugging the coastline, down to Tripoli. This indirect route, made necessary by the British base at Malta which lay directly between Sicily and Tripoli, was some 600 miles in length, and once ashore, the tonnage had to be carried over immense distances from the port to the troops either by road or by a few coastal vessels. From Tripoli to El Alamein was 1,400 miles, and even from Benghazi, the nearest port safe from air attack in August 1942, it was 750 miles. Moreover, the supply route was in constant danger of attack by enemy submarines, warships, and aircraft. The island fortress of Malta dominated the supply route, and it was in enemy hands. Losses were considerable. When Italy entered the war, one-third of her merchant fleet had been lost through internment; by September 1942 half the remainder had been lost through enemy action; between June 1940 and May 1943 the enemy sank more than sixteen per cent of the Axis cargoes. Tobruk, small as it was as a port, was of some help to the Panzer Army after its capture in June 1942. However, this was severely limited; because of the vulnerability of its approach routes, and of its own location, to enemy action, the Axis suffered high losses in ships. Thus, in August, the Italian navy refused to continue to send its vessels into Tobruk; it was a severe blow to Rommel. Furthermore, the distances over which motor transport was expected to supply the Panzer Army were huge, too great for the resources allocated to North Africa. OKH believed that 200 miles was the largest distance a motorised army might expect to be effectively supplied. At any one time, thirty five per cent of supply trucks were under repair and, when Rommel was at El Alamein, between thirty-five and fifty per cent of the Panzer Army's fuel was used in bringing the supplies to the front. Moreover, the Italian navy was hampered through lack of fuel oil, a shortage of coastal vessels, and the limitations of cargo-handling facilities at the ports. In the face of such harsh realities, OKH believed that the proper supply of Rommel's force in attack was impossible; the only solution was to refrain from any advance. Furthermore, the Army leaders argued, it was the Italians who were responsible for the transport of supplies; North Africa was their theatre of war, and complaints should be addressed to them. As Halder wrote on 29 July 1941: 'North Africa is an Italian theatre of operations. Bastico is in full command there. . . . Safeguarding of transport on North African route is the responsibility of the Italians.'[36]

But Rommel would have none of this. Certainly he acknowledged that the inefficiency and inadequacy of the Italians had much to answer for; thus far he agreed with OKH. He later wrote: 'In Rome one excuse after the other was found for the failure of the supply organisation which was supposed to maintain my army. It was easy enough back there to say: "It can't be done", for life and death did not depend on finding a solution.'[37] From the beginning, the Italians had been reluctant to allow a strong German presence in what was, after all, their own theatre of operations. This situation was worsened by the poor relations that Rommel enjoyed with their military leaders, for whom he exhibited a strong contempt. Certainly, the men in whose hands the over-all direction of supplies lay were far from inspiring. Rommel's description of Cavallero, the Chief of Staff of the Commando Supremo, contained much truth: 'Marshal Cavallero belonged to the type of intellectually fairly well-qualified, but weak-willed, office-chair soldier. The organisation of supplies, the command of men, anything in any way constructive requires more than intellect; it requires energy and drive and an unrelenting will to serve the cause, regardless of one's personal interests.'[38]

Thus, the Germans in North Africa were not well-served by their allies, important though they were to them. Rommel wrote that 'As a result of his discussions with the Italian authorities, Gause had gained the impression that it would be difficult to persuade them to agree to further German forces being shipped to North Africa, for they feared that the German element would then gain a preponderance . . . and be in a position of advantage vis-à-vis their own.'[39] This reluctance extended to the supplying of units already in Africa. Rommel knew that during the vital month of August 1942, when Panzer Army Africa contained approximately two Germans for every one Italian, the Commando Supremo shipped across the Mediterranean only 8,200 tons for the German troops and 25,700 for their own, of which 800 tons were to satisfy civilian needs. But he possessed no influence over the shipping lists, or the rate at which the Italians would work. For example, some 2,000 trucks earmarked for the panzer army stood waiting in Italy for more than a year. Rommel's frustration was expressed in a letter to his wife on 9 April 1942: 'Kesselring came yesterday. His news . . . wasn't very cheerful. They're just riddled with bureaucracy in anything and everything, and on top of that there's a complete lack of understanding of the demands of modern warfare. The whole tempo of the supply organisation is completely inadequate. And that with Malta neutralised as never before.'[40] Moreover, Rommel saw, as did Halder, that as long as the British held Malta any offensive towards Suez was bound to be a difficult affair. The island must at least be neutralised by air attack, or at best occupied, for success to be guaranteed.

Although he might acknowledge the very considerable difficulties, Rommel could not believe they were insuperable. He was firm in his advocacy that 'If everybody had pulled together in a resolute search for ways and means, and the staff work had been done in the same spirit, the technical difficulties could, without any doubt, have been overcome.'[41] His solutions to the practical problems of supply and reinforcement were simple. He wrote in 1944:

'The following steps were all that would have been necessary to release sufficient troops for North Africa, and to safeguard their transport to Libya and their supply: (a) The creation of an adequate air concentration in the Mediterranean area, by moving Luftwaffe formations from France, Norway, and Denmark (taken in relation to the total war effort, the establishment of air mastery over the Mediterranean would have more than compensated for a weakening of German air power in the countries concerned). (b) Transfer to the North African theatre of several of the armoured and motorised formations which were lying idle in France and Germany [for example, in March 1942 two new panzer divisions were sent to the Eastern Front, one of which had been formed from occupation troops in Norway, and in June there were three army armoured divisions in France for rest and refits; any one of these could have been sent to North Africa in time for the drive into Egypt]. (c) Malta should have been attacked and taken. (d) The appointment of one man to take charge of supplies, with full powers over all Wehrmacht authorities concerned in their handling and protection. He would have required full support at all times on political matters (to overcome Italian intransigence). These measures had nothing extraordinary about them, and would have been quite normal action to take, yet they would have conclusively decided the war in Africa in our favour.'[42]

Not one of these conditions was met, and a continually critical supply problem was the result.

Rommel understood that the single most important inhibiting factor in the battle for supplies was not the island of Malta or the Italian Command; it was his own Führer who, together with the High Command, prevented any attempt to fulfil his four conditions. He wrote of this in bitter terms, recalling the time in 1942 when his force was approaching the heart of Egypt:

'It was obvious that the High Command's opinion had not changed from that which they had expressed in 1941, namely, that Africa was a "lost cause", and that any large-scale investment of material and troops in that theatre would pay no dividends. A sadly short-sighted and misguided view. For, in fact, the supply difficulties which they were so anxious to describe as "insuperable" were far from being so. All that was wanted was a real personality in Rome, someone with the authority and drive to tackle and clear away the problems involved. No doubt this would have led to friction . . . but this could have been overcome by an authority unencumbered with other political functions. Our government's weak policy towards Italy seriously prejudiced the German-Italian cause in North Africa.'[43]

Here lay the rub. The Army High Command, preoccupied with events in the Soviet Union, regarded North Africa as only a minor concern and, being unable to see the potential success that it offered, placed easy relations with the Italians above Rommel's requirements, salving their consciences by constant repetition that his difficulties were self-induced by his disregard of their warnings and directives. Halder's admission after the war sets out the insuperable nature of the problem:

> 'As far as I was concerned, the North African affair was largely a political decision. We realised that it was important to Italy that the African coastline be prevented from falling into enemy hands, but with the English commanding the sea I insisted that the utmost we could send, and keep supplied, were three to four divisions. With so small a force all we could hope to do was to defend Italian territory for as long as possible. Of course, if the opportunity for offensive action presented itself we would take it. But on the whole we regarded the matter as a fight for time. Sooner or later things were bound to turn out badly for the Italians, but the longer we could postpone that from happening – perhaps for years – so much the better. To achieve that purpose, the outlay of three to four divisions might not prove too costly.'[44]

The attitude of Albert Kesselring, a Luftwaffe Field-Marshal, was also of considerable importance to Rommel. As Commander-in-Chief, South, he had under his control all Luftwaffe units in Africa, Italy, and Greece. The direction of the German naval force in the Mediterranean was later added, followed, at the beginning of 1943, by the over-all command of the army in Africa and Italy. Thus, the support Kesselring could give to the ground troops, in terms both of the influence he had with Hitler and of ensuring command of the air and security of the supply-line, was potentially considerable. Westphal held him in high opinion:

> 'No other Air Force commander could outdo Kesselring in his efforts to support the ground troops. That his resources were often inadequate and had to be spread out thin is another story. . . . Neither weather nor threat of enemy action could prevent him repeatedly flying to Africa in order to give what help he could, or, when necessary, to mediate between rival German and Italian requirements. He paid as little attention to his own person as did Rommel. He made as many as two hundred flights over areas endangered by the enemy, and was shot down five times in his Stork alone.'[45]

Rommel, too, although his relations with Kesselring were sometimes bad, could write: '. . . he had considerable strength of will, a first-class talent for diplomacy and organisation, and a considerable knowledge of technical matters.'[46] But Kesselring had one great failing, which was fatal to the panzer army: he was over-optimistic about the future and failed to recognise the crucial significance of the problems of supply. This was recognised by Warlimont, who remembered: 'The views of . . . Kesselring had a considerable influence on Hitler's attitude. He was optimistic about further developments both in Tunis and as regards the seas supply situation.'[47]

Nor was Hitler, the man in whose hands the ultimate fortune of Panzer Army Africa lay, any better than his Army Command. Delighted by Rommel's successes and generous in his recognition of them, (Rommel was elevated from *Generalleutnant* to *Generalfeldmarschall* in only eighteen months, and was later awarded the diamonds to the swords and oak-leaves of the Knight's Cross, Germany's second-highest military decoration), Hitler nonetheless failed to appreciate the military realities of the situation. Other factors weighed more heavily with Hitler the politician, high among them good relations with the Italians. Warlimont wrote: 'In spite of all his fine words, and in spite of all possible pressure from OKW, Hitler always put Mussolini's susceptibilities ahead of the military requirements.'[48] As a result, all the Führer was prepared to do was to order the Luftwaffe to take measures to protect the convoys to North Africa. It was clear that Hitler had no clear idea of just what his aims in this area were, a lack of vision that affected all those responsible for the Reich's war effort. As Halder noted in his diary on 23 September 1941: 'North Africa: It is not quite clear what we really want there.'[49] Instead of setting out the objectives to be gained, and providing the resources necessary for their realisation, Hitler let events dictate his policy (and therefore that of OKH and OKW), with the result that no careful logistical planning was ever undertaken. To the Führer, the amount of ground gained obscured all else from his vision, including the crippling material losses. Warlimont described the haphazard nature of Hitler's planning:

'At the beginning of 1942, Supreme Headquarters [OKW] had no influence on these [land operations in North Africa] whatsoever; Rommel's sudden new breakthrough eastward came as just as much of a surprise to Hitler in East Prussia as it did to Mussolini in Rome. Rommel later found it necessary to call for German help for the later stages of his offensive, by-passing the Italian authorities who had other views; at the same time, Kesselring reported that, after months of bombing, he considered that he had almost completed his task of "eliminating" the installations of the British base on Malta, and that the island was cut off from all reinforcement by sea. Only when all this had happened did Hitler and Mussolini, with their immediate advisers, meet in Berchtesgaden at the end of April in order to decide on a timetable and objectives for future strategy in the Mediterranean area in the summer of 1942.'[50]

Two meeting held between Rommel and Hitler well illustrate the problems faced by the long-suffering field commander. Before the battle of El Alamein Rommel had flown first to the Duce, who 'still did not realise the full gravity of the situation',[51] and then to the Führer to plead for more supplies and reinforcements. He recorded the outcome thus:

'His headquarters had obviously been very impressed by the panzer army's successes and now wanted to force a decision in the Mediterranean area. . . . I concluded my report with the following words: "I quite realise that, with the present strategic sea and air situation in the Mediterranean, a very great effort will be required to ensure a safe and uninterrupted German supply to Africa. It will make the utmost demands. . . ." '

However, like the Duce, Hitler and his advisers failed to understand the intense urgency of Rommel's plea. He continued: 'During the conference I realised that the atmosphere in the Führer's H.Q. was extremely optimistic. Göring in particular was inclined to minimise our difficulties.' Hitler, in a burst of enthusiasm, announced a considerable increase in supplies in the next few weeks, but their failure to arrive caused Rommel to note that 'many of these promises had been given in a moment of over-optimism and on the basis of incorrect production figures'.[52] The next time Rommel was to see his Führer was on 28 November, at the end of the initial retreat from El Alamein, when he argued that:

'. . . since experience indicated that no improvement in the shipping situation could now be expected, the abandonment of the African theatre of war should be accepted as a long-term policy . . . if the army remained in North Africa, it would be destroyed. I had expected a rational discussion . . . [but] the Führer flew into a fury and directed a stream of completely unfounded attacks on us. Most of the . . . staff officers present, the majority of whom had never heard a shot fired in anger, appeared to agree with every word the Führer said. . . . We were accused, among other things, of having thrown our arms away. . . . I began to realise that Adolf Hitler simply did not want to see the situation as it was, and that he reacted emotionally against what his intelligence must have told him was right.'[53]

This chronic inability on the part of Hitler to comprehend the realities of Rommel's position was noted by others. After the war Westphal wrote:

'For various reasons, Hitler was unwilling to quit the African war theatre voluntarily. He therefore tried to draw the help so sorely needed by the Army from the Army itself, with the result that the organisation most in need of relief became still more strained. The repeated requests for aid from the two sister arms, partly by protection of the lines of communication, and partly by immediate support in battle, could not be granted. Instead, Hitler had new battalions and regiments flown over. Finally, it became a vicious circle. Here also a large part was played by that underestimation of the enemy, overestimation of our own resources, and neglect of reality which first appeared at Dunkirk and later occurred so often on the Eastern

Front. Hitler wanted to be stronger than mere facts, to bend them to his will. All attempts to make him see reason only sent him into a rage. In November 1942, he burst out with the words: "Even in Africa the Army leaders can see nothing but difficulties, instead of taking positive action against them, like Göring and the others." [54]

One short order from Hitler would have sufficed to alleviate significantly Panzer Army Africa's material difficulties once and for all; but it was not to come, despite all Rommel's efforts. Instead, the Führer offered a strange and dangerous mixture of encouragement and neglect. His culpability becomes all the greater because of his failure to deal with the question of Malta, the great thorn in the side of the Axis supply line. The best opportunity for its capture had been passed unheeded by the dictator in April 1941. Then, despite the argument of his OKW advisers, Hitler chose Crete for airborne invasion. The decision appears to have been taken as a result of pressure from the Luftwaffe chiefs, who believed that a base in Crete would provide them with far-reaching possibilities for air action in the eastern Mediterranean. Furthermore, capture of the island would ensure the closure of the Aegean sea and at the same time offer a stepping-stone in a further advance to the Suez area (although it later proved impossible to supply Rommel's force via Crete because of the poor railway facilities in Greece and the lack of shipping). On 20 May the invasion took place, and although the island was won by the end of the month the casualties among the German paratroop and air-landing troops were so high, and the loss of transports so great, that a similar invasion of Malta was an impossibility for some time to come. The cost of the attack on Crete had severely weakened Hitler's faith in the ability of such forces to undertake independent action on a large scale. The Führer had also been disturbed by the fact that the amphibious part of the Cretan operation had been an utter fiasco owing to the efforts of the Royal Navy based at Alexandria. These doubts boded ill for the future. Then came the invasion of the Soviet Union, and the attention of the Luftwaffe was turned to the Eastern Front, with the result that only the X Air Corps was left in southern Europe. Throughout May this formation had furiously attacked Malta, but, despite this, by the beginning of June the island's air defences and naval forces were stronger than they had ever been.

The invasion of Malta again became a possibility in the first half of 1942. The Luftwaffe in the south under Kesselring had been reinforced, and during the spring had managed to gain a measure of air superiority over the Mediterranean. Rommel remembered gratefully that 'The heavy Axis air raids against Malta, in particular, were instrumental in practically neutralising for a time the threat to our sea routes. It was this fact which made possible an increased flow of material. . . . [and] the reinforcement and refitting of the German-Italian forces thereupon proceeded with all speed.' [55] By the end of April, largely through the efforts of Raeder, Hitler had been persuaded of the need to capture the island, and preparations were set in train for a combined Italian-German airborne-seaborne invasion. Rommel, although anxious that Malta should be taken, was also concerned to begin a fresh advance now that his forces had been replenished. He saw the need to attack the enemy before they moved against him with superior strength and with all the advantage of the initiative. Hitler and Mussolini agreed, but with the provision that, as soon as Tobruk fell, the panzer army should stand on the defensive and allow the Axis to concentrate its resources on Malta. The invasion was set for August.

In the event, the plan for the attack on Malta was abandoned. Rommel achieved brilliant success in the Gazala battles, and on 21 June, the day he was promoted to Field-Marshal, the fortress of Tobruk capitulated. Yet the panzer army did not halt; instead, while his advance units were speeding towards the Egyptian frontier, Rommel sent personal messages to both Hitler and Mussolini asking that he be allowed to continue the fight. The advice given to the Führer by Kesselring, von Rintelen, and the naval staff all ran counter to Rommel's request; but an elated Hitler, already doubtful about the fighting capacity of the Italian Navy and Army in the event of a seaborne invasion, and fearful of the possibility that the German airborne troops might be left without aid as in Crete, decided to condone his field commander's action. The Führer signalled to the Duce: 'It is only once in a lifetime that the Goddess of Victory smiles.'[56] Malta was abandoned and the destruction of the British Army in the Near East was made the prime task for Axis effort.

Rommel has often been criticised for thus forcing the strategic direction of the Mediterranean theatre. It is argued that he thereby ensured the failure of the panzer army through the material exhaustion largely brought about by the disruption caused by Malta to the Axis supply line. But this is to mistake the realities of the situation on three counts. First, it was unfortunate that the air and sea operation against Malta should have been made conditional upon the halting of the ground forces in the desert; the Axis commands should have founded their plans on surer foundations than that. Second, it would have been militarily foolish to impose a halt on the victorious panzer army, even in its weakened state, when the enemy were on the run, and when it had Egypt within its grasp; in an advance, time is of the essence, and no retreating army should be given a respite in which to regain its strength, to build up its defence, or to mount a counter-attack. And third, the decision whether or not to invade Malta was Hitler's and Mussolini's responsibility (in practice, the former's), not Rommel's. Although Rommel had every right to advance his arguments, it was for the supreme leadership, and not the field commander, to take such grand strategic decisions as were necessary. Had Hitler sent an order to halt, then Rommel would have obeyed; that the Führer did not, but instead sent encouragement for further advance, is a matter of fact. The responsibility was his, not Rommel's.

The most telling argument that reveals the fatal passivity of the German leadership over the Mediterranean theatre, and that goes far to prove

Rommel's assertion that, with a certain amount of goodwill and effort, adequate supplies could have been delivered to the panzer army, is the fact that, after the Allied landings in Tunisia on 8 November 1942, the amount of material and reinforcements sent to Africa by the Axis was significantly increased. In October only 80,000 tons had been sent to North Africa, of which 45,600 tons arrived; in November, however, 115,200 tons were sent and 94,045 arrived, of which 30,309 went to Tunisia. The previous best that year had been in July, when 95,000 tons had been sent. Rommel recorded:

> '. . . in Tunisia – when, of course, it was too late – it became perfectly possible to double our supplies; but by that time the fact that we were up to our necks in trouble had penetrated even to the mainland. . . . Whet we found really astonishing was to see the amount of material that they were suddenly able to ship to Tunisia, quantities out of all proportion to anything we had received in the past. . . . All at once it was found possible to ship anything up to 60,000 tons a month to Tunis [until March 1943], in spite of the fact that the British and Americans then had a far tighter grip on the Mediterranean than they had in 1941–42.'[57]

Furthermore, all this was at a time when the German involvement in the wide spaces of the Soviet Union had never been greater, and when the disaster of Stalingrad was daily growing nearer. On 12 November the 5th Paratroop Regiment began to arrive, followed by panzergrenadiers and engineer units, as well as a company of tanks. By the end of the month, some 17,000 troops had arrived. On the 15th, seven days after the landings, OKH ordered that a combined command be instituted in Tunisia and, on the 19th XC Army Corps was formed out of *Stab Nehring*. Later that month the 10th Panzer Division, which had been resting and refitting in France since May, moved to Tunisia, and a number of independent units were formed into Division von Broich (later renamed Division von Manteuffel). This was followed late in December by the motorised 334th Infantry Division, and by a number of other formations, included among which was the heavy 501st Panzer Battalion equipped with the new Tiger tanks, and 190th Panzer Battalion. Units of the élite motorised infantry Luftwaffe division, 'Herman Göring', began to arrive in November, and by early March 1943 the majority had disembarked. In late March and early April, a further motorised infantry division, the 999th Light Africa Division, also landed. On 8 December 1942 the 5th Panzer Army under the command of General Jurgen von Arnim had been formed out of XC Corps to take control of all the formations now in Tunisia. To coordinate the 5th Panzer Army and Panzer Army Africa, both of which were then in Tunisia, Army Group Africa was instituted on 23 February 1943 under Rommel. Simultaneously, Panzer Army Africa was renamed 1st Italian Army, and was given to the command of an Italian, General Messe. Thus, within a few months, during the hardest period of fighting that Germany had known till then, the German leadership proved quite capable of doubling the number of German formations in North Africa. So much for the 'insuperable' difficulties of supply.

Yet even then, Rommel's panzer army was to be neglected. He remembered that he was forced to draw:

> '. . . attention to the fact that practically the whole of our shipping space was being used for the 5th Panzer Army, and that my army was not even receiving the necessities of life, although it was carrying the main burden of the fighting. The most likely reason for this was the interest that the Luftwaffe and various other Rome authorities had in supplying the 5th Army for an offensive to the west. . . . I was not best pleased when it turned out that Kesselring had diverted to Tunis a number of the latest type 8.8cm guns, which the Führer had promised us and which we urgently required [Kesselring was forced to reverse his decision].'[58]

What made the whole affair even more galling to Rommel was that he had always been aware of the strenuous efforts being made by the British to master the supply problem. He wrote: 'Our . . . difficulties were in reality far easier to overcome than those which the British were facing, for they had to carry all their material over a 12,000-mile sea route round the Cape.'[59] Further difficulties for the enemy were caused by German submarine warfare, although no concentrated effort was made to disrupt the convoys, and no serious attention was given to the British supply ports by the Luftwaffe. The build-up of men and material for Montgomery's 8th Army before El Alamein particularly attracted Rommel's attention, and he noted: 'The peril of the hour moved the British to tremendous exertions, just as always in a moment of extreme danger things can be done which had previously been thought impossible.' And, as if in reference to future German action in Tunisia, he added: 'Mortal danger is an effective antidote for fixed ideas.'[60]

And so, in Rommel's words, 'Concerning the over-all strategic situation in the Mediterranean area, the OKW and OKH showed a passivity nothing short of irresponsible.'[61] Von Thoma in his report to Hitler in October 1940 had been correct: if a German force was to be sent to North Africa it had to be adequate for its task. If those units actually provided were to act merely as a 'stiffener' for the Italians in defence of Tripolitania, then indeed they would have been adequate, at least for some time; if, however, they were to be allowed, or even encouraged, to undertake offensive action with, as their aim, the Axis domination of the Near East, then clearly the three German divisions sent before August 1942 were grossly under-strength for the task. In that case it was the duty of Hitler and the Army High Command to ensure, by all the means at their disposal, that, at the very least, the few units under Rommel's command were kept adequately supplied with men and material. If this were impossible, then he should not have been allowed to undertake his offensive action; difficult subordinate though he was, a direct order by the Führer would have sufficed to stop him. Had he then disobeyed, dismissal would have solved the problem. Instead, however, a field commander was allowed to precipitate the Axis into taking the initiative in North Africa, at times even being encouraged to do so by the Führer. No order to halt ever came from the supreme leadership; but neither did the supplies nor reinforcements that might have allowed Rommel to achieve ultimate success. On the contrary, the inaction of the higher command ensured the material starvation and, at times, the complete exhaustion of the force it had allowed to take the offensive. Thus, it was his own high command that robbed a brilliant panzer leader of victory, and ensured the withering and the downfall of the armoured idea in the vast deserts of Africa, its most ideal setting.

23

North Africa – The Campaign

For the moment we're only step-children,
and must make the best of it.

FIELD-MARSHAL ERWIN ROMMEL
Commander, Panzer Army Africa,
29 September 1941

The history of Rommel's panzer army becomes not so much the record of brilliant advances and deft withdrawals, as much as the sad story of neglect and incompetence in the provision of supplies and reinforcements. The causes of Rommel's failure were outside his control, and lay in shortages of men, equipment, munitions, and petrol rather than in any weaknesses of his tactical or strategic thought. Victory was denied him not because he was out-generalled, or out-fought, but because his own superiors allowed his command to exhaust itself on the deserts of Egypt, Libya, and Tunisia.

At first, all went well; the German formations, small as they were, possessed an abundance of skill and determination. Although at the beginning of the offensive in April 1941, Rommel's fifty tanks were opposed by double that number, his machines were, on average, superior to those of the enemy. However, his small force of Germans and Italians proved quite inadequate to sustain an operation along the North African coast further than Sollum, especially when the port of Tobruk was stubbornly holding out in its rear, and a halt was ordered on 11 April, the twelfth day of the advance. In his diary for 23 April Halder wrote: '. . . the piecemeal thrusts of weak armoured forces have been costly. . . . His motor vehicles are in a poor condition and many of the tank engines need replacing. . . . Air transport cannot meet his senseless demands, primarily because of lack of fuel. . . . It is essential to have the situation cleared up without delay.'[1] The next day he noted: 'Telegraph to Rommel, spelling out to him that he cannot count on any help and so must shape his decisions accordingly.'[2] Thus very early on Rommel was forced to accept such physical restraints on his capability to mount an offensive, admitting on 2 May that 'we were not strong enough to mount the large-scale attack necessary to take the fortress [Tobruk]'.[3] He prepared for the inevitable enemy counter-attack, later recalling: 'Unfortunately our petrol stocks were badly depleted, and it was with some anxiety that we contemplated the coming British attack, for we knew that our moves would be decided more by the petrol gauge than by tactical requirements.'[4] Furthermore, by that time the British tanks outnumbered the German by roughly four to one, while the Italians had none in Africa to contribute to Rommel's defence. In mid-June the British under General Wavell struck, but were outmanoeuvred by Rommel. He remembered: 'The battle made a great impression on our superior commands. . . . the Italian High Command realised the necessity of considerably reinforcing the Axis forces in North Africa. The German element was to be brought up to four mechanised divisions and the Italian to an armoured corps of three divisions, with a further two to three motorised divisions. Their zeal, unfortunately, did not last long.' Rommel went on to write: 'If these reinforcements had in fact come to Africa in the autumn of 1941, with their supplies guaranteed, we could have beaten off the British winter offensive in the Marmarica. . . . We would have been strong enough to destroy the British in Egypt in the spring of 1942. . . .'[5]

Rommel was not to be strong enough; although he was preparing for a November advance, his battle-strength remained low. Between September and October, for example, there was a drop in deliveries of fifty per cent in supplies and armament, and seventy-five per cent in vehicles. Against the British 'Crusader' offensive, which began in November, Rommel could field only 249 German tanks, of which five were PzKw Is and seventy PzKw IIs, supported by 146 inferior Italian models, to face 738 British machines (including those within Tobruk). Moreover, whereas the enemy possessed a further 500 tanks in reserve or in transit, Rommel had none. His only advantage lay in his anti-tank guns, two-thirds of which were of the new 5cm variety and considerably superior to the British 2-pounders. Nevertheless, in spite of his numerical inferiority, Rommel managed to stay the enemy offensive, beating it simply by superior manoeuvre. Tactically, the Germans had won; strategically, victory belonged to the British, for in the end it was to be their reserves that decided the outcome. On 7 December, having been notified that reinforcements would not arrive until the following year, Rommel decided to withdraw from the battle. A new British attack opened the next day. Bayerlein wrote: 'In view of the great numerical superiority of the enemy and the condition of our own troops, Rommel now decided to give up Tobruk completely and beat a fighting retreat to the Gazala position. It was a painful decision to have to take . . . but to have stayed any longer . . . would merely have led to the steady attrition of our already weakened forces.'[6] Fuel had almost run out; the Africa Corps had only forty-six tanks left, and, by the time the retreat had passed through Gazala and ended at Agedabia, this number had been almost halved. Rommel wrote to his wife on 22 December: 'Retreat to A[gedabia]. You cannot imagine what it's like. . . . Little ammunition and petrol, no air support. Quite the reverse with the enemy.' Their superiority in armour was now of the order of 7:1.

By the end of 1941 the position had become so bad that every arrival of a transport at Tripoli was regarded as a triumphant success. Of this period, which was marked by Rommel's well-conducted withdrawal, which surprisingly the enemy failed to exploit, Bayerlein remembered:

> 'There was one more major "victory" to record before the retreat was over – on 19 December a convoy from Italy arrived in Benghazi carrying two German panzer companies, a number of artillery batteries and supplies. These were the first ships carrying arms which had arrived since the beginning of the British offensive in mid-November. However, part of the convoy had been sunk during the crossing and two panzer companies and one battery lost.'[7]

It took only a few of these 'victories' for Rommel to decide to attack again. The beginning of 1942, as in 1941, was to be good for the panzer army. Supplies, though they were by no means abundant or even satisfactory, were at least adequate. Bayerlein described how little proved enough to suffice the hungry: 'On 5 January 1942 a convoy of ships carrying fifty-five tanks and twenty armoured cars, as well as anti-tank guns and supplies of all kinds, arrived safely in Tripoli. This was as good as victory in battle, and Rommel immediately began to think of the offensive again.'[8] On 21 January, much against the wishes of the Italians, he mounted his counter-stroke with some 110 tanks, and by the 28th he had pushed the enemy back over 100 miles to Gazala. There the front stabilised for a time; the race to build up supplies for the next offensive began.

At the end of these 'winter' battles, the Germans were in the unusual, but fortunate, position of continuing to increase their strength, and by the beginning of May Rommel was prepared to resume the attack. He wrote: 'Compared with what was to come . . . the balance of power was quite tolerable – even though only three German and three Italian divisions were fit to use in the offensive, while the remainder, due to their lack of mobility, had to remain almost entirely in the background. A further factor was that two weak Italian motorised divisions, due to their poor armament, could be used only under German protection.'[9] On 26 May, the day the Axis offensive was launched, Rommel possessed 332 German and 228 Italian tanks to face about 900 British machines. Only the nineteen up-gunned PzKw IIIs (nineteen more were on their way from Tripoli) possessed armament superior to the best of those of the enemy. PzKw IIs still numbered fifty in all, and there were only forty PzKw IVs. The Africa Corps, 90th Light, and XX motorised Italian Corps (two divisions) had between them only 10,000 vehicles. Some units had sixty trucks out of their official strength of 400. Moreover, manpower was low; the German formations were short of 12,000 men on establishment, 90th Light going into battle with an average of only fifty riflemen per company. The Italian motorised divisions had personnel complements which belonged more properly to a brigade, and the infantry divisions were little more than regiments. Nonetheless, Rommel believed that this was the time to strike; after May his enemy would be too strong.

The Gazala battles of May were considerable victories for Rommel; the enemy's armoured force was virtually destroyed and Tobruk was taken. The attack continued. By 30 June the panzer army had reached El Alamein, only sixty miles from Alexandria, and the end of the British presence in the Near East seemed imminent. However, that was not to be. Rommel sadly recorded: 'In winning our victory at Tobruk we . . . had expended the last of our strength.'[10] Only captured material ensured that the offensive could continue; in June eighty-five per cent of all German transport had formerly been used by the enemy, but it was not enough. By 25 June the Africa Corps was down to fifty tanks, and the XX Corps to only fourteen; on 5 July the Germans possessed barely thirty ready for action. Rommel later wrote: 'After three days vainly assaulting the Alamein line, I decided that I would call the offensive off for the moment, after the next day's attack. Reasons for my decision were the steadily mounting strength of the enemy, the low fighting strength of my own divisions, which amounted by that time to no more than 1,200 and 1,500 men, and above all the terribly strained supply situation.'[11] Keitel later commented: 'One of the biggest occasions we passed by was El Alamein. I would say that, at that climax of the war, we were nearer to victory than any time before or after. Very little then was needed to conquer Alexandria and to push forward to Suez and Palestine.'[12]

In the lull that followed, Rommel strove desperately to build up his forces. But on 8 July, as he was about to attempt one more thrust, the Africa Corps and 90th Light together possessed only fifty tanks and fifty anti-tank guns, whereas their nominal strength was 371 tanks and 466 anti-tank guns. The infantry strength was also extremely low; each panzer division had only one rifle regiment of 300 men, while 90th Light had four regiments amounting in all to 1,500 men. The German element of the panzer army was down to a total of only 2,100 infantrymen. Indeed, in a report to OKH on 21 July Rommel estimated that the Germans were down to thirty per cent of their effective strength. The strength of the Italians was similarly depleted, their two armoured and one motorised divisions possessing only fifty-four tanks, forty anti-tank guns, and 1,600 men. No wonder Rommel could remember that his formations 'no longer merited the title of divisions'. Facing them, the enemy had some 200 tanks. Forestalling the German attack, the British advanced on the 9th but achieved little, as did Rommel's counter-thrust. Both sides were exhausted, and Rommel was now reluctantly forced to the conclusion that 'There could be no question of launching any large-scale attack in the immediate future'.[13] Writing to his wife on 17 July, he revealed that his despondency had reached a low level: 'Things are going downright badly for me at the moment, at any rate in the military sense. The enemy is using his superiority, especially in infantry, to destroy the Italian formations one by one, and the German formations are much too weak to stand alone. It's enough to make one weep.'[14] He later recalled that 'Our forces were now so small in comparison with the steadily growing strength of the British that we were going to have to count ourselves lucky if we managed to go on holding our line at all.'[15]

'So ended', in Rommel's words, 'the great campaign of the summer. It had begun with a considerable victory. But, after the capture of Tobruk, the immense strength of the British Empire had begun to tell again.'[16] However, the panzer army in Africa, exhausted though it was, prepared itself for one last attempt to push on to the Suez Canal. August was the crucial month; it was, again, to be a race against time. If the Germans could build up their battle strength to an acceptable level, victory might yet belong to them. But at this time the German supply lines were undergoing constant attack from the RAF; no ship bringing material up to Tobruk, Bardia, or Marsa Matruh was safe from harassment. As Rommel remembered:

> 'During the early part of August the supplies we received barely covered our daily requirements. [He later stated that all the supplies brought across the Mediterranean between 1 and 20 August were sufficient for only half the consumption of the German component of the panzer army.] Replenishment was hardly to be thought of, and a build-up out of the question. The situation of vehicles was particularly worrying; the bad state of the roads and the continual heavy demands we were having to make on our transport were resulting in a steady thirty-five per cent of our vehicle strength being in for repair. As some eighty-five per cent or so of our transport still consisted of vehicles of British or American manufacture, for which we had no great stocks of spares, it is easy to imagine the difficulties our repair shops were having to contend with. The units of the 164th Division and Italian Folgore Parachute Division which were just then arriving possessed no vehicles of their own and were thus becoming a load on the transport columns of other formations.'[17]

In addition, the state in which Rommel's men found themselves was equally deplorable, 19,000 of the Germans having been in Africa since March 1941, and all of them suffering severely from the effects of the climate and from battle fatigue. The four German divisions, which with their supporting units amounted to 90,000 men and 12,600 vehicles, were short of 17,000 soldiers, General Bayerlein estimating that the German fighting strength at that time was only 34,000 men.

At the end of August, during which month the panzer army had been able to exist only because of the large British supply dumps in Marmarica and western Egypt that had fallen into its hands, Rommel had managed to increase his force to 203 German gun-armed tanks (the majority of which had come from the repair shops) and 243 Italian machines, half of which were worn out, to face 700 of the British. Qualitative superiority lay only with the seventy-four PzKw IIIs with long 5cm guns and the twenty-seven PzKw IVs with the long 7.5cm guns. Furthermore, the Germans were deficient of at least 1,600 trucks, more than eighty-five per cent of their existing vehicles having been captured from the enemy and thirty per cent standing in need of repair. Ammunition, too, was desperately short, as was petrol, enough being available for an advance of only eighty miles. It was known that early in September the British expected a 100,000 tons convoy to arrive at Suez, laden with the latest weapons of war with which to begin an offensive; time, therefore, was of the essence. Yet Rommel consistently had to postpone the attack because of the acute lack of petrol and the failure of the authorities at home to send the amounts required. By the end of August sufficient had still not arrived, and in the last few days of that month four more tankers were sent to the bottom of the sea. By now, no further delay could be countenanced; the moon, so indispensable to the plan of attack, was on the wane. To postpone the offensive for a month would have meant the end of German hopes. Therefore, Rommel gave the order to advance, and at the same time he notified OKH that shortages in fuel and ammunition would severely restrict the scope of his operations. On the night of 30–31 August, the Axis troops set out on their last attempt.

The second battle of El Alamein, commonly known as the battle of Alam Halfa, was, perhaps inevitably, a failure for Rommel. By the evening of 1 September the whole panzer army had only one issue of petrol left, enough for sixty-two and a half miles over fairly easy terrain; by the evening of the following day Rommel had decided to call off the attack and retire to a better defensive position, a movement which had been completed by the 6th. He later wrote: 'After three days vainly assaulting the Alamein line, I decided that I would call the offensive off for the moment after the next day's attack. Reasons for my decision were the steadily mounting strength of the enemy, the low fighting strength of my own divisions, which amounted by that time to no more than 1,200 to 1,500 men, and, above all, the terribly strained supply situation.'[18] Thus ended the battle nicknamed by the defeated troops the 'Six-day race'. It was Rommel's last chance of gaining Suez. He wrote: 'We could now expect that the full production of British industry and, more important, the enormous industrial potential of America, which, consequent on our declaration of war, was now fully harnessed to the enemy cause, would finally turn the tide against us.'[19]

During, and after, the battle of Alam Halfa, there developed apace two further factors in the desert war: enemy air power and qualitative superiority. The Luftwaffe had lost the battle of numbers with the RAF, who took undisputed possession of the air. Now, it was not just the supply lines that were disrupted; the manoeuvres of field units were subject to ever-growing interference. According to the German estimate, the RAF had dropped no less than 1,300 tons of high explosive on the battle area over the six days, far greater than anything that had been experienced previously. Between 30 August and 4 September the panzer army was bombed twenty-four hours a day, every day; a total of 9,200 bombs fell on its formations, for the loss of 110 soldiers killed and 305 wounded, 170 vehicles (including one tank) destroyed and 270 (including two tanks) damaged. According to Rommel this 'had pinned my army to the ground and rendered any smooth deployment or any advance by time schedule completely impossible'.[20] It had had a 'paralysing effect' on the motorised forces, rendering useless the tenets of the armoured idea. Speed, manoeuvre, and concentration to offset numerical inferiority, upon which the panzer force had relied for so long, were now severely limited, and only a 'balance of power in the air would have made the old rules of warfare valid again . . . with certain tactical restrictions'. Thus Rommel was brought forcefully to the conclusion that 'Anyone who has to fight, even with the most modern weapons, against an enemy in complete command of the air, fights like a savage against modern European troops, under the same handicaps and with the same chances of success. . . . In every battle to come, the strength of the Anglo-American air force was to be the deciding factor.'[21]

Loss of control of the air came at a time when the Germans also lost their qualitative superiority in tanks. Of the importance of this superiority, Bayerlein wrote:

> '. . . the extent of either a victory or a defeat can be measured by the numbers of tanks destroyed. But it is not only the quantity of tanks which matters, even more important is their technical performance, manoeuvrability and the range and calibre of tank guns. For the main thing in the open desert is to bring the enemy under effective fire and start hitting him before he is in a position to hit back. What matters is to be further away from the enemy than he is from you.'[22]

Until the beginning of the summer of 1942 the German machines had possessed that superiority over their opponents; although the Africa Corps had within it a certain number of obsolete PzKw IIs, it began the African venture with a high proportion of PzKw IIIs, all armed with the 5cm gun, and PzKw IVs. Both tanks had been given extra frontal armour, although, on their first arrival, not all machines were so equipped. In destructive power, protection, and mobility they outclassed their opponents, the only exception being the armour on the Matilda tank. However, by May 1942 matters were different. Although some PzKw IIIs and IVs had been better armed and armoured, being provided with longer versions of the 5cm and 7.5cm guns respectively, their numbers were insufficient to have any great impact on the Gazala battles. More important, the British by then possessed quantities of the new Grant tank, armed with a 75mm gun corresponding to the German short 7.5cm, and a 37mm anti-tank gun. Rommel wrote:

> 'Up to May of 1942 our tanks had in general been superior in quality to the corresponding British types. This was now no longer true, at least not to the same extent. The American-built Grant tank, which appeared for the first time in the summer battles, undoubtedly had a match in our long-barrelled Panzer IV, but only four of these latter were on African soil during our [Gazala] offensive. There was, in any case, no ammunition for them, so that they were in fact unable to take any part.'[23]

The qualitative balance turned ever more against the Germans as time went on. Although the PzKw III and IV 'Specials' at Alam Halfa were in greater proportions than before, seventy-three and twenty-seven respectively out of totals of 166 PzKw IIIs and thirty-seven PzKw IVs, the British were by then being equipped with the Churchill tank (the Mark III armed with an effective 6-pounder) and the Sherman, a well-protected, well-armed machine with a 75mm gun. Unquestioned qualitative superiority was regained by the Germans only with the introduction of the Tiger tank armed with the formidable 8.8cm gun at the very end of 1942; it came too late and in too few numbers to have any effect. However, in anti-tank guns the Germans maintained a distinct superiority with their 5cm Pak until December 1942, when the British 17-pounder arrived. Some sort of parity was maintained by the introduction of the new 7.5cm Pak, and until the end the famous 8.8cm dual-purpose anti-aircraft/anti-tank gun was to wreak havoc among the enemy.

As in the air, so on the ground; the initiative had passed to the enemy. The brilliant German armoured tactics, which till then had brought them so much success, were over. Whereas before Alam Halfa, Rommel in defence, as in attack, had always relied on mobility and freedom of manoeuvre in the open spaces of the desert, he was now forced to order his troops to dig in behind a barrier of half a million mines, with their left flank resting safely on the Mediterranean and their right protected by the Qattara Depression, a vast area of burnt desert, impenetrable by a modern army. Outflanking manoeuvres and descents on their rear were thus rendered impossible, and a frontal assault was the only course left open to the enemy. Further factors served to reinforce the static nature of the German defence, described by Rommel thus:

> 'The relative strengths in motorised divisions had become too unequal; while our opponents were receiving a steady flow of motorised reinforcements, we received only non-motorised, which were as good as useless in the open desert. Consequently we were forced to choose a form of warfare in which they, too, could play their part. The British air superiority . . . created severe limitations on the tactical use of motorised forces. . . . We were permanently short of petrol. I did not want to get myself into the awkward situation of having to break off a battle because we were out of petrol. In a mobile defensive action, shortage of petrol spells disaster. For all these reasons, we now had to try to base our defence on a fortified and infantry-held line.'[24]

The armoured idea was now but a desert memory. This was exemplified by the disposition of the four Axis armoured divisions: grouped in two pairs in two separate areas, they were divided into battle-groups capable of acting independently of each other. This dissipation of strength, ordered by, of all people, Rommel, was necessitated by the limited tank strength of the panzer army in comparison with that of its enemy, and by the acute lack of petrol, both of which reasons made it imperative to avoid a major armoured battle of manoeuvre. The battle-groups were designed merely to plug the gaps should enemy penetrate the infantry defence line. The Germans could not risk fighting as they had done before.

The final, and most famous, battle of El Alamein began on 23 October. For the Axis it was a 'battle without hope'. There had never been any chance that they would manage to build up sufficient strength at a rate equal to, or greater than, their enemy, and despite repeated requests, few supplies came through to the panzer army. Frustration was intense. After he had been handed his Field-Marshal's baton by a grateful Führer, Rommel remarked to his wife: 'I would rather he had given me one more division.'[25] The panzer army possessed fewer than 104,000 men, of whom only 50,000 were German, 496 tanks, 290 of which were Italian and 33 PzKw IIs, 500 guns, and 850 anti-tank guns. The actual battle strength of the German force was even lower: only 24,173 were fighting soldiers. Individual units were extremely weak – 15th Panzer, for example, had only 3,840 men – and more than one-third of all vehicles were undergoing repair. Against such a force, Montgomery, the new British commander, could field 195,000 men and 1,029 gun-armed tanks (with another 1,000 in workshops), 908 guns, and 1,451 anti-tank guns. Moreover, the enemy troops were well-fed and cared for, whereas those of the Axis were undernourished and easily susceptible to sickness. But most damaging to Rommel's prospects was the fact that at the opening of the battle there were just seven issues of petrol remaining in Africa, and only three issues with the panzer army – enough for a movement of 180 miles per vehicle. When it is realised that the minimum amount regarded as essential for effective operations was thirty issues, Rommel's dismay becomes understandable. The result was, he recorded, that 'We would be completely prevented from taking the correct tactical decisions and would thus suffer a tremendous limitation in our freedom of action. I was bitterly angry. . . .'[26] By the 26th the supply situation was:

> 'approaching disaster. . . . There was only enough petrol left to keep supply traffic going between Tripoli and the front for another two or three days, and that without counting the needs of the motorised forces, which had to be met out of the same stocks. What we should really have done now was to assemble all our motorised units in the north in order to fling the British back to the main defence line in a concentrated and planned counter-attack. But we had not the petrol to do it. . . . I reported to the Führer's H.Q. that we would lose the battle unless there was an immediate improvement in the supplies. . . .'[27]

In the battle the strength of the panzer army began to diminish fast. By the fourth day, the 26th, the number of German tanks had fallen from 206 to 137, and by the following day to 114. Reinforcements and supplies were not, of course, reaching Rommel. By 2 November, the eleventh day of the battle, the supply shortage was 'absolutely desperate'.[28] In that one day alone the panzer army had fired off 450 tons of ammunition, and received only 190 tons to replenish stocks. By the evening the Germans had thirty-two tanks left, and the Italians 120, to face more than 800 of the enemy. In a letter to his wife, Rommel wrote: 'Very heavy fighting again, not going well for us. The enemy, with his superior strength, is slowly levering us out of our position. That will mean the end. You can imagine how I feel. Air raid after air raid after air raid!'[29] At this point, Rommel decided to withdraw to take up a new defensive position at Fuka, some sixty miles to the rear, and signalled to Germany accordingly.

Now came one final event which, although it was to make no difference to the failure of the panzer army, was to bring about its physical exhaustion: Hitler's intervention. At 1.30p.m. on 3 November Rommel received a message from his Führer:

> 'The German people join with me in following, with full confidence in your leadership and in the bravery of the German and Italian troops under your command, the heroic defence in Egypt. In your present situation nothing else can be thought of but to hold on, not to yield a step, and to throw every weapon and every fighting man who can still be freed into the battle. Strong air reinforcements will be sent to the Supreme Commander South in the next few days, and the Duce and Commando Supremo will do their utmost to provide you with the means to carry on the struggle. Despite his superiority the enemy must also have exhausted his strength. It would not be the first time in history that the stronger will has triumphed over the enemy's strong battalions. You can show your troops no other road than to victory or death.'[30]

Rommel was stunned. He later acknowledged that 'for the first time during the African campaign I did not know what to do'.[31]

Although Hitler's interference in operational matters had long become standard practice in Europe, this was the first time he had ever taken charge of events in North Africa. The German soldiers there now lost their freedom of action as surely as had their comrades on the Russian front. Rommel recorded that:

> 'A kind of apathy took hold of us as we issued orders for all existing positions to be held on instructions from the highest authority. I forced myself to this action, as I had always demanded unconditional obedience from others and, consequently, wished to apply the same principle to myself. Had I known what was to come I should have acted differently, because from that time on, we had continually to circumvent orders from the Führer or Duce in order to save the army from destruction.'[32]

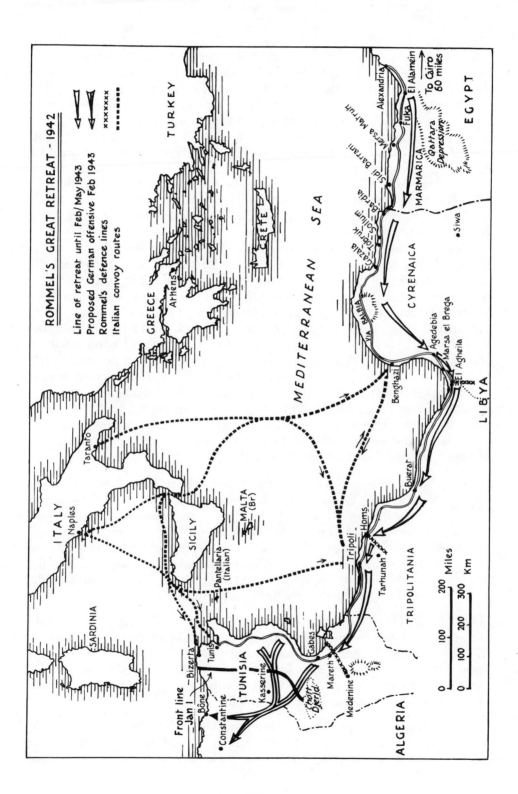

ROMMEL'S GREAT RETREAT - 1942

Line of retreat until Feb/May 1943
Proposed German offensive Feb 1943
Rommel's defence lines
Italian convoy routes

TURKEY

GREECE

Athens

CRETE

MEDITERRANEAN SEA

ITALY

Naples

Taranto

SARDINIA

SICILY

MALTA (Br)

Pantellaria (Italian)

Bizerta

Tunis

Bône

Constantine

ALGERIA

TUNISIA

Kasserine

Shott Djerid

Medenine

Mareth

Gabes

Front line
Jan 1

TRIPOLITANIA

Tarhunah

Tripoli

Homs

Buerat

Benghazi

Agedabia

Marsa el Brega

El Agheila

LIBYA

VIA BALBIA

CYRENAICA

Agedabia

Siwa

Tobruk

Sollum

Bardia

Sidi Barrani

Mersa Matruh

MARMARICA

Fuka

El Alamein

To Cairo
60 miles

Alexandria

Qattara Depression

EGYPT

0   100   200 Miles
0   100   200   300 Km

The movements which had already been begun towards the west were halted, and the troops, inspired by their Führer's order, prepared to sacrifice themselves in a final, desperate effort. Rommel then sent a signal to Hitler, which included the passage: 'All the available German forces have already been thrown in. Up to now German losses in infantry, anti-tank men, and engineers amount to about fifty per cent, in artillery about forty per cent. Twenty-four tanks are at present available to the German Africa Corps. Of XX Corps, the Littorio and Trieste divisions have been practically wiped out. . . . Every last effort will continue to be made to hold the battlefield.'[33] That evening Rommel sent an officer to Germany to report his view that if the Führer's order were upheld, the total destruction of the panzer army would be only a matter of days.

On 4 November was witnessed the most disturbing deterioration of the near-static panzer army; by the early afternoon its front had been decisively broken and the enemy armour was moving into its rear. There were now no reserves with which to counter the enemy. Only twelve tanks remained fit for action. The commander of the Africa Corps, von Thoma, was captured by the British while attempting a vain counter-attack. At 11.15a.m. Rommel signalled to Hitler: '. . . our losses are so high that there is no longer a connected front. . . . We cannot expect any new German forces . . . the Italian troops have no more fighting value. . . .'[34] He concluded by asking permission to withdraw to the Fuka position. Before receiving Hitler's reply, Rommel ordered the move west at 3.30p.m., attempting to save from extinction what little was left of the motorised part of the panzer army; it was not until the next morning that the Führer's approval for the move came through. Of this, Rommel remembered:

> 'The authorisation for the retreat, which had now arrived [5 November] – far too late – from the Führer and Duce, charged us with the duty of extricating all German and Italian troops, especially the non-motorised units. We could do nothing but shrug our shoulders, for extricating the infantry was precisely what the original order had prevented us from doing. Moreover, had we waited for the authorisation, we would have lost not only the infantry but also the armoured and motorised divisions.'[35]

The delay had been fatal. His obedience to the 'victory or death' order of the 3rd was regarded by Rommel as his one mistake of the battle. Had he circumvented it, he believed that his army 'would in all probability have been saved, with all its infantry, in at least a semi-battle worthy condition'.[36] As it was, Panzer Army Africa was materially exhausted. Of its strength on the evening of the 5th, Rommel recorded:

> 'Our fighting power was very low. The bulk of the Italian infantry had been lost. . . . As for the XX Italian Motorised Corps, it had been practically wiped out on 4 November. . . . The only forces

which retained any fighting strength were the remnants of the 90th Light Division, the Africa Corps' two divisions – now reduced to the strength of small combat groups – the Panzergrenadier Regiment Africa, and a few quickly scratched together German units, the remains of the 164th Light Division. Tanks, heavy Flak guns, heavy and light artillery, all had sustained such frightful losses at El Alamein that there was nothing but a few remnants left.'[37]

By 9 November the panzer army had a fighting strength of 2,500 Italians and 5,000 Germans, equipped with thirty-five German and a few Italian anti-tank guns, sixty-five German field guns and a small number of Italian types, and eleven German and ten Italian tanks. Some 10,000 other German troops and a greater number of Italians were without any equipment, and 35,000 Axis soldiers had been either killed or captured at El Alamein.

Hitler's interference on 4 November boded ill for the future. During the long and agonising retreat Rommel was never allowed the operational freedom he so desperately required, and the movement of the panzer army was determined largely by the Commando Supremo and Führer Headquarters. Retreat, as Rommel knew but Hitler was unable to comprehend, is not an unmitigated disaster for an army; if a general is able to keep the fighting power of his force intact and receive adequate supplies, he can seize on any of a number of favourable tactical opportunities with which he will inevitably be presented. As the enemy advances, his problems mount: his supply-line lengthens, and his fighting strength diminishes. The retreating army, on the other hand, contracts its supply route and concentrates its force, so that, in Rommel's words, 'the moment must eventually come when the retreating force is locally superior to its enemy. If at that moment it has access to an adequate supply of petrol and ammunition, it has a wonderful opportunity. It can turn and strike at the advancing enemy force, and destroy it. . . .'[38] Thus, when it became clear to Rommel that he had lost the battle of El Alamein, he by no means believed, to paraphrase Sir Winston Churchill, that this was the beginning of the end. Had he withdrawn from the battle before the destruction of his motorised units (units that were vital to cover the retreat of the infantry), had he been able to build up his supplies, especially petrol, and had he been allowed to retreat as far as he thought necessary before turning on his assailant, then the story of the North African campaign might well have been different. But the Italian and German High Commands ensured that this was not to be so. Rommel's motorised force was destroyed at El Alamein; throughout the retreat, his supply problems remained acute; and at no time was he allowed to determine the pace, or the distance, of his withdrawal. Ironically, apart from the outstanding endurance and fighting qualities of the troops, the greatest advantage possessed by the panzer army lay not in any strength of its own, but in the weaknesses of the enemy, or, to be more precise, in Montgomery's excessive caution. Of this Rommel recorded: 'Montgomery had an absolute mania for always bringing up adequate reserves behind his back and risking as little as possible. The speed of reaction of the British command was comparatively slow.'[39] Added to this, the advance of 8th Army was slowed down after the first few weeks because of heavy rains. Only twice, at Buerat and Tripoli, was Montgomery to show the energy required to encircle Rommel's force, but both times and with great effort, the 'Desert Fox' managed to elude destruction. Thus, it might be argued, it was the Axis military leaders who lost North Africa, not Montgomery who won it.

Hitler's attitude towards the fighting in the desert was typical of his whole ill-advised interference in military matters. Far from the realities of battle, and surrounded by men often unsympathetic to Rommel, the Führer proved incapable of understanding the plight of the panzer army. The atmosphere in the Führer headquarters was far from conducive to any comprehension of reality. Even after the war, Kesselring was unable to recognise the extent to which supplies dominated the North African campaign. Of the battle of Alam Halfa he wrote:

> 'Despite my assurance that I would put 500 cubic metres of high-grade aviation petrol at the disposal of the Army, the petrol problem remained acute; the more so as even this quantity was, for reasons incomprehensible to me, never delivered. I accept the responsibility for this – although I knew nothing of it till after the war – but I cannot grant that this omission was decisively important. The fact that all our motorised forces were engaged in more or less mobile defensive operations until 6 September, relying on the supplies which were still available at that time, is sufficient proof that there would have been petrol enough for the continuation of the offensive, especially as it may reasonably be assumed that, as in previous cases, stocks would have been replenished by captured stores. The defeat may be attributed to causes of a more psychological nature. I had at the time the conviction that this battle would have presented no problem to the "old" Rommel. Had he not been suffering in health from the long strain of uninterrupted campaigning in Africa, he would never have pulled out when he had already completely encircled the enemy – the British "Last Hope" position, as it was called, had already been outmanoeuvred. I know today that his troops were unable to understand the order to retire.'[40]

After the battle, in the period before the enemy attack, Kesselring fully believed that 'The Axis forces were kept fed, equipped, and reinforced to the limit of their requirements. . . .'[41] No wonder that Rommel could write bitterly:

> 'We had lost the decisive battle of the African campaign. . . . The astonishing thing was that the authorities, both German and Italian, looked for the fault not in the failure of supplies, not in our air

inferiority, not in the order to conquer or die at Alamein, but in the command and troops. . . . Our old ill-wishers particularly – men who had always resented our success – drew from our defeat the courage to vilify us, where previously they had had to keep silent.'[42]

Certain instances reveal Hitler's ill-formed, highly emotive views concerning events in North Africa. During the last stages of El Alamein, Rommel had sent his aide, Lieutenant Berndt, who in civilian life was a senior Party official and a member of the Propaganda Ministry, to explain the seriousness of the situation caused by the Führer's victory or death order. Of this meeting, Warlimont noted that Hitler:

> '. . . refused to recognise that the battle in the North African desert was now governed by the availability of equipment and that with American aid on one side and the catastrophic sea transport situation on the other, the Axis powers had not the smallest possibility of keeping level. The last despairing efforts of Hitler's "leadership" were to move a few heavy tanks to Italian harbours and then make the most frequent use of the words "forthwith" and "super-urgent movement"; but this could not affect the situation.'[43]

Rather more than a month later, during a conference on 12 December 1942, Hitler revealed his remarkable ignorance of military matters in general, and of conditions in North Africa in particular, when he replied to Jodl's assertion that Rommel was prevented from conducting mobile or offensive operations because of an acute fuel shortage:

> 'I must say he has an enormous army and it seems to have had enough fuel to get back here from the Alamein position. They didn't do that on water. The whole time they've apparently had practically no fuel. If they'd brought the fuel up instead of going back themselves they could have operated up front. No doubt about that. It would have been simpler to operate up front merely with a couple of divisions. After all, all that's necessary are the tanks and a little artillery. They've gone back a thousand miles taking with them household stuff and everything else they could lay their hands on. . . . But really I think one shouldn't leave a man too long in a position of such heavy responsibility. Gradually he loses his nerve. It's different if one's in the rear. There, of course, one keeps one's head.'

Jodl, however, stood by the field commander [as, despite Rommel's assertion, did a majority in OKW, who realised that the position was hopeless], pointing out to the Supreme Commander: 'I don't think you can argue much about what he's done. He's like someone who's been living on a diet of milk and bread and is then asked to take part in the Olympic Games. He hasn't had any supplies for weeks. In the east they scream if they're two trains short. His intention is to go back step by step in order to gain time for the construction of the position here; in view of the fuel situation he can't do anything else.'[44]

At this time, Warlimont asserted, Hitler was even toying with the idea of complete evacuation from North Africa, but he added: 'Nevertheless, no precautionary action was taken in North Africa to avert the impending disaster.'[45] The utter bankruptcy of the Führer's thinking on the campaign is revealed by an entry in the OKW Operations Staff war diary of 7 December 1942, which read: 'Just now the Führer considers it a positive advantage that for the moment Rommel's army has insufficient fuel to enable it to withdraw further.'[46] A few days later the Supreme Commander laid before von Arnim his vision of the future in North Africa, a vision which saw the Allies being hurled back into the sea from whence they came, and he quoted Göring's bland assurance that it was only a short hop to Tunis by aeroplane, and that in future the supply lines across the Mediterranean would be secure. Warlimont noted sourly: 'This being the atmosphere and climate of opinion at the top, it is hardly to be wondered at that Supreme Headquarters scarcely noticed, let alone made use of, the fact that an opportunity now existed to avert almost certain catastrophe in North Africa by timely withdrawal.'[47]

Hitler's 'victory or death' order had been fatal to the panzer army; it provided the *coup de grâce*, and it turned a planned, orderly withdrawal into a headlong retreat past the Fuka position, past Marsa Matruh, Sidi Barrani, Marsa el Brega, Buerat, Tripoli, across the Libyan border into Tunisia, back 1,400 miles in three months to the Mareth line. Rommel angrily remembered: 'On orders from the Führer and Duce, we were compelled to go on doing battle with the British on 3 and 4 November. And these two days decided our future fate, for they cost us very nearly 200 tanks – almost all our remaining armour – and a large part of the Italian formations. They robbed us of all chance of engaging in mobile warfare during the retreat, for the army was now so shattered that there was nothing for it but continued withdrawal.'[48] As a result, the great retreat from 5 November 1942 to 15 February 1943, on which date Rommel's rearguard finally gained the transient safety of the Mareth line, was a great ordeal for the panzer army. Undoubtedly, the troops performed magnificently. As General Westphal wrote, the retreating force:

> '. . . was restricted to a single road, attacked from the air by day and night, insufficiently motorised, and frequently short of essential petrol, so that it often happened that, simply through lack of fuel, opportunities favourable for minor counter-attacks could not be exploited. Living as it was from hand to mouth in all things, it is astonishing that the panzer army was able to carry out the great withdrawal movement over almost fifteen hundred kilometres without internal or external disintegration.'[49]

For Rommel it was an agonising experience. On 8 November, when he learnt that an Anglo-American task force had landed in Tunisia, all hopes for the future ended. It was a severe psychological blow. 'This', he realised, 'spelt the end of the army in Africa.'[50]

Although Rommel succeeded in eluding Montgomery's clumsy clutches, the condition of his force during the retreat improved only slightly. On 6 November he wrote: Conditions on the road were indescribable. Columns in complete disorder – partly of German, partly of Italian vehicles – choked the road between the minefields. Rarely was there any movement forward, and then everything soon jammed up again. Many vehicles were on tow and there was an acute shortage of petrol, for the retreat had considerably increased consumption.'[51] Petrol remained scarce, and restricted the panzer army to an average rate of withdrawal of only six to seven miles a day. Rommel's memoirs are full of references to this:

> 'Next day [14 November] we were faced with a grave petrol crisis, when the Luftwaffe flew across only sixty tons instead of our full day's demand of 250, which Kesselring had promised. . . . On 15 November the petrol crisis took an even more acute turn, when several petrol ships on the way to Benghazi were turned back, and a tanker left Benghazi with 100 tons of petrol still on board. Added to this, the Luftwaffe was still flying only very small quantities across. Lack of petrol prevented the Africa Corps from getting under way until midday, and by evening it was halted again without a drop in its tanks.'[52]

The potential that adequate supplies of motor fuel would have presented Rommel is shown by his remembrance of an action on 17 December: '. . . after a few tons of petrol had at long last arrived, a counter-attack was launched . . . and twenty British tanks were shot up in heavy fighting.'[53] The restrictions imposed on the panzer army's freedom of movement was, according to Rommel, 'particularly deplorable, as the enemy presented us repeatedly with excellent tactical opportunities for such a move. . . . The speed of reaction of the British command was comparatively slow. In the earlier stages of the retreat their outflanking column was too weak, and we could have attacked and destroyed it on several occasions if only we had had the petrol.'[54]

However, optimism about the future of Panzer Army Africa still remained in the higher commands. In Italy and in Germany, Rommel was regarded as an emotional pessimist 'cock-a-hoop in victory, but a prey to despair in defeat'.[55] As early as 13 November, and without reference to Rommel, Cavallero and Bastico had decided that the area Marsa el Brega-El Agheila should be held at all cost. Mussolini then delivered himself of the belief that no situation was serious unless the commander felt it to be so, a curious remark for any intelligent man to make, and on 22 November Hitler ordered that the position be held to the last. Rommel was in despair. He saw that it was impossible to hold the new defence line against any determined attack; the whole front covered 110 miles, a greater distance than at El Alamein, with only 30,000 mines to form a barrier, and with the open flank guarded by a single, unreliable Italian colonial battalion. The so-called 'strongpoints' were often as much as five miles apart, and not mutually supporting.

By mid-November, when the panzer army had reached the temporary and uneasy safety of the Marsa el Brega-El Agheila line, Rommel had become convinced of the hopelessness of his position. He had 5,000 men, less than one-third, of the German fighting troops he had possessed before El Alamein: 'The remains of the army represented in fighting strength approximately one weak division.'[56] In this connexion, the real and the nominal strengths of the African Corps are worth noting: instead of 371 tanks, it possessed thirty-five; instead of 100 armoured cars, sixteen; instead of 246 anti-tank guns, twelve; and instead of sixty field howitzers, twelve. The panzer army required 400 tons of supplies every day, but only fifty tons could be brought up to the front: 'We had neither supply dumps nor stocks, and lived, in the truest sense of the word, from hand to mouth.'[57] Only four issues of petrol were left in Africa. Some troops had gone for a week without bread. Writing bitterly, Rommel later expressed himself of the opinion that: 'The mismanagement, the operational blunders, the prejudices, the everlasting search for scapegoats, these were now to reach the acute stage. And the man who paid the price was the ordinary German and Italian soldier. . . . There was . . . only one course open to us – never to accept battle . . . [which was exactly what the Axis High Command was making inevitable].'[58] The only alternative to destruction that Rommel now envisaged was an immediate retreat to the Gabes line, followed by a complete evacuation to Europe. But this, no one would countenance. In Rommel's interview with Hitler on the evening of 28 November, when the Field-Marshal illustrated, in the blackest of terms, the condition of his force (10,000 men of which were without weapons), the Supreme Commander ended any hope of even a limited, strategic withdrawal by stating that his decision not to yield an inch in the winter of 1941–42 had saved the situation on the Eastern Front, and that the same would apply in North Africa. In ending the meeting, Hitler gave the expansive, but empty, assurance that he would do everything he could to get supplies to Rommel, and then promptly ensured that this would never be by placing Göring in charge of the operation. Of this appointment Rommel wrote:

'After leaving the Führer's H.Q. Göring and I travelled . . . to Rome. I was angry and resentful at the lack of understanding displayed by our highest command and their readiness to blame the troops at the front for their own mistakes. My anger redoubled when I was compelled to witness the antics of the *Reichsmarschall* in his special train. The situation did not seem to trouble him in the slightest. He plumed himself, beaming broadly at the primitive flattery heaped on him by the imbeciles from his own court, and talked of nothing but jewellery and pictures.'[59]

Despite the resistance to a withdrawal that came from the Axis military leaders, events were to force such a move. The long-awaited resumption of the offensive by the British came on the night of 11 December, by which time Rommel had already moved back his non-motorised units from Marsa el Brega. The next evening the mechanised forces, still hampered by lack of petrol, began their withdrawal, thus eluding what should have been a fatal outflanking move by Montgomery's force. Once again the retreat was on, with Rommel doing everything he could to avoid accepting battle with the immeasurably stronger 8th Army. Lack of petrol remained the greatest single problem, determining the speed and the quality of the retreat. Of ten large ships that set out for Tripoli, nine were sunk and the tenth carried not a drop of petrol. The only chance for Rommel's sadly depleted force was to reach the safety of the Gabes line, 120 miles west of the Tunisian border, a defensive position which covered a narrow twelve miles between the sea and a chain of lakes and marshes known as the Chott Djerid. It was to the Gabes line, secure from outflanking movements from the south, and which did not lend itself to motorised warfare, that Rommel had looked so longingly since the great retreat had begun, seeing its defence as the only prospect for saving the German and Italian forces. His plan was simple: a careful, but fast, retreat to Gabes, which would have been aided by the caution of the British commander, with the motorised forces acting as cover for the slower infantry. Once behind Gabes, the main weight of the fight would have been transferred to the non-motorised infantry, who then could have held the line for several months while Montgomery was assembling enough material to assure him of success in the assault. Meanwhile, the motorised force, refitted with whatever supplies arrived, would unite with 5th Panzer Army and strike against the Anglo-American forces on the wide-open western front in Tunisia, partially destroy it, and drive the remnants back to Algeria. This accomplished, a quick redeployment would enable the Axis forces to push Montgomery back to the east. By such methods, Rommel believed, he could so delay the inevitable Allied victory in North Africa that an evacuation of all the valuable, battle-tried troops to Europe would be possible. Thus, just as were the Germans at Dunkirk, the Allies would be robbed of the full fruits of victory.

However, such a daring, far-seeing plan, with, it must be said, all its attendant risks and the recognition of ultimate defeat in North Africa, never had the slightest hope of acceptance by either Germany's or Italy's leadership. Neither could accept the idea that failure was inevitable, that prestige and an empire had to be lost for the future good of the two countries. Added to this, there was the 'stand or die' mentality that had gripped Hitler's mind and stultified German strategic thinking, as had been revealed so disastrously at El Alamein. The order had come to resist to the end at Marsa el Brega, and, after a brief flirtation by Göring with Rommel's Gabes plan – he was dissuaded from it by Kesselring's arguing that the evacuation of Tripolitania would be disastrous for the Luftwaffe and ruin the strategic air situation in Tunisia – the further retreat to Gabes was ruled out of the question. Rommel commented:

> 'The fact that our higher authority had refused to think from the outset in terms of a final unavoidable evacuation of Tripolitania had cost us much time and material. Thus the entire work of fortifying the Buerat line had, in the end, been useless; likewise the fortifications at Tarhunah-Homs. If only the Italian infantry had gone straight back to the Gabes line and begun immediately with its construction, if only all these useless mines we had laid in Libya had been put down at Gabes, all this work and material could ultimately have been of very great value.'[60]

Even after the inevitable withdrawal from Marsa el Brega, Gabes was still rejected by the two High Commands, Mussolini sending a message on 19 December which read roughly: 'Resist to the uttermost, I repeat, resist to the uttermost with all troops of the German-Italian Army in the Buerat position.'[61] Inadequately fortified, and open to the ever-threatening southern flanking movement, it was a hopeless mission, which would have ended in the total destruction of Rommel's command. Furthermore, the Field-Marshal was becoming increasingly concerned at the possibility of the Anglo-American forces attacking Gabes from southern Tunisia and driving a wedge between his force and 5th Panzer Army, a fear made all the worse by the lack of information about the state of von Arnim's command. Furthermore, the supply problem remained as disastrous as ever; only 152 tons of petrol arrived each day to meet the daily need of 400 tons, with the result that ninety-five per cent of the petrol received was used either in withdrawing or in getting the fuel to the motorised formations. Hundreds of trucks remained stationary at the side of the road for want of fuel, while the enemy's Long-Range Desert Group skilfully disrupted the supply lines in the rear; and all the time the British and Commonwealth forces were bringing up thousands of tons of petrol and munitions for their forthcoming offensive. The panzer army was a spent force, with shortages of fifty per cent in personnel, eighty per cent in tanks and anti-tank guns, seventy per cent in guns, and forty per cent in lorries. On 28 December, Rommel wrote to his wife: 'Our fate is gradually working itself out. . . . What is to happen now lies in God's hands.'[62] The next day all his troops had withdrawn behind the Buerat line; the waiting for the forthcoming offensive began. On the 31st, in consequence of Rommel's strong arguments, Commando Supremo ordered that further retreat from Buerat would be allowed if the army were threatened by a powerful offensive. On 6 January, Cavallero announced that, because it was impossible to supply properly both the Tunisian and the Libyan theatres, it had been decided that, as Tunisia was of more importance to the Axis, Tripolitania should be evacuated. However, it was stipulated that the withdrawal to Mareth should not be quick but, instead, take about two months to achieve; in the meantime the enemy was to be kept at bay by a number of counter-attacks. Rommel was thus ordered to conduct a long-drawn-out, aggressive withdrawal, for which he simply had not the resources: still the Axis commands could not bring themselves to face the inevitable.

Fortunately for Rommel, while he was plagued by a stubborn and strategically insensitive High Command, he was at the same time faced by an over-cautious enemy who placed the build-up of men and material before the advantages of speed and surprise. Montgomery had the initiative, but he chose not to exploit it; instead, he granted the Germans yet another valuable reprieve. Once again the inadequate supply prevented Rommel from exploiting this pause: for example, between 1 and 8 January fifty tons of ammunition and 1,900 tons of petrol were used at the front, and only thirty tons and 800 tons respectively arrived to replace them. Worse still, the threat of the Anglo-American attack on Gabes became so acute that on 13 January Rommel was forced to detach 21st Panzer Division, minus its tanks and most of its artillery, to 5th Panzer Army. Two days later, on the morning of the 15th, Montgomery began his long-awaited attack on the Buerat position: 450 British tanks faced thirty-six German and fifty-seven obsolete Italian machines, while Rommel's artillery, numbering seventy-two German and ninety-eight Italian pieces, was outnumbered by Montgomery's 360. The panzer army held fuel for only 150 miles, rations for five days, and two-thirds of an issue of ammunition. That evening, Rommel ordered the withdrawal. Still the pressure mounted; the readings of the petrol gauges dropped. Rommel feared for his southern flank, and a continued retreat became necessary past the Tarhunah-Homs line and beyond. Tripoli, the capital of the Italian North African Empire, was entered by the 8th Army on 23 January, exactly three months after the battle of El Alamein had begun. In that time, Rommel had been forced to retreat 1,400 miles. Two days later the Field-Marshal wrote to his wife: 'I simply can't tell you how hard it is for me to undergo this retreat and all that goes with it. Day and night I'm tormented by the thought that things might go really wrong here in Africa. I'm so depressed that I can hardly do my work.'[63] The next day, the 26th, his headquarters moved across the frontier into Tunisia, and on 13 February the last of his soldiers left Libya. By this time the great retreat was almost over, and Rommel's German formations were left with half their establishment in troops, one-third in tanks, and one-quarter in anti-tank guns. Of the 130 tanks in the panzer army, only half were fit for action.

From the final crossing of the Tunisian border, it took but two days for the retreat to come to an end, when on 15 February the rearguard of the 15th Panzer Division crossed into the Mareth line, eighty miles within the Tunisian border. This was intended by the Commando Supremo to be the last point beyond which no further withdrawal would take place. The Mareth line, formed of old French frontier fortifications, left much to be desired, for, in Rommel's opinion, it was capable of being outflanked. Instead he urged, once more with no success, the further withdrawal into the Gabes line, which had a totally secure southern flank. Forty miles were all that separated them, but the Commando Supremo was not prepared to entertain the idea of a further loss of ground, however small. Thus, ultimately, the value of the Mareth line was to be rendered nought, and the only time German troops were to see Gabes was when they passed through it, in retreat.

Behind the Mareth line, however insecure, the Axis fortunes in North Africa temporarily took a turn for the better. The slow advance of the Anglo-American forces from Algeria had allowed 5th Panzer Army to consolidate and extend its bridgehead and by February 1943, although there was a critical shortage of artillery, it had proved possible to build up von Arnim's force to a strength of two panzer and three infantry divisions. At that time, with the union of 5th Panzer Army with the German-Italian panzer army in Tunisia, and with the advantage of interior lines of communication, the Axis forces felt themselves able to go over to the offensive once again. By mid-February there were 100,000 Axis fighting troops in Tunisia, 74,000 of whom were German, and 280 tanks. The aim of the proposed attack was to eliminate the threat to Tunisia from the Allied forces in Algeria by smashing their assembly areas, and then to turn on, and defeat, Montgomery in Libya. This was a modification of Rommel's original 'Gabes Plan'. The outcome was the battle of the Kasserine Pass, which aimed at dislocating the Anglo-American supply lines in Algeria, cutting off their forward troops, and piercing as far as the bases of Constantine and Bône. It was a daring strategy, fully consonant with the principles of the armoured idea. Recognising the risks, Rommel wrote: 'No doubt the operation we were planning would have been fraught with great dangers for us if the Anglo-American command had made its correct operational move and launched the mass of its force against our long flank. . . . But commanders whose battles have so far all been fought in theory tend as a rule to react directly rather than indirectly to the enemy's moves.'[64] Von Arnim was not prepared to accept the plan, and nor was the Commando Supremo. An important modification was made, one born of hesitation and caution, which forced Rommel to thrust not against the enemy's main command and communication centres, but to attack the immediate rear, closer to the front and nearer to the enemy's reserves. It was a move expected by the Allied generals, an example of the classic battle of encirclement. On 14 February, 156 German and 23 Italian tanks moved into the attack. Initially, much success was achieved, but failure was brought about because of the Commando Supremo's modification to the plan and the strength of the Allies. The battle ended on the 23rd with the Axis calling off the offensive and withdrawing behind the Kasserine Pass. Of the battle, Rommel later wrote:

'And so ended the battle of Sbeitla-Kasserine. It had begun with a great victory for the German armour over the "green" Americans, an advantage which should have been exploited by a thrust deep into enemy territory to collapse the whole of their Tunisian front. Unfortunately the orders which the Commando Supremo had sent us . . . took no account of this great aim, and the attack was directed into the reach of the Anglo-American reserves. The stubborn American defence of the Kasserine Pass and the delayed arrival of the 5th Army's forces [held back, in part, through von Arnim's rivalry] prevented us from making a surprise break-in to the enemy hinterland, and the enemy was thus given time to organise his defence in the rear and bring his reserves up to the critical spot.'[65]

Consequently, the last chance for a great German victory in North Africa came to nothing; the only difference from previous occasions was that this time the armoured idea was frustrated not so much by lack of supplies but by lack of daring.

However, the limited success gained at Kasserine had been something of a personal triumph for Rommel. Previously, his prestige had been on the wane, and his days in command numbered. Defeat, for whatever reason, is no friend of a military leader, and Rommel had had his fair share of reverses since El Alamein. By his acceptance of the need to yield up Tripoli without a firm fight, a defeat which had a shattering effect on the Italians, Rommel had laid himself open to the opprobrium of both Hitler and Mussolini. The Duce had insisted that the Tarhunah-Homs line be held for at least three weeks (something Rommel would have been prepared to attempt had he been given enough supplies), and on the 20th, the day after the German and Italian troops had moved back through that position, Rommel received a 'severe rebuke'[66] from Marshal Cavallero, which, inspired by Mussolini, expressed displeasure at the Field-Marshal's actions. Six days later, on the 24th, he was informed by the Commando Supremo that, once he had shepherded the panzer army into the Mareth line, eighty miles inside Tunisia, he was to be relieved of command 'for reasons of health', and replaced by an Italian, General Messe, a former leader of the Italian Expeditionary Corps in Russia. The actual date of the handover was to be left to Rommel himself. In one sense this came as a relief to him; he wrote on 28 January that he 'had little desire to go on any longer playing the scapegoat for a pack of incompetents'.[67] However, the arrival of Messe caused him to change his mind, for he perceived in this general a dangerous over-optimism, and he decided not to relinquish command of his troops until he could secure their position for some time to come. On 7 February he wrote to his wife: 'My whole being cries out against leaving the battlefield so long as I can stand on my feet.'[68] Furthermore, General Messe displayed no great eagerness to take control of the panzer army. In such a situation Rommel decided not to yield command until specifically ordered to do so. That the orders would not have been long in arriving cannot be doubted, but before they were sent the Axis forces had undertaken the Kasserine operation. The results of that offensive, limited though they were, proved to be sufficient to raise Rommel's status and to cause Ambrosio, the new Italian Chief of Staff, and Kesselring to offer him a new command – Army Group Africa. At first he rejected it, knowing that Hitler wanted von Arnim for the post and having no wish to continue under the control of Kesselring and the Commando Supremo; however, on orders from Rome which arrived on 23 February, he accepted. He later wrote:

> 'I received the news with mixed feelings. On the one hand I was glad I would again be able to have some wider influence over the fate of my men – General Messe having shortly before assumed command over the Mareth front [the panzer army now renamed 1st Italian Army]; on the other hand, I was not very happy at the prospect of having to go on playing whipping-boy for the Führer's H.Q., the Commando Supremo, and the Luftwaffe.'[69]

Rommel's new command was doomed to be a short one. The failure at Kasserine was followed by a defeat at Medenine, where on 6 March the three panzer divisions of the army group failed to break through to Montgomery's assembly areas and were repulsed with great loss. Had the attack taken place a week earlier, when the British 8th Army was off-balance as a result of undertaking a local offensive designed to relieve pressure on the 1st Army, then success might well have been achieved by the Germans; as it was, after a few days of frantic preparation, the British and Commonwealth troops were waiting in strength for Rommel's expected move. Of this defeat, Rommel wrote: '. . . the cruellest blow was the knowledge that we had been unable to interfere with Montgomery's preparations. A great gloom settled over us all. The 8th Army's attack was now imminent and we had to face it. For the army group to remain longer in Africa was now plain suicide.'[70] Supplies were short. On 8 January Rommel's and von Arnim's staffs had estimated that approximately 150,000 tons per month were required for Tunisia; on 12 January Kesselring had informed Hitler that 60,000 tons could be delivered, a figure later confirmed by Ambrosio. In January 73,000 tons were delivered, in February, 63,000 tons, whereas a minimum of 70,000 tons was required just for maintaining the armies at subsistence level. Losses in transit were as high as forty-one per cent. Von Arnim was as persistent as Rommel in describing this situation as catastrophic.

In March 1943 the task facing Army Group Africa was a formidable one: the defence of a front of 400 miles, 350 of which were held only lightly and, in some places, not at all. Against this, Rommel estimated that the Allies (composed of 1st English Army, II US Corps, 8th Army, and three French divisions) could hurl 1,200 tanks, and 210,000 fighting troops. He himself had nearly one third of a million troops in Tunisia, with a proportion of two Italians to one German, but of this total, only 80,000 Germans and 40,000

Italians were fighting soldiers. The rest, apart from the Luftwaffe, formed a massive administrative 'tail', mostly of Italians, that had been organised for a large colonial African Empire, and of rear-echelon units of divisions that had long since been taken prisoner. Thus, Army Group Africa, with just one and a half per cent of its battle requirement, and a half per cent of its ammunition needs, had at its disposal thirty-four German and fourteen Italian battalions, together with forty-three batteries, which meant a distribution of strength of roughly one battalion to every eight miles. Between them, the three German panzer divisions possessed 142 tanks. Rommel therefore reported to his superiors on 1 March that it would prove impossible to hold the bridgehead should the enemy launch an all-out attack, and consequently he urgently recommended that the front be shortened to 100 miles as soon as possible in order to avoid total destruction. Evacuation was now proposed as the only course of action. But Rommel's suggestion met with no sympathy. Mussolini and Hitler refused to face up to reality and, when Rommel flew to argue his case on 9 and 10 March, he met with an unyielding opposition. The Duce, he found, still lacked 'any sense of reality in adversity',[71] and Hitler, depressed at the Stalingrad débâcle, was so deluded that all he could envisage was a counter-offensive to throw the enemy out of North Africa. Tunisia, the Führer argued, had to be held at all costs for two reasons: to tie up enemy soldiers and shipping which might be used elsewhere, and to command the Sicilian Narrows and thereby prevent an Allied landing in southern Europe. These were all that were left to Hitler for the army group's continued existence. After his interview with Rommel, Hitler ordered him to take immediate sick leave; he was never to return to Africa.

No further offensive action was mounted by Army Group Africa, now under the command of von Arnim, and the Axis forces in Tunisia waited for their end. Von Arnim constantly asked that his line be shortened, but to no avail; he was merely told that the morale of the troops had suffered by the many withdrawals. When the field commander emphasised the shortage of ammunition, he was informed that 12,000 tons of ammunition had been abandoned at El Alamein, despite the cry of shortage that had so often been heard, and that he should be able to make do with his stocks. On 17 March came the order from Commando Supremo: '. . . the task of the army group is to hold its ground in Tunisia . . . the Mareth Zone is to be defended to the last.'[72] On the 20th the Allied offensive began. Orders to hold to the last man were meaningless; the resources to maintain the defence were simply not there. Throughout March only 51,000 tons arrived in Tunisia, and on the 29th von Arnim sent a report to OKW in which he stated: 'Supplies shattering. Ammunition only available for one to two more days, no more stocks for some weapons such as medium field howitzers. Fuel situation similar, large-scale movement no longer possible. . . .'[73] On the 31st the supply returns for the army group indicated that the troops had, on average, four and a half days' rations, two and a half issues of ammunition, and enough fuel to cover thirty miles per vehicle. In April the position became even worse, only 34,000 tons arrived, and on the 25th von Arnim estimated that there was sufficient ammunition to last for only three days' fighting, and fuel for seventeen miles. His conclusion was that 'even without the Allied offensive, I should have had to capitulate by 1 June at the latest because we had no more to eat'.[74] By the end of April, the Army Group was even having to distil low-grade wine into motor-fuel.

The end was near. By late April, the two Axis armies, with barely 100,000 fighting troops (60,000 of which were German) and fewer than 100 tanks, faced Allied forces of up to 300,000 men on their combat strength, and 1,400 tanks. By 12 May Axis resistance was over. The next day, the headquarters of the Africa Corps signalled to the army group: 'Ammunition shot off. Arms and equipment destroyed. In accordance with orders received the German Africa Corps has fought itself into the condition where it can fight no more. . . .'[75] With the fall of Tunisia, more than 230,000 Axis prisoners, almost half of them German, passed into Allied captivity.

24

Italy

For the want of a nail, a kingdom was lost. . . .

TRADITIONAL NURSERY RHYME

The destruction of the Axis forces in Tunisia in May 1943 was a disaster of far greater magnitude than just the loss of North Africa or of nearly a quarter of a million soldiers; it severely impaired the ability of Germany to continue the war, and had consequences that were to remain with Hitler until the very end. The irony of it was that the loss of North Africa, caused by the reluctance to allocate the relatively small, but essential, resources of men and material, brought about the very situation that Hitler and his high commands had hoped to avoid – the diversion of valuable fighting units from the main theatres of war (the east and, later, the west) to one of secondary importance, the Mediterranean – and this time on a far larger scale than had ever been envisaged. Had Hitler given Rommel that extra support so consistently and vigorously demanded, then victory, not defeat, might well have greeted the Axis efforts in the Near East (with all the attendant advantages, such as oil); instead, parsimonious neglect from 1940 to 1942 resulted in the employment of a high proportion of scarce resources in south Europe (Italy and the Balkans) from 1943 to 1945, at a time when pressure on Germany was daily growing more intense. In 1941 or 1942, five or six well-supplied German divisions, or even less, could have cleared Egypt of British presence, whereas in 1943 and 1944, some twenty-four divisions were needed in Italy alone; a further twenty were positioned in the Balkans, largely to ward off an expected enemy invasion.

The collapse of the Axis bridgehead in Tunisia in early May 1943 was, rightly, regarded at Führer headquarters as a catastrophe. The capture of eight Axis divisions in Tunisia, kept there at Hitler's insistence, had left Italy and her islands with no immediate prospect of adequate defence. Quite clearly, the Allies would not restrict their success to the African coast; landings on the mainland of Europe, either in Italy or in the Balkans, could be expected at any time. Warlimont later wrote that OKW was quite aware that: 'Now . . . the Tunisian bridgehead was gone, the theatre of war was no longer a comparatively restricted area of the North African coastline but the entire sweep of the Mediterranean. Major Allied forces had now become available for employment elsewhere.'[1] The question was, where would the Allies land, and how best to prepare for them? The Italians and OKW believed it would be in Sicily; Hitler thought otherwise, and named Sardinia, as well as the Peloponnisös and Dodecanese. He considered that Sardinia would provide an easy stepping stone to Corsica, which, in its turn, would allow an invasion of the mainland of either France or Italy; this opinion was strengthened by a clever deception perpetrated by British Intelligence. Thus, Hitler increased the German forces in Greece to four divisions (to support Italian 11th Army), placed a division in Sardinia (to cooperate with four Italian divisions), moved two parachute divisions to the south of France, and ordered four armoured divisions to Italy. Two divisions (one grenadier, the other panzer), both of which had suffered losses in North Africa, were in Sicily (with the four divisions of the Italian 6th Army). Up to that time, Mussolini had been reluctant to allow any large number of German troops in Italy, and had refused offers of divisions. However, by the time the Allies landed, it seems that Hitler had despatched as many units to that country as he could spare. Even so, the Italians refused to allow the two German divisions in Sicily to be used as a corps and distributed them among their own formations, thereby dissipating their strength and usefulness.

On 10 July the Allies landed eight divisions in Sicily, keeping four more in reserve in North Africa. By 17 August the last Axis soldier had been evacuated from the island; 40,000 Germans, together with 60,000 Italians and much equipment, were successfully ferried across the straits of Messina. Hitler's confidence in the ability of the Italians to defend their homeland had been shattered, and he had lost his first battle in western Europe. Had he listened to his advisers, his preparations to meet the invasion might well have been more thorough; but he had chosen to ignore them, and the transfer of two divisions to the island after the invasion had begun was to no avail. (Kesselring believed that they would have been 'decisive' had they been deployed there from the beginning.) The invasion of the mainland was now inevitable.

But where in southern Europe? Hitler was convinced that it would be in the Balkans, an area where he particularly feared an attack. In Directive No. 48, dated 29 July, he declared: 'The enemy's measures in the eastern Mediterranean, in conjunction with the attack on Sicily, indicate that he will shortly begin landing operations against our strong line in the Aegean, Peloponnese-Crete-Rhodes, and against the west coast of Greece with offshore Ionian islands. . . . The enemy's conduct of operations is also based on the bandit movement, which is increasingly organised by him in the interior of the south-east area.'[2] Even after the Allied landings on the mainland of Italy in early September, Hitler continued to expect the main attack to take place in the Balkans. Warlimont wrote:

'. . . Hitler not only clung to his determination to defend the outer coastal perimeter, but now wanted to include the island outpost chain. . . . He continually reverted to his preoccupation over the Romanian oil area, and now produced numerous additional political and military arguments such as the prevention of an Allied line of communications to Russia through the Aegean and the Dardanelles, and the necessity of countering enemy pressure on Turkey and her entry into the war.'[3]

However, the Commander-in-Chief, South-East (from mid-July 1942, von Weichs), and the Commander-in-Chief of the Navy, together with OKW, felt that with the limited resources available it was impossible to hold the outer perimeter stipulated by Hitler. The only defensive line against an enemy invasion of Greece, they argued, was one east and west through Salonika, which would provided the flank protection for the front in the northern Adriatic; 'only by such a reduction of commitments would it be possible to bar the enemy's advance into the heart of Europe'.[4] Hitler, however, rejected their arguments, although accepting that they were based on sound military principles, and stated that, for political considerations, the whole of the Balkan area, including the islands, must be held. Not until September 1944, when Bulgaria declared war on Germany and thereby threatened the communications of the troops occupying Greece, did Hitler allow the evacuation of the Aegean islands; the order for the withdrawal from Greece, southern Albania, and southern Macedonia followed on 2 October. One month later, this movement was completed, although, owing to lack of transport, 22,000 men were left on Crete, Rhodes and Lemnos.

The invasion of Sicily brought with it one other major consequence: the fall of Mussolini and the defection of the new Italian government from the Axis alliance. On 25 July, while the battle for Sicily was at its height, Mussolini was dismissed after a vote of no confidence by the Fascist Grand Council the day before, and was replaced as Prime Minister by Marshal Badoglio. Negotiations were at once entered into with the enemy, and a secret act of surrender was signed on 3 September, the day the Allies landed at Reggio on the toe of Italy. On the 8th, the Italian surrender was made public, and the following day the Allies landed at Salerno and at Taranto. The Germans, aware that the Axis was on the point of disintegrating, were well-prepared, and immediately took steps to occupy key centres and to disarm Italian troops. At this time, Kesselring had only seven German divisions in the centre and south of Italy with which to check the Allied landings and to deal with the Italians. However, a further eight divisions had arrived in northern Italy, and several more were on their way. The skill of the German troops, and the acquiescence of their former partners, together with the extreme caution of the Allied commanders, enabled Kesselring to halt the invaders in November, only 70 miles beyond Salerno, and 100 miles south of Rome. It was to be eight months before Italy's capital was occupied.

Kesselring's success in checking the Allies in the south of Italy had a profound effect on Hitler. Before hearing of it, he had intended to hold only the Apennines in north Italy, turning them into an impregnable defensive line garrisoned by twenty-one German divisions under the command of Rommel; afterwards, his customary reluctance to yield even a foot of ground reasserted itself and he determined to halt the enemy south of Rome. On 21 November Hitler ordered Kesselring to take over the supreme command of the Italian theatre, with the new designation 'Commander-in-Chief, South-West'. He was, of course, still responsible to OKW.

On 22 January 1944 the Allies renewed their attempt to reach the Italian capital by landing at Anzio, twenty-five miles south of Rome. But, mainly because of the slowness of the Allied commanders, the Germans managed to contain any breakout from the small bridgehead, and at the same time to block a renewed assault in the south. After yet another pause, this time of four months, the Allies again began their offensive, using to the full their overwhelming air power, and on 5 June, the day before the invasion of Normandy, they at last entered Rome. However, a masterly withdrawal by Kesselring established the German forces in the mountain line north of Florence, and deadlock returned to the Italian front. The onset of winter brought an end to the Allied endeavours in Italy for 1944. Not until April 1945 was the over-stretched German front in Italy broken by fresh blows, and the last German troops driven from the country. In spite of their material superiority, it had taken the Allies twenty months to clear Italy.

The extreme length of the campaign is understandable only when the following factors are taken into consideration: the skill and determination of the German defenders, who were well-aided by the difficult, mountainous country south of the Po valley; the extreme caution shown by the Allied commanders, which, among other things, prevented them from taking advantage of the long Italian peninsula to execute a strategic outflanking manoeuvre from the sea; and the Allied command's relegation of Italy to the status of a secondary theatre of war, and their switching of resources to the main front in western Europe (which meant that Allied superiority in the front line in Italy dropped from sixty per cent in the very early days to minus twelve per cent in the last stages of the campaign). However, to view the war in Italy only in terms of ground lost or gained and time taken misses the real significance of the campaign. It caused the Germans to divert valuable fighting formations to a secondary front when their generals on both the Eastern and the Western Fronts were crying out for reinforcements. The Allied Commander in Italy, Field-Marshal Alexander, believed that his campaign, despite and because of its slowness, 'fulfilled its strategic mission'. He argued that:

'Our role was subordinate and preparatory. Ten months before the great assault in the west, our invasion of Italy, at first in very moderate strength, drew off to that remote quarter forces that might have turned the scale in France. As the campaign progressed, more and more German troops were drawn in to oppose us . . . when the value of our strategic contribution was at its greatest [in the period before and during the invasion of Normandy], fifty-five German divisions were tied down in the Mediterranean by the threat, actual or potential, presented by our armies in Italy. The record of comparative casualties tells the same story. On the German side they amounted to 536,000. Allied casualties were 312,000.'[5]

Alexander's view was shared by most of the German generals. Writing of the period after the landings at Anzio, Warlimont made the point: 'Now there seemed little doubt that the strategy behind the Allied offensive was to prevent any move to German forces from Italy to the west. Hitler's continued determination to cling "to every inch of territory", and his alarm at the loss of prestige which the imminent fall of Rome would entail, meant that he conformed to the enemy's plan even more exactly than might have been expected.'[6] Thus, on 1 June 1944 Italy absorbed twenty-seven divisions and the Balkans a further twenty-five, around eighteen per cent of all divisions within the Army, the Air Force, and the Waffen SS; a year previously the percentage had been only nine. Almost one in five of Germany's divisions, therefore was kept tied to the south of Europe in 1944 and 1945; their absence was painfully felt elsewhere.

After the war, there was much discussion among those most closely involved as to whether or not, after the fall of Tunis, Hitler's over-all Mediterranean policy was sensible. Warlimont, for example, was convinced that it was not. He wrote:

> 'The struggle in northern Italy was an exhausting one, and no doubt it held the enemy for a considerable period, but from the German point of view in the fifth year of the war it was totally unjustified, particularly since the long, exposed coast of Italy offered the Allies opportunities for landings which could at any time have brought upon us a new catastrophe. Furthermore, both the eastern and western theatres were deprived of forces which could have been made available in considerable numbers if a timely withdrawal to the northern Apennines had been made. . . . Hitler's Mediterranean strategy threw a far greater strain on the German war potential than the military situation justified, and no long-term compensating economies were made in other theatres. . . . the Supreme Command had only one object, to defend the occupied areas everywhere on their outermost perimeter and on other fronts to plug such holes as appeared as quickly as possible.'[7]

Kesselring, however, held a different view:

> 'To evacuate the whole of Italy and to defend the Reich from positions in the Alps would not have been to economise our effec-

tives; it would have given the enemy untrammelled freedom of movement in the direction of France and the Balkans, have meant sacrificing an indispensable deep battle-zone and unleashing the air war on the whole of southern Germany and Austria. Similarly, to have evacuated southern and central Italy and held the Apennines and Alps only, would not have resulted in any saving of men and materials, nor have appreciably lessened the danger of sea and airborne landings or the extension of the air war as above.'[8]

In his appraisal, Kesselring is probably correct; there is no evidence to suggest that a withdrawal to the north of Italy would have saved the commitment of German forces – indeed, when Hitler was seriously considering this course of action, he was prepared to allocate no fewer than twenty-one divisions for the defence of that front. The question of the Balkans, however, is somewhat different. There was no Allied invasion of Greece, although one was seriously contemplated, and the force employed for coastal protection never came into contact with the enemy. A significant proportion of the German effort in the Balkans was occupied in dealing with the partisans, which proved to be a fruitless task involving large losses (as, indeed, it was also in Italy, where between four and seven divisions were employed in internal security duties). The proposals put to the Führer for a partial withdrawal of the Balkans were justified both by events and by military prudence (which Hitler himself admitted); however, a substantial force would in any case have had to remain to guard the German south-east flank, wherever it was situated. The reality of the situation was that whatever strategy Hitler might choose to adopt, the failure to hold North Africa had forced the Germans to commit large numbers of troops to the Mediterranean theatre, troops they could not spare without great loss to their other fronts, but troops which had to be found nevertheless.

Hitler's interference in the conduct of military operations in Italy became as marked as it was on other fronts, although Kesselring later claimed that he did not find it too restricting. He wrote: 'Even though I received repeated injunctions from the OKW not to surrender so much territory, I had to operate in the main as I thought necessary in the light of my own more accurate knowledge of the situation. . . . I do not remember a single occasion when I was "on the mat" for acting "autocratically" [i.e. independently], apart from the evacuation of Sicily.'[9] But Westphal, Kesselring's chief of staff, disagreed:

'At first, Hitler had allowed commanders in Italy a certain limited freedom of action. However, after the Nettuno [Anzio] landing had upset the precarious balance, he began to intervene more and more drastically. From now on the commanders were on leading-strings, continually pestered with trivialities. Hitler now concerned himself with numberless details, and prescribed answers to all sorts of questions which could only properly be weighed up and decided on the spot.'[10]

Westphal admitted that Kesselring, partly because of his able defence in southern Italy, and partly because he was a Luftwaffe and not an Army commander, did enjoy a certain favour with the Führer, and that he 'had a knack which often enabled him to get his own way in most skilful fashion'. However, he went on:

'All the same, the steadiness of the local Army commanders could not fail to be affected by the intervention of OKW in the daily conduct of affairs, and by Hitler's wakeful suspicions that something was being hidden from him, that an order had not been carried out, or that a favourable opportunity had not been exploited. The necessary and incessant occupation with all kinds of details, which was intensified by Hitler's daily questionings, often made it difficult to see the wood for the trees. That is why it cannot be denied that the German leadership in the Italian war theatre was frequently inhibited and sometimes rather cramped.'[11]

Hitler's interference was to prove fatal on three occasions during the Italian campaign: during the initial landings, during the battle for the Anzio bridgehead, and during the last stages of the fighting in northern Italy. The first arose out of Hitler's original intention of abandoning southern and central Italy, and of making a firm defence in the northern Apennines. As a result, the command structure in Italy was divided between Rommel, who was charged with the defence of the north, and Kesselring, who had command of the German troops to the south. Despite frequent protests by the latter, Hitler refused to combine the two commands until the middle of November, well after the Allied landings had taken place, when it was clear that a line south of Rome could be held. Of this Westphal wrote: 'The duality that had long bedevilled the German leadership in Italy was now ended. It was immaterial who the commander was; now at last there was a single commander who had all the forces at his disposal.' For all that, it was too late; the consequences of the delay were already disastrous. Westphal continued:

'Such a commander-in-chief would have been able to conduct the Salerno battle [the most important Allied landing] quite differently from the way Kesselring had been able to do with his own forces. In the case of need, the two mobile and particularly battle-worthy divisions [under Rommel] in upper Italy near Mantua could have been spared from the task of disarming Italian troops. If these high-quality troops had been set in motion towards the front on 9 September . . . they would in all probability have arrived to throw their weight into the battle which reached its crisis on 13 September. . . . An immediate request to this effect from the Commander-in-

Chief, South [Kesselring] had been turned down by OKW. Later, Jodl himself admitted that this refusal of Kesselring's urgent appeals was a serious mistake.'[12]

In January 1944 came the landing at Anzio. Hitler, perturbed by the threat both to Rome and to all the forces to the south, immediately took direct control of the situation; his desire was to throw the enemy back into the sea and thereby have an adverse affect on the plans for the invasion of the west. But he made the 'error of giving the local command exact instructions as to how they were to conduct the attack'.[13] Hitler himself laid down the precise plans of the German counter-attack, and insisted on them, even though they were opposed by the commander on the spot, General von Mackensen. The supreme warlord decreed that inexperienced troops were to attack across unfamiliar terrain in the evening when light was bad. Failure was the result. Had the field commanders had their way, it is not inconceivable that the assault would have been carried. Kesselring and von Mackensen were convinced that it would, and both later admitted their error in allowing Hitler to dictate the course of action.

The final defeat of the German forces in northern Italy in early 1945 was assured by Hitler's continual insistence on the principle of 'no withdrawal'. Once the northern end of the Apennines had been reached at the end of 1944, it was clear to Kesselring that the line could not be held there for long, especially as its left flank had been pushed back almost as soon as it had become established. He therefore pressed for an immediate withdrawal to the Alps, a move made all the more urgent by the threat to his rear from the Balkans, where the Russians were daily advancing and had become potentially dangerous. Hitler would not agree, and finally decided on 5 October that 'the Apennines front should be held, not merely until late autumn, but permanently, and northern Italy thereby retained.'[14] Warlimont remembered Hitler's views, as translated by Jodl: 'It was a "dangerous principle" ... to try to stop a breakthrough by defence in depth. Voluntary withdrawals weakened our own forces rather than the enemy. That way one might save a couple of divisions but endanger a couple of arhies.'[15] This rigid attitude persisted all through the winter and into the early spring of 1945, surviving intact despite the strong protests of General von Vietinghoff, Kesselring's successor (the Field-Marshal had been transferred to the west on 10 March 1945). As a result, when the Allied offensive began in early April, the defenders, rigidly holding their positions, were unable to indulge in even limited mobile defence (petrol was very short), let alone a withdrawal; encirclement was the inevitable result, and the conquest of north Italy by the Allies was achieved by the beginning of May. There was by then no hope that a stand could be made in the Alps; the forces for it simply did not exist. On the 2nd the Commander-in-Chief, South-East, signed an agreement for unconditional surrender, six days before his counterparts did so in the west.

25

The East – The 1942 Summer Campaign

*Although methods may change with the battle, it is
the maintenance of the aim that is the essence of
military operations.*

ALFRED VON SCHLIEFFEN

Chief of the General Staff 1891–1903

The German Field Army in the spring and early summer of 1942 was in sorry shape. An OKH report, dated 30 March, indicated that of a total of 162 combat divisions facing the Red Army, only eight were available for any mission, three were capable of offensive operations after a period of rest, forty-seven were ready for limited offensive operations, seventy-three were suited for defence, and twenty-nine for only limited defensive operations; two were not in a condition for any commitment to battle whatsoever. Of sixteen panzer divisions in the east, only 140 serviceable tanks were available between them. Few divisions were more than twenty per cent mobile. It was a situation which Halder was correct in describing as 'disastrous'.

Time was not to improve matters greatly; the German Army was never to recover from its reverse in 1941. Although it increased its strength by twenty-three divisions, from 203 in June 1941 to 226 by July 1942, owing to its high losses in that period – 367,000 killed, 50,000 missing – its total manpower grew but little, from 3,800,000 to 3,948,000 men. This was not sufficient to cope with its widening responsibilities in the four corners of Europe and in North Africa. The result was that there was a decrease of 359,000 in the number of men available for the Eastern Front, despite the fact that the number of divisions employed there had increased by twenty-nine to 177. Thus, at the opening of the 1942 summer campaign, only 2,847,000 German soldiers were in the Soviet Union, and no fewer than 1,101,000 were elsewhere, 971,000 of them in OKW theatres of war. Hitler's dispersal of the limited strength available forced him to rely more and more on his allies in any forthcoming offensive in the east, however much the introduction of non-German formations might introduce an element of unreliability into operations not known before.

Because of the shortage of men, infantry divisions were reorganised on a basis of seven battalions instead of nine, and the battle-strength of companies was fixed at eighty soldiers instead of 180. No newly designed equipment arrived to increase fire-power, although the 5cm anti-tank gun continued to replace the out-dated 3.7cm type. The shortage in motor transport was especially severe, and between 1 November 1941 and 15 March 1942 only 7,500 vehicles arrived to replace the 75,000 lost. Reconnaissance battalions even began to use bicycles. In an OKW paper prepared by Warlimont, it was noted that 'Mobility is considerably affected by shortage of load-carrying vehicles and horses which cannot be made good. A measure of demotorisation is unavoidable.'[1] However, this was to prove difficult, for the shortage of horses (180,000 had died in the winter months, to be replaced by 20,000) was especially severe, and the available reserves of some 200,000 were not adequate. Fuel oil, too, was still in short supply (its availability in 1942 was expected to be barely one third that of 1941), and it was stated that 'Ammunition difficulties must be reckoned with in August 1942; they may be sufficient to affect operations.'[2]

The condition of the panzer arm was as bad, if not worse. Losses of tanks between 22 June 1941 and 1 March 1942 had amounted to 3,424 on all fronts, while only 2,843 had come from the production lines. From that time, the strength of the armoured divisions was governed more by such shortages than by any tables of theoretical organisation. The number of tanks possessed by the Army had dropped from 5,262 on 1 June 1941 to 4,462 on 1 March 1942, which was lower than at any time since January of the previous year, fifteen months past. Furthermore, only 2,468 were considered fit for frontline service (the PzKw IIs and 38(t)s having joined the PzKw Is and 35 (t)s as officially obsolete). By 1 July, with tank output running at an average of only 356 units per month, the numbers had increased to only 5,663 and 3,471 respectively, and by 1 December to 5,931 and 3,939 for use in North Africa as well as for employment over the 2,000-mile Eastern Front. Moreover, no effort was made to concentrate the limited armoured strength available. In late 1941, two more panzer divisions had been created, followed in 1942 by another four – two in February, and two in the autumn – bringing the total of such formations to twenty-seven. A further dissipation was brought about by the addition of tank battalions to Army and Waffen SS motorised infantry divisions, and, at the end of the year, a further five panzer divisions were formed, in practice if not in name, by the expansion of the Waffen SS tank battalions into regiments (to be followed by yet one more in the spring of 1943). All this was at a time when the panzer divisions allocated to the northern and central sections of the Eastern Front could be equipped with only enough tanks for one, sometimes two, weak battalions each (approximately 40–60 machines). Only by starving other formations could the relatively few panzer divisions allocated to the major offensive in 1942 be brought up to strength, and even then they averaged only 135 machines each. Captured foreign vehicles were used to a greater extent than before, one panzer division, stationed in Norway, being equipped solely with French tanks.

Just as important as the numerical shortages was the marked qualitative inferiority of the German tanks compared with the best possessed by the enemy. The unexpected appearance of the Soviet KV Is and T34s during the early days of 'Barbarossa' had had an immense psychological impact on the minds of soldiers who, till then, had been accustomed to nothing but armoured superiority. For the first time they had come up against machines that could shoot from any visible range and could penetrate their thickest armour at 1,000 yards, whereas they, in their turn, had to close to within 200 yards to make a kill. The Army High Command was reported 'dumbfounded' by the realisation that in tank technology they lagged far behind their major enemy; ambitious plans for expanding the panzer arm to a total of thirty-six divisions equipped with 7,992 PzKw IIIs and 2,600 PzKw IVs were immediately abandoned. Hitler even stated his belief that the days of the tank were numbered, and doubts were now continually expressed as to the efficacy of the armoured force. New, heavy tanks were ordered, and, as an interim measure, the PzKw IIIs and IVs were up-gunned and up-armoured. They were given long-barrelled (and more powerful) 5cm and 7.5cm guns respectively, and both had their armour thickness doubled. (This arming of the PzKw III was the belated fulfilment of an order, given by Hitler after the campaign in the West, which the OKH Weapons Department had chosen to ignore, much to the Führer's anger when he discovered it.) By such means, the PzKw IV was given a measure of equality with the contemporary T34, although it continued to suffer from inferior mobility. The only other improvements in the quality of the armoured divisions lay in the provision of an 8.8cm anti-aircraft, anti-tank gun battalion, and in the greater use of half-tracked armoured personnel carriers, which, at that time, equipped one of the four infantry battalions.

The nature of German armoured warfare was thus changing rapidly. Although in the 1942 summer campaign the superior tactics and organisation of the panzer divisions were still to dominate in spite of the fire-power, protection, and mobility of the enemy's tanks, the shock administered by the KV Is and T34s in 1941 had proved to be the final nail in the coffin of the armoured idea. Emphasis on manoeuvre was to be increasingly replaced by reliance on material; factors such as the muzzle velocity of tank guns and the thickness and angle of tank armour came to outweigh superior training, sophisticated organisation, and brilliant tactics. In the years after 1942 the German panzer force was to witness a revolution in tank design, the result being that the last machines to be produced during the war resembled mobile fortresses, intended for power and impregnability in defence rather than for speed and versatility in attack. Moreover, the concept of infantry-support as the main role of armour took on a new lease of life. Panzer divisions were distributed among infantry armies; infantry divisions were used to a greater extent in panzer armies; tank battalions were given to motorised infantry formations; and production of the assault-gun was increased at the expense of the tank. By 1 July 1942, the number of assault-guns in stock (780) was almost one-quarter of the front-line strength of tanks.

At the same time, more powerful assault-guns were ordered, and 'tank-hunters', self-propelled, well-armoured anti-tank guns, were designed. It was not long before the tank became just one of a number of armoured fighting vehicles, its former position of superiority gone for ever.

As for 'Barbarossa', so for the Eastern offensive in 1942, there was a conflict between Hitler and his Army leaders as to the operational objectives of the campaign. Had the generals had their way, a resumption of a full-scale attack would not have taken place; there was even a proposal that, once the Soviet counter-offensive was over, the Army should withdraw to its original front in Poland. Heusinger recorded that:

> 'For a long time Halder examined the idea of whether we should not definitely go over to the defensive in the East, since further offensive operations seemed to be beyond our strength. But it is impossible even to mention this to Hitler. What then? If we let the Russians get their second wind and the menace of America increases, then we have surrendered the initiative to the enemy and shall never get it back again. We can therefore do only one thing – try once more in spite of all drawbacks.'[3]

Warlimont noted that such was Halder's discomfort at the prospect of Hitler's proposed offensive, that it 'could be felt almost physically'.[4]

The Führer was firm in his opinion that the attack should be resumed. He had, he argued, already occupied forty-seven per cent of the inhabited places of the Soviet Union, so why should he not go on to conquer the rest? Von Blumentritt, who became Deputy Chief of the General Staff early in January 1942, wrote of:

> 'Hitler's hope of obtaining in 1942 what he had failed to obtain in 1941. He did not believe that the Russians could increase their strength, and would not listen to evidence on this score. There was a "battle of opinion" between Halder and him. The Intelligence had information that 600 to 700 tanks a month were coming out of the Russian factories in the Ural mountains and elsewhere. When Halder told him of this, Hitler slammed the table and said it was impossible. He would not believe what he did not want to believe. Secondly, he did not know what else to do – as he would not listen to any idea of a withdrawal. He felt that he must do something, and that something could only be offensive. Thirdly, there was much pressure from economic authorities in Germany; they argued that it was essential to continue the advance, telling Hitler that they could not continue the war without oil from the Caucasus and wheat from the Ukraine.'[5]

As early as 3 January 1942, when the Soviet winter counter-attack showed no signs of abating, the Führer revealed his intentions, telling the Japanese ambassador that 'the object is to resume the offensive towards the Caucasus as soon as the weather allows. This is the most important direction for an offensive; we must reach the oilfields there and also in Iran and Iraq. Once we have got there we hope that we can assist the rise of the freedom movement in the Arab world. Naturally, we shall also do all we can to obliterate Moscow and Leningrad.'[6] As time went on Hitler proceeded to communicate his views to the Army Command; it became clear to Halder and his aides that what was proposed was an offensive that revealed traces of the Führer's original idea for 'Barbarossa' – namely, an attack on both flanks with the centre being held back. Leningrad was to be taken, but, in contrast with the previous year's plan, the emphasis from the outset was to be placed in the south, in the Ukraine and the Caucasus.

However, there was no consensus as to what form Hitler's proposed offensive in the south should take. The view of OKW, summed up by Warlimont, was: 'the prospect of economic gains in the south, especially of wheat, manganese and oil . . . to cut off the Russians from these goods, allegedly indispensable for their continuation in the war. . . .'[7] In this, the acquisition of the Caucasus, with its vital oilfields and its position on the direct route to Iran and Iraq, was seen as the central aim of the whole campaign. On 1 April Hitler had emphasised the importance of this operation to von Kleist, who was to lead the armoured drive into the Caucasus. The general remembered: 'Hitler said we must capture the oilfields.by the autumn because Germany could not continue the war without them.'[8] OKH, however, held a different view as to what Hitler's intention was; Stalingrad on the Volga, not the Caucasus, was the principal objective. Halder explained:

> 'In Hitler's written order to me to prepare an offensive in south Russia in the summer of 1942, the objective given was the River Volga at Stalingrad. The operational order of the OKH, therefore, emphasised this objective and held only a protection of the flank south of the River Don to be necessary. This flank protection was to be achieved, firstly by blocking the eastern part of the Caucasus – which was to be reached by attack; secondly, by holding a strong mobile force at Armavir [180 miles south-east of Rostov], and on the high ground eastwards, which was to afford security against possible Russian attack between the High Caucasus and the River Manych.'[9]

This, only partial, advance into the Caucasus was to be secondary to the main offensive towards Stalingrad.

Where, then, lay Hitler's true intentions? Perhaps, nowhere. At no time did the Supreme Commander express himself clearly and precisely as to which of the objectives in the south should be given priority. His mind, never very orderly, was a confusion of aims: the defeat of the Soviet forces in the bend of the Don; the acquisition of Caucasian oil and, possibly, that of Iran and Iraq as well; the occupation of the major industrial, armament, and communication centre of Stalingrad (only forty miles east of the Don), an occupation which would make possible an advance to the Urals or a move northwards to take Moscow and its defenders in the rear. But however these objectives were to sort themselves out in the future, one thing is clear: that when OKH presented its proposals for the campaign as described, Hitler raised no objection; Stalingrad was to be the first objective. However, Halder did note that in the Führer's 'over-estimation of his own forces, and under-estimation of the enemy forces – so typical of him – he was, early on, inwardly opposed to the limitation in the choice of objectives ordered by the OKH south of the River Don. I remember some critical remarks made just at that time, about the lack of daring and initiative on the part of the General Staff. But Hitler did not [outwardly] connect them with the restriction shown on the subject of objectives south of the River Don.'[10]

The Führer's attitude was set out in his Directive No. 41, dated 5 April, which, drafted in large part by Hitler himself, accepted the operational premises of the OKH proposal while at the same time preparing the way for an advance into the Caucasus: 'Our aim is to wipe out the entire defence potential remaining to the Soviets, and to cut them off, as far as possible, for their most important centres of war industry.' Under the heading of 'The main operation on the Eastern Front', Hitler gave little attention to how an advance into the Caucasus should be conducted; instead, he spent some time in explaining how the attack to the Volga was to be undertaken. He noted that the aim of operations within the bend of the Don was 'to destroy the enemy armies', and stipulated that 'every effort will be made to reach Stalingrad itself, or at least to bring the city under fire from heavy artillery, so that it may no longer be of any use as an industrial or communications centre'. However, elsewhere, the Caucasus was specified as the major objective: 'In pursuit of the original plan for the eastern campaign ,the armies of the central sector will stand fast, those in the north will capture Leningrad and link up with the Finns, while those on the southern flank will break through into the Caucasus. . . .' As yet, there was no conflict between Hitler and OKH. Certainly Hitler had extended the campaign beyond the limits intended by the generals, but at the same time he had made the acquisition of the Caucasus, the *prime* objective, dependent on success in the bend of the Don and at Stalingrad, the *first* objective. He stated: 'The purpose is . . . to occupy the Caucasus front by decisively attacking and destroying Russian forces stationed in the Voronezh area [300 miles north of Rostov, the 'gateway' to the Caucasus] to the south, west, or north of the Don.'[11] Only after the Red Army in that area had been destroyed, and Stalingrad dominated, would the attack on the oilfields begin.

Thus Stalingrad was of considerable importance to both the Army leaders and Hitler, although their reasons differed. For OKH, the destruction of the Soviet forces in the Don Bend and the acquisition of Stalingrad was an end in itself: it would represent a considerable victory for the Germans; it would provide an excellent anchor for a defensive line; and it would open the way for future operations in any direction – east to the Urals, south to the Caucasus, or north to behind Moscow. With this Hitler concurred, but added one other and, to him, more important condition: the occupation of Stalingrad would ensure the protection of the north-east flank of a drive into the Caucasus; without the domination of the Don-Volga area, the German advance south to the oilfields would be dangerously exposed to a Soviet counter-attack in its rear. It was this that was to prove fatal. Stalingrad might be important in Hitler's eyes, but it was but a means to an end – the end being the occupation of the Caucasus. He sounded this warning note in his directive: 'The swift progress of the movements across the Don to the south, in order to attain the operational objectives, is essential, in consideration of the season.'[12] In this lay the seeds of a grave defeat. Hitler once again wanted to do everything all at once with only limited resources.

The plan for the 1942 offensive took no account whatsoever of the principles of the armoured idea. Indeed, steps were taken to guard against their use. On this point, Hitler's Directive No. 41 was quite specific. The Führer stated: 'It must not happen that, by advancing too quickly and too far, the armoured and motorised formations lose connexion with the infantry following them; or that they lose the opportunity of supporting the hard-pressed, forward-fighting infantry by direct attacks on the rear of the encircled Russian armies.'[13] With this, OKH was in full agreement. Encirclement was to dominate, although, and here the Army leaders were more sceptical, not in the grand, classic manner. Hitler believed that 'Experience has sufficiently shown that the Russians are not very vulnerable to [large] operational encircling movements. It is therefore of decisive importance that, as in the double battle of Vyazma-Bryansk, individual breaches of the front should take the form of close pincer movements. We must avoid closing the pincers too late, thus giving the enemy the possibility of avoiding destruction.'[14] Therefore, instead of there being one massive encirclement of all the Soviet troops within the bend of the Don, as might have been attempted the previous year, Hitler envisaged two, to be undertaken by three separate attacks. The first phase of the offensive, code-named 'Blue I', was to consist of an attack by 2nd Army, 2nd Hungarian Army, and 4th Panzer Army from the area of Kursk eastwards to the east bank of the Don. There, the infantry would consolidate the front, while the 4th Panzer Army moved south, along the river. The second attack, 'Blue II', would take place two days after the first from the Kharkov area; 6th Army would move east, almost to the Don, where it would turn south-eastwards on the right flank of 4th Panzer Army. The third thrust, 'Blue III' would begin a few days later from the area around Taganrog, whence 1st Panzer Army, 17th Army, and 8th Italian Army would move along the lower Don to Stalingrad. Thus, 4th and 1st Panzer Armies would meet somewhere east of the Don near Stalingrad, thereby closing the outermost pincers, and within this area 400 miles wide and 300 miles deep, two major cauldron battles would be fought, owing to the attack of the large 6th Army, which disected the advance of the two panzer armies. However, this plan was considerably amended because of the limited power of attack of the 'Blue III' force; 1st Panzer Army was directed to advance nearer to 6th Army, and was moved 150 miles to the north of Taganrog, near Artemovsk, while 17th Army and 8th Italian Army were left to confine the enemy in the area of the Sea of Azov. Stalingrad was still the objective of 1st Panzer Army, but the change meant that the cauldron battles effected between it, 6th Army, and 4th Panzer Army would be considerably reduced; the plan of operation had degenerated further into one for a few small tactical encirclements.

The units that were to undertake the attack had been brought up to almost full personnel strength at the expense of the formations along the rest of the front, which averaged about fifty per cent of their manpower. They were led and composed as follows. Army Group South, under von Bock, which was to prepare the offensive and conduct its opening stages, was to be divided into two new Army Groups – A and B – shortly after the attack opened. Army Group B, in the north, commanded by von Bock, consisted of 6th Army, under von Paulus (two panzer, one motorised infantry, and fifteen infantry divisions) and Group von Weichs, under the general of that name, made up of 2nd Army, under von Weichs (one motorised infantry, four German, and two Hungarian infantry divisions), 2nd Hungarian Army under Jany (four Hungarian infantry divisions), and 4th Panzer Army, under Hoth (three panzer, two motorised infantry and six infantry divisions). To the south, Army Group A, commanded by List, was composed of 1st Panzer Army under von Kleist (three panzer, two motorised infantry, seven German and four Romanian infantry divisions) and Group Ruoff, made up of 17th Army under Ruoff (one panzer, one motorised infantry, six German and four Romanian infantry divisions), and 8th Italian Army under Gariboldi (six divisions). At the beginning of the offensive there were seventy-four divisions, of which fifty-four were German, six Hungarian, eight Romanian and six Italian. Of these, nine were panzer and seven motorised infantry (two of them Waffen SS). There were 1,495 tanks, 133 with the long 7.5cm gun, available for the attack, supported by 1,500 of the 2,750 aeroplanes in the east. A further two German and six Allied divisions were on their way to the front – the only formations that could be called reserves.

Behind this force, however, there was an inadequate supply line: the railway was still working at low capacity, and there were too few railheads in the requisite areas to support the armies. Nor could much reliance be placed on motor transport, for the availability of trucks and fuel was, as always, limited. Even the spearhead divisions had only 85 per cent of their organic motor transport, and the infantry divisions much less. There was a considerable shortage of tank and truck drivers in the armoured divisions, and a great lack of prime movers for towing artillery. Horses would, once again, sustain the advance. Moreover, it is interesting to note how the limited mechanised strength (just over one fifth) of the attacking force was deployed. Instead of being concentrated within the two panzer armies, three of the nine panzer divisions were given to two infantry armies, and three of the seven motorised infantry divisions were distributed among three infantry armies. Thus, more than one-third of the mechanised units were dissipated instead of concentrated. Moreover, the panzer armies themselves included large numbers of infantry divisions within their orders of battle – 4th Panzer Army had six of its eleven divisions mainly reliant on horses, and 1st Panzer Army had eleven of its sixteen, and four of these were Romanian. This would slow down the pace of the panzer armies in the forthcoming offensive. Lastly, 4th Panzer Army, initially at least, was placed under a higher, intermediate command, that of von Weichs, commander of 2nd Army, a fact reminiscent of the first eastern campaign. Concentration of force, and independence from infantry, were again to be denied to the panzers.

Before the 1942 summer campaign, a number of events had taken place: the Crimea had been almost completely occupied by von Manstein's 11th Army, and the Soviet Balakleya-Izyum salient near Kharkov had been captured by 6th Army and 1st Panzer Army, the Soviets, who attacked first, losing 214,000 men as prisoners alone, and the Germans gaining a valuable area from which to begin the new offensive. To the north, Army Group Centre had begun operations to eliminate Soviet salients on its front, and Army Group North was still investing Leningrad. The Balakleya-Izyum battle had marked Hitler's first, and only, personal victory as a military commander. The Soviets had launched an attack towards Kharkov on 12th May, pre-empting a German strike, code-named 'Fredericus' in the same area by six days, and by the evening were barely fifteen miles from Kharkov. The German field commanders were stunned, and von Bock urged Halder that 'Fredericus' would have to be abandoned in favour of a frontal defence in front of Kharkov. But calmer views were being taken in Führer headquarters and OKH. Neither Hitler nor Halder believed that plans should be changed to repair 'minor blemishes', as the former put it; despite repeated warnings from the men in the field, the high command stood firm, and merely ordered that 'Fredericus' begin one day earlier, on the 17th May. Counter-attack, not defence, was believed to be the best solution. It was; by the 22nd the enemy was encircled between von Kleist's and Paulus' armies, and a great victory achieved. Never again would the supreme command act in this way.

It was in the south that the decisive stroke was mounted. At 2.15a.m. on 28 June the first assault of Operation Blue struck the enemy; 4th Panzer Army, supported by 2nd Army, advanced on Voronezh. Two days later 6th Army attacked the Soviet front, and by 2 July, the fourth day of the campaign, the first envelopment was completed at Star Oskol. Soviet resistance was fast collapsing. On the 6th Hoth's army was over the Don and had seized Voronezh, more than 100 miles from the original front-line; most of the Red Army was still west of the river, and the Soviet Command, believing that the

German objective was Moscow, began to move its forces in the east accordingly. Thus far, all appeared to be going well for the attackers. But then Hitler began again to interfere in the operational conduct of the Army. Warlimont wrote: 'No one could have foreseen how Hitler was to exercise his power of supreme command; in fact, he proved more overbearing and less open to advice than ever before, and it was this which was the decisive factor in bringing about the awful crisis of the second Russian winter 1942–43.'[15]

By the time the Germans had reached Voronezh, the only resistance to be met came from that area; to the south, in the corridor between the Donets and the Don, the Red Army was hardly to be seen. Von Bock, therefore, was reluctant to move his troops down to the south-east before the large enemy forces on his flank had been subdued; he sent one corps of the 4th Panzer Army south-east, but it was insufficient to envelop the Soviet armies escaping east across the Don. Two days after reaching Voronezh, he released further armoured units, but within a day or so they ran out of fuel and came to a halt. Hitler was furious at von Bock's delay; he wanted Hoth's 4th Panzer Army to move with all speed down the banks of the Don to entrap the Soviet forces between it and 6th Army. And in order to meet such enemy pressure as was being exerted on Voronezh, he had ordered, from the start, a heavy concentration of anti-tank guns on that particular area of the front, which was to be held by 2nd Hungarian Army. Halder wrote on 6 July: 'At the Führer situation conference there was another fearful scene over the control of the offensive by the army group; loud insistence on holding all forces together in conformity with the southward objectives; prohibition to strike towards Voronezh.'[16] It was beginning to look as if the entire offensive within the Don Bend would be a failure, and that, because of von Bock's caution, made worse by lack of petrol and by cloud-bursts, the mass of the Red Army would escape east over the river. Measures had to be taken. On the 7th Army Group A was ordered to advance, despite the fact that Army Group B was still too far away; on the 9th Hitler directed Hoth to move south, instead of south-east along the Don, with one panzer corps to execute a short encircling movement in conjunction with 1st Panzer Army in the area of Kamensk-Shakhtinskij. This was the first modification of the plan, a desperate attempt to cut off the retreating enemy. But von Bock had already ordered the panzer corps south-east, along the Don, and so, by the time it had been turned back and had met up with von Kleist's forward units, only 14,000 enemy soldiers were taken in the encirclement. It was not until the 13th that 4th Panzer Army managed to reach Boguchar, 150 miles south of Voronezh and 200 miles from Stalingrad. Only some 130,000 Soviet troops had been captured up to this time, and it was obvious that most were escaping across the Don.

At this point, in a desperate, but misplaced, attempt to save the situation, Hitler ordered another, and a major, departure from the original plan. Certain that the Red Army must have withdrawn to the lower Don, north of Rostov, where they were maintaining a stiff resistance against 17th Army, he

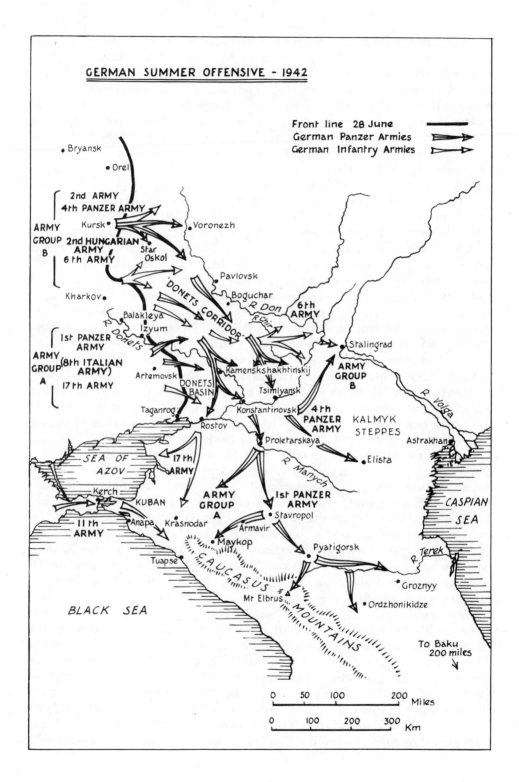

GERMAN SUMMER OFFENSIVE - 1942

Front line 28 June
German Panzer Armies
German Infantry Armies

Bryansk

Orel

2nd ARMY
4th PANZER ARMY
ARMY
GROUP
B
Kursk
2nd HUNGARIAN
ARMY
6th ARMY

Voronezh

Star
Oskol

Pavlovsk

Kharkov

Boguchar

Balakleya
Izyum

DONETS CORRIDOR

R Don

6th
ARMY

R Chir

1st PANZER
ARMY
ARMY
GROUP (8th ITALIAN
ARMY)
A
17th ARMY

R Donets

Stalingrad

Artemovsk

Kamenskshakhtinskij

ARMY
GROUP
B

DONETS
BASIN

Tsimlyansk

R Volga

Taganrog

Konstantinovsk

4th
PANZER
ARMY

KALMYK
STEPPES

Rostov

Proletarskaya

Astrakhan

SEA OF
AZOV

17th
ARMY

R Manych

Elista

Kerch

KUBAN

ARMY
GROUP
A

1st PANZER
ARMY

CASPIAN
SEA

11th
ARMY

Anapa
Krasnodar

Stavropol

Armavir

Maykop

Pyatigorsk

R Terek

Tuapse

CAUCASUS

Mt Elbrus

MOUNTAINS

Groznyy

Ordzhonikidze

BLACK SEA

To Baku
200 miles

0   50   100   200   Miles

0   100   200   300   Km

disregarded any idea of reaching Stalingrad and instead ordered a great encirclement battle to take place north of the mouth of the Don. On 13 July he transferred Hoth's 4th Panzer Army from von Bock's command to List's, and ordered it to cross the lower Don at Konstantinovsk and then move west towards Rostov and the Sea of Azov; von Kleist's 1st Panzer Army would meanwhile right about-turn, cross the Donets once again, and move west along the northern bank of the lower Don. Subsequently, on the 13th, both panzer armies began the move away from Stalingrad in a last attempt to find the retreating enemy; it was a move that was to end in one of the greatest defeats suffered by German arms during the entire war.

The diversion of 4th Panzer Army from Stalingrad to the lower Don was a fatal mistake; it achieved nothing on the Don. Von Kleist remembered: 'The 4th Panzer Army was advancing . . . on my left. It could have taken Stalingrad without a fight, at the end of July, but was diverted south to help me in crossing the Don. I did not need its aid, and it merely congested the roads I was using. When it turned north again, a fortnight later, the Russians had gathered just sufficient forces at Stalingrad to check it.'[17] The other armies of Army Group B, now under the command of von Weichs (von Bock having been sent into retirement on the 14th) could make no progress against Stalingrad in the absence of 4th Panzer Army. The 2nd Army was occupied with Soviet counter-attacks around Voronezh; the 2nd Hungarian Army was defending 100 miles of front along the Don between Voronezh and Pavlosk; and the 6th Army was left to cover the flank from Pavlovsk and, at the same time, advance over 250 miles into the Don Bend to Stalingrad. It was a task beyond its resources, even when 8th Italian Army arrived to take over the sector of the front south-east of Pavlovsk.

By 18 July, Hitler again modified his plans. On that day Halder wrote: 'Yesterday I made a suggestion which was peremptorily turned down in favour of a senseless concentration on the northern bank of the Don against Rostov. Today at the Führer's conference my suggestion was suddenly accepted, and an order issued by the "All Highest" that the Don should be crossed on a wide front and the battle of Stalingrad began.'[18] Thus, when the 4th Panzer Army crossed the Don, it would not turn west towards Rostov, but instead move north-east towards Stalingrad. However, the advance to the Lower Don would continue, despite the fact that by then it was clear that the enemy was withdrawing as fast as it could, and that by the time the two panzer armies arrived the Don crossings would be virtually undefended. Owing to fuel shortages and rainfall, it was not until 22 July that units of 4th Panzer Army formed bridgeheads across the river. Still, there was much dissatisfaction at OKH. On the 23rd Halder wrote: '. . . It must now be clear even to the amateur that there is a senseless concentration of mobile formations in the Rostov area, and that the vital outer flank at Tsimlyansk [130 miles east of Rostov] is going short. I gave emphatic warnings that both of these things would happen. Those on the spot, where victory is within their grasp, are furious with the High Command and reproach it bitterly.'[19]

On 23 July Hitler issued Directive No. 45. Its contents represented a considerable extension in the scope of the offensive; now, two objectives, the Caucasus and Stalingrad, were to be pursued simultaneously. Its opening paragraph stated erroneously:

'In a campaign which has lasted little more than three weeks, the broad objectives outlined by me . . . have been largely achieved. Only weak enemy forces . . . have succeeded in avoiding encirclement and reaching the further bank of the Don.'

The task of Army Group A was to be:

'. . . to encircle enemy forces which have escaped across the Don in the area south and south-east of Rostov, and to destroy them. . . . [Following this] the most important task of Army Group A [in reality, 17th Army] will be to occupy the entire eastern coastline of the Black Sea, thereby eliminating the Black Sea ports and the enemy Black Sea fleet. . . . At the same time, a force composed chiefly of fast-moving formations [1st Panzer Army] will give flank cover in the east and capture the Groznyy area [more than 200 miles from the Black Sea]. . . . thereafter the Baku area will be occupied by a thrust along the Caspian coast.'[20]

This was a considerable objective. From Rostov to Baku is more than 700 miles as the crow flies, and the width of the front across the line of the Caucasus was 800 miles. The terrain was flat, the cornfields immediately south of the Don giving way to a waterless, hot steppe stretching as far as the Caucasus mountains, which are, in places, up to 15,000 feet in height. For this task, Army Group A which, owing to Hitler's interference, had already lost the use of two élite motorised divisions – the *Leibstandarte* and *Grossdeutschland* – was reinforced by only a Romanian mounted corps. Moreover, a large part of 11th Army, which had completed its task of subduing Sevastopol, was sent to Leningrad instead of being used in the south where it was needed. At the same time Army Group B was ordered 'to develop the Don defences and, by a thrust forward to Stalingrad, to smash the enemy forces concentrated there, to occupy the town, and to block the land communications between the Don and the Volga as well as the Don itself. Closely connected with this, fast-moving forces will advance [south-east] along the Volga with the task of thrusting through to Astrakhan and blocking the main course of the Volga in the same way'.[21] Thus, 4th Panzer Army was to advance 175 miles to Stalingrad and then a further 250 miles to Astrakhan, over ground subject to rainfall, while the four infantry armies held a defensive front more than 700 miles in length against what was certain to be heavy enemy pressure. The resources of the two army groups were simply not sufficient for such simultaneous tasks. The objectives laid down in Directive No. 45 were the result of two factors: the need to secure the north-east flank by taking Stalingrad, a task which had not been achieved earlier simply because of the Führer's decision to order 4th Panzer Army to proceed to the lower Don; and Hitler's insistence that the Caucasus should be occupied, and that this be done before the onset of bad weather, thus making it imperative that the advance be begun by the beginning of August at the latest. In such a way, was the fateful decision of 13 July, to proceed south to Rostov instead of concentrating on Stalingrad, compounded, and failure ensured.

As List's Army Group A burst into the Caucasus, and its armies fanned out across the peninsula, across a front 300 miles wide, it appeared that the German advance there had become a pursuit. Rostov fell on 23 July, and on the 25th the attack from the Don bridgeheads began. On the right flank Group Ruoff managed, admittedly with some difficulty, to reach the Black Sea coast at Anapa on 28 August, having covered a distance of more than 250 miles. But it was on the left, 200 miles away, where von Kleist's 1st Panzer Army advanced, that events appeared so spectacularly successful. Its offensive began in earnest on 28 July, and on the 29th Proletarskaya, seventy-five miles from the Don, was taken. By 9 August the oil centre of Maykop, 200 miles south-east of Rostov, was entered, and at the same time Pyatigorsk, 150 miles to the south-east of Maykop, was occupied. The foothills of the Caucasian mountains had been reached after only twelve days. But then the pace of the advance slowed dramatically; it took until 2 November, another eighty-five days, to advance a further 125 miles to within a few miles of Ordzhonikidze, the most southerly point reached by the German forces. German Jägers (Riflemen) might plant the Reich's war flag on Mount Elbrus, but the enemy still held the passes. Meanwhile, on the right, 17th Army had managed to push only some sixty miles up the Black Sea coast before being forced to a halt in early October. Baku still lay 300 miles distant from the German forces.

The reasons for the failure of Army Group A in the Caucasus were not difficult to understand. Von Kleist believed: 'We could still have reached our goal if my forces had not been drawn away bit by bit to help the attack at Stalingrad. Besides part of my motorised forces, I had to give up the whole of my Flak corps and all my air force except the reconnaissance squadrons.' Other factors also were important: 'The primary cause of our failure was shortage of petrol. The bulk of our supplies had to come by rail from the Rostov bottleneck, as the Black Sea route was considered unsafe. A certain amount of oil was delivered by air, but the total which came through was insufficient to maintain the momentum of the advance, which came to a halt just when our chances looked best.'[22] Sometimes for days on end the armoured forces were stopped for lack of fuel. There were other reasons. As the spearheads advanced, the spacious plains gave way to difficult, hilly, and wooded country; resistance from local troops and guerrilla forces determined to defend their homes hardened, and harassment from Soviet aircraft increased. By the end of August, when the attacking force consisted of only eight divisions, von Kleist was faced by a force of forty divisions and brigades. No reinforcements could be expected from Army Group B fighting at Stalingrad; it served only as a further drain on his resources. The failure in the Caucasus was a classic example of a Supreme Commander attempting too much, with too little, all at once.

26

The East – Stalingrad

Above all, maintain freedom of operations.

NAPOLEON

While von Kleist was pushing deep into the Caucasus, the battle for Stalingrad was developing. The city was subjected to a two-pronged attack, one from the north-west by 6th Army, and the other from the south-west by 4th Panzer Army. The importance of the objective was recognised by Hitler and his closest advisers. On 30 July, the day after 4th Panzer Army had begun its move north-east, Halder wrote: 'At the Führer's conference, General Jodl took the floor. In solemn tones he stated that the fate of the Caucasus would be decided at Stalingrad. Forces must therefore be diverted from Army Group A to Army Group B; so the idea which I put to the Führer six days ago, but which was then understood by none of the great brains of OKW, has now been served up afresh and accepted.'[1] However, 6th Army under von Paulus made slow progress at first because the bulk of its transport had been diverted to Army Group A as a result of the Führer's directive of 23 July. It took ten days, during which time von Paulus's force was severely restricted in action, for this mistake to be rectified. Because of this – as well as the strong resistance already exhibited by the enemy, the need to detach more and more units to cover the extending flanks, and the time required for Hoth to fight his way up from the south-west – it was not until 19 August that the first serious attempt to take Stalingrad was begun. For this, von Paulus was given over-all command of the two armies. On the 23rd a panzer corps of 6th Army managed to penetrate to the city's outskirts; the battle intensified, and then developed into the longest-drawn-out, most terrible struggle of the whole war.

The tactical events during the battle of Stalingrad need not be dealt with here; suffice it to say that strong Soviet resistance gradually brought the Germans to a halt by 6 September, when they were already in the city. On 19 November the enemy mounted counter-attacks north and south of Stalingrad, and by the 21st they had encircled 6th Army and half of 4th Panzer Army. The attackers were now the attacked; the 280,000 soldiers isolated in a pocket thirty miles across from east to west, and twenty-five miles from north to south, were in danger of death or capture. On 31 January 1942, after a siege lasting seventy-three days, von Paulus and his remaining 91,000 men surrendered.

Stalingrad had always interested Hitler. In his Directive No. 41, dated 5 April 1942, he had seen it as an important objective that would have to be dominated before a successful operation in the Caucasus could be carried out; in his Directive No. 45 of 23 July, he placed its acquisiton on a level equal with the occupation of the Black Sea coast and the exploitation of the Baku; soon after, he had arrived at the conclusion that the taking of the city was of such crucial importance that units could even be takn from the Caucasian thrust for the purpose. Stalingrad came to dominate his thinking; nothing mattered but its occupation. For the Führer, the city that bore the name of the Soviet dictator took on a political significance greater than any military consideration; defeat at its gates would be unthinkable. At Stalingrad, it was the world's assessment of Germany's power, and of Hitler's leadership, that was at stake. On 28 September, and again on 8 November, he publicly staked his reputation on gaining Stalingrad, declaring 'I will remain on the Volga'. The city quickly assumed a symbolic importance; its name was linked with that of Verdun in the First World War. There, in 1916, the German Army had called off its attack, when just one more month would have sufficed to destroy the whole French Army. This, Hitler was adamant, would never happen again. To this end, he ordered on 14 October that 'Every leader . . . must be convinced of his sacred duty, to stand fast come what may, even if the enemy outflanks him on the right and left, even if his part of the line is cut off, encircled, overrun by tanks, enveloped in smoke, or gassed'.[2] This was prophetic. When it became clear that the attackers would be the encircled, and that the only hope for their salvation lay in a timely withdrawal, Hitler refused to countenance such a course of action. His 'instinct' had proved correct the year before, or so he thought; it would be justified again. His 'will' would triumph once more over the cautious professionalism of his generals; there would be 'no withdrawal'; resistance would be maintained to the last man. Over Stalingrad, then, Hitler exhibited a military wrong-headedness that was plain for all to see. Reason appeared to play little part in his thinking; a cool, detached assessment of the conditions on the battlefield had no place in his deliberations.

The battle of Stalingrad need never have taken place. Had Hitler adhered to his original plan, the city would have been taken in mid-July; as it was, when it had become clear that the dogged Soviet resistance would make its capture extremely costly, if not impossible, the attack should have been called off, and a more mobile form of warfare resumed. Von Manstein maintained that:

> 'The risk which the German Command ought to have taken, after the summer offensive had merely won us more territory without

bringing about the decisive defeat of the Soviet southern wing, consisted in returning to mobile operations between the Caucasus and middle reaches on the Don – with due advantage being taken of the large bend in the river – in order to prevent the enemy from attaining the initiative. But to substitute one risk for another was not in Hitler's mentality. By failing to take appropriate action after his offensive had petered out without achieving anything definite, he paved the way to the tragedy of Stalingrad.'[3]

A number of realities stared Hitler in the face, but he refused to see them. He could not understand that the more his armies converged on the city, and the more they concentrated their effort on its small area, the less their superiority in manoeuvre and flexibility counted and the greater their shortages of men and supplies told. The moment 6th Army and 4th Panzer Army became locked in combat outside Stalingrad, the theories, lessons, and possibilities of *Vernichtungsgedanke*, let alone of the armoured idea, were thrown overboard, and a large part of Germany's Field Army was condemned to fight a costly slogging-match of attrition, the very form of warfare its generals had been trained to avoid. And it was the Germans, not their enemies, who were least able to bear the terrible losses that were the inevitable consequence of such a battle.

If Hitler disregarded the need for manoeuvre, he also neglected to safeguard his flanks. It is ironic that the man, who in 1940 and 1941 had been so obsessed with ensuring proper flank protection for his advances, now forgot it so completely. The armies within the Don Bend formed a massive, 600-mile salient jutting into Soviet territory. To the north and south of Stalingrad, to Voronezh and to Rostov, the Don sweeps back sharply to the west and thereby left the north-east and south-east flanks of the German armies dangerously exposed. The situation was made worse by the fact that, when the 1st and 4th Panzer Armies had parted company with each other on the lower Don in late July, they had advanced on divergent courses, one to the south-east, the other to the north-east, leaving a dangerous angular front between them; a gap 190 miles wide yawned between the two army groups in the Kalmyk Steppes, guarded by one one division. Hitler feared an attack on this salient, but would do nothing about it. As early as August, OKH had warned of the dangers of this front. Von Blumentritt recorded:

> 'The danger to the long-stretched flank of our advance developed gradually, but it became clear early enough for anyone to perceive it who was not wilfully blind. During August, the Russians by degrees increased their strength on the other side of the Don, from Voronezh south-eastward. A number of short and sharp attacks on their part explored the weakness of the German defence along the Don. These exploratory attacks showed them that the 2nd Hungarian Army was holding the sector south of Voronezh, and the 8th Italian Army was holding the sector beyond that. The risk became worse after Sep-

tember, when the Romanians took over the more south-easterly sector as far as the Don Bend, west of Stalingrad, and held a front of 250 miles with only thirty-three battalions. There was only a slight German stiffening in this long "Allied" line. . . . I . . . made a written report to the effect that it would not be safe to hold such a long defensive flank during the winter. The railheads were as much as 200 kilometres [125 miles] behind the front, and the bare nature of the country meant that there was little timber available for constructing defences. Such German divisions as were available were holding frontages of fifty to sixty kilometres [31 to 37 miles]. There were no proper trenches or fixed positions. General Halder endorsed this report and urged that our offensive should be halted, in view of the increasing resistance that it was meeting, and the increased signs of danger to the long-stretched flank. But Hitler would not listen.'[4]

Instead, he even withdrew units that were protecting the flank to send against Stalingrad. Von Manstein, no admirer of the fighting qualities of either the Romanians or the Italians, was adamant about Hitler's folly. He wrote: '. . . to leave the main body of the army group at Stalingrad for weeks on end, with inadequately protected flanks, was a cardinal error. It amounted to nothing less than presenting the enemy with the initiative we ourselves had resigned on the whole southern wing, and it was a clear invitation for him to surround 6th Army.'[5]

At the same time as concern was growing over the manning of the salient, Hitler withdrew forces from the front. Warlimont believed this to be 'the ultimate cause of the failure'. He continued: 'Even before the slanting drive down the corridor between the Don and the Donets began, an entire panzer corps . . . was assembled in the rear and put at the disposal of Army Group Centre. The main reason for that was that it seemed impossible to supply petrol for more than a certain amount of mechanised forces in the southern region'.[6] Thus, two panzer divisions from Army Group B were detached in the first days of the campaign – to be followed later in July by two élite motorised infantry formations, *Grossdeutschland* and *Leibstandarte,* taken from Army Group A, both of which were to be transferred to the west as a security measure against any British landing. In the event, only the *Leibstandarte* made the journey; the *Grossdeutschland* became involved in the Soviet counter-attack on the central sector and was forced to stay there. All these moves were carried out in the face of strong opposition from the generals, including Jodl; they were a significant blow to both offensives in the south.

Even when the German armies were embroiled in the battle of attrition in the streets and alleyways of Stalingrad, expending their strength in a series of localised attacks against ferocious opposition, and when the Soviets had overcome the Romanians north and south of the city and had encircled the German attackers, Hitler still refused to acknowledge reality. If withdrawal had been the correct course before mid-November, how much more was it so as the enemy was drawing the ring around 6th Army. Yet the Führer would not allow such a course. Von Manstein commented:

> 'What must be made perfectly clear . . . is that it was the Supreme Command's business to issue an order affording 6th Army the opportunity to acquire operational elbow-room and thereby to avoid being surrounded. . . . When the Soviets unleashed their big offensive across the Don and south of Stalingrad on 19 November, the German leaders must have known what was coming. From that moment onwards it was inadmissible to wait until the enemy had overrun the Romanians, for even if their armies had not been carved up so quickly, it would still have been necessary to use 6th Army in a mobile role in order to master the situation. . . .'[7]

But no such order came. When on 19 November, 1,300 miles away in his mountain retreat at the Berghof, Hitler heard of the Soviet counter-attack, he angrily dismissed the proposal of Army Group B headquarters that 6th Army be withdrawn. On the 21st he attempted to improve the fast-deteriorating situation on Army Group B's front by the creation of a new army group. Von Manstein and the headquarters of the 11th Army, then in the Vitebsk area, received an order from OKH stating that 'for the purpose of stricter coordination of the armies involved in the arduous defensive battles to the west and south of Stalingrad', they were to take over-all control of 4th Panzer Army, 6th Army, and 3rd Romanian Army. The new command was to be known as Army Group Don, and its immediate task was 'to bring the enemy attacks to a standstill and recapture the positions previously occupied. . . .'[8] On the 27th Army Group Don took over its new command. However, von Manstein's freedom of action was severely restricted by the exacting conditions imposed by Hitler on the most important force in the army group: 6th Army. On 23 November, by which time the Soviets had moved thirty-four divisions across the Don, von Weichs had sent a signal to Führer headquarters in which he stated that it was impossible to supply nine-tenths of 6th Army's requirements by air, and that, because it was unlikely that a relief operation could be mounted before 10 December, he asked that von Paulus be ordered to break out immediately. The losses in men and equipment thereby occasioned would be preferable to their being starved into submission. That night von Paulus himself, with the agreement of both von Weichs and all his corps commanders of 6th Army, had sent a radio message to Hitler asking that he be allowed to act on his own initiative, and stating that only by a concentration and a withdrawal could his force survive. Ammunition was low, and only immediate action could prevent the early destruction of 6th Army.

At Führer headquarters the tension mounted. After the war, the new Chief of the General Staff, Zeitzler, maintained that he had strongly supported the arguments coming from Army Group B, and that on 23 November Hitler had given verbal approval for a breakout. Whether or not that were so cannot be ascertained, but, if it were, the Führer must have repented of his decision by the next day. On the morning of the 24th Göring arrived to promise Hitler that, as at Demyansk, the Luftwaffe would supply the encircled forces at Stalingrad from the air. Hitler immediately declared the city to be a 'fortress', and the troops received an order to stay on the Volga. This was followed on the 26th by a personal message from him to all soldiers of 6th Army, in which he ordered them to stand fast and promised to do all in his power to support them. Hitler's decision being final, the fate of the 284,000 men cut off in the besieged city was dependent on three essential conditions: that they could be properly supplied from the air; that there should be a continuous flow of reinforcements to the relief force; and that 6th Army must leave Stalingrad. Although Hitler endorsed these proposals on 3 December, it soon became clear, as von Manstein recorded, that he 'had not the slightest intention of releasing 6th Army from Stalingrad'.[9] Nor would the other two prerequisites for the success of the operation be fulfilled.

The air support of 6th Army was a failure from the beginning. The belief of von Paulus and his generals appears to have been that if they were properly supplied from the air, their chances of holding out were good: 550 tons each day were the minimum required to supply 6th Army with the rations, clothing, equipment, and munitions needed for effective defence, but only once was even half that figure achieved. The largest delivery for one day was 290 tons, on 7 December; the average in mid-December was 140 tons, and by mid-January this had fallen to 60 tons, rising to 80 tons at the end of that month. Such figures bore little relation to requirements. Even in the first days of the encirclement the 6th Army had only enough rations left for six days, and ammunition for two days, many batteries being without shells at all. By mid-January, when the temperature had fallen to −30°C, the daily ration for the troops had sunk to 200 grammes of horse meat, 75 grammes of bread, and 12 grammes of fat or margarine. Von Paulus, no longer able to feed his prisoners-of-war, had ordered that they should be released.

The responsibility for this state of affairs lay with Hitler. Both von Weichs and von Manstein had pointed out to him the difficulty of providing adequate support by air, and the former had been correct when he had warned on 23 November that the Luftwaffe was not capable of delivering a tenth of 6th Army's needs. But Göring had thought otherwise; his wildly optimistic appreciation of his Air Force's capability, as well as his inept handling of the operation, meant inevitably that the 6th Army slowly starved to death. However, it was Hitler who had decided that the Luftwaffe should be employed at Stalingrad; von Manstein wrote of the importance of this decision:

'Only if a guarantee of air supplies were given . . . could we afford to delay a breakout until the intervention of relief forces improved the army's chances of escape. By refusing to sanction Paulus's request for a breakout . . . Hitler had to all intents and purposes already given that guarantee. His refusal had been based on an assurance from Göring. . . . Nevertheless, Hitler should still have checked up on the reliability of his statements. Besides knowing what sort of person Göring was, he was also well aware of the strength of the Luftwaffe.'[10]

Hitler, the Supreme Commander, had insisted on taking full responsibility during the years of victory; now, during defeat, it remained with him still.

Failure in the air was matched by failure on the ground. Von Manstein wrote: 'The fact that we ultimately failed in our mission [to rescue the 6th Army] was primarily due to the extraordinary preponderance of the enemy's forces and the deficient strength of our own.'[11] According to promises made by OKH, von Manstein expected that his relief force would amount to four armoured, four infantry and mountain, and three Luftwaffe field divisions, which 'might conceivably suffice to make temporary contact with 6th Army and to restore its freedom of movement. In no event, however, could they administer a defeat big enough to enable us . . . to "reoccupy the positions held prior to the attack".'[12] But the troops, even for this small force, were not forthcoming despite von Manstein's repeated protests. Owing in large part to the low efficiency of the railways and to the thaw that had begun in the Caucasus having turned the roads into seas of mud, there were delays in finding units to replace those which had failed to arrive, and in transporting them to their assembly areas; two divisions were diverted to support the Third Romanian Army which was facing collapse, half a mountain division was moved by OKH to Army Group A and the other half was retained by Army Group Centre; one panzer division was so depleted that it proved incapable of offensive action; the army artillery from Army Group A did not arrive at all; a Luftwaffe Field Division was late in forming, and the others were found to be too weak to include in the attacking force. Hitler made no effort to provide von Manstein with more formations; he still wanted to do everything at once, and thus avoid deciding on priorities. Von Manstein argued that:

> 'There were two possible ways of effecting this reinforcement. Army Group Don repeatedly asked to be given Army Group A's III Panzer Corps of two armoured divisions, which should not have been used in mountainous country anyway. On each occasion the request was refused because Army Group A claimed it could not release the corps unless it were allowed to evacuate a salient projecting far into the Caucasus – a measure which Hitler, in turn, would not countenance. We were just as unsuccessful in our attempts to get an Army Group A regiment to relieve 16th Motorised Division at Elista, where it was covering the deep flank of 1st Panzer Army [it was later released, but too late]. . . . The second possible way . . . lay in the provision of new forces by OKH. At the time in question, 17th Panzer Division and

the newly established 306th Infantry Division were . . . on their way to Army Group Don. . . . Unfortunately OKH had the [panzer] division detained as its own reserve behind the left wing of the army group because – not without reason – it feared a large-scale attack was impending there. Yet OKH could not have it both ways: success for 4th Panzer Army *and* security against a crisis which – if it did arise – 17th Panzer Division could not master anyway. While we preferred success for 4th Panzer Army, Hitler opted for the security. . . . The upshot was that when Hitler did release the division, after 306th Infantry Division had caught up [to become the OKH reserve] it arrived too late for the first phase of the relief formation. Possibly this was where the decisive opportunity was thrown away . . . it may seem surprising, in view of the number of enemy formations confronting the army group, that we still continued to believe in the possibility of relieving 6th Army at all.'[13]

To make matters worse, on 4 December the Soviets, who were keeping up their pressure on the Don front, attacked on the lower Chir, north-east of 4th Panzer Army and the point nearest to Stalingrad. One panzer and one infantry division of Army Detachment Hollidt, its best formations earmarked for the relief of 6th Army, became occupied in defensive fighting well before the operation was mounted and were never able to take part in the attack. Thus, 4th Panzer Army, or, to be more precise, one of its panzer corps – the only formation capable of offensive operations – was left to make the attack towards Stalingrad alone. Just two panzer divisions, one of which had only thirty tanks, and an assault-gun brigade were expected to advance eighty miles against heavy Soviet opposition. Moreover, delays in the assembly of the divisions had caused the attack to be postponed from 3 December until the 12th, by which time enemy strength had increased. German intelligence reported that the enemy formations ranged against Army Group Don at that time amounted to eighty-six rifle and eleven cavalry divisions, seventeen rifle, fifty-four tank, and fourteen motorised brigades, plus a number of independent tank regiments and battalions.

The attack that opened on 12 December was a failure. By the 17th the 57th Panzer Corps of 4th Panzer Army, totalling 230 tanks, and the assault-gun brigade had reached to within thirty-five miles of the city, but were to advance little further. On that day the 17th Panzer Division at last arrived, but too late. The next day, the 18th, was, according to von Manstein:

'. . . a day of crisis of the first order. East of the Don, despite the arrival of 17th Panzer Division . . . [4th Panzer Army] had still not fought to a point which offered any prospect of its being able to thrust swiftly into the vicinity of Stalingrad and create the conditions needed for 6th Army's breakout. On the contrary, it looked as though the corps would be forced on the defensive, since the enemy was continuing to throw forces in its path from the siege round the city. On the lower Chir [now to the west-north-west of 4th Panzer Army], heavy fighting [which had begun on 4 December] was still in progress, although the enemy had not so far succeeded in penetrating our front. On the left wing of the army group, on the other hand, a most serious crisis was taking shape, the enemy having begun a major attack against Army Detachment Hollidt and the Italian Army forming the right wing of Army Group B.'[14]

Here the Romanians and the Italians proved unequal to their task of holding the line, and the flank of Army Group Don was broken. Now 4th Panzer Army itself was in danger of encirclement.

Von Manstein and Hoth, however, still persevered. The army group commander asked OKH to allow 6th Army to break out of Stalingrad to meet 4th Panzer Army. He remembered that:

> 'There was still a chance that once 17th Panzer Division had made its presence fully felt, 57th Panzer Corps could win further ground in the direction of the pocket. In other words, one could still hope for a favourable outcome of the struggle east of the Don. Yet how much easier this could have been achieved if only 17th Panzer and 16th Motorised Divisions (of which the latter was still tied up at Elista) could have been available for 4th Panzer Army's relief operation from the very outset!'[15]

Now Hitler, having by his actions made certain that there were not to be enough troops for the advance to Stalingrad, made the final error; he ordered that 6th Army should stay put. If 4th Panzer Army could not reach it, it was not to move tc 4th Panzer Army. At the same time, OKH informed von Manstein that all units moving up would be sent to Army Group B to help stabilize its front. The fate of 6th Army was finally sealed by the refusal of von Paulus to countenance a breakout in defiance of Hitler's order. On 19 December one of von Manstein's officers arrived in the Stalingrad fortress to communicate the views of his chief to von Paulus and to argue for a withdrawal. Von Manstein wrote:

> 'Paulus himself had not been unimpressed . . . though he did not fail to emphasise the magnitude of the difficulties and risks which the task . . . would imply. The army's Chief of Operations and Quartermaster-General likewise stressed these difficulties . . . but both men also declared that in the circumstances it was not only essential . . . but also entirely feasible. What ultimately decided the attitude of 6th Army headquarters was the opinion of the chief of staff, Major-General Arthur Schmidt [an enthusiastic believer in the Führer's genius]. He contended that it was quite impossible for the army to break out just then, and that such a solution would be "an acknowledgement of disaster". . . . While the army commander was probably a better-trained tactician and a clearer-thinking man, it

looked as if his chief of staff was the stronger personality of the two. And so the upshot of the talks was that General Paulus himself ended by pronouncing the breakout a sheer impossibility and pointing out that the surrender of Stalingrad was forbidden "by order of the Führer".'[16]

However, von Manstein was not to be defeated so easily. On 19 December the reinforced 57th Panzer Corps had advanced to within thirty miles of Stalingrad. Von Manstein wrote:

> 'The moment for which we had longed since the take-over had arrived. If 6th Army now began its breakout while 4th Panzer Army either continued the attack northwards or at least drew off further forces from the siege front, the enemy in between would find himself between two fires, and there would at last be a prospect of establishing enough contact to provide 6th Army with the fuel, ammunition, and food it needed for continuing its breakthrough. For this purpose, the army group had assembled transport columns loaded with 3,000 tons of supplies behind 4th Panzer Army, in addition to tractors for mobilising part of the 6th Army artillery. They were all to be rushed through to the beleagured army as soon as the tanks had cleared a route, however temporary.'[17]

Time, however, was crucial, for Army Group Don could hold the front for a short time only against the Soviet attacks west of Stalingrad. Accordingly, at noon on the 19th von Manstein signalled an urgent appeal to Führer headquarters to allow 6th Army to breakout. With no immediate response forthcoming, at 6.00p.m. von Manstein himself ordered von Paulus to begin an immediate drive to the south-west, and at the same time to evacuate Stalingrad.

But 6th Army did not move. Von Paulus was concerned at the risks involved, especially in view of the weakened condition of his force, and doubted whether it would be possible to disengage his troops, who were already subject to constant attack. It was true that 4th Panzer Army still lay thirty miles distant, and certainly 6th Army's 100 remaining tanks had not sufficient fuel for an advance of more than twenty miles; but it was also sensible to surmise that, once von Paulus had launched his attack, the progress of Hoth's units would be greatly eased, and that would allow them to cover at least the remaining ten to twelve miles. However, von Manstein admitted that:

> '. . . the army commander was faced with a tremendous gamble. . . . While a breakout certainly offered the army a chance of rescue, it could equally well lead to its destruction. Should the first attempt to break through the enemy's siege front prove unsuccessful, should 6th Army get stuck halfway while 4th Panzer Army were unable to make any further progress, or should the enemy manage to overrun the

German troops shielding the breakout from the rear and flanks, then 6th Army's fate would be sealed in no time at all.'

But, as the army group commander realised:

'. . . the fact remained that this was our one and only chance of saving the army. Not to utilise it – however great the risks – meant to resign all hope of salvation.'[18]

Whatever von Paulus's objections – and they were not inadmissible – it was unthinkable that he would have disobeyed a direct order from his senior commander, especially in this last chance to save his army, had it not been for one factor: Hitler. Although the Führer had at last been convinced of the necessity for 6th Army to attack south-east to join 4th Panzer Army, he at the same time insisted that Stalingrad be held. On this point he remained adamant. His intention was that a corridor be formed by which the army could be supplied for as long as was necessary. This ensured that von Paulus could never mount his breakout, for it was impossible for 6th Army to attack south-west as well as hold its present front at Stalingrad. In its weakened state, and with the overwhelming strength of the enemy, there could be no question of it maintaining its position in the city while simultaneously keeping contact with 4th Panzer Army. Furthermore, the Soviet counter-attacks against Army Groups Don and B no longer allowed two armies to be tied down east of the Don. Along the whole of the north-eastern flank, nearly 200 miles, von Manstein's army group was already retreating in disarray, overwhelmed by an enemy whose superiority was nearly sixfold. By remaining within thirty miles of the city, the 4th Panzer Army was running every conceivable risk, and the threat of yet another major encirclement was daily growing nearer. When von Manstein attempted to reason with Hitler along these lines, he was told that a breakout was an impossibility in any case: had not 6th Army 'only enough petrol for fifteen to twenty miles at the most?'[19] But even had Hitler not had this 'reason' to hide behind, it was probable that he would not have allowed any evacuation of the city; von Paulus, and even less, Schmidt, would not have disobeyed the Führer, especially in view of their grave doubts as to the feasibility of any breakout operation. Von Paulus, then, decided against the venture. He was dubious of von Manstein's plan, recognised the impossibility of Hitler's, and was, in any case, incapable of disobeying the Führer. Stalingrad would be held. Thus was the fate of 6th Army sealed.

From 23 December Stalingrad began to recede as the primary concern of Army Group Don, which concentrated its attention on the rest of the front. On that day, owing to the intensity of the Soviet attacks to the north-east, one panzer division was taken from 4th Panzer Army's spearhead to re-inforce the units on the Lower Chir. Von Manstein commented: 'The army group had only taken this agonising decision to deprive the . . . relief group of a whole division when it became clear that 6th Army could no longer be expected to break out in time. . . . And so, in the battleground east of the Don, too, the hour now came for the initiative to pass to our opponents.'[20] On the 27th, the same day on which Hitler rejected von Manstein's proposals for its reinforcement, 4th Panzer Army began the withdrawal. By the last day of 1942 more than 100 miles separated 6th Army from the nearest German units. On 8 January the Soviets offered the chance of capitulation to the encircled troops, but on Hitler's orders it was refused. Four days later, 6th Army sent a report in which it stated: 'Reserves are no longer available; nor can any be formed. Heavy weapons now immobilised. Severe losses and inadequate supplies, together with cold, have also considerably reduced troops' power of resistance. If enemy maintains attack in present strength, fortress front unlikely to hold more than a few days longer.'[21]

On 22 January von Paulus asked Hitler's permission to open negotiations for surrender. His troops were suffering intense deprivation; ammunition and rations were almost at an end. Resistance was proving impossible. Von Manstein recorded:

> 'In this connexion I had a long argument with the [Führer] . . . by telephone. I urged him to authorise a capitulation, my belief being that though every day's reduction of the army's resistance must aggravate the army group's situation as a whole, the time had now come to put an end to this valiant struggle. In bitter fighting, the army had expended its last ounce of strength to hold a far stronger enemy, thereby decisively contributing to the salvation of the Eastern Front that winter. From now on, the army's sufferings would bear no relation to any advantage which could be derived from continuing to tie down the enemy's forces.'[22]

Hitler, however, would have none of it; 6th Army was to continue to fight to the last. His reason was identical with that which von Manstein had put forward but rejected. Nevertheless, the end was near. On the 24th, von Paulus radioed to OKH:

> 'Fortress can be held for only a few days longer. Troops exhausted and weapons immobilised as a result of non-arrival of supplies. . . . Heroism of officers and men nevertheless unbroken. In order to use this for the final blow, shall give orders just before final break-up for all elements to fight through to south-west in organised groups. Some of these will get through and sow confusion behind Russian lines. Failure to move will mean the end of everyone, as prisoners will also die of cold and hunger. Suggest flying out a few men, officers and other ranks, as specialists for use in future operations.'[23]

Hitler refused the request for evacuation, and reserved for himself the final decision as to the breakout. On the 31st, by which time the wounded of 6th Army were receiving no rations, Hitler made von Paulus a field-marshal. No German field-marshal had been captured since the unification of Germany in 1871, but that very day von Paulus and his staff surrendered. The next forty-eight hours saw the last of the fighting.

An army of 280,000 men had been destroyed; more than 200,000 were killed or captured. Of the 91,000 that entered Soviet captivity in those last days, only a few thousand would return to Germany after the war. Von Manstein's lines bear eloquent testimony to the struggles of the ordinary German soldiers: 'By their incomparable bravery and devotion to duty, the officers and men of the army raised a memorial to German arms which, though not of stone and bronze, will nonetheless survive the ages.'[24]

The significance of Stalingrad was immense, but it has grown out of proportion with the passage of time. In the words of von Manstein:

> 'While the eyes of all Germany were on Stalingrad at the turn of 1942–43, and anxious hearts prayed for the sons who fought there, the southern wing of the Eastern Front was simultaneously the scene of a struggle even greater than that being waged for the lives and freedom of the 6th Army's gallant two hundred thousand. The issue was no longer the fate of a single army but of the entire southern wing of the front and, ultimately, of all the German armies in the east.'[25]

The situation of the German southern flank in November 1942, immediately before the Soviet counter-offensive, was critical. The front, with its right wing on the Black Sea, continuing through the northern Caucasus up to the Kalmyk Steppes east of Elista, up to the Volga and Stalingrad, and then back to the Don and up to Voronezh, stretched over some 800 miles. Two army groups, A and B, occupied this area, but they were not directed against one single objective; instead, Hitler had ordered them to pursue divergent lines of advance, one eastwards towards Stalingrad, the other south-east into the Caucasus. As a result, the area of divergence, centred on the Kalmyk Steppes, was one of considerable weakness in the German line, especially as it was guarded by only one motorised infantry division. An attack on this area by the enemy would place the Germans in serious trouble and face them with the prospect of complete dislocation. The situation was made much more dangerous by the close proximity to the front line of Rostov, the gateway to the Caucasus, the Don crossing through which ran the line of communications of Army Group A, as well as of 4th Panzer and 4th Romanian Armies. This town, so vital to the Germans, was but 185 miles from the nearest Soviet formations on the Don, which were themselves opposed only by the unreliable Romanians and Italians of Army Group B, whereas 375 and 250 miles respectively separated it from the left wing of Army Group A and from 4th Panzer Army. Further to the west lay the Dnepr crossings of Zaporozhye and Dnepropetrovsk, through which ran the lines of communication for almost the entire German southern wing; these were 260 miles from the enemy on the Don, but 440 miles from 6th Army and 560 miles from the spearheads of 1st Panzer Army. If the Soviets, now in considerably

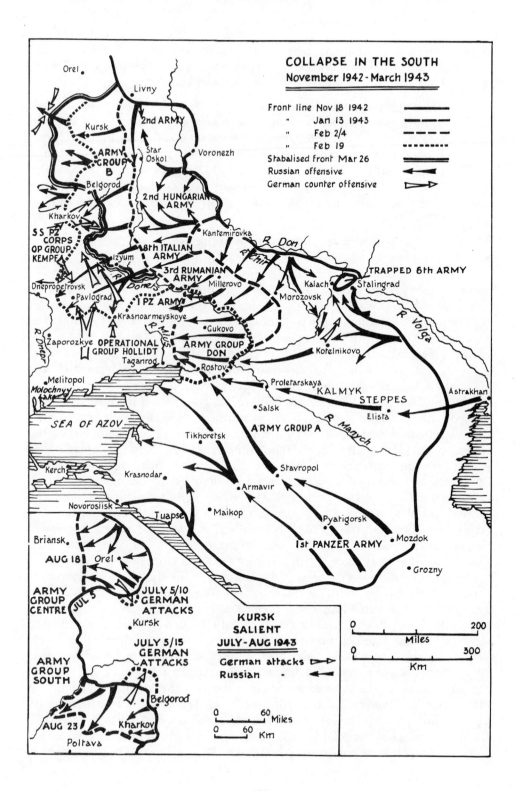

COLLAPSE IN THE SOUTH
November 1942 - March 1943

Front line Nov 18 1942	
" Jan 13 1943	
" Feb 2/4	
" Feb 19	
Stabalised front Mar 26	
Russian offensive	
German counter offensive	

Orel

Livny

2nd ARMY

Kursk

ARMY GROUP B

Star Oskol

Voronezh

Belgorod

2nd HUNGARIAN ARMY

Kharkov

SS PZ CORPS OP GROUP KEMPF

Kantemirovka

R. Don

8th ITALIAN ARMY

R. Chir

Izyum

3rd RUMANIAN ARMY

Millerovo

Kalach

TRAPPED 6th ARMY

Dnepropetrovsk

R. Donets

1 PZ ARMY

Morozovsk

Stalingrad

Pavlograd

Krasnoarmeyskoye

Gukovo

ARMY GROUP DON

R. Volga

R. Mius

Zaporozkye

OPERATIONAL GROUP HOLLIDT

Kotelnikovo

R. Dnepr

Taganrog

Rostov

Proletarskaya

KALMYK STEPPES

Astrakhan

Melitopol

Molochnyy Lake

Salsk

Elista

SEA OF AZOV

Tikhoretsk

ARMY GROUP A

R. Manych

Kerch

Krasnodar

Stavropol

Armavir

Novorosiisk

Tuapse

Maikop

Pyatigorsk

1st PANZER ARMY

Mozdok

Briansk

Grozny

AUG 18 Orel

JULY 5/10 GERMAN ATTACKS

ARMY GROUP CENTRE

JUL 5

Kursk

JULY 5/15 GERMAN ATTACKS

KURSK SALIENT
JULY - AUG 1943

German attacks
Russian

0		200
	Miles	
0		300
	Km	

ARMY GROUP SOUTH

Belgorod

AUG 23

Kharkov

Poltava

0	60	Miles
0	60	Km

greater strength than their enemy, could gain Rostov or, better still, the Dnepr crossings, and cut off the German armies from their life-lines, then a major victory would be theirs. As von Manstein wrote:

> 'What this situation could mean in practice I knew only too well from personal experience, having in summer 1941 covered the odd 190 miles from Tilsit to Dvinsk in four days with LVI Panzer Corps. I had done so, moreover, against opposition that was certainly tougher than anything the Italian and Hungarian armies could offer on the Don. At that time the Russians had also had very many more reserves behind their front than were available to us in the winter of 1942.'[26]

The point at issue now was nothing less than the survival of Army Groups A and B.

For the Germans, the outcome of the winter battles of 1942–43 depended on their ability to keep open the Rostov and Dnepr crossings or, failing that, to escape a Soviet encirclement. Considering the overwhelming numerical superiority of their enemy, the weakness of their allies who were holding vital sectors of the front, and the proximity of the Soviets to their objectives, it was remarkable that only 6th Army was caught in the onslaught; it was especially remarkable when, to the numerous disabilities under which the Germans laboured, is added Hitler's interference in operational matters.

Throughout the Soviet counter-offensive, complete inflexibility characterised Hitler's direction of the German southern flank, finding expression in the oft-repeated words, 'no withdrawal'. Stalingrad, the Don Bend, the Caucasus, the Donets Basin; all, at one time, had to be 'held to the last' – that is, until circumstances proved stronger than Hitler's will. The destruction of 6th Army was the result, and the annihilation of Army Groups A and Don (renamed South on 14 February 1943, when it incorporated elements of Army Group B, which was disbanded) was always likely. When the Red Army launched its attack on 19 November, it was clear that a successful defence of the existing front-line was an impossibility. The German Command was, therefore, faced with a choice between two courses of action: to bring back 6th Army to the west of the Don immediately in order to reinforce the Allied formations with Germans, and to consolidate the position in the Don Bend; or, as von Manstein proposed, to execute a strategic withdrawal of all the forces from the Don Bend and the Caucasus and to establish a strong defensive line behind the lower Dnepr. This latter alternative would have resulted in a considerable shortening of the front, thus concentrating the previously over-extended forces, which could then have launched a counter-attack against the exposed right flank of the advancing enemy. A classic battle of envelopment would result, and defeat would be turned into victory. But 'no withdrawal' precluded both plans. Von Manstein recorded: '. . . Hitler was not the man to embark on a course which initially committed him to relinquish the conquests of summer 1942 and would unquestionably

have entailed considerable operational hazards. . . . With his lack of experience in operational matters, he may even then have hoped to restore the
situation on the southern wing by throwing in the SS Panzer Corps which
was moving up to Kharkov.'[27] Thus, because of the Führer's inability to
understand that yielding ground as part of an operational plan is no crime,
and that, on the contrary, it might be a necessary pre-condition to success,
the newly composed Army Group Don was forced 'to devise one stop-gap
after another to meet a danger which arose from the original strategic
situation and grew increasingly acute as time went on: the danger that the
entire southern wing would be tied off '.[28] Hitler, by his obstinacy, had given
the initiative to the enemy; as a result, all his troops could do was to react to
the moves of the Soviets.

Despite all the disadvantages suffered by the Germans, foremost among
which was Hitler's intransigence, their southern flank, though it lost ground,
survived the Soviet assault. On 19 November the Red Army attacked north
and south of Stalingrad, overwhelmed the Romanians and in five days had
encircled the 6th Army; by 12 December, on which date von Manstein
launched his ill-fated relief operation, the Red Army had penetrated to a
depth of more than 100 miles; on the 16th it began its potentially most
dangerous operation when it struck down from the middle Don and put the
Italians of Army Group B to flight. Rostov then lay just 125 miles away, due
south; on Christmas Eve it broke through on the Chir front and the Kalmyk
Steppes, also in the general direction of Rostov; by New Year's Eve it had
extended its attack by seventy miles, and all that separated it from Rostov
was 4th Panzer Army, which itself was in constant danger of encirclement.
Only two days earlier Hitler had ordered Army Group A, whose escape
route was close to being cut off, to withdraw, but by only seventy-five miles;
by 7 January the Soviets were but thirty miles from Rostov, and the severance of Army Group A from the rest of the German front seemed imminent.
Not until 27 January would Hitler give the order for the final evacuation of
the Caucasus; by 1 February most of the army group had passed through
Rostov, which fell to the Soviets a few days later. Only 17th Army remained
in the Caucasus; according to Hitler's order, it was to defend, at all costs,
the Taman peninsula and the Kuban bridgehead – a foothold was to be
maintained, however hopeless the possibility of a future advance to the
oilfields might seem to the generals.

The danger still remained, however, that 1st Panzer Army might be
encircled. In mid-January the Soviets had resumed their attack south from
the central Don towards the area behind Rostov, and at the same time had
moved down the corridor between the Don and the Donets as well as
thrusting at Army Group B below Voronezh. There, the Red Army penetrated 100 miles in one week, and covered half the distance to Kharkov. In the
last week of January the enemy resumed the move westward towards Kursk,
which he captured on 7 February; Kharkov fell on the 16th, much to Hitler's
displeasure, as he had ordered that the city be held to the last man. But a

greater danger was the continued southward push from the Donets towards the Sea of Azov; by 12 February Krasnoarmeyskoye, on the main line from Rostov to Dnepropetrovsk, had been reached: the Dnepr lay less than 100 miles away, and the retreat of the forces that had just escaped the Caucasus was in danger. The race was now on to see which side could be the first to reach the Dnepr crossings. By the 17th the Red Army was within thirty miles of the river; but, just as it was on the verge of victory, its advance was crippled by lack of transport, shortage of supplies, and an early thaw. The Germans took swift advantage of this. On the 19th von Manstein launched his daring counter-stroke aimed at the Soviet salient; by the first week of March the Germans had reached the Donets, and on the 15th Karkhov was retaken. On the 19th, when Belgorod, more than fifty miles north-east of Kharkov, had been re-occupied, the German offensive came to an end in the slush of the spring thaw. No great destruction of the enemy was achieved in this the last successful attack to be mounted on the Eastern Front, but, by it, von Manstein had saved the army group from annihilation.

Both sides exhausted, the front now stabilized along a line from Taganrog on the Sea of Azov, up the Mius to the Donets, along to Belgorod, where the large enemy salient at Kursk began, to Orel. The Caucasus had been lost, as had the Don Bend and part of the Donets Basin, vital economic areas central to Hitler's endeavour in the east; 6th Army had been destroyed, and four allied armies were broken. Stalingrad was now 500 miles from German troops. But the front had held. That the Germans had not met with total disaster was due to three factors: the skill of the German commanders and the bravery of their soldiers; the reluctance of the Soviet attackers to take the risks required to turn success into a decisive victory; and the valiant fight of 6th Army to the very end of its strength.

   Von Manstein believed that the reason the southern front was saved was because:

> '. . . the army and army group staffs adhered firmly to two well-established German principles of leadership: (i) Always conduct operations elastically and resourcefully; (ii) Give every possible scope to the initiative and self-sufficiency of commanders at all levels. Both principles, admittedly, were greatly at variance with Hitler's own way of thinking. . . . The German fighting troops, convinced of their superiority as soldiers, stood their ground in the most desperate situations, and their courage and self-sacrifice did much to compensate for the enemy's numerical preponderance.'[29]

But professionalism and bravery alone were not enough to stem the enemy onslaught; the failings of the Soviets themselves played their part. Although their winter counter-offensive was launched with overwhelming numerical strength, which, by early 1943, had reached a proportion of 7:1 on some sectors of the front, they achieved no decisive result apart from the destruction of 6th Army. The Red Army, despite the weaknesses of its enemy, especially in the nature of his front and in the collapse of his allied armies, proved unable to effect a battle of encirclement after Stalingrad. One reason was that it lacked the resources in artillery and transport to coordinate its breakthrough operations; thus they had to be staggered, and as a result their full effect was lost because the Germans were able to concentrate on each one individually instead of being overwhelmed by the three at once.

The Soviets also revealed a certain reluctance to exploit their successes, especially after the swift and complete collapse of the allied armies. The Soviet commander, Zhukov, was wary of over-extending his offensive and laying himself open to counter-attack; he knew that the training and experience of his officers and men were unequal to the rigours of mobile warfare as waged by the Germans. Caution, rather than daring, marked the Soviet attack. Von Manstein believed:

> '. . . with the exception of Stalingrad, the Soviet command never managed to coordinate strength and speed when hitting a decisive spot. In the first phase of the winter campaign it undoubtedly tied down unnecessarily large forces against 6th Army in order to make doubly sure of its prize. In doing so, it let slip the chance to cut off the German southern wing's supply lines on the lower Don. The forces that attacked the Chir front were certainly strong, but they did not act in concert. After the breakthrough on the Italian front, the Soviet command similarly failed to stake everything on quickly reaching the Donets and Rostov. . . . Even after the successful breakthrough against the Hungarian Army, which tore open the German front from the Donets to Voronezh, the Soviet command still failed to press on with sufficient speed and strength in the decisive direction – towards the Dnepr crossings.'[30]

Because of Hitler's refusal to allow a strategic withdrawal along the whole southern front, the capacity of 6th Army to hold Stalingrad became a crucial factor for the fortunes of the German southern wing. Approving Hitler's decision to reject the Soviet offer of capitulation made on 9 January, von Manstein wrote:

> 'By 19 January, ninety of the 259 formations reported to be facing Army Group Don were committed around 6th Army. What would have happened if the bulk of these ninety formations had been released through a capitulation of 6th Army on 9 January is plain enough. . . . Every extra day 6th Army could continue to tie down the enemy forces surrounding it was vital as far as the fate of the entire Eastern Front was concerned. . . . It was the cruel necessity of war which compelled the Supreme Command to demand that one last sacrifice of the brave troops at Stalingrad.'[31]

And, even had a successful relief operation been mounted, and von Paulus's troops had escaped west, von Manstein admitted that:

> '. . . at the same time as the extricated elements of 6th Army might have been joining 4th Panzer Army, the entire enemy siege forces would have been released. With that, in all probability, the fate of the whole southern wing of the German forces in the east would have been sealed. . . .'[32]

True though this was, Hitler's insistence that Stalingrad be held till the last is no evidence of good generalship on his part; it arose solely out of his total inability to regard strategy in terms other than the area of ground occupied or the number of prisoners captured, and from his narrow idea that 'will-power' alone could create victory out of the near-certainty of defeat. It was not the sign of an able military mind to make the sacrifice of a first-class army the main means by which a front might be saved; 6th Army would have been of far greater use, for far longer, if it had been ordered to undertake an orderly withdrawal immediately the Soviet counter-offensive showed signs of effecting its encirclement. Moreover, after the 6th Army had assumed its 'fortress' role, when the fortunes of the entire southern front were placed on it, Hitler signally failed to keep its troops adequately supplied either by air or by ground for their crucial task. Indeed, his mean allocation of units to the relieving force was to result in its inability to reach the city and so enable its starving defenders to prolong their resistance (which, at the time, they themselves believed could have been continued into the spring if enough rations and munitions were received). The sacrifice of the 280,000 men of 6th Army in the winter fighting of 1942–43 was perhaps the most striking example of the bankruptcy to which Hitler's military ineptitude had sunk.

27

The Crisis of 1943

I cannot understand it; what has happened?
ADOLF HITLER
March 1943

The latter half of 1942 and the first quarter of 1943 was marked also by a further deterioration in the relationship between Hitler and his generals; by March 1943 Goebbels could write in his diary: 'The Führer's experiences with the generals have embittered him beyond measure. He even becomes unfair and condemns decent officers as well as en masse. . . . After the war he wants to cheerfully put on his brown Party uniform again and have as little as possible to do with generals.'[1] Indeed, Hitler's desire to minimise his contact with his chief military 'advisers' was marked even in June 1942, during the planning of the summer campaign. He spent long periods away from his headquarters, seeing Halder perhaps only once a week, and had few discussions about the forthcoming offensive. At the same time, Hitler took to by-passing the Chief of the General Staff and establishing direct contact with the generals at the front. His amateur's approach to the 'little matter' of commanding the Army revealed itself in a number of ways: he accepted only those intelligence reports that suited him, and he refused even to listen to unpalatable information; he had no idea of the basic elements of strategy – time and space; he disregarded the principle of concentrating strength at the decisive point; he wanted to do everything at once, and based his actions on wishful thinking rather than on reality; he proved incapable of taking even the most urgent decisions in time, and yet he became less and less prepared to allow his field commanders to act on their own initiative. In short, he exhibited qualities the very opposite of those required of a warlord, and his demands on the Army proved ruinous. As Halder remarked: 'A man, with dynamic intellect, energy, and bold daring may go beyond what the average military mind sees as the limits of possible achievement, but he will never fail to recognise and heed the fact that ultimately such limits do exist. He will not, as did Hitler, base all his actions on wishful thinking rather than on what can be achieved.'[2]

By 1942, suspicion obsessed Hitler; his behaviour was characterised by a complete absence of self-criticism and an overriding compulsion to see the worst in others, especially in his generals. His mistrust was shared by his closest confidants; in March 1942 General Schmundt even criticised Halder for his 'apparent lack of confidence in the Führer',[3] to which Halder replied that no one could arouse confidence in others if he were not prepared to show it to them. Two months later, on 24 June, in despair Halder entered in his diary: 'In OKW . . . the campaign against the General Staff is in high gear again. The unfortunate Reichel affair [an officer, travelling by plane, crashed into no-man's land carrying with him plans for the forthcoming offensive which fell into the enemy's hands] seems to have crystallised ill-feelings of apparently long-standing. We only have to brace ourselves now for the explosion.'[4] A month later, when Army Groups A and B were advancing in the Don Bend, and after the furious scenes over the advance to Voronezh, in which Keitel could discern a leadership crisis looming up, Halder recorded the effects on Hitler of the excessive build-up of armour around Rostov – the result of his own order:

> 'Now that the result is so palpable, he explodes in a fit of insane rage and hurls the gravest reproaches against the General Staff. This chronic tendency to underrate the enemy's capabilities is gradually assuming grotesque proportions and develops into a true danger. The situation is getting more and more intolerable. There is no room for any serious work. This so-called "leadership" is characterised by a pathological reaction to the impressions of the moment and a total lack of any understanding of the command machinery and its possibilities.'[5]

Quite clearly the relationship between Hitler and his Chief of the General Staff was becoming intolerable, a situation made no better by the move of the Führer headquarters in mid-July to Vinnitsa in the Ukraine. Here the heat was stifling; Warlimont remembered that 'Hitler . . . was particularly affected by it. This probably contributed to the disagreements and explosions which reached an unprecedented height in the weeks and months which followed.'[6] The crisis of confidence between the two most important men in the Army grew. Keitel noted:

> 'Although Hitler had tolerated cooperating with Halder more from common sense than from a sense of trust or even personal inclination, one could detect a marked estrangement between them, an increasing tension manifested partly by his abrupt treatment of Halder, partly by unfavourable criticism of him, and occasionally even by violent quarrels. We all saw how Hitler vented his disillusionment over the way the offensive had seized up and about the cries of help from Army Groups North and Centre . . . cries which Halder was underlining and emphasising to him. . . . His criticisms of Halder became increasingly frequent: he was a pessimist, a prophet of doom, he was infecting the commanders-in-chief

with his wailing and so on. It was then that I knew that the wheel had turned full circle again: a scapegoat was being sought, somebody else to be sent into the wilderness.'[7]

The climax of the 'explosive atmosphere', as Warlimont called it, came on 24 August, when Halder urged Hitler to allow Army Group Centre to withdraw some of its forces which were in danger of being cut off during the Soviet attack on the Rzhev salient. Halder's strong advocacy of an action that went so much against Hitler's cardinal principle of 'no withdrawal' clearly annoyed the dictator, who turned on his Chief of the General Staff with the words:

'You always come here with the same proposal, that of withdrawal. . . . I expect commanders to be as tough as the fighting troops.'

With that, Halder retorted in a raised voice:

'I am tough enough, my Führer. But out there brave men and young officers are falling in thousands simply because their commanders are not allowed to make the only reasonable decision, and have their hands tied behind their backs.'

Hitler, taken aback, replied:

'Colonel-General Halder, how dare you use language like that to me! Do you think you can teach me what the man at the front is thinking? What do you know about what goes on at the front? Where were you in the First World War? And you try to pretend to me that I don't understand what it's like at the front. I won't stand that! It's outrageous!'[8]

The final breach between the two men was not far off.

The next month was a harrowing time for Halder; his duty as a soldier was tested to the very limits of endurance. At the same time as he withstood the Führer's abuse, he was trying to mitigate the worst effects of Hitler's misguided directions. On 30 August he wrote: 'Today's conference with the Führer was again an occasion for abusive reproaches against the military leadership abilities of the highest commands. He charges them with intellectual conceit, mental inadaptability, and utter failure to grasp the essentials.'[9] On 9 September Halder was visited by Keitel, who hinted that he would be removed; on the 24th, the day he was relieved by General Zeitzler, he wrote his final entry in his diary: 'After the situation conference, farewell by the Führer. My nerves are worn out, also his nerves are no longer fresh. We must part. [Hitler spoke of] the necessity for educating the General Staff in fanatical faith in the Idea [of National Socialism]. He is determined to enforce his will also in the Army.'[10] With that, an able successor to von Moltke and von Schlieffen went into retirement.

Halder's dismissal, although the most important, was but one of several changes during the 1942 offensive. On 15 July von Weichs had taken over command of Army Group B from von Bock, whose advance on Voronezh had so much displeased Hitler; and on 9 September List, commander of Army Group A, had been relieved of his post for failing to conduct his advance to the Führer's liking. Hitler himself took over command of Army Group A, and directed its operations from Vinnitsa, almost 1,000 miles away from the troops on the field. To his duties of Leader of the Party, Head of State, Supreme Commander of the Wehrmacht, and Commander-in-Chief of the Army, Hitler now added the direct command of an army group in the field. This special responsibility lasted until 22 November, when he gave over control of the force in the Caucasus to von Kleist. During the Stalingrad débâcle, Hitler's disenchantment with his field commanders intensified, and his control over their actions became ever more strict. For example, on 23 November, erroneously believing that the commander of LI Corps, von Seydlitz-Kurzbach, was more reliable than von Paulus, Hitler detached him and his unit from the control of 6th Army and made them responsible for the defence of the north-east part of the Stalingrad pocket. (Ironically, it had been von Seydlitz himself who had begun the withdrawal for which von Paulus received the blame.) By mid-January 1942 the Führer's relations with von Manstein had become so strained that the Field-Marshal, frustrated by the restrictions on his operational freedom, asked the new Chief of the General Staff to have him relieved; he suggested that he be replaced by a 'sub-directorate'[11] of the kind maintained by the Quartermaster-General, which existed only to carry out direct instructions from the central directorate – in this case, Hitler. The Führer, for his part, was annoyed at von Manstein's independence of mind and by 17 February had resolved to dismiss him but had refrained from doing so then because of the serious threat posed by the Red Army to the Dnepr crossings.

Hitler's distrust of the generals spread from OKH to OKW. The immediate cause of the rift between the Führer and his Wehrmacht aides was their support of List's action in the Caucasus, about which he was so dissatisfied. On 31 August the army group commander reported to Hitler at Vinnitsa, bringing with him a map with a scale of only one to one million and devoid of any unit dispositions. Although the dictator treated List with courtesy, he clearly found the lack of an adequate map depicting troop deployments to be highly irritating, and when the general left his presence he gave vent to his feelings. When Keitel pointed out that List was merely acting in accordance with Hitler's own order that no detailed maps be carried by officers when travelling by plane, the Führer rounded violently on his unfortunate Chief of OKW, 'shouting that Göring had also been at the conference . . . and had been very shocked by it all'.[12] A few days later, on 7 September, Keitel sent Jodl to the army group to see how matters were, and to report accordingly. On his return the same night, Jodl told the Führer that List was adhering to the instructions that he had received, and, moreover, that he himself agreed with the view of the army group as to further moves in the Caucasus. Keitel records the impact of this on a suspicious Hitler, who promptly flew for the first time into a rage with Jodl: 'Here again the damage had been done by the crisis of confidence and by his pathological delusion that his generals were conspiring against him and were trying to sabotage his orders on what were in his view pretty shabby pretexts.'[13] From that time on, Hitler's mistrust revealed itself in a number of ways, which entirely transformed the atmosphere at his headquarters. He no longer took his meals with his OKW chiefs; he transferred the location of his daily conferences from the map room to his own hut, and limited the attendance to the smallest number possible (the passage of time was to see the briefing conferences resume their former nature); at military discussions he had shorthand-typists take down every word; and for more than four months he refused to shake hands with either Jodl or Keitel. He even let it be known that he proposed to have Keitel replaced by Kesselring and Jodl by von Paulus, and, although these changes never materialised because of the deepening crises in North Africa and at Stalingrad, relations never fully recovered. Jodl made matters worse by arguing that Halder should be kept on as Chief of the General Staff. Hitler remained distant and suspicious until the end, in spite of Keitel's continual reassurances and Jodl's declared intention never again to contradict the dictator. To Warlimont, who had himself been relieved of his post by Hitler for a few days in early November because of an error on the part of one of his staff, Jodl said: 'Keep yourself out of the briefing conferences from now on; it's too depressing having to go through that.'[14]

The position in which the OKW leaders now found themselves was exascerbated by Hitler's choice of Kurt Zeitzler as the new Chief of the General Staff. Zeitzler had always been a particular favourite of the Führer; when he had held the post of senior Army staff officer in the National Defence Section of OKW, he had been energetic in pursuing the policy of a unified command of the Wehrmacht, and his friendship with Schmundt had ensured his being noticed by Hitler, who then, and subsequently, took the unusual step of receiving him for personal discussions. In the middle of April 1942, after having received a number of other appointments which included being chief of staff to Group Kleist in May 1940, Zeitzler was made chief of staff to Commander-in-Chief, West, as the result of a proposal from Schmundt and as the personal choice of Hitler. The Führer was impressed by his enthusiasm, expressions of loyalty and obvious ability, and his good opinion of him increased after the repulse of the British-Canadian raid on Dieppe in August 1942. A few days later, after his major collision with Halder over the Rzhev salient, Hitler remarked that he wished to have by his side as the Chief of the General Staff 'someone like this chap Zeitzler'.[15] On 24 September Hitler's wish became reality, and the forty-seven year old Zeitzler, promoted *General der Infanterie*, took Halder's post. Young, and relatively inexperienced in high command, he did not possess that air of authority in the eyes of the senior army and army group commanders that was essential for the Army's highest executive officer. Moreover, he was regarded universally as 'the Führer's creature'. This might suit Hitler, but not the generals; some, including Keitel, had wanted von Manstein as the replacement, but Hitler, probably realising that he possessed too strong a personality to be dominated, refused to consider it.

Zeitzler was, at the beginning, Hitler's man; even so, he found it difficult to influence his Führer. After the war, he looked back on his role:

> 'As the Chief of the General Staff had only an advisory position, he did not have the power of command for the Eastern Front. . . . This was exercised by Adolf Hitler himself. He signed the basic orders and instructions himself or copied them out. Occasionally – particularly when he noticed that I was of a different opinion – he even drafted or dictated them himself. I have in a few cases refused to counter-sign orders in the hope of perhaps preventing their being issued. Apart from one single case where, annoyed, he put the draft aside and never returned to the subject again, they were issued all the same via the Adjutant.'[16]

However, Zeitzler refused to be intimidated by his Führer. The 'Thunderball', as he was nicknamed, had no patience when Hitler described him as a 'mere staff officer' who knew nothing about troops, and often asked him never to use derogatory expressions about German officers in his presence. Hitler unquestionably had an admiration for Zeitzler's strength of character, and his relations with him were not marked with that bitterness which had had so detrimental an effect upon Halder.

Because of Zeitzler's past record, the OKW chiefs hoped that he would straightway foster a spirit of close cooperation between OKH and OKW. His first address to the officers of the Army Command betokened well for such a development: 'I require the following from every staff officer: he must believe in the Führer and in his method of command. He must on every occasion radiate this confidence to his subordinates and those around him. I have no use for anybody on the General Staff who cannot meet these requirements.'[17] As a mark of confidence, almost immediately after the appointment the Führer and his immediate entourage left the stifling atmosphere of Vinnitsa for the coolness of Berlin, placing the immediate direction of affairs on the Eastern Front in Zeitzler's hands. The new Chief of the General Staff, not unnaturally, saw fit to exploit his position of favour with Hitler, and instead of cooperating with OKW sought to reacquire for OKH its former authority. He was dissatisfied with his role, which in reality was no more than that of a chief of staff for the Eastern Front, and was jealous of the OKW's control over all other theatres of war. Keitel wrote:

> 'It was our first and most grievous disappointment when we saw exactly the opposite of what we had hoped for taking place: Zeitzler not only dissociated himself from us, but was intent on excluding us to an increasing degree . . . from decision-making on the Eastern Front, by means of frequently briefing Hitler on the Eastern Front . . . alone . . . it was obvious that he considered Jodl solely interested in the other theatres of war; and it was even more obvious that he feared our influence on the Führer – a very regrettable and narrow-minded point of view.'[18]

Although Zeitzler never had any hope of seeing the end of the OKW theatres of war (unless Hitler had believed it to be necessary), he nevertheless did manage to exclude OKW from the Eastern Front; he even went so far as to forbid members of the Army Operations Section to give any information whatsoever to OKW, a mean action not reciprocated by the Wehrmacht leaders. The result was that the direction of land operations was divided between two authorities, one of which steadfastly refused to cooperate with the other. This was the final step in the disintegration of the organisation of the higher command of the Armed Forces, and was to prove disastrous to Germany's conduct of a successful defence in west, east, and south during the last year of the war. As Warlimont noted: 'The only "victor" who emerged from this wreckage . . . was Hitler, who as a result became, in the literal sense of the words, the only man fully informed regarding all theatres of war.'[19] Such an illogical division of authority well-suited the Führer, who thereby reigned supreme.

The period between November 1942 and May 1943 was, for the Germans, a time of crisis. In July 1942 Hitler had declared, 'The Russian is finished',[20] and at the same time he had seen his troops close to within a few miles of the Suez Canal. Within four months these high hopes had been shattered. In November, with the British attack at El Alamein, the Allied landings in North Africa, and the Soviet offensive beginning round Stalingrad, it became clear that Germany had lost the initiative. At the end of January, the destruction of 6th Army, with the loss of 280,000 men, was complete. By the middle of March, the Germans had suffered a great loss of territory in the east. By the middle of May, the Axis presence in North Africa had been eliminated, and about 300,000 Germans and Italians had gone into Allied captivity. Catastrophes of this magnitude had far-reaching repercussions upon Hitler and his generals, and sufficed to shatter completely any last remnants of mutual confidence that might have survived from the halcyon days before 1938. The Führer's reaction to von Paulus's surrender at Stalingrad was immediate and bitter. The record of the midday conference on 1 February 1943 revealed the depths to which Hitler's opinion of his military leaders had sunk. He was totally unable to comprehend that von Paulus, Schmidt, von Seydlitz, and other generals had actually surrendered to the enemy:

> 'When you think that a woman has got sufficient pride, just because someone has made a few insulting remarks, to go and lock herself in and shoot herself right off, then I've no respect for a soldier who's afraid to do that but would rather be taken prisoner. . . . I can't understand how a man like Paulus wouldn't rather die. The heroism of so many tens of thousands of men, officers, and generals is cancelled out by a man like this who hasn't the character when the moment comes to do what a weakling of a woman can do.'

Von Paulus he dismissed as a 'characterless weakling', von Seydlitz was 'fit to be shot', and professional officers as a whole were classified as 'intellectual and mental acrobats and athletes'. And in a final fury against all generals, irrespective of their merit, the Führer declared: 'There will be no more field-marshals in this war. We'll only promote them after the end of the war. I won't count my chickens before they are hatched.'[21] He ended his policy of giving senior generals large gifts from his own purse (von Kluge, for example, had received a quarter of a million reichsmarks on his sixtieth birthday in October 1942), and decorations and promotions were henceforth more difficult to come by for those who had not won his favour.

In his rationalisation of the defeats in the east and North Africa, Hitler exhibited a curious contradiction. On the one hand, he took all responsibility himself, declaring to von Manstein: 'I alone bear the responsibility for Stalingrad!'[22] The fate of 6th Army he justified in relation to events on the rest of the Eastern Front; the loss of his forces in Tunisia, instead of their prompt evacuation, he deemed necessary because their fight delayed the Allied invasion of south-east Europe by six months and kept Italy within the Axis. And yet on the other hand, he blamed the generals for the disasters. He proved unable to realise that he had imposed impossible conditions on them, and felt, quite simply, that they had failed him. In his diary for 9 May 1943 Goebbels recorded Hitler's attitude:

> 'He is absolutely sick of the generals. He can't imagine anything better than having nothing to do with them. His opinion of all the generals is devastating. Indeed, at times it is so caustic as to seem prejudiced or unjust, although on the whole it no doubt fits the case. . . . All generals lie, he says. All generals are disloyal. All generals are opposed to National Socialism. All generals are reactionaries. . . . He just can't stand them. They have disappointed him too often.'[23]

Speer remembered 'Blunt statements that the officers were without honour, without intelligence, that they were liars, that he was dealing with a bunch of crooks, were often made by him in the presence of numerous army officers. He could not be moved to adopt a more conciliatory tone, instead he became even more offensive.'[24]

The General Staff, in particular, came in for continual condemnation, and its officers were constantly to see the diabolical side of Hitler's nature. He and his adjutant, Schmundt, the Chief of the Army Personnel Office, (to whom Hitler had made over the responsibility for the personnel of the General Staff) together evolved a policy whereby the dominance of the General Staff in the higher appointments of the Army would be brought to an end. Faster promotion for the battle-tried, younger field commanders was introduced, and able officers not educated in the General Staff were given special training to qualify for advancement. It was the declared intention of both men to ultimately abolish the distinctive wine-red trouser stripes and silver collar tabs peculiar to the General Staff, together with the mysticism and élitism of that body. There was to be only one officer corps within the German Army. Tradition, such as that which the General Staff represented, was regarded as dangerous, a cause of inhibition rather than of strength, and in direct conflict with the fanatical, 'revolutionary' qualities of National Socialism. For that reason, even the older generals of fifty years of age or above were considered unreliable; their crime was that they had served for too long in the old Army.

Hitler's disillusion with the Army had been developing since the bitter winter battles of 1941–42; it found expression in his attitude towards the armed SS. Until that time, the Waffen SS (as it was called from the end of 1940) had grown only slowly; by June 1941 it numbered only 165,000 men, roughly three per cent of the whole Army. The commitment of the armed SS to the field of battle had represented no alteration in its relationship with the Wehrmacht. In the Polish campaign, the SS regiments had been distributed throughout the invasion force and were subject to military command and discipline. After the destruction of Poland, there occurred the only substantial alteration in the Army's control over the armed SS to take place during the entire war: on 17 October 1939 the Ministerial Council for the Defence of the Reich issued a decree which freed all SS-VT members from the legal jurisdiction of the Armed Forces; although they were still subject to the provisions of the military penal code, they were to be tried not by military courts-martial but by special SS courts whose members were appointed by Hitler at the suggestion of Himmler. In other areas, however, military control remained as tight as ever; for example, OKW established a low upper limit of recruitment to the SS-VT, refused to consider service in the SS *Totenkopfverbände* security units (distinct from the *Totenkopf* division) as military service, and was equally unwilling to allow the establishment of a peacetime SS reserve, except under joint SS and OKW administration.

All this well-suited Hitler, and he continued to look on his armed SS simply as 'militarised state police'. In August 1940, he emphasised this role in his secret 'Statement on the Future of the Armed State Police', which was circulated to Army Commands:

> 'In its final form the Greater German Reich will include within its frontiers peoples who will not necessarily be well-disposed towards the Reich. Outside the borders of the Old Reich, therefore, it will be necessary to create an armed state police capable, whatever the situation, of representing and enforcing the authority of the Reich in the interior of the country concerned. This duty can only be carried out by a state police containing within its ranks men of the best German blood and identified unquestionably with the ideology upon which the Greater German Reich is founded. Only a formation constituted along these lines will be able to resist subversive influences in times of crisis. . . . The Waffen SS formations will return home having proved themselves in the field and so will have

the authority required to carry out their duties as State police. Such use of the Waffen SS at home is in the interests of the Wehrmacht itself. . . . In order to ensure the quality of men in the Waffen SS remains high, the number of units must remain limited . . . and should not, in general, exceed five to ten per cent of the peacetime strength of the Army.'[25]

However, after the Soviet winter counter-offensive in 1941, when the fighting qualities of the SS divisions had so much impressed Hitler, the Führer acceded to requests from the Waffen SS generals to strengthen the force. To him, it personified his belief in the triumph of the will above all adversity: 'At the present time we have it confirmed that every division of the SS is aware of its responsibility. The SS knows that its job is to set an example . . . and all eyes are upon it.'[26] As a result, in May 1942 he authorised the formation of an SS Corps (previously, the SS divisions had been distributed singly throughout the Army), and approved the reorganisation of the existing divisions, including the addition of tank battalions and, later, of tank regiments. He also ordered that further units should be raised; by September 1943 the Waffen SS contained fifteen divisions (three of which were composed of Bosnian, Galician, and Latvian volunteers), 280,000 men were in field units, and 70,000 in training or in reserve. The soldiers of the armed SS amounted to more than five per cent of the strength of the entire German Army. Of the thirty-two armoured divisions then in existence, no fewer than seven, more than one-fifth, belonged to the Waffen SS (they were designated 'panzer' divisions in October, but their tank strength was not altered, and remained equal to, or better than, that of the Army divisions). During 1943 six SS corps commands were formed, to be followed by a further seven by 1945. By the end of the war, no fewer than forty SS divisions had been raised at one time or another (twenty-seven of which were composed of foreigners) and the number of men under the SS oath had risen to nearly 700,000 – more than one-tenth of the total of the entire German Field Army.

This very considerable expansion of the Waffen SS at the expense of the Army cannot be seen as evidence that Hitler intended to supplant the military by a political force. Until the end the Waffen SS units remained under the operational control of the Army; this fundamental principle was never breached, and the highest position ever reached by a Waffen SS officer was that by Sepp Dietrich, who commanded 5th and 6th Panzer Armies from late 1944 to the end of the war. Steiner's charge of 'Army Group Steiner' in the very last few days of the war was a paper command only. Himmler was made Commander of the Upper Rhine and then of Army Group Vistula at the end of the war, but this was such a disaster that he voluntarily gave up the post. His command of the Reserve Army after July 1944 was a political move on the part of Hitler, and had no bearing on the role of the Waffen SS. Hitler's ideas concerning the future peacetime employment of the armed SS never changed; even at the end of 1944, when it had grown almost to the size of the pre-war Army, he was still able to declare that its heavy casualties would 'mould and train the survivors for their demanding security tasks in the post-war years'.[27] Just as his commitment of the SS-VT to the field of battle in 1939 had arisen from his desire to train it as his future state police and from his need for well-trained field units, so his expansion of the Waffen SS after the winter of 1941–42 was due not to his aim to supplant the army, but to his pressing need for élite fighting formations and his disillusion with the Army generals. The sole causes of the expansion of the Waffen SS were Hitler's recognition of the very high fighting qualities of the best of his SS men, and his admiration for the exploits of their senior officers, both of which he believed were due in large part to the National Socialist indoctrination that was then lacking in the Army.

A further indication of Hitler's lack of any respect for his Army came in the autumn of 1942, when OKW, alarmed at the losses being suffered on the Eastern Front, proposed that the Navy should make over 20,000 men and the Air Force 200,000 to the Army. The dictator at first agreed, but Göring objected and stated that 'he was not going to let his good young National Socialists be dressed up in the grey (meaning reactionary) uniform of the Army'.[28] Instead, he proposed that Luftwaffe Field Divisions composed entirely of Luftwaffe personnel be raised. Hitler then immediately acquiesced to his *Reichsmarschall,* and twenty-two Luftwaffe Field Divisions were formed, much to the dissatisfaction of the Army. Had the Air Force personnel been used to fill the gaps in the seasoned Army divisions, they would have been of great value; as it was, they were wasted, because the new formations into which they were concentrated suffered from serious deficiencies. Insufficient training, inexperienced leadership, and, to a certain extent, unsuitable equipment tended to make them a liability in battle. Hitler, however, would seldom acknowledge this, and when in October 1943 OKW finally managed to get these divisions incorporated within the Army, it proved impossible to raise their fighting efficiency by a significant amount. Such was the inevitable result of the disregard for the Army's interests.

The early spring of 1943 saw the German Army facing a supreme crisis which threatened its continued existence. Defeats on the Eastern Front and in North Africa had inflicted shattering losses on the field force of more than half a million men. The destruction of divisions between January and May had been severe: twenty were lost in Stalingrad, and six (of which two were Luftwaffe) outside, and another six in Tunisia – a total of thirty Army formations, roughly one-eighth of all those, including the Waffen SS, in the German order of battle, a figure made all the worse by the addition of the divisions engaged in occupation in the south-east and in the west, which were hardly fit for operations in any case. General Thomas stated that, whereas the total losses in the eastern campaign up until Stalingrad were equivalent to the equipment required for about fifty divisions, in the battle of Stalingrad alone enough for forty-five divisions were lost. In March 1943 the

Eastern Front was 470,000 men below establishment, and the whole Field Army 700,000. The condition of the front-line units was critical, and there was no prospect of adequate replacements. Divisional strengths were reduced from nine to six battalions, equipment levels were low, and casualties were particularly high among experienced officers and NCOs.

The state of the panzer arm was particularly deplorable, with the divisions but shadows of their former selves; no fewer than eight had been destroyed either in the snows of the Ukraine or in the desert of North Africa. On 23 January 1943 it was revealed that only 495 tanks remained fit for service along the entire length of the eastern Front, and these, apart from a few new Tigers with their heavy armour and lethal 8.8cm guns, consisted mainly of PzKw IIIs and IVs, which, despite their many improvements, were still inferior to the enemy T34s. Since the beginning of the struggle with the Soviet Union 7,800 tanks had been destroyed. Losses in battle and from obsolescence had considerably exceeded production; the destruction of tanks in the first three months of 1943 totalled 2,529, well over half the 4,278 produced in 1942. As a result, total stocks available to the Germans declined from 5,463 on 1 February to 3,643 on 1 May – the lowest for more than two years – while those classified as 'front-line' fell from 4,261 to 2,504. Captured foreign tanks, which had always played their part in equipping the Reich's armoured force, were still in use – by 31 May 1943 a total of 822 on all fronts, of which 126 were in the east. Assault-guns and 'tank-hunters' had played a major role in the fighting; assault guns numbered 1,048 on 1 May, and 'tank-hunters' and armoured anti-aircraft guns around 1,000 whereas there had been none the year previously. Although the majority of assault-guns remained outside the framework of the panzer divisions, an increasing number were incorporated in tank regiments to make up for the crippling deficiencies. Moreover, the morale of the panzer troops, so long a decisive factor in their success, was low, aware as they were that they were members of a badly mauled and neglected force; their confidence in the High Command, which had constantly misused them, was non-existent. Such was the state of the Reich's panzer arm after three and a half years of war; the armoured initiative now lay with its enemies. Total collapse seemed imminent.

The German Army was never to recover from this crisis; never again would it be capable of mounting a successful major offensive. Desperate measures were called for if it were even to survive. Only by a prodigious increase in the production of munitions and equipment, and by a tight restructuring of the field units, could the forces in the field be ready to resist the enemy advances in the east, south, and west. The necessary output of armaments was achieved, but the reorganisation of the Army was not. Even before 1943 the Reich's production had been increasing; the Minister of Armaments, Fritz Todt, had begun the strict rationalisation required, and even before his death in February 1942 the economy had been adapting itself to the rigours of total war. Albert Speer, his successor, carried on and extended his work, so that the armament output of 1942 exceeded by two-fifths that of 1941. Nonetheless, this was still low, both in comparison with the production in enemy countries and in relation to what was to come. Armed with wide-ranging powers, Speer began yet another increase in armament production, which in 1943 was fifty-six per cent higher than in 1942, and more than twice as high as in 1941. By mid-1943 this improvement was beginning to reveal itself; on 1 July, for example, there were 3,452 front-line tanks, almost 1,000 more than at the worst point of the crisis.

In the reorganisation of their depleted forces, the Germans were less successful. The high rate of casualties and the lack of reserves made it impossible to bring the infantry divisions up to full strength; consequently, divisions should have been merged in order to restore a reasonable ratio of men employed in combat to those employed in auxiliary services. Such a method would have made it possible to introduce measures which had become increasingly necessary for economising in officers, NCOs, and specialists, as well as in motor vehicles, horses, and equipment. But this was not to be. All intentions were frustrated. Hitler, the military illiterate, continued to view military strength in terms of numbers rather than in quality. Therefore, he preferred to dilute the fighting strength within the divisions so as to maintain the numbers of such formations constant; he even ordered that every one of the 'Stalingrad divisions' be reconstituted, along with four of the six lost in Tunisia. At the same time, new Waffen SS divisions were added to the German order of battle; between 1 July 1942 and 1 July 1943 the number of field divisions in the Army, the Luftwaffe, and the Waffen SS rose by fifty-five. The German Army then had 243 divisions: 174 infantry, sixteen fortress, seven mountain, eleven security, twelve panzer-grenadier (the new title for motorised infantry), and twenty-three panzer; the Waffen SS possessed eleven: two mountain, one cavalry and eight panzergrenadier (seven of which could be counted as panzer), and the Luftwaffe had twenty-two: nineteen field, one panzergrenadier, and two paratroop – a grand total of 276. This increase in divisions was brought about only by a decrease in their individual combat strengths; the result was a wasteful and dangerous inflation in the ratio of administrative to fighting soldiers, and a loss in the quality of the formations. By 1 July 1943, when the Field Army totalled 4,480,000 men, its 243 divisions and independent units (army troops) were 616,000 men below on establishment. This low ratio of combat to administrative troops would become particularly marked when the fighting was resumed, for then the losses would be borne mainly by the fighting soldiers, and the spearheads would tend to shrink out of proportion to the tail. All this would go far to nullify any improvements in the quality of equipment.

An indication of the gravity of the crisis facing the Army was seen in Hitler's decision to recall Guderian to active service, his task being 'the future development of armoured troops along lines that will make that arm of the service into a decisive weapon for winning the war'.[29] As such, he was given control of the organisation, training, manning, and equipment of all panzer and panzergrenadier units. Having learnt from his past struggles with the General Staff, Guderian made it a condition of his return that he be made entirely independent of OKH (he was asked only to 'consult'[30] with Zeitzler), and answerable to Hitler alone. Moreover, the Luftwaffe and Waffen SS armoured units were also to come under his control. Thus was created yet one more military agency outside the influence of the Chief of the General Staff, and over which only the Führer had control. On 1 March 1943 Guderian took up his post as Inspector-General of Armoured Troops; as he recorded: 'I was not surprised that the General Staff, particularly its Chief, and the OKH were so markedly unenthusiastic about this assignment of duties, which they regarded as an encroachment upon their own hallowed rights. One result was that I became involved in difficulties and held up by lack of cooperation from certain quarters over and over again.'[31] Clearly, the exigencies of total war and the experiences of the past few years had not lessened antipathy towards an independent panzer arm. One aspect of this manifested itself in the retention by the artillery arm of the majority of assault-guns under its control (Guderian was limited to 'heavy' assault-guns, which then were only just coming into production). This was serious, for assault-guns were needed to reinforce the sadly depleted armoured divisions; at that time they constituted nearly one-third of total output of armoured vehicles, and were well on the way to overtaking tank production (which they did by September 1944). When, at a Führer conference, Guderian proposed that all assault-guns be placed under his command, he met with immediate and total opposition. As he remembered:

> 'All those present except Speer disapproved, in particular of course the gunners; Hitler's chief adjutant also spoke up against me, remarking that the assult artillery was the only weapon which nowadays enabled gunners to win the Knight's Cross. Hitler gazed at me with an expression of pity on his face, and finally said: "You see, they are all against you. So I can't approve either". . . . It was nine months before Hitler was convinced that a mistake had been made, and even by the end of the war it had not proved feasible to supply all the divisions with the urgently needed defensive weapons.'[32]

Old prejudices died hard, to the detriment of the armoured force.

Despite all this, Guderian set about his task with his customary energy. He straightway countered a proposal favoured by Hitler and the General Staff that all tank production be abandoned in favour of concentrating on the new Tigers and Panthers; such a proposal would have limited Germany to a total output of only twenty-five Tigers a month for some time to come; this, as Guderian noted, 'would have certainly led to the defeat of the German Army in the near future'.[33] Within three weeks of his appointment he had produced an outline plan for a revitalised force. Asserting that 'a panzer

Left: Field Marshal Erich von Manstein, commander of Army Group Don. *Below:* A scene during the vain relief operation to save 6th Army.

Far top left: A German machine-gunner waits patiently for the inevitable Soviet attack, summer 1943. *Far bottom left:* An 8.8 cm gun in action in south USSR late 1943. *Left:* A horsed despatch rider gives a message to the commander of a 'Rhinoceros' tank-hunter, an 8.8 cm gun mounted on a PzKw IV chassis, 1944. *Below:* Waffen SS troops in action, central front 1944.

Left: A Panzer regiment prepared to counter-attack the
advancing Soviets, winter 1944.
The tanks are PzKw IVs. *Bottom
left:* Field Marshal Model, the
'saviour' of the Eastern Front.

Above: A PzKw V 'Panther', introduced in 1943. Some 6,000 of these tanks were produced in the last two years of the war. *Left:* A PzKw VI 'King Tiger' in the streets of Budapest, 1945. Over 450 of these machines were produced.

Above left: The last defence: German troops in a barge patrol the Vistula river, early 1945. *Above right:* The Atlantic Wall in the area of Calais; only here was it strong enough to have a good chance of withstanding an invasion. The Allies, however, attacked elsewhere. *Below:* A PzKw VI 'Tiger' moving up to the front in Normandy. 1,343 of these formidable defensive machines were produced in the war.

Above right: A member of the 'Ost-truppen' in the West. The POA insignia on his arm indicates that he is a member of the 'Russian Army of Liberation' *Above left:* Hitler alive and well on the afternoon of the Bomb Plot. Only a few hours after he had been involved in the explosion, Hitler met Mussolini (extreme left) who was visiting the Führer Headquarters. Next to the Duce is Martin Bormann; behind Hitler is Grand Admiral Dönitz; on his left is Göring. *Below:* A PzKw IV and panzer grenadiers in Belgium, September 1944.

Left: The increased political indoctrination of the Army was revealed in many ways; one of them was the raising of the 'Feldherrnhalle' division, formed from many SA members and named after an elite SA unit. *Below left:* General Kurt Zeitzler, Chief of the General Staff from 1942 to 1944. *Below right:* Hitler reviews the remnants of his forces, boys from the Hitler Youth, Berlin, April 1945.

division has complete combat efficiency only when the number of its tanks is in correct proportions to its other weapons and vehicles',[34] he went against Hitler's disastrous 1940 reorganisation and sought to establish a target of 400 tanks in each division. Other proposals included better crew training, an increase in the number of half-track vehicles, improved reconnaissance units, and a greater use of assault-guns within panzer divisions as a stop-gap measure before a greater number of tanks became available. Guderian also envisaged the future employment of the two new tanks then just coming off the production lines – the Tiger and the Panther. The product of the panic in the summer of 1941, both were powerful machines well-suited to the new defensive role of the panzer force. The PzKw VI 'Tiger', which first emerged in August 1942, weighed 56 tons and had a top speed on roads of 23mph; more important for the Germans at that time was the fact that it was well-protected and possessed excellent destructive power, being armed with the anti-tank version of the famous 8.8cm anti-aircraft gun. An equal to the Soviet machines in achieving the combination of maximum fire-power, protection, and mobility was the PzKw V 'Panther', which, armed with a long 7.5cm gun of considerable penetrating ability, protected by relatively thick, sloped armour (which proved much more difficult to pierce than the ordinary vertical plates) and weighing 45 tons, could achieve on roads a top speed of 34mph. After overcoming its teething troubles, which included a somewhat alarming tendency to catch fire while rolling peaceably along the road, the Panther proved to be the best-designed tank of the war. These two machines gave the panzer force a distinct qualitative superiority over its enemies for the first time since 1939, and this was further buttressed by the continual up-gunning of the PzKw IIIs and IVs (by the end of the war each tank carried weapons of roughly three times the power of those they had at the beginning). Moreover, improved assault-guns and tank destroyers were also appearing. In the hands of experienced crews these machines would go a long way to offset Germany's numerical inferiority.

After the exhaustion of the German counter-attack in the muddy season of mid-March 1943, a period of calm descended on the Eastern Front; both sides had battled to the end of their strength, both needed to rest, re-equip, and reorganise. For the Germans, with their lower reserves of manpower and production of armaments, this was especially important. In Guderian's view, this period of consolidation should have been a long one. At a conference with Hitler on 9 March the Inspector-General of Armoured Troops told the gathering: 'The task for 1943 is to provide a certain number of panzer divisions with complete combat efficiency capable of making limited objective attacks.' Only in 1944 would the German Army be prepared 'to launch large-scale attacks'.[35] This feeling was shared by most, if not all, generals, and even by Hitler, from whom no ambitious plans emanated. It was best summed up by von Manstein:

'The question now was how the German side should continue the struggle the following summer. Obviously, after so many major formations had been lost, there would no longer be the forces available to mount another crucial offensive on the scale of 1941 and 1942. What did seem possible – given proper leadership on the German side – was that the Soviet Union could be worn down to such an extent that it would tire of its already excessive sacrifices [some eleven million men killed or captured] and be ready to accept a stalemate. At the time in question [March] this was far from wishful thinking.'[36]

The commander of Army Group South ruled out any purely defensive, static strategy, for there were simply not enough divisions to cover the whole front from the Baltic to the Black Sea. Moreover, a delay in taking the initiative might allow the Soviets to mount an offensive when German attention was focussed on the expected Allied landings in Europe, the danger of which had become acute as a result of events in North Africa. Plans had to be evolved to deal with the certainty of a Soviet attack. Von Manstein concluded his argument by stating: 'The German command thus had very little time left in which to force a draw in the east. It could do so only if it succeeded . . . in dealing the enemy powerful blows of a localised character which would sap his strength to a decisive degree. . . . This pre-supposed an operational elasticity on our part which would give maximum effect to the still-superior quality of the German command staffs and fighting troops.'[37] Zeitzler, too, held similar views, which were presented to Hitler on a number of occasions after 19 March. The Führer, for his part, had been impressed by the success of von Manstein's counter-stroke at Kharkov, and was eager to see it done again. The question was, how and when could it take place?

After Kharkov, von Manstein presented Hitler with two alternatives; the first and, from his point of view, the better was to wait for the Soviet attack, which would certainly be launched in the south Ukraine, give ground before it, and then with all possible strength mount a decisive counter-attack on its exposed northern flank with the aim of encircling its forces. This was the 'backhand' method. The other, the 'forehand', would be to mount concentric attacks to cut off the large Soviet salient at Kursk and there destroy the enemy's reserves of armour before turning south to roll up his front in the south Ukraine. If the latter were chosen, time was of the essence, for it was vital to make the attempt before the Red Army could recover from its winter losses. The best month, von Manstein suggested, would be in April, when the enemy was still refitting his units and the ground drying out just sufficiently to allow the passage of armour.

Hitler, true to form, rejected taking the risks and the loss of territory involved in the 'backhand' stroke, and decided in favour of the 'forehand'. The plan evolved between him and Zeitzler was for concentric attacks to be mounted to the north of the Kursk salient by Model's 9th Army of Army

Group Centre, and from the south by Hoth's 4th Panzer Army of Army Group South. The objective was strictly limited – the destruction of the enemy forces within the salient – and the plan possessed only the vaguest references to its exploitation and to any further operations. But at the same time as accepting von Manstein's and Zeitzler's proposal thus far, Hitler completely disregarded the central element on which their plan rested: time. Hitler's doubts concerning the operation, which, he admitted, caused his stomach to turn over whenever he thought of it, were fuelled by Model, who believed that the enemy was preparing deep and strong defensive positions in exactly those areas the attack was to be mounted. The Führer was anxious that there should be no failure at Kursk, for he regarded a successful outcome to the battle as politically vital, in order to prove to the German people, his allies, and the world at large that neither he nor his Reich was finished. Victory at Kursk, he believed, would cause the disintegration of the enemy coalition. At a conference on 2 May, in which Model and Guderian (who feared heavy casualties which would be impossible to replace) spoke out strongly against the proposed offensive, Hitler decided to postpone the operation from Mid-May until June 'by which time he hoped', according to von Manstein that:

> '. . . our armoured divisions would be stronger still after being fitted out with new tanks [the Tiger and Panther]. He stuck to his decision even after it had been pointed out to him that the unfavourable developments in Tunisia could mean that if "Citadel" [the code-name of the operation] were put off any longer, there would be a danger of its coinciding with an enemy landing on the Continent. Nor would he recognise that the longer one waited, the more armour the Russians would have. . . . As a result of delays in the delivery of our own new tanks, the army group was not ultimately able to move off on "Citadel" until the beginning of July, by which time the essential advantage of a "forehand" blow was lost. The whole idea had been to attack before the enemy had replenished his forces and got over the reverses of the winter.'[38]

Whether or not the Kursk operation as originally proposed by von Manstein and Zeitzler ever had any prospect of success is a purely hypothetical question; certainly they thought so, as also did von Kluge. Von Kleist said after the war: 'If it had been launched six weeks earlier it might have been a great success – though we no longer had the resources to make it decisive. But in the interval the Russians got wind of the preparations. They laid deep mine-fields across their front, while withdrawing their main forces further to the rear, so that comparatively few were left in the bag that our high command had hoped to enclose.'[39] After Hitler's postponement, both Zeitzler and von Manstein became ever more sceptical as to the prospects for 'Citadel'. Guderian remained set against the operation, seeing nothing but disadvantages in the Führer's proposed use of the new tanks before they were ready in sufficient numbers, or had overcome their teething troubles. On 9 March he had told Hitler: 'New equipment must be held back . . . until the new weapon is available in sufficient quantities to ensure a decisive surprise success. Premature commitment of new equipment simply invites the enemy to produce an effective defence against it by the next year, which we shall not be able to cope with in the short time then available.'[40]

The delay imposed on 'Citadel' by Hitler's desire to attack with the new tanks was crucial. The errors that had been committed at Stalingrad were repeated, and the Germans, instead of creating conditions in which man-oeuvre predominated, threw away their tactical advantage of speed and manoeuvre, meeting the enemy on ground that suited him. With all hope of surprise gone, they proceeded to assault head-on what had by then become the strongest fortress in the world. No fewer than forty-three divisions, of which seventeen were armoured, two tank brigades, and a number of independent assault-gun battalions, were ranged against the Kursk salient in two armies – 9th and 4th Panzer. Of the 2,269 tanks and 997 assault-guns then in service in the east, 1,850 tanks and 530 assualt-guns were committed in the slogging match that became known as the 'death ride of the panzers'. They were launched on 5 July in the, by then, predictable pincer movement against a salient 100 miles wide and 150 miles deep which had been turned into a defensive system the very purpose of which was to wear down an armoured-led attack. The Soviet line consisted of six defended belts com-posed of anti-tank posts, thick mine-fields, and 3,500 miles of trenches backed by 3,306 tanks and 20,220 guns. To make matters worse for the attackers, torrential rain had turned the southern flank over which 4th Panzer Army was to advance into a bog. Thus, the attack inevitably degen-erated into a bitter and costly battle of attrition, the very opposite of what had been intended. It shattered forever all hopes of the use of the armoured idea in the German Army.

Whether or not the Germans were ever near to success at Kursk, as von Manstein thought they were, is open to debate. One thing is certain: even had the two German armies gained open country and completed the en-circlement, they would have been so materially exhausted as to render any further advance impossible. On the sixth day of the battle, 10 July, when 9th Army could make no further headway, the Allies landed in Sicily as von Manstein had warned; on the 13th, the day after the greatest tank battle in history in which 1,500 machines had taken part, and 4th Panzer Army had advanced twenty-five miles at a cost of 350 armoured vehicles and 10,000 men, Hitler called his army group commanders to him. He told them that, as the Italians were not even attempting to fight, Sicily was likely to be lost, and further landings, this time on the mainland, must be expected. It was therefore necessary to build up new armies in Italy and the western Balkans, made up of forces drawn from the Eastern Front. 'Citadel' would have to be discontinued. The only concession he made was that 4th Panzer Army, which appeared on the verge of success, could continue the attack with the sole aim of smashing the enemy's armoured reserves; but even this was only a temporary concession, for a few days later he ordered that several armoured divisions should be sent to Army Group Centre. On 17 July Hitler called off the assault; the Germans withdrew to their former front-line.

Even though the enemy at Kursk had lost heavily in men and equipment, possibly four times as much as that sustained by the attackers, the last German offensive in the east had been, in von Manstein's words, 'a fiasco'. Von Mellenthin wrote that at Kursk the 'panzer divisions had been bled white'.[41] The SS Panzer Corps, which had begun the battle with 425 tanks and 110 assault guns, ended it with only 183 and 64 respectively. As Guderian wrote:

> 'By the failure of "Citadel" we had suffered a decisive defeat. The armoured formations, reformed and re-equipped with much effort, had lost heavily both in men and in equipment and would now be unemployable for a long time to come. It was problematical whether they could be rehabilitated in time to defend the Eastern Front; as for being able to use them in defence of the Western Front against the Allied landings that threatened next spring, this was even more questionable. Needless to say the Russians exploited their victory to the full. There were to be no more periods of quiet on the Eastern Front. From now on the enemy was in undisputed possession of the initiative.'[42]

The losses sustained by the Soviets were, on the other hand, far less serious; their reserves of manpower appeared inexhaustable. On 12 July, even during the Kursk offensive, the Red Army had begun its 'backhand' counterstroke aimed at 9th Army and at Orel (which itself was in a salient). The great German retreat was on.

28

The East – The End

The continual demand that the almost impossible shall be made possible is in itself a brake on action.

GENERAL SIEGFRIED WESTPHAL

From mid-1943 until the end of the war the German field commanders in the east had two battles to fight: one with an enemy numerically superior; the other with Hitler. The first was clearly out of the Army's control; the Germans had lost the initiative and were subjected to a continual rhythm of offensive operations suited to the Soviet's still limited mobility and poor communications and their liking for mass-attack. Liddell Hart described the Red Army's offensives as an 'alternating series of strokes at different points, each temporarily suspended when its impetus waned in face of stiffening resistance, each so aimed as to pave the way for the next, and all timed to react on one another. . . . In that offensive process, the Russian losses were naturally heavier than the Germans' but the Germans lost more than they could afford, following the costly failure of their own offensive.'[1] The strategic problem for the Germans was now how to provide sufficient forces in relation to space, the ability to effect enough local strength and operational freedom to counter the Soviet attacks wherever they came. Yet it was precisely this that Hitler succeeded in preventing. Against his interference, the generals were forced to wage a second battle; it took up much time and nervous effort which properly should have been spent elsewhere, and it, like the battle against the Soviets, ended in their defeat.

Hitler's policy of 'no withdrawal' had its origins in the winter battles of 1941–42, which, he believed, fully justified his insistence that not an inch of ground should be yielded voluntarily. Never was he to repent of this belief, and, until the end of the war, he firmly rejected the idea of strategic manoeuvre in defence. At a conference on 10 January 1945, for example, he declared: 'I always have a horror when I hear that in some spot or other we have had to disengage or withdraw in order to get operational freedom. For two years now I've been hearing about this, and the result is always disastrous.'[2] Indeed, for Hitler, 'no withdrawal' was elevated from a strategic principle to a soldierly ethic, even a moral one. The adherence to the concepts of 'no surrender' and 'fight to the last man', which permeated all his orders in the last years of the war, was for him the ultimate commitment that a soldier could make to his Fatherland. Only he, the Führer, the arbiter of the nation's destiny, could make the decision whether to yield ground or not. In August 1944, a special issue of OKW's 'Notes for the Officer Corps', inspired by Hitler, declared: 'This decision [to surrender] is obviously for the OKW alone, and for no other. . . . the word of the Führer alone can be given in explanation of the apparently senseless sacrifice involved in fighting to the last man.'[3] Nine months later, the day before he committed suicide in the shattered remains of Berlin, Hitler made a point of stipulating in his last will and political testiment: 'May it be in the future, a period of honour with German officers, as it already is in our Navy, that the surrender of a district or town is out of the question, and that, above everything else, the commanders must set a shining example of faithful devotion to duty until death.'[4]

Von Manstein encapsulated the conflict of attitudes between Hitler and the generals at the end of his memoirs, aptly entitled *Lost Victories*:

> 'What had weighed most heavily of all on my staff and myself – to say nothing of the commanders and staffs of our subordinate armies – was the perpetual struggle we had to wage with the Supreme Commander to get operational necessities recognised. Our repeated demands for the establishment of *a clear focal point of effort at the decisive spot* . . . and for *operational freedom of movement* in general . . . were merely outward manifestations of the struggle. The basic issue was between two incompatible conceptions of strategy and grand tactics: *Hitler's,* which arose from [his] personal characteristics and opinions . . . [and those] based on the traditional principles and outlook of the German General Staff. On one side we had the conceptions of a dictator who believed in the power of his will not only to nail down his armies wherever they might be, but even to hold the enemy at bay. The same dictator, however, fought shy of risks because of their inherent threat to his prestige and who, for all his talent [sic], lacked the groundwork of real military ability. On the other side stood the views of military leaders who, by virtue of their education and training, still firmly believed that warfare was an *art* in which clarity of appreciation and boldness of decision constituted the essential elements. An art which could find success only in mobile operations, because it was only in these that the superiority of German leadership and German fighting troops could be maintained.'[5]

Von Manstein recognised that the proposals he constantly put before the Führer would have involved great risks in other theatres of the war and other sections of the Eastern Front, as well as serious drawbacks in the political and economic spheres, but he argued that it was the only way to exhaust the Soviet Army's strength and bring about a stalemate in the east. Hitler's would end in failure.

Von Manstein's belief was shared by the vast majority of the generals. Concerning a specific situation at the end of 1943, Guderian wrote:

> 'So far as all the others were concerned, it would have been better to give them [the Dnepr bridgeheads] up and retire behind the broad river line. Thus reserves could have been built up . . . and with such reserves it would have become possible to fight a mobile war and to pursue an operational plan. But if Hitler heard the word "operational", he lost his temper. He believed that whenever his generals spoke of operations they meant withdrawals; and consequently Hitler insisted with fanatical obstinacy that ground must be held, all ground, even when it was to our disadvantage to do so.'[6]

Hitler's fear of leaving the western front vulnerable by moving forces to the east, his desire to hold every inch of territory with over-extended, understrength units, his almost pathological rejection of operational withdrawals, led him to disregard any idea of forming a strategic reserve. Halder commented that it was 'characteristic of Hitler's lack of strategic understanding that he never understood the slightest interest in the disposition and movement of reserves . . .',[7] and Guderian commented acidly that 'All attempts to assemble reserves behind the most immediately threatened sectors of the very tense Eastern Front foundered on the rocks of Hitler's and Jodl's incomprehension. . . . Ostrich politics were here combined with ostrich strategy.'[8] This failure certainly played an important part in the German defeat.

Other generals were equally forthright in their condemnation of Hitler's policy. Zeitzler was fundamentally opposed to it, as was the whole of the General Staff. General Heinrici, an expert in defensive tactics, believed that the defeat in the east was:

> '. . . due to one main reason – that our troops were compelled to cover immense spaces without the flexibility in the command that would have enabled them to concentrate on holding decisive points. Thus they lost the initiative permanently. I doubt whether we could have worn down the Russians by pure defence, but might well have been able to turn the balance by a more mobile kind of warfare, and by shortening our front so as to release forces that could be used for effective counter-strokes. . . . Hitler always tried to make us fight for every yard, threatening to court-martial anyone who didn't.'[9]

Another general in the east, von Tippelskirch, describing the Soviets' summer offensive of 1944, remembered:

> 'It would have been much wiser strategy to withdraw the whole front in time. The Russians always needed a long pause for preparation after any German withdrawal, and they always lost disproportionately when attacking. A series of withdrawals by adequately large steps would have worn down the Russian strength, besides creating

opportunities for counter-strokes at a time when the German forces were still enough to make them effective. . . . The root cause of Germany's defeat was the way that her forces were wasted in fruitless efforts, and above all in fruitless resistance at the wrong time and place. That was due to Hitler. There was no strategy in our campaign.'[10]

Von Manteuffel, also a brilliant tactical general, said:

'There is no doubt that the advance of the Red Armies in the various phases of the war would have resulted differently if our defence had been more mobile and with a delaying resistance. Time and time again this form of fighting [on a tactical level] has brought me success even against numerical superiority.'[11]

And, finally, General Dittmar, in whose judgement Liddell Hart placed much faith, thought that it was possible to wear down the Russians:

'I believe we could, and the advantages of an elastic defence were clear, but our military chiefs could not apply it properly because of Hitler's objections. . . . The policy of clinging on at all costs in particular places repeatedly changed the campaign for the worse. The attempt to cement one threatened breach in the general front repeatedly caused fresh breaches. In the end it proved fatal.'[12]

On 12 July 1943 the Soviets began their counter-offensive, this time aimed against the Orel salient. Army Group Centre, reinforced by units from von Manstein's force, put up a bitter defence, and the enemy advance was checked; Orel was held. Ironically it was Hitler, for the only time in his career, who brought about a timely withdrawal by giving a direct order to evacuate the salient. However, the reason behind his decision was not operational, but political, and founded on events many miles from Orel. On 25 July Mussolini had been arrested and a provisional government set up in Italy. Although the new government immediately affirmed its allegiance to the Axis partnership, Hitler had his doubts, and the next day he informed von Kluge that the Orel salient would have to be evacuated so as to make troops available for Italy. On 1 August, after hearing of a conversation between Churchill and Roosevelt concerning Italy's defection from the Axis, the Führer ordered an immediate withdrawal. Von Kluge, anxious about the effects this would have on his Russian helpers, and concerned about the lack of prepared defensive positions to the rear, reluctantly translated his master's wish into action.

The Orel offensive was the beginning of the constant pressure maintained by the Soviets on an ever-weakening Army Group Centre. By the end of September it was forced back beyond Smolensk, and by the end of November across the Berezina. As the summer merged into autumn, von Kluge and his men became increasingly depressed. Their feeling of neglect mounted, and by the middle of October von Kluge was so desperate that he even sent a personal

THE EAST - 1944

Leningrad

Front line
Dec 22 1943

Front line
Jan 11 1945

Intermediate
Russian lines

Trapped
German forces

International Bdys

Pre-war Russian/
Polish Bdy

ESTONIA

Luga

Pskov

Courland
Peninsula

AUG 29

Riga   LATVIA

MAR

Memel   LITHUANIA   Dvinsk

Vitebsk

Smolensk

Königsberg   Vilnius   Orsha   R Dnepr

Danzig

EAST PRUSSIA   Grodno   Minsk

R Vistula   Bobruysk

Bialystok   RUSSIA

R Bug   Brest Litovsk   PRIPYAT   Mozyr

Warsaw   VULA   MARSHES   R Pripet

POLAND   Lublin   Kovel   Korosten

Baranov   Rovno   Kiev

Lvov   Tarnopol   Berdichev   Cherkassy

Vinnitsa   R Dnepr

CARPA   R Dnestr   Uman   Kremenchung

SLOVAKIA   Kolomyya   Kirovograd

THIANS   Yampol   Krivoy Rog

HUNGARY   APL 15   Nikopol

Budapest   Lower Bug   Nikolayev

SEPT 24   Jassy   Kherson

Odessa

Foesani

BLACK
SEA

Galatz

ROMANIA   R Danube

Belgrade   Turnu
Saverin   Ploiesti

Bucharest

0   200
          Miles
0   300
          Km

letter to the Führer, pointing out that failure was inevitable when the strength of his forces was continually dwindling, and the strength of the enemy always rising. His army group was 200,000 men short of establishment, and the few replacements he had received were generally of low quality. No answer to his letter was received, and on 27 October von Kluge was invalided from his post as a result of a motorcycle accident. His successor, Busch, inherited a situation that was dire; the fighting strength of his over-stretched divisions was so low that some units had only one man for every eight yards of front. By the end of October the strength of his most important formation – 3rd Panzer Army – had dwindled from 292,000 in May to under 200,000, and each division was forced to cover a frontage of 25,000 yards instead of the normal 15,000.

To the south, where the Soviets mounted their main offensive, the situation was even more critical. Even as early as August, von Manstein's thirty-eight infantry divisions in Army Group South had a fighting strength of only eighteen, his fourteen panzer divisions of only six, and these were expected to cover a front of 610 miles. By October, when he was on the Dnepr, von Manstein reported that, in each division in the south, the average number of soldiers fit for front-line combat was reduced to 1,000, and would not rise above 2,000 even after promised replacements had arrived. These 1,000 men were responsible for holding a front of up to twelve miles (one man to cover twenty-one yards). The condition of the panzer divisions was just as lamentable. Immediately before the Kursk offensive, the average number of tanks in von Manstein's eleven panzer divisions was ninety-five (of which seventeen were obsolete models), and those fit for action seventy-eight; almost six months later it was revealed that the total had sunk to eighty, and those actually serviceable to twenty. One army division had six tanks in the field with which to face the enemy. No wonder von Manstein could write after the war: 'Henceforth Army Group South found itself waging a defensive struggle which could not be anything more than a system of improvisations and stop-gaps. . . . To maintain ourselves in the field [and avoid the fate of 6th Army at Stalingrad], and in doing so to wear down the enemy's offensive capacity to the utmost, became the whole essence of this struggle.'[13]

The crucial Soviet offensive in 1943 against Army Group South may be divided into five distinct phases. First was a probing diversionary attack near Izyum on the Donets (300 miles south-east of Orel) begun on 17 July, which was stopped by the Germans, although to no avail. Despite von Manstein's argument that the Donets area was untenable in the long-term. Hitler insisted on it being maintained, thus causing the army group to move substantial armoured units from its north flank around Kharkov to the south in order to restore the situation on the Mius front. As von Manstein recognised later, this was fatal; appeals to OKH to reinforce the northern flank went unheeded, and on 3 August the Red Army attacked towards Belgorod. The second and most dangerous phase had begun. In two days the town was taken; by the 13th the Soviets had arrived at Kharkov, twenty-five miles from the former front-line, and on the 23rd the city, which again Hitler had ordered was to be held to the last (because its fall, he believed, would have an unfavourable effect on the attitudes of Bulgaria and Turkey), was evacuated by the Germans. Here lay the greatest threat to Army Group South, for, by forcing its northern flank, the enemy was clearly making a bid to break through south-east to the Dnepr and thereby encircle the whole of von Manstein's force (a repetition of the previous winter's plan). As early as 8 August the army group commander had told Zeitzler that there were two ways of avoiding such an outcome: either to evacuate the Donets area immediately and thereby release units for the northern wing, or to transfer divisions from other fronts outside the army group's control to the threatened sector. No action was taken by OKH. On the 23rd a sharp counter-attack managed to halt the enemy, but only temporarily. On 26 August further Soviet attacks began to develop along the line of junction between Army Groups Centre and South, west of what had been the Kursk salient. The situation was becoming critical, especially as thirteen days earlier, on 13 August, the Red Army had launched another attack in the Donets Basin – the third phase. Taganrog was taken and, by the 27th, the 'position in the Donets area became more perilous than ever'.[14] Von Manstein thereupon demanded that the Führer should either provide his southern wing with further forces or else give him the freedom to move back so as to halt the enemy on a shorter line.

At a meeting with Hitler on 27 August, von Manstein and his generals painted a dark picture, 'with special reference to the condition of the troops, who had long been suffering from overstrain'.[15] Von Manstein made the point that there had been only 33,000 replacements for 133,000 casualties, and that, by comparison, the enemy possessed a wealth of reserves. He again presented Hitler with the two alternatives: reinforcement or withdrawal. The dictator listened, promised to provide units if at all possible, departed, and did nothing. No reinforcements arrived; the two other army groups to the north claimed that they could not spare a single division, and Hitler refused to consider denuding other theatres until he knew where the Allies would land next in Europe. Von Manstein noted wryly: 'Unfortunately, the Russians paid not the slightest heed to this desire of Hitler's to put off his decision. They went on attacking, and the situation became increasingly difficult.'[16] It was not until the evening of the 31st that Hitler was finally forced by events to allow the withdrawal from the Donets Basin, the area so 'essential' to the economic health of the Reich, 'provided that the situation absolutely demands it and there is no other possible alternative'.[17] That morning von Manstein had already given the orders for a partial evacuation. He noted:

> 'If only it had been given this freedom of movement a few weeks earlier, the army group would have been in a position to fight the battle on its southern wing more economically. It could have freed formations for the vital northern wing and still halted the enemy advance on a shortened front, possibly even forward of the Dnepr. Now, however, freedom of movement served only to preserve the

southern wing from defeat. Even so, it remained doubtful whether a proper front could still be established forward of the river.'[18]

The situation, temporarily eased in the south, grew worse again in the north. The attack begun on 26 August at the junction of Army Group Centre and South was, by 3 September, beginning to threaten the flanks of both formations. On that day, the two army group commanders flew to see Hitler, von Manstein realising that it was essential to form a strong army in front of Kiev, now being threatened. The forces necessary for this would come from other theatres. Von Manstein recorded: 'I am sorry to say that the talk von Kluge and I had with Hitler proved quite profitless. Hitler declared that no forces could be spared either from other theatres or from Northern Army Group.'[19] Even when, a few days later, von Manstein pointed out that the enemy was reinforcing his Ukrainian front at the expense of other sectors, and that therefore it would be safe for the Germans to do the same, he made no impact. A second meeting with Hitler took place on the 8th, the day that Krasnoarmeyskoye in the south was taken, and Bakhmach in the north threatened. Von Manstein emphasised that the position on his southern flank could not be restored east of the Dnepr, and that in order to find the necessary forces for the northern wing, a similar withdrawal behind the river by Army Group Centre was also required. He wrote:

> 'Hitler now accepted in principle the need to take the right wing of the army group [South] back on to the Melitopol-Dnepr line, though he still hoped to avoid doing so by bringing up new assault-gun battalions. As usual, he thought the use of technical resources was sufficient to halt a development which in fact could have been averted only by throwing in several divisions. As for acquiring forces from Army Group Centre by taking it back to the upper Dnepr, Hitler maintained that it was impossible to withdraw that distance at such short notice. The muddy season would be upon us before a movement of those dimensions [at the furthest, it would be 275 miles] could be completed, and, as had already happened in the evacuation of the Orel salient, too much equipment would be lost in the process. The best one could hope for was to withdraw to some intermediate line. This, of course, would not have achieved the man-power economy we were after.'[20]

However, the Führer did admit the necessity of strengthening Army Group South, and directed von Kluge to assemble a strong force on the boundary in front of Kiev. Moreover, he even agreed to the evacuation of 17th Army from the Kuban bridgehead, the last German toehold in the Caucasus.

However, except for the Kuban evacuation, the dictator failed to keep his promises; the danger of encirclement from the north grew nearer day by day, and on 14 September von Manstein told OKH that the following day he would be forced to give the order to retire behind the Dnepr, a distance of some 100 miles from the front line. The next day Hitler was told by his army group commander that the crisis that had developed on the northern wing might well prove fatal not just to the southern sector but to the whole Eastern Front. Von Manstein argued that:

> 'This crisis was the consequence of Army Group Centre's failure to hand over forces. . . . it seemed quite intolerable that a transfer of forces which the Supreme Command itself had acknowledged to be urgently necessary could not be enforced. . . . The reason why Hitler had not got his way with Army Group Centre in this case was, of course, that he had failed to give timely consideration to the need to shorten the front there, and had not demanded prompt execution in spite of all the objections raised.'[21]

As a result, Hitler immediately ordered that von Kluge should move four divisions to von Manstein, promised infantry units and replacements from the west, and allowed the withdrawal to the Dnepr. But, by then, because of the Führer's procrastination, Army Group South was forced to withdraw under enemy pressure from a front of 450 miles and converge on five major crossings – Dnepropetrovsk, Kremenchug, Cherkassy, Kanev, and Kiev – with the ever-present danger that the Soviets would already be there.

The Red Army pursued von Manstein's troops vigorously; on 21 September it reached the Dnepr, and between the 22nd and 30th, numerous crossings were made on a 300-mile stretch between the Pripyat Marsh and the area north of Zaporozhye. On the 22nd it even began an attack on Kiev, but by the 27th that had been repulsed. Thus, despite the magnificent exploits of the German troops, the withdrawal to the Dnepr had brought them little respite. When the Red Army chose to resume the offensive it would be in an excellent position to do so. Hitler had not allowed any work to be done to fortify the Dnepr until 12 August, partly because of the detrimental effect this would have had on the 'retreat-minded' generals, and partly also because of the effort then being put into the construction of the Atlantic Wall. Thus, at the end of September when the exhausted troops arrived, they found few ready-made defences for their protection. Moreover, as von Manstein remembered, 'German formation strengths had fallen off to a frightening degree in the incessant fighting of the past two and a half months, and the replacements of personnel and weapons – especially tanks – came nowhere near filling the gaps. To a very large extent this was due . . . to Hitler's persistence in setting up new divisions back home.'[22] Even before the Dnepr had been reached, the army group had told Führer headquarters that, in view of these weaknesses, it was unlikely that the line could be held for any length of time; and now, with the Red Army across the river at so many points, this appeared even more unlikely. Urgent appeals for reinforcement for the thirty-seven infantry and seventeen panzer or panzergrenadier divisions went unheeded; Army Group Centre's front had been shortened by one-third, and, although it was expected to be under relatively little pressure, no units came from that quarter.

Likewise, no preferential treatment was given in the matter of supplies and replacements. As von Manstein noted:

> '. . . the question was whether the German Supreme Command still had the forces and means available to win the struggle in the part of the Eastern Front where the enemy was intent on bringing matters to a head in 1943. . . . Obviously it [the Supreme Command] could do so only if it made up its mind to accept considerable risks in other sectors of the Eastern Front and other theatres of operations. Provided such action was taken, an abortive Soviet offensive against Army Group South would probably wear down the enemy's attacking power to a conclusive degree – a success which might decisively influence further the course of the war.'[23]

Despite getting support from Zeitzler, von Manstein did not receive even a part of the force he needed. Hitler rejected any evacuation from the Crimea of von Kleist's Army Group A, whose life-line with the rest of the Eastern Front, the Zaporozhye-Melitopol-Molochnyy Lake triangle, was in danger of being occupied by the Soviets (the evacuation would have given von Manstein 200,000 troops but, the Führer argued, would have provided the Soviets with an air base from which to bomb the Romanian oil fields); he was also reluctant to take any divisions from the west. In an effort to concentrate his limited forces, von Manstein asked to be allowed to withdraw from the bridgehead of Dnepropetrovsk east of the Dnepr; Hitler refused – indeed he even specified that it be further enlarged.

The fourth phase of the 1943 offensive began on 10 October with an attempt to cut off the Crimea from the rest of the front. On 14 October Zaporozhye was taken, followed on the 23rd by Melitopol. By the beginning of November the Red Army had advanced a further seventy miles westwards, and 17th Army of Army Group A had been cut off, the Perekop peninsula had been entered, and a bridgehead established on the north coast of the Crimea. The enemy advance had been so fast that a proposed counter-attack to relieve 17th Army had no chance of being mounted. Owing the the Führer's reluctance to countenance an earlier withdrawal (he had even counter-manded von Kleist's order for evacuation in late September), an army consisting of a quarter of a million men (half of them Romanian) were left, useless, in the Crimea for six months, until May 1944. When Hitler finally allowed the evacuation by sea and air in face of a strong Soviet attack, no fewer than 80,000 casualties, of whom almost half were prisoners, were suffered, and nearly all 17th Army's equipment was lost in the withdrawal.

In mid-October, the fifth phase of the Soviet offensive began: the attempt to cut off the two German armies in the Dnepr Bend. It was closely linked with the attack against the Crimean flank. The first attempt, initiated on 16 October, penetrated forty miles into the German rear to Krivoy Rog by the 23rd. Such was the seriousness of the situation that Hitler made one infantry and five armoured divisions available to the army group for the specific task of defending the bend, the retention of which he regarded as essential for the German war effort. However, von Manstein could not wait until they had arrived ('how different things might have been if these five armoured formations had been at the army group's disposal four weeks earlier!'[24]) and he was forced to mount a counter-attack with his existing forces. It was a success, and the Red Army was pushed back twenty miles; the situation was saved, for the moment.

On 3 November the enemy resumed its attack on the vital northern wing of the army group. The position soon became desperate; on the 6th Kiev was taken, followed on the 12th by Zhitomir and on the 17th by Korosten. The enemy had penetrated ninety miles, and 4th Panzer Army was on the verge of disintegration. Hoth was relieved of his command by Hitler, and replaced by Raus. The next day, the 18th, a counter-attack towards Kiev was begun with insufficient strength; it retook Zhitomir, but petered out in the rain on the 26th. As before, the threat to the northern flank had been severe, but again Hitler had been reluctant to allocate reserves to that part of the front. The five panzer divisions he had made available for the Dnepr Bend were to be used only in that area; he wished von Manstein to pursue the success he had had there, to preserve the deposits of manganese found at Nikopol, and to relieve Army Group A and so deprive the Soviets of the Crimea, which they would use as a basis for aerial warfare against the Romanian oilfields. Moreover, the Führer believed that the loss of the Crimea would provoke a change of heart in Turkey, Bulgaria, and Romania. (His obsession was such that on 6 February 1944 he even took 6th Army [the southern-most unit of Army Group South] from von Manstein's control and placed it under Army Group A in order to send two of its divisions to the Crimea. Events prevented this, however.) Von Manstein argued that this might be so, but if his north flank were turned all the success in the world in the Dnepr Bend would be rendered useless. Thus, with difficulty, he managed to obtain for his counter-attack in the north a panzer division from von Kluge, three of the five armoured divisions originally made available for the Dnepr Bend, and several other units. As events were to prove this was too small a force; more was needed. However, the Dnepr Bend had to be maintained; no strategic withdrawal in order to shorten the line and make more units available to the decisive sector would be allowed.

While the fighting was continuing around Zhitomir, the Red Army made its second attempt to cut off the forces in the river bend. Against the masses of men and material thrown against the army group here, von Manstein had no chance; certainly there was no question of releasing units from the vital northern flank. On 20 November he submitted a memorandum to OKH in which he stated:

> 'The army group would have to get through the winter holding a front which far exceeded the resources of its almost completely exhausted divisions. It would not have enough reserves to take effective action against any major enemy attacks, particularly if called upon to do so at

several places at once. Operationally, therefore, the army group would remain completely at the enemy's mercy. ... The prior condition for successfully prosecuting this struggle, we insisted, was a sufficiency of hard-hitting reserves. If these could not be transferred from other theatres, they must be created by radically shortening the front of the German southern wing (including a seaborne withdrawal of 17th Army from the Crimea). The army group could not last the winter if it had to fight without reserves.'[25]

During the rest of November and December the Soviet attacks continued, and, as every day passed, the truth of von Manstein's words became more obvious. Yet still Hitler refused to face reality; still he insisted on the importance of the manganese deposits and the Crimea; still he believed that the enemy would bleed itself to death as, he thought, it had done in the winter of 1941–42. What he failed to recognise was that the Soviets' losses, although high, could be sustained, whereas those of the Germans could not. If the battle of attrition lasted much longer, the forces under von Manstein's command would be brought to utter exhaustion, and would be simply overrun. A second Stalingrad was well in the making.

On Christmas Eve the northern flank again came under pressure; the next day von Manstein again asked OKH for permission to withdraw his right wing from the Dnepr in order to halve the frontage to be covered and thereby to provide reserves for the north; again Hitler refused. As a stop-gap measure, von Manstein proposed that 1st Panzer Army, leaving behind half its forces in the Dnepr Bend, should be transferred to the north, next to 4th Panzer Army. When no decision was forthcoming from Führer headquarters, he took the matter into his own hands; on the 29th the orders for the transfer of 1st Panzer Army were issued. Another attempt by von Manstein to get Hitler to change his mind took place on 3 January, but with the same result. Throughout the rest of the month, the struggle for the Dnepr Bend continued; the heroism of the troops and the skill of their commanders managed to hold the enemy – but only just. To the north, however, the situation was daily deteriorating. The Soviets reoccupied Berdichev and they exploited the wide gaps that were appearing not only between Army Groups Centre and South, but also between von Manstein's 1st and 4th Panzer Armies. Still the extensive withdrawal of the southern wing was prohibited, and von Manstein was forced to launch a limited counter-attack to restore the situation in the north. In the end, it was only enemy pressure that forced the Führer to yield up the bend. On 31 January the Red Army launched a heavy attack east of Krivoy Rog; within three days a decisive breakthrough was made on the northern front of 6th Army (now under Army Group A) and a number of formations were almost cut off. Hitler then had to agree to the evacuation of the land east of the Dnepr and the Nikopol bridgehead. Von Manstein commented: 'Had this bastion been given up at the proper time, it would not only have been possible to withdraw all the forces inside it in good order, but also to free divisions for the far more important northern wing of the army group. Instead, 6th Army's formations had been expended in the wrong place operationally, and one doubted whether they could ultimately withstand the pressure of the pursuing enemy.'[26]

In 1944 Hitler's operational failures of 1943 bore fruit. His poor timing of the Kursk offensive and his dogged insistence on the principle of 'no withdrawal' had allowed 1943 to slip by without the achievement of a stalemate on the Eastern Front. Instead, he had succeeded in dissipating still further the limited German strength to no avail; much ground had been lost, and the enemy, despite his high sacrifices at the hands of the German troops, had not been exhausted – indeed, he was now poised to take the war into the very heart of the Reich. The expected Allied invasion in the middle of the year would prove the final blow to all German hopes.

The German southern flank was to be the first to face the Soviet onslaught in 1944. At the end of January the inevitable occurred, and two corps (including one panzer division), some 60,000 men, were encircled at Cherkassy, in the middle of von Manstein's front. Immediately, a relief force was formed and, in conjunction with a breakout by the trapped soldiers, some 30,000 men succeeded in escaping westwards. Hitler's first reaction had been to prohibit any such withdrawal, but he was finally forced by events to give his consent. However, although these men, lacking most of their heavy equipment, were extricated by the end of February, the two experienced corps had been destroyed as fighting formations. The next set-back came in early February, with the Soviet occupation of Rovno, on the northern sector of von Manstein's front, an area left weakly held because of Hitler's continued refusal to form a new army to cover the flanks of Army Groups Centre and South. By this move, the Soviets were now well within the 1939 borders of Poland. In the south, the Soviets attacked and pushed the Germans out of the Nikopol salient on 8 February, and from Krivoy Rog a fortnight later. It was clear that the Soviets now possessed far greater mobility than the defenders, this being due in no small measure to the vast numbers of American four- and six-wheel drive trucks now in use. Both in men and in armaments the Soviets were daily increasing their numerical superiority, as much through the dwindling strength of the Germans as by their own reinforcements; by March 1944 the average Red Army tanks corps possessed between fifty to a hundred tanks, whereas the German equivilent, the panzer division, had, at best, thirty fit for action. Von Manstein reckoned that, between July 1943 and January 1944, the Soviets in the south had received 1,080,000 men and 2,700 tanks (including assault-guns) to take the place of 405,409 killed, wounded, or missing and an unknown loss of armoured vehicles. All Hitler could provide were empty promises and assurances that the enemy's exhaustion was imminent. In that, once more, he was wrong.

On 3 March, the Soviets again attacked with overwhelming strength the northern wing of von Manstein's army group. By the 7th, after covering 100 miles, they were astride the Odessa-Warsaw railway line near Tarnopol, and by the 28th Nikdayev on the Bug had been captured. In the south, another Soviet attack had taken Kherson at the mouth of the Dnepr by the 13th, and had cornered parts of the German forces in this area. A third attack, launched in the centre from Uman against the hard-pressed Germans, managed to reach the Bug by the 12th; by the 18th the Dnestr had been crossed at Yampol and other places. The Germans had retreated 150 miles, but their ordeal was far from over. Further advances to the west meant that by the end of March the Soviets were brought close to the foothills of the Carpathians. The frontier of Hungary was about to be breached.

At about this time, Hitler evolved a new version of his 'no withdrawal' strategy. His Führer Order No. 11, dated 8 March, specified that henceforth 'Fortified Areas' and 'Local Strongpoints' would be instituted with the intention of holding the enemy advance on the Soviet borders of pre-September 1939. It read:

> 'The "Fortified Areas" will fulfil the function of fortresses in former historical times. They will ensure that the enemy does not occupy these areas of decisive operational importance. They will allow themselves to be surrounded, thereby holding down the largest possible number of enemy forces, and establishing conditions favourable for successful counter-attacks. "Local Strongpoints" are strongpoints deep in the battle area, which will be tenaciously defended in the event of enemy penetration. By being included in the main line of battle, they will act as a reserve of defence and, should the enemy break through, as hinges and corner-stones for the front, forming positions from which counter-attacks can be launched. Each "Fortified Area Commandant" should be a specially selected, hardened soldier, preferably of general's rank. He will be appointed by the army group concerned. . . . Only the commander-in-chief of an army group in person may, with my approval, relieve the 'Fortified Area Commandant" of his duties, and perhaps order the surrender of the fortified area.'[27]

The generals had little faith in such a 'Stalingrad' policy, as they called it. Von Manstein commented: 'In practice they [the fortresses] required more troops to defend them than was worth devoting to their retention. . . . Later in 1944, this method of Hitler's led to considerable losses.'[28] One of the first casualties was 1st Panzer Army which, at the end of March, became encircled around Tarnopol. The area was immediately designated by the Führer a 'fortress'; after a long argument, Hitler finally agreed with von Manstein to provide extra units for a relief force, and to allow 1st Panzer Army to fight its way to the west. By 9 April it had succeeded in reaching the main German line; more than 200,000 men were saved to fight another day, but large quantities of their heavy equipment and weapons had been lost. It had been yet another costly mistake of Hitler's 'no withdrawal' mentality.

At the beginning of April, when the seasonal floods began with the accompanying mud, the Soviet offensive, by then at the very end of its over-stretched supply and transport organisation, came to a temporary halt. Except in the Crimea, where 80,000 men and equipment for 200,000, were lost owing to Hitler's refusal to sanction an evacuation until the very last moment, a general lull descended over the Eastern Front. In the Baltic region in January, the Germans had been forced back from Leningrad to Lake Peipus; from there, the line ran due south via Vitebsk and Bobruysk to the Pripyat Marsh, where it turned abruptly westwards to just beyond Kovel (almost to Brest-Litovsk), uncovering the right flank of Army Group Centre, thence to the Carpathians at Kolomyya, then south-east to Iasi (Jassy) and west of Odessa. The Soviets were only fifty miles from the part of the Bug from which Hitler had launched his invasion almost three years previously. The front line, with all its indentations, ran for 1,650 miles. Busch, the commander of Army Group Centre, had only one division of about 2,000 men to every sixteen miles of his 650-mile front. Nervously, the Germans waited for the resumption of the Soviet offensive, knowing full well that when it did break their numerical inferiority could not be offset by operational mobility. Busch thought that he would be the next to bear the main brunt of the attack; Hitler, believing that Stalin would wish to gain the Romanian oilfields, argued otherwise, and reinforced Army Groups North Ukraine (formerly South) and South Ukraine (formerly A) with panzer and panzergrenadier formations. All warnings that the enemy were preparing to assault the central sector of the front, where the Germans still had a large foothold on Soviet soil, were dismissed at Führer headquarters as unrealistic. Moreover, the construction of rearward defences on the line of the Berezina was forbidden.

On 6 June 1944 the Allies landed in Normandy; on 22 June, the third anniversary of the eastern campaign, when all attention was focussed on the west, the Soviets attacked Army Group Centre, as Busch had prophesised. Most of 3rd Panzer Army was destroyed within a few days, largely through Hitler deciding too late that Vitebsk need not be held to the last. At the beginning of July, a further 100,000 men were encircled at Minsk, and by the 8th it was clear that Army Group Centre had been destroyed. Total German casualties were put as high as 300,000 men; a breach 250 miles wide had been made through the front, and the way to East Prussia and the Baltic States lay open. It was a disaster greater even than that of Stalingrad.

The Soviets continued, and their advance thrust towards all points of the compass except east. Dvinsk, Vilna, Grodno, Bialystok and Brest-Litovsk all fell within a short time, and by the middle of July the Germans had been swept out of Belorussiya and half north-eastern Poland; Army Group North's flank was being turned as the enemy thrust into Lithuania, and it was in danger of encirclement when, at the same time, an offensive was begun at Pskov. On 14 July another attack opened, supported by overwhelming air strength, this time south of the Pripyat Marsh against Army Group North Ukraine; within days the enemy had moved on to Lvov and Lublin. By the 26th some units of the Red Army had even reached the Vistula; by the 31st a suburb of Warsaw had been penetrated, and the next day Polish patriots began their uprising in the capital. In little more than one month, the Germans had been pushed back over 200 miles. To the north, Tukums on the Gulf of Riga was occupied, and Army Group North, standing firm in pursuance of Hitler's order, saw its land escape route cut off. On 2 August the Red Army secured a major bridgehead over the Vistula near Baranow, 130 miles south of Warsaw. In the west, the Allies were breaking out of the Normandy bridgehead into the open plains beyond. Total German collapse seemed imminent.

Once again, Hitler's policy had been the main cause of the catastrophic German failure. The Soviet commander, Zhukov, was surprised at the ineptitude of the German defence, especially on the central front. He argued, correctly, that as soon as the offensive broke, the Germans should have retired to a rearward defence line and then mounted mobile flanking attacks on the advancing Soviets. That they did not pursue this policy resulted in the destruction of the central front. What Zhukov did not realise, however, was that such an operational withdrawal was prevented not by Busch's ineptitude but by Hitler's intransigence. Only when Model came to command the remnants of Army Group Centre was any tactical flexibility achieved, and this was due not to the Führer's change of mind, but to his having a soft spot for the new commander, which led him to overlook the Field-Marshal's frequent minor contraventions of the principle of 'no withdrawal'. Hitler's total inability to comprehend the realities of the war was most evident in his directions to Army Group North. Because of his insistence that the Baltic States be held to the last (which he justified by saying that their evacuation would have a disastrous impact on Finland, and, when it made peace with the Soviets in late August, on neutral Sweden), Army Group North's line of retreat was cut off by the Soviets on 31 July. By 21 August a narrow corridor had been pierced through to the pocket from the west, but Hitler refused to allow the troops to withdraw through it; instead he sent two divisions from Army Group Centre to reinforce the defenders. By mid-October, after further enemy attacks, Army Group North was cornered in the Courland peninsula (a province of Latvia surrounded on three sides by the Baltic Sea). Despite repeated protests, especially from Guderian, Hitler refused to countenance a seaborne evacuation of Courland, his argument always being that Army Group Courland (as it was retitled in January 1945) had an essential role to play in pinning down Soviet forces that might otherwise be released for the main attack westwards. But this 'Stalingrad' mentality was barren of results. For the Soviets, the resources required to invest this position were available; for the Germans, fighting for their very survival on other fronts, the troops in Courland were an irretrievable loss that could never be made good. There, two armies, the 16th and 18th, (initially twenty-six divisions, reduced later to twenty-two) would remain until the end of the war, a living example of Hitler's wasteful intransigence.

August 1944 was to witness an unexpected, but memorable, German revival on the central sector of the Eastern Front, a revival due to several factors, of which the skill and bravery of the German troops and their commanders was one (and this even though the enemy had noticed a marked decline in both these qualities, caused by the costly defeats of the past years which had taken great toll of both experience and leadership). Other factors were that the Soviets, having advanced 500 miles in five weeks, had outrun their supply lines, and had also suffered heavy losses. The scanty German reserves, hastily assembled on the central sector, and ably led by Model (who had replaced Busch on 28 June), just managed to hold the Soviets, and by the second week in August were able to mount a number of counter-attacks. The Germans were now enjoying the advantages of the combined effect of their own contracted front and the attackers' over-extended communications. Moreover, it seems that Stalin deliberately halted his troops in front of Warsaw to allow the Germans to subdue the armed resistance within the city (which they did by 2 October, after a ferocious fight lasting two months, in which the SS more than lived up to their unpleasant reputation) and thereby see eliminated any potential opposition to his rule in the future Soviet-dominated Poland. The Red Army maintained its position along the Vistula and the borders of East Prussia for nearly six months before it mounted a major offensive, which took it to the outskirts of Berlin. This delay was far longer than required by military considerations, and was probably the result of Stalin's cold political calculations. He knew that for Germany the war was lost, and that, wherever he attacked, it was only a matter of time before the Allies achieved total victory. He knew, also, that it was possible to end the war in 1944 by a direct drive into the heart of the Reich. That, he did not choose to do; he wanted to place the countries of the Balkans under Soviet dominance and to prevent them going over to the western allies, as might happen if German occupation were ended by the collapse of the Reich rather than by Soviet occupation. Thus it was to the Balkans that the centre of gravity shifted in late 1944. This saved Germany for another six months.

On 20 August the Soviets struck unexpectedly at Romania. Army Group South Ukraine was a poor command. Of the 800,000 troops dispersed over a front of 400 miles, only 360,000 were German and the rest Romanian; although the twenty-three German divisions possessed what were then considered to be high personnel strengths of up to 10,000 men each, only fifteen per cent of the soldiers had had any experience of battle and the efficiency of the reinforcements, many of whom were over-age, was low. Moreover, the infantry divisions possessed only 400 motor vehicles each, and some 6,000 horses; shortages of guns and equipment were widespread and severe. Of the 120 tanks available, more than half belonged to the Romanians, although there were in addition 280 assault-guns. Perhaps the most serious weakness was that nearly all air and panzer reserves had been removed, as OKH had not expected an offensive on the Romanian front. That a large part of this force would soon be destroyed was due to Hitler's insistence that when the attack came there should be no withdrawal into Romania, although such a move had been suggested by the Romanian Marshal, Antonescu. The attackers, numbering some 900,000 men with 1,400 tanks, quickly broke through the Romanian defenders, who gave way without a fight, and by the 23rd the whole of 6th Army, some twenty German divisions, had been encircled in a great pocket between the Dnestr and the Prut. Hitler had not given permission to withdraw until 22 August—far too late. On the 26th, after further encirclements of German troops, the supreme warlord ordered Army Group South Ukraine to take up defensive positions from the mouth of the Danube to Galatz, Focsari, and the Carpathians—the same line that had been urged on him by all concerned before the Soviet offensive began. But by then such a front was not longer tenable; the Soviets had already passed beyond it. Within nine days more than 180,000 Germans were lost, and a further 50,000 soon suffered the same fate. On the 27th Soviet tanks moved through Galatz; on the 30th the Ploiesti oilfields were occupied; and on the 31st the Romanian capital, Bucharest, was entered. The enemy had covered 250 miles in twelve days; in the next six he was to cross a further 200 miles to the Yugoslav border at Turnu Severin. From there the Soviets embarked on a great flanking manoeuvre to take the Germans on their now exposed south-eastern flank in Hungary. On 8 September Bulgaria declared war on Germany; by 24 September the south-east salient of Hungary had been taken, and the enemy had advanced to within 100 miles of Budapest, the capital. In the south, Belgrade, the Yugoslav capital, was liberated on 20 October, and on 4 November the suburbs of Budapest were reached. The Hungarian capital was stubbornly defended until mid-February, and the Soviets were forced to encircle it and to consolidate and extend their south-western flank. Although in the early days it would have been possible for the defenders to break out to the west, attempts to relieve the encircled force in Budapest came to naught. The German position in the Balkans disintegrated within four months, and the Soviets had won their second great victory in 1944.

By the end of the year it was clear to OKH that the Red Army would soon resume its offensive against the central sector of the Eastern Front guarding the approaches to Germany; it was little more than 300 miles from Berlin—less than five weeks campaigning judging by their previous performance. Yet the German preparations to meet this inevitable, and crucial, onslaught were woefully inadequate. Once again the root cause of the trouble was Hitler, backed by Jodl, for whom the OKH theatre of war was of secondary importance. The two men were too much absorbed by their offensive in the Ardennes, begun on 16 December and designed to shatter the Allied armies in the west, to bother over-much about future events in the east. After the stabilisation of the central front in August, the new Chief of the General Staff, Guderian, wrote:

'In general, the long front from the Carpathians to the Baltic was relatively quiet so that the building of fortifications and the withdrawal of panzer and panzergrenadier divisions to form a mobile reserve was successfully carried out. All the same, twelve weak divisions could provide only a very inadequate reserve for such an enormous front, approximately 725 miles long [far shorter than it had been before, however], and against such vast superiority of strength as the Russians now possessed.'[29]

Much work needed to be done on the fortifications in the east. Tactical experience had shown that two lines were needed, the major line of defence to be well-camouflaged twelve miles behind the front line. In the event of a major attack, the bulk of the German forces would be withdrawn to this major line; the Soviet assault would waste its energy on the rearguard in the front line of defence, and, when it then came unexpectedly on the major defence system, would suffer a severe set-back. Hitler, however, would have none of this stratagey. Guderian wrote:

'There can be no doubt that this theory was absolutely correct. I approved it, and submitted it to Hitler. He lost his temper, saying that he refused to accept the sacrifice of twelve miles without a fight, and ordered that a major defensive line be built from one to two miles behind the main line of defence. He was basing his ideas on the conditions prevailing in the First World War when he gave these nonsensical orders, and no arguments could bring him to see reason. This mistake of his was to cost us dear when the Russians broke through in January 1945 and our reserves – again on a direct order of Hitler and against my judgement – were once again too close to the front. Main line of defence, major defensive positions, reserves, all were buried beneath the tidal wave of the initial Russian breakthrough and lost to us.'[30]

At the end of December, when the German Army was expending its strength in the fruitless Ardennes offensive, which became bogged down on the 23rd, there came growing evidence that the Soviets were preparing for an imminent, major offensive. German intelligence calculated correctly that the attack would begin on 12 January, and that the enemy possessed a superiority of 11:1 in infantry, 7:1 in tanks, and 20:1 in guns. Guderian remembered:

'I was faced with the problem of whether in fact what was now demanded of our soldiers was humanly feasible. . . . for us the question was, simply, "to be or not to be". And no alternative [to destruction] existed unless, and until, the impending Russian offensive was somehow, somewhere, brought to a standstill. To do this it was necessary immediately to transfer forces from the west to the east, to build up a strong reserve army in the Lodz-Hohensalza area, and to force the Russian armies which broke through to fight a war of movement, for this was the type of battle in which the German commanders and soldiers, despite the long war and their consequent exhaustion, were still superior to the enemy.'[31]

The rigid principles on which Hitler had so far conducted the defensive war had merely played into the hands of the Soviets, forcing his troops to conduct a form of battle which was tailored not to their own strength but to that of their enemy. Now, as the New Year was approaching, Hitler had his last chance of adopting the strategic principles that had for so long been advocated by his generals. But, once again, he rejected them. No forces would be withdrawn either from Courland or from the west, where success was still expected; the intelligence estimates of Soviet strength were 'rubbish'; and the eastern armies would not yield an inch of ground voluntarily. After a meeting with Guderian on Christmas Eve, Hitler astonished his Chief of the General Staff by saying that 'the Eastern Front must take care of itself '.[32] The very next day, Christmas Day, he further weakened the Eastern Front by ordering two strong SS divisions that were in reserve in the area north of Warsaw to be transferred to Budapest in a vain attempt to relieve the encircled city. Of this, Guderian wrote:

> 'All protests remained fruitless. In Hitler's opinion the relief of Budapest was more important than the defence of Eastern Germany. He advanced reasons of external politics when I asked him to reverse this ill-starred order, and turned down my request. Thus, two of the fourteen and a half panzer or panzergrenadier divisions assembled as a reserve against the impending Russian attack were sent to a secondary front. Only twelve and a half remained for a front of approximately 750 miles.'[33]

Guderian, however, was reluctant to give up the fight at Führer headquarters. He ascertained from von Rundstedt and Westphal that there were three divisions in the west and one in Italy that could be made immediately available to the east and, moreover, were near railheads. A warning order was despatched to the units in question, and the Chief of Field Transport was told to make the necessary preparations. On New Year's Eve, armed with these facts, Guderian went to see Hitler and obtained his approval for the transfer. However, it was but a partial victory, for, as Guderian remarked, 'even this wretched pittance was to go, by Hitler's orders, to Hungary'. On 9 January, three days before the Soviet onslaught, Guderian warned the Führer: 'The Eastern Front is like a house of cards. If the front is broken through at one point, all the rest will collapse, for twelve and a half divisions are far too small a reserve for so extended a front.' Hitler's parting remark was again: 'The Eastern Front must help itself and make do with what it's got.'[34]

On 12 January 1945 the Soviets launched their attack from the Vistula on the German central front; by the 31st they were on the lower Oder, barely fifty miles from Berlin. All had gone exactly as Guderian had predicted. The enemy fell on the seventy divisions of Army Group Centre and Army Group A, commanded by Reinhardt and Harpe respectively, and the main thrust was made on the line Warsaw-Berlin, exactly where the German mechanised forces were weakest. Because of Hitler's interference, seven of the eighteen panzer divisions in the east were in Hungary, four in East Prussia, two in Courland, and only five in the centre, covering Brandenburg. Within a few days the German front was breached to a width of 200 miles, through which gap poured nearly 200 enemy divisions; on the 17th Warsaw fell, and two days later the frontier of Germany was reached. At the end of the first week of the offensive, the Soviet breach had widened to nearly 400 miles over over a depth of 100 miles. On 19 January the first enemy troops set foot on German soil.

Hitler's reaction to this direct threat to the Thousand-year Reich, the invasion of the sacred borders of Germany by the hated Bolshevik-Slav horde, was truly amazing. His first act was to order, on the 15th, the transfer of the strong Panzer Corps *Grossdeutschland* 150 miles south from East Prussia to Kielce, a town that had already been taken. Guderian was strong in his opposition, arguing that in face of the Soviet flood this corps alone, moved so late, could achieve nothing, and that it would be far better employed where it already was, protecting East Prussia at a time when the enemy's attack there was about to become 'highly dangerous'.[35] However, Hitler had his way, and the panzer corps was moved, being forced to retreat immediately it de-trained at Lodz. On 16 January the dictator returned to Berlin, for the last time, and established his headquarters in the area of the partly-bombed Reich Chancellery. Not surprisingly, in order that forces could be made available for the broken Eastern Front he decided that the Western Front should go over to the defensive (it had already been forced to do so by enemy action). But he still refused to countenance any evacuation of Courland – all he was ever to release from there were two panzer and four infantry divisions. The 6th SS Panzer Army and a number of other units were to be transferred from the west to fight the Red Army. Guderian had already prepared plans for such a force to be deployed east of the Oder river, with the aim of attacking the flank of the Soviet offensive that was now aimed directly at the heart of the Reich and halting it. Hitler, however, had other ideas; the 6th SS Panzer Army was to go to Hungary, some 350 miles south of the Soviet breakthrough. Guderian later recorded:

> 'On hearing this [from Jodl] I lost my self-control, and expressed my disgust to Jodl in very plain terms. . . . During my ensuing conference with Hitler, I expressed my views and my disagreement with the proposed course of action. Hitler could not accept my opinions and reaffirmed his intention to attack and to relieve Budapest. An argument that was to last for several days now began on the subject of this ill-begotten plan. After I had disposed of the military reasons that he advanced, he produced economic ones: since the bombing of the German synthetic oil plants, our retention of the Hungarian oilfields

and refineries became essential to us, and assumed a decisive importance for the outcome of the war. "If you don't get any more fuel, your
tanks won't be able to move and the aeroplanes won't be able to fly.
You must see that. But my generals know nothing about the economic
aspects of the war." He was completely infatuated with this idea, and
it was impossible to persuade him that it was incorrect.'[36]

Thus, the forces that were transferred from the west were divided; one group,
the smaller, went to the front defending the capital, Berlin, the other, the
larger and of better quality, was sent to the south-east, to Hungary. Not until
17 February was 6th SS Panzer Army to be used in action against the Soviets
near Budapest, and within six weeks its last man was to leave Hungarian
territory. But that was in the future; for the present the north-central sector of
the Eastern Front was facing total disintegration. The advance to the Oder
was developing into a race. Of Army Group A, the remnants of 4th Panzer
Army and 9th Army had been left far behind, and only 17th Army had
managed to retire with any semblance of order. On the 22nd the Soviets
reached the upper Oder, north of the industrial area of Upper Silesia, near
Breslau; on the 31st enemy spearheads reached the lower Oder, near Kustrin.
Only 40 miles were between them and Berlin. The western Allies lay 380 miles
away. To the north, Army Group Centre was also in dire straits, and by the
26th its three armies, 3rd Panzer Army, 4th Army, and part of 2nd Army, had
been cut off in East Prussia after a Soviet advance of 125 miles in twelve days.
Again, the Führer's reluctance to sanction a withdrawal while there was still
time had been the main contributory factor to this new 'Stalingrad'. Once the
encirclement was complete, Hitler reacted as expected, and, instead of
ordering a breakout or, better still, a seaborne evacuation, he declared that
East Prussia was to be held to the last. The troops fell back to the ancient city of
Königsberg, which was thereupon given the title 'fortress'.

By the end of January the German position in the east was grave indeed;
total defeat could not be long delayed. Guderian wrote: 'The appalling month
of January had justified all our fears of what this new great Russian offensive
would bring.'[37] In the northern tip of Courland, Army Group Courland, with
twenty infantry and two armoured divisions, was isolated; in East Prussia,
Army Group North (known until 25 January as Army Group Centre), with
nineteen infantry and five armoured divisions, had been forced into the
narrow strip of Samland, into Königsberg and into Ermland, and could be
supplied only by air or by sea; from the Vistula between Graudenz and Elbing
to the Oder between Schwedt and Grünberg, Army Group Vistula (a new
command), with twenty-five infantry and eight armoured divisions, held a
thin line vulnerable to further attack; from Silesia to the Carpathian mountains, Army Group Centre (the new name for Army Group A given on 25
January), too, with twenty infantry and eight armoured divisions, held on to a
precarious line. From the Carpathians to the Drava, Army Group South, with
nineteen infantry and nine armoured divisions and awaiting the arrival of 6th

FINAL COLLAPSE OF THE REICH
ADVANCE FROM EAST TO WEST

LITHUANIA

Königsberg

Insterburg

EAST PRUSSIA

Danzig

Elbing

Koslin

POMERANIA

Graudenz

Tannenberg

Mlawa

R Narek

Rozan

Settin

Pyritz

Arnswalde

Hohensalza

R Vistula

Plock

R Bug

GERMANY

Schwedt

Landsberg

Warsaw

Berlin

Kustrin

Poznan

R Warthe

POLAND

Lodz

Magnuszev

Frankfurt

Guben

Grünberg

Kalisz

R Pilica

Radom

R Elbe

R Neisse

SILESIA

Breslau

R Oder

Kielce

Leipzig

Dresden

Baranov

Katovice

R Vistula

Prague

Jaslow

CZECHOSLOVAKIA

GERMANY

R Danube

Vienna

AUSTRIA

Budapest

HUNGARY

Front line Jan 11 1945
"   "   Feb 2
"   "   Feb 24
British/US front May 7

0   100 Miles

0   160 Km

482

SS Panzer Army, prepared for a vain counter-offensive either side of Lake Balaton with the aim of retaking the right bank of the Danube to secure the southern flank of the whole Eastern Front and to ensure the retention of the Hungarian oilfields. In the east the German Army and Waffen SS possessed 103 weak infantry divisions and thirty-two equally frail panzer and panzer-grenadier divisions. Owing to Hitler's concept of military operations, no fewer than thirty-nine infantry and seven armoured divisions, one-third of the total, were encircled behind the northern flank of the Soviet advance, and so were of little or no use to the defence of the German Reich. Such was the numerical and material preponderance of the Red Army that a delay such as the 6th Army at Stalingrad had imposed on the 1942–43 winter offensive could not be repeated by the combined efforts of Army Groups Courland and Vistula. Because of Hitler's obsession with the southern sector of the front, which was of secondary importance in comparison with the areas of Pomerania and Silesia, only forty-five infantry and sixteen armoured divisions remained to defend the approaches, more than 700 miles in extent, to the centre of Germany and to Berlin. The Soviets, for their part, were increasing their forces on the Oder by about four divisions every day.

Guderian, understandably, was alarmed. He later recorded:

> 'In view of this general situation, I decided once again to urge Hitler that he postpone the offensive in Hungary and that instead he attack the Russian spearhead which had reached the Oder at a point between Frankfurt and Kustrin; the flanks of this spearhead were still vulnerable if attacked from a line Cologne-Guben in the south and Pyritz-Arnswalde in the north. I hoped by such an action to give increased protection to the capital and interior of Germany, and to win time for armistice negotiations with the western powers. The necessary preconditions for this operation were prompt evacuation of the Balkans, Italy, Norway, and particularly of Courland.'[38]

Hitler again disagreed: the troops in all these areas were to remain, especially in Courland. All that he would allow was a limited attack from Arnswalde, with the aim of defeating the Soviets north of the Warthe, and of retaining Pomerania. The counter-offensive, which began on 15 January, was spearheaded by six panzer divisions; after four days, it petered out.

The final advance by the Soviets into Germany was but a matter of time; nothing anyone could do would alter the outcome of the war. To be sure, by the sacrifice of the defence on the Rhine to the needs of the Oder, the Germans managed to check the Soviet advance on the Oder-Neisse line in the third week of February; between the 17th and 22nd of that month, Army Group South eliminated the Soviet bridgehead across the Gran; and from 3–8 March, German troops mounted a successful counter-attack to recapture the railway east of the Riesengebirge between Berlin and Silesia. But these successes only delayed the inevitable by a few weeks. The offensive in Hungary, begun on 6 March, met initially with some success but ultimately with failure, and within ten days the Soviets launched a massive counter-attack. By the end of the month German troops had left Hungarian soil, and by 6 April the outskirts of Vienna were reached by the Red Army. The city finally fell on the 13th. In all, half of Austria was occupied by the Soviets. Meanwhile, the Red Army swept through Czechoslovakia to within fifty miles of its western border. To the north, too, the Soviet colossus rolled relentlessly on. In early March the bridgehead over the Oder was enlarged, and by the end of the month Silesia was fully occupied. Hitler was still sure that the enemy was at the end of his strength; but on 16 April, just five days after the western Allies had voluntarily halted on the Elbe, sixty miles from Berlin, the Soviets began their final attack, launching 193 divisions against fifty weak German ones. By the 25th, Berlin had been completely encircled, and on the 27th the Soviets joined hands with the Americans on the Elbe. On the afternoon of the 30th, with the enemy little more than 1,000 yards from his underground bunker, Hitler committed suicide; three days later, resistance ended in the Reich's capital. At midnight on 8 May the war in Europe officially ended. Since 22 June 1941, German losses in the east had numbered more than 1,015,000 dead, 4,000,000 wounded, and 1,300,000 missing. The Red Army's casualties had amounted to more than fourteen million, of which more than ten million were dead.

29

Military Demise

I need more divisions.

ADOLF HITLER,

1944

In the twenty-odd months from the battle of Kursk until the end of the war, the state of the German Army went from bad to worse. Losses rose dramatically. On the Eastern Front, where the Army had been under-strength since the first months of the invasion of Russia in 1941, no fewer than 1,686,000 men were either killed, wounded, or missing between 1 November 1942 and 31 October 1943, whereas the number of replacements was only 1,260,000. In that period, nearly one million were lost permanently to the Army as a result of death, serious wounds, or capture, a loss that was made particularly alarming by the fact that a high percentage were experienced soldiers, whereas their replacements were relatively ill-trained and of lower-grade. In 1944 the position degenerated even further. The manpower of the German Field and Replacement Armies dropped continuously, from a peak of 6,550,000 in 1943 to 5,300,000 by the end of the war, and losses increased, especially in the number of those taken prisoner; between June and November 1944, the German Army lost in the east 214,000 killed and 626,000 missing, and in the west, 54,000 killed and 339,000 missing. This loss, of some 1,200,000 men, equalled the total loss from September 1939 until, and including, the defeat at Stalingrad, and took no account of the number of wounded, many seriously, which was generally thought to be three times that of the dead. In 1944 no fewer than 106 divisions were destroyed, three more than the number mobilised by Germany in September 1939.

The resources of manpower within Germany could not cope with such a drain. A number of expedients were used: men up to fifty years old were made eligible for service in the front line; personnel fit for combat duty were taken from depots and military staffs and exchanged for those at the front who were less fit; units not employed in combat were forced to make do with fewer men; Luftwaffe and Navy personnel were transferred to the Army; workers in industry were made available for service by the introduction of women and foreign labourers; women were employed in signals units, on high-level staffs, and in anti-aircraft batteries; and there was an increased recruitment of volunteers from the eastern territories into the Army. Hospitals and convalescent homes were scoured for those strong enough to carry a rifle, and special units were formed from men who had hitherto been thought unfit for active duty; 'stomach' battalions were instituted, made up entirely of those who were suffering from stomach troubles (one whole division in the west was nicknamed the 'White Bread Division' because of the main diet of its soldiers), and 'ear' battalions, from men whose hearing was either partly or wholly deficient.

However, these desperate measures could not materially alter the situation. Manpower continued to fall, and divisional strengths to retract. New divisional organisations were introduced with fewer battalions or regiments, which provided for lower personnel complements, and the number of fighting troops in each division was decreased. On 2 October 1943 a new pattern for infantry divisions was introduced, with an establishment of 10,708 men (plus 2,005 Hiwis – *Hilfswillige,* former Soviet prisoners-of-war who had volunteered to help with non-combatant duties), between 5,000 and 7,000 fewer than that at the beginning of the war; later the number was increased to about 12,000. As usual, however, field strengths were often considerably lower. Moreover, the number of 'army troops' declined, much to the detriment of the efficiency of the armies and army groups in the field. In June 1941, there had been 111 artillery and fifty-four pioneer 'army troop' battalions, whereas two years later there were only seventy and forty-nine respectively. Only in the number of coastal batteries, which rose from 173 to 513 in the same period, was there any increase in the German Army's auxiliary units.

Problems of manpower were paralleled by problems of equipment, despite the fact that in 1943 the import and production of steel, coal, oil, and other basic materials had never been higher, and the production of arms had reached unprecedented levels; by December 1943, output was 150 per cent higher that it had been in February 1942. This was to continue into 1944, when production again increased dramatically, before it fell, equally as spectacularly, from September onwards owing to territorial losses, shortages in raw materials, and Allied strategic bombing. The sizeable achievement in the years 1943 and 1944 is best illustrated by a glance at the average monthly production figures for armoured vehicles (tanks, assault-guns, etc.) for each year of the war: 1939: 62; 1940: 136; 1941: 316; 1942: 516; 1943: 896; 1944: 1,524; and the first three months of 1945: 1,258. In the tonnage of armoured vehicles produced, the result was even more significant; from 2,901 tons per month in 1940, output was increased to a monthly average in 1944 of 45,746 – roughly a fifteen-fold increase. However, these improvements, though essential to the continued fighting ability of the German Army, had come too late; severe shortages continuously plagued the field formations. Simultaneously with the increase in output there was a decline in efficiency because important spare parts were frequently lacking. The shortage of certain types of ammunition such as armour-piercing shells, certain arms such as artillery pieces, petrol, spare parts, optical instruments, and prime-movers became increasingly obvious. Often were the occasions when the troops received weapons that were not fit for use at the front. For example, on 31 October 1943, of the 2,300 tanks in the east (the invasion force had begun with 3,332 in June 1941), only about one-third were fit for service against the 5,600 armoured vehicles that the Soviets had facing the Germans.

The number of panzers lost during 1943 increased to 6,362 tanks and 1,705 assault-guns compared with 2,648 and 330 respectively in 1942; on 1 December 1943, Germany's stock of tanks was only 5,158, some 500 fewer than in January, and front-line machines totalled only 3,355, some 1,000 fewer. The nominal tank strength of an army panzer division at the outbreak of the war had been 328 tanks; in 1943 it was 160. Actual strengths were even lower. At the beginning of the Kursk offensive, the average strength of an army panzer division was seventy-three tanks, of which twenty-six were obsolete, while the number fit for action was only sixty-four; the Waffen SS divisions were better off, averaging 131 tanks and thirty-five assault-guns, with fewer unfit for action, while the élite *Grossdeutschland* division had most of all, 165 and thirty-five respectively. Almost six months later, on 20 November, a return of strengths revealed that the fourteen panzer divisions in Army Group South had between them 977 tanks, of which only 280 were fit for action; the highest establishment was that of the much-favoured *Leibstandarte* SS 'Adolf Hitler', with its 155 tanks, and the lowest the 23rd Panzer Division, with a mere twenty-seven. Qualitative improvements no greater than those of the enemy could not compensate for this numerical contraction. Other equipment was similarly deficient. Artillery and ammunition remained in extremely short supply, with the result that more reliance was placed on the mortar. The state of mechanisation remained critical, and, despite an increase in production, the number of trucks and passenger cars available to the German Army fell from their peak of 715,000 in January 1943 to 670,000 by the end of that year, and to 400,037 by the end of 1944. Similarly, unarmoured half-tracks fell from 28,420 in December 1943 to 11,000 a year later. The reliance on horses had never been greater; only sixteen per cent of the German divisions were fully mechanised. All that could be sent to the troops in abundance were exhortations to fight to the last. Typical of the fine but empty phrases that continually came from the Führer Headquarters in lieu of weapons was the following, dated August 1944: 'The OKW will henceforth often be no longer able to meet demands, however urgent and justifiable, for air, armour, and artillery support, even when enemy superiority is overwhelming. Any shortage of weapons, therefore, must be made good by strengthening the morale of the troops.'[1]

The year of 1944 was a dismal one for the panzer force, despite prodigous increases in production, the build-up of stocks to unprecedented levels (on 1 July 1944 the German Army possessed 7,447 tanks, of which 5,807 were suitable for front-line service, and 4,167 assault-guns, of which 3,960 were front-line), and the creation of one Waffen SS and two army armoured divisions (this brought the number of panzer divisions to thirty-one, roughly eleven per cent of the field divisions). Unit strengths continued to decline appreciably, so that a division was fortunate if it possessed more than sixty tanks. The opening of a second major front in June 1944 took an enormous toll of the panzer arm; losses of tanks and assault-guns in the first half of 1944 averaged 650 each month, but after the Allied landings in Normandy losses rose to 1,154. Furthermore, an increasingly high proportion of tanks were undergoing repairs, many being rushed into service before they had been run-in; in January 1944, for example, no fewer than 2,261 went through the workshops, more than one-fifth of the total available to the Army. Moreover, the strategic and tactical bombing carried out by the enemy, which cost the Germans an estimated fifth of their potential production of armoured vehicles, prevented the proper movement of machines from the factories to the depots, and from there to the troops in the field. The air offensive aimed directly against the German transport system destroyed a considerable amount of material in transit, and, by the end of 1944, had caused the marshalling capacity of the railway to drop by forty per cent. Thus, although 2,199 tanks were produced by German factories in September, October, and November, only 1,371 reached the troops to replace the 1,575 lost.

As in 1943, because of the severe shortages and high losses, the nominal number of tanks in a tank company was reduced during 1944 from twenty-two to seventeen, and, at the beginning of 1945, to fourteen; the paper strength of a panzer division was brought down to only 120 tanks. In March 1945, a reorganisation laid down the total of tanks in each division as fifty-four – one-sixth the number with which the panzer divisions had invaded Poland five and a half years before. The actual field strengths of the armoured divisions remained far lower than the nominal. By the end of the war, the exhaustion of the panzer force was complete. On the Eastern Front in mid-April 1945, the twelve commands had between them only 2,698 panzer vehicles of all kinds left in the field, and of these only a half were tanks, many of which could not move through lack of fuel. Even the much-favoured 6th SS Panzer Army, in which were such formations as the *Leibstandarte* and *Hitler-Jugend* panzer divisions, was left with a total of only forty-two tanks fit for action – an average of slightly more than five in each division.

The other components of the panzer division showed some improvement in the last two years of the war; to compensate for the decrease in tank strength, the motorised infantry (renamed in 1942 'panzergrenadiers') built up a formidable fire-power, illustrated by a comparison of weapon scales for 1939 and 1944. In 1939, three battalions of riflemen possessed between them ninety-three light and forty-two heavy machine-guns, twenty-seven light and eighteen medium mortars, six light infantry guns, and nine 3.7cm anti-tank guns. In 1944, the four battalions of panzergrenadiers had 354 light and fifty-one heavy machine-guns, no light but thirty medium and sixteen heavy mortars, no light but twelve heavy infantry guns, thirty-nine 2cm anti-aircraft guns, and twelve 7.5cm guns (its anti-tank guns had been given to the division's anti-tank battalion). Additional fire-power was given to the artillery regiment, and more anti-aircraft guns were distributed throughout the division. However, in terms of mobility, the panzer division improved but little; an average of only one panzergrenadier battalion in four was mounted in armoured, half-track personnel carriers, and of the 3,690 vehicles in the 1944 model division, only 785 were tracked, either fully or partially.

The breakdown of the German Army was exacerbated by Hitler's actions. Until the end, he refused to understand the need for reducing the number of divisions so as to increase their fighting efficiency and economise on non-combatant support units. On the contrary, the number of divisions available to the Army, the Luftwaffe, and the Waffen SS continued to rise. In September 1939, there had been 103 divisions; in June 1941, 208; in July 1943, 276; and by June 1944, 284, 257 of which belonged to the Army, twenty-one to the Waffen SS and six to the Luftwaffe. Because he was fascinated by numbers, and desired to mislead the enemy as to the true strength of his forces, Hitler insisted that for every division that was destroyed, another would be formed. Thus, when forty-one divisions were lost in the east between the battle of Kursk, in July 1943, and May 1944, no fewer than fifty-two others were created; during the rest of 1944, ninety-six divisions were either destroyed or had to be disbanded, and ninety-nine were formed; and in the first four months of 1945, a further forty were instituted, all that could be found to replace the, by then, constant destruction of units in the field.

Such was Hitler's desire to raise new divisions, that, at the end of 1942, he had changed the function of the Replacement Army. Until then, it had been based on a number of replacement battalions affiliated to regiments in the field, through which new personnel went to the front as reinforcements. The reorganisation separated the training and replacement functions of the Replacement Army; replacement was still carried out by the special replacement battalions, but training was undertaken by newly formed reserve battalions, reserve divisions, and reserve corps, which often trained in occupied Europe. In the east, some of these formations were converted into field-training divisions and employed under the control of army groups. In October 1943, there were no fewer than thirty-one replacement divisions in the Reich, their significance being administrative rather than tactical, as well as four field-training and seventeen reserve divisions. However, owing to Hitler's insistence on the creation of new fighting formations, a number of these divisons were converted either into field or into static divisions and sent into battle; as a result, by mid-1944 the old established system of replacement broke down completely and a new organisation had to be built up. Later, in the latter half of 1944, after Himmler had assumed control of the Replacement Army, new formations called *Volksgrenadier* (People's Grenadier) divisions were formed from replacement units, shattered divisions, depot staffs, and such like. Each, composed of only some 8,000 men, and poorly trained, the *Volksgrenadier* divisions were of little use in the field, despite Himmler's assertion that their close identity with the Waffen SS, Party ideology, and the people was of more value than military professionalism.

Measures were sometimes ordered that were dangerous in their self-deception. Entirely disintegrated divisions, with the strength of a regiment or even less, were designated 'division-groups', three of which were designated a 'corps-groups'. Impracticable organisations such as armoured, assault-gun, and engineer brigades, the strength of which amounted to one or two battalions, and which had nothing to do with the term 'brigade', were also established. In late January 1945 Hitler even ordered the formation of a tank-destroyer division; high-sounding title though it had, the division was to consist merely of bicycle companies equipped with anti-tank grenades. This was all that was left to send against the T34s and the Shermans. The old units that still remained were but shadows of their former selves; to the ravages of war had been added the burden of Hitler's neglect. For example, in September 1944, of the 26,000 machine-guns and 2,090 80mm mortars produced, only 1,527 and 303 respectively were sent to front-line units, while 24,473 and 1,947 went to divisions then being formed. As Speer remembered: 'New divisions were formed in great numbers, equipped with new weapons and sent to the front without any experience of training, while at the same time the good battle-hardened units bled to death because they were given no replacements of weapons or personnel.'[2] Thus, the divisions in the field were ultimately sacrificed on the altar of Hitler's obsession with numbers, an obsession that had scarred the German Army since the earliest days of rearmament.

30

The West 1944–1945 – Invasion

*There was no plan any longer. We were merely
trying, without hope. . . .*

GENERAL GUNTHER VON BLUMENTRITT

On 6 June 1944 the western Allies landed in Normandy; the long-feared
invasion of Hitler's Europe had begun. Five weeks later they landed in
southern France. By the middle of August the Americans had broken out of
the hard-fought-for Normandy bridgehead; on 25 August Paris was liberated, and by 15 December the Germans had been pushed out of France,
Belgium, and a part of Holland. The German Army had won the west in
1940 in four weeks; in 1944 it took six months to lose it. From the outset, its
forces were considerably inferior, both numerically and qualitatively, to
those of the invaders. Against the two million Allied soldiers under
Eisenhower allocated for the invasion, the Germans could deploy just fifty-
nine, largely low-standard, divisions. To make matters worse, not knowing
where the invasion would take place, these formations had to be deployed
over a distance of 3,000 miles from the German/Dutch border in the north to
the Italian frontier in the south. This was one great weakness; another,
perhaps more decisive, was the failure to deploy those limited units in
accordance with sound principles of strategy and command. For both these
failings, Hitler, the supreme warlord, was responsible.

Because of the division of operational responsibility between OKW and
OKH, with OKH being confined to the Eastern Front, Hitler was the only
man who could control the movements of German units in all the theatres of
war. Only he could take an over-all strategic view; only he could order the
movement of even one battalion from east to west. Had the Führer proved
himself an able Supreme Commander, this might not have been of much
importance; but, as he completely lacked either the mental training or the
stability of character required for this demanding role, it was disastrous. His
failure to bring about a stalemate in the east, and his dispersal of his limited
forces over all parts of Europe, was made worse by his inability to act
according to long-term considerations. He was moved more by immediate
events than by well-laid plans. He was no longer the master of the war, but

its servant. He failed to form a strategic reserve, preferring instead to send his divisions hither and thither to any sector of the front threatened with collapse – a collapse brought about by his refusal to allow his field commanders operational freedom, including their ability to effect a strategic withdrawal when the occasion demanded. Thus, the attempt to build up the strength of the German forces in the west was doomed to failure from the outset. However much Hitler might fear an Allied invasion in the future, his actions would be determined by present events in the east.

The concern for the west that Hitler showed in 1944 was a relatively new phenomenon. Certainly, he had always been anxious lest the British invade Norway, and thus had always kept a relatively high proportion of his forces there (as many as fourteen divisions by the middle of 1943), but at first he dismissed an attack on the Continent as impossible. In his Directive No. 32, dated 11 June 1941 and entitled somewhat optimistically 'Preparations for the period after "Barbarossa" ', he did not even deal with the idea of an invasion. Its opening paragraph stated: 'After the destruction of the Soviet Armed Forces, Germany and Italy will be military masters of the European continent. . . . No serious threat to Europe by land will then remain.'[1] No possible invasion from the west was even mentioned.

Then, at the end of 1941, failure on the Eastern Front, increasing opposition from the populations of the occupied countries, and the entry of the United States into the war dramatically increased the threat of the Western Front; what Great Britain alone might be unable to achieve, partnership with the United States might well make possible while Germany was bogged down in the Soviet Union. From that time, the threat of invasion hung like the Sword of Damocles over the Führer's head. On 14 December 1941 he gave orders for the defence of the Atlantic coastline. Warlimont wrote: '. . . Hitler decided, entirely on his own, that an order should be prepared for the construction of a "new West Wall" to assure the protection of the Arctic, North Sea, and Atlantic coasts. The strategic object was laid down as being "to assure protection against any landing operation even of very considerable strength with the employment of the smallest possible number of static forces".' Norway was still regarded as taking precedence, but the coasts of Belgium and France assumed a greater importance than hitherto. Warlimont added: 'In the light of subsequent developments, and looked at over-all, this order, whether intentionally or not, marks the beginning of the period when, stategically, Germany was forced on to the defensive.'[2]

In the week after Christmas 1941, Hitler's fears were partially realised by the small Commando raids on the Norwegian coast, and on 23 March 1942 his Directive No. 40 warned: 'The coastline of Europe will, in the coming months, be exposed to the danger of an enemy landing in force.'[3] As if to fulfil his prophecy, five days later the raid on St Nazaire took place, with as its main object the destruction of the only dry-dock on the Atlantic coast capable of taking the German battleship *Tirpitz*. This was followed in August by the raid at Dieppe, the biggest undertaken by the British, as much a demonstration of strength as a reconnaissance in force of the Atlantic Wall. In Hitler's mind, the importance of the Dieppe raid was magnified out of all proportion, and served as a constant reminder of the vulnerability of his western flank. In November 1942 Vichy France was occupied by the Germans so as to secure the southern flank. Then, in May 1943, Tunis fell; a landing in the south of France now became a possibility, all the more so after the occupation of Sicily in July and the invasion of Italy in September. At the same time, Hitler feared landings in Norway, Holland, Belgium, northern France down to Brittany, and even in Spain and Portugal. The generals, while agreeing with the rumours that an invasion would come, nevertheless restricted the possible landing areas to Belgium and northern France. During 1943 the feeling of uncertainty and insecurity about the threat from the west grew, made worse by the increasing activity of the resistance movements in the occupied countries, by the obvious successes of Allied forces in the Mediterranean, and by the ever-increasing heavy bombing raids on the Reich. The material superiority of the western enemy was no longer in doubt. On 3 November Hitler issued his Directive No. 51, the culmination of his worry of the previous few years; it was, as Warlimont noted, 'the starting point and framework on which the German Wehrmacht prepared for its great task of defence against the forthcoming attack on western Europe. . . .'[4] It began:

> 'The hard and costly struggle against Bolshevism during the last two and a half years . . . has demanded extreme exertions. The greatness of the danger and the general situation demanded it. But the situation has since changed. The danger in the east remains, but a greater danger now appears in the west: an Anglo-Saxon landing! In the east, the vast extent of the territory makes it possible for us to lose ground, even on a large scale, without a fatal blow being dealt to the nervous system of Germany. It is very different in the west! Should the enemy succeed in breaching our defences on a wide front here, the immediate consequences would be unpredictable. Everything indicates that the enemy will launch an offensive against the Western Front of Europe, at the latest in the spring [of 1944], perhaps even earlier. I can, therefore, no longer take responsibility for further weakening in the west, in favour of other theatres of war. I have therefore decided to reinforce its defences, particularly those places from which the long-range bombardment [by the V.Is] of England will begin. For it is here that the enemy must and will attack, and it is here – unless all indications are misleading – that the decisive battle against the landing forces will be fought.'[5]

Hitler then went on to order the adequate equipping of all motorised units, the provision of anti-tank guns, and the general increase of weapons in all units in the west. Moreover, he stated categorically: 'No units or formations stationed in the west and in Denmark [where an attack was thought possible], nor any of the newly raised self-propelled armoured artillery or anti-tank units in the west, will be withdrawn to other fronts without my approval.'[6] And the following month, he admitted: 'if they attack in the west, that attack will decide the war. . . . they have made their decision. The attack . . . will take place any time from the middle of February or early March.'[7]

Typically, Hitler's actions failed to live up to his words. The distractions of the other fronts, and the false sense of security that his much-vaunted Atlantic Wall gave him, ensured that the divisions assigned to the west were deficient both in numbers and in quality. The Atlantic Wall, begun early in 1942, was potentially an impressive system of fortification and strongpoints at important ports (fortresses) but it was in no condition to meet a determined invasion. Indeed, in the Normandy area only eighteen per cent of the planned defences had been completed by the time the invasion came, despite the vigour with which Rommel, in charge of the defences, had pursued the task. Von Rundstedt, the Commander-in-Chief, West, said of the Wall:

> 'Strategically, the value of these fortresses was insignificant because of their inability to defend themselves against a land attack. . . . We subsequently lost more than 120,000 men in these concrete posts when we withdrew from France. . . . As for the Atlantic Wall itself [the 'cord' between the 'knots' of the fortresses] it had to be seen to be believed. It had no depth and little surface. It was sheer humbug. . . . Once through the so-called Wall, the rest of these fortifications and fortresses facing the sea were of no use at all against an attack from behind. I reported all this to the Führer in October 1943, but it was not favourably received.'[8]

Von Rundstedt had touched Hitler on a particularly sensitive spot. The Atlantic Wall, with its numerous 'pill-boxes', gun emplacements, coastal batteries and fortresses, represented an ideal to Hitler; it stood for strength and security, completely denying the enemy any part of the Continent. It was, in short, the epitome of 'no withdrawal'. As Hitler had boasted to Guderian: 'I am the greatest builder of fortifications of all time.' The panzer leader later commented: 'Hitler had remained a man of the 1914–18 trench warfare epoch, and had never understood the principles of mobile operations.'[9]

And so, trusting implicitly in his 'Atlantic Wall', Hitler succumbed to the pressures of other fronts. The slogging-match at Kursk had put paid to any hopes Guderian and others might have for the formation of large armoured formations in the west; and the Soviet offensives, together with the Allied invasions of Sicily and Italy and the threat to the Balkans, ensured that no build-up of formations behind the Atlantic Wall was possible. In Warlimont's words, the result was that 'Hitler continued, literally up to the day before the invasion, to prejudice the defensive preparations in the west in favour of the east or even of Italy'.[10] On 1 July 1943 there had been 186 divisions on the Eastern Front, seven in Italy, and forty-four in the west; on 1 June 1944, five days before the invasion, after the destruction of Army Group Centre in the east, there were 156 divisions in the east, twenty-seven in Italy, and only fifty-four in the west, nineteen per cent of all those available to Hitler. Indeed, in addition to being regarded as a convalescent home for the rest and reorganisation of units shattered on the Eastern Front, the west assumed a new role as a pool from which fresh formations could be sent to other fronts as the situation demanded. Warlimont recorded:

> 'Up to the beginning of 1944 . . . the continued discrepancy between what German Supreme Headquarters intended and what it actually did had resulted in the forces available for the west, measured in battle-worthy army formations, being actually smaller than in the previous autumn. If the situation maps of 7 October 1943 and 11 January 1944 are compared, they show a loss of four divisions against an increase of seven untrained "battle-groups" of regimental strength.'[11]

Moreover, it proved only too easy for OKH to frustrate the desired movement of formations from east to west, especially as OKW appeared to take little active interest in the matter. Transfers were constantly deferred and delayed by inserting in movement orders phrases like 'as soon as the battle situation makes this possible'.[12] 'Battle-groups' containing the best fighting elements were often left behind in the east, while the 'division', but a shell of its former self, would make its way to Belgium or France. As von Rundstedt remarked: 'often I would be informed that a new division was to arrive in France direct from Russia, or Norway, or central Germany. When it finally made its appearance in the west it would consist, in all, of a divisional commander, a medical officer, and five bakers.'[13]

The opening of 1944 brought with it no improvement in the situation, even though Hitler was sure that an invasion would be mounted in the early spring. On 21 January Jodl noted in his diary: 'equipment now available in depots for *Panzerjäger* (anti-tank) battalions of divisions in the west, to go to the east.' [14] On 22 January the Allies landed at Anzio in an attempt to take Rome, and, in reaction, two motorised divisions earmarked for the west were retained in Italy, an infantry division and a tank battalion were sent from France, and a number of units were moved from the Reich. In late February Hitler decided to occupy Hungary, and a corps headquarters, certain 'army troops', and the Panzer Lehr division (an excellent, well-equipped division formed by Guderian in November 1943 out of the demonstration units of panzer training schools, with the specific intention of defending the west) were sent in March from von Rundstedt's command to the east. Only with great difficulty did OKW manage to get the formations back before the invasion, and then most of them had been severely mauled in battle. In March, so dire was the situation on the southern sector of the Eastern Front (thanks to the Führer's inflexibility) that Hitler 'began raiding the resources of the west in earnest'.[15] On 24 and 25 March it was deprived of three assault-gun battalions, one Luftwaffe and one infantry division, and two SS panzer divisions. Warlimont noted:

> '. . . the west was now left without a single battle-worthy, fully operational armoured division at a moment when the invasion might come any day. It is true that Hitler reached this decision only after deliberating on it for some days; it is also probably true that, without this assistance, the 1st Panzer Army . . . could not have escaped encirclement. This does not alter the fact, however, that, in view of the threat hanging over the west, the German Supreme Command ought never to have let things get to such a pass.'[16]

The final major loss to the west took place on 2 June, just four days before the Allied landings, when a number of heavy tank units and a Luftwaffe field division were moved to Italy in reaction against a severe threat to Rome.

The condition of von Rundstedt's force on 6 June was lamentable. He had at his disposal more than 850,000 soldiers and 1,552 tanks, organised into fifty-nine divisions, five more than on the 1st of the month, of which forty-eight were infantry, one panzergrenadier, and ten panzer. Two further panzer divisions, both SS, were 'on loan' to the east, and were ordered to return six days after the invasion. The forces were divided into two army groups, B and G. The more important, B, was commanded by Rommel, and was made up of 15th and 7th Armies covering the crucial area from Holland to the Loire: the other, G, with 1st and 19th Armies, was under von Blaskowitz, and occupied the area from the Loire to the Alps. Of the infantry divisions, (half of which were coast-defence or training formations) von Rundstedt considered that no more than a quarter had either the personnel or the equipment commensurate with the title 'division'; many, for example, classified as 'fortress divisions' possessed no transport and were given a multiplicity of captured foreign arms. The infantry contained a high proportion of older men, convalescents, and inexperienced officers. Considerable reliance was placed on foreign volunteers, especially in the supply and administrative services, and the infantry divisions contained numbers of Russians, Hungarians, Poles, Yugoslavs, Czechs, Romanians and Dutch, to name but a few of the nationalities in German service. Pay books were issued in eight different languages just to deal with the various peoples from the Soviet Union, of whom there were some 60,000 in France. Their fighting value, however, was negligible; the problem of administrating them considerable. Von Rundstedt believed them to constitute 'a menace and a nuisance to operations in France'.[17] And, although the panzer divisions in the west represented almost one-third of the total then available to the Germany Army, their strength was illusory. Three had never seen action before, and the rest had been in the west at the most only since January (two of them had returned from the east only a few days before the invasion). Warlimont asserted that, because of the usual OKH dilatoriness, four of the armoured divisions still had substantial remnants left in the east, and were not considered operational by the time of the invasion. Average battle strengths were low – some seventy-five battle-ready tanks to each division – and many of the soldiers were in need of rest after the rigours of the Eastern Front. Von Rundstedt had demanded seventy well-trained and well-equipped divisions as the absolute minimum with which he could hope to defend the west; he received fifty-nine, with an effective strength of no more than thirty-two. The question was: how was this force to cover 3,000 miles of coastline? The solution decided was disastrous; it contributed to the German failure every bit as much, and probably even more, than did their paucity of forces.

As in the east, so in the west; from the beginning the panzer force was not to be used to advantage. All agreed that it would play the decisive role in defeating the forthcoming invasion, but there existed two distinct schools of thought as to exactly how it was to be employed. The struggle between these schools was, in essence, the struggle that had bedevilled all German defensive operations since the winter of 1941–42. Should the defenders seek to defeat the enemy immediately on landing, or should they mount massive, well coordinated counter-attacks on the enemy's bridgehead, even though the assembly of the forces for such an action might take some time to effect? In other words, should rigidity or manoeuvre dominate the German strategy.

Surprisingly, it was Rommel, the field-marshal who had once been the master of manoeuvre, who was now the arch-proponent of inflexibility. The experiences of North Africa had left him a changed man; gone was the daring armoured commander; in his place was the stubborn defender for whom material superiority and rigid lines counted for all. In a conversation with Bayerlein in July 1943, Rommel expounded his new views: 'We have just learnt in Russia for the first time that dash and over-optimism are not enough. We must have a completely new approach. There can be no question of taking the offensive for the next few years . . . and so we must try to make the most of the advantages which normally accrue to the defence. . . . We must fight on interior lines. In the east we must withdraw as soon as possible to a suitable, prepared line.' He thought that the main hope lay in an overwhelming superiority of anti-tank guns which would bring any attack to a halt: 'Our last chance in the east lies in equipping the Army thoroughly for an unyielding defence.' In the west, 'the place that matters',[18] Rommel believed that mobile warfare was no longer the answer to defence simply because the overwhelming Allied material superiority, especially in the air, had made it impossible.

In another talk with Bayerlein concerning the defence of the west, Rommel remarked:

'Our friends from the east cannot imagine what they are in for here. It's not a matter of fanatical hordes to be driven forward in masses against our line . . . here we are facing an enemy who applies all his native intelligence to the use of his many technical resources. . . . Dash and doggedness alone no longer make a soldier . . . he must have sufficient intelligence to enable him to get the most out of his fighting-machine. . . . You have no idea how difficult it is to convince these people [his colleagues]. At one time they looked on mobile warfare as something to keep clear of at all costs, but now that our freedom of manoeuvre in the west has gone, they are all crazy after it. Whereas, in fact, it's obvious that if the enemy once gets his foot in, he'll put every anti-tank gun and.tank he can into the bridgehead and let us beat our heads against it, as he did at Medenine. To break through such a front you have to attack slowly and methodically, under cover of massed artillery, but we, of course, thanks to the Allied air forces, will have nothing there in time. The day of the dashing cut-and-thrust tank attack of the early war years is past and gone – and that goes for the east too, a fact which may, perhaps, by this time, have gradually sunk in.'[19]

In a report made to the Führer after a tour of the Atlantic coast, Rommel declared that the 'focus of the enemy landing operation will probably be directed against 15th Army's sector (the Pas de Calais)', and proposed the following method of defence:

'With the coastline held as thinly as it is at present, the enemy will probably succeed in creating bridgeheads at several different points and in achieving a major penetration of our coastal defences. Once this has happened, it will only be by the rapid intervention of our operational reserves that he will be thrown back into the sea. This requires that these forces should be held very close behind the coast defences. If, on the other hand, our principal reserves have to be brought up from well back inland, the move will not only require a great deal of time – time which the enemy will probably use to reinforce himself at his point of penetration and either organise his forces for defence or press the attack farther inland – but will also be under constant danger from the air. Bearing in mind the numerical and material superiority of the enemy striking-forces, their high state of training and tremendous air superiority, victory in a major battle on the Continent seems to me a matter of grave doubt. British and American superiority in the air alone has again and again been so effective that all movement of major formations has been rendered completely impossible, both at the front and behind it, by day and by night. . . . I therefore consider that an attempt must be made, using every possible expedient, to beat off the enemy landing on the coast and to fight the battle in the more or less strongly fortified coastal strip.'[20]

Mobility and manoeuvre on the part of the defenders had given way in Rommel's mind to the rigid impregnability of underwater obstacles, vast belts of mines, wire, fortifications, massed anti-tank weapons and machine-guns, backed by infantry and armoured formations in linear defence.

An entirely opposite point of view was taken by von Rundstedt, Guderian, and Geyr von Schweppenburg (commander of Panzer Group West, responsible for training matters). They vigorously opposed Rommel's ideas, pointing out that, owing to the uncertainty prevailing as to exactly where the Allies would land, the deployment of the armoured formations along 3,000 miles of coastline would make it impossible to react to the enemy move and to concentrate an adequate force quickly at the critical point. They certainly recognised the significant limitations imposed on the freedom of manoeuvre by Allied air power, but they rejected any idea that movement was now rendered impossible. They believed that the only chance of success lay not in the dispersal of force but in its concentration, not in rigidity but in manoeuvre. To this end, they proposed that the panzer forces be grouped some distance behind the coast, north and south of Paris, from where they would be able to converge on the landing area once it was clear where the enemy was making his main effort. He could then be attacked from the flanks and wholly destroyed. This was similar to von Manstein's 'backhand' strategy that he had so often advocated in the east. They knew that time was of the essence, but rejected the suggestion that the enemy would be so strong within a couple of days of landing as to be able to defeat any counter-attack mounted by the massed panzers. After the war, Guderian wrote:

> 'We [von Rundstedt, Geyr von Schweppenburg, and Guderian] were in complete agreement that enemy sea and air superiority made our task more difficult. Allied air supremacy must in particular affect our ability to move our forces. It seemed likely that in order to achieve sufficient speed and concentration we should have to move only by night. Our opinion was that it all depended on our making ready adequate reserves of panzer and panzergrenadier divisions: these must be stationed far enough inland from the so-called Atlantic Wall, so that they could be switched easily to the main invasion front once it had been recognised: these moves must be facilitated by repairs to the French road network and by the construction of alternative river crossings, underwater bridges, or bridges of boats.'[21]

Which school of thought was correct, it is now impossible to tell, for neither had its own way in the end. The Supreme Commander made certain of that. Hitler's view had always been straightforward: the defeat of the invaders in as short a time as possible. As early as 23 March 1942, he had stipulated in his Directive No. 40: 'The Commander . . . will use [his forces] so that the attack collapses *if possible before it can reach the coast, at the latest on the coast itself*. Enemy forces which have landed must be destroyed or thrown back into the sea by immediate counter-attack.'[22] This was the whole reason for building the Atlantic Wall; not an inch of ground should be allowed to the enemy, not a moment of time given him. Hitler constantly repeated this theme. In an address to the commanders in the west on 20 March 1944, he declared: 'The enemy's entire landing operation must under no circumstances be allowed to last longer than a matter of hours or, at the most, days.'[23]

But Hitler's simple aim was in no sense a coherent strategy. Certainly, his view of defensive war, which might be summed up as the 'the Atlantic Wall' or 'no withdrawal' mentality, had much in common with Rommel's proposals. Hitler was adamant that, as on the Eastern Front, every part of the Atlantic and the Mediterranean coasts in the west should be held by troops, and that no area should be divested of units in order to form a strategic reserve or to reinforce the more likely areas of invasion. As a result, the infantry and coastal-defence divisions were tied to the coast, from the Hook of Holland to the borders of Italy, and the armoured divisions were dissipated from the Meuse estuary in the north to the mouth of the Rhône in the south. Guderian, von Rundstedt, and others had no cause to thank the Führer for any sympathy for their proposals. Nor had Rommel; on 23 April, he wrote to Jodl:

> 'My only real anxiety concerns the mobile forces. Contrary to what was decided at the conference of 21 March they have not been put under my command [von Rundstedt still retained a reserve for his own use]. Some of them are dispersed over a large area well inland, which means that they will arrive too late to play any part in the battle for the coast . . . any large-scale movement of motorised forces to the coast will be exposed to air attacks of tremendous weight and long duration. . . . The most decisive battle of the war, and the fate of the German people itself, is at stake. Failing a tight command in one single hand of all the mobile forces available for defence, failing the early engagement of all our mobile forces in the battle for the coast, victory will be in grave doubt. If I am to wait until the enemy landing has actually taken place, before I can demand, through normal channels, the command and despatch of the mobile forces, delays will be inevitable. This will mean that they will probably arrive too late to intervene successfully in the battle for the coast and prevent the enemy landing.'[24]

After a meeting with Geyr von Schweppenburg in early May, Hitler further weakened Rommel's position, arriving at a compromise between the two schools of thought which satisfied neither and merely exacerbated an already confused situation. Perhaps as a partial acknowledgement of the validity of the arguments of Guderian and von Schweppenburg, or perhaps because he wished to take a direct hand in the forthcoming battle, Hitler created an OKW Reserve of four armoured divisions (one was the panzer-grenadier division) out of the eleven in the west, to be used when, and how, he alone thought fit.

As to where the main emphasis of the defence should lie, Hitler, in common with his generals, believed that the Allied invasion would take place in the area north of the Seine, probably around the Pas de Calais. Here was by far the shortest sea-route; here were long stretches of coast suitable for landing, and several large ports; and here the enemy air force could operate to the greatest effect. It was also the nearest point to the Ruhr, the industrial heart of Germany, the occupation of which would quickly bring the war to an end. As a result, Hitler ordered that the defenders, while holding the entire 3,000 miles, should concentrate in the area about 200 miles in length between the Scheldt and the Seine. Sixteen infantry and coastal-defence divisions and four panzer divisions were positioned there. However, in the spring of 1944, Hitler suddenly, and without apparent reason, included Normandy as a probable enemy objective (indeed, since November 1943, OKW had suspected an enemy attempt there). However, he was by no means convinced that this was the only place the Allies would attack. Warlimont remembered that 'he [Hitler] believed . . . previous to, and a long time after, the invasion that a second, and probably the main, landing would take place on the Channel coast'.[25] As a result, although he ordered that the northern coast of Normandy be reinforced at the utmost speed, at the same time he stipulated that there was to be no weakening in the area north of the Seine. And, as the front south of Normandy was already very sparsely held – twenty-five divisions (four armoured) to defend well over 1,000 miles – few formations could be found for the newly specified danger area. By 6 June, only one extra division and certain anti-aircraft units had been sent to Normandy. Thus, when the invaders struck along the 150 miles from the Cherbourg peninsula to the Seine, there were only six infantry divisions, four of which were merely coastal-defence formations, and one armoured division, to meet them. Von Blumentritt later recorded: 'The dispositions would more truly be described as "coast protection" rather than as "defence"! As we did not anticipate that any landing would be made on the west side of the Cherbourg peninsula, that sector was held very lightly – we even put Russian units there.'[26] In May OKW, with Hitler's approval, had refused Rommel's request that the two panzer divisions of the OKW Reserve, which lay seventy-five and 110 miles respectively from the Normandy beaches, be brought in closer to the sea. This was in accordance with the policy of keeping back the reserve for intervention wherever the main attack was delivered. It was a decision which was to have momentous consequences.

Thus, when the Allies began their invasion of Europe on 6 June, they found their landing areas weakly defended. This was entirely due to Hitler: he had starved the west of divisions and resources; he had decided which areas should be most heavily defended, and yet had failed to provide Normandy with the forces he said its importance demanded; and it was he who had ordered that two of the strongest panzer divisions should not be positioned near the landing areas where they could intervene at once, but instead should be held back in reserve far from the beaches, and therefore subject to attack from the air should they attempt to move forward. To make matters worse, no fewer than three of the five German commanders most deeply concerned with the deployment of the armoured forces were away from their headquarters during those decisive hours when the landings began. Rommel was in Germany visiting his home; Dollmann, commander of 7th Army, was at Rennes taking part in war games; and Dietrich, commander of 1st SS Panzer Corps, the most important component of the OKW Reserve, was absent in Brussels. Only von Rundstedt, who had no authority to commit the reserves, and Geyr von Schweppenburg, who had no operational command, were àt their battle stations. Hitler, for his part, was asleep, and was only informed of the invasion at midday.

By the evening of the first day of the invasion, the Allies had gained four bridgeheads on the Normandy coast, the largest being ten miles wide and three to six miles deep. The local German reserves had been thrown into the battle, and their ammunition was running low. Only one panzer division, the 21st, had intervened in the fighting, and its success is indicative of what might have occurred had more been able to do so. Although, because of Rommel's absence in Germany, the division did not actually engage the enemy until the afternoon, its action frustrated Montgomery's hope of capturing the key point of Caen that day, and part of it actually pierced the British front and drove on to the coast. Owing to a lack of support it was forced to withdraw for fear that enemy counter-action would result in its encirclement.

It has often been alleged that Hitler's command of the two divisions of the OKW Reserve nearest the beaches, and the delay that resulted in acquiring his authorisation to use them, was fatal. Owing to the Führer's habit of sleeping late, and Jodl's refusal to authorise any movement of the divisions until he knew whether or not the landings were merely a feint, it was not until 4.00p.m. that they were released to join in the battle; by then it was far too late for them to have any effect on the fighting that day. Yet this is to mistake the reality of the situation. Had the two panzer divisions been released twelve hours earlier, at 4.00a.m., when von Rundstedt had first asked for them, there can be no doubt that, by moving in daylight, they would have suffered such high casualties that their value as fighting formations would have ended. The enemy's undisputed air superiority made impossible any daylight movement even in rearward areas, as the experience of both these divisions the next day was to prove. The panzer divisions would have been of use only if they had been brought up either before the invasion when Rommel had asked for them, or on 5 June when the Intelligence Service had reported the interception of enemy radio messages which, it was correctly believed, signified the start of the invasion. As it was, Hitler's refusal to grant Rommel's request, and OKW's inexplicable inaction after receiving the radio messages, prevented the two strongest panzer divisions in the west, 12th SS and Panzer Lehr, from playing the role that had been expected of them, perhaps with decisive results. By the time they actually reached the fighting zone on the 7th, the 12th SS in the early morning, and the most advanced elements of Panzer Lehr in the afternoon, they had both suffered badly as a result of Allied air attack. Panzer Lehr was unable to attack until the 9th, and the 12th SS, which, owing to the intensity of air attack at times had averaged only four miles an hour, ran out of fuel as soon as it arrived on the scene.

By failing to defeat the invasion within the first twenty-four hours, the Germans had, unbeknown to them, lost the entire battle. The failure was due to the material superiority of the Allies, to the dispositions of the Germans, and to Hitler's intransigence. Of the Allied superiority both in the air and on the ground, little need be said. Their superiority in the air was complete. On 6 June, for example, the Allied air forces flew no fewer than 10,585 sorties, the Luftwaffe only 319. On 11 June, Rommel reported to OKW:

> 'Our operations in Normandy are. . . rendered exceptionally difficult, and in part impossible to carry out, by the following factors: the exceptionally strong and in some respects overwhelming superiority of the enemy air force . . . the enemy has complete command of the air over the battle up to about 100 kilometres behind the front and cuts off by day . . . almost all traffic on roads or by-roads or in open country. Movements of our troops on the field of battle by day are thus almost entirely prevented, while the enemy can operate freely.'[27]

Rommel also mentioned the effects of heavy naval artillery, the material superiority of the Allied divisions, and the actions of paratroop and air-landing units. By 18 June the Allies had landed twenty divisions; facing them, the Germans could muster only eighteen, and, in fighting strength these were barely equivalent to fourteen.

Of more importance were the disadvantages arising from the disposition of the German troops before D-Day; the armour could arrive only piecemeal, usually having sustained heavy punishment from the air and, on occasions, from partisans. The plight of Panzer Lehr and 12th SS has already been described. Of the others, the 2nd Panzer Division had to travel 160 miles from the Seine and after its arrival on 13 June it took seven days before it could muster its strength to go into action as a complete division; the 17th SS Panzergrenadier Division arrived on the 17th after covering 200 miles from Bayonne; the main body of the 2nd SS Panzer Division arrived on the 26th after moving over 450 miles from Toulouse through country alive with guerrillas, and its tanks, hampered by lack of fuel, did not arrive until a few days later; two SS divisions, 9th and 10th SS Panzer, reached Normandy from the Eastern Front on 25 June; the mass of the 1st SS Panzer Division did not go into battle until 9 June, and the 116th Panzer Division not until late July (having been kept on the coast between Abbeville and Dieppe in anticipation of a second landing); and it was not until early August that 19th Panzer in the south was transferred to Normandy.

Moreover, because the German commanders (until the end of the second week) and Hitler (for seven weeks) feared that the Normandy landings might be a feint to draw away forces from the intended main invasion in the Pas de Calais, the front was not reinforced to the extent that was desirable. Nor would Hitler allow any evacuation of the south of France either. The infantry divisions, like the panzer, arrived piecemeal, often severely damaged by air attack. Losses by far exceeded replacements, and by the end of July the Germans had lost 127,247 men, and received only 14,594. Thus, the new formations had to be sent in to the fighting as, and when, they arrived; no coordinated counter-attack with fresh units was ever made. On 7 and 8 June any concerted action by the panzers divisions had proved impossible – many had not arrived, and others were prevented from moving by lack of petrol. The few attacks that were mounted were failures. The next day, the 9th, Rommel decided that 'there should be a return to the defensive in the sector between the Vire and the Orne and that the counter-attack should be postponed until all preparations have been completed' (in other words, until the necessary formations had arrived)'.[28] The race now began between the two sides as to who would be ready first. On the 10th the headquarters of Geyr von Schweppenburg, appointed to command the armoured counter-attack, was destroyed by Allied bombing, and, on the 11th, after evidence that the enemy ground-forces were massing for an assault on Caen, all idea of a counter-offensive was dismissed. When Rommel told Dietrich that he should attack, back came the answer, 'But with what? We haven't enough troops. We need another eight or ten divisions in the next day or two or we are finished.'[29]

Once the Allies had established their bridgehead, von Rundstedt realised that there was only one course left open. After the war, he said:

> 'I knew all along that the German position in France was hopeless, and that eventually the war would be lost. But if I had been given a free hand to conduct operations, I think I could have made the Allies pay a fearful price for their victory. I had planned to fight a slow retiring action, exacting a heavy toll for each bit of ground that I gave up. I had hoped that this might have brought about a political decision which would have saved Germany from complete and utter defeat. But I did not have my way. As commander-in-chief in the west my only authority was to change the guard in front of my gate.'[30]

From the beginning Hitler exercised a strict control over the Normandy battlefront; no movement could take place without his approval. On 3 July Rommel forwarded a memorandum to him which contained the complaint:

> 'After the enemy had succeeded in gaining his foothold on the Continent, it was the intention of Army Group B, when its re-

inforcements had arrived, first to wipe out the bridgehead north of Carentan, thus eliminating all danger to the Cotentin peninsula and the fortress of Cherbourg, and not until then to launch an attack on the enemy between the Orne and Vire [in the centre and right of the German front]. The OKW [Hitler], however, did not agree and gave orders for our main weight to be shifted to the eastern flank at the Orne estuary [around Caen].'[31]

Just as the field commander's initial course of action was rejected by Führer headquarters, so was his second. After the 11th it was clear that the Germans had lost the battle to destroy the bridgehead, and that nothing but disaster could result from the policy of holding the ring around it and sending in the odd division as, and when, it arrived. Between them, von Rundstedt and Rommel evolved a new scheme of operations. Von Rundstedt described the plan:

> 'To concentrate enough tanks for a decisive blow, it was imperative that infantry be available to replace the armour that had been rushed up to hold the line. I recommended to Berlin that the fifteen or twenty infantry divisions in southern France and along the Atlantic coast be pulled back and sent north of the Loire. With these divisions I planned to hold a position along the Loire and the Orne rivers, relieve the panzer divisions, and with them push forward with a counter-offensive. Such a policy, of course, meant the abandonment of all of France south of the Loire, and this decision was considered politically impossible. . . .'[32]

The 'no withdrawal' orders had already emanated from Führer headquarters. Even before the invasion had begun, Hitler told his troops in an Order of the Day, dated 13 May 1944: 'Here there can be no weakening and no manoeuvring, here a halt must be made, to stand fast or to die. Every leader, every commander of a strongpoint, of an island, of a fortress, or of a ship must pledge to me his honour that he will never surrender, that he will continue the struggle to the last fighter, to the last grenade, to the last cartridge.'[33] On 10 June Hitler told 7th Army: 'There can be no question of fighting a rearguard action nor of retiring to a new line of resistance. Every man shall fight or fall where he stands.'[34] On the 16th Hitler, insisting that ground in the Cotentin peninsular be held at the cost of defending Cherbourg, began a course of events which ensured that it would be in full Allied control by the 29th; a properly conducted withdrawal, as proposed by Rommel, might well have meant that this vital port would have been denied to the enemy for many more weeks to come. On the 17th, when the Führer met von Rundstedt and Rommel in France, he rejected the plan described by von Rundstedt and insisted that there should be no withdrawal. He seemed to believe that it was still possible to push the Allies back into the sea without changing his strategy, and he placed his hope for the future on a strengthening of the Luftwaffe and the devastation that his V-weapon offensive would cause in Great Britain. On the 20th he ordered Rommel to launch an offensive immediately after the arrival of the four SS panzer divisions then moving to Normandy; the plan was to drive a corridor to Bayeux and the coast, and then isolate and destroy the British around the area of Caen. On 29 June, the 23rd day of the invasion, the panzers were at last ready to launch their long-awaited, decisive counter-attack. It was too late. Their strength had decreased while that of the enemy had increased; the resistance the Germans met proved to be too great, and on the 30th the attack was called off. A final attempt was made on 1 July, but it also came to naught, and only a few miles covered by the German tanks. As the SS men were actually moving into the attack on the 29th, von Rundstedt and Rommel were at Berchtesgaden seeing Hitler. Their vain hopes that they could make their Führer see reason were frustrated; he merely used the occasion to try to fire them with optimism, and ended by ordering them to 'hold out in all circumstances'. His argument ran: 'We must not allow mobile warfare to develop since the enemy surpasses us by far in mobility. . . . Therefore, everything depends on our confining him in his bridgehead, by building up a front to block him off, and then go on fighting a war of attrition to wear him down and force him back.'[35] That Hitler, after all recent German experience, could still believe that such action could win a war, reveals the heights of illusion to which he was then subject.

The position in which the Germans in Normandy found themselves at that time was well summed up by von Kluge (who succeeded von Rundstedt early in July). He wrote to Hitler on the 21st:

'. . . there is no way by which, in the face of the enemy air force's complete command, we can find a strategy which will counterbalance its positively annihilating effect without giving up the field of battle. . . . I came here with the fixed determination of making effective your order to stand fast *at any price*. But when one has to see by experience that this price must be paid by the slow but sure annihilation of the force . . . when one sees that the material supplies coming up in almost all areas are at times completely insufficient . . . and that fighting material . . . is largely insufficient for the demands of the command, with the result that the brunt of the defence falls on the good will of the brave troops, anxiety about the immediate future of this front is only too well justified. . . . in spite of intense efforts, the moment has drawn near when this front, already so heavily strained, will break.'[36]

In his letter, he enclosed observations by Rommel, dated 15 July (two days before he was wounded and invalided back to the Reich), which contained the following:

'. . . our own losses are so high that the fighting strength of the divisions is sinking fast. Reinforcements from home arrive very scantily and, with the difficult transport situation, reach the front only after weeks. About 97,000 men . . . in losses – that is to say a daily average rate of 2,500 to 3,000 men – as against 10,000 in reserve (of whom about 6,000 have arrived). The material losses of the troops engaged are also exceptionally high, and have been replaced so far only to a very small extent, for example, of about 225 tanks [lost] only seventeen [have arrived] so far. The newly brought-up infantry divisions are inexperienced in battle, and with the smallest provision of artillery, anti-tank weapons, and means of attacking tanks at close quarters, are not in a position to ward off successfully for long hostile major attacks made after many hours of drum fire and heavy bombing. . . . The supply situation is so difficult . . . that only what is most essential can be brought up. . . . No forces worth mentioning can be brought to the Normandy front without weakening the front of 15th Army on the Channel or the Mediterra-nean front in southern France. . . . On the enemy's side new forces and masses of war material are flowing to the front daily . . . no mobile reserves to defend against . . . a breakthrough are at the disposal of 7th Army. . . . The force is fighting heroically every-where, but the unequal combat is nearing its end. It is in my opinion necessary to draw the appropriate conclusions from this situation.'[37]

But no withdrawal resulted. The month of July passed with the Germans conducting merely passive defence. Nor was any reinforcement of their position made, for Hitler still continued to fear an Allied landing in the Pas de Calais; he also found it impossible to withdraw units from the Eastern Front, which was then undergoing considerable pressure on its central sector. And so the scene was set for a sequence of events which, within a month, led to the destruction of the German forces south of the Seine, and to the evacuation of most of France.

From as early as 9 June, when Rommel had ordered that there should be a temporary return to the defensive, the initiative had lain with the Allies, who were able to conduct the battle according to their wishes. Thus, Mont-gomery was able to fulfil his strategic aim of drawing the majority of the panzer divisions to his front around Caen, thereby allowing the Americans considerable scope for their breakout on the German left wing. Because of Hitler's insistence on no withdrawal, the Germans were forced to hold the Caen area strongly, for a British breakthrough there would mean the end of the German armies west of the Seine; as a result, their left flank was kept weak and vulnerable. On 25 July the Americans attacked the sparsely held line in front of them at St Lô, where there were no panzer divisions to oppose them. On the 31st Avranches was captured; the breakout from the Nor-mandy bridgehead was well under way, and the chief of staff to Army Group B telephoned von Kluge to tell him 'the left flank has collapsed'. Von Kluge immediately informed the Führer:

'Whether the enemy can still be stopped at this point is questionable. The enemy air superiority is terrific, and smothers almost every one of our movements. . . . Losses in men and equipment are extraordinary. The morale of the troops has suffered very heavily under constant murderous enemy fire, especially since all infantry units consist only of haphazard groups which do not form a strongly coordinated force any longer. In the rear areas of the front, terrorists, feeling the end approaching, grow steadily bolder. This fact, and the loss of numerous signal installations, makes an orderly command extremely difficult.'[38]

The American breakout continued between 1 and 13 August, as Patton's 3rd US Army fanned out from Avranches west to Brest, south to Nantes, and east of Le Mans and beyond. It was obvious that the German left flank was disintegrating beyond repair, and that it was in danger of being 'rolled up'.[39] Accordingly, von Kluge advocated a withdrawal to the Seine, or further. But Hitler, far from conceding that such a move should take place, instead ordered a counter-attack; he was now behaving exactly as Stalin had in 1941, when he ordered the Red Army either to stand firm or to push forward, thus facilitating the German aim of encirclement. The only concession Hitler made to reality was to allow the transfer of infantry divisions from the Pas de Calais to Normandy. But in his fantasy he saw the breakout by the 3rd US Army as providing a golden opportunity for a decisive counter-attack. The German armour would be massed against Mortain and would smash east through the weakly held flank to the sea at Avranches; the annihilation of Patton's force would result. Von Kluge was sent detailed plans accordingly, but no reserves of tanks came with them. By that time, of the 1,400 tanks which had been thrown in against the Allied bridgehead, more than 750 had already been lost, so that the six panzer divisions to be employed in the counter-attack were equivalent to only three. Hitler wanted to wait until sufficient force had been built up, but von Kluge, fearing the continual Allied build-up around his flank, decided on an early attack. On the 7th, it began; at first the tanks were successful, and an elated Hitler issued orders that the entire Allied position in Normandy should be rolled up, but strong resistance, including devastating air attack, brought the German attack to a halt after an advance of only ten miles, just one-third of the way to Avranches. On the same day, American counter-measures began, and by the 9th the Germans had retreated to their starting-point.

Of more concern to von Kluge was the deep out-flanking movement now threatening his southern front. An attack west, instead of a withdrawal east, had brought the Germans perilously close to envelopment. To the south, for 100 miles from Domfront to the Loire at Angers, the Germans had only one panzer, and one infantry division and several security battalions, a force further weakened when, on the evening of the 8th, von Kluge ordered the armoured division to be sent to Mortain for one further attempt at

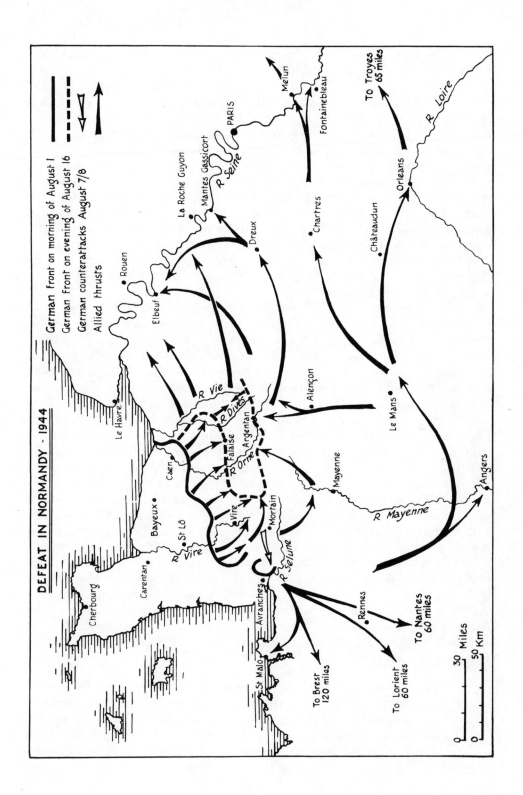

DEFEAT IN NORMANDY · 1944

German front on morning of August 1
German front on evening of August 16
German counterattacks August 7/8
Allied thrusts

To Troyes
65 miles

R. Loire

Melun

Fontainebleau

PARIS

Mantes Gassicort

R. Seine

La Roche Guyon

Chartres

Orleans

Dreux

Châteaudun

Rouen

Elbeuf

Alençon

Le Mans

R. Vie

R. Dives

Argentan

Falaise

R. Orne

Mayenne

Angers

Le Havre

Caen

Vire

R. Mayenne

Bayeux

St Lô

Mortain

R. Vire

R. Selune

Cherbourg

Carentan

Avranches

Rennes

To Nantes
60 miles

St Malo

To Brest
120 miles

To Lorient
60 miles

30 Miles

50 Km

509

Avranches which was planned for the 10th. Although the local commander, SS General Hausser, protested that this move, 'at the moment when strong enemy tank units are thrusting at our flanks, would deal a death blow not only to 7th Army but also to the entire Wehrmacht in the west', von Kluge replied, 'It is the Führer's order'[40] and insisted upon its execution. At the same time, the northern sector around Caen, weakened because of the withdrawal of the panzer divisions for the Mortain counter-attack, was giving way under heavy enemy pressure. The salient, from which von Kluge was vainly attempting to reach the coast, became a trap. On the 10th, just as the counter-attack was to be renewed at Mortain, reports reached von Kluge that, encouraged by the German attack on the 7th, the Americans, instead of advancing east as before, were now pushing north and north-east towards Alençon, 7th Army's main supply centre. Only four German battalions stood in the way. Clearly the situation called for prompt action, but von Kluge knew that to ask permission to withdraw, the only sensible course, would be regarded as breaking the Führer's orders (the defeat on the 7th had already been received with bad grace, Hitler having remarked: 'Success only failed to come because Kluge did not want to be successful').[41] Therefore, von Kluge asked merely that the panzer divisions be 'temporarily transferred from the Mortain area to . . . destroy the enemy spearheads thrusting northwards. . . . to render possible the prosecution of the decisive offensive [towards Avranches]'.[42] Hitler treated this request with grave suspicion, and gave no answer. The Allied armies pressed forward; twenty German divisions were being encircled. On the 11th Hitler was reluctantly forced to admit that the switch of panzer forces to Alençon was necessary, but he stipulated that the plan for the attack on Avranches should be adhered to. Still he would not consider any general withdrawal; still he envisaged a counter-attack to the sea which would defeat the enemy. As Warlimont wrote: 'This was a completely unrealistic object, but the Supreme Commander clung to it, issuing a bewildering series of orders following each other with ever-increasing rapidity, and with equal rapidity being overtaken by the even faster-moving course of events.'[43] By the 13th the southern and northern jaws of the Allied pincers were only twenty miles apart, the gap being centred around Falaise, and on the 14th Hitler authorised a limited withdrawal of the 7th Army from the western end of the pocket. That day, von Kluge sent his weekly situation report, which stated blandly: 'The enemy's first main objective . . . is to outflank and encircle the bulk of the 5th Panzer Army and 7th Army on two sides.'[44] In an appended report from Hausser, the following point was made:

'As a result of the breakthrough by enemy armoured formations through the left part of the army front, a large part of the divisions . . . which were in the fighting uninterruptedly without rest and without any great bringing-up of reserves since the beginning of the invasion, have been split into groups. These fought their way separately back through the enemy lines . . . in an easterly or south-easterly direction. . . . Condition of these straggling sections mostly very bad. Weapons are only brought with them in part (only rifles, pistols, and machine-pistols). Motor and horse-drawn sections still have a few machine-weapons and heavy infantry weapons, which, however, are mostly badly in need of repair. Condition of clothing appalling. Many without headgear, without belts, and with worn footwear. Many go barefoot. In so far as they cannot get supplies from the supply centres they live on the country without considera-tion for property. Hatred and terrorist activity is thus intensified among the population. . . . Morale . . . badly shaken. The enemy command of the air has contributed specially to this. . . .'[45]

On the 16th, Falaise was entered by the Allies, but still no order for the withdrawal had been received from the Führer. On his own initiative, von Kluge had extricated a badly mauled 2nd SS Panzer Corps, and had told Hausser to evacuate his motor transport and administrative troops; but he would go no further. The tone of the orders from the Führer had grown curter with the days; von Kluge feared arrest at any moment, and on the 17th he was relieved of his command, to be replaced by Model, the 'saviour' of the Eastern Front. Even this was little use to the almost-encircled German troops, who, hour by hour, were suffering intensive Allied air attack. By the evening of the 17th the gap had closed to just six miles; 100,000 German troops were within a pocket twenty miles wide and ten miles deep. Among them were many of the best of those then in the west. The slaughter and the confusion was appalling. On the 18th, without consulting his Führer, Model ordered a withdrawal, and on the 19th the pocket was closed; only a few remnants were to break out the following day. Some 10,000 Germans were killed and 50,000 captured in the battle; thousands of trucks and around 500 armoured vehicles were either abandoned or destroyed. A third of 7th Army, less most of its heavy equipment, had eluded the trap, due mainly to Montgomery's slowness in closing the northern pincer. Nevertheless, it was a considerable victory for the Allies, for which they had to thank Hitler.

31

The West 1944–45 – The End

It was now just a question of time – and lives.
FIELD-MARSHAL GERD VON RUNDSTEDT
Commander-in-Chief, West

On 15 August, while the battle for the Falaise gap was at its height, the Allies landed in southern France; the inferiority of the German defence on the Mediterranean coast at once became apparent, and on the 16th Hitler was forced to allow Army Group G to disengage from the enemy and retreat to the area of Dijon. Also on the 15th, 3rd US Army's offensive to the Seine began in earnest, brushing aside the few German forces in its way; on the 25th Paris was liberated, and on the 29th the last German troops escaped a second encirclement and crossed the Seine. The skill of the German field command had prevented this retreat from becoming a rout, and bad weather had stopped the Allied air forces from keeping up their onslaught on the Seine crossings. Nevertheless, thousands of foot-bound or horse-driven Germans had been overtaken by fast-moving Allied columns, and had had to leave behind nearly all their heavy equipment. Dietrich remembered that 'From the point of view of equipment abandoned, the Seine crossing was almost as great a disaster as the Falaise pocket'.[1] Only 100 to 120 armoured vehicles were brought back over the Seine; 2,200 were left behind in Normandy either destroyed or abandoned, the result of ten weeks' bitter fighting. Almost half the total number of German troops engaged in the battle of Normandy had been either killed or wounded (240,000) or captured (210,000). About fifty divisions had been in action; now, fewer than ten could be classed as reasonable fighting divisions. In three months, the battle of Normandy had cost the Germans almost twice as many men as had Stalingrad. On the 29th, the day the last of his troops were crossing the Seine, Model reported to the Führer in the most dismal of terms. His command was finished.

'The divisions which were taken back from Normandy across the Seine under extreme difficulties and hardest fighting are armed only with a few medium weapons, in general only carbines etc. The supply of the personnel and material replacement required is absolutely insufficient. . . . The panzer divisions, at present, each have five to ten tanks ready to be employed. In regard to artillery, only isolated guns are left with the infantry divisions and isolated troops with the panzer divisions. . . . The low degree of manoeuvrability of the infantry divisions, caused by the fact that they have been made mobile only by temporary expedients (horses), had a particularly unfavourable influence in the unequal fight with the motorised enemy, all the more as the necessary reserves of assault-guns and other heavy anti-tank guns are completely missing. Consequently, there was an absolute tactical inferiority of the formations still available.'[2]

The defence of the Seine was now an impossibility; Model was given no respite. Immediately, the Allies attacked across the river, and by 2 September they had reached the Belgian border. The position of von Blaskowitz's Army Group G was little better, and it found itself retreating as fast as it could through France along the Swiss border. The Germans left behind them 160,000 men defending the Atlantic and Channel ports from Ostend to the Gironde estuary, in the belief that the denial of these facilities to the Allied armies would cause grave problems to their supply lines, as well as cause them to expend large numbers of troops in their investment. At the same time, 34,000 men were isolated in the Channel Islands. The number of prisoners that fell to the Allies became embarrassing, for they had not the administrative facilities to deal with them. In the two weeks after the fall of Paris, a further 140,000 Germans became prisoners-of-war. By early September, Model's opinion was that the seventy-four German divisions available for the 480-mile front from the North Sea to the Swiss border were equivalent to a fighting strength of only twenty-five. The defence that they had been able to put up had been negligible. Guderian wrote:

'While our panzer units still existed, our leaders had chosen to fight a static battle in Normandy. Now that our motorised forces had been squandered and destroyed, they were compelled to fight the mobile battle that they had hitherto refused to face. Favourable chances that the boldness of the American command occasionally offered us, we were no longer in a position to exploit. The original intention – to counter-attack the southern wing of the advancing American armies – had to be given up.'[3]

It was clear to the German generals that their Army in the west was not simply about to face total defeat; it was actually experiencing it. The war could be brought to an end in September – the time required for the Allies to drive, almost unhindered, into the Reich. Describing the condition of the German forces in the west at the beginning of September, General Westphal, the chief of staff to von Rundstedt, wrote:

'There could be no question of systematic supplies . . . not only because of the speed of the withdrawal, but because of the destruction wrought by air attack on the rail and telephone network, and the absence of any sort of preparation for a retreat. Such lack of providence contained the gravest dangers. To give a single example: an important message with the highest degree of priority still required, in the middle of September, twelve or sometimes twenty-four hours to reach an army group from the headquarters of the Commander-in-Chief, West. . . . The over-all situation in the west was serious in the extreme. A heavy defeat anywhere along the front, which was so full of gaps that it did not deserve this name, might lead to catastrophe, if the enemy were to exploit his opportunity skilfully. A particular source of danger was that not a single bridge over the Rhine had been prepared for demolition, an omission which took weeks to repair. . . . The Allied armoured forces were four times our own, while their superiority in the air was many times greater still. . . . The West Wall . . . was no longer in a defensible state because of the . . . removal of weapons, ammunition, wire, and mines to the fortifications on the Atlantic coast. Sometimes even the keys for individual emplacements were missing. It was at least six weeks before even the essential preparations could be laboriously made. Until the middle of October, the enemy could have broken through at any point he liked, with ease, and would then have been able to cross the Rhine and thrust deep into Germany almost unhindered.'[4]

On 7 September, three days after his reinstatement as Commander-in-Chief, West, von Rundstedt was even more specific; he reported to OKW 'for the special attention of the Führer':

'Our own forces are tied up in battle, and in part severely mauled. They are short of artillery and anti-tank weapons. Reserves worthy of mention not available. The numerical superiority of the enemy's tanks to ours is incontestable. With Army Group B at the present time there are some 100 tanks available for action. The enemy air force dominates the battle area and rear communications deep into the rearward terrain. . . . In order to be able to command with any prospect of success, I again request, in addition to the immediate forces five to ten divisions solicited for the region of Aix-la-Chapelle for the defence of the Rhine-Westphalian industrial zone, the immediate bringing-up, regardless of everything, of all available armoured vehicles . . . as well as an urgent special supply of all available anti-tank weapons. . . .'[5]

At least two panzer divisions, the 2nd and 2nd SS, each had only three tanks left, and, between them, only fifty guns of all types with virtually no ammunition. To relieve this chronic plight, little help came from Führer head-quarters. As Blumentritt, Model's chief of staff, remembered: 'During all this chaos, the only instructions that came from Berlin were "Hold! Hold! Hold!" ' On 4 September, Model had told Führer headquarters that the front from Antwerp to the Franco-Luxembourg border 'must be manned by twenty-five divisions with an adequate armoured reserve of five to six panzer divisions . . . otherwise the gateway into north-west Germany will be open'.[6] However, there were simply no fresh divisions to be had. What was needed was a miracle, and this is precisely what occurred.

At the beginning of September, the Allies were advancing almost unhindered. Along the whole Western Front, the Germans could dispose of only 100 serviceable tanks; Allied material superiority had now reached 20:1 in armour and 25:1 in aircraft. There was simply no opposition left to prevent the continued advance into Germany. On 3 September, for example, British armoured units covered seventy-five miles, took Brussels, and drove on to Antwerp, which it captured the following day. The Ruhr, the industrial heart of the Reich, the occupation of which would have made further German resistance impossible, was only 100 miles away, and between it and the British was a 100-mile gap devoid of German forces. As the paratroop general, Student, later remembered:

> 'The sudden penetration of the British tank forces into Antwerp took the Führer's headquarters utterly by surprise. At that moment we had no disposable reserves worth mentioning either on the Western Front or within our own country. I took over command of the right wing of the Western Front on the Albert Canal on 4 September. At that moment I had only recruit and convalescent units and one coast-defence division from Holland. They were reinforced by a panzer detachment of merely twenty-five tanks and self-propelled guns.'[7]

And yet, during the next two weeks, the Allies made very little further progress, and after three months the furthest they had succeeded in advancing was only fifty miles in Holland, and seventy miles in France. The front stabilized along a line from the coast to near Arnhem, down the Dutch border to Aachen, across the Ardennes, along the Luxembourg and French borders to the Rhine, and then, following the river almost all the way, down to Switzerland. Not until May 1945 was the war brought to an end, a full seven months after the opportunity to do so presented itself in September 1944. The cost to the Allied armies was to be 500,000 casualties; the cost to the German people and to the miserable prisoners in Hitler's concentration camps was incalculable. What were the reasons?

Quite simply, despite its overwhelming successes, the Allied Command was not prepared either materially or mentally to exploit the potential offered by the complete German collapse. By early September they had reached a position which, when planning the invasion, they had not expected to gain until May 1945. The advance, conducted over a broad front, was experiencing considerable logistical difficulties. The extreme length of the supply lines, the growing mechanical failures of the motor transport, and the continued occupation by the Germans of the Channel and the Atlantic ports, leaving Cherbourg as the only relatively large port open to the Allies, meant that adequate supplies could not be transported to the armies to allow them to pursue their energetic advances simultaneously. This situation was made particularly serious by the fact that, whereas German divisions required only 200 tons of supplies a day, those of the Allies required 700 tons, so lavish were their ammunition, equipment, and rations. Eisenhower, the Allied Supreme Commander, was forced to distribute his resources between two main attacks – one by the British to the north-east and the other by the Americans to the east; he decided first to do all he could to facilitate the advance in the north-east until Antwerp was taken, after which he would attack over a broad front, giving equal weight to both thrusts. Thus, on 30 August, as Patton's spearheads reached the Moselle, the main body of his 3rd US Army, restricted at that time to a petrol consumption of just 32,000 tons a day instead of the normal 400,000, was halted through lack of fuel. The Rhine crossings lay only seventy miles away, and yet Patton's tanks were forced to remain stationary for five days; time enough for the Germans to build up their forces on the Moselle front.

On 4 September Antwerp fell; and it was then the turn of the British to be unable to exploit their opportunity. Resources were at once taken from Montgomery's command and placed at the disposal of the Americans, in compliance with Eisenhower's strategy. At the same time, other difficulties came to the fore, which, together, were of much greater importance than the diversion of supplies. Most important of all was the self-imposed halt to rest, refit, and refuel after reaching Brussels and Antwerp between 4 and 7 September (the British had covered no fewer than 250 miles in one week). Once the Allies had broken into Belgium their self-confidence grew, and with it came a tendency to relax. In the face of the German collapse, speed seemed to have lost some of its urgency. A well-coordinated, well-supplied advance now seemed of more importance than a hectic thrust. Even so, it is difficult to excuse the inexplicable neglect to capture the bridges over the Albert Canal in the suburbs of Antwerp before they were blown by the Germans on 4 September. Against the resumed advance, the newly arrived German parachutists put up a tenacious defence in the swampy heath country that was out of all proportion to their weak numerical strength, and the British managed to push on only a further eighteen miles before coming to a halt. Other difficulties arose from the six-day stoppage in air supply – owing to preparations for an airborne offensive in Belgium (never carried out) – which prevented the transport of roughly one and a half million gallons of petrol, enough to get all the Allied armies on to the Rhine; from the large number of defective British lorries; from the excessive allocation of ammunition and other supplies to transport at the expense of petrol; from the entanglement of 1st US Army in the fortified Aachen area, at the behest of Montgomery who wanted his right flank protected, thus delaying the Americans five weeks, until 21 October, and necessitating the diversion of a large amount of supplies; and from the failure to eliminate the German troops on the Scheldt estuary until early November, which meant that the first Allied convoy to use the port of Antwerp, so vital to the continued supply of the Allies for their advance into Germany, did not arrive until the 28th of that month. The result was that, as Eisenhower later admitted, 'the life-blood of supply was running perilously thin through the forward extremities of the Army'.[8]

Time lost by the Allies was time gained by the Germans, time in which to reinforce the Western Front before the onslaught was renewed. In the last weeks of August, every division that could be found had been sent to the southern part; only ten panzer brigades being formed in the Reich remained available for further deployment. The Replacement Army was raising its *Volksgrenadier* divisions, but during August and September only six of these were transferred to the west. Only by raiding garrisons, fortress battalions, training schools, depot staffs, convalescent homes, and even the police and the Todt Organisation could a motley gathering of 135,000 men be made available to garrison and to rebuild the West Wall. As fighting men, ill-equipped and often of low standard, they proved of little value. Only from the unexpected quarter of the Luftwaffe did any real help come. To the surprise of OKH, on 4 September Göring revealed the existence of six parachute regiments, and the possibility of raising another two, a total of 20,000 soldiers. Together with a further 10,000 men from redundant ground staff and air crews of the Luftwaffe, this force was organised into the 1st Parachute Army (with the equivalent strength of only two divisions) and assigned to a front of sixty miles in Holland. The idea of forming an armoured reserve remained still-born; there were simply not sufficient stocks of armour at the Army's disposal. While Hitler had ordered that the entire production of Tiger IIs and Jagdpanthers be sent to the west (in September, eighty machines were produced) he had at the same time directed almost all the medium armour to go to the Eastern Front (a total of 700). During September, the only substantial armoured reinforcements that arrived were the ten newly formed panzer brigades (each equipped with thirty-three Panthers and eleven assault-guns, or with forty-eight Panthers and forty-eight PzKw IVs), formations that were hastily thrown together, ill-trained, and equipped with large numbers of tanks fresh from the factories and subject to a high rate of mechanical failure. As a result, these brigades were easily out-fought by the enemy divisions, and were later disbanded. The tanks and men they absorbed would have been far better used had they been allocated to the existing panzer divisions, as von Rundstedt had advocated. By 27 September, the total number of armoured weapons available to Army Group B had increased from 100 to 239; they were opposed by 2,300. The condition of the troops was still lamentable, as Model pointed out to von Rundstedt in a report dated 27 September:

> 'The operations of Army Group B were particularly unfavourably influenced by the following factors: almost unlimited air superiority of the enemy . . . superiority of the enemy artillery . . . preponderance of the enemy panzer weapons . . . insufficient replacements of personnel [from 1 to 25 September casualties amounted to 75,000 men, reinforcements to 6,500]. . . . I am reporting the above-mentioned points, although they are already known, because the result of the present decisive battles depends on more consideration being given to them.'

Model also considered that 'the reverses in the west are primarily due to allowing the panzer divisions to be exhausted'.[9]

However, in the northern area leading to the Ruhr, their most vulnerable sector of the front, the Germans had managed to plug the gap. The positioning of two SS armoured divisions in the area of Arnhem was particularly fortunate; it frustrated the Allied airborne attempt to get across the Rhine that began on 17 September. This was followed by a series of counter-attacks which, as Model intended, served to keep the British on the defensive in the salient directed towards the river. The successful defensive actions undertaken by the Germans at Arnhem, Aachen, and Antwerp, made possible by failings in the Allies' strategy, won for the Germans a vital breathing-space. Along the rest of the front that marked the Reich's frontier, the build-up of German units progressed faster than that of the Allies. The Germans were now benefiting from the considerable advantages of a relatively short, interior line of communications, whereas their enemy was forced to bring his troops and supplies across the gale-torn Channel and over some 300 to 400 miles of land. In mid-November, a general offensive launched along the 600-mile front by all the Allied armies in the west brought but small gain at high cost. Only in Alsace was the Rhine reached, to little avail. In the north, thirty miles still separated the British from the river and the Ruhr, thirty miles that were not covered until the early spring of 1945.

Historians have made much of Hitler's Ardennes counterstroke mounted in December 1944; but it was nothing more that the involuntary death throe of a dying man. Not for one moment had it any hope of success, and at no point was it near to achieving victory. All it succeeded in doing was to exhaust the last reserves of strength remaining to the German Army so that it collapsed in January 1945 when the Soviets struck in the east. The Ardennes offensive was simply Hitler's last desperate gamble, the ultimate folly of the most irresponsible warlord known to history.

Ever since the Allied landings in June 1944, Hitler had been anxious to seize the initiative and to mount a massive counterstroke that would dramatically turn the tide in his favour. The fruitless Mortain attacks in early

August, which brought about the destruction of most of 7th Army in the Falaise encirclement, were the first manifestation in the west of this principle of 'attack at all costs'. They were followed in mid-September by a vain counter-attack against the Americans in Lorraine (not the most vital sector of the front) which caused the loss of more than half the 350 Panthers and PzKw IVs that had been sent there especially for the attack. While the Lorraine counter-offensive was being won and lost, at Hitler's behest OKW was busily drawing up preparations for a major offensive. This was the first time that it had been called upon to undertake such planning, and it was totally unequipped for the task. The Commander-in-Chief, West, was not consulted, and even during the battle itself OKW commanded the armies in the field by means of telephone and wireless; no reports were made from 6th Panzer Army to von Rundstedt – instead, they were sent direct to OKW, who then passed on the information to Model when sending him orders. By the end of September, preliminary studies had shown that the Monschau-Echternach area in the Ardennes offered the best prospects for the offensive. Hitler then stipulated that the vital port of Antwerp should be the aim of the main thrust, and that the attack would take place at the end of November. On 9 October, without having had the benefit of any advice from von Rundstedt or the other senior field commanders on whose expertise the success of the attack depended, Jodl presented OKW's plans to Hitler. Warlimont remembered:

> 'Comparatively little is known about this stage of the procedure, but it is clear that even on this occasion Hitler made it his business to alter the objectives in many respects, and, as always, to widen them. Jodl notes in his diary: "the Führer orders: 1. Left flank to be extended to include Bastogne and Namur; 2. A second attack from north of Aachen southwards along the Meuse; 3. There must be a flank guard. The flank guard is to act offensively." It seems more than likely that on this day, and no later, the objective of the operation was finally laid down; it was to drive in one sweep through the Eifel and Ardennes, across the Ourthe and Meuse and right through Belgium to the Channel coast at Antwerp. Hitler was clearly trying to resurrect in miniature the basic concept of the offensive in the west of May 1940, though the miniature was far too large for the existing circumstances.'[10]

In themselves, the principles on which the Ardennes counterstroke was based had much to commend them. The Germans were to concentrate their forces at the point where the enemy was weakest (the Germans massed more than 240,000 men to attack an area defended by only 80,000); surprise was to be a vital element, the assault taking place at a time and a place the Allies least expected; and there was to be a speedy exploitation of the attack towards objectives some 110 miles distant, avoiding enemy strongpoints and without undue concern about extended flanks. The paralysis of the enemy, not his physical destruction, was the aim, to be achieved by dividing his forces and occupying his vital command and supply centres of Brussels and Antwerp (the largest port in Europe). This, Hitler hoped, would set the stage for the annihilation of twenty to thirty enemy divisions, and inflict a crippling defeat on the Allies on the Continent. Even if it did not result in a compromise peace, the Germans would gain time – time in which to switch forces to meet the invader from the east, to rebuild the Reich's bombed factories under the protection of the winter weather, and to develop further the war-winning weapons on which the Führer's hopes for the future so much depended: the V rockets, the jet fighters, and the electro U boats.

The plan had one overriding weakness: it had no contact with reality. On 24 October it was unveiled in all its detail to the generals who would have to carry it out. As Westphal remembered:

> 'The following week was spent by the Commander-in-Chief, West, and Army Group B in searching calculations and study. The results confirmed our initial apprehensions, namely that the forces [three armies of some twenty divisions attacking along an initial front seventy-five miles wide] would be inadequate for a thrust to Antwerp. If a penetration were effected over the Meuse in a northwesterly direction, the flanks of the wedge would lengthen as more ground was gained. It appeared to be out of the question that the 7th Army would be strong enough to protect the southern flank for long. Nor would the Allied troops adjacent to the breakthrough front be expected to stand politely back and make way for the attackers. What would happen if they stood fast, or, as was probable, launched counter-attacks? In a word: with the forces which could be expected to be at our disposal, the attack across the Meuse appeared to be too risky. Even if Antwerp were reached, it would be impossible to hold on to the ground covered by the advance.'[11]

On 3 November Jodl, 'speaking in Hitler's name', briefed the senior commanders in the west on OKW's plans for the offensive. Warlimont wrote:

> 'From the outset, Jodl left no doubt that these directions came from the Führer and were therefore unalterable. Nevertheless, as one man, the assembled commanders protested, primarily against the distance of the objective – over 125 miles away. The forces proposed, they said, even if they could be concentrated and more or less adequately equipped in time, which recent experience showed was improbable, were nothing like adequate, particularly under winter conditions. During the discussion, a counter proposal was made for a "limited solution". It consisted merely of eliminating the enemy breakthrough at Aachen, which had meanwhile fallen to the Americans on 21 October and as a result recovering the neighbouring forts of the Siegfried Line [the West Wall]. In the most favourable situa-

tion it might then be possible to advance to the Meuse. Only if, contrary to all expectation, the subsequent situation allowed, would it be possible to consider a rapid regrouping of forces and an advance to a more distant objective.'[12]

Jodl would have none of this. The Führer, he argued, had rejected any 'limited solution', and would not countenance any postponement of the attack from November to December. Nevertheless, the next day, the generals communicated their alternative plan to Führer headquarters, where it was disregarded. Jodl wrote that 'The Führer has decided that the operation is unalterable in every detail'.[13] Hitler's mind was not to be influenced by his field commanders.

After the war, the generals maintained their unanimous rejection of Hitler's plan. Von Rundstedt said:

> 'I strongly object to the fact that this stupid operation in the Ardennes is sometimes called the "Rundstedt offensive". That is a complete misnomer. I had nothing to do with it. It came to me as an order complete to the last detail [Hitler had even written on the plan in his own handwriting: 'NOT TO BE ALTERED']. . . . The forces at our disposal were much, much too weak for such a far-reaching objective. I suggested that my plan against the Aachen salient be used instead, but the suggestion was turned down, as were all my other objections. It was only up to me to obey. It was a nonsensical operation, and the most stupid part of it was the setting of Antwerp as the target. If we reached the Meuse we should have got down on our knees to thank God – let alone try to reach Antwerp.'[14]

Model was also opposed to Hitler's plan, and made no fewer than four attempts to persuade his Führer of its weakness. Their disillusion was also shared by the SS general, Dietrich, commander of the new 6th (SS) Panzer Army (given the honorific 'SS' after the offensive) which, together with the 5th Panzer Army and 7th Army, was to undertake the operation. He later recounted with a trace of irony:

> 'All I had to do was to cross a river, capture Brussels, and then go on and take the port of Antwerp. And all this in December [the operation was delayed from November because of delays in assembling the necessary forces], January, and February, the worst three months of the year, through the Ardennes where the snow was waist deep and where there wasn't room to deploy four tanks abreast, let alone six armoured divisions; when it didn't get light until eight in the morning, and was dark again at four in the afternoon, and my tanks can't fight at night; with divisions that had just been re-formed and were composed chiefly of raw, untrained recruits; and at Christmas time.'[15]

Only the commander of 5th Panzer Army, von Manteuffel, had any success with Hitler, and even then he managed only to get some points of tactical detail changed: the exact hour of the attack, the timing of the artillery barrage, and the deployment of the armour. The strategic basis of Hitler's plan remained intact.

The condition of the attacking force was grave indeed. In 1940, the advance through the Ardennes to the Channel had been undertaken by a force which, starting with forty-four divisions, had increased to seventy-one by the time it had reached its objective. Now, in late 1944, only twenty-eight divisions were committed to the battle, of which nine were armoured. The enemy, for his part, was now far more able to react to German moves than he had been in 1940. The two breakthrough armies had 1,200 tanks and assault-guns between them, an illusory strength when it is remembered that these machines could not operate without petrol, and that, when the offensive began, the Germans possessed only one-quarter of the fuel they regarded as the absolute minimum, and most of this was kept east of the Rhine, too far back. Many tanks were to come to a halt simply through lack of fuel. Moreover, the recovery and repair system was woefully inadequate. Eight promised divisions, including two armoured, were not available for the attack, and the later movement of reserves was to be severely hampered because of the petrol shortage. The flanking armies, 7th and 15th, were denied their intended reinforcements owing to dangerous enemy pressure in the east and to the American attacks around Aachen in November, which absorbed divisions originally earmarked for the offensive. As a result, the flanks of the operation, so important for its success, were weakly held. The infantry divisions, especially the *Volksgrenadiers,* were far from uniform in quality, and many lacked formation training and experienced officers and NCOs. An unnecessary handicap under which the attackers had to labour was the obsessive secrecy which, on Hitler's orders, surrounded the operation. Front-line officers were not even informed of their objectives until the day before the attack, and most divisional commanders had only a few days' notice. As a result, numerous mistakes occurred when the offensive began, for commanders simply had not had sufficient time to study the problem, reconnoitre the ground, and make their preparations; the first day's attack was a masterpiece of confusion. The postponement of the offensive from late November to 16 December, owing to the delays in assembling the necessary units, was to prove disastrous. The original dates had been chosen to take full advantage of the seasonal bad weather which would allow ground movement but prevent effective enemy air activity. But by mid- and late December the weather had the opposite effect, and despite Göring's promises the Luftwaffe proved quite unable to wrest even temporary command of the air from the Allies. Only from 16 to 23 December, when fog impeded the enemy air forces, was the weather a help to the Germans; thereafter, the clear days enabled the Allies to make movement by day virtually impossible, and the snow and ice on the roads caused movement by night to be extremely dangerous and slow.

Finally, the attacking force suffered from one other great disadvantage, again brought about by Hitler's dominance over the planning of the operation. The basis of the plan was to execute a turning movement from the Ardennes to the north-west in the direction of Liège and Antwerp. Therefore, as all the generals except Dietrich argued, the main strength should have been placed on the left flank, on the outer side on the wheel which had to travel the farthest. But Hitler would not view it that way. The 6th Panzer Army under Dietrich, containing four SS panzer divisons [including two in the OKW reserve], was to be given the major role, and it was on the right (inner) flank of the wheel, nearest Antwerp. On the left, the 5th Panzer Army, under von Manteuffel, which had the advantage of advancing over easier ground, with more roads and a weaker defence, achieved the greater success during the early days of the offensive, but it was never given the strength needed to exploit it. Even when Dietrich's attack was bogged down, and the only hope of victory lay in reinforcing von Manteuffel, Hitler ordered that reserves be sent to Dietrich instead, a move which seems to have been for political rather than military reasons. Hitler preferred to see his plan and the SS troops succeed at the expense of the Army formations, even if it risked the chance of achieving victory. Von Rundstedt was right when he declared that this was a 'fundamental mistake which unbalanced the whole offensive'.[16]

At 5.30a.m. on 16 December the Ardennes counter-offensive began; the Allies were taken completely by surprise, and some early success was achieved despite muddle on the German side. However, as early as the second day the advance began to founder; by the 20th, 6th Panzer Army could advance no further; by the 24th, Christmas Eve, a panzer spearhead of 5th Panzer Army had made the furthest penetration – sixty miles to Celles, except that there it had to remain; the battalion had run out of petrol! Enemy resistance in the path of the advance was dogged, particularly at St Vith and Bastogne, where American troops acted as a block past which the Germans were diverted. These points began to hold back an ever greater proportion of the attacking force; delay was inevitable. St Vith fell on 22 December, but not Bastogne. According to OKW's plan, it should have been reached at the latest on the second day of the offensive; instead, it was not reached until the third, and not by-passed until the sixth. Time, so vital to the advance, was lost to the Germans, but gained by the Allies. Had Bastogne fallen immediately, von Manteuffel would have had an easy race to the Meuse, for on 19 December there were only two battalions of engineers and some armoured cars to oppose his advance. The delay, however, gave the Americans time to stiffen their defence east of the river, and the Germans never came nearer to it than four miles. The attackers were suffering also from Hitler's determination to place the weight of the advance on Dietrich's 6th Panzer Army. Although it was soon clear that faulty leadership, difficult terrain, shortage of fuel, and enemy resistance had prevented the SS troops from making satisfactory progress, in contrast with 5th Panzer Army which was still forging ahead, it was not until the 20th that Hitler would consider shifting the emphasis of the attack to von Manteuffel. Not until the evening of the 25th did two divisions of the OKW Reserve arrive at 5th Panzer Army's front (having been held up for thirty-six hours owing to lack of fuel), and by then it was too late. The following day, when von Manteuffel was promised further reserves, the German front began to contract. Moreover, on the flanks of the advance, enemy reaction was far quicker than OKW had expected: on the 20th the Allies regrouped their front, and on the 22nd began mounting a counter-attack from the south, to be followed on 3 January by one from the north. On 23 December, when the weather began to improve, the Allied air forces began to join the battle, soon to inflict such damage on the enemy that von Mellenthin could write: 'The Ardennes battle drives home the lesson that a large-scale offensive by massed armour has no hope of success against any enemy who enjoys supreme command of the air.'[17] On the 26th, the eleventh day of the offensive, the German troops were forbidden to make any large moves by day. By then, however, the advanced units were already beginning to fall back.

To the German field commanders, united in their pessimism about the outcome, the failure of the Ardennes offensive was clear almost from the beginning. Westphal remembered: 'As early as 22 December, Rundstedt had urged Hitler to call off the offensive. He pressed the request the more vigorously because it was clear to him that forces would soon have to be surrendered by the western Army in favour of the Eastern Front [where the new Soviet offensive was about to open]. Hitler said no. He still hoped that Bastogne might be taken.'[18] On the 24th Model and von Manteuffel again proposed the 'limited solution' to Hitler, who, although not agreeing to the substitution of Aachen for Antwerp, accepted that the occupation of the Namur-Liège sector of the Meuse had to be made the primary objective before any further advance could be undertaken. He would still not contemplate the failure of his undertaking. On the 28th he told von Rundstedt that, although the counter-offensive had 'not resulted in the decisive success which might have been expected . . . a tremendous easing of the situation has come about. The enemy has had to abandon all his plans for attack.'[19] At the same time, he prepared to unleash a secondary attack with eight divisions southward from the Saar, the success of which, he believed, would bring about the collapse of the American threat to the Ardennes offensive on the left flank, which could then be resumed with every prospect of success. On 1 January 1945 that attack was delivered but was brought to a halt without any dislocation of the Allied dispositions. The abortive battle in the Ardennes continued, with no prospect of success. On 3 January von Rundstedt informed his commanders that the only sensible course of action was to withdraw and save what was possible of men and material. Hitler would not agree. On the 5th all idea of taking Bastogne was abandoned, and on the 8th the Führer permitted Model to give up the area west of Houffalize, barely twenty miles from the German starting-point on 16 December. Still he refused to sanction a full withdrawal. Westphal wrote:

> 'The proper action now, in view of the urgent necessity for economis-
> ing our forces, would have been to withdraw as rapidly as possible
> behind the West Wall. But Hitler would not agree to this either, for
> he feared that the enemy might follow on all too rapidly. He would
> not listen to representations to the effect that, although the enemy
> might indeed act in this way, a withdrawal of our own troops in one
> bound would still be more economical. It was therefore the middle of
> January before the German forces, greatly exhausted, arrived
> behind the frontier rivers, Our and Sauer. The last two weeks in
> particular, with their perfect flying weather, resulted in ir-
> replaceable sacrifices.'[20]

Von Manteuffel later remembered that, by 5 January, 'the situation was so serious that I feared that Montgomery would cut off our armies. Although we managed to avoid this danger, a large part of them was sacrificed. Our losses were much heavier in this later stage than they had been earlier, owing to Hitler's policy of "no withdrawal". It spelt bankruptcy, because we could not afford such losses.'[21]

The Ardennes offensive, and its unnecessary prolongation, had two major consequences. First, its preparation and continuance severely diminished the resources available to the armies in the east (for example, in November and December, while 2,299 armoured vehicles, new and refitted, had gone to the west, only 921 had been sent to the east); this clearly favoured the Soviet offensive which began in mid-January. Guderian was particularly annoyed by Hitler's intransigence in the face of all advice, recalling that:

> 'A sensible commander would . . . have remembered the dangers
> looming on the Eastern Front which could only be countered by a
> timely breaking-off of the operation in the west that was already a
> failure. But not only Hitler, but also the High Command . . . during
> these fateful days, could think of nothing save their own Western
> Front. The whole tragedy of our military leadership was revealed
> once again towards the end of the war in this unsuccessful Ardennes
> offensive.'[22]

It took ten days after the beginning of the Soviet offensive for the Führer to approve the move of reinforcements from west to east. Second, the Ardennes venture had resulted in high casualties, which the Germans were in no position to afford – no fewer than 130,000 men, of which 19,000 were killed. Between them, 5th and 6th Panzer Armies had lost 600 panzer vehicles, some divisions being left with fewer than twenty tanks. Most of the *Volks-grenadier* divisions were badly mauled, and at least one was reduced to only 1,000 men. Ammunition was so low that there was enought for only five rounds each day for every gun in the west. These losses were particularly serious as they were virtually irreplaceable; the Allies made good theirs within two weeks. A high percentage of the German losses occurred during the month when all hope of winning the battle had disappeared. Had von Rundstedt's advice been taken, and had a withdrawal taken place soon after 22 December, not only would the Germans in the west have conserved much of their strength while at the same time inflicting a not insignificant blow to the enemy, but also reinforcements could have been made available for the east either before, or immediately after, the beginning of the Soviet offensive.

Hitler's counterstroke may have delayed the further Allied advance by six weeks, but it did not prevent it. On 8 February the enemy attacked, with the aim of destroying the German positions west of the Rhine. The German forces were in no condition to put up an adequate defence. To their harsh losses in the Ardennes was added the reduction in their strength by the withdrawal of roughly one-third of their divisions (and their best ones at that) to the east. In all, sixteen divisions and a large quantity of artillery were moved, and most of the new equipment diverted, to ward off the Soviets. In February, for example, 1,675 armoured vehicles went to the east, and only sixty-seven to the west. Against such overwhelming Allied superiority on the ground and in the air, a rigid defence was both impossible and dangerous, but Hitler demanded it nevertheless. In January, in an attempt to prepare the German defences for the inevitable resumption of the enemy attack in the west, von Rundstedt had proposed that the whole of Holland west and south of the Ijssel Sea should be given up in order to use fewer troops. Hitler, true to form, declared that Holland was to be held to the last, and it was later designated a 'fortress', in which a whole army would be trapped by early April. Von Rundstedt, with the full agreement of Model, then proposed a particular course of action for the defence. Westphal wrote:

> 'In words of particular urgency, he declared that the only aim of decisive importance was to maintain coherence of the front and to prevent a breakthrough on a strategic scale. In the face of this necessity, the policy of clinging to every foot of German soil in the rigid form in which it had been ordered till now, must be abandoned. Moreover, it was now indispensable to make extensive preparations for the organisation of the defence on the east bank of the Rhine. Even though rivers no longer presented the same obstacles as in earlier times, the Allies, in their methodical way, were sure to make careful preparations for crossing the Rhine. Staying too long west of the river would increase the danger of the enemy's following closely on the heels of the German troops. Would Hitler preserve his freedom of action? . . . Hitler persisted in his demand that every foot of soil should be defended.'[23]

He rejected any idea that the sparsity of forces demanded a shortening of the front; he pointed out that the West Wall was strong enough to meet any attack (a myth: the troops themselves had little faith in the obsolete fortifications, and there were not enough soldiers to man every bunker or pill-box; von Rundstedt called it a 'shameful fabrication'[24]); and he forbade the surrender of even the smallest outpost without his permission. The Rhine, Hitler argued, was the vital link between the Ruhr and the rest of Germany; withdrawal to its east bank would 'merely mean moving the catastrophe from one place to another'.[25]

It was this 'no withdrawal' order which, with the marked inferiority in strength, was to characterise the end of the campaign in the west, as, indeed, it had done throughout. Warlimont wrote: 'Hitler's orders remained as rigid as ever. . . . So, in spite of its courage and self-sacrifice, the remnants of the German Army were to a great extent expended forward of the Rhine.'[26] Von Manteuffel was equally explicit: 'After the Ardennes failure, Hitler started a "corporal's war". There were no big plans, only a multitude of piecemeal fights.'[27]

By 3 March, the twenty-sixth day of the renewed Allied offensive, fifteen German divisions were threatened with destruction west of the Rhine; Hitler still forbade a withdrawal, and not until the 10th did he allow an evacuation; too late. By 25 March, when the last resistance west of the Rhine had collapsed, the Germans had lost 350,000 men. One-third of Hitler's troops in the west had been captured. On the 23rd the Allies crossed the Rhine on a broad front (having already gained a bridgehead at Remagen on the 7th); within a week the majority of Model's Army Group B, twenty-one divisions in all, had been surrounded in the Ruhr, which Hitler had ordered to be held at all costs, and by 18 April 325,000 men surrendered. A few days later Model shot himself. At the same time as the Ruhr was being subdued, the Allies plunged into the interior of the Reich, sweeping aside the few scattered units that could be brought up to oppose them. Of those days, Jodl remembered: 'We could no longer talk of a general conduct of the war. We had no reserves and could exert no control over the situation.'[28] In the west, a front could not be said to exist; the Allies could advance at will. On 11 April, after an advance of fifty-seven miles since dawn, the Allies reached the Elbe, fifty-three miles from Berlin, and were ordered not to go any further eastwards. On 18 April, the day the Ruhr pocket surrendered, Hitler's last new army, the 11th, was encircled in the Harz mountains. During the thirty days of April, the Allies took more than 1,650,000 prisoners, which brought the total since the beginning of the campaign in June 1944 to almost 3,000,000. On 4 May the German forces in north-west Europe formally surrendered, and on the 5th all their units in the west laid down their arms.

32

The Final Ignominy

I am no ordinary soldier-king but a war lord —
probably the most successful in history.

ADOLF HITLER

1943

By mid-1943, the characteristics of Hitler's military leadership were well-established: his child-like obsession with numbers, his unrivalled capacity for self-delusion, his suspicion of the professional military caste, his oft-expressed belief in the power of a fanatical will, his fear of taking risks, his disinclination for long-term plans, his propensity to place political before military considerations, and his inability to distinguish between the important and the trivial. To these was now added his reaction to defeat. Failure at Stalingrad and Tunis had been heavy blows to his belief in his own infallibility. In the east, in the skies over the Reich, and in the west, Germany was outnumbered; the tide had indeed turned. Perhaps Hitler began to see that, beneath the transient vision he had created of himself as Führer and warlord, there was the reality of the son of a petty Austrian official, the gassed corporal of the trenches, the military illiterate who read, but failed to understand, Frederick the Great, von Clausewitz, von Moltke, and von Schlieffen. He knew that he was the man whom the generals followed, yet despised. His nerves began to falter, and he found an outlet for his frustration in frequent outbursts of rage that reminded witnesses of the fits of a spoiled child unrequited in his desires. There were always others, such as the General Staff, to blame, and straws at which to clutch, such as the exhaustion of the 'Russian bear', the terrible destructive power of Germany's new rocket weapons, or the break-up of the enemy alliance. But that was all that was left to Hitler. His Army was being beaten before his very eyes, and he had not the wit to put a stop to it.

All this had, over the years, brought about a situation in which, as Westphal put it:

'The gulf between the Führer and the German Army leaders was absolute and unbridgeable. It arose from the always irreconcilable conflict between concrete and abstract thinking, between sober objectivity and the chasing of fantasies, between logical calculation based on facts and the attempt to force the facts to fit impossible desires. It was an intense spiritual torment for every thinking German soldier to be unable to ward off the impending military and moral disaster, to have to look on while everything was wasted and squandered. But in the Third Reich the motto was "Death to the Expert", particularly the soldier. Not only Hitler, but almost every Party leader believed himself to possess a more soundly based judgement in all questions concerning the conduct of the war than that possessed by the leaders of the Army. To these Party strategists we may apply the ironical words of the ancient Romans: *Dulce bellum inexpertis* [War is delightful to the inexperienced].'[1]

Attempts were made by the generals to correct the ever-more apparent defects in the military leadership of the Reich caused by Hitler's character, but they were doomed to failure. Von Manstein, for example, tried on no fewer than three occasions to persuade Hitler: '. . . to leave the conduct of military operations in all theatres of war to *one* responsible Chief of Staff and to appoint a special Commander-in-Chief for the Eastern Theatre', although at the same time to retain the title of Supreme Commander. Von Manstein even went so far as to tell Hitler that 'One thing we must be clear about . . . is that the extremely critical situation we are now in cannot be put down to the enemy's superiority alone, great though it is. It is also due to the way in which we are led.'[2]

Zeitzler, exasperated by OKW and the limitations of the Army's freedom of action in the east, proposed a radical reorganisation of the High Command, but to no avail. His plan involved complete independence for the commanders in the Eastern Front; the fusion of OKH and OKW into a single body, which would have the Waffen SS under its control; the placing of all questions of armament under the Quartermaster-General; and the taking of military power from Hitler and putting it back in the hands of the generals (although, again, leaving Hitler with his title of Supreme Commander). Later, Guderian attempted to enlist the unlikely aid of Goebbels to persuade Hitler to appoint a Chief of the Wehrmacht General Staff, who would control the conduct of operations, but when Guderian suggested this to the Führer, he, like von Manstein and Zeitzler, met with a point-blank refusal. Subsequently, Hitler was often to say to Guderian, rather pathetically, 'I can't understand why everything has gone wrong for the past two years', to which the reply was always: 'Change your methods'.[3] The advice was ignored. Hitler, having gained supreme control, was hardly the man to relinquish it.

The frustration of the generals was immense. In mid-1943 von Manstein felt it necessary to write to Zeitzler:

'If my misgivings about coming developments are disregarded, and if my intentions as a commander, which aim merely at removing difficulties for which I am not responsible, continue to be frustrated, I shall have no choice but to assume that the Führer had not the necessary confidence in this headquarters. I am far from believing myself infallible. Everyone makes mistakes. . . . As long as I remain at this post, however, I must have the chance to use my own head.'[4]

Six months later, he felt himself again forced to express himself thus: 'If any leadership is to be successful, it must be based on a harmonious coordination of policy at all levels. . . . If the Supreme Command remains dumb as well as deaf to the conclusions drawn by the army group in its own limited sphere of activity, a coordinated policy will be quite out of the question.'[5] However, what kept von Manstein, in common with a number of less aggressive generals, in his post was his fear that he would be replaced by someone less able than himself and more responsive to Hitler's will, with disastrous results for the troops.

Zeitzler, however, reached a point where he could work no more with Hitler. He realised shortly after his appointment as Chief of the General Staff that Hitler did not want an adviser but merely a man who would forward his views and orders without criticism. This did not suit the energetic Zeitzler, and his admiration for the Führer soon turned to disillusion. Guderian remembered: 'He did not hesitate to give Hitler his views, and he fought hard for his point of view. Five times he offered to resign his post, and five times his offer was refused, until at last [in July 1944] Hitler's distrust of him grew so great that he finally let him go. He did not succeed in persuading Hitler to change his attitude.'[6] After the war, Zeitzler told his interrogators how his break with Hitler began when he demanded that 6th Army be withdrawn before it was encircled at Stalingrad:

> 'Adolf Hitler refused point-blank, and, for the first time, was exceedingly rude to me at this interview. As I, in my temperamental way, spoke up for my views very loudly and sharply, a severe row was the consequence. Adolf Hitler tried again and again to make me come round, but I, at a private interview, for the first time asked to be relieved from my post. Although he was impressed by this, he refused point-blank.'

From this time on, relations between the two men grew from bad to worse. Severe rows became ever-more frequent, although Zeitzler realised that he was achieving little. He remembered:

> 'I became convinced that verbal resignations were useless, and in the spring of 1944, at a new measure which went against my conscience, tendered my resignation in writing. As I learned afterwards, this impressed him considerably, as he was not used to such a thing. In the following night he sent for me and told me the following: "You should not write such letters to me. A general cannot leave his post.

He must hold out. I too must hold out." All counter-arguments were useless.'[7]

Finally, in desperation over the encirclement of Army Group Courland, Zeitzler offered his resignation for the fifth time, and once again had it rejected. He could take no more. On 10 June 1944 he reported himself sick, and Heusinger, Chief of the Operations Department of the General Staff, took over his duties. Zeitzler never returned to service.

Hitler's method of handling the Army had degenerated into two expedients: the dismissal of individuals, and the political indoctrination of the masses. No senior commander was secure from Hitler's wrath. On 29 January 1944 the commander of Army Group North, von Küchler, was retired after withdrawing one of his armies to save it from encirclement, and was replaced by Model; on 30 March the commanders of Army Group South and A, von Manstein and von Kleist, were dismissed as a result of their repeated attempts to use their own initiative on the battlefield, and were replaced by Model and Schörner (at the same time, the army groups were renamed North Ukraine and South Ukraine respectively); and on 28 June, during the disastrous Soviet offensive, the commander of Army Group Centre, Busch, was removed, and Model took over his position. On 3 July Model's successor as commander of Army Group North, Lindemann, was dismissed for refusing to attack, instead proposing a withdrawal, and he was replaced by Friessner. Thus, in six months, the entire senior leadership on the Eastern Front had been changed completely. Moreover, on 6 July 1944, exactly one month after the Allies had landed, the Commander-in-Chief, West, von Rundstedt, was dismissed for the second time and was replaced by von Kluge. Von Rundstedt's faults were that he had been critical of Hitler's policy of 'no withdrawal', and that, when Keitel had asked, 'What shall we do?' he had replied: 'Make peace, you fools, what else can you do?'[8] Other senior commanders, too, felt Hitler's wrath at what he considered to be either disobedience to his expressed will or unwarranted failure in the field. Hoth, commander of 4th Panzer Army, was one of them; in mid-November 1943 he was replaced for being 'tired', and in part responsible for the defeat of Army Group Centre. Others included Hollidt, commander of 6th Army; Lanz, commander of Group 'Lanz'; Kempf, commander of Group 'Kempf'; Jordan, commander of 9th Army; Ruoff, commander of 17th Army; Jaenecke, his successor; and Schmidt, commander of 2nd Panzer Army.

At the same time that Hitler was trying to beat the generals into submission, he was also planning to imbue the mass of the Army with National Socialism, a 'spirit' which, from the early 1930s, he had believed was compatible with good soldiering. On 26 July 1943, for example, he declared: 'These young men are fighting like fanatics because they come from the Hitler Youth, who ... generally fight more fanatically than the older people.'[9] The reason for this, he was sure, lay in the political indoctrination of the past years. Hitler must also have realised that, for as long as he could retain the loyalty, if not the affection, of the great majority of junior officers, NCOs and men, then the generals would find that their means of rebellion, which, after all, consisted solely of the soldiers prepared to follow them, were denied to them. Without men, the generals were powerless. Security, therefore, lay in a National Socialist Army. At the end of 1943 Hitler instituted the OKW National Socialist Leadership Organisation, which was designed to inspire the Wehrmacht with National Socialist ideology and to increase its determination to resist. Hitler himself took part in the education of his Army to the extent that he normally made the closing address at the regular 'National Socialist Courses of Instruction' for senior generals. Von Manstein, who, together with all other army group and army commanders on the Eastern Front, was summoned to one of Hitler's meetings in early 1944, wrote: 'The more difficult the military situation became, the greater importance he attached to "faith" as a guarantee of victory. It was an attitude which he sought to apply more and more in the selection of senior officers for posts down to divisional commander.'[10] Political attachment now came to be of greater importance to a military career than professional expertise.

The history of the German opposition to Hitler from 1939 had been a sad one. The conspirator's plans were frustrated by the early successes of Hitler's aggression, the hesitations of his generals, the strict nature of his police state, and the tight security that surrounded his person. Death had come to be seen as the only way by which Hitler's tyranny could be removed, but not until the tragedy of Stalingrad, followed hard by defeat in Tunisia, did conditions appear favourable for such a coup. As Halder remarked in 1939, only failure abroad offered any hope for the underground opposition. During 1943 there were several attempts on the Führer's life, but all came to nothing: on 13 March a bomb, placed in his aircraft by a group of officers at von Kluge's headquarters, failed to go off; later that month Hitler's vacillation over whether to visit the War Museum in Berlin caused a suicide bomb attempt to be cancelled; some time afterwards, an officer who managed to get into the Führer's presence was, because of his junior rank, placed too far from the dictator to be able to shoot him; in November another suicide mission misfired, owing to Hitler's non-appearance; and in December a further bomb attempt was frustrated because of Hitler's last-minute cancellation of a conference.

Apart from a number of abortive attempts, 1943 had also seen a new leadership coming to the fore in the underground military opposition. Of the former conspirators Halder had withdrawn, Beck was getting old and tired, von Witzleben although still active had been retired from the Army, von Hammerstein was dead, Canaris, who from early 1944 was no longer Head of the Abwehr (which had been incorporated into the SS system) preferred to play his own game, and Oster, under suspicion from the Gestapo, was useless. By 1944 the new men were the most active. Foremost among them were Colonel Count Claus von Stauffenberg, a handsome, educated, brave officer in his late thirties who had sustained severe injuries in early 1943 and was now Chief of Staff to the Reserve Army; General Friedrich Olbricht, a deeply religious man and Head of the Supply Section of the Reserve Army; and Henning von Tresckow, Chief of Staff of Army Group Centre. Still playing their part were Heinrich von Stülpnagel, then military governor of France, and the ever-active civilian Carl Goerdeler. In the first half of 1944 these officers and civilians built up a new organisation capable of taking over the government as soon as Hitler had been removed by either bomb or bullet; the plan they evolved was code-named 'Valkerie'. After the dictator's death, the key installations in Berlin, such as the radio, power, and railway stations, would be occupied by the military, the SS would be disarmed, and all Army units at home and abroad would be informed that, as the Führer and Supreme Commander was dead, the Army had been empowered to form a new government with Beck at its head and with von Witzleben as the Commander-in-Chief of the Wehrmacht, supported by Olbricht as his Chief of Staff. At the same time, all senior Party, SS, and Police officials would be arrested and precautionary measures taken against the militarised political formations.

On 20 July 1944 von Stauffenberg placed a bomb, concealed in a brief-case, under the table at a midday conference in the Führer's East Prussia headquarters, to which he had been asked to give a report. Having already left the room, he made his escape after the resulting explosion, but thanks to the small amount of charge used, to the flimsy construction of the hut in which the conference was being held, and to the action of another officer, who inadvertently pushed the bomb away from the target behind a heavy wooden plinth supporting the table, Hitler was not killed, but merely shocked. Failure at the Führer headquarters was matched by failure in Berlin; hours were lost through vacillation, bad organisation, and ill-luck. At 6.45p.m., six hours after the explosion, the news of Hitler's survival was broadcast throughout the Reich, and all attempts at a coup came to an abrupt end. Only in Paris did the plan succeed, and then only momentarily; von Stülpnagel succeeded in rounding up all the SS and Gestapo, but, lacking the support from his commander, von Kluge, and hearing that Hitler had survived, he was forced to release them.

Hitler's revenge was immediate and terrible. At midday on the day after the bomb explosion, he broadcast to the German nation:

> 'If I speak to you today, it is first in order that you should hear my voice, and should know that I am unhurt and well, and secondly that you should know of a crime unparalleled in German history. A very small clique of ambitious, irresponsible and, at the same time, senseless and very stupid officers had formed a plot to eliminate me and the command of the German Wehrmacht. The bomb . . . exploded two metres to my right. . . . I myself sustained only some very

minor scratches, bruises, and burns. I regard this as a confirmation of the task imposed upon me by Providence. . . . The circle of these conspirators is very small and has nothing in common with the spirit of the German Wehrmacht and, above all, none with the German people. I therefore order now that no military authority, no leader of any unit, no private in the field is to obey any orders emanating from these groups of usurpers. I also order that it is everyone's duty to arrest, or, if they resist, to kill at sight anyone issuing or handling any such orders. . . . This time, we shall get even with them in the way that we National Socialists are accustomed.'[11]

How many people were executed in the ensuing purge, carried out with efficiency by Himmler's security services, is unknown. One estimate, based on the names of individuals known to have perished, sets the number at 250, but another states that some 10,000 were sent to concentration camps, gassed, shot, or hanged. At least two field-marshals and sixteen generals met their end, among whom were Rommel, von Witzleben, Fellgiebel, Chief of Army Communications, von Hase, commandant of the Berlin garrison, Hoepner, Olbricht, Oster, Stieff, Chief of the Army Organisation Office, and von Stülpnagel, as well as Colonel von Stauffenberg and Goerdeler. Beck, von Tresckow, and Wagner, the Army Quartermaster-General, cheated the hangman by committing suicide. Canaris also died at the hand of the SS. In the wake of the intense suspicion that the bomb plot had engendered, Fromm was arrested and, in due course, done away with (despite the fact that he had been responsible for the killing of conspirators on 20 July), and von Kluge, recalled from the Western Front owing to Hitler's fear that he was meeting with the enemy, took poison rather than face certain arrest, humiliation, and death in Berlin. Many other officers were imprisoned, foremost among whom were Halder, together with his wife, von Falkenhausen, and Thomas. A number of important changes also took place. Zeitzler was dismissed from the Army and deprived of the right to wear uniform; Heusinger, who had had some contact with the conspirators, was arrested and replaced by General Wenck; Guderian, who happened to be in the right place at the right time and was untainted by any suspicion of contact with the plotters, was made the acting Chief of the General Staff on the night of 20 July (in default of General Bühle, the Chief of the Army Staff within OKW and Hitler's first choice, who had been seriously injured in the explosion). At the same time, the faithful Himmler replaced Fromm, and the ardently National Socialist General Burgdorf took over the position of Schmundt, who had died as a result of the bomb. In early September Warlimont, who had been hurt in the blast, was given sick leave and never employed again.

Hitler's reaction to the Bomb Plot had been predictable; but what of the Army's? The first indication as to what it would be came with its unquestioning acceptance of the *Reichsführer* SS as the new Commander-in-Chief of the

Replacement Army; Himmler, the man who, above everyone else in Germany, was disliked by the officer corps, was given one of the most important posts in the German Army without a word of protest being uttered. Indeed, von Brauchitsch even bestirred himself from his retirement and, whether or not under compulsion is unknown, published a statement in August condemning the traitors of 20 July and welcoming Himmler's new appointment as a sign of closer cooperation between the SS and the Army. On 23 July the new Chief of the General Staff issued an Order of the Day, in which he described the conspirators as 'a few officers, some of them on the retired list, who had lost courage and, out of cowardice and weakness, preferred the road to disgrace to the only road open to an honest soldier – the road of duty and honour'.[12] The loyalty of a unified Army was then pledged to the Führer. The next day, it was announced that the service salute had been done away with, and the 'Führer salute', of outstretched right arm, was made obligatory for all members of the Wehrmacht; in Göring's words, this was seen as a special 'indication of the unshakable loyalty to the Führer and of the close bonds of comradeship between Wehrmacht and Party'.[13] So concerned was the Army leadership to express its recognition of Hitler as its Führer and Supreme Commander that it did all that it could to prove its allegiance to his creed – National Socialism. On 29 July Guderian, no doubt prompted by Hitler, issued the following order, which was intended to ensure that the German Army no longer resisted National Socialism, but actually preached it:

> 'Every General Staff officer must be a National Socialist officer-leader, that is, not only by his knowledge of tactics and strategy, but also by his model attitude to political questions, and by actively cooperating in the political indoctrination of younger commanders in accordance with the tenets of the Führer. . . . In judging and selecting General Staff officers, superiors should place traits of character and spirit above mind. . . . I expect every General Staff officer immediately to declare himself a convert or adherent to my views and to make an announcement to that effect in public. Anybody unable to do so should apply for his removal. . . .'[14]

The new Chief of the Army Personnel Office, Burgdorf, then proceeded to do all that he could to ensure that the spirit of this order applied to the whole of the force. At the same time, the activities of the OKW National Socialist Leadership Organisation were increased, and its permanent organisation began to extend down even to battalions. At all of this came not a word of protest; indeed, at least one field-marshal, Model, actually requested a Waffen SS officer as an aide-de-camp, and ordered that a political officer be attached to the headquarters of Rommel's old command, Army Group B.

The final abeyance of the Army leadership came on 4 August, when, in reply to a 'request' from the Army, Hitler instituted a 'court of honour' to cleanse its ranks of traitors and thereby to vindicate its honour. Von Rundstedt was appointed president, and Keitel and Guderian were two of the four other generals whose task it was to investigate the conduct of officers arrested on suspicion of complicity in the plot, and, if found guilty, to dismiss them from the service and to hand them over to the Gestapo for trial (and certain condemnation) in a 'People's Court'. Guderian remembered the unpleasant duty he was ordered to perform: 'During these melancholy sessions, one was constantly beset by the most difficult problems of judgement and of conscience. Every word uttered had to be most carefully weighed, and in setting one man free there was always the danger that this would bring misfortune to others whether unsuspected or not yet arrested.'[15] Such a duty was made even more onerous by the knowledge that four days before, on 1 August, it had been decreed that the relatives of officers or soldiers found guilty of treason should share the responsibility and, therefore, the penalty for that act.

The 20 July Bomb Plot, instead of destroying Hitler, had only hardened his will to resist. Although he was obviously a sick man, bent and shuffling, the explosion appeared to have released a source of hither-to untapped energy; the new Chief of the General Staff believed that 'All the forces that had lurked within him were aroused and came into their own. He recognised no limits any more.'[16] Warlimont wrote of the dictator's new spirit: 'He was presumptuous enough to consider that it was "providence" which had preserved him on 20 July, and now expected that other "miracles" would give the war a new turn, although in earlier days he had heaped scorn upon the heads of any enemy leaders who had used this sort of language.'[17] And, during interrogation after the war, Guderian gave this account:

> 'Hitler's mistrust now reached extremes, and the miracle of his survival gave him greater faith than ever in his mission. He shut himself up in his bunker, engaged in no further private talks, and had every word of his conversations recorded. He lost himself more and more in a realm of the imagination which had no basis in reality. Every free expression of opinion and every objection to his frequently incomprehensible views, evoked an outburst of rage on his part. He lost his capacity to listen to a report to the end. His criticisms became stronger, and his actions more drastic, with every passing day. He felt that he alone had the right to hold opinions upon which decisions would be based. He was convinced that he alone possessed clear perception concerning all fields of human activity. Accordingly, he condemned generals, staff officers, diplomats, government officials, and, towards the end, even Party and SS leaders as armchair strategists, weaklings, and finally as criminals and traitors.'[18]

But, beneath the façade, Hitler was a broken man. He refused to face reality, turning aside from all gloomy reports, and declaring: 'Anyone who speaks to me of peace without victory will lose his head, no matter who he is or what his position.'[19] When informed that, for their forthcoming January 1945 offensive, the Soviets had an over-all superiority of 15:1 on the ground and 20:1 in the air, he described this as a bluff, 'the greatest imposture since Genghis Khan'.[20] He once confided to Guderian, after having refused to see Speer to hear his gloomy warnings about the future: 'Now you can understand why it is that I refuse to see anyone alone any more. Any man who asks to talk to me alone always does so because he has something unpleasant to say to me. I can't bear that.'[21] His only solace was to plan grand offensives with non-existent armies, to hear the gross flattery of his closest Party associates, and to bolster himself with remembrances of what had been. He refused to learn from others. 'There's no need for you to try to teach me', he would tell his soldiers. 'I've been commanding the German Army in the field for five years, and during that time I've had more practical experience than any gentleman of the General Staff could ever hope to have. I've studied Clausewitz and Moltke and read the Schlieffen papers. I'm more in the picture than you are.'[22]

Together with the political indoctrination of the Army came its final, and complete, emasculation. It began immediately after the abortive Bomb Plot. On 20 July Reichsführer SS Heinrich Himmler, Chief of the SS and Police, and Minister of the Interior, whose security service had, in May, taken control of the OKW Abwehr department, became Commander-in-Chief of the Replacement Army, with control of all military forces within Germany and the training of new formations for the field. This was followed by his appointments as Commander-in-Chief, Upper Rhine (from 2 December 1944 to 24 January 1945) and as Commander of Army Group Vistula (from 24 January to 31 March 1945), for both of which he was singularly ill-equipped; Guderian called the appointment to Army Group Vistula 'idiocy'.[23] At last, even Hitler was forced to realise that Himmler had neither the time, the training, nor the character for such a demanding task; he acceded to Guderian's request for an Army general to be appointed to the Reichsführer SS's headquarters to supervise a forthcoming attack. Only after further demonstrations of his military incompetence was Himmler prevailed upon by Guderian to give up his field command; Hitler would never have relieved him of it otherwise.

Further encroachment by the Party into military affairs came with the establishment of the German home guard. The idea had been suggested some time before by Heusinger, when Chief of the General Staff Operations Department, but it had been turned down by Hitler. Now, however, he accepted that, as the frontiers of the Reich were already breached, some form of civilian defence was necessary, and the *Volkssturm* was established on 25 September. All males between the ages of sixteen and sixty, not in the Armed Services but capable of bearing arms, would be conscripted into its ranks. But the *Volkssturm* was not to be a part of the Army. Although it was trained and equipped along military lines, under the supervision of the commander of the Replacement Army, Himmler, and although designed to fight in battle, it was the Party, not the Army, that was charged with its leadership and levy. Guderian records the result:

> 'Bormann [Head of the Party Chancery and Hitler's closest adviser and confidant] did nothing to begin with; after repeated urgings on my part he did finally instruct the Gauleiters . . . to proceed with the undertaking. . . . the *Volkssturm* was expanded to an undesirable extent, since there were neither sufficient trained commanders nor an adequate supply of weapons available for so large a force – quite apart from the fact that the Party was less interested in the military qualifications than in the political fanaticism of the men it appointed to fill the responsible posts. My old comrade-in-arms, General von Weitersheim, was a member of the rank and file of a company commanded by some worthless Party functionary. As a result, the brave men of the *Volkssturm* . . . were in many cases drilled busily in the proper way of giving the Hitler salute instead of being trained in the use of weapons of which they had no previous experience.'[24]

Even Hitler, in an order dated 28 January 1945, was forced to admit: 'Experience . . . has shown that *Volkssturm*, emergency and reserve units have little fighting value when left to themselves, and can be quickly destroyed. The fighting value . . . is immeasurably higher when they go into action with troops of the regular army in the field.' Hitler therefore ordered that, wherever possible, such units were to be combined with regular troops into mixed battle-groups under unified command so as to be given 'stiffening and support'.[25] Party dogma could not for long withstand military reality.

Another source of tension between Army and Party came with the division of responsibility between the two when the fighting reached the territory of the Reich itself. On 13 July, Hitler had decreed that:

> 'The military commander-in-chief, to whom I delegate plenary powers, will address his demands concerning civil matters arising out of the military situation to the Reich Commissioner for Defence [who, at the same time, was a Gauleiter] in the area of operations. In the immediate battle areas, whose limits will be defined by the Commander-in-Chief in agreement with the Reich Commissioner for Defence in the area of operations, senior military commanders are empowered to issue direct instructions to civilian authorities. . . .'[26]

If matters concerned the NSDAP, exactly the same procedure was followed, with the exception that the military commander dealt directly with the local Gauleiter. After the Bomb Plot, Hitler amended his order. The plenary powers were taken from the military commander and given to the Reich Commissioner for Defence. This enabled the latter, in the area of operations (although not the immediate battle areas), to take any measures necessary because of threatened enemy attack; to give instructions to all state and local authorities; and to issue regulations having the force of law. Thus, only on the battlefield were the soldiers to be allowed to act without interference from the Party. In the wider theatre of operations, an area just as important militarily as the frontline, especially during a defensive war, it was the Party through the state organisation that reigned supreme – the local Army headquarters had no function other than to act as expert advisers.

This was but a reflection of the state of affairs that had been, for so long, the custom at national level. There, it was Hitler the politician who took full responsibility for the conduct of the Army in war, with OKW and OKH operating merely as advisers and executives. The new Chief of the General Staff, Guderian, found his role, already limited to the Eastern Front, even more constrained than his predecessor's had been. After putting the General Staff into working order again after the momentous event and consequences of 20 July, he remembered that it was only possible to:

> '. . . function in a very cumbersome and slow fashion, since Hitler insisted on approving every detail and refused to allow the Chief of the General Staff the most limited powers of decision. I therefore requested that I be given the right to issue instructions to the eastern army groups on all matters that were not of fundamental importance. I also asked that I be permitted to give directions to all General Staff Corps officers of the Army on such subjects as concerned the General Staff as a whole. Both requests were refused by Hitler. Keitel and Jodl were in agreement with him. . . . Jodl countered my remonstrances with the remark: "The General Staff Corps ought actually to be disbanded".'[27]

Jodl merely echoed Hitler's sentiments. On 31 August, for example, the Führer told his listeners: '. . . if there is not an iron will behind it, the battle cannot be won. I accuse the General Staff of failing to give the impression of iron determination, and so of affecting the morale of the officers who have come here from the front; and when General Staff officers go up front I accuse them of spreading pessimism.'[28] When the garrison of four battalions evacuated Warsaw on 17 January on instructions of their commandant, but in direct contradiction to Hitler's order that it be held to the last man, the Führer gave full vent to his frustration and anger with the General Staff. Guderian remembered:

> '. . . Hitler's rage knew no bounds. He completely lost all comprehension of, and interest in, the frightful general situation, and thought of nothing save the misfortune of losing Warsaw . . . and to punishing the General Staff for what he regarded as its failure. . . . Hitler told me to arrange that the General Staff officers responsible for issuing the reports and signals connected with the withdrawal from Warsaw be held for interrogation. I made it quite clear to him that I alone was responsible for the events of the previous day, and

therefore it was I whom he must arrest and have interrogated, and not my subordinates. He replied: "No. It's not you I am after, but the General Staff. It is intolerable to me that a group of intellectuals should presume to press their views on their superiors. But such is the General Staff system, and that system I intend to smash." '29

It took him just another three months to put his threat into practice.

Hitler's first act following on the evacuation of Warsaw was to have the Chief of the Army Operations Section, Colonel von Bonin, and two of his senior staff officers arrested; Guderian himself was put under interrogation by two of the most senior SS and Gestapo chiefs. Relations between Hitler and the Chief of the General Staff grew worse. Guderian recounts one meeting on 13 February when he tried to get the Führer to place an experienced general at Himmler's Army Group Vistula headquarters to lead a vital attack: 'And so it went on for two hours. His fists raised, his cheeks flushed with rage, his whole body trembling, the man stood there in front of me, beside himself with fury and having lost all self-control. . . . He was almost screaming, his eyes seemed to pop out of his head, and the veins stood out on his temples.'30 Guderian was forced to attend, on average, two briefings a day with his Führer, which he described as 'simply chatter and a waste of time'. When Guderian attempted to argue with Hitler, the usual retort was, 'How dare you speak to me like that? Don't you think I'm fighting for Germany?'31 On one occasion, a witness even had to pull Guderian back by his jacket from an enraged Führer, so convinced was he that the Chief of the General Staff was about to be a victim of physical assault. On 28 March, the final break came. Guderian defended a certain General Busse, whom Hitler had unjustly blamed for the failure of a counter-attack at Küstrin. During the dictator's tirade, the Chief of the General Staff had interjected: 'Permit me to interrupt you. I explained to you yesterday thoroughly – both verbally and in writing – that General Busse is not to blame for the failure of [the] Küstrin attack. 9th Army used the ammunition that had been allotted it. The troops did their duty. The unusually high casualty figures prove that. I therefore ask you not to make any accusations against General Busse.' Hitler then, quite quietly, told Guderian: '. . . your physical health requires that you immediately take six weeks' convalescent leave', and later added, 'Please do your best to get your health back. In six weeks the situation will be very critical. Then, I shall need you urgently.'32 But in six weeks, the General Staff, on Hitler's order, was to exist no more. Indeed, it had but twenty-eight days left.

Guderian was replaced by General Krebs, a close friend of Burgdorf, to whom he owed his promotion. Although he lacked experience of command, he was a highly capable staff officer who had shown himself skilled at adaptation and accommodation. His task was merely 'to advise on the Eastern Front',33 but his position was not to last long. On 25 April, at the instigation of Jodl, who had finally realised that the dangerous division between the two High Commands should end, Hitler signed an order 'for the command organisation and the centralisation of the staffs'. It read: 'The OKW ... will command in accordance with my directives which I will transmit through the Chief of Staff, OKH, who is with me.'[34] Hitler terminated the command function of OKH, and undertook to direct the battle on the ground solely through the OKW Operations Staff in the north, and the newly instituted 'Command Staff B' in the south. The command of all forces was given to Admiral Dönitz in the north and Field-Marshal Kesselring in the south. No general held a Wehrmacht command, and on no front was the Army supreme.

At the same time as Hitler was putting an end to the influence of the Army in military affairs, he was also concerned to restrict the initiative and freedom of action of the officers, senior and junior, in the field. The dismissal of commanders continued; in the west, the two successive commanders-in-chief, von Kluge and von Rundstedt (for the third time) were removed; in the east, Harpe, commander of Army Group A, Reinhardt, commander of Army Group North, and Raus, commander of 3rd Panzer Army, were among the most important to go. At the end of the war, the five army group commanders on the Eastern Front had, on average, fewer than two months' experience of their position; in the west it was little better. Only three field-marshals remained in service: Keitel, Busch, who had been recalled to service in mid-April, and Schörner.
As well as dismissals, Hitler had taken to demotion. Guderian recorded:

> 'Tried and trusted officers at the front were, in the heat of the moment and without any proper enquiry being made, demoted by one or more ranks. . . . I often intervened on behalf of unfortunate individuals who, for some reason or another – usually a ridiculous one involving them in disagreement with the Party functionaries – had suddenly found themselves incarcerated in a concentration camp or sent to a penal unit. Unfortunately, it was only rarely that one even heard of such cases.'[35]

During March 1945, after the Americans had captured intact the bridge over the Rhine at Remagen, Hitler instituted a 'Flying Special Tribunal West', under a fanatical National Socialist, General Hübner. Westphal wrote:

> 'Hitler's headquarters at once began to ask who was to blame. . . . The western commanders were in no doubt that – apart from a train of unhappy chances – the bridge had been lost because of the senseless extension of the front. But that put the blame on OKW, and Hitler had never acknowledged a mistake of his own. Keitel had already told me when we met at the conference of 6 March that Hitler had long been dissatisfied with the "lax" discipline in the west. Hitler now decided to have the guilty ones sought out and

punished by an organ of his own. . . . Hübner was made responsible
to Hitler alone, and was provided with wider powers than any
judiciary in the German Army before. He could not only try a soldier
of any rank by court martial, but he could confirm his own judgement and execute it without delay. His position was a judicial
monstrosity. The Special Tribunal West did not disappoint Hitler
. . . [those it found guilty] were the victims of Hitler's demand that an
example should be made which would create courage through
fear.'[36]

Hitler's determination to direct the German war effort took him to absurd
lengths, and totally inhibited the Army. On 21 January 1945, just two days
after the Warsaw incident, Hitler issued what came to be known as his
'shackling order'[37]:

'I order as follows:
1. Commanders-in-Chief, Commanding Generals, and Divisional
Commanders are personally responsible to me for reporting in good
time: a) Every decision to carry out an operational movement. b)
Every attack planned in divisional strength and upwards which does
not conform with the general directives laid down by the High
Command. c) Every offensive action in quiet sectors of the front,
over and above normal shock-troop activities, which is calculated to
draw the enemy's attention to the sector. d) Every plan for dis-
engaging or withdrawing forces. e) Every plan for surrendering a
position, a local strongpoint, or a fortress. They must ensure that I
have time to intervene in this decision if I think fit, and that my
counter-orders can reach the front-line troops in time.
2. Commanders . . . are responsible to me that every report made to
me either directly, or through the normal channels, should contain
nothing but the unvarnished truth. In future, I shall impose draco-
nian punishment on any attempt at concealment, whether deliberate
or arising from carelessness or oversight. . . .'[38]

Of this order, Warlimont noted: 'Hitler's intention . . . must have been to
achieve his long-sought end, completely to muzzle the Wehrmacht – or
rather the Army. By the contemptuous terms in which it was couched, he
was clearly giving full expression to his hatred of General Staff officers and
their traditional intellectual independence.'[39]

Orders now emanating from the Führer's headquarters ended with
warnings of dire retribution in case of failure; for example, to a tactical
directive to Army Group Vistula, dated 21 April, Hitler added: 'Officers
who do not accept this order without reservation are to be arrested and shot
instantly!'[40] This was taken to its ultimate conclusion three months later; on
28 April, only two days before his suicide, Hitler placed his final shackle on
the generals when he ordered 'that basic decisions are to be presented to the

Führer with thirty-six hours notice. Independent decisions are to be justified in detail.'[41] The Führer could go no further in the process that he had begun in 1938. The German Army in defeat was, indeed, Hitler's.

At the close of the war, the supreme warlord lived out his last remaining days in a bunker under his Reich Chancellery, which was already being hit by Soviet artillery fire. Berlin, so long the subject of heavy air attack, was but a shell of its former self. But Hitler remained connected by telephone and by the Berlin radio tower to all his formations remaining in the field. Still he issued orders, demanded reports, dismissed commanders, and moved shattered divisions as if they were fresh formations; still he could think only of fighting to the end, a fight which now seemed to have taken on a mystical significance. On 18 March, in reaction to attempts to stop his 'scorched-earth' policy, he told his listeners:

> 'If the war is to be lost, then the nation, too, will be lost. . . . There is no need to consider the basic requirements that a people need in order to continue to live a primitive life. On the contrary, it is better ourselves to destroy such things, for this nation will have proved itself the weaker, and the future will belong exclusively to the stronger eastern nation. Those who remain alive after the battles are over are in any case only inferior persons, since the best have fallen.'[42]

And on those few occasions when he was forced to admit all was lost, he blamed those around him. On 18 April, for example, he declared: 'If the German people loses the war, it will have proved itself unworthy of me.'[43]

Warlimont has left a fine description of the last days of Hitler's military leadership:

> 'So in this final phase of the war, German Supreme Headquarters and its strategy was torn in all directions – between east and west – between attempts at ambitious operations for which neither forces nor resources were available, and the pitiless march of events which continuously overtook their planning; between the grizly heroism of a determination not to recognise the approach of catastrophe, and day-to-day activity in a dream-world of armies, divisions, and regiments capable of fighting. The determination of one man possessed of the devil governed everything; the machinery of command churned out orders in normal form though there might be no one to receive them. . . . Hitler's leadership was therefore now without object or objective, but the last crazy orders continued to issue forth stamped with his own faults and his own phraseology.'[44]

The, by now, meaningless exhortations of 'no withdrawal', 'fanatical resistance', and 'fight to the last' permeated all his directives and thought. He even proposed the withdrawal from the Geneva Convention protecting prisoners so as to stimulate last-minute resistance. At the beginning of March, he issued the threat that if soldiers were taken prisoner unwounded, their relatives at home would suffer for it; a few days later, he ordered that, before another yard of German territory be yielded up, all industrial establishments and supply depots should be destroyed regardless of even the bare necessities of life. On 15 April, he called on his troops on the Eastern Front to arrest, and, if necessary, kill on the spot, anyone ordering a retreat, no matter what his rank. His final admonition to his soldiers was devoid of all relevence: 'Form yourselves into a sworn brotherhood, to defend, not the empty conception of a Fatherland, but your homes, your wives, your children, and, with them, our future. In these hours, the whole German people looks to you, my fighters in the east, and only hopes that, thanks to your resolution and fanaticism, thanks to your weapons, and under your leadership, the Bolshevik assault will be choked in a bath of blood.'[45] Only fourteen days later Hitler shot himself, and a week later, on 7 May, the fighting in Europe was over. The German Army under its Commander-in-Chief, Adolf Hitler, had lost the war.

33

The Great Folly

*The possibility of a repetition of the absolute
command by one, ungifted amateur, surrounded by
weaklings, must be prevented for all time to come.*

GENERAL LUDWIG BECK
Chief of the General Staff, 1933–38

The Army's failure to mount any significant opposition to Hitler during the war has been subject to almost as much unfavourable comment by historians as has the lack before the war. Sir John Wheeler-Bennett is particularly damning; he condemned most of the generals for not having had anything to do with rebellion, and described their reaction after the Bomb Plot as 'a nadir of supine degradation'. He continued:

> 'To such a measure of abasement had attained that corps of whose independence of thought and action Ludendorff, in victory, and Seeckt, in defeat, had been so justly proud. The Nemesis of power, the destiny which its own ambition and lack of intellectual integrity had shaped, had at last overtaken it. And in how base a guise. . . . The futile failure of a few of their number to carry out what all had known to be necessary had left the corps fawning and frightened; fearful and unwilling to exercise any further claims to mental freedom. So had the mighty fallen.'[1]

Fine words, indeed, but misplaced. For the fault of the German generals, and fault there was, was not that they renounced the idea of a politically inspired coup, but that they forsook their military duty and allowed an amateur to direct even minor operations, ill-fitted though they knew him to be, both by training and by temperament, for this role.

In western society, a soldier is not a political animal; indeed, one of the fundamental pre-conditions of his service is that he should leave aside all forms of political activity. This idea was as strong in the Germany of the Third Reich as it is in Great Britain today. The German generals, imprisoned by their tradition, inhibited by their inexperience, and disadvantaged by the speed and decisiveness of events around them, had proved incapable of mounting any significant opposition to Hitler's tyranny before 1939;

during the war, this continued. Indeed, it was then less likely that the Army would attempt a coup; even defeat did not provide the opportunity for which the conspirators had waited with such expectation. The attitude of the great majority of generals may be understood by the following passage, taken from a document dated 19 November 1945, signed at Nuremberg by von Brauchitsch, Halder, von Manstein, Westphal, and Warlimont, the purpose of which was to provide 'in all frankness, a complete survey of all facts and events which were of importance for the German Army in the pertinent period before and during the war'. Part of it read:

> 'A group of officers decided to effect a radical change by killing Hitler [in July 1944]. The question whether this was the way to save Germany had undoubtedly been asked by many. Officers who had been educated in the Christian faith – and they were the overwhelming majority, particularly in the older generation – did not find a place in their creed for breaking their oath of allegiance or for murdering their commander. Others followed these considerations: the nation had given Hitler its confidence, and the majority in all probability still believed in him; therefore, a change of government would not result in a liberation leading to a democratic form of government, but to another form of coercion; the Army as a whole was not against Hitler; the SS, which had numerous units in the Army, was certainly closely bound to the NSDAP, therefore a civil war on the front and at home was inevitable, and that in face of the enemy. Germany's defeat would undoubtedly have been attributed to the Army. It could not be the task of the leading officers to break the backbone of the Army. It is the responsibility of a man who undertakes to change the government of his country to provide a new and better government, a new leader. The Army had been trained since the last war to keep entirely out of politics. It had now, in the hour of emergency, neither the men nor the means to take the political leadership of the nation into its hands.'[2]

As before the war, so during it; practical objections combined with moral ones to make all idea of a coup appear hopeless. Von Manstein, never a man to refrain from speaking his mind to the Supreme Commander, typified the dilemma of a senior officer:

> '. . . as one responsible for an army group in the field, I did not feel I had the right to contemplate a *coup d'état* in wartime because in my own view it would have led to an immediate collapse of the front, and, probably, to chaos inside Germany. Apart from this, there was always the question of the military oath and the admissibility of murder for political motives. As I said at my trial: "No senior military commander can for years on end expect his soldiers to lay down their lives for victory and then precipitate defeat by his own hand." '[3]

The generals, then, were quite incapable of mounting a coup against their Head of State; to expect them to have been otherwise is quite unreasonable. War, whether under conditions of victory or defeat, is not the time for soldiers to act in such a manner; its practice demands from them the most rigid adherence to their tradition of being above, and apart from, politics. War demands loyalty to the Head of State; it demands obedience and the elevation of the sanctity of the oath to even higher importance than in peace. If the German generals were non-political in the years up to 1939, how much more so would they be after, when their energies and concerns were so completely engaged in the serious and all-consuming business of fighting.

It can never be established with certainty just how much, during the war, the German generals knew of Hitler's dictatorship, which was taking on an ever-more hideous aspect. In 1941 the 'Final Solution' of European Jewry was begun, and the concentration camps became centres of mass extermination. At the same time security within the Reich was stricter, the prisons of the Gestapo were never fuller, and the power of the SS grew as each month passed. But few soldiers were aware of this. When far from home and in a foreign land, the general did not stop to consider for long, if at all, the plight of the slave labourers in the factories of the Reich who were turning out the weapons and munitions so vital for the troops who were being killed for the lack of them. Indeed, the general probably had little idea of conditions on the home front. Because of Hitler's order that no one was to be told anything other than that which directly concerned him, commanders hardly knew of events or plans beyond the flanks of their own commands, let alone of what was happening within the Reich. Rumours there might have been, but facts were few, and information came mainly from Goebbels's skilful propaganda machine. The soldier might feel that things were not all as they should be, but, like the mass of the German people, he did not know with certainty. He was denied the historian's advantage of hindsight, the ability to read the terrifying diatribes given by the Führer at his dinner table, the opportunity to look into the neat files of the Reichsführer SS, or the chance to visit Auschwitz, Treblinka, or a host of similar death camps.

However, the Army's knowledge of crimes within areas of its own competence was more definite. In Poland, for example, von Brauchitsch and Halder had known that the SS were sending in their *Einsatzgruppen* (Action Groups) with the aim of 'house-cleaning: Jews, intelligentsia, clergy, nobility'.[4] Such was General Blaskowitz's revulsion at what he saw in Poland that he made strong representations which incurred Hitler's lasting displeasure. Although an extremely able general, he was never again to receive promotion. In the Soviet Union, the soldiers witnessed many terrible atrocities by the SS and Party administrators. Indeed, the Army itself was not immune from the taint of the baser aspects of National Socialist ideology. As early as March 1941, the Army leaders understood from Hitler that the invasion of the east was a 'Clash of two ideologies. . . . Communism is an enormous danger. . . . This is a war of extermination. . . . We do not wage war to preserve the enemy.'⁵ The Army allowed the SS *Einsatzgruppen* into their area of operations, and accepted Hitler's notorious Commissar Order, which called for the immediate liquidation of captured Soviet political officials and leaders, if necessary by German soldiers. A month before the start of 'Barbarossa', OKH had drawn up an order which provided for the 'shooting in action or while fleeing' of all people 'who participate or want to participate in hostile acts, who by their behaviour constitute a direct threat to the troops, or who, by any act of theirs, resist the German Armed Forces',⁶ and on 6 June OKW instructed that:

> 'In the struggle against Bolshevism, the enemy's conduct will not be based on the principles of international law or humanity. In particular, hate-inspired, cruel and inhuman treatment of our prisoners-of-war must be expected from political commissars of all grades, who form the hard core of enemy resistance. These commissars are the originators of barbarous, Asiatic methods of warfare, and they must therefore be dealt with with all possible severity and dispatch . . . whether captured during battle, or whilst offering resistance, they must be shot at once.'⁷

Thus was the stage set for the war in the Soviet Union. In contrast with the practice in the west and in North Africa, brute hostility towards the innocent or the defenceless was not unknown in the German Army in the east. In October 1941, for example, von Reichenau ordered that 'Feeding inhabitants and prisoners of war, who do not work for the German Armed Forces, from army messes, is as much an act of misplaced humaneness as giving away bread or cigarettes. . . . The terror of German counter-measures must be greater than the menace of struggling Bolshevik remnants. . . .'⁸ In 1941 von Manstein, together with Küchler, von Reichenau, and Hoth, issued orders which stated: 'The soldier in the east is not merely a fighter according to the rules of war, but also a protagonist of a merciless racial idea, who must fully understand the necessity for hard, but just, punishment of Jewish sub-humanity'; he also insisted that 'the Jewish-Bolshevik system must be wiped out once and for all', and that the German soldier was to act 'as avenger for all the cruelties committed against him and the German people'.⁹ Although the generals did not propose mass extermination as a solution, many, aware of the actions of the SS *Einsatzgruppen,* preferred to turn a blind eye to its practice. Von Rundstedt, for example, issued an order forbidding his soldiers to watch or to photograph executions, and Busch, it is reported, when told that men and women were being shot outside his headquarters, merely told his adjutant to pull the curtains. Instances of active cooperation with the SS murder squads are more difficult to come by, although they are not unknown; for example, one report from the SS in the Ukraine, stated that the majority of their 55,432 executions recently carried out were Jewish prisoners-of-war handed over by the Army.

In its treatment of the five million Soviet prisoners-of-war, the German

Army was also ordered to mete out harsh treatment. An OKH instruction, dated 25 July 1941, laid down: 'In line with the prestige and dignity of the German Army, every German soldier must maintain distance and such an attitude with regard to Russian prisoners-of-war as takes account of the bitterness and inhuman brutality of the Russians in battle. . . . In particular, fleeing prisoners-of-war are to be shot without preliminary warning to stop.'[10] Three months later, the headquarters of 6th Army ordered that 'All prisoners who are slackers will be shot'.[11] Conditions within the camps in the first year of the invasion were indescribable; the Wehrmacht had not the resources to feed or clothe adequately its own fighting troops, let alone the three million Red Army prisoners taken in the five months up to December. Disease, starvation, and ill-treatment were rife; cannibalism was even resorted to by the prisoners. During the entire war, some three and a half million Soviet soldiers perished in captivity. Even the Party and the SS officials complained of this ill-treatment; one of them, the infamous 'Gestapo' Müller, wrote in November 1941 that 'The commandants of concentration camps complain that from five to ten per cent of the Soviet Russians slated for execution arrive in the camps dead or half-dead.'[12]

But there was a reverse side to the coin. Apart from isolated individual incidents, the German soldiers generally behaved well towards the conquered peoples of the east (or as well as any conscript army does in wartime). Military courts applied the letter of the law concerning pillage and maltreatment, often with considerable severity. Von Manstein issued orders which stipulated that 'The population of the occupied eastern territories . . . are to be treated as allies',[13] and ensured that appropriate agrarian, social welfare, educational, and administrative reforms be initiated. The Army economic authorities ordered that 'Care must . . . be taken that the working population in the countryside is treated decently and justly . . .'.[14] And, in early 1943, von Kleist also directed that 'The inhabitants of the occupied eastern territories in the area of Army Group A are to be treated as allies. Treatment as inferiors strengthens the enemy's will to resist and costs German blood.'[15] Such orders were indicative of the reaction by the Army to the methods with which it had begun the campaign. That it was, however, more for practical than for moral reasons, was indicated in May 1943, by the chief of staff to 2nd Army 'thus: 'We can master the wide Russian expanse which we have conquered only with the Russians and Ukrainians who live in it, never against their will.'[16] Terror was found to be counter-productive.

Many generals had been fearful of the consequences of the policy of harshness from the very beginning. Von Bock noted in his diary for 4 June 1941: 'An OKW order . . . framed in such a way as to give every soldier the right to shoot, from in front or behind, any Russian whom he suspects of being a guerrilla . . . is not acceptable and is not compatible with military discipline.'[17] On 8 June, von Brauchitsch ordered that commissars were to be dealt with only when it had first been shown that the individual in question had quite clearly acted against the Wehrmacht. On 11 June General Müller, employed for 'special duties' by the Commander-in-Chief of the Army, warned that harsh measures must not degenerate into a blood-bath. During 'Barbarossa' many field units neglected to implement the Commissar Order, and frequent protests at its application were made. Von Tresckow, for example, persuaded von Bock to ask the Army Command to have it revoked, and in September 1941 2nd Army reported that 'the effect of the punitive orders in regard to commissars and politicians was responsible, in part, for the enemy's tough resistance'.[18] Later that month, OKH asked OKW for some relaxation of the Commissar Order, but Hitler refused. By May 1942, however, he was forced to admit that the commissars should be spared 'in order to strengthen the inclination of the encircled Russian forces to desert and surrender'.[19] When he issued his Commando Order in October 1942, providing for the execution of those taking part in commando raids, Hitler recognised that this would arouse opposition within the Army, and that many would not carry it out. This was, he declared, the fault of OKH 'which wanted to turn professional soldiers into clergymen'.[20] Indeed, he was quite correct; in the desert Rommel destroyed the order on receipt, and in the west it was not implemented. When, in the autumn of 1941, Hitler issued orders concerning the shooting of hostages, the Army boycotted them; at Hitler's insistence that they should be observed, OKH declared that each case should be thoroughly investigated before the decision was taken. This procedure took a long time, and often no results were forthcoming. When Hitler specifically ordered that persons should be shot for a particular reprisal, commanding officers often chose those who had, in any case, been sentenced to death for other offences. As a result, it became necessary for the SS authorities to take such matters out of the Army's control.

The policy carried out by the Army in the east was a product of the general sickness that had affected all German society during Hitler's dictatorship. Communism was seen as a deadly enemy, the most serious threat to Germany; the Jews were understood to be its leaders, and the Slavs had, traditionally, been regarded with some suspicion, if not hostility. The Army's policy was initially motivated by these beliefs, and was designed to ensure success in the field and security in the rear areas. As von Manstein put it, 'the population must be more afraid of our reprisals than of the partisans'.[21] Thus, Hoepner, no friend of the National Socialists, could order his panzer group in 1941 to carry out the Commissar Order, and report on 10 July 1941 that his men had 'liquidated' no fewer than 101 commissars. If a man such as he, who was to pay with his life for his opposition to Hitler, ending his days hanging by piano wire from a meat-hook, could apply the Führer's orders in the Soviet Union, how much more could the rest of the strictly non-political generals?

But if, as Beck did in 1938, certain of the senior generals had understood the moral depravity of the National Socialist régime they served, and the depths to which they themselves were forced to sink, and if, thereupon, they had succeeded in breaking free from their tradition and had resolved upon destroying Hitler's tyranny, what could they have done? The answer must be: very little. Isolation and condemnation would have been their lot. Gone long-since was the close-knit unity of their class. As General Geyr von Schweppenburg wrote after the war:

> 'One thing is certain: during the last two hundred years of Prussian-German military history, no body of generals was ever so thoroughly divided, watered down, disunited and internally disintegrated as it was in the Third Reich. And this applied in hardly less measure to all the other classes and the professions. The people left it to the generals to perform the surgical task of healing. The people overlooked, and still do today, the fact that they themselves, their politicians, their intelligentsia, did too little to oppose, and so helped create the situation.'[22]

Even during the terrible years of defeat, when the Allied bombers pounded the Reich day and night, when reverse after reverse was reported from the front, and when the newspapers were full of lists of the dead, the German people did not desert their Führer. Disaffection grew, but remained very much with a minority. The vast majority of the junior officers and troops, who knew nothing of Hitler's military stupidity, and of the population, who remembered his achievements, still believed in the mystic aura of invincibility that had been created around him; the successes and victories of the years 1933 to 1942 could not be easily disregarded, and even some generals had fallen prey to the myth of the Führer's 'genius' in operational command. As late as mid-1944 defeat was by no means widely regarded as inevitable, and even for those who understood reality, the Allies' strong demand for 'unconditional surrender' made them stiffen their resolve to continue the fight. By comparison with Hitler's prestige, the generals knew that their own reputation in the nation was low. Without the promise of support from their troops, with the certainty of opposition from the SS and the Luftwaffe (which controlled the large number of anti-aircraft batteries within the Reich), and with the probability of their being rejected by the people, the military conspirators would have been foolish to move. The fear remained that, as in 1933, any attempt to remove Hitler might easily result in the horrors of an internecine struggle within the Reich; and this time it would come during a war, with the very real fear of a consequential collapse at the front – most dangerous of all, a collapse in the east, and the dominance of central Europe by the Soviets. This was a possibility even more abhorrent to the senior officers than the continuance of National Socialism as they knew it. Guderian wrote in his memoirs:

> 'Of course, one question will always be asked: what would have happened had the assassination succeeded? Nobody can answer this. Only one fact seems beyond dispute: at that time the great proportion of the German people still believed in Adolf Hitler and

would have been convinced that with his death the assassin had removed the only man who might still have been able to bring the war to a favourable conclusion. . . . The people's hatred and contempt would have turned against the soldiers who, in the midst of a national struggle for existence, had broken their oath, murdered the head of the government and left the storm-wracked ship of state without a captain at the helm. It also seems unlikely that our enemies would have treated us any better in consequence than they actually did after the collapse.'[23]

Thus, the Army did nothing to counter Hitler's dictatorship.

But if the generals had neither the reason nor the opportunity to mount politically inspired opposition to Hitler, there still remained a sound military cause for action against him. In late 1939 Hitler, the Head of State, broke with tradition by breaching the operational autonomy of the Army; he laid down how the generals were to conduct the campaign, first against the west, and later, against the Soviet Union. In December 1941, he made himself Commander-in-Chief of the Army, and came to control even the minor movements of the troops in the field. As von Rundstedt admitted in spring 1944: 'You see that guard posted outside. If I want to post him on the other side of the house, I must first ask permission of Berchtesgaden.'[24] Perhaps the most eloquent testimony of the military impotence of the generals is a conversation recorded between von Leeb and Halder during the Soviet winter counter-offensive of 1941–42. Von Leeb was protesting at Hitler's 'no withdrawal' policy which, he was sure, would lead to defeat if rigidly applied.

'Do you know, Halder', he said, 'that one can lose an army corps this way?'

Halder replied, lamely, 'Yes'.

Von Leeb continued:

'Do you know that one can lose a whole army this way?' to which came the answer, 'Yes'.

Pushing home his argument, von Leeb added: 'Do you know that one can lose a war this way?'

'Yes', Halder then replied with an air of tired resignation. 'But you know how it is, Herr Field-Marshal. . . . Nothing that you and I have had to learn counts for anything today.'[25]

The generals' acceptance of Hitler's dominance of operations was against both their tradition and their duty. Certainly, the Prusso-German officer had always accorded unlimited loyalty to his Head of State and titular Supreme Commander, but he had never given unquestioning submission to his military superior. Blind obedience, although a part of his political outlook, had no place in his soldierly ethic. This is illustrated by the story of General von Seydlitz, who, when ordered by Frederick the Great to attack the unbroken Russian infantry during the battle of Zorndorf in 1758, had refused, replying: 'Tell His Majesty that my head will be at his disposal after the battle, but that as long as the battle lasts I intend to use it in his service.'[26] A responsibility was laid upon each staff officer and commander to make known to his superiors his reasoned objections to orders, for it was held that such intellectual independence was healthy for both the development of his military abilities and for the progress of the Army in the field. It accorded with his understanding of duty, a duty which was owned not simply to his superiors, but to the troops under his own command. Responsibility and conscience counted for as much as obedience – that, after all, was why he had been made an officer in the first place. Thus, while a German officer had traditionally accepted the submergence of his individuality for the greater good of the Army, he did not hold that, in questions of military authority, he was a mere automaton.

But, within OKW before the war and in the Army during it, this tradition was debased. The personal oath the soldiers had sworn to Hitler as Head of State in August 1934 – at a time when his interference in the operational affairs of the Army was quite properly nil and appeared very likely to remain that way – came to be interpreted as obliging them as a point of honour to accept every order, however dangerous, made by Hitler as a military commander. The generals failed to distinguish between their political duty to Hitler as a Head of State, which demanded obedience, and their military duty as soldiers, which did not. Ever since Frederick the Great, the Head of State and Supreme Commander had taken no part in directing military operations; this, he had invariably left to his generals, the men whose training and experience uniquely qualified them for the job. The monarch and the politician might decide on which country to declare war, but they certainly did not order how the war should be fought. Political goals and military methods were vastly different. But this tradition, this logical and, hitherto, accepted division of responsibility, was ignored by Hitler, and made a mockery of. That he should have attempted to take over military command from his generals is not surprising; that they allowed him to do so with such ease is inexcusable.

The reasons for the German generals' abnegation of their military duty, and the betrayal of their tradition, are many. Certainly, the oath of loyalty sworn to Hitler held great significance for them, and they might not have cared to make such a firm distinction between political and military obedience; after all, the step from formulating grand strategy to directing military strategy, although significant, can also be relatively short, and, once taken, as it was in late 1939, it is difficult to reverse. Perhaps, too, there was a weakness of character common to the senior officers at that time, one hinted at by Guderian, who wrote: '. . . it is possible that [in selection] intellectual ability was sometimes overvalued in comparison to strength of character and particularly to warmth of personality. . . .'[27] Such men might well have been overawed by the speed and decisiveness of events, and, after 1938, by their continual harassment by Hitler; moreover, they might have become used to his dominance in those early years when his judgment always appeared right, and their own so mistaken. The occupation of the Rhineland, the annexation of Austria, the Czechoslovak affair, and the campaign in the west showed that Hitler's action had, in the short term, proved superior to their hesitation; it was only in the longer term, when it was too late, that the disastrous effects of the rushed rearmament and the embarking upon war, of which the generals had constantly warned, were to prove them to have been right. But by then Hitler had assured himself of his position over them; he had taken that short, yet vital, step from grand strategy to military strategy, and they had not opposed him. Some realised what had happened, but were powerless.

Thus it was that, with one exception, no senior serving general acted openly against Hitler during the war; not one corps, army, or army group commander was sufficiently convinced that the evil likely to result from a coup would be less than the actual evil of Hitler remaining in control. A number of generals and field-marshals were approached by the conspirators, and one in particular, von Kluge, was under constant pressure to declare his opposition and to act accordingly, but nothing came of it. In early 1942, a scheme had been conceived of by Beck, Goerdeler, and a number of others by which, they hoped, the field-marshals would declare against Hitler without violating their oath to him as Führer and Supreme Commander. The plan was that, at a prearranged moment, the field-marshals in the east, followed by those on other fronts, would assert their intention not to accept military orders given by Hitler in his new capacity as Commander-in-Chief of the Army. Thereupon, while the field-marshals fought on, the confusion would allow the Replacement Army to seize control of the Reich, depose Hitler, dissolve the National Socialist state, and restore the independence of the Army. Of all the senior commanders, only von Witzleben, Commander-in-Chief, West, was prepared to act, and to do so even without the support of his colleagues in the east; but his intention came to nothing because, when he took sick leave on account of haemorrhoids, Hitler decided to retire him and place him on the reserve. Von Witzleben was thus relegated to the distinguished company of men such as Beck, von Hammerstein, and Hoepner – men committed to action but without the power of command.

A second attempt to goad the field-marshals into action was taken against the background of the disaster at Stalingrad; the conspirators hoped that the defeats in the east and in North Africa would make it clear to both the generals and to the German people that the war was lost, and that the only hope for the future lay in the overthrow of Hitler's government while the German Army still remained intact. The plan called for von Paulus, before surrendering at Stalingrad, to exhort the German Army and people to destroy the régime that was so wantonly sacrificing thousands upon thousands of men in a fruitless struggle. Von Manstein and von Kluge were then to demand from Hitler that the command of the Eastern Front henceforth be vested in them, after which the already planned action in the west and in the Reich would follow. In the end, von Paulus did not cooperate, and von Manstein, disgusted by the way the commander of 6th Army had conducted operations while encircled, reaffirmed his allegiance to Hitler, as also did von Kluge, who was, as usual, fearful for the safety of his family.

The only senior general who acted as his conscience and military duty dictated was Zeitzler. A man neglected by historians, he was, nevertheless, one of the bravest of the generals who faced Hitler – perhaps the bravest. He alone took his disillusion with Hitler's military command to its logical conclusion: a refusal to continue in service. After the war, Zeitzler told his captors:

> 'After a few months in my new position I realised that in the Chief of the General Staff Adolf Hitler did not want an adviser in the proper sense, but a man who forwarded only his (Hitler's) views and orders unconditionally, who fought for his ideas without criticism, and made propaganda for him and his leadership. This filled me – a young general – with deep anxiety for the future, and I foresaw bitter struggles in my position, as I . . . could not and would not take part in anything against my inner conviction and against my conscience.'[28]

By the spring of 1944, Zeitzler had come to the conclusion that he could continue in his position no more. The immediate cause of the break was over the impending encirclement of Army Group Courland, which Hitler, with his insistence on 'no withdrawal', was making inevitable against all advice from his Chief of General Staff. At the end of June and the beginning of July, Zeitzler had several private interviews with his Führer, the last of which he recalled thus:

> 'I told him that I could not be a party to the encirclement of the Army Group Courland. It would be lost to no purpose in the same way as the Stalingrad Army and parts of the army in Crimea, where I had been against his policy right from the start. This made him lose his temper. He became very loud, and broke off the interview with the words: "I bear the responsibility and not you." I replied just as loudly: "In the same way as you, my Führer, are responsible to the German people, I am responsible to my conscience. And nobody can relieve me of that responsibility, not even you, my Führer." He thereupon became pale with rage. I was prepared for anything. However, he tried to make me come round, and wanted to break off the interview. I did not permit this, and told him something like this: Even though I was not the adviser on over-all strategy, I nevertheless had to regard the position in the east in the light of over-all strategy, and I therefore considered it my duty to tell him that it was impossible to win the war by military means. Something had to be

done. (I meant some political action.) He then started roaring. Because nobody had told him that before. He spoke of defeatism and railed at the General Staff. I told him just as excitedly, that I had asked him already four times to be allowed to resign, now I demanded for the fifth time to be sent away at last, as I could not take part in all this any longer. Then he said to me: "I see, criticism from below, and no criticism from above." That in his eyes was a serious offence against a basic principle of National Socialism. That was the end. It was the last time that I saw and spoke to Adolf Hitler. From that moment onward I did not do any more duty. I reported sick immediately.'[29]

Five months later Zeitzler was discharged from the Army, and, as a punishment, deprived of the right to wear uniform. But Zeitzler's act, however brave, was, like Beck's six years before, isolated and achieved nothing. New men could always be found to fill their places, men who might argue but never act.

In 1944, the only serving field-marshal who seemed prepared to act against Hitler was Rommel. After his unhappy experience of the Führer's interference during the North African campaign, and on his return to Europe in March 1943, where he came to the conclusion that total victory was now beyond Germany's grasp, Rommel became increasingly disillusioned. The conspirators went to work on him at the end of 1943, after he had become commander of Army Group B in the west, and by March 1944 it seemed as if Rommel was set against Hitler. However, he differed from the conspirators by believing that it was foolish to do away with Hitler, fearing that the Führer's aura and also his political aides would still remain strong after his death; instead he argued that, once it was clear that the Allies had secured a foothold on the Continent, the soldiers in the west should negotiate a surrender and allow an immediate Allied occupation which would keep the Soviets out of Germany. Such was his plan, and he described the attempt of 20 July as 'stupid'.[30] How Rommel would have acted, however, is pure speculation, for, on 17 July, he suffered severe wounds from an air attack and was invalided home. After the Bomb Plot, evidence was gathered that revealed his links with the conspirators, and Hitler ordered his death; on 14 October, two generals arrived at Rommel's home, took him away in their car, and gave him poison with which to kill himself. To avoid difficulties for his family, the Field-Marshal did as he was requested. For propaganda reasons the real cause of his death was kept secret, and the German nation, told that he had finally succumbed to his wounds, was treated to the spectacle of his state funeral.

After the war, a number of generals attempted to justify their quiescent role. Westphal, for example, wrote:

'It was by no means the case that the Army commanders took everything without resistance. . . . If this had been so, Hitler would have had no reason to mistrust them. . . . A proof that the Army leaders were not all blind yes-men is given by these figures: of eighteen field-marshals of the Army, nine were, one after the other, dismissed from their posts . . . three more paid the death penalty after 20 July . . . and only two – Keitel and Schörner – remained in service to the end. . . . The Generalobersts were in a similar case. . . . only a few remained in service to the end without being called to book [twenty-one had been dismissed, three of whom were executed after 20 July].'

Westphal dismissed their failure thus:

'Of course, they believed that a limit was set to their resistance to Hitler by their duty of military obedience, which, in Montgomery's opinion, too, remains undivided. According to law, all officers . . . were liable to service [and] . . . could no more refuse service than could the ordinary soldier or conscripted reservist. If they are reproached with not having thrown away their arms, then in fairness the same reproach must be levelled against the scientists and inventors who worked for the war effort, the munition workers, the railwaymen etc., because they did not go on strike. It was their fate that they were delivered over, like the whole nation, into the hands of a man who was a master in exploiting the loyalty, faith, and political inexperience of the people.'[31]

But Westphal was wrong; there were limits to military obedience, and the position of the generals was not similar to that of scientists or railwaymen, especially not in relation to Hitler's interference. That interference resulted in the deaths of hundreds of thousands of men, and, ultimately, in the defeat of the nation.

Whether or not action against Hitler for purely military reasons would have been successful is hypothetical. There were the same practical restraints on an armed coup as pertained to one on political grounds, and, certainly, individual actions such as the offers of resignation of von Brauchitsch, Zeitzler, von Leeb, and others had no effect – the dictator would heed such actions only if it suited him. Some form of collective move was required, such as a mass resignation or a unanimous refusal to acknowledge Hitler's position as Commander-in-Chief. General Dittmar believed that 'Perhaps Hitler's destructive influence could have been held in bounds if he had from the first step been up against a counter-poise of the highest military leadership, one with a united front, firmly holding to its traditions and acting according to its conviction.'[32] Apologists have pointed to the many inhibitions to such a course in reality, foremost among which was the lack of unity among the generals, but that is not the point at issue here. What is a fact is that, in the face of this direct threat to their position and responsibility, the generals failed to unite and mount any opposition to

Hitler's usurpation. Indeed, as far as the evidence shows, such a move was not even discussed by the Army leaders after 12 November 1939, when Halder's plans for a coup were dropped so hastily. Thus, apart from a very few, isolated exceptions, the German generals failed to distinguish between their duty to their Head of State and their duty to their profession. The rigid obedience that they held should guide their actions perverted their sense of responsibility, distorted their tradition, strained their honour, and dulled their conscience. Although they were men of great professional experience and, on the whole, of high standards of personal morality, they prostituted their talent to Hitler's megalomaniac will, and allowed the militarily unskilled dictator to disregard their ethics and to neglect their well-founded strategic principles. For this, they received nothing but his contempt. Their knowing acceptance of the substitution of his dangerous amateurism for their sound expertise deserves also the contempt of history. There lay the greatest folly in the history of the German Army.

FINIS

APPENDIX

Organisation of the German Army, September 1939

On mobilisation in 1939, in accordance with the division of the Army into Field and Replacement Armies, the OKH also split into a field headquarters and a home command based in Berlin. The Commander of the Replacement Army (*Befehlshaber des Ersatzheeres*) was appointed to take control of the home command. The field headquarters comprised the Army General Staff and the Army Personnel Office, while the Commander of the Replacement Army had control of the General Army Office, the Army Ordnance Office, the Army Administration Office, the Inspector of Officer Cadet Courses, the Inspectors of Arms and Services (removed from the General Army Office on mobilisation), and the Chief of Army Judicature (a new post held by the same man as headed the Army Legal Branch in the General Army Office). The office of Chief of Mobile Troops was disbanded.

There were differences in the wartime organisation of the Army General Staff. The *Oberquartiermeister* I no longer had any branches directly subordinated to him but instead became deputy to the Chief of the Army General Staff and represented him in his absence; he was assigned specific duties from time to time. In addition, *Oberquartiermeisters* II and III were removed from the establishment altogether. Such reorganisation necessitated many changes, among which was the elevation of the Operations Branch to the status of an independent agency within the General Staff. Previously it had been linked with the branches of transport, supply and administration, topography, and fortifications under the *Oberquartiermeister* I. Furthermore, the General Staff also was divided into two – a field headquarters and a rear echelon.

The organisation of the Field Army was logical and simple. The highest field command was the *army group,* composed of two or more *armies,* each formed of two or more *army corps,* which, in their turn, were made up of two or more *divisions*, the largest homogeneous units of the Army capable of acting independently. Flexibility was the outstanding characteristic of this organisation, with divisions, army corps, and armies frequently being moved from one grouping to another as operational requirements and opportunities dictated. Seldom were there more than three divisions in one army corps, more than four army corps in one army, or more than three armies in one army group. Attached to the army corps, armies, and army groups were service, administrative, and fighting troops (army troops), including heavy artillery and engineers, required to support large formations in the field. Some divisions and army corps were held in reserve, either under the control of army groups or armies, or under the direct supervision of the Army High Command for allocation to the field commands as circumstances dictated.

The most important field unit of the Army was the division, the largest possible self-contained formation with a balanced composition of arms able to support itself in the field. In 1939 there were five distinct types of division – infantry, motorised infantry, mountain, light, and armoured. The thirty-five First Wave infantry divisions each had a total strength of 17,700 men, the majority of whom were distributed among three infantry regiments, each of three battalions, an infantry gun company, and an anti-tank company. The battalions were four-company organisations, the fourth filling the role of a heavy weapons company. The other divisional units consisted of an artillery regiment, and anti-tank, reconnaissance, pioneer, signals, and replacement battalions, and supply, administrative, and medical services. Thus, an infantry divison of the First Wave possessed armament of 378 light and 138 heavy machine-guns, 93 light and 54 medium mortars, 20 light and 6 heavy infantry guns, 75 anti-tank guns, 36 light and 12 heavy field howitzers, 12 light anti-aircraft guns and 3 armoured cars. Divisions of the Second Wave varied little from this, but possessed 2,460 fewer men, 33 fewer light and 24 fewer heavy machine-guns and, in common with the Third and Fourth Waves, no mortars, heavy infantry guns, or light anti-aircraft guns. (The First Wave were the only divisions in the entire Army to possess heavy infantry guns.) Only in light infantry guns were the Second Wave superior to the First, having 26 instead of 20. The formations of the Third and Fourth Waves, while varying from the thirty-five 'model' active divisions, possessed the basic organisation common to all infantry divisions. The Third Wave divisions had 17,900 men, the Fourth only 15,020; both had exactly the same equipment levels as those of the Second Wave with the only exceptions being in the number of machine-guns and in the complete lack of armoured cars.

The three mountain divisions resembled the standard infantry divisions, but were not organised uniformly. The authorised strength of such formations was 17,180, and the scale of equipment was considerably lower than that of First Wave divisions – only 275 light and 72 heavy machine-guns, 66 light and 36 medium mortars, 12 light and no heavy infantry guns, 48 anti-tank guns, 16 light (mountain) and 8 heavy field howitzers, and no anti-aircraft guns or armoured cars. The four motorised infantry divisions were smaller than the First Wave formations by some 1,280 men, although organised along almost identical lines, and they had a lower scale of equipment in all but light infantry guns (24) and armoured cars (30).

The four light divisions differed from the infantry in their organisation quite considerably, their strengths being approximately 11,000, the lowest for any similar formation. Basically, however, they might be considered as low-strength motorised infantry divisions with a 'stiffener' of eighty-six tanks organised into a tank battalion. The six armoured divisions likewise differed considerably in their organisation, but essentially they consisted of one tank brigade of two four-battalion, regiments, one motorised infantry brigade of one regiment, and one motorcycle battalion, as well as an artillery regiment (devoid of heavy field artillery), an anti-tank battalion, a reconnaissance battalion, an engineer battalion, and signal, supply, administrative, and medical units. The average of 11,790 men were equipped with 328 tanks, 101 armoured cars, 180 light and 46 heavy machine-guns, 30 light and 18 medium mortars, 8 light infantry guns, 48 anti-tank guns, 16 light and 8 heavy field howitzers, four 10cm cannons (the only formations so armed), and 12 light anti-aircraft guns. Thus, apart from special equipment, general armament levels of the panzer divisions were on the low side.

A Note on Sources

I have relied upon a wide range of sources, both original and secondary, and have drawn as much on many of the well-known works on the period as on the fine collections of documents found in the archives of the Imperial War Museum (IWM), the Public Record Office (PRO) and the Liddell Hart Papers (LHP). Of particular use have been the collection of captured German documents found in the IWM, and the interrogation reports and translations of documents prepared for the War Crimes Military Tribunal in 1945 and 1946, found in the LHP.

I have made extensive use of quotations, and would like to place on record my indebtedness to the following published works which must be regarded as basic texts for all students of the German Army:

Heinz Guderian, *Panzer Leader*, Michael Joseph, 1952.
Wilhelm Keitel, *Memoirs*, with introduction and epilogue by Walter Görlitz, William Kimber, 1965.
Albert Kesselring, *Memoirs*, Kimber, 1953.
B. H. Liddell Hart, *The Other Side of the Hill* (revised), Cassell, 1951.
Erich von Manstein, *Lost Victories*, Methuen, 1958.
Erwin Rommel, edited by B. H. Liddell Hart, *The Rommel Papers*, Collins, 1953.
Walter Warlimont, *Inside Hitler's Headquarters*, Weidenfeld and Nicolson, 1964.
Siegfried Westphal, *The German Army in the West*, Cassell, 1951.

My quotations from men such as Halder, Jodl and Zeitzler come from translations of captured documents and interrogation reports.

I also owe a great deal to the information contained in books by the following authors: B. H. Liddell Hart, J. F. C. Fuller, R. O'Neill, J. Wheeler-Bennett, K. Demeter, H. Deutsch and H. Rosinski.

I should also like to thank two Americans, John Calder and Otto Kuhn, for making available to me their, as yet, unpublished manuscripts on the German Army 1933 to 1939; although much of their material can be found in published works, their compilations are of considerable value to a researcher.

Notes

PART 1   *The Political Destiny of the German Army, 1933–39*

1   *Political Heritage*

1. Gordon Craig, *The Politics of the German Army 1640–1945*, London, 1955, p. 229.
2. *Official Record of the Trial of the Major War Criminals before the International Military Tribunal*, Nuremberg, 1947–49, Vol. 22, p. 522.
3. Walter Warlimont, *Inside Hitler's Headquarters 1939–45*, London, 1964, pp. ix–x.
4. B. H. Liddell Hart, *The Other Side of the Hill*, London, 1951, p. 51.
5. LHP, files on German generals.
6. Ibid., quoted from Wolfgang Forster, *Ein General Kämpft gegen der Krieg*, Munich, 1949, p. 39.
7. John Wheeler-Bennett, *Nemesis of Power*, London, 1964, p. 9.
8. Plato, *Laws XII*, taken from OKW, *Glückhäfte Strategie*, Berlin, 1942.
9. Karl Demeter, *The German Officer Corps in Society and State, 1650–1945*, London, 1965, p. 168.
10. Berghahn, *The Approach of the First World War*, London, 1973, p. 10.
11. Author's collection, Gestapo interrogation of Hans Oster, 1944 (also in Demeter).
12. Demeter, p. 165.
13. Author's collection, Oster interrogation.
14. Herbert Rosinski, *The German Army*, New York, 1966, p. 165 (quoting Seeckt).
15. Demeter, p. 357.
16. Hans von Seeckt, *Thoughts of a Soldier*, London, 1930, pp. 79–80.
17. Author's collection, Oster interrogation.
18. Siegfried Westphal, *The German Army in the West*, London, 1951, p. 4.
19. Demeter, p. 358.
20. Ibid., p. 357.
21. Westphal, p. 3.
22. Author's collection, Oster interrogation.
23. Wilhelm Keitel, *The Memoirs of Field-Marshal Keitel*, London, 1965, p. 243.
24. Demeter, pp. 195–6.
25. Rosinski, pp. 131–2.
26. LHP, files on German generals.
27. Author's collection, Oster interrogation.
28. Craig, p. 388.
29. Wheeler-Bennett, p. 200.
30. Ibid., p. 213.
31. Ibid., p. 225.
32. Ibid., pp. 285–6.

2   First Years

1. LHP, extracts from Hitler's speeches etc.
2. Adolf Hitler, *Hitler's Secret Book*, New York, 1952, p. 85.
3. Hermann Rauschning, *Hitler Speaks*, London, 1939, p. 20.
4. Ibid., p. 16.
5. Ibid., p. 20.
6. Heinz Guderian, *Panzer Leader*, New York, 1957, p. 384.
7. Ibid., p. 387.
8. Joachim Fest, *The Face of the Third Reich*, London, 1972, p. 362.
9. Ibid., p. 358.
10. Ibid., p. 358.
11. Wheeler-Bennett, p. 291.
12. Craig, p. 470.
13. Friedrich Hossbach, *Zwischen Wehrmacht und Hitler*, Hanover, 1949, p. 103.
14. Robert O'Neill, *The German Army and the Nazi Party, 1933–39*, London, 1966, pp. 141–2.
15. Ibid., p. 93.
16. Adolf Hitler, *My New Order* (Speeches), New York, 1941, p. 397.
17. Fest, p. 358.
18. Unpublished manuscript, Otto Kuhn, dated 1973, concerning the SA and SS 1920–39; also quoted in Heinz Höhne, *Order of the Death's Head*, London, 1969.
19. Ibid.
20. Ibid.
21. Ibid.
22. O'Neill, p. 63.
23. Demeter, p. 202.
24. O'Neill, pp. 66–8.
25. Höhne, p. 96.
26. O'Neill, p. 70.
27. Ibid., p. 81.
28. Ibid., p. 138.
29. Hossbach, p. 76.
30. Telford Taylor, *Sword and Swastika*, London, 1953, p. 154.
31. Warlimont, p. 10.
32. LHP, files on German generals; also quoted by O'Neill.
33. O'Neill, p. 48.
34. Harold Deutsch, *Hitler and his Generals*, Minneapolis, 1974, pp. 25–6.
35. O'Neill, p. 50.
36. Westphal, p. 45.

3   Alliance

1. Taylor, pp. 117–8.
2. Westphal, p. 7.
3. Fest, p. 360.
4. Demeter, p. 203.
5. Ibid., p. 203.
6. O'Neill, p. 76.
7. Wheeler-Bennett, p. 394.
8. Demeter, pp. 152–3.
9. O'Neill, p. 86.
10. LHP, files on German generals.
11. O'Neill, p. 90.
12. Ibid., p. 96.
13. Ibid., p. 96.
14. Unpublished collection, dated 1970, of Reichswehr and Wehrmacht Orders and Decrees, by John Calder; also quoted by O'Neill.
15. Ibid.
16. Ibid.
17. Demeter, p. 210.
18. Calder; also quoted by O'Neill.
19. Ibid.
20. O'Neill, p. 112.
21. Ibid., p. 113.
22. Calder; also quoted by O'Neill.
23. Ibid.

4   Independence

1. Adolf Hitler, *Hitler's Secret Conversations*, 1941–44, New York, 1953, p. 403.
2. Taylor, pp. 117–8.
3. Erich von Manstein, *Lost Victories*, London, 1958, p. 77.
4. Hossbach, p. 77.
5. Taylor, pp. 153–4.
6. Alan Bullock, *A Study in Tyranny*, London, 1962, p. 405.
7. Ibid., p. 339.
8. Taylor, p. 119.
9. Bullock, p. 307.
10. Deutsch, p. 31.

11. Ibid., p. 23.
12. Wheeler-Bennett, p. 325.
13. Kuhn, unpublished manuscript.
14. Ibid.
15. George Stein, *The Waffen SS,* Oxford, 1966, p. 11.
16. O'Neill, p. 149.
17. Kuhn, unpublished manuscript.
18. Helmut Krausnick *et al., Anatomy of the SS State,* Collins, 1968, pp. 262–3 (Chapter 2, by Hans Buchheim).
19. Taylor, p. 121.
20. Westphal, p. 6.
21. Ibid., p. 8.
22. Calder, unpublished manuscript; also quoted by O'Neill.
23. O'Neill, p. 112.
24. Calder, unpublished manuscript.
25. O'Neill, p. 253.
26. Ibid., p. 144.
27. Calder, unpublished manuscript; also quoted by O'Neill.
28. O'Neill, p. 101.
29. Calder, unpublished manuscript; also quoted by O'Neill.
30. LHP, files on German generals.
31. O'Neill, p. 127.
32. Fest, p. 363.
33. O'Neill, p. 129.
34. Fest, p. 363.
35. Calder, unpublished manuscript; also quoted by O'Neill.
36. O'Neill, p. 172.
37. Ibid., p. 172.
38. Ibid., p. 180.
39. Ibid., p. 180.
40. Ibid., p. 181.
41. Herbert Mason, *The Rise of the Luftwaffe,* London, 1925, p. 97.
42. Ibid., p. 210.
43. Bullock, p. 345.
44. Deutsch, p. 38.
45. Wheeler-Bennett, p. 290.
46. Manstein, p. 78.
47. Keitel, pp. 36–7.
48. Warlimont, p. 10.
49. Author's collection, Hossbach memorandum.
50. Ibid.
51. Warlimont, p. 10.

5 Crisis

1. Höhne, p. 243.
2. Ibid., p. 243.
3. Deutsch, p. 115.
4. Höhne, p. 245.
5. Ibid., p. 245.
6. Warlimont, p. 13.
7. Wheeler-Bennett, p. 367.
8. Höhne, p. 244.
9. Fest, p. 365.
10. Wheeler-Bennett, p. 694.
11. Guderian, p. 30.
12. Westphal, p. 24.
13. Fest, p. 557.
14. Guderian, p. 30.
15. Kenneth Macksey, *Guderian: Panzer General,* London, 1975.
16. Guderian, p. 28.
17. Deutsch, p. 417.
18. O'Neill, p. 199.
19. Deutsch, p. 420.
20. Guderian, p. 30.
21. Deutsch, p. 250.
22. Walter Schellenberg: *Schellenberg,* London, 1958, pp. 14–5.
23. Deutsch, p. 213.
24. Ibid., p. 417.
25. Harold Deutsch, *The Conspiracy against Hitler in the Twilight War,* Minneapolis, 1968, p. 62.
26. Deutsch, *Hitler and his Generals,* p. 254.
27. Wheeler-Bennett, p. 393.
28. Deutsch, *Hitler and his Generals,* p. 404.
29. Ibid., p. 403.
30. Ibid., p. 404.
31. Ibid., p. 405.
32. Ibid., p. 410.
33. Fest, p. 365.
34. Deutsch, *Hitler and his Generals,* p. 408.

6 The First Shackles

1. Wheeler-Bennett, p. 372.
2. Mason, p. 96.

3. Manstein, p. 75.
4. Ibid., pp. 75–6.
5. Deutsch, *Hitler and his Generals*, p. 221.
6. Ibid., p. 230.
7. Deutsch, *Twilight War*, p. 34.
8. Ibid., p. 34.
9. Deutsch, *Hitler and his Generals*, p. 280
10. O'Neill, p. 207.
11. Calder, unpublished manuscript: also quoted by O'Neill.
12. O'Neill, p. 160.
13. Warlimont, p. 8.
14. Ibid., p. 9.
15. Ibid., p. 17.
16. Guderian, pp. 387–8.
17. Keitel, p. 52.
18. Deutsch, *Hitler and his Generals*, p. 132.
19. Ibid., p. 214.
20. Keitel, p. 15.
21. Albert Speer, *Inside the Third Reich*, London, 1971, p. 164.
22. Ibid., p. 339.
23. Ibid., p. 339.
24. Hugh Trevor-Roper, *The Last Days of Hitler*, London, 1952, p. 61.
25. Keitel, p. 28.
26. Warlimont, p. 13.
27. Guderian, p. 388.
28. Percy Schramm, *Hitler: The Man and the Military Commander*, London, 1972, p. 193.
29. Speer, p. 339.
30. Westphal, p. 52.
31. Jodl, KTB, 10 Aug. 1938.
32. Warlimont, p. 59.
33. Ibid., p. 46.
34. U.S. War Department, *Handbook of German Military Forces*, Washington, 1941, p. 15.
35. Warlimont, p. 3.
36. Guderian, pp. 364–5.
37. Warlimont, p. 17.
38. Ibid., p. 14.
39. Ibid., p. 17.
40. Ibid., p. 21.
41. Ibid., p. 25.

7 Road to War

1. Keitel, p. 58.
2. Ibid., pp. 58–9.
3. William Shirer, *The Rise and Fall of the Third Reich*, London, 1964, p. 437.
4. Bullock, p. 446.
5. Wheeler-Bennett, p. 398.
6. Ibid., p. 399.
7. O'Neill, p. 219.
8. Wheeler-Bennett, p. 401.
9. Ibid., p. 400.
10. Ibid., p. 404.
11. O'Neill, pp. 200–1.
12. Keitel, p. 66.
13. Shirer, p. 454.
14. Barry Leach, *German Strategy against Russia, 1939–41*, London, 1973, p. 33.
15. Manstein, p. 80.
16. Deutsch, *Twilight War*, p. 31.
17. Ibid., p. 34.
18. Manstein, pp. 80–1.
19. Warlimont, p. 18.
20. Keitel, p. 69.
21. O'Neill, p. 229.
22. Deutsch, *Twilight War*, p. 38.
23. Bullock, p. 464.
24. Shirer, p. 554.
25. Karl Bracher, *The German Dictatorship*, New York, 1970, p. 392.
26. Shirer, p. 554.
27. Ibid., p. 554.
28. Deutsch, *Hitler and his Generals*, p. 395.
29. Bracher, p. 489.
30. Ibid., p. 490.
31. Westphal, p. 23.
32. Ibid., p. 23.
33. Keitel, p. 73.
34. Ibid., p. 246.
35. O'Neill, p. 226.
36. Manstein, p. 77.
37. Warlimont, p. 16.
38. Ibid., p. 17.
39. Wheeler-Bennett, p. 425.
40. Shirer, p. 570.
41. Ibid., pp. 590–2.

42. Ibid., p. 605.
43. Wheeler-Bennett, p. 228.
44. Manstein, pp. 23–4.
45. Shirer, pp. 641–5.

46. Keitel, p. 87.
47. Manstein, p. 30.
48. Wheeler-Bennett, p. 451.
49. Ibid., p. 451.

PART 2 *The Battle of Ideas*

8 *The Myth*

1. Winston S. Churchill, *History of the Second World War*, Vol. 1, London, 1949, pp. 3–4.
2. Tom Wintringham, *New Ways of War*, London, 1940, p. 5.
3. F. O. Miksche, *Blitzkrieg*, London, 1941, p. 24.
4. J. R. Lester, *Tank Warfare*, London, 1943, p. 64.
5. B. H. Liddell Hart, *History of the Second World War*, London, 1970, p. 22.
6. Ibid., p. 66.
7. J. F. C. Fuller, *Decisive Battles of the Western World*, Vol. 3, London, 1956, pp. 381–2.
8. LHP, letter from Liddell Hart to Guderian, dated 7 Oct. 1948.
9. Larry Addington, *The Blitzkrieg Era and the German General Staff*, New Brunswick, 1971, p. 234.
10. Guderian, p. 385.
11 Hermann Rauschning, *Hitler Speaks*, London, 1939, p. 182.
12. Max Werner, *Military Strength of the Powers*, London, 1939, p. 154.
13. J. Benoist-Méchin, *Sixty Days That Shook the West*, London, 1963, p. 43.
14. B. H. Liddell Hart, *The Other Side of the Hill*, London, 1951, p. 27.
15. Ibid., p. 23.
16. Mason, p. 90.
17. Demeter, p. 51.
18. Erich von Ludendorff, *The Nation At War*, London, 1936, pp. 87–9.
19. Adolf Hitler, *My New Order*, New York, 1941, pp. 116–7.

9 *The War Lord*

1. Wheeler-Bennett, p. 290.
2. Rauschning, p. 230.
3. Adolf Hitler, *Mein Kampf*, London, 1938, pp. 523–31.
4. Ibid., p. 11.
5. Wheeler-Bennett, p. 290.
6. Schramm, p. 197.
7. John Strawson, *Hitler as a Military Commander*, London, 1971, p. 241.
8. Franz Halder, *Hitler as Warlord*, London, 1950, p. 70.
9. Schramm, p. 103.
10. Ibid., p. 108.
11. Manstein, p. 276.
12. LHP, file on Hitler and his generals.
13. Hermann Rauschning, pp. 16–21.
14. J. F. C. Fuller, *Machine Warfare*, London, 1942, p. 28.
15. J. F. C. Fuller, *Conduct of War*, London, 1961, p. 244.
16. Rauschning, p. 17.
17. Ibid., pp. 15–6.
18. Craig, p. 441.

10 *Strategic Tradition*

1. Wheeler-Bennett, p. 338.
2. Shirer, p. 352.
3. Fuller, *Conduct of War*, pp. 117–8.
4. Ibid., p. 118.
5. Edward Mead Earle, *Makers of Modern Strategy*, London, 1948, p. 180.
6. Ibid., p. 183.
7. Liddell Hart, *The Other Side of the Hill*, p. 29.
8. Seeckt, pp. 63–4.
9. Ibid., p. 24.

10. Liddell Hart, *The Other Side of the Hill*, p. 29.
11. LHP, letter from von Manstein to Liddell Hart, dated 25 Jan. 1958.
12. OKH, *Die Truppenführung*, HDV 300, 1937, p. 1, para. 2.
13. Ibid., para. 339.
14. E. Middeldorf, *Taktik im Russland-feldzug*, Berlin, 1956, p. 10.
15. OKW, *Glückhäfte Strategie*, Berlin, 1942, p. 92.
16. Fuller, *Machine Warfare*, pp. 39–40.

11 *Strategic Revolution*

1. Wintringham, pp. 28–9.
2. Fuller, *Conduct of War*, p. 243.
3. Liddell Hart, *The Other Side of the Hill*, pp. 65–75.
4. Guderian, p. 13.
5. Werner, p.
6. Guderian, 1937, reprinted in *Armor*, Nov.–Dec. 1952, pp. 54–6.
7. Guderian, p.
8. Erwin Rommel, *Rommel Papers*, London, 1953, p. 299.
9. Guderian, *Militär Wissenschaftliche Rundschau*, 15 Oct. 1936, p. 10.
10. LHP, Guderian, 1936.
11. Guderian, 1937, reprinted in *Armor*, Nov.–Dec. 1952, pp. 54–6.
12. Fuller, *Conduct of War*, p. 257.
13. LHP, Guderian, 1936.

14. Guderian, pp. 383–4.
15. Liddell Hart, *The Other Side of the Hill*, p. 122.
16. Rommel, p. 517.
17. Guderian, pp. 21–2.
18. Liddell Hart, *The Other Side of the Hill*, p. 69.
19. Guderian, p. 20.
20. Westphal, p. 37.
21. Guderian, p. 69.
22. Ibid., p. 21.
23. Macksey, p. 58.
24. Guderian, pp. 62–3.
25. Guderian, *Militär Wochenblatt*, 28 Oct. 1934.
26. Rommel, p. 517.
27. Liddell Hart, *The Other Side of the Hill*, p. 66.
28. Ibid., p. 71.
29. Halder, *Kriegstagebuch* (KTB), 27 Aug. 1941.
30. Guderian, p. 24.
31. Ibid., p. 17.
32. Ibid., p. 26.
33. Ibid., p. 44.

12 *Unreadiness*

1. Demeter, p. 107.
2. LHP, files on German generals.
3. Westphal, p. 36.
4. Ibid., pp. 36–9.
5. Ibid., p. 37.

PART 3 *The Years of Victory*

13 *Poland*

1. Friedrich Heiss, *Der Sieg im Osten*, Berlin, 1940, p. 19.
2. Ibid., p. 15.
3. IWM, AL 1446.
4. Heiss, p. 119.
5. Ibid., p. 18.
6. Ibid., p. 18.
7. Manstein, pp., 62–3.
8. LHP, letter from Guderian to Liddell Hart, dated 20 Dec. 1949.

9. Liddell Hart, *History of the Second World War*, pp. 29–30.
10. IWM, AL 1448.
11. Ibid.

14 *Military Impotence*

1. Warlimont, p. 5.
2. Halder, *Kriegstagebuch* (KTB), 24 Aug. 1939.
3. Ibid., undated entry at end of the first volume (ends 10 Sept. 1939).

4. Ibid., 25 Sept. 1939.
5. Ibid., 27 Sept. 1939.
6. IWM, War Directive No. 6.
7. Ibid., No. 1.
8. Hitler, *My New Order*, p. 102.
9. Halder, KTB, 29 Sept. 1939.
10. Ibid., 8 Oct. 1939.
11. Keitel, p. 99.
12. Warlimont, pp. 36–7.
13. Manstein, p. 72.
14. Ibid., pp. 72–84.
15. Warlimont, p. 57.
16. Manstein, p. 93.
17. Keitel, p. 100.
18. Halder, KTB, 4 Oct. 1939.
19. Deutsch, *Twilight Conspiracy*, p. 72.
20. Halder, KTB, 11 Oct. 1939.
21. Manstein, p. 85.
22. Keitel, p. 102.
23. Manstein, p. 87.
24. Deutsch, p. 229.
25. Wheeler-Bennett, p. 459.
26. Deutsch, *Twilight Conspiracy*, p. 197.
27. Ibid., p. 235.
28. Ibid., p. 240.
29. Ibid., p. 246.
30. Halder, KTB, 7 Jan. 1940.
31. Wheeler-Bennett, p. 492.
32. Deutsch, *Twilight Conspiracy*, p. 259.
33. Guderian, p. 64.
34. Taylor, *The March of Conquest*, New York, 1958, p. 57.
35. Manstein, p. 88.
36. Deutsch, *Twilight Conspiracy*, p. 262.
37. Halder, KTB, 23 Nov. 1939.
38. Guderian, p. 66.
39. Ibid., p. 66.
40. Ibid., p. 66.
41. Jodl, KTB, 18 Oct. 1939.
42. Warlimont, p. 45.
43. Ibid., pp. 56–8.
44. Ibid., p. 62.
45. Ibid., p. 56.
46. Ibid., p. 79.
47. Jodl, KTB, 13 Dec. 1939.
48. Warlimont, p. 71.
49. Ibid., p. 72.
50. Halder, KTB, 21 Feb. 1940.
51. Ibid., 21 Feb. 1940.

52. Warlimont, **pp. 75–6.**
53. Jodl, KTB, 19 April 1940.
54. LHP, files on German generals.
55. Warlimont, p. 76.
56. Ibid., pp. 79–80.
57. LHP, Wavell.
58. Jodl, KTB, 14 April 1940.
59. Halder, KTB, 14 April 1940.
60. Jodl, KTB, 17 April 1940.
61. Ibid., 19 April 1940.
62. Craig, p. 502.

15 *The West – The Plans*

1. IWM, War Directive No. 6.
2. Ibid., No. 10.
3. Taylor, *The March of Conquest,* p. 162.
4. Manstein, p. 97.
5. Author's collection, Operation Yellow, second version.
6. Manstein, p. 98.
7. IWM, War Directive, No. 8.
8. Taylor, *The March of Conquest,* p. 165.
9. Jodl, KTB, 30 Oct. 1939.
10. L. F. Ellis, *The War in France and Flanders*, London, 1953, p. 338.
11. IWM, War Directive No. 8.
12. Jodl, KTB, 13 Feb. 1940.
13. IWM, AL 7956.
14. Ibid.
15. Ibid., AL 795C.
16. Manstein, p. 108.
17. Halder, KTB, 21 Jan. 1940.
18. IWM, AL 795.
19. Ibid. AL 795B.
20. Ibid.
21. Ibid.
22. Ibid.
23. Ibid.
24. Ibid., AL 1092.
25. Ibid., AL 7950.
26. Guderian, p. 74.
27. Ibid., p. 72.
28. IWM, AL 795B.
29. Halder, KTB, 6 Mar. 1940.
30. Guderian, p. 69.
31. Ibid., pp. 69–70.
32. Halder, KTB, 14 Feb. 1940.
33. Manstein, p. 100.
34. Guderian, pp. 70–1.

35. Halder, KTB, 17 Mar. 1940.
36. Guderian, p. 70.
37. Halder, KTB, 4 Feb. 1940.
38. Ibid.
39. Ibid., 28 Apr. 1940.
40. Ibid, 2 May 1940.
41. Addington, pp. 85–6.

16 *The West – The Campaign*

1. Fuller, *Conduct of War*, pp. 258–9.
2. Ibid., pp. 257–8.
3. Liddell Hart, *History of the Second World War*, p. 66.
4. LHP, letter from Guderian to Liddell Hart dated 24 Jan. 1949.
5. Halder, KTB, 12 May 1940.
6. Liddell Hart, *The Other Side of the Hill*, p. 173.
7. Guderian, p. 71.
8. H. A. Jacobsen, *Dokumente zur Vorgeschichte des Westfeldzuges, 1939–40*, Vol. 2, Göttingen, 1956, p. 32.
9. Liddell Hart, *The Other Side of the Hill*, pp. 177–8
10. Halder, KTB, 16 May 1940.
11. Jacobsen, p. 34.
12. Ibid., p. 38.
13. Liddell Hart, *The Other Side of the Hill*, p. 179.
14. Ibid., pp. 178–9.
15. Jacobsen, p. 40.
16. Ibid., p. 42.
17. Halder, KTB, 17 May 1940.
18. Halder, KTB.
19. Jodl, KTB, 18 May 1940.
20. Ibid.
21. Halder, KTB, 18 May 1940.
22. Ibid.
23. Ibid.
24. LHP, file on invasion of the West.
25. Jacobsen, p. 47.
26. Guderian, p. 89.
27. Jodl, KTB, 20 May 1940.
28. Liddell Hart, *The Other Side of the Hill*, p. 184.
29. Ellis, p. 95.
30. Ibid., p. 96.
31. Jacobsen, p. 61.
32. Guderian, pp. 91–2.

33. Ellis, p. 158.
34. Ibid., p. 158.
35. IWM, 1L 1092B.
36. LHP, file on invasion of the West.
37. Ellis, p. 151.
38. Ibid., p. 138.
39. Ibid., p. 348.
40. Ibid., p. 348.
41. Warlimont, p. 98.
42. Jacobsen, p. 74.
43. Jodl, KTB, 24 May 1940.
44. Ellis, p. 139.
45. IWM, War Directive No. 13.
46. Guderian, p. 94.
47. Halder, KTB, 24 May 1940.
48. Ibid.
49. Jacobsen, p. 74.
50. Ellis, p. 150.
51. Ibid., p. 150.
52. Halder, KTB, 25 May 1940.
53. Jodl, KTB, 25 May 1940.
54. Ellis, p. 150.
55. Ibid., p. 151.
56. Jacobsen, p. 56.
57. Halder, KTB, 26 May 1940.
58. Ibid.
59. Jodl, KTB, 26 May 1940.
60. Halder, KTB, 26 May 1940.
61. Guderian, p. 96.
62. Ellis, p. 192.
63. Ibid., p. 191.
64. Ibid., p. 192.
65. Ibid., p. 208.
66. Jacobsen, pp. 147–51.
67. Halder, KTB, 30 May 1940.
68. Guderian, p. 99.
69. Albert Kesselring, *Memoirs*, London, 1953, p. 60.
70. Guderian, p. 104.
71. F. W. Mellenthin, *Panzer Battles 1939–45*, London, 1955, p. 22.
72. Liddell Hart, *The Other Side of the Hill*, p. 168.
73. Halder, KTB, 6 June 1940.
74. Ibid., 10 June 1940.
75. Ibid., 13 June 1940.
76. Ibid., 19 June 1940.
77. Guderian, p. 105.

78. LHP, file on invasion of the West.
79. Ibid.

17 *Decisions*
1. Manstein, p. 150.
2. Halder, KTB, 3 Sept. 1940.
3. Taylor, *March of Conquest,* p. 346.
4. Halder, KTB, 23 May 1940.
5. Keitel, p. 110.
6. Warlimont, pp. 89–90.
7. Leach, p. 52.
8. Ibid., p. 53.
9. Halder, KTB, 22 June 1940.
10. Ibid., 15 June 1940.
11. IWM, War Directive No. 16.
12. Halder, KTB, 6 Aug. 1940.
13. Westphal, p. 89.
14. LHP, file on Operation 'Sealion'.
15. Manstein, p. 167.
16. IWM, War Directive No. 19.
17. Halder, KTB, 27 Mar. 1941.
18. IWM, War Directive No. 26.
19. Halder, KTB, 22 July 1940.
20. Leach, p. 54.
21. Halder, KTB, 4 July 1940.
22. Ibid., 3 July 1940.
23. Ibid., 13 July 1940.
24. Ibid., 30 July 1940.
25. Ibid., 5 Dec. 1940.
26. Ibid., 31 July 1940.
27. IWM, War Directive No. 18.
28. Halder, KTB, 5 Dec. 1940.
29. IWM, War Directive No. 21.
30. Halder, KTB, 28 Jan. 1941.
31. Leach, p. 141.
32. Ibid., p. 141.
33. Ibid., p. 142.
34. Ibid., p. 159.

18 *'Barbarossa' – The Plans*
1. Halder, KTB, 3 July 1940.
2. Ibid., 22 July 1940.
3. Ibid., 31 July 1940.
4. Ibid., 26 July 1940.
5. Ibid., 1 Aug. 1940.
6. Author's collection, Marcks Plan.
7. Leach, p. 106.
8. Halder, KTB, 5 Dec. 1940.
9. Author's collection, Lossberg Study.

10. IWM, War Directive No. 21.
11. Halder, KTB, 9 Jan. 1941.
12. Warlimont, p. 138.
13. Ibid., p. 140.
14. Author's collection, OKH Deployment Plan.
15. Ibid.
16. Halder, KTB, 3 Feb. 1941.
17. Ibid., 17 Mar. 1941.
18. Leach, p. 163.
19. Ibid., p. 164.
20. Warlimont, pp. 141–2.
21. Author's collection, OKH Deployment Plan.
22. IWM, War Directive No. 21.
23. Author's collection, OKH Deployment Plan.
24. Ibid.
25. Halder, KTB, 3 Feb. 1941.
26. Leach, p. 106.
27. Guderian, p. 117.
28. Liddell Hart, *The Other Side of the Hill,* p. 272.
29. Author's collection, OKH Deployment Plan.
30. Ibid.
31. Guderian, p. 122.
32. Halder, KTB, 14 Mar. 1941.
33. Ibid., 19 Mar. 1941.
34. Ibid., 27 Mar. 1941.
35. Leach, p. 135.
36. Halder, KTB, 20 May 1941.
37. Ibid., 13 June 1941.
38. Ibid., 1 July 1940.
39. Ibid., 29 Sept. 1940.
40. Ibid., 5 May 1941.
41. Liddell Hart, *The Other Side of the Hill,* pp. 254–5.
42. Ibid., p. 251.
43. Leach, p. 94.

19 *'Barbarossa' – The Campaign*
1. Halder, KTB, 22 June 1941.
2. Ibid., 9 June 1941.
3. Warlimont, p. 135.
4. Keitel, p. 127.
5. Leach, p. 144.
6. Manstein, p. 177.
7. Halder, KTB, 24 June 1941.

8. Guderian, p. 129.
9. Halder, KTB, 23 June 1941.
10. Guderian, p. 131.
11. Halder, KTB, 24 June 1941.
12. Ibid., 29 June 1941.
13. Ibid., 29 June 1941.
14. Ibid., 2 July 1941.
15. Guderian, pp. 131–5.
16. Halder, KTB, 24 June 1941.
17. Guderian, p. 132.
18. Ibid., p. 134.
19. Liddell Hart, *The Other Side of the Hill*, p. 272.
20. Halder, KTB, 3 July 1941.
21: Liddell Hart, *The Other Side of the Hill*, p. 272.
22. Halder, KTB, 9 July 1941.
23. Guderian, p. 149.
24. Halder, KTB, 26 July 1941.
25. Guderian, p. 150.
26. Ibid., p. 154.
27. Purnell's *History of the Second World War*, p. 702.
28. Ibid.
29. Manstein, pp. 184–5.
30. Ibid., p. 186.
31. Halder, KTB, 28 June 1941.
32. Ibid., 8 July 1941.
33. Manstein, p. 193.
34. Ibid., p. 193.
35. Halder, KTB, 11 July 1941.
36. IWM, War Directive No. 33.
37. Ibid., No. 33a.
38. Ibid., No. 40.
39. Halder, KTB, 23 June 1941.
40. Ibid., 25 June 1941.
41. Ibid., 29 June 1941.
42. Ibid., 5 July 1941.
43. Ibid., 7 July 1941.
44. Ibid., 9 July 1941.
45. Ibid., 10 July 1941.

20 *'Barbarossa' – The Failure*

1. Halder, KTB, 3 July 1941.
2. Ibid.
3. Ibid., 11 July 1941.
4. Ibid., 12 July 1941.
5. Ibid.
6. Ibid., 13 July 1941.
7. Ibid., 12 July 1941.
8. Ibid., 15 July 1941.
9. Ibid., 16 July 1941.
10. Ibid., 13 July 1941.
11. Ibid., 20 July 1941.
12. Author's collection, OKH Memorandum.
13. Halder, KTB, 28 July 1941.
14. Warlimont, p.
15. Halder, KTB, 8 July 1941.
16. Jodl, KTB, 5 July 1941.
17. IWM, War Directive No. 33.
18. Ibid.
19. Halder, KTB, 23 July 1941.
20. Ibid., 26 July 1941.
21. Ibid., 30 July 1941.
22. IWM, War Directive No. 34.
23. Halder, KTB, 30 July 1941.
24. Ibid., 31 July 1941.
25. Guderian, p. 151.
26. Ibid., p. 153.
27. Keitel, p. 150.
28. Warlimont, p. 187.
29. Ibid., p. 187.
30. Halder, KTB, 8 Aug. 1941.
31. Halder, KTB, 11 Aug. 1941.
32. IWM War Directive No. 34, Supplement.
33. Halder, KTB, 13 Aug. 1941.
34. Ibid., 15 Aug. 1941.
35. Author's collection, OKH Memorandum.
36. Ibid., Hitler's reply to Memorandum.
37. Ibid., OKH Deployment Directive.
38. Halder, KTB, 8 July 1941.
39. Warlimont, p. 180.
40. Halder, KTB, 22 Aug. 1941.
41. Ibid., 22 Aug. 1941.
42. Warlimont, pp. 191–2.
43. Halder, KTB, 30 Aug. 1941.
44. Guderian, pp. 158–62.
45. Ibid., p. 162.
46. Ibid., p. 157.
47. Halder, KTB, 25 Aug. 1941.
48. Ibid., 27 Aug. 1941.
49. Ibid., 28 Aug. 1941.
50. Ibid., 29 Aug. 1941.
51. Ibid., 31 Aug. 1941.
52. Guderian, p. 165.

53. Ibid., p. 166.
54. Halder, KTB, 4 Sept. 1941.
55. Guderian, pp. 167–8.
56. IWM, War Directive No. 35.
57. Guderian, pp. 173–4.
58. Ibid., p. 174.
59. Halder, KTB, 8 Oct. 1941.
60. Guderian, pp. 179–82.
61. Ibid., p. 186.
62. Ibid., p. 188.
63. KTB, 11 Nov. 1941.
64. Liddell Hart, *History of the Second World War*, p. 168.
65. Guderian, pp. 189–90.
66. Ibid., p. 192.
67. Ibid., p. 194.
68. Halder, KTB, 29 Nov. 1941.
69. Ibid., 1 Dec. 41.
70. Guderian, p. 193.
71. Halder, KTB, 27 Nov. 1941.
72. Ibid., 30 Nov. 1941.
73. Ibid., 5 Dec. 1941.
74. Ibid., 6 Dec. 1941.
75. IWM, War Directive No. 39.
76. Guderian, p. 199.
77. IWM, War Directive No. 39.
78. Halder, KTB, 16 Dec. 1941.
79. Keitel, p. 166.
80. Halder, KTB, 2 Feb. 1942.
81. Liddell Hart, *The Other Side of the Hill*, pp. 289–90.
82. Halder, KTB, 19 Dec. 1941 – 20 Jan. 1942.
83. Halder, *Hitler as Warlord*, p. 51.

21 *The New Commander-in-Chief*

1. Keitel, p. 145.
2. Author's collection, von Bock memorandum.
3. Kesselring, p. 78.
4. LHP, von Rundstedt file.
5. Ibid.
6. Halder, KTB, 1 Dec. 1941.
7. Ibid.
8. Liddell Hart, *The Other Side of the Hill*, p. 278.
9. Halder, KTB, 7 Dec. 1941.
10. Halder, *Hitler as Warlord*, p. 49.
11. Warlimont, p. 212.
12. Ibid., p. 213.
13. Halder, KTB, 30 Nov. 1941.
14. Ibid., 2 Jan. 1942.
15. Ibid., 3 Jan. 1942.
16. LHP, Warlimont file.
17. Warlimont, pp. 216–7.
18. Ibid., p. 142.
19. Ibid., p. 142.
20. Ibid., p. 179.
21. Ibid., p. 214.
22. Ibid., p. 196.

PART 4 *The Years of Defeat*

22 *North Africa – The Scene*

1. Desmond Young, *Rommel, the Desert Fox*, London, 1950, pp. 89–90.
2. Erwin Rommel, *The Rommel Papers*, London, 1953, p. 191.
3. Winston Churchill, *History of the Second World War*, Vol. IV, London, 1951, p. 59.
4. Westphal, pp. 127–8.
5. Ibid., p. 126.
6. LHP, file on Rommel.
7. Rommel, p. 252.
8. Ronald Lewin, *Rommel as a Military Commander*, London, 1968, p. 143.
9. Liddell Hart, *The Other Side of the Hill*, p. 247.
10. Ibid., pp. 235–6.
11. IWM, War Directive No. 18.
12. Ibid., No. 22.
13. LHP, file on Rommel.
14. Rommel, p. 111.
15. Lewin, p. 31.
16. Rommel, pp. 105–6.
17. Halder, KTB, 3 April 1941.

18. Ibid., 15 April 1941.
19. Ibid., 22 April 1941.
20. Ibid., 23 April 1941.
21. Ibid., 3 May 1941.
22. Ibid., 7 May 1941.
23. Ibid., 8 July 1941.
24. Ibid., 11 May 1941.
25. Ibid., 20 May 1941.
26. Rommel, p. 139.
27. Ibid., p. 140.
28. Ibid.
29. Ibid.
30. IWM, War Directive No. 32.
31. LHP, file on Rommel.
32. Westphal, p. 130.
33. Rommel, p. 133.
34. Ibid., p. 327.
35. LHP, Halder, interrogation.
36. Halder, KTB, 29 July 1941.
37. Rommel, p. 243.
38. Ibid., p. 352.
39. Ibid., p. 139.
40. Ibid., p. 187.
41. Ibid., p. 243.
42. Ibid., p. 513.
43. Ibid., p. 192.
44. LHP, Halder, interrogation.
45. Westphal, p. 128.
46. Rommel, pp. 268–9.
47. Warlimont, p. 308.
48. Ibid., p. 309.
49. Halder, KTB, 23 September 1941.
50. Warlimont, pp. 235–6.
51. Rommel, p. 294.
52. Ibid., pp. 294–5.
53. Ibid., pp. 365–6.
54. Westphal, p. 133.
55. Rommel, p. 112.
56. F. W. von Mellenthin, *Panzer Battles 1939–1945*, London, 1955, pp. 118–9.
57. Rommel, pp. 192, 358, 513.
58. Ibid., p. 368.
59. Ibid., p. 513.
60. Ibid.
61. Ibid., p. 513.

23 *North Africa – The Campaign*

1. Halder, KTB, 23 April 1941.
2. Ibid., 24 April 1941.
3. Rommel, p. 141.
4. Ibid.
5. Ibid., p. 148.
6. Rommel, pp. 171–2.
7. Ibid., p. 176.
8. Ibid., p. 180.
9. Ibid., p. 197.
10. Ibid., p. 233.
11. Ibid., pp. 248–9.
12. LHP, Keitel, interrogation.
13. Ibid., p. 253.
14. Ibid., p. 257.
15. Ibid.
16. Ibid., p. 260.
17. Ibid., p. 265–6.
18. Ibid., p. 248–9.
19. Ibid., p. 283.
20. Ibid., p. 283.
21. Ibid., pp. 285–6.
22. Ibid., p. 185.
23. Ibid., p. 196.
24. Ibid., p. 298.
25. Ibid., p. 232.
26. Ibid., p. 304.
27. Ibid., pp. 304–8.
28. Ibid., p. 318.
29. Ibid., p. 317.
30. I. S. Playfair, *The Mediterranean and Middle East*, Vol. 3, London, 1954, pp. 475–6.
31. Rommel, p. 321.
32. Ibid., pp. 321–2.
33. Playfair, p. 476.
34. Ibid., pp. 476–7.
35. Rommel, p. 338.
36. Ibid., p. 327.
37. Ibid., p. 340.
38. Ibid., p. 395.
39. Ibid.
40. Albert Kesselring, *Memoirs*, London, 1953, p. 152.
41. Ibid., p. 157.
42. Rommel, p. 327.
43. Warlimont, pp. 269–70.
44. Ibid., pp. 297–9.
45. Ibid., p. 307.
46. Ibid., p. 308.
47. Ibid.

48. Rommel, p. 395.
49. Westphal, p. 120.
50. Rommel, p. 345.
51. Ibid., p. 340.
52. Ibid., pp. 351–2.
53. Ibid., p. 375.
54. Ibid., p. 395.
55. Ibid., p. 364.
56. Ibid., p. 363.
57. Ibid., p. 359.
58. Ibid., p. 358.
59. Ibid., p. 366.
60. Ibid., p. 396.
61. Ibid., p. 377.
62. Ibid., p. 380.
63. Ibid., p. 391.
64. Ibid., p. 401.
65. Ibid., p. 408.
66. Ibid., p. 389.
67. Ibid., p. 391.
68. Ibid., p. 395.
69. Ibid., p. 408.
70. Ibid., p. 416.
71. Ibid., p. 418.
72. Playfair Vol 4 p. 331.
73. Ibid., p. 359.
74. Liddell Hart, *History of the Second World War*, p. 426.
75. LHP, file on Rommel.

24 *Italy*

    Warlimont, p. 317.
2. IWM, War Directive No. 48.
3. Warlimont, p. 383.
4. Ibid., p. 385.
5. W. G. F. Jackson, *The Battle for Italy*, London, 1967, p. 317.
6. Warlimont, p. 416.
7. Ibid., pp. 386–7.
8. Kesselring, p. 267.
9. Ibid., p. 249.
10. Westphal, p. 164.
11. Ibid., pp. 164–5.
12. Ibid., p. 154.
13. Ibid., p. 159.
14. Warlimont, p. 474.
15. Ibid.

25 *The East – The 1942 Summer Campaign*

1. Warlimont, p. 240
2. Ibid.
3. Ibid., p. 227.
4. Ibid., p. 230.
5. Liddell Hart, *The Other Side of the Hill*, pp. 295–6.
6. Warlimont, p. 226.
7. Liddell Hart, *The Other Side of the Hill*, p. 312.
8. Ibid., p. 301.
9. Ibid., pp. 310–1.
10. Ibid., p. 311.
11. IWM, War Directive No. 41.
12. Ibid.
13. Ibid.
14. Ibid.
15. Warlimont, p. 243.
16. Halder, KTB, 6 July 1942.
17. Liddell Hart, *The Other Side of the Hill*, p. 306.
18. Halder, KTB, 18 July 1942.
19. Ibid., 23 July 1942.
20. IWM, War Directive No. 45.
21. Ibid.
22. Liddell Hart, *The Other Side of the Hill*, p. 303.

26 *The East – Stalingrad*

1. Halder, KTB, 30 July 1942.
2. LHP – collection of extracts from Führer orders.
3. Manstein, pp. 293–4.
4. Liddell Hart, *The Other Side of the Hill*, pp. 308–9.
5. Manstein, p. 295.
6. Liddell Hart, *The Other Side of the Hill*, p. 313.
7. Manstein, pp. 302–3.
8. Ibid., p. 294.
9. Ibid., p. 328.
10. Ibid., pp. 315–6.
11. Ibid., p. 312.
12. Ibid., p. 319.
13. Ibid., pp. 327–9.
14. Ibid., pp. 331–2.
15. Ibid., p. 332.

16. Ibid., pp. 333–4.
17. Ibid., pp. 335–6.
18. Ibid., p. 341.
19. Ibid., p. 340.
20. Ibid., pp. 345–6.
21. Ibid., p. 355.
22. Ibid., p. 360.
23. Ibid., p. 358.
24. Ibid., p. 365.
25. Ibid., p. 367.
26. Ibid., p. 370.
27. Ibid., p. 373.
28. Ibid.
29. Ibid., pp. 382–441.
30. Ibid., p. 440.
31. Ibid., p. 354.
32. Ibid., pp. 307–8.

27 *The Crisis of 1943*

1. Goebbels, diary, 9 March 1943.
2. Halder, *Hitler as War Lord*, p. 21.
3. Warlimont, p. 230.
4. Halder, KTB, 24 June 1942.
5. Ibid., 23 July 1942.
6. Warlimont, p. 246.
7. Keitel, pp. 182–3.
8. Warlimont, pp. 251–2.
9. Halder, KTB, 30 August 1942.
10 Ibid., 24 September 1942.
11. Manstein, p. 386.
12. Keitel, p. 180.
13. Ibid., p. 181.
14. Warlimont, p. 258.
15. Ibid., p. 259.
16. LHP, Zeitzler, interrogation.
17. Warlimont, p. 260.
18. Keitel, p. 184.
19. Warlimont, p. 264.
20. Halder, KTB, 20 July 1942.
21. Warlimont, pp. 301–5.
22. Manstein, p. 365.
23. Goebbels, diary, 9 May 1943.
24. LHP, Speer, interrogation.
25. Author's collection.
26. *Hitler's Secret Conversations*, p. 178.
27. Kuhn, unpublished manuscript.
28. Warlimont, p. 265.
29. Guderian, p. 227.
30. Ibid., p. 228.

31. Ibid., p. 230–1.
32. Ibid., p. 237.
33. Ibid., p. 222.
34. Ibid., p. 236.
35. Ibid., p. 234.
36. Manstein, p. 443.
37. Ibid.
38. Ibid., p. 447.
39. Liddell Hart, *The Other Side of the Hill*, p. 318.
40. Guderian, p. 235.
41. Mellenthin, p. 240.
42. Guderian, pp. 251–2.

28 *The East, the End*

1. Liddell Hart, *History of the Second World War*, p. 492.
2. LHP, extracts from Hitler's speeches etc.
3. LHP, intelligence summary, SHAEF, dated September 1944.
4. LHP, typescript of Hitler's last will and testament.
5. Manstein, pp. 547–8.
6. Guderian, p. 256.
7. Halder, *Hitler as War Lord*, p. 31.
8. Guderian p. 280.
9. Liddell Hart, *The Other Side of the Hill*, pp. 324–5.
10. Ibid., pp. 326–7.
11. Ibid., p. 327.
12. Ibid., p. 327–8.
13. Manstein, p. 450.
14. Ibid., p. 458.
15. Ibid., p. 459.
16. Ibid., p. 460.
17. Ibid.
18. Ibid.
19. Ibid., pp. 461–2.
20. Ibid., p. 463.
21. Ibid., p. 466.
22. Ibid., p. 472–3.
23. Ibid., p. 474.
24. Ibid., p. 482.
25. Ibid., pp. 491–2.
26. Ibid., pp. 513–4.
27. IWM, Führer Order No. 11.
28. Manstein, p. 530.
29. Guderian, p. 304.

30. Ibid., p. 305.
31. Ibid., p. 310.
32. Ibid., p. 312.
33. Ibid.
34. Ibid., p. 315.
35. Ibid., p. 320.
36. Ibid., p. 321.
37. Ibid., p. 329.
38. Ibid., p. 341.

29 *Military Demise*
1. LHP, intelligence summary, SHAEF, dated September 1944.
2. LHP, Speer, interrogation.

30 *The West 1944–45 – Invasion*
1. IWM, War Directive No. 32.
2. Warlimont, p. 199.
3. IWM, War Directive No. 40.
4. Warlimont, p. 400.
5. IWM, War Directive No. 51.
6. Ibid.
7. Warlimont, pp. 401–3.
8. LHP, von Rundstedt, interrogation.
9. Guderian, pp. 259–264.
10. Warlimont, p. 401.
11. Ibid., p. 405.
12. Guderian, p. 257.
13. LHP, von Rundstedt, interrogation.
14. Jodl, KTB, 21 January 1944.
15. Warlimont, p. 414.
16. Ibid.
17. LHP, von Rundstedt, interrogation.
18. Rommel, pp. 451–3.
19. Ibid., p. 468.
20. Ibid., p. 453–5.
21. Guderian, p. 261.
22. IWM, War Directive No. 40.
23. Rommel, p. 465.
24. Ibid., pp. 68–70.
25. Liddell Hart, *The Other Side of the Hill*, p. 396.
26. Ibid., p. 398.
27. LHP, translation of Army Group B and C-in-C West reports.
28. Ibid.
29. Shulman, Milton, *Defeat in the West*, London, 1947, p. 153.

30. LHP, von Rundstedt, interrogation.
31. LHP, translations of Army Group B and C-in-C West reports.
32. LHP, von Rundstedt, interrogation.
33. LHP, file on the invasion.
34. Ibid.
35. Chester Wilmot, *The Struggle for Europe*, 1952, p. 346.
36. LHP, translations of Army Group B and C-in-C West reports.
37. Ibid.
38. Ibid.
39. Ibid.
40. Wilmot, p. 404.
41. Liddell Hart, *The Other Side of the Hill*, p. 421.
42. Wilmot, p. 416.
43. Warlimont, p. 450.
44. LHP, translation of Army Group B and C-in-C West reports.
45. Ibid.

31 *The West 1944–45 – The End*
1. Wilmot, p. 434.
2. LHP, translation of Army Group B and C-in-C West reports.
3. Guderian, p. 299.
4. Westphal, pp. 173–4.
5. LHP, translation of Army Group B and C-in-C reports.
6. Ibid.
7. Liddell Hart, *The Other Side of the Hill*, p. 429.
8. Wilmot, p. 540.
9. LHP, translation of Army Group B and C-in-C West reports.
10. Warlimont, p. 481.
11. Westphal, p. 179.
12. Warlimont, pp. 481–2.
13. Westphal, p. 180.
14. Shulman, pp. 289–90.
15. Ibid., pp. 290–1.
16. Ibid., p. 288.
17. Mellenthin, p. 332.
18. Westphal, p. 184.
19. Wilmot, p. 605.
20. Westphal, p. 185.
21. Liddell Hart, *The Other Side of the Hill*, p. 464.

22. Guderian, pp. 308–9.
23. Westphal, p. 190.
24. Ibid., p. 194.
25. Wilmot, p. 673.
26. Warlimont, p. 506.
27. Manteuffel, p. 301.
28. Shulman, p. 357.

32   *The Final Ignominy*
1. Westphal, p. 656.
2. Manstein, pp. 287, 504.
3. Guderian, p. 260.
4. Manstein, p. 453.
5. Ibid., p. 510.
6. LHP, Guderian file.
7. LHP, Zeitzler, interrogation.
8. Wilmot, p. 347.
9. Warlimont, p. 359.
10. Manstein, p. 511.
11. Wilmot, pp. 378–9.
12. Wheeler-Bennett, p. 678.
13. Warlimont, p. 422.
14. Shulman, pp. 181–2.
15. Guderian, p. 276.
16. Ibid., p. 273.
17. Warlimont, p. 462.
18. LHP, Guderian, interrogation.
19. Warlimont, p. 462.
20. Guderian, p. 310.
21. Ibid., p. 336.
22. Ibid., p. 305–6.
23. Ibid., p. 332.
24. Ibid., p. 288.
25. H. R. Trevor-Roper, *Hitler's War Directives*. London, 1966, pp. 290–1.
26. Ibid., p. 243.
27. Guderian, p. 277.
28. Warlimont, p. 453.
29. Guderian, pp. 324–5.
30. Ibid., p. 343.
31. Ibid., p. 337.
32. Ibid., pp. 356–7.
33. Warlimont, p. 513.
34. E. F. Ziemke, *Stalingrad to Berlin*, Washington, 1957, p. 481.
35. Guderian, pp. 336–7.
36. Westphal, pp. 195–6.
37. LHP, Guderian, interrogation.

38. H. R. Trevor-Roper, *Hitler's War Directives*, pp. 289–90.
39. Warlimont, p. 501.
40. Ziemke, p. 478.
41. Schramm, p. 145.
42. Guderian, p. 352.
43. Schramm, p. 176.
44. Warlimont, p. 497.
45. H. R. Trevor-Roper, *Hitler's War Directives*, p. 301.

33   *The Great Folly*
1. Wheeler-Bennett, p. 677.
2. LHP file on V. Brauchitsch.
3. Manstein, pp. 287–8.
4. Halder, KTB, 19 September 1939.
5. Ibid., 30 March 1941.
6. Alexander Dallin, *German Rule in Russia, 1941–45*, London, 1947, p. 31.
7. Helmut Krausnick et al., *Anatomy of the SS State*, p. 520 (chapter by Buchheim).
8. Dallin, p. 71.
9. Dallin, pp. 259–60.
10. Ibid., p. 410.
11. Ibid., p. 418.
12. Ibid., p. 416.
13. Ibid., p. 530.
14. Ibid., p. 359.
15. Ibid., p. 263.
16. Ibid., p. 550.
17. Krausnick et al., p. 519 (chapter by Buchheim).
18. Ibid., p. 522.
19. Ibid.
20. Ibid., p. 523.
21. Dallin, p. 260.
22. Schweppenburg, p. 202.
23. Guderian, p. 276.
24. Schweppenburg, p. 223.
25. Görlitz, p. 409.
26. Ibid., p. 4.
27. Guderian, p. 382.
28. LHP Zeitzler, interrogation.
29. Ibid.
30. Rommel, p. 486.
31. Westphal, pp. 62–3.
32. LHP, Dittmar, interrogation.

Select Bibliography

ADDINGTON, LARRY H.: *The Blitzkrieg Era and the German General Staff, 1865–1941*. New Brunswick: Rutgers, 1971.
ALLEN, WILLIAM SHERIDAN: *The Nazi Seizure of Power*. New York: Watts, 1965.

BAUER, EDDY: *Panzer Krieg* (2 Vols.) Bonn: Offene Wörte, 1965.
BECKER, CAJUS: *The Luftwaffe War Diaries*. London: Macdonald and Jane's, 1967.
BELFIELD, E. and ESSAME, A.: *The Battle for Normandy*. London: Batsford, 1965.
BENOIST-MÉCHIN, J.: *Sixty Days that Shook the West*. London: Jonathan Cape, 1963.
BERNHARDT, WALTER: *Die Deutsche Aufrüstung, 1934–39*. Frankfurt am Main: Bernard und Graefe, 1969.
BLAU, GEORGE E.: *The German Campaign in Russia: Planning and Operations, 1940–42*. Washington D.C.: U.S. Department of the Army, 1955.
BLUMENSON, MARTIN: *Breakout and Pursuit*. Washington D.C.: U.S. Army Military History Department, 1961.
BLUMENTRITT, GÜNTHER: *Von Rundstedt, The Soldier and The Man*. London: Odhams, 1952.
BRACHER, KARL: *The German Dictatorship*. New York: Praeger, 1970.
BRACKMANN, ALBERT *et al.*: *Unser Kampf in Polen*. Munich: Bruckmann, 1959.
BROSZAT, MARTIN: *German National Socialism 1919–1945*. Santa Barbara, California: American Bibliographical Center-Clio Press, 1966.
BULLOCK, ALAN: *Hitler, A Study in Tyranny*. New York: Harper & Row, 1964.

CARREL, PAUL: *Hitler's War on Russia*. London: Harrap, 1964.
　　Scorched Earth. London: Harrap, 1970.
CECIL, ROBERT: *Hitler's Decision to Invade Russia 1941*. New York: David McKay, 1976.
CHAPMAN, GUY: *Why France Fell*. London: Cassell, 1968.
CHURCHILL, WINSTON S.: *History of The Second World War*. London: Cassell, 1949.

CLARK, ALAN: *Barbarossa*. London: Hutchinson, 1965.
COLE, HUGH M.: *Ardennes and the Battle of the Bulge*. Washington D.C.: U.S. Army Military History Department, 1965.
COOPER, MATTHEW, and LUCAS, JAMES: *Panzer, The Armoured Force of the Third Reich*. London: Macdonald and Jane's, 1976.
CRAIG, GORDON: *The Politics of the Prussian Army 1650–1945*. New York: Oxford University Press, 1964.
CREVELD, MARTIN VAN: *Hitler's Strategy 1940–41*. New York: Cambridge University Press, 1973.

DALLIN, ALEXANDER: *German Rule in Russia, 1941–45*. London: Macmillan, 1951.
DELARUE, JACQUES: *The Gestapo*. New York: William Morrow, 1964.
DEMETER, KARL: *The German Officer Corps in Society and State, 1860–1945*. London: Weidenfeld and Nicolson, 1965.
DEUTSCH, HAROLD: *The Conspiracy against Hitler in the Twilight War*. Minneapolis: University of Minnesota, 1968.
    Hitler and His Generals, The Hidden Crisis. January – June 1938. Minneapolis: University of Minnesota, 1974.
DÖNITZ, Admiral KARL: *Memoirs*. London: Weidenfeld and Nicolson, 1958.

EARLE, EDWARD MEAD: *Makers of Modern Strategy*. Princeton: Princeton University Press, 1943.
EBELING, Dr. H.: *The Political Role of the German General Staff between 1918 and 1938*. London: New Europe, 1945.
ELLIS, L. F.: *The War in France and Flanders*. London: H.M.S.O., 1953.
    Victory in the West (2 Vols.) London: H.M.S.O., 1968.
ERICKSON, JOHN: *The Road to Stalingrad*. New York: Harper & Row, 1975.

ESEBECK, HANNS GERT Von: *Afrikanische Schicksalsjahre*. Wiesbaden: Limes, 1950.
ESSAME, H.: *Battle for Germany*. London: Batsford, 1969.

FEST, JOACHIM: *The Face of the Third Reich*. New York: Pantheon 1970.
    Hitler. New York: Random, 1975.
FRANK, FRIEDRICH, *et al.: Unser Kampf in Holland, Belgien und Flandern*. Munich: Bruckmann, 1941.
FRIED, HANS ERNEST: *The Guilt of the German Army*. New York: Macmillan, 1943.
FULLER, Major-General J. F. C.: *Armoured Warfare*. London: Eyre and Spottiswoode, 1943.
    Conduct of War. New York: Funk & Wagnalls, 1961.
    The Decisive Battles of the Western World (3 Vols). London: Eyre and Spottiswoode, 1956.
    Machine Warfare. London: Hutchinson, 1942.
    The Second World War. New York: Hawthorn, 1969.

GAULLE, CHARLES De: *The Army of the Future*. London: Hutchinson, 1940.
GEYR Von SCHWEPPENBURG, L.: *The Critical Years*. London: Allen Wingate, 1952.

GILBERT, FELIX: *Hitler Directs His War*. Hauppauge, N.Y.: Universal Publishing, 1971.
GOEBBELS, JOSEF: *The Goebbels Diaries*. (Ed. Louis P. Lochner). Westport, Conn.: Greenwood Press, repr of 1948 ed.
GÖRLITZ, WALTER: *The German General Staff*. London: Hollis and Carter, 1953.
GREINER, E.: *Die Oberste Wehrmachtführung, 1939–1943*. Wiesbaden: Limes, 1951.
GRUNBERGER, RICHARD: *A Social History of the Third Reich*. London: Weidenfeld and Nicolson, 1971; Penguin, 1974.
GUDERIAN, HEINZ: *Panzer Leader*. New York: Ballantine, 1957. abr ed. 1976.
    Mit dem Panzern in Ost und West. Göttingen: Volk und Reich, 1942.

HALDER, FRANZ: *Hitler as Warlord*. London: Putnam, 1950.
    Kriegstagebuch, 1939–1942.
HARRISON, G. A.: *Cross Channel Attack*. Washington D.C.: Army Military History Department, 1951.
HEIDEN, KONRAD: *Der Führer*. New York: Howard Fertig, repr of 1944 ed.
HEISS, FRIEDRICH: *Der Sieg im Osten*. Berlin: Volk und Reich, 1940.
HIGGINS, TRUMBALL: *Hitler and Russia*. London: Macmillan, 1966.
HILLGRUBER, ANDREAS: *Hitlers Strategie*. Frankfurt am Main: Bernard und Graefe, 1965.
HINSLEY, F. H.: *Hitler's Strategy*. Cambridge: Cambridge University Press, 1951.
HITLER, ADOLF: *My New Order* (Speeches). New York: Octagon Books, repr of 1941 ed.
    Table Talk. (Ed. H. Trevor-Roper). London: Weidenfeld and Nicolson, 1953.
    War Directives, 1939–45 (Ed. H. Trevor-Roper). London: Sidgwick and Jackson, 1964; Pan, 1966.
HOFFMANN, PETER: *The History of the German Resistance, 1933–1945*. Cambridge, Mass.: M.I.T. Press, 1976.
HÖHNE, HEINZ: *The Order of the Death's Head*. New York: Coward, McCann & Geoghegan, 1970.
HORN, A.: *To Lose a Battle*. London: Macmillan, 1969.
HOSSBACH, FRIEDRICH: *Zwischen Wehrmacht und Hitler*. Göttingen: Vardenhoek und Ruprecht, 1965.
HOTH, HERMANN: *Panzer Operationen*. (Die Wehrmacht im Kampf, vol. II) Heidelberg: Vowinkel, 1956.
HOWARD, MICHAEL: *The Mediterranean Strategy in the Second World War*. London: Weidenfeld and Nicolson, 1968.
HUNTINGTON, SAMUEL P.: *The Soldier and the State*. Cambridge, Mass.: Harvard University, 1957.

INTERNATIONAL MILITARY TRIBUNAL: *The Trial of the German Major War Criminals: Proceedings of the International Military Tribunal Sitting at Nuremberg, Germany* (23 Vols.). London: H.M.S.O., 1949–51.
IRVING, DAVID: *Hitler's War*. New York: Viking Press, 1977.

JACOBSEN, H. A.: *Dokumente zur Vorgeschichte des Westfeldzuges, 1939–1940* (2 Vols.). Göttingen: Musterschmidt, 1956.
    Fall Gelb: der Kampf um den deutschen Operationsplan der Westoffensive, 1940. Wiesbaden: Steiner, 1957.

JACOBSEN, H. A. and ROHWER, J.: *Der Zweite Weltkriege in Chronik und Dokumentum.* Darmstadt: Wehr und Wissen, 1961.

JODL, ALFRED: *Kriegstagebuch 1938–1945* – fragments prepared by the International Military Tribunal.

KEILIG, WOLF: *Das Heer* (3 Vols.). Bad Neuheim: Podzun, 1956 and various dates.

KEITEL, WILHELM: *The Memoirs of Field-Marshal Keitel,* with an introduction and epilogue by Walter Görlitz. London: William Kimber, 1965.

KENNEDY, R. M.: *The German Campaign in Poland, 1939.* Washington D.C.: Department of the Army, 1956.

KESSELRING, ALBERT: *Kesselring.* Westport, Conn.: Greenwood Press, repr of 1954 ed.

KRAUSNICK, HELMUT et al.: *Anatomy of the SS State.* London: Collins, 1968.

LAFFIN, JOHN: *Jackboot.* London: Cassell, 1965.

LEACH, BARRY A.: *German Strategy against Russia, 1939–1941.* New York: Oxford University Press, 1973.

LESTER, J. R.: *Tank Warfare.* London: Allen and Unwin, 1943.

LEWIN, RONALD: *Rommel as a Military Commander.* London: Batsford, 1968.

LIDDELL HART, B. H.: *The Other Side of the Hill.* London: Cassell (revised and enlarged), 1951.

   A History of the Second World War. New York: Putnam, 1971.

   Strategy. New York: Praeger (revised), 1961.

   The Tanks – The History of the Royal Tank Regiment 1914–45 (2 Vols.). London: Cassell, 1959.

LUDENDORFF, ERICH: *The Nation at War.* London: Hutchinson, 1936.

MACKSEY, KENNETH: *Guderian: Creator of the Blitzkrieg.* New York: Stein and Day, 1976.

MANSTEIN, ERICH Von: *Lost Victories.* London: Methuen, 1958.

MASON, H. M.: *The Rise of the Luftwaffe, 1918–1940.* New York: Dial, 1973.

MELLENTHIN, F. Von: *Panzer Battles.* Norman, Okla.: University of Oklahoma Press, 1972.

MIDDELDORF, E.: *Taktik im Russlandfeldzug.* Berlin: E. S. Mittler und Sohn, 1956.

MIKSCHE, F. O.: *Blitzkrieg.* London: Faber and Faber, 1941.

MILWARD, ALAN S.: *The German Economy at War.* Atlantic Highlands, N.J.: Humanities Press, 1965.

MÜLLER-HILLEBRAND, B.: *Das Heer, 1933–1945* (3 Vols.) Frankfurt am Main: E. S. Mittler und Sohn, 1954, 1956, 1969.

   The Organisational Problems of the Army High Command and their Solutions, 1938–1945. U.S. Army, Europe, Historical Division, 1953.

MUNZEL, O.: *Die Deutschen Gepanzerten Truppen bis 1945.* Hertford: Maximilian, 1965.

   Heinz Guderian – Panzer Marsch. Munich: Schild, 1955.

   Panzertaktik. Heidelberg: Vowinkel, 1959.

NEHRING, W.: *Die Geschichte der deutschen Panzerwaffe, 1916 bis 1945.* Berlin: Propyläen, 1969.

OBERKOMMANDO DES HEERES: *Jahrbücher des deutschen Heeres, 1940, 1941, 1942.* Leipzig: Breitkopf und Härtel, 1940, 1941, 1942.

    Die Truppenführung. HDV 300.

OBERKOMMANDO DER WEHRMACHT: *Glückhäfte Strategie.* Berlin: 1942.

    Kriegestagebuch (5 Vols.) Frankfurt am Main: Bernard und Graefe, 1961–63.

    Sieg über Frankreich. Berlin: 1940.

    Der Sieg in Polen. Berlin: Andermann, 1940.

    Sieg im Westen. Berlin: 1940.

    Die Wehrmacht, 1940, 1941. Berlin: Die Wehrmacht, 1940, 1941.

OGORKIEWICZ, RICHARD M.: *Armour.* New York: Arco, 1970.

O'NEILL, ROBERT: *The German Army and the Nazi Party, 1933–39.* New York: Heineman, 1967.

ORLOW, DIETRICH: *The History of the Nazi Party.* Vol. 1 – 1919–33, Vol. 2 – 1933–45. Pittsburgh: University of Pittsburgh Press, 1969, 1973.

PHILIPPI, ALFRED, und HEIM, FERDINAND: *Der Feldzug gegen Sowjetrussland, 1941–45.* Stuttgart: Kohlhammer, 1962.

PIELALKIEWICZ, JANUSZ: *Pferd und Reiter im II Weltkrieg.* Munich: Sudwest, 1976.

PLAYFAIR, I. S.: *The Mediterranean and Middle East.* (4 Vols.) London: H.M.S.O., 1954.

RAUSCHNING, HERMANN: *Hitler Speaks,* London: Butterworth 1939.

REITLINGER, GERALD: *The Final Solution.* London: Vallentine, Mitchell, 1953.

RICH, NORMAN: *Hitler's War Aims.* (2 Vols.) New York: Norton, 1973, 1974.

ROBERTSON, E. M.: *Hitler's Pre-War Policy and Military Plans, 1933–39.* London: Longmans, 1963.

ROHER, J. *et al.*: *Decisive Battles of World War II: The German View.* London: Deutsch, 1965.

ROMMEL, ERWIN: *Papers.* (Ed. B. H. Liddell Hart) New York: Harcourt Brace Jovanovich, 1953.

ROSINSKI, HERBERT: *The German Army.* New York: Praeger, 1966.

SCHRAMM, PERCY ERNST: *Hitler: The Man and the Military Leader.* New York: Watts, 1971.

SCHRAMM, WILHELM RITTER Von: *Conspiracy among Generals.* New York, Scribner, 1957.

SEATON, ALBERT: *The Russo-German War, 1941–45.* London: Barker, 1971.

SEECKT, HANS Von: *Thoughts of a Soldier.* London: Benn, 1930.

SENFF, H.: *Die Entwicklung der Panzerwaffe im deutschen Heer zwischen der beiden Weltkriegen.* Berlin: E. S. Mittler und Sohn, 1969.

SENGER und ETTERLIN, Dr. F. Von: *Die deutschen Panzer 1926–45.* Munich: Lehmanns, 1959.

    Die Panzergrenadiere. Munich: Lehmanns, 1961.

SHIRER, WILLIAM L.: *Berlin Diary.* New York: Knopf, 1941.

    The Rise and Fall of the Third Reich. New York, Simon and Schuster, 1960; London: Pan, 1964.

SHULMAN, MILTON: *Defeat in the West.* Westport, Conn.: Greenwood Press, repr of 1948 ed.

SIEGLER, F.: *Die höheren Dienstellen der deutschen Wehrmacht, 1933–45.* Stuttgart: Deutsche Verlagsanstalt, 1953.

SPEER, ALBERT: *Inside the Third Reich.* New York: Macmillan. Sphere, 1971.

SPEIDEL, H.: *We Defended Normandy.* London: Jenkins, 1951.

STEIN, GEORGE H.: *The Waffen SS.* Ithaca, N.Y.: Cornell University Press, 1966.

STRAWSON, JOHN: *Hitler as a Military Commander.* London: Batsford, 1971.

TAYLOR, A. J. P.: *The Origins of the Second World War.* New York: Atheneum, 1962.

TAYLOR, TELFORD: *Sword and Swastika.* Magnolia, Mass.: Peter Smith, repr of 1953 ed.

TOLAND, JOHN: *Adolf Hitler.* New York: Doubleday, 1976.

TREVOR-ROPER, H. R.: *The Last Days of Hitler.* New York: Macmillan, 3rd ed 1962.
    Hitler's War Directives. London: Sidgwick and Jackson, 1964; Pan, 1966.

U.S. GOVERNMENT PRINTING OFFICE: *Nazi Conspiracy and Aggression* (10 Vols.). Washington D.C., 1946.

U.S. WAR DEPARTMENT: *Handbook of German Military Forces.* Washington D.C., 1941.

WARLIMONT, WALTER: *Inside Hitler's Headquarters, 1939–45.* London: Weidenfeld and Nicolson, 1964.

WERNER, MAX: *The Military Strength of the Powers.* London: Gollancz, 1939.

WERTH, ALEXANDER: *Russia at War, 1941–1945.* New York: Dutton, 1964.

WESTPHAL, SIEGFRIED: *The German Army in the West.* London: Cassell, 1951.

WHEELER-BENNETT, JOHN: *The Nemesis of Power.* New York: St. Martin, 1964.

WILLIAMS, JOHN: *The Ides of May. The Defeat of France May–June, 1940.* London: Constable, 1968.

WILMOT, CHESTER: *The Struggle for Europe.* Westport, Conn.: Greenwood Press, repr of 1952 ed.

WINTRINGHAM, TOM: *New Ways of War.* London: Penguin, 1940.
    Peoples' War. London: Penguin, 1942.

YOUNG, Brigadier DESMOND: *Rommel, The Desert Fox.* New York: Harper & Row, 1951.

ZESKA, Major Von: *Das Buch vom Heer.* Berlin: Borg, 1940.

ZIEMKE, E. F.: *The German Northern Theatre of Operations, 1940–45.* Washington D.C.: Department of the Army, 1959.
    Stalingrad to Berlin. Washington D.C.: Department of the Army Historical Series, 1968.

Index